LEGAL SECRETARY'S
COMPLETE HANDBOOK

LEGAL SECRETARY'S

COMPLETE HANDBOOK

by

BESSE MAY MILLER

CO-AUTHOR
COMPLETE SECRETARY'S HANDBOOK

PRENTICE-HALL, INC.
Englewood Cliffs, N. J.

Preface

THIS BOOK gives you a full understanding of law office duties and is a guide to their intelligent and craftsmanlike performance. It will help you to develop into a competent legal assistant —will help you to become the lawyer's "partner" by sharing his responsibilities, thereby saving him many hours of explanation and dictation.

In whatever state you may work, this book will be useful to you. Numerous 49-state tables give the practices in each state, where practicable. For example, a table shows the requirements in each state for the number of witnesses to a will, so that the secretary may type the proper number of lines for witnesses' signatures without instructions. The specimen legal forms are easily adapted to the requirements of a particular state. They illustrate standard phraseology as well as a professional manner of setting up the document.

Since this book is a *complete* handbook, it takes you through the gamut of law office duties—from filing to keeping account records; from typing letters to typing briefs; from filling in printed deed forms to preparing a closing statement; from attending to the execution of a document to attending to the details of organizing a corporation.

The last part of the book contains reference material that throws light on the terminology of the profession. The chapter on the law library covers all of the standard law books and tells how to use them. The list of Latin words and phrases and the easy-to-understand definitions of law terms enable you to grasp quickly the meaning of the legal words and phrases used by the lawyer.

The book is useful for the beginner and for the experienced secretary. The beginner will find step-by-step explanations and

v

instructions to guide her; the experienced secretary will find suggestions that will enable her to assume more responsibility and to increase her proficiency.

The practices and instructions given are necessarily arbitrary to some extent, but they are based upon the practices of successful law firms, both large and small. The user of the handbook must remember, however, that each lawyer has the prerogative of determining how a task shall be done and what responsibilities the secretary shall assume.

The author is deeply grateful to the members of the Advisory Committee and of the Legal Committee, who are listed on the following pages. The Advisory Committee were most generous in making available to me the experiences and practices that lead to success in their careers. The Legal Committee were never-failing sources of information about matters in their respective states. The cooperation of the National Association of Legal Secretaries is also gratefully acknowledged.

The author is especially grateful to Lillian Doris for her valuable cooperation and assistance and for her constant encouragement.

BESSE MAY MILLER

Advisory Committee

LIBBY KRAUSE, First Vice President of National Association of Legal Secretaries and Secretary to Mr. Kenneth Sperry, Long Beach, California

CATHERYNE W. CLOUSE, Past President of Nashville Legal Secretaries Association and Secretary to Mr. Charles L. Cornelius, Jr., of the firm of Cornelius & Collins, Nashville

CAROLYN CONLAN FRICK, Supervisor of Stenographers, Cadwalader, Wickersham & Taft, New York City

WILDA E. FLEMING, Secretary to Mr. Robert H. Anderson of the firm of Loftin Anderson Scott McCarthy & Preston, Miami, Florida

PHYLLIS F. CASTLE, First President of Berrien County Legal Secretaries Association, Niles, Michigan

CATHERINE HANDSCHU, Secretary to Mr. Arthur H. Boettcher of the firm of Brown, Jackson, Boettcher & Dienner, Chicago

CELIA KESSLER, formerly Secretary to Honorable George J. Beldock, Justice of the Supreme Court, Appellate Division of the State of New York, Kings County

BEATRICE J. LONGSTREET, Secretary to Mr. Irving M. Engel of the firm of Engel, Judge, Miller, Sterling & Reddy, New York City

HELEN MACMILLAN, Secretary to Mr. Reginald Heber Smith of the firm of Hale & Dorr, Boston

ERNESTINE G. PICKETT, Secretary to Mr. Howard L. Williams of the firm of Hering, Morris, James & Hitchens, Wilmington, Delaware

EILEEN G. WELLS, Secretary to Mr. Hugh C. Bickford of the firm of Bickford & Weston, Washington, D.C.

Legal Committee

ALABAMA—Mabel Wheeler, Secretary to Mr. Douglas Arant of the firm of White, Bradley, Arant, All & Rose, Birmingham

ALASKA—Martha M. Rivers, Secretary to The Honorable Ralph J. Rivers, United States Representative from Alaska, Washington, D.C.

ARIZONA—Jean Burger, Secretary to Mr. Walter E. Craig of the firm of Fennemore, Craig, Allen & McClennen, Phoenix

ARKANSAS—Dorothy M. Orsini, Executive Secretary of the Arkansas Bar Association, and Mildred S. Brown, Secretary to Mr. Edward L. Wright of the firm of Harrison, Lindsey & Upton, Little Rock, and President of Greater Little Rock Legal Secretaries' Association.

CALIFORNIA—Oliva C. Abegglen, former Secretary to Mr. Stanley W. Reckers of the firm of Butler & Reckers, Sacramento

COLORADO—Shirley A. Bown, former Secretary to the firm of Strickland, Strickland & Tull, Denver

CONNECTICUT—Ellen C. Strom, Secretary to Mr. Richard T. Steele of the firm of Steele, Collins & Maxwell, Hartford

DELAWARE—Ernestine G. Pickett, Secretary to Mr. Howard L. Williams of the firm of Hering, Morris, James & Hitchens, Wilmington

FLORIDA—Louise Bosdell, Secretary to Mr. Thomas E. Camp, III, Vice President and Trust Officer, The Barnett National Bank of Jacksonville

GEORGIA—Marilyn C. Barcroft, Secretary to Mr. Alex P. Gaines of the firm of Gaines and de Give, Atlanta

IDAHO—Ferne Witt, Secretary to the firm of Anderson, Kaufman and Anderson, Boise

ILLINOIS—Helen T. White, Secretary to the firm of Brown, Hay and Stephens, Springfield

INDIANA—Emma N. Moore, Secretary to the firm of Ross McCord Ice & Miller, Indianapolis

IOWA—M. Joy Eastman, Secretary to Mr. Thomas B. Roberts of the firm of Brody, Parker, Miller, Roberts & Thoma, Des Moines

KANSAS—Della Zoe Fisher, Secretary to Mr. Ralph E. Gilchrist of the firm of Gilchrist & Buck, Wichita

KENTUCKY—Beatrice S. McDonald, Secretary to the firm of Hobson and Meigs, Frankfort

LOUISIANA—Eleanor K. Strain, formerly Secretary to Mr. Charles E. Dunbar, Jr. of the firm of Phelps, Dunbar, Marks & Claverie, New Orleans

MAINE—Pauline F. Church, Secretary to the firm of Goodspeed & Goodspeed, Augusta

MARYLAND—Roberta L. Bromelsick, Secretary to the firm of White, Page & Lentz, Baltimore

MASSACHUSETTS—Barbara M. McAllister, formerly Secretary to Mr. Sargent H. Wellman, Boston

MICHIGAN—Alyce R. Galligan, Secretary to the firm of Jennings, Fraser, Parsons & Trebilcock, Lansing

MINNESOTA—Florence M. Walstrum, Secretary to the firm of Doherty, Rumble, Butler & Mitchell, Saint Paul

MISSISSIPPI—Mary Ella Barnett, Secretary to the firm of Butler, Snow, O'Mara, Stevens and Cannada, Jackson

MISSOURI—Betty L. Ashlock, Secretary to the firm of Keyes & Bushman, Jefferson City

MONTANA—Fern L. Baker, Secretary to Wellington D. Rankin and Arthur P. Acher, and Melba Gibbs, formerly Secretary to Mr. William A. Brown, Helena

NEBRASKA—Pauline Hultquist, Secretary to the firm of Davis, Healey, Davies & Wilson, Lincoln

NEVADA—Betty Hill, Secretary to Mr. William J. Crowell, Carson City

NEW HAMPSHIRE—Selma A. Nordstrom, Secretary to the firm of Booth, Wadleigh, Langdell, Starr & Peters, Manchester

NEW JERSEY—Isabel Miller, Secretary to the firm of Homan, Philips & Gold, Trenton

NEW MEXICO—Amalia P. Salazar, Secretary to Mr. Henry J. Hughes, Santa Fe

NEW YORK—Florence H. Townsend, Secretary to the firm of Halter, Sullivan & Rehfuss, Albany

NORTH CAROLINA—Norma G. Hamrick and Jewell Freeman, Secretaries to the firm of Smith, Leach, Anderson & Dorsett, Raleigh

NORTH DAKOTA—Ethel B. Freeman, Secretary to the firm of Zuger, Zuger & Pearson, Bismarck

OHIO—Evelyn T. Madlener, formerly Secretary to Mr. Richard V. Willcox of the firm of Willcox, Horst, Park & Hoffman, Columbus

OKLAHOMA—Athilene Kennedy, Secretary to the firm of Emery & Emery, Oklahoma City

OREGON—Sallie Clinton, Secretary to Mr. George Black, Jr. of the firm of Black, Kendall & Tremaine, Portland

PENNSYLVANIA—Maxine H. Goldstrom, Secretary to the firm of Thorp, Reed & Armstrong, Pittsburgh

RHODE ISLAND—Sandra B. Grady, former Secretary, and Nancy E. Wilbur, present Secretary to the firm of Worrell and Hodge, Providence

SOUTH CAROLINA—Ethel W. McCants, former Secretary, and Jennie M. Culley, present Secretary to Mr. Clarke W. McCants, Jr., Columbia

SOUTH DAKOTA—D. Iris Clow, Secretary to the firm of Martens, Goldsmith & May, Pierre

TENNESSEE—Mattie Lee McCauley, Secretary to the firm of Taber, Chambliss, Swafford & Claunch, Chattanooga

TEXAS—Leona Lindau, Secretary to Mr. Arthur P. Bagby, Austin

UTAH—Ethel A. Farrell, Secretary to Mr. C. C. Parsons of the firm of Dickson, Ellis, Parsons & McCrea, Salt Lake City

VERMONT—Barbara A. Foster, Secretary to Mr. William H. Edmunds of the firm of Edmunds, Austin & Wick, Burlington

VIRGINIA—Phyllis N. Troy, Secretary to Mr. John C. Goddin of the firm of Shewmake, Gary, Goddin & Blackwell, Richmond

WASHINGTON—Rhea Baker, Secretary to Mr. Harry Henke, Jr. of the firm of Skeel, McKelvy, Henke, Evenson & Uhlmann, Seattle

WEST VIRGINIA—Virginia C. Field, Secretary to Mr. Robert S. Spilman, Jr. of the firm of Spilman, Thomas, Battle & Klostermeyer, Charleston

WISCONSIN—Betty L. Schansberg, formerly Secretary to Mr. Thomas N. Burke, Madison

WYOMING—Mae Townsend, Secretary to the firm of Ellery & McClintock, Cheyenne

Table of Contents

PART I

Usual Duties in a Law Office

1. YOU, THE LAWYER, AND THE LAW OFFICE   3

You and the Lawyer: The secretary as a partner 3. The secretary's ethics 3. Survival of the fittest 4. Requirements for admission to the bar 4. Law degrees 5. Specialization in the law field 5. Building a practice 6. The lawyer's outside activities 8. The lawyer's relation with his client 9. Fees 9.

Organization and Personnel of a Law Firm: Kind of business organization 10. Personnel in a law office 10. The secretary's duties 11. The secretary's deportment 11.

The Law Office: Layout 13. The furniture 13. Decoration 14. Equipment 14. Stationery supplies 15.

A New Matter: New case report 16. What the secretary does 17. Routing of new case report 19.

2. CONTACTS WITH CLIENTS AND OTHER CALLERS   20

The secretary's introduction to the client 20. Basic precepts 21.

Contacts in Person: Contacts in person with clients 21. Client calls without an appointment 22. Stranger who wants legal advice 24. A client is early for an appointment 25. Hysterical clients 25. Invitations from clients 25. Presents and payment for work 25. Client wants to see a file 26. Salesmen 26.

Contacts over the Telephone: Importance of telephone contacts 27. Rules of telephone courtesy 27. Placing calls for the lawyer 28. Long distance, or toll, calls 29. When clients place toll calls 29. Answering calls for the lawyer 30. Making notes of incoming calls 30. Screening calls for the lawyer 31. Finding the purpose of a call 32. An irate client calls 33. Client or prospective client asks what a fee will be 34. Your telephone conversation 34. Desk telephone lists 34.

3. REMINDER SYSTEMS AND PRACTICES   37

The Diary: What is a diary 37. Diaries that you should keep 39. How to make up diaries 39. How to make entries about legal work 40. How to obtain information for entries 40. Checklist of entries to make in diary 41. Tickler card file 43. Use of tickler card file with diary 43. Checklist of entries of work accomplished 43.

Follow-up Files: Necessity for follow-up files 44. Checklist of material to be placed in follow-up files 44. Equipment for follow-up system 45. Arrangement of folders for follow-up 45. Operation of the follow-up system 45. How to handle material in the daily follow-up file 47. Follow-ups on a small scale 47. Tickler card file for follow-up 47.

Reminding the Lawyer of Things to Be Done: Necessity for reminder 47. How to remind the lawyer of appointments 48. Reminders showing appointments for a month 48. How to remind the lawyer of things to be done 49. How to remind the lawyer of court work 49.

4. *FILING IN THE LAW OFFICE*   52

Classification of files 52.

Numerical System of Filing Applied to Clients' Files: What is the numerical system of filing 53. How to use the numerical system in a law office 53. Assigning numbers according to type of case 57. How to transfer numerical files 57.

Alphabetical System of Filing Applied to Clients' Files: What is the alphabetical system of filing 58. How to use the alphabetical system 59. How to transfer alphabetical files 59.

Other Files: Personal file 60. General correspondence file 60. Periodicals, bulletins, etc. 61.

Physical Setup of Files: Preparation of material for filing 61. How to type index tabs and labels 62. How to arrange the papers in the file folders 63. Preparation for closing a file 64. Extra copies and printed papers, drafts 65. Control of material taken from the files 65.

5. *CORRESPONDENCE AND TELEGRAMS IN THE LAW OFFICE*   66

Styles of letter setups 66. Opinion letters 70. Punctuation 70. Subject line 70. How to type the date line 71.

The Address: The addressee's name 71. Titles 71. Business titles or position 73. Forms for addressing women 74. How to type the street address 75.

Salutations: How to type the salutation 76. Forms of salutation 76. Forms of salutation in letters addressed to women 77.

The Complimentary Close: 78.

Signature: How to type the signature 78.

Miscellaneous Suggestions About Correspondence: Envelopes 79. Attention line 80. Responsibility or identification line 80. Personal notation 80. Mailing notation 80. Enclosure mark 81. Carbon copy distribution notation 81. Postscript 81. Heading on succeeding pages 82. Enclosures 82.

Some Concrete Aids in Letter Writing: Suggested techniques 83. Trite terms to be avoided 83. Unnecessary words and phrases 86. Two words with the same meaning 87. Favorite words and expressions 88. Big words versus one syllable words 88. Sentence length 88.

Telegrams: How to send a telegram 89. How to type a telegram 89. How to send the same message to multiple addresses 90. How to send a telegram to a person on a train 90. How to send a telegram to a person on a plane 90. Punctuation 90. Paragraphing 91. Mixed groups of letters and figures 91. How to type a telegram when work is in the machine 91.

6. HOW TO ADDRESS PERSONS HOLDING HONORARY OR OFFICIAL POSITIONS   92

United States government officials 93. State and local officials 97. Court officials 99. United States diplomatic representatives 100. Foreign officials and representatives 102. Officers of the armed forces—Army 104. Officers of the armed forces—Navy 105. Catholic faith 106. Jewish faith 109. Protestant faith 110. College officials 112.

7. HOW TO KEEP ACCOUNT RECORDS IN THE LAW OFFICE   113

How to Keep Books in the Law Office: System of bookkeeping in the law office 113. Books required 113. Basic principles of double entry bookkeeping 114. Simple rules to remember 114. Cash journal 115. General ledger 116. Subsidiary ledger 117. Posting to the general ledger 119. Explanation of cash journal entries and posting 119. Trial balance 129. Taking a trial balance of accounts receivable 129. Profit and loss statement 130. Drawing account 130. Pay-roll record 130. Capital account 132.

Time and Cost of Professional Services: Records required to find time and cost of service 132. Finding the cost of a lawyer's time 132. Daily time sheet 133. Posting the time charges 136.

Billing the Client: Preparation of the bill 138. Charges made to clients 138. How the amount of the bill is calculated 138.

PART II

Preparing Legal Instruments and Documents

8. DISTINCTIVE FEATURES OF DICTATION AND TYPING   143

The secretary's loose-leaf notebook 143.

Dictation in the Law Office: Importance of understanding dictated material 144. Errors in the dictation 144. Pairs of words that cause confusion 145. Recurring phrases, clauses, and paragraphs 146. Special outlines for unusual words 147. Take-ins 147. Testimony 149.

How to Prepare Legal Papers: Number of copies 150. Paper 153. How to align paper in typewriter 153. Margins 154. Paragraphs 155. Numbering pages 155. Marginal and tabular stops 155. Tabulated material 156. Responsibility and distribution line 156. Line spacing 157. Standard rules for spacing 157. Space for fill-ins 158. Underscoring 158. Quotations and other indented material 158. Drafts 161. Copying 162. Collating 163. Conforming 163. Ditto marks 163. Legal backs 164. How to make corrections on bound pages 165. Printed law blanks 166.

9. BASIC INFORMATION ABOUT LEGAL INSTRUMENTS 168

What is a legal instrument 168. Parties to an instrument 168. How to type legal instruments 169.

Execution of an Instrument: What is "execution" of an instrument 169. Testimonium clause 169. Signatures 170. How to fit the signatures on the page 171. Sealing an instrument 172. Attestation clause 176.

Acknowledgments: Importance of acknowledgments in the law office 176. Laws governing acknowledgments 177. Essentials of an acknowledgment 179. How and where to type the acknowledgment 182. Who may make an acknowledgment 182. Who may take an acknowledgment 183. Authentication 183.

Notaries Public: What is a notary public 185. Following the letter of the law when you notarize a paper 187. Details to observe when you notarize a paper 189.

Recording Legal Instruments: Purpose in recording instruments 189. Distinction between recording and filing 190. What the secretary does 190.

10. SPECIFIC INSTRUMENTS: AFFIDAVITS; POWERS OF ATTORNEY; WILLS 193

Affidavits: What is an affidavit 193. Distinction between affidavit and acknowledgment 193. Essentials of an affidavit 194. Authentication 194. Preparation of affidavit 194.

Powers of Attorney: What is a power of attorney 196. Parties to a power of attorney 196. Forms of powers of attorney 196. Statements and clauses 196. Directions for the preparation of a power of attorney 197.

Wills: What is a will 198. Who are the parties to a will 198. Forms and kinds of wills 199. Printed forms of wills 199. Pattern of the contents of wills 200. Title 200. Introductory paragraph 200. Revocation clause 200. Text, or body 201. Payment of debts and funeral expenses 201. Dispositive clauses 201. Trust provisions 201. Residuary clause 202. Appointment of executor 202. Appointment of guardian 202. Testimonium, or signature, clause 202. Attestation clause and witnesses' signatures 202. Typing a will 204. Signature page and preceding page of a will 206. How to gauge and test the page length 208. Witnessing a will 209. Certifying copies of wills 209. Capitalization and punctuation 210. "Do's and don'ts" in preparing a will 211. Codicil 213. Suggestions for red-inking a will 213.

PART III

Courts and Litigation

11. COURTS AND THEIR FUNCTIONS 217

The word "court" 217. Court procedure 218. American court system 218. Jurisdiction 229. Inferior courts 230. Superior courts 230. Courts of special jurisdiction 231. Courts of intermediate review 231. Supreme appellate courts 232. Distinction between equity and law 232. Judges and justices 234. Clerk of the Court 235. Clerk's index system 235. Clerk's permanent record book 236. Clerk's minute books 236. Court calendar and calendar number 237. Calendar call 237.

12. *BASIC INFORMATION ABOUT LITIGATION PAPERS*   239

Parties to an Action: Party bringing a law suit 239. Party defending a law suit 239. Parties to a cross action 240. Party intervening 240. Parties on appeal 241. Amicus curiae 241. Who may be parties to a law suit 241.

Verifications: What is a verification 243. Who may verify a pleading 244. Forms of verification 244. How to type a verification 244. How to administer the oath to person verifying a pleading 246.

How to Type Court Papers: Paper 249. Heading or caption 249. How to type the caption 250. Captions on papers filed in Federal district courts 258. Indentations 259. Number of copies 259. Numbering pages 259. Conforming copies 259. Legal backs for court papers 259. Folding 262. Printed litigation blanks 262.

Practice and Procedure: The secretary's responsibility 263. Variations in practice and procedure 263.

13. *SPECIFIC COURT PAPERS: WHAT THEY ARE AND HOW TO PREPARE THEM*   267

Summons and Complaint: Plaintiff's first pleading 267. Analysis of a complaint 268. How to prepare the complaint 269. The summons 271. How to prepare the summons 271. Return day of summons 273. Alias summons; pluries summons 274. What the secretary does about the summons and complaint 274.

The Answer: Defendant's first pleading 275. Analysis of an answer 275. How to prepare the answer 276. Methods of service of answer on plaintiff's attorney 279. What the secretary does about the answer 280.

Notice of Appearance: Analysis of a notice of appearance 281. How to prepare a notice of appearance 281. What the secretary does about the notice of appearance 281.

Notice of Trial; Note of Issue: Noticing a case for trial 284. When the notice must be served 284. Note of issue—preparation 285. Notice of trial—preparation 286. What the secretary does about the notice of trial or note of issue 288.

Stipulations: Analysis of a stipulation 288. How to prepare a stipulation 289. What the secretary does about stipulations 289.

Demurrers: Analysis of a demurrer 291. How to prepare the demurrer 291. What the secretary does about a demurrer 295.

Demand for Bill of Particulars, Bill of Particulars, Interrogatories, and Motion to Make Pleading More Definite: Demand for bill of particulars 296. Parts of demand for bill of particulars 296. How to prepare the demand for bill of particulars 296. What the secretary does about the demand for bill of particulars 299. Parts of bill of particulars 299. How to prepare the bill of particulars 299. What the secretary does about the bill of particulars 302. Interrogatories 302. Motion to make the pleading more definite 302.

14. *SPECIFIC COURT PAPERS: WHAT THEY ARE AND HOW TO PREPARE THEM (CONT'D)*   303

Notices: Discussion 303. How to prepare a notice 303. Backing and binding of notices 304. Service of notice 306.

Motion and Notice of Motion: What is a motion 309. Return day of motion 310. Information you need to prepare a notice of motion 310. What the secretary does about the notice of motion and affidavit 312.

Affidavit for Use in Court: Discussion 312. How to prepare an affidavit for court use 313.

Orders: Discussion 315. How to prepare an order 315. What the secretary does about an order 317.

Findings of Fact and Conclusions of Law: What the "findings of fact and conclusions of law" are 320. How to prepare findings of fact and conclusions of law 320. What the secretary does about findings of fact and conclusions of law 321.

Instructions to the Jury: What an instruction to the jury is 321. How to prepare an instruction to the jury 321.

Judgments and Decrees: What judgments and decrees are 322. How to prepare a judgment or decree 322. Number of copies 322. What the secretary does about a judgment or decree 325.

15. *HOW TO KEEP A PROGRESS RECORD OF COURT MATTERS*   326

Physical features of a suit register 326. Loose-leaf binder for the suit register 326. File folder used for progress record 327. Portable tray or cabinet for the suit register 328. How to file the record sheets 329. When and how to open a case in the suit register 329. What to enter 329. Form and sufficiency of record 332. Closing the record of a case 333.

16. *WHEN A CASE IS APPEALED: RECORDS, BRIEFS, CITATIONS*   335

Rules of the reviewing court 335. Methods for review by a higher court 336. Diary entries 336. Change in caption of case 337. Designation of parties to an appeal 337. Notice of appeal 339. Service on opposing counsel 340.

Contents and Preparation of the Record on Appeal: What is a record on appeal 340. Assignment of errors and instructions to the clerk 342. Who prepares the record 342. How to prepare the record 342. Format and make-up of record 343. Binding, volumes, and title 343. Certification, filing, and service 343.

The Brief: Nature of a brief 344. Preliminaries to preparing the brief 344. Time element 345. Preparation of the brief 345. Application for oral argument 352. Procedure when having a brief printed 352.

Citations: What is a citation 354. How to take citations in shorthand 354. Accuracy of citations 354. Official reports and the National Reporter System 354. How to cite a constitution 358. How to cite statutes and codes 358. How to cite cases in official reports and reporters 361. Named reporters 363. String citations 363. How to cite an unpublished case 363. How to cite slip decisions 363. How to cite treatises 364. How to cite law reviews 364. How to cite legal newspapers 364. Underscoring and italicizing 364. Spacing of abbreviations 365. Placement of citations 365. Illustrations of citations 365.

17. *HANDLING MATERIAL FOR PRINTING*   367

Preparing the Manuscript for the Printer: Typing rules for manuscript 367. Checking the manuscript 368. Marking copy 369. Planning 369. How to mark copy 370. How to estimate length of copy 370.

Correcting Galley and Page Proofs: Procedure 373. Importance of correcting galley and page proofs 373. Proofreader's marks 374. Reading the proof 376.

PART IV

Assisting in Specialized Practice

18. *ORGANIZING A CORPORATION*   379

What is a corporation 379. Steps in the organization of a corporation 380. Who may form a corporation 381. State of incorporation 381. Memorandum preliminary to preparation of incorporating papers 382. Reservation of name 383. Charter 384. Preparation of charter 385. Execution of the charter 389. Filing the charter and payment of fees 390.

Organization Meetings: Necessity and purpose of organization meeting 391. The secretary's preparation for the organization meeting 391. Corporate outfit 391. Waiver of notice of organization meeting 392. Preparation of by-laws 393. Minutes of first meeting of incorporators 394. Minutes of first meeting of directors 395. Resolution opening a bank account 395. Preparation of stock certificates 395.

19. *ACTING AS CORPORATE SECRETARY*   418

Information folder 418.

Corporate Meetings: Kinds of meetings 419. Preparations for meetings 419. Meeting folder 419. Notice of stockholders' meeting 420. Waiver of notice of stockholders' meeting 420. Quorum at a stockholders' meeting 421. Proxies and proxy statement 421. Notice of directors' meeting 422. Quorum at directors' meeting 422. Preservation of notice 423. The agenda 423. Reservation and preparation of the meeting room 423. Directors' fees 424. Material to take to meetings 424. Drafting resolutions before meetings 425. Preparations for taking notes at meetings 425. Taking notes at meetings 426.

Minutes: The minute book 428. Arrangement of contents of combined minute book 428. Preparation of draft of minutes 429. How to prepare minutes in final form 429. Correction of errors in minutes 430. Certified extract of minutes 430. Indexing of minutes 432.

Issuance and Transfer of Stock of a Small Corporation: Authority to issue certificate 433. Stock certificate book 433. Original issue and transfer of stock 433. Taxes on stock 433. Issuance of certificate of stock 435. Transfer of certificate 436. Separate form of assignment 437.

The Corporation Calendar: Need for a corporation calendar 438. How to keep the corporation calendar 438. Where to get dates for the corporation calendar 439.

Change of Corporate Name: Details when corporate name is changed 440.

Specimen Corporate Forms: Minutes of first meeting of incorporators of a Delaware Corporation 440. Waiver of notice of first meeting of incorporators 442. Waiver of notice of first meeting of directors 442. Notice of annual meeting of stockholders 443. Notice of special meeting of stockholders, indicating purpose of meeting 443. Affidavit of secretary that notice of annual meeting of stockholders was mailed 443. Affidavit of secretary of publication of notice of stockholders' meeting 444. Proxy for special meeting of stockholders; purposes of meeting not indicated 444. Notice of special meeting of directors, specifying purposes 445. Minutes of annual meeting of directors 445. Resolution of directors authorizing sale and issue of stock to persons determined by executive committee 447. Resolution of directors amending a particular by-law upon authorization of stockholders 447. Directors' resolution accepting resignation of a member of board 447. Directors' resolution accepting resignation of officer 448. Directors' resolution expressing gratitude for services of resigning officer 448. Blanket resolution of directors authorizing issuance of duplicate certificate in event of loss 448. Excerpt of minutes showing adoption of minutes of previous meeting as corrected 448. Resolution of directors (or stockholders) extending sympathy upon death of associate 449.

20. *REAL ESTATE PRACTICE: DEEDS; MORTGAGES; LEASES*   **450**

Pattern followed for each instrument 450.

Real Property Descriptions: How land is described 451. Section and township description 451. Metes and bounds description 453. Lot and block description 454. How to type real property descriptions 454. How to check land descriptions 456.

Deeds: What is a deed 456. Parties to a deed 456. Forms of deeds 457. Kinds of deeds 458. Printed forms of deeds 458. Checklist of information needed to fill in form 458. Typed deeds 461. Statements and clauses in deeds 461. Revenue stamps 463. State tax 464. Recording 464. "Do's" and "don'ts" in the preparation of a deed 464.

Mortgages: What is a mortgage 465. Parties to a mortgage 466. Forms of mortgages 466. Purchase money mortgage 467. Printed mortgages 468. Checklist of information needed to fill in mortgage or deed of trust 468. Typed mortgages and deeds of trust 469. Statements and clauses in mortgages 469. State tax 472. "Do's" and "don'ts" in the preparation of a mortgage 472.

Leases: What is a lease 474. Parties to a lease 475. Classification of leases 475. Printed forms 476. Standard lease clauses 476. Checklist of standard clauses in commercial leases 479. Style of typed lease 480. Execution, acknowledgment, and recording of lease 480. "Do's" and "don'ts" in the preparation of a lease 481.

21. *REAL ESTATE PRACTICE (CONT'D): CONTRACTS OF SALE AND CLOSINGS* 483

Contract of Sale: Necessity for a contract of sale 484. Types of contracts of sale of land 484. Parties to a contract 484. How to prepare a contract of sale 485. Checklist of information necessary to fill in form 485. Earnest money 486. Escrow for the sale of real property 486.

Title Closings and Evidence of Title: What is a title closing 487. Evidence of title 487. Abstract of title 487. Opinion of title 489. Certificate of title 490. Title insurance policies 490. Torrens certificate 490. Preparations for closing 491.

Preparation of Closing Statement: What is a closing statement 492. How to calculate adjustments 494. Example of calculation of tax adjustment 494. Example of calculation of interest adjustment 495. Example of calculation of insurance adjustment 495. Example of calculation of rent adjustment 495. Miscellaneous payments 495. Suggested form of closing statement 496.

22. *FORECLOSURE ACTIONS* 500

Papers necessary for institution of foreclosure action 500. Information needed to prepare papers in foreclosure action 500. Venue 501. Parties to a foreclosure action 501. Fictitious names 501. Description of note or bond 502. Description of mortgage 502. Description of property 502. When is a mortgage considered in default 503.

Procedure in Foreclosure Action: Title search for foreclosures 503. Preparation of complaint 503. Number of copies 504. *Lis pendens* 505. Preparation of notice of *lis pendens* 505. Preparation of summons 508. Filing and service of summons, complaint, and *lis pendens* 508. Follow-up of process service 508. Party sheet 508. Other steps in foreclosure proceedings 509. Checklist of what to do in foreclosure action 510.

23. *PROBATE AND ESTATE ADMINISTRATION* 511

Distinction between executor and administrator 511. The lawyer's part in the administration of an estate 512.

Probate of Will: The executor's right to act 513. Probate of will 513. Parties to a probate proceeding 513. Copy of will and affidavit 515. Petition for probate of will 515. Transfer tax affidavit 523. Citation and waiver in probate proceeding 523. How to prepare a waiver of citation 524. How to prepare a citation 524. Preparations for hearing 527. Notice of probate 527. Deposition of witnesses to the will 529. Oath of executor 529. Decree admitting will to probate 529. Letters testamentary 530. Notice to creditors 530.

Appointment of Administrator: Application for letter of administration 531. Parties 531. Who has prior right to letters of administration 532. Necessary papers in application for letters of administration 532. How to prepare petition; oath; designation of clerk 532. Renunciation 537. Citations 537. Notice of application for letters of administration 538. Letters of administration 539.

24. *HANDLING COMMERCIAL COLLECTIONS*   540

Commercial law lists 540. Office procedures affecting collections 541. How to file collection matters 541. Follow-up system 541. Acknowledgment of claim 542. Collection letters 544. Reports to the forwarder 545. Installment payments 545. Record of collections 545. Remitting 546. Fees 546. Forwarding an item for collection 546.

Uncontested Suit: When the lawyer recommends suit 548. Summons and complaint 548. Preparation and service of summons and short-form complaint 548. Checklist of information needed to draw summons and complaint in suit on a collection item 549. Judgment by default 549. How to prepare a judgment by default 550.

PART V

Reference Material

25. *THE LAW LIBRARY AND HOW TO USE IT*   553

Statutes and Codes: Compilations of laws 553. How to find a law 554.

Reports of Decided Cases: Scope and organization of reports 554 How to use the reports and reporters 555. Purpose of the blue book and the blue and white book 556. How to use the blue book 557. How to use the blue and white book 557. Other publications of decisions 557.

Books That Classify the Law: 559.

American Digest: Organization of American Digest system 559. How to use the digest system 560. Table of cases 561.

Shepard's Citations: Purpose of Shepard's Citations 562. Abbreviations used 562. How to use Shepard's Citations 563.

Illustrative Case: 563.

Corpus Juris Secundum System: Scope and organization of system 566. How to use Corpus Juris Secundum System 566. How to cite 567.

Form Books: Practice manuals 567. Books of legal forms 567.

Reference Facilities for Checking Names and Addresses: 568.

26. *LATIN WORDS AND PHRASES*   569

27. *LAW TERMS AND MISCELLANEOUS PROCEDURES EXPLAINED*   577

Part I

Usual Duties in a Law Office

---

1. You, the Lawyer, and the Law Office   3
2. Contacts with Clients and Other Callers   20
3. Reminder Systems and Practices   37
4. Filing in the Law Office   52
5. Correspondence in the Law Office   66
6. How to Address Persons Holding Honorary or Official
   Positions   92
7. How to Keep Account Records in the Law Office   113

1

You, the Lawyer, and the Law Office

AN UNDERSTANDING of what a law office is like—how it functions—its personnel—is needed as a basis for an intelligent
performance of your duties as secretary to a lawyer. This chapter
describes (1) what is expected of you as a secretary in a law
office; (2) the training and effort necessary for a lawyer to build
a worth-while practice; (3) the organization and personnel of
a law firm; (4) the physical aspects of a law office; and (5) the
customary processing of a new matter when it is received by a
law firm, before any work is done on it.

You and the Lawyer

The secretary as a partner. The lawyer likes to look upon his
secretary as his partner. He and she are a team, each pulling a
share of the heavy load. To be worthy of the partnership, the
secretary must strive to gain knowledge of the lawyer's work,
must take an interest in and think about it, so that she will
be able to do a little more than what is expected of her. She must
be loyal and discreet, and be governed by high standards in all of
her actions. In addition to being able to take shorthand rapidly
and transcribe it accurately, she must have initiative, administrative ability, judgment, and a deep sense of responsibility.

The secretary's ethics. The law secretary is bound by the same
code of ethics as her employer. She cannot solicit business for
him; she must regard everything she knows about a client or a
case as confidential. She never divulges the contents of a written
document in the office, without permission from the lawyer. It
is a cardinal sin for a law secretary to talk outside of the office

3

about a case, even if the talk is merely an anecdote. Frequently she is tempted to entertain her friends with interesting tidbits about socially prominent clients, but she always resists the temptation. Irreparable harm can result from mentioning anything about what is transpiring in a case. For example, suppose a lawyer dictates an application for injunction against removal of certain property from the county, so that he can levy upon it. If the secretary should mention this, the owner of the property, especially in a small town, might hear about it and remove the property before the judge signs the injunction. Information received from clients by a secretary in the course of her work is a *privileged communication* (see page 9).

Survival of the fittest. The law is a "jealous mistress" and an "exacting master." There is no royal road to fame in the profession. The necessary education is long, gruelling, and expensive; competition is keen; practice is arduous for almost all lawyers and not particularly lucrative. The profession is overcrowded in large metropolitan areas; every year thousands drop out of the race and go into business or another profession because they cannot earn a living in the practice of law. Yet, undaunted by the experience of others, thousands and thousands of young men and women enter law school every year, with the hope of eventually achieving a foothold in this honorable and fascinating profession.

The man or woman who, in spite of all the obstacles, becomes a respected member of the bar deserves the influential position he or she undoubtedly occupies in the community. And from you, his secretary, he deserves strenuous effort and cooperation, prompted by heartfelt respect and admiration.

Requirements for admission to the bar. Each state has its own requirements for admission to the bar. In every state, the requirements include these four factors: academic training, legal training, moral character, and belief in and loyalty to the form of the United States Government.

In almost all states the applicant for admission to the bar must take an examination, even though he is a graduate of a law school. Graduates of a few schools are admitted without examination in some of the states. Admission to practice in one state does not license the attorney to practice in another state. He must comply with the rules that state has for admission of an "attorney applicant." However, almost all of the states will admit an attorney from another state without examination after he has practiced a specified length of time, provided he meets other requirements. A few states require the attorney applicant to take an examination.

License to practice in one or more states does not admit the lawyer to practice in the Federal courts. To be admitted to the United States Supreme Court, an attorney must have practiced three years in the highest court in his state or territory. A member of the bar moves the attorney's admission in open court. Requirements for admission to the Federal courts of appeals and district courts vary with the circuit and the district.

An attorney may obtain special permission to argue a particular case before a court in which he is not licensed to practice. This often happens in criminal cases when the accused wants a nationally famous criminal lawyer to represent him in the state in which he is to be tried.

Law degrees. The law degrees obtainable and the abbreviations of them follow. Notice that in some cases the abbreviation of the Latin *juris*, meaning law, is used.

Bachelor of Laws	LL.B.; B.L.
Bachelor of Civil Law	J.C.B.; B.C.L.
Master of Laws	LL.M.; M.L.
Doctor of Laws	LL.D.; J.D.
Doctor of Law	Jur. D.
Doctor of Civil Law	J.C.D.; D.C.L.
Juris Civilis Doctor	J.C.D.
Doctor of Jurisprudence	J.D.
Juris Doctor	Jur. D.
Jurum Doctor	J.D.
Doctor of Juristic Science	J.S.D.
Doctor of Both Laws	J.U.D.

Specialization in the law field. General practitioners in law, as in medicine, are gradually disappearing, although specialization in law is not yet as extensive as it is in medicine. Again as in the medical field, specialization in law is more prevalent in large cities than in small places. If you are secretary to a specialist or assigned to a particular department in a large firm, your work will probably be in only one field: corporation law (Chapters 18 and 19); real estate matters and foreclosures (Chapters 20, 21, and 22); probate matters (Chapter 23); taxation (Chapter 27, page 617); or some other specialized field.

The trend toward specialization results from the lawyer's inclination and liking for a special field and from the human impossibility of becoming expert in every field. Specialization is a great timesaver for the lawyer and his secretary. The lawyer who handles a tax matter as an incident to his other practice must spend hours doing research on a problem that a tax specialist could dispose of in a few minutes, because the specialist meets the same problem every day.

Building a practice. Graduating from law school and being admitted to the bar do not mean that the lawyer will succeed in building a worth-while practice. He must have not only the necessary training and knowledge of law, but a personality that will attract clients, gain their confidence, and hold them.

It is not ethical for a lawyer to advertise for business. All that he can do is to send out an announcement card, stating that he is engaged in the practice of law at a certain address. He also sends these announcement cards when he joins a new firm, or moves his offices. Figure 1 illustrates an announcement when the

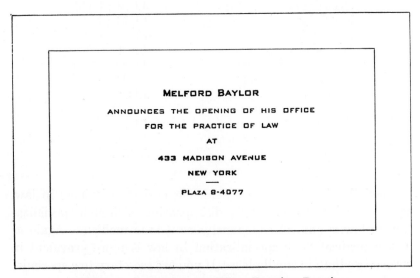

Figure 1. Announcement When Entering Practice.

lawyer first enters practice; Figure 2, when he resumes practice; Figure 3, when he moves his offices.

Twenty Pine Street
New York 5, N. Y.

John R. Brown, having completed his term as a Justice of the Supreme Court of the State of New York, announces his return to the practice of law with the firm of

Brown & Hartung

January 15, 1952   *Hanover 2-4483*

Figure 2. Announcement When Resuming Practice.

BEGEL, BUDGE & MILLER

ANNOUNCE THE REMOVAL OF THEIR OFFICES TO

52 VANDERBILT AVENUE

NEW YORK 17, N. Y.

WHERE THEY WILL CONTINUE THE GENERAL PRACTICE

OF LAW UNDER THE FIRM NAME OF

BEGEL, BUDGE, MILLER & STEBLING

AUGUST 1, 195-   LEXINGTON 2-5200

Figure 3. Announcement of Removal of Offices.

These cards cannot be mailed out indiscriminately to people whom the lawyer does not know. You can be very helpful in compiling and maintaining a permanent list of people to whom announcements may be sent. Keep the list on 3″ by 5″ index cards, and enter regularly any additions or changes that come to your attention.

The cards may be mailed to the groups listed below.

1. *Friends and acquaintances.* You will have to depend largely upon the lawyer to compile this list originally, but you can maintain it by adding the name of contacts he makes that you know about; also by keeping the addresses on the list up to date.

2. *Members of the local bar.* You can probably obtain this from the classified telephone directory. Volumes I and II of *Martindale-Hubbell Law Directory* contain a list of lawyers and their addresses in the United States and Canada. Every law library (Chapter 25) and almost every law office contain this directory.

3. *County officials.* Each state publishes a "bluebook," directory, register, or roster, which contains the names of county officers, state officers, judges, members of the senate and house. and names of departments and administrative offices. Probably a more accessible source for the names of county officials is the clerk's office in the county courthouse.

4. *Classmates.* You can get the names and addresses of the lawyer's college classmates from the permanent secretary of his class. If there is no permanent class secretary, write to the Alumni Secretary who will refer you to the proper source for the information or send it to you.

5. *Other lawyers.* The names of lawyers in other localities with whom your employer is personally acquainted should be put on the announcement list.

6. *Clients.* The name of each client should be added to the announcement list.

The lawyer's outside activities. The legal profession is a public service; its purpose is the administration of justice. Therefore, the lawyer's first interest in outside activities is usually the work of his bar association—that is his duty as a member of the profession. But he also takes a wholehearted interest in civic affairs—the school, church, charities, and any movement that will improve the community in which he lives. His position in the community demands that he participate in its affairs. Participation is the lawyer's duty; the secretary should make it hers. You, as his secretary, should read the reports of the bar association and

keep abreast of what is going on locally and nationally. Be always on the alert for news items that will interest him and call them to his attention. You will soon learn that the lawyer appreciates your interest and your willingness to help him by doing things that are beyond the scope of your actual duties.

The lawyer's relation with his client. A lawyer is a fiduciary. His relation with his client is one of trust and confidence. He represents that client's interest to the best of his ability and does not use his position of trust and confidence to further his own private interests. He never discusses the client's business with outsiders but considers it strictly confidential. So sacred is the relation between lawyer and client that information given to the lawyer by the client is a "privileged communication"—that is, the lawyer cannot be compelled to testify concerning it.

Fees. A fairly standard charge is made in many communities for certain items of work, including drawing deeds, mortgages, examining abstracts, evicting tenants, obtaining default divorces, foreclosing mortgages, organizing small corporations, and probating estates, providing these matters have no unusual complications. Otherwise, there is no standard basis for determining the amount of a fee; each office has its own method. The time element is a large factor. For that reason, an accurate record of the time spent on each item is important.

The type of fee charged is important to you for record and bookkeeping purposes (Chapter 7). Fees are classified as follows:

1. *Single retainer.* The client retains the lawyer for a specific case and agrees to pay a specified fee. Frequently part of the retainer is paid in advance.

2. *Yearly retainer.* Many organizations are constantly in need of legal advice and have numerous legal matters to be looked after. They retain lawyers on an annual basis. When a client is on a yearly retainer basis, you should know whether a specific matter is covered by the retainer or is to be charged for separately.

3. *Contingent fee.* Lawyers occasionally agree to take a case for a client for a percentage of the amount recovered. The fee is contingent upon the successful outcome of the case. Contingent fees are customary in personal injury cases, especially if the client is unable to pay for the lawyer's time except out of the damages he might recover.

4. *Forwarding fee.* Frequently a case is referred to a lawyer by an out-of-town firm. Often, though not always, a percentage of the fee earned is sent to the forwarding attorney.

5. *Collection charges.* The collection of commercial items is a special branch of law practice (Chapter 24). There is a standard charge for collection items, based on a percentage of the amount collected, with an additional fee if suit is necessary.

Organization and Personnel of a Law Firm

Kind of business organization. A lawyer either practices law alone or enters into a partnership agreement with one or more lawyers. The state statutes do not permit him to incorporate—the corporation is too impersonal where personal service is important. The law firm frequently consists of a senior partner or partners, a junior partner or partners, and associate lawyers. Even if a lawyer does not have a partner, he frequently has associates. They are paid a salary and do not share in the firm's profits, nor are they responsible for its obligations. You will notice that when lawyers' names are listed on the letterhead of a law firm or on the door of a law office, a line separates one group of names from another group. The names below the line are the names of associate lawyers who are not members of the firm.

In any law firm, whether large or small, a designated partner is responsible for the smooth functioning of the organization. Generally this partner is called the "managing partner." All of the service departments—stenographic, accounting, filing, maintenance of court docket and court calendar—are under his supervision. In large offices he will have a managing clerk and office manager under him to look after the details, but the responsibility is his.

Personnel in a law office. One of the many compensations of working in a law office is the type of people with whom you are associated. The prestige and dignity of a law office demand that every position in the firm be filled by a person of intelligence and refinement. The personnel might consist of:

Partners
Associate lawyers
Law clerks
Managing clerk

Office manager
Supervisor of secretaries and stenographers
Secretaries
Stenographers
Proofreaders
Receptionist
Bookkeepers
Clerks
File Clerk
Mail Clerks
Telephone operators
Office boys and pages

The number of persons in each position depends upon the size of the firm and the volume of work. Several of the positions are filled by the same person if the volume of work is small.

The secretary's duties. In a small law office, the work and responsibilities of all the service departments fall on the secretary. In a large office, some of the responsibilities are hers; in any event, she should be familiar with them so that she can cooperate properly with other departments. In addition to stenographic work, the secretary in a law office has some or all of the following duties and responsibilities:

1. Writing letters (Chapter 5)
2. Making appointments (Chapters 2 and 3)
3. Taking telephone calls (Chapter 2)
4. Filing (Chapter 4)
5. Maintaining the diary and tickler (Chapter 3)
6. Keeping account of charges, disbursements, and collections (Chapter 7)
7. Following office cases on court calendars (Chapter 15)
8. Proofreading (Chapter 17)
9. Maintaining the court docket or suit register (Chapter 15)

The secretary's deportment. It goes without saying that the dignity of a law firm should be maintained at all times by its secretaries. An impression of refinement is reflected in (1) knowledge of professional customs and practices; (2) good manners, and (3) personal appearance.

The customs and practices in the legal profession that the secretary should know are covered throughout this book.

Figure 4. Cabinet for Documents. Printed Forms, and Ledgers, Which Serves as Room Partition.

It can be taken for granted that anyone who has aspired to be a secretary to a lawyer has learned good manners and that politeness, friendliness, graciousness, and consideration for others are well-established habits.

The Law Office

Layout. The ideal suite of law offices consists of a reception room, a workroom, a library, a file room, a conference room, and a series of private offices. The reception room, workroom, and file room may be combined as a general office; the law books may be in various offices; there may be no conference room, but each lawyer *always* has a private office. The confidential nature of legal matters and the desire of clients for privacy demand this. Glass partitions so common to business offices are not used in law offices because they do not insure privacy. Large law offices usually have a series of private suites, consisting of an office for the lawyer and an office for the secretary who is assigned to him. Lawyers sometimes share an office suite, each lawyer conducting his practice as a sole practitioner.

Here are some suggestions you can make about the layout of a suite of law offices when you are asked for ideas:

1. If the workroom is also the waiting room, separate the waiting room from the work portion with a rail. At least arrange the furniture so that it is not necessary for people passing in and out of the general office to enter the part used as a workroom. Figure 4 illustrates a cabinet with filing facilities, which is appropriate for separating the work space from the waiting room.

2. The secretary should be located as near as possible to the lawyer to whom she is assigned.

3. A private exit from the lawyer's private office is desirable so that a client does not have to leave through the waiting room where other clients are waiting. It also affords the lawyer an opportunity to go and come without being observed.

The furniture. The only furniture in a law office that requires special comment is the *legal blank cabinet*. Every law office uses a large variety of printed legal blanks. They must be kept in good condition and must be quickly available for use. A cabinet has been designed for this special purpose. It consists of shallow drawers the length and width of the blanks. See the lower left-hand corner of Figure 4.

As in any office, secretarial desks are preferable to typewriter desks if the person using the desk has any clerical work to do.

Decoration. Dignity should mark the decoration and furnishings of the law office. When you are asked to make suggestions about decorating the office, remember:

1. Decorations should be subdued. Select draperies with a self-colored design, not a gaily colored floral design.

2. Carpets should be a monotone, preferably dark.

3. If a general office is used for the waiting room and the workroom, suggest rubber tile for the floor.

4. Portraits of famous judges and lawyers, with a few etchings, are appropriate. Avoid unframed pictures and unnecessary calendars.

5. It is customary to hang on the wall framed diplomas and certificates of admission to the bar of firm members. Clients seem to gain confidence from them.

Equipment. In addition to the equipment found in almost every office, two items are practically indispensable in a modern law office: a copyholder and an electric typewriter. A copyholder has an adjustable line-spacing attachment that decreases the possibility of skipping or repeating lines when you are doing copy work. The attachment is operated by depressing a lever with the right little finger. This movement soon becomes as automatic as depressing the space bar on a typewriter. Another advantage of the copyholder is that it is placed back of the typewriter and holds the paper in front of you, thus avoiding the strained position necessary when copying from material placed on the side of the desk. There are several makes of copyholders, but they all work on the same general principle.

An electric typewriter is not only less fatiguing than one operated manually, but the operator is able to make many more legible copies at one time. Numerous copies are frequently necessary in legal work. Typewriters with pica instead of elite type are standard in law offices, because court papers must be written in the larger type. A few offices have typewriters with elite type for correspondence and for filling in printed forms, but the majority of offices use the pica typewriter for all purposes.

Stationery supplies. In addition to the usual stationery used for correspondence, law offices have many kinds of paper for legal work. The stationery supplies used for various purposes in a typical law office follow.

"Legal cap" is white paper, 8″ by 13″ or 8½″ by 14″, with a wide ruled margin at the left and a narrow ruled margin at the right. It is used for court papers and for legal instruments, such as agreements, contracts, and the like. Substance 16 is used for the original or ribbon copy. Legal cap, substance 20, is preferable for the original of wills; substance 13 for the carbon copies. In some states, legal cap has numbers along the left margin.

Bond or onion skin legal cap is used for the carbon copies, substance 13 or 9 if no more than 8 copies are made; substance 9, for more than 8 copies. Some offices use substance 16 (same as ribbon copy) for the office copy because it is more durable.

"Legal-size" paper, plain without the ruled margins, same substance as the legal cap, is also used for legal instruments of various kinds and for court papers in some jurisdictions. See Table VII in Chapter 12 for those jurisdictions in which plain legal-size paper is used for court papers.

Short white paper, approximately 8″ by 10½″, with ruled margins, substance 16, is used for the ribbon copy of briefs and law memoranda; substance 9 or 13 for the carbon copies.

Short white paper, approximately 8″ by 10½″, plain without ruled margins, is used for legal documents that are not written on long paper. The choice varies with the office.

"Manuscript covers" are of a heavy colored paper, usually blue, about 25 per cent cotton fiber. Legal instruments and court papers are bound in them.

Legal-size covers, with or without the firm name, are used for binding legal instruments and court papers. Legal-size covers with a printed panel are frequently used for binding court papers. These covers are referred to as *backs,* because they cover only the back of the paper bound in them.

White covers, with or without the firm name engraved on them, are used for binding wills.

Short covers, with or without the firm name, are used for binding briefs, law memoranda, and legal instruments that are typed on short paper. They are double and are bound at the side.

Legal-size yellow manifold is used for drafts.

Legal scratch pads are pads of 8½″ by 12½″ yellow paper, with ruled margin and lines. See that there is always one on the lawyer's desk and one in his brief case. He uses the pads for making notes, writing drafts in longhand, and the like.

"Firm letterheads," 8½″ by 11″, substance 24, 20, or 16, are used for the original of firm correspondence. Some firms also have an 8½″ by 7½″ letterhead for short letters.

"Continuation sheets," loosely called second sheets, of the same substance as the letterheads are used for additional pages of a letter. They do not have a letterhead on them but usually have the firm name engraved or printed on them.

"Firm letterheads," marked "copy," on unglazed onion skin, substance 9, are used for copies of correspondence.

Colored onion skin or yellow manifold is used for the file copy of correspondence.

"Executive letterheads," 6″ by 7″, engraved with the attorney's name, is used for the attorney's personal correspondence. This paper frequently has a kid finish.

"Monarch" size envelopes, 3⅞″ by 7½″ are used with the executive stationery. No. 6¾ (3⅝″ by 6½″) and No. 10 (4⅛″ by 9½″) envelopes fit the 8½″ by 11″ letterheads.

Envelopes of heavy manila stock (about 40 pounds), 3½″ bottom flap, 3½″ top flap gummed solid, with a ¾″ scored shoulder also gummed, are used for mailing bulky documents and papers that can be folded.

A New Matter

New case report. When a new matter is received in a law office, it must be processed in a routine manner before the lawyer actually begins to work on it. In the well-organized law office, a new case report is made immediately on every matter received. The lawyer who interviews the client obtains from him the following information:

1. Name, address, and telephone number of the client.
2. Name of opposing party, and his address and telephone number, if known.
3. Attorney for opposing party, if any.

Occasionally these data are given to the secretary by the client as he leaves the office, but it is usually more diplomatic for the lawyer to make a note of the information.

What the secretary does. The secretary's first job is to get the information from the lawyer as soon as the client leaves the office, so that she can make up a new case report. The reports also call for one or more of the following items of information, which the lawyer should indicate to the secretary.

1. The general nature of the case, whether general litigation, probate, foreclosure, etc.
2. Whether the case is on an annual retainer basis or is a single case. This affects the bookkeeping (Chapter 7).
3. Whether the client is new or old.
4. Whether stenographic services are to be billed separately or included in the over-all fee.
5. Name of the junior partner or associate, if any, to be assigned to the case.

Printed forms are provided for new case reports, or they may be mimeographed. Frequently the lawyer himself makes out the reports, because they call for very little writing. Two types of forms are illustrated in Figures 5 and 6. Notice that the form

MORGAN, BURBANK & CHAMBERS
REPORT OF NEW CASE OR MATTER
MUST BE TYPEWRITTEN

Date:
Name of Client:

CLASSIFICATION
☐ General Litigation
☐ Corporate and Financial
☐ Indiv. Pers., Trust

Address:
Title of Case or Matter:

☐ Estate and Litigation as to Estate

REAL ESTATE
☐ General
☐ Certiorari

Court:
Member in Charge:
Assistant:

☐ Dispossess
☐ Foreclosure

(CHECK AND RETURN PROMPTLY)

1. Charge Register:............................ 2. Managing Clerk:............................ 3. Bookkeepers:............................
4. Budget Committee:............................ 5. Files:............................

Figure 5. New Case Report.

HALL and DOBB
NEW CASE REPORT

File No.

Received by...

For Credit of..   Date..

Attorney receiving a new case will fill out this blank, sign it, and then send it to Files.

Files will assign the file number, index under the names given in 1 to 4; note any instructions as to filing in 5; initial

here...................and send to Assistant Managing Partner.

Assistant Managing Partner will assign attorneys, initial, etc. and send to the Accounting Department.

Accounting Department will see that the report is properly filled out, service ledger cards made, open a service ledger

account, and initial here..   ....
                                               Submitted by   Verified by

Accounting Department will list on weekly summary and initial here...

Estimated Value of Case $_____	Add to Firm Announcement List		Billing		Client	
	Yes ☐ No ☐		Retainer or Continuing	Single Cases	New	Old
Nature of Case			☐	☐	☐	☐

1. Name of Client...

   Address...

   ....

2. Title of Case...

   ....

3. Opposing Party...

   Address...

   ....

4. Additional Names (if any)...

   that should be indexed...

   (Additional names should be given where the name of the person referring the case or the name of a person with whom there is to be much correspondence does not appear in 1, 2, or 3 above.)

5. Filing Instructions (if any)...

6. Remarks...

Received by Assistant Managing Partner:...................Date...................at...................

Attorney Responsible...   Will case be litigated?

Assistant Assigned...   No   ☐

Junior Assigned...   Yes   ☐

2800 2-51 C.8.P. FORM 1A   Doubtful ☐

From Reginald Heber Smith, Law Office Organization. *Courtesy American Bar Association Journal.*

Figure 6. New Case Report—Another Form.

illustrated in Figure 6 even has a space in which the attorney indicates whether or not the client is to be added to the firm announcement list described on page 7.

When the report is filled out, it is ready to be routed.

Routing of new case report. The routing procedure varies with the office, but the following order of routing is practical and can be adapted to the requirements of any office. If you are a secretary in a small office, instead of routing the new case report you will take the steps indicated by this procedure.

1. File department. File number is assigned and a file opened. File clerk initials. (Chapter 4.)

2. Accounting department. Ledger sheet for the client and case is opened, after which disbursements may be made for and charged to the case. (Chapter 7.) Bookkeeper initials.

In an extremely large firm, there might be other departments or committees to which the report should be routed.

The new case is then returned to the filing department and filed. The mechanics of processing the case have been completed, and the attorney and his secretary are ready to work on it. The matter might consist of drawing an instrument (Part II), in which event the file will soon be closed (Chapter 4); or it might involve litigation (Part III) that extends over a period of years; or it might be a matter in a specialized field of law (Part IV), such as organizing a corporation (Chapter 18). Regardless of the nature of the case, you, as secretary, will have dictation and typing about it (Chapter 8), and, very probably, you will have contact with the client either in person or by telephone (Chapter 2).

The subsequent chapters of this book will show you how to do in a professional manner any task that might arise in connection with the case.

2

Contacts with Clients and Other Callers

THE LAWYER's secretary has far more contacts with clients, both in person and over the telephone, than the secretary in a business office usually has with customers. Furthermore, every caller is a potential client, and every client with a small claim is a potentially valuable client. You can appreciate, therefore, the importance of your attitude and conduct in your relations with clients and callers.

Certain situations requiring tact and diplomacy arise repeatedly in the course of the secretary's contacts with clients and other callers. Basic precepts govern the handling of these situations, but the application of the precepts varies with the secretary's personality, the office in which she works, and the individual client or caller. In this chapter, we give fundamental instructions and make suggestions about how to handle certain difficult phases of contacts in person and over the telephone.

The secretary's introduction to the client. In law offices where the "team" spirit prevails, the lawyer always introduces the client and the secretary, in the same manner that he makes a social introduction. He presents a man client to the secretary; he presents the secretary to a woman client. He explains to the client that the secretary always knows where to reach him; that if the client telephones when he is out, the secretary will answer his questions or get the answer from another member of the firm. In an emergency she will get in touch with him. The lawyer further explains to the client that he has the utmost confidence in the secretary and that she necessarily knows about the client's problem. The client gradually comes to know the secretary personally and to have a high regard and respect for her efficiency.

The secretary's contacts thus promote the goodwill of the client and are of inestimable value to the lawyer.

Basic precepts. Good manners, judgment, and discretion should control your attitude in your contacts with clients and other callers. Your tone of voice should always be warm, cordial, and respectful, without subservience. The tone of voice is especially important over the telephone, because you cannot show your interest by your facial expressions. Guard against the tendency to let your voice become mechanical and without expression.

On a new job the lawyer will probably give you explicit instructions about certain clients, but he will expect you to observe the following precepts without instructions from him.

1. Find out the name of a caller and the purpose of his call.

2. Never discuss with one client the affairs of another.

3. Guard against letting your knowledge of a client's legal difficulties color your attitude toward the client.

4. Never give legal advice.

5. Maintain the goodwill of the caller and make his contact with the firm pleasant and satisfactory.

6. Judge which clients the employer will welcome, which he wants to avoid, which should be seen by another lawyer in the firm, and which you should take care of yourself.

7. Make explanations to those callers whom the lawyer will not see, without antagonizing the caller.

Contacts in Person

Contacts in person with clients. You should be prepared to handle certain situations that occur frequently in law offices. You might make a mistake, but you may be sure that the lawyer will back you up in presence of the caller. If he thinks you made a mistake, he will tell you so privately and will point out to you how you should have handled the matter. These situations are:

1. A client calls without an appointment, and the lawyer cannot see him.

2. A client calls without an appointment, but the lawyer will see him.

3. A stranger wants legal advice.

4. A client is early for an appointment.

5. A client is hysterical.

6. A client invites you to dinner.
7. A client gives you a present or offers payment for work done for him.
8. A client wants to see a file.
9. A salesman wants to see the lawyer.

Suggestions are given here on how to meet the foregoing situations.

Client calls without an appointment. The client, Mr. Edwards, calls to see Mr. Rogers, the attorney.

Secretary: Good afternoon, Mr. Edwards. Is there something I can do for you?

Mr. Edwards: I'd like to see Mr. Rogers. Is he in?

Lawyer cannot see the client

Secretary: Yes, he is here, but he will be unable to see you this afternoon, Mr. Edwards. He expects to be busy with the gentleman who is with him now until after closing time. I'm sorry. Can anyone else help you?

Mr. Edwards: No, I have to see him. I'm from out of town. I didn't make an appointment because I didn't know when I'd get here. It would only take a little while.

Secretary: I'm very sorry, but he asked me not to disturb him or to make any more appointments for this afternoon. Could you come some other day? I'd be glad to make a future appointment.

Mr. Edwards: Well, I don't know when I will be back this way again, and it's very important.

From this point, the secretary must depend on her own judgment as to whether the client is someone the lawyer would want to make an exception for or whether she should dismiss him as inoffensively as possible. If she has been the secretary for a long time, she may be able to induce him to see another lawyer in the office or to handle the matter temporarily herself. The important thing is to follow orders without offending the client.

If she is a new secretary, she should probably excuse herself and ask another lawyer in the firm to come out and speak to Mr. Edwards. The other lawyer could also tell her whether or not Mr. Rogers would like to be notified that Mr. Edwards has called. The new secretary should hesitate to take the responsibility of turning away an out-of-town client. Under the circumstances, no reasonable attorney could censure her for letting him know that the client is calling. If the client were not from out of town, she should insist politely but firmly that she cannot disobey her instructions.

Lawyer will see the client

Secretary: I'm sorry I failed to note your name on Mr. Rogers' appointment book for today. What time did you have an appointment?

The secretary knows Mr. Edwards did not have an appointment, but this is a diplomatic way of bringing to his attention that he should always make an appointment before calling. It also prompts him to tell the secretary the amount of time the interview will require. Of course, the secretary's voice should be especially friendly and courteous.

Mr. Edwards: I didn't have an appointment today, but I'll take only a few minutes of his time.

Secretary: I'm sure Mr. Rogers will be glad to see you for a few minutes, Mr. Edwards. Won't you have a seat? Would you care to look at the paper while you are waiting?

The phrase "for a few minutes," said without emphasis, lets the client know that the lawyer has other appointments and that he should be brief.

If Mr. Rogers is alone when Mr. Edwards calls without an appointment, after asking the caller to be seated, take the file to Mr. Rogers and tell him that Mr. Edwards is waiting and would like to see him for a few minutes.

If Mr. Rogers is in conference and you know that he will be finished within a short time, inform the client of this and ask him to wait. If you expect Mr. Rogers to be busy for some time and you know that it is all right for you to interrupt him, ring him on the interoffice phone and ask him if he would come outside to see Mr. Edwards for a few minutes. If Mr. Rogers cannot be interrupted for some time, make this suggestion to the client:

Secretary: I'm sorry but Mr. Rogers will be unable to see you for about an hour, Mr. Edwards. Do you have some other business in town that you could attend to and then come back in about that length of time?

Stranger who wants legal advice. A man whom the secretary has never seen before comes into the office. The following conversation might take place.

Secretary: How do you do. May I help you?
Mr. Jones: I'd like to see Mr. Rogers.
Secretary: May I have your name, please?
Mr. Jones: Jones—Robert A. Jones.
Secretary: I don't believe you have an appointment, do you, Mr. Jones?
Mr. Jones: No.
Secretary: Have you consulted Mr. Rogers before?
Mr. Jones: No, I haven't.
Secretary: May I ask who referred you to him?

Up to this point, the secretary does not know whether Mr. Jones is calling about a legal matter or not, but the answer to her last question should enable her to classify the caller.

Mr. Jones: A friend of mine, George King—Mr. Rogers handled a case for him once.
Secretary: Oh, yes, Mr. King. And may I ask the nature of your problem, Mr. Jones?
Mr. Jones: I had an automobile accident last week.
Secretary: I'm sorry to hear that. I am sure that Mr. Rogers can help you, but he is busy right now. Could I make an appointment for you to see him later today, say, 4:45 this afternoon?
Mr. Jones: Couldn't I wait now?
Secretary: I'm afraid he will be busy for some time, and then he has another appointment. It would be better if you could come back. Would tomorrow be more convenient?
Mr. Jones: No, I guess this afternoon would be better.
Secretary: I'm sorry that he can't see you now. It's too bad you didn't telephone for an appointment. I'll put you down for 4:45 this afternoon.
Mr. Jones: I'll be here then.
Secretary: Good-by.

You should also get the telephone number of the caller so that if the lawyer cannot keep the appointment you can notify the caller. When the appointment is made for several days in advance, give the caller the attorney's card as a reminder. The telephone conversation with the stranger who telephones for an appointment (page 32) is also applicable to a call in person.

A client is early for an appointment. A nuisance in a law office is the client who always arrives considerably ahead of appointment time and expects to carry on a conversation with the secretary until time for the appointment. You should offer the client a paper or a magazine and continue with your work. Discussion with the client not only is a waste of your employer's time; it is not good form. Of course, this suggestion does not mean that you should be unfriendly or refuse to acknowledge remarks made by the client; it does mean that you should discourage the client from conversing with you.

Hysterical clients. It sometimes happens that a distraught woman client becomes hysterical in the office. If so, take her to the rest room and make an effort to calm her. Then suggest that perhaps she would like to postpone the appointment until she feels better. Since the hysteria is sometimes brought on by discussing the case with the secretary while waiting for the appointment, the secretary must try to direct the conversation away from the client's immediate concern.

Invitations from clients. A basic rule of office conduct is that office life and social life must be kept apart. This rule is particularly applicable to the contact between a lawyer's secretary and his clients. If the social contact proves disagreeable in any way, the unpleasantness may be reflected in the professional contact, and may even result in loss of the client. The secretary, therefore, should not accept social invitations from clients whom she has met in the lawyer's office. You may make an exception to this rule and accept an invitation from a client whom you have known a long time, provided you first ask the lawyer if he thinks it is all right for you to accept the invitation.

Presents and payment for work. Oftentimes the secretary is required to do some special work for out-of-town clients or associate counsels and is offered a present or payment for the work. Gifts of candy, cigarettes, and the like may be accepted without permission from the lawyer. It is also appropriate to accept Christmas presents, with your employer's consent, provided they are not very expensive. You should never accept expensive personal gifts from a client.

You do not accept payment for work done for a client or associate counsel when the work is done on the lawyer's time.

When client or counsel requests you to work overtime or at night on a special job that is not connected with your work, you are entitled to payment. You should consult your employer before agreeing to do the work. The acceptance of payment for work done after hours on a matter that is connected with your job requires careful consideration. It is permissible, though not always desirable, to accept payment, provided you are offered a lump sum and are not asked the price of your services, and provided your employer is willing. Many secretaries feel that extra payment by the client or associate counsel is in the nature of a gratuity and do not wish to accept it for this reason. On the other hand, clients and associate counsel are genuinely appreciative of the extra effort on their behalf and are merely trying to show their gratitude. Refusal of their offer might easily offend them. You, of course, should be guided entirely by the extent of the service and your employer's views.

Client wants to see a file. Frequently a client stops in the office to look over papers in a file. It is not usually necessary to disturb the lawyer for this reason. Ask the client exactly what papers he would like to examine, remove them from the file, and hand them to him, if he is entitled to see them. He is entitled to examine papers that are his, such as a mortgage or deed. He is also entitled to examine other papers of which he has personal knowledge or which are of public record, such as court papers and transcripts of testimony taken in his presence. He is not entitled to examine the lawyer's working papers, correspondence about his case, or any other papers of which he does not have personal knowledge. Never hand an entire file to a client without express permission. Of course, he is not supposed to take any of the papers out of the office, unless the lawyer says that he may.

Salesmen. Salesmen are frequent visitors to law offices. You will soon learn to distinguish between those whom the lawyer is interested in seeing and those who are not welcome.

Law book salesmen. Law books, services, and periodicals are tools with which a lawyer works, and he buys them readily. Almost all lawyers are interested in seeing the salesmen who sell this equipment, if time permits. You soon become familiar with the names of the various publishing houses and with their salesmen. Unless otherwise instructed, you can let the law book salesman see the lawyer at the time of his call, if convenient, or you can make a future appointment for him. It is to the advantage of the salesman to talk to the lawyer when he is not distracted or pressed for time. If you make an appointment that the lawyer cannot keep, be punctilious in notifying the salesman before he comes to the office. Remember that the salesman's time is worth money and that his services are useful to the lawyer.

Magazine salesmen, peddlers, and the like. Although practically all office buildings have large signs prohibiting magazine salesmen, peddlers, and the like, they occasionally get into your office. They read the name of the firm on the door and walk in and ask to see one or more members of the firm. Often there is no visible means of detecting that the caller is in this class. When you ask the stranger who referred him to the attorney (see page 24), he will probably be evasive if he is selling and will tell you that he will require only a few minutes time. A rule that must be strictly observed is: Never let a stranger into the lawyer's private office unless you are positive he is not a magazine salesman or peddler.

Contacts over the Telephone

Importance of telephone contacts. Telephone contacts are of paramount importance in a law office. The secretary must know how to answer and make calls smoothly, how to talk into the instrument, and how to take messages for the lawyer, as well as what to say. Here, in addition to the fundamentals of telephone techniques, examples are given on handling telephone calls in the following situations:

1. A stranger calls for an appointment but is reluctant to divulge the nature of his business.
2. An irate client telephones while the lawyer is out.
3. A client or prospective client asks the fee for certain services.

Rules of telephone courtesy. The following simple rules constitute the basis of courteous and efficient telephone usage:

1. Answer calls promptly.
2. When you leave your desk, arrange for someone to take your calls.
3. Keep pad and pencil handy.
4. In asking a caller to wait, say, "Will you please hold the

line while I get the information," and wait for the reply. When you return to the telephone, thank the caller for waiting. If it will take you some time to get the information, offer to call back.

5. If you have to put the receiver down for any reason, put it down gently.

6. Do not interrupt or be impatient. Listen attentively. Do not make the other party repeat because of your inattention.

7. Do not try to talk with a cigarette or pencil in your mouth.

8. When you have finished talking, say, "Thank you, Mr. Smith," or "Good-by," pleasantly and replace the receiver gently. Let the caller hang up first.

Placing calls for the lawyer. The correct practice to follow when you place calls for the lawyer has developed from expediency. When *you* place the call, it is your privilege to get the person called on the wire before connecting your employer. Assume that you are calling Mr. Wilson for the lawyer, Mr. Rogers. When you get Mr. Wilson's secretary on the wire, you say, "Is Mr. Wilson there, for Mr. Rogers?" Then Mr. Wilson's secretary will put her employer on and trust to your good judgment and care to see that Mr. Rogers comes on the line promptly. (When she calls your employer, you reciprocate the courtesy.) When Mr. Wilson comes on the line, say to him, "Here is Mr. Rogers, Mr. Wilson," and establish the connection between the two men at once.

You must be extremely careful not to keep the person called waiting for the lawyer to take the call. On the other hand, it is your job to see that he does not hold the phone needlessly. When you are calling a person whose secretary is cooperative and dependable, there is no difficulty because you and she can connect your employers simultaneously.

There is an exception to this procedure. If you call a close friend or a person to whom deference is due by the lawyer, connect him as soon as you talk to the secretary at the other end of the line. Tell the lawyer that the person he is calling will be on the line immediately and let him receive the call direct. Some secretaries follow this procedure at all times. However, the practice described above is preferred because the person making the call is alert to take it and, therefore, time for both the caller and the person called is saved in the long run.

Long distance, or toll, calls. A record must be kept of every long distance, or toll, call that is placed from your office. These calls are usually made on behalf of a client and are charged to his account. Always ask the operator to tell you the amount of the charge and make a memorandum immediately. Figure 7 illustrates a useful printed form. After you fill in the details, give it

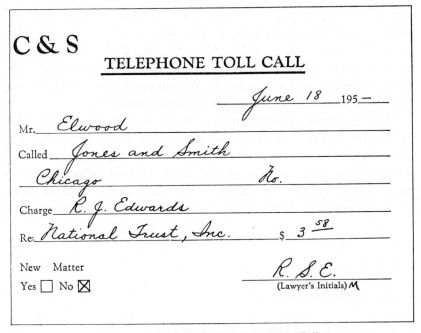

Figure 7. Record of Toll Telephone Call.

to the lawyer who made the call so that he can initial it. As his secretary, you will probably have the authority to initial it for him. The illustration shows that the secretary initialed the form for the lawyer and placed her own initial beneath his initials. The form is then sent to the bookkeeper. If you keep the books, you should have a folder for telephone call memoranda, against which you can check the bill and make the charges to clients' accounts.

When clients place toll calls. Clients frequently ask permission to place a telephone call. Quite often these calls are toll calls and the question of payment for them might present an embarrassing situation. The thoughtful client immediately suggests payment, but many excellent clients simply do not think about payment. Keep a record of these calls and bill the client for them, unless special circumstances make it more diplomatic for the law firm to charge the call to overhead.

Answering calls for the lawyer. If a secretary calls and tells you that her employer wants to speak with a certain lawyer in your office, ask her to wait a moment and announce the call to the lawyer. Say to the secretary, "One moment, please," and tell the lawyer that "Mr. Wilson of ABC is calling." The lawyer will then pick up the phone and wait until Mr. Wilson is connected with him. Or perhaps the other secretary has learned that you are cooperative and she puts Mr. Wilson on the line at the same time that you connect the call with your employer.

Making notes of incoming calls. It is important that the lawyer be informed of every call that comes in for him, whether the caller leaves a message or not. Do not depend upon memory for this, but make a note immediately. If your office does not have printed forms for this purpose, you might suggest that some be ordered. They are not expensive and are convenient,

---

C & S

....195.......

TELEPHONE MESSAGE for Mr...

Mr...called at...................o'clock

He was told that you were:	He said (left):
out....................................☐	no message................................☐
not in to-day.....................☐	he will call again...................☐
not in your room.............☐	he is answering your call ☐
talking on telephone......☐	please call him.......................☐
out of town......................☐	please see him........................☐
to call him back.............☐	it is urgent.............................☐

His telephone number is..

Additional remarks:..

....

....

....

Figure 8. Telephone Message Memo.

easy-to-read, and neat. Figures 8 and 9 illustrate useful forms. Keep a pad of the form on your desk—and on the desk of everybody in the office who takes telephone messages.

Form No. 30

Telephone Call Memo

Date_____.

Place this slip under telephone instrument on desk of

Mr._____

_____

Mr. _____

Tel. No._____

Called you at_____M.

Message:

Refused Name

No Message

Please Call

Will Call

Please See

_____

Telephone operators are expected to report on this form every call which does not reach the person called, regardless of instructions from the person calling. If no message, so state.

Figure 9. Telephone Message Memo—Another Form.

Screening calls for the lawyer. A lawyer usually expects his secretary to screen his calls; otherwise his calls do not go through the secretary but are put through directly to him.

A polite way of asking who is calling is, "May I tell Mr. Rogers who is calling?" Or, "May I ask who is calling?" A legitimate caller seldom objects to giving his name.

If the caller does not want to give his name, you have the right to insist, politely but firmly, that he do so. As a matter of fact, you have no right to put through calls without first screening them, when this is expected of you, and without learning that the lawyer is willing to talk. If the caller insists upon withholding his name you might say, very politely, "I'm very sorry, but Mr. Rogers has someone with him at the moment. If you cannot tell me who is calling, may I suggest that you write to him and mark your letter 'personal'? I'll be glad to see that he gets it promptly."

Finding the purpose of a call. A secretary is usually expected to find out why a person wants an appointment with her employer. This frequently poses a delicate problem in the law office, because callers are often reluctant to disclose the nature of their legal business. However, knowledge of what the client wants frequently enables the secretary to save considerable time, not only for the lawyer but also for the prospective client. This situation is illustrated by the following conversation between a secretary and Mr. Wilson, the caller.

Secretary: Rogers & Williams. (The practice in answering the telephone varies. In some offices, the practice is to answer the telephone with the number.)

Mr. Wilson: This is James Wilson. I'd like an appointment to see Mr. Rogers, please.

Secretary: I am Mr. Rogers' secretary, Mr. Wilson, and I'll be pleased to arrange an appointment for you. Approximately what date and time would you like to see Mr. Rogers?

Informing the caller that you are the lawyer's secretary gives him an opening to tell you the nature of his business. But this caller did not respond in the manner the secretary desired.

Mr. Wilson: I would like to see him on Tuesday afternoon, say around 2 o'clock.

Secretary: Mr. Rogers will be busy part of the afternoon on Tuesday, Mr. Wilson. About how long will you require for your appointment?

This gives the caller another opportunity to state the nature of his business, but Mr. Wilson is rather elusive.

Mr. Wilson: I will not require more than an hour of his time. How about two to three?

Now comes the difficult part. You must find out what he wants and you must do it diplomatically. The "voice with a smile" is especially important here.

Secretary: In connection with a client's visit, Mr. Wilson, it is often necessary for Mr. Rogers to have certain forms or information available. In order that I may have everything in readiness for your appointment on Tuesday, could you give me a general idea about the nature of your business? I do not need to know any of the details, of course, just a brief statement.

By giving him a good reason for your inquiry and assuring him that you are not interested in details, you have asked him, in a gracious and courteous manner, for a statement concerning his appointment.

Perhaps he says he wants a divorce. You know that Mr. Rogers will not handle the case but that it will be turned over to a junior member of the firm.

Secretary: Mr. Davis of this office usually handles matters of that kind and confers with Mr. Rogers regarding them when necessary. It would really be better for you to see Mr. Davis on Tuesday. If agreeable to you, I'll arrange the appointment with Mr. Davis instead of Mr. Rogers.

Or perhaps Mr. Wilson says that he has a small collection matter he would like Mr. Rogers to handle. Your office does not handle collections except for retainer clients.

Secretary: I'm sorry, Mr. Wilson. As much as Mr. Rogers would like to help you, he does not handle collections. However, Mr. Robert Ames, a young member of the Bar located in this building, would be pleased to handle the matter for you. Would you like his telephone number?

There are innumerable situations, but by exercising discretion and diplomacy you will soon be able to handle them all.

An irate client calls. Occasionally a client who is annoyed about something telephones while the lawyer is out. It is usually advisable to avoid making explanations to him. Simply tell him that you will ask the lawyer to call as soon as he returns—and make sure that you tell the lawyer about his call. No matter how good a secretary you are, how tactful and diplomatic, some things must be handled by the lawyer, and annoyed clients belong at the top of the list.

Client or prospective client asks what a fee will be. Many clients and prospective clients try to find out over the telephone what the lawyer will charge for certain services. A lawyer's secretary should *never* quote fees; that is for the lawyer to do. As a matter of fact, the lawyer himself does not like to quote fees until he is thoroughly familiar with the amount of work involved. For example, the fee for drawing a simple will is not as much as the fee for drawing a will that involves a trust. When a client asks you what a fee will be, offer to make an appointment for him with the lawyer. If he does not want an appointment, offer to have the lawyer call him.

Your telephone conversation. If you have to make a telephone call for the lawyer, plan your conversation before placing the call. Know your facts. Know the points you want to cover. If necessary, have an outline of them before you while you talk. Have all records and other material before you. This is particularly important on out-of-town calls.

Identify yourself immediately to the person to whom you are speaking, thus, "This is Miss Smith, Mr. Roger's secretary," or, "This is Miss Smith of the firm of Rogers and Williams." It is neither necessary nor desirable to give your first name.

Keep your telephone conversation brief but not to the point of curtness. Take time to address people by their names and title and to use expressions of consideration, like "Thank you," "I am sorry," and "I beg your pardon."

Desk telephone lists. You should keep on your desk an up-to-date directory of the name, address, and telephone number of the following:

Law Business Numbers

Attorneys associated in current cases (temporary listing)
Attorney available for various kinds of matters that your
    office does not handle

Attorneys on opposite side of current cases (temporary listing)
Auctioneers
Bonding companies
Collection agencies
Consuls
Court reporters
Courts
Custodians
Deputy sheriffs
Detectives
Engineers
Engravers
Investigators
Law journals
Law stationers
Libraries
Marshals
Mimeographers
Newspapers
Photographers
Printers
Process servers
Translators

Office Administration Numbers

Airlines
Building manager or superintendent
Emergency calls (Fire, Police, Ambulance, etc.)
Express office
Messenger service
Post Office
Railroads
Residence of employees in your office
Stationer (office supplies)
Telegraph office
Time of day
Typewriter repairs
Weather

Lawyer's Personal Telephone Numbers

Bank
Dentist
Doctors
Family (residence and business)
Florist
Friends whom he calls frequently
Garage
Organizations to which he belongs
Services (dry cleaner, tailor, etc.)
Stores that he trades with
Travel agency
Theater ticket agency

3

Reminder Systems and Practices

EVERY SECRETARY in a law office has the responsibility of seeing that certain things are done at certain times. The need for an infallible system of reminders is imperative, because failure to take legal action at the time required might have irreparable consequences. *For any reminder system to function properly, the secretary must keep it accurately and must refer to it each day.*

Three reminder systems are described in this chapter: (1) the diary, (2) the card tickler, and (3) follow-up files, none of which is a complete substitute for the other. Suggestions are also made for methods of reminding the lawyer of his appointments and things to do.

The Diary

What is a diary? A diary is not only a record of future appointments and work to be done but also a daily record of what is actually accomplished. It is kept from year to year and furnishes a permanent record of appointments, dates that cases were tried, and time spent with clients in or out of office or in court. The diary has a separate page printed for each day in the year. Many standard yearbooks are designed for lawyers and are entirely satisfactory—the important thing is that they should have space for work actually done and the time consumed doing it as well as space for appointments and matters to be attended to. In many law offices, especially those in which several attorneys practice, time records and charges are kept on charge sheets (see Chapter 7). In such instances it is not necessary to use a diary that provides space for work done and time consumed

Figure 10 illustrates a page from a lawyer's diary. See also the Daily Page, illustrated in Chapter 7 (Figure 23), which serves as an appointment book and as a convenient place to record all services and charges connected with a client's business. Chapter 15 describes suit registers, or court dockets. These are progress

Saturday, APRIL 21		112th Day

9:45 – Dept. 2 – King V. Smith – Trial

11:00 – Mr. S. A. Murray (Tr. 7491)

(ax.– 7230 – chg. Smith V. City)

4:30 – Harbor Committee Meeting

Last day to file Op. Br. – Allen V. City
Pay jury fee Deposit – Linn V. Fall

Clients Name and Address	Work Done	Time
King (Arthur L.) 207 Sunset Ave.	Briefing Trial	2 hrs. 4 hrs.

Figure 10. Page from Lawyer's Diary.

records of litigation; advance entries in the diary are essential as reminders to take the necessary action.

Diaries that you should keep. Two diaries are required, one for the lawyer and one for you, but the entries are not completely duplicated. In the lawyer's diary, enter all of his appointments and important days he should remember, such as his wife's birthday. If the important days are not noted, he may inadvertently make conflicting engagements. Do not enter in his diary items that are merely reminders to you, such as days on which checks should be written. Watch his diary closely for appointments he makes without telling you.

In your own diary, enter notations of your own business activities and appointments, as well as the lawyer's appointments and the things that you will have to remind him about.

If you are responsible for following court cases for more than one lawyer, as well as being responsible for personal matters for a member of the firm, it will be less confusing to keep all court matters in a separate diary.

How to make up diaries. Keep a list of items that go in the diary year after year (see checklist below). As soon as diaries for the forthcoming year are available, enter all of the recurring items, events, and appointments under the appropriate date. In preparing the diaries, work from the list, not from the previous year's diary, because dates for events change. For example, if the board meetings of a corporation client are held on the first Monday of every month, the actual dates vary from year to year. In making an entry, be certain that the date is not Sunday or a holiday. Enter notations of additional appointments and things to do as soon as you learn about them.

Enter time-consuming tasks that must be done by a certain date sufficiently *in advance* to permit the work to be finished on time. Also make an entry under the date on which the action must be taken. The practice of making advance entries is very important and will save you and the lawyer the strain of having to prepare material on short notice. It is not usually necessary to make advance entries in the lawyer's diary—you can remind him of work to be done. (See page 49.) Underline important due dates and deadlines in red.

When dates call for presents or cards, enter a reminder in

your diary, about ten days before the date, as well as on the date. Christmas presents and card lists should be brought up about six weeks before Christmas, the exact time depending upon local shopping conditions.

Advance notice of payments of large sums should also be entered in the diary. The lawyer's funds might be low, or he might want to negotiate a renewal of a loan.

How to make entries about legal work. Under the date upon which a step must be taken, make an entry setting forth (1) the title of the matter, (2) the time and place for the step, and (3) the nature of the act to be performed, fully described. If you keep the diary for more than one lawyer, also include the initials of the lawyer or lawyers interested. The third example of entries, below, indicates that a brief must be prepared. This entry should also be made under an advance date (see above), with a notation of the date the briefs must be ready. Form the habit of making entries in the diary immediately upon learning that they should be made. *Allow no telephone calls or other interruptions to interfere.*

Examples of entries:

> Joan Wilson Estate—pay on account New York Estate Tax to obtain benefit of 5% discount.   RSF

> International Jones Co.—Clerk's Office, U. S. Court House, Foley Square—Order to show cause returnable why certain claims should not be compromised.   NEL

> Richards v. Rogers (both actions)—Last day to serve and file reply briefs.
>   RSF:NEL

How to obtain information for entries. Information necessary to make these entries is obtained in various ways:

1. Observe the dates and the places mentioned in papers that your firm prepares and in those served on it by opposing counsel. For example, an order in the International Jones Co. case would read, in part:

"ORDERED that the plaintiff or his attorney show cause, . . . at the office of the Clerk of the United States District Court for the Southern District of New York in the United States Court House, Foley Square, Borough of Manhattan, City of New York, on the 18th day of July, 19.., at 10:30 o'clock in the forenoon. . . ."

Obviously, you know that a diary entry should be made under date of July 18 and that the place is the Clerk's Office, U. S. Court House, Foley Square.

2. Observe the date a notice is served on your office, or your office serves a notice.

3. Calculate the time prescribed by law or rules of law for answering, replying to, or moving to dismiss or correct a pleading when a pleading is served on your office. You can get this information from the practice rules of the court.

4. Calculate the time for taking any step when the time limit for that step runs from some other act of which you have notice.

5. *Ask the lawyer for diary dates whenever you do not have them or do not know how to calculate them.*

It would be impossible to set forth here all of the instances and time limits that affect litigation; not only are they numerous, but they vary with the state. Knowledge of them is gained by experience and study. The lawyer is responsible for knowing them and instructing you accordingly; *you* are responsible for making notations in the diary in accordance with his instructions and for asking him to give you those instructions. A few diaries have an appendix of timetables of procedure and court rules for specific states, which are very helpful to the legal secretary.

Checklist of entries to make in diary. Here is a checklist of the items that the secretary usually enters in the appropriate diary:

Appointments
   Clients, in and out of office
   Doctor and dentist
   Social, evening and daytime

Court Work
   Return dates on summons
   Deadlines for filing pleadings and serving copies on opposing counsel
   Deadlines for serving notices in probate court

Hearings
Pre-trial conferences with court and opposing counsel
Trial dates

Family Dates

Anniversaries
Birthdays
Mother's Day
Father's Day

Holidays

Christmas
Easter
Election Day
Independence Day
Labor Day
Religious holidays
Thanksgiving
Valentine's Day

Meetings

Board meetings
Club meetings
Committee meetings
Stockholders' meetings
Bar association meetings

Payment Dates

Bar association dues
Contributions
Insurance premiums
Interest on notes payable and maturity dates
Periodic payments, such as salaries, rent, allowances to children, tuition, and the like

Renewal Dates

Automobile license
Hunting and fishing licenses
Subscriptions to periodicals

Tax Dates

Federal income tax returns and payment dates for clients and for the lawyer's personal tax
Federal estate tax returns for clients
Social security tax returns and payments

State and local taxes
Unemployment tax returns and payments
Withholding tax returns and payments

Tickler card file. A tickler card file has a tabbed guide for each month of the year and 31 tabbed guides, one for each day of the month. The daily guides are placed behind the current month guide. Memoranda are made on cards or slips, which are filed behind the daily guide according to the date on which the matter is to be brought up.

Use of tickler card file with diary. Generally, secretaries in law offices do not like to depend upon tickler cards as reminders for deadlines, hearings, trial dates, and other legal work. It is too easy to lose or misplace a small 3″ by 5″ card or slip, and the resulting damage might be irreparable. Furthermore, tickler cards do not constitute a permanent record of the day's activities as a diary does.

Tickler cards can be used in conjunction with a diary very satisfactorily. They reduce the work necessary in making diary entries. Recurring items can be put on one card, and the card can be moved from week to week, month to month, or year to year. Thus, if a certain check is made out each Friday, you can make one card and move it each week, instead of making 52 entries in your diary. Also, you can put all necessary information on the card so that you or anyone else can attend to the task without referring to any other material. Tickler cards are also particularly useful for indefinite date follow-ups. If the lawyer has told you he wants to do a certain job sometime within the next few months, you can make a card and move it from time to time if he does not do the task when you first bring it to his attention.

A tickler card file *does not* take the place of a diary for noting appointments. All appointments, even regularly recurring ones, should be entered in the diary; otherwise, whenever you want to make an appointment you will have to look not only in the diary but also at the tickler.

Refer to the diary every afternoon for the following day and to the tickler each morning.

Checklist of entries of work accomplished. The purpose of making entries in the diary of work accomplished and time consumed is to charge the client for the work. Therefore, any time consumed in behalf of a client should be entered unless a separate time sheet is kept. This time includes:

Dictation
Appointments
Conferences
Closings
Interviewing witnesses
Trials
Hearings
Arguments
Research
Some telephone calls
Some stenographic work

Follow-up Files

Necessity for follow-up files. If all the matters in a law office that had to be followed were entered in the diary, it would become so cluttered it would lose its usefulness. Therefore, follow-up, or tickler, files are a useful supplement to the diary. A notation or reminder, usually a carbon copy, is placed in the tickler file while the material itself remains in its proper place in the regular files. If the material itself is placed in the follow-up file instead of in the regular file, it cannot be located if it is needed before the follow-up date.

Checklist of material to be placed in follow-up files. Court cases are preferably followed through the diary, but the following matters are generally followed through follow-up files rather than through the diary:

1. Matters that are referred to other lawyers or law clerks in the office for information, comment, or action.

2. Correspondence or memoranda awaiting answer.

3. Collection letters (see also Chapter 24).

4. Covering letters enclosing documents sent by registered mail, until receipt is received.

5. Requests for acknowledgments of documents, etc.

6. Receipts for documents left with court clerks or other officials for recording.

7. Letters to Register of Deeds, or other officials, enclosing

papers for recording, to be kept until papers are returned and delivered to client.

8. Letters to abstract company.

Equipment for follow-up system. Numerous styles of equipment for follow-up purposes are on the market, but many secretaries to busy lawyers have found the follow-up file system described here to be practical, efficient, and time saving.

The only equipment necessary is a file drawer and file folders. Make a set of file folders consisting of (a) 12 folders labeled from January through December, (b) 31 folders labeled from 1 through 31, and (c) 1 folder marked "Future Years." If you have a heavy volume of follow-up material, it is advisable to have two sets of folders labeled by days—one for the current month and one for the succeeding month.

Tabbed guides marked 1 through 31 and removable separators tabbed with the months will make it easier to locate a particular folder, but these are not necessary to the efficient functioning of the system.

Arrangement of folders for follow-up. Arrange the folders labeled by days in numerical order in the front of the file. Place in these the follow-up material for the current month. The folder labeled for the current month is at the back of the other monthly folders ready to receive any material to be followed up in the same month next year. Immediately following the numerical daily folders is the folder for the coming month, followed by the folder for the succeeding month, and so on.

Operation of the follow-up system. 1. Make an extra copy of correspondence or memoranda that require a follow-up, preferably on paper of a different color. Mark on the extra carbon the date on which it is to be followed up. When there is no carbon copy of material for follow-up, write a brief memo for the tickler file. For example, if your employer gives you a newspaper clipping and tells you to bring it to his attention on the 30th of the month, prepare a tickler memo (on the same color paper as the follow-up carbon copy of correspondence) for follow-up on the 30th, but file the clipping so that you can put your hands on it if your employer wants it before the 30th. The memo should indicate where the material is filed. File any pertinent papers in the regular files.

2. Place material that is to be followed up in the current month in the proper date folders. Each day transfer the empty daily folder back of the folder for the coming month. Thus you always have 31 daily folders for follow-ups, part of them for the remaining days in the current month and part of them for the first part of the coming month. Place material that is to be followed up more than 30 or 31 days in the future in the proper month folder, regardless of the day of follow-up. See Figure 11, which is a diagram of the arrangement of folders on April 15. On that day, material to be followed up from April 16 through May 15 is

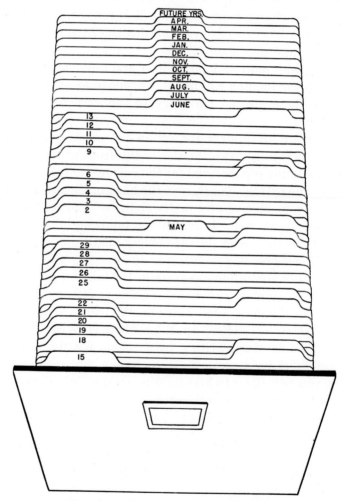

Figure 11. Diagram of Follow-Up Files.

placed in daily folders; material to be followed up after May 15 is placed in the proper month folder.

3. On the first of each month, transfer the material from the folder for that month into the folders labeled by days. To avoid filing material for follow-up on Saturdays (if the office closes), Sundays, or holidays, reverse the folders for those days so that the blank side of the label faces the front of the file. Notice in Figure 11 that the folders for April 16, 17, 23, 24, 30 and 31 (since April has only 30 days), and May 1, 7, 8, and 14 are blank. The empty folder for the current month is then transferred to the rear of the other month-by-month folders.

How to handle material in the daily follow-up file. Each day when you examine your follow-up file you will find that a large part of the material has been answered without a follow-up. Destroy these carbons or memoranda. If a heavy schedule keeps you from giving attention to all the material in the daily folder, mark the less important items for follow-up at a later date.

Move indefinite follow-ups forward from week to week until a definite date is established or until the matter is completed. This procedure is often referred to as "combing-back."

Follow-ups on a small scale. When you have only a small amount of correspondence or other matters to follow up, a set of follow-up file folders is not necessary. Mark the carbons with the follow-up date and file them chronologically in one folder, with those marked for the earliest follow-up on top.

Tickler card file for follow-up. A tickler card file is as useful as follow-up file folders for any type of material except correspondence. You can type a notation for yourself on a card and place it in a tickler card file as easily as you can type a memorandum and put it in a file folder. But it is a waste of time to make a card notation of correspondence when you can make an extra carbon at the time of transcription. Therefore, unless you have only a small amount of correspondence to follow up and handle it as described in the preceding paragraph, use follow-up file folders instead of a tickler card.

Reminding the Lawyer of Things to Be Done

Necessity for reminder. It is advisable for a secretary in a new job to ask the lawyer if he likes to be reminded of things to be done and if he has a preference as to the method. His diary shows his appointments and the things he has to do. For many lawyers, placing the diary, open at the current date, in a conspicuous place on his desk is sufficient.

Suggestions for other methods of reminding the lawyer of things to do follow.

How to remind the lawyer of appointments. In the late afternoon, or the first thing in the morning, place on the lawyer's desk a typed schedule of his appointments, giving him all the pertinent information. Memorandum paper about 6″ by 9″ is desirable for this purpose. Before the time of the appointment give the lawyer the file and other material that he will need for it.

Reminders showing appointments for a month. Many lawyers like to see the month's engagements at a glance. There are calendars designed for this purpose, usually on cardboard about 9″ by 11″. Figure 12 is an illustration of such a calendar. Note that under the arrangement of dates on this calendar, every Sunday in the month is on the top row, every Monday on the next row, and so on.

NOVEMBER

	Sunday, 6th	Sunday, 13th	Sunday, 20th	Sunday, 27th
	Monday, 7th	Monday, 14th	Monday, 21st	Monday, 28th
Tuesday, 1st	Tuesday, 8th	Tuesday, 15th	Tuesday, 22nd	Tuesday, 29th
Wednesday, 2nd	Wednesday, 9th	Wednesday, 16th	Wednesday, 23rd	Wednesday, 30th
Thursday, 3rd	Thursday, 10th	Thursday, 17th	Thursday, 24th Thanksgiving Day	
Friday, 4th	Friday, 11th	Friday, 18th	Friday, 25th	CALENDAR 19__
Saturday, 5th	Saturday, 12th	Saturday, 19th	Saturday, 26th	

Figure 12. Appointment Calendar for a Month.

How to remind the lawyer of things to be done. To remind the lawyer of a task that he should do, place the file on his desk, with a memorandum if necessary. For example, if a real estate closing is scheduled for the 29th and papers must be drawn for it, put the file on his desk about the 27th with a memo that the closing is scheduled for the 29th.

If the lawyer told you that he wants to do a certain thing in connection with a matter, attach a reminder to the file. For example, suppose he told you, "If we do not receive that information from Robinson by Friday, I want to obtain a stipulation postponing his case another week." On Friday, if the information has not been received, you type a memo, "You wanted to obtain a stipulation to postpone this case," and attach it to the Robinson file before placing it on the lawyer's desk. It might be even better for you to type the stipulation and give it to him with the file. This procedure would depend on your experience and the lawyer's wishes in connection with delegating such duties to you.

Some lawyers make a practice of calling their secretaries into their office the first thing every morning to dispose of the correspondence and to discuss pending matters and things to be done. This is the ideal arrangement. For the discussion, you take with you a list of things to be done and any material pertaining to them, as well as your notebook.

How to remind the lawyer of court work. In a large office a diary of court cases is maintained by the managing clerk under the supervision of the managing attorney. Although each lawyer in charge of a matter is presumed to know its status, it is the duty of the managing clerk to follow the status of the matter, to furnish information regarding the status, and to aid in securing prompt and orderly disposition of court matters. In a comparatively small office, you, as secretary to the senior partner or to the managing partner, will probably have this responsibility.

From your diary records, send a written notice to the lawyer in charge, sufficiently in advance to permit him to make preparations necessary to take the indicated step. Figure 13 is a printed form, filled out, that is used for this purpose. Mimeographed or typed slips would serve the purpose. The lawyer in charge of

MORGAN, BURBANK & CHAMBERS
Managing Clerk's Department

To ..... Mr. Edwards ....

Reference   Wilson   vs.   Green

Time: October 22,   19 -- . at 10 AM.

Place: County Court House, Department B

Action

    Last day to

    Motion for order dismissing complaint

    Settlement of

    Examination of

    Hearing

    Trial

    Argument

    ....

                           ESR
           ....
                 Managing Clerk

Dated..... October 19 ...., 19 --

(Please note below disposition of matter and return to
Managing Clerk.)

Attended and argued in support of motion.
Decision reserved.

                         J. T. E.

Figure 13. Notice of Diary Entry.

the matter should return the written notice to you with a notation of the action taken.

Another method of reminding the lawyers in your office about pending court work is to type the entries from your diary each week for two weeks in advance, making as many copies as necessary to circulate among the lawyers. In an office with numerous attorneys, the list would be mimeographed. Each lawyer then checks the cases in which he is interested. You will recall that the diary entries include the initials of the interested lawyers.

If you are secretary to a lawyer who receives a notice from the managing clerk, or from the secretary to the managing partner, check your diary and see that preparations necessary to take the required action are made.

4

Filing in the Law Office

LAWYERS usually want specific file folders, papers, or letters in a hurry, and one of your most important duties is to produce them promptly. No matter what system of filing you use, the accuracy with which you file determines whether you will be able to find the desired material without extended searching and fumbling. Remember that a paper misplaced even temporarily causes embarrassment to you and to the lawyer and can mean a lost client.

Your filing system should be so well organized that someone besides you can find papers when needed. You might know where a paper is because you put it there, but no one else will be able to locate it. "Memory" filing is not a filing system.

In this chapter we classify the material to be filed and describe the methods appropriate to the material. We also tell how to prepare the material for filing and how to arrange the papers so that disorderly files and unnecessary searching will be avoided.

Classification of files. It is expedient to segregate files pertaining to clients' business from files pertaining to personal and office administration matters. The following classification of files is appropriate for the typical law office:

1. *Clients' business.* Files in this category include all matters relating to clients, with the exception of commercial collections when handled in volume. Some offices separate the material into litigation and non-litigation matters. Other offices segregate files relating to a particular field of law if a large part of the practice is in a specific field. Still other offices segregate matters relating to a retainer client with a large volume of business. The least con-

fusing method, however, is to keep all the files of each client together.

Since clients' files constitute by far the major part of the files in a law office, the detailed explanations in this chapter of the numerical and alphabetical systems of filing relate to clients' files.

2. *Commercial collections.* Where a fair volume of commercial collections is handled, the files are segregated from other clients' business because of the close follow-up on these cases. Chapter 24, "Handling Commercial Collections," describes fully the system of filing used for these cases.

3. *Personal files.* The lawyer's personal file contains material relating to the lawyer's personal business matters, correspondence, and outside activities, such as bar association committees.

4. *General correspondence files.* This is the miscellaneous or "catch-all" file. It contains all material not relating to clients' business or to the lawyer's personal matters. Office administration material, such as personnel applications and records, correspondence about office equipment, correspondence with law book publishers, and the like would be placed in this file. Correspondence about a case that the lawyer does not accept would be filed here.

5. *Periodicals, bulletins, etc.* Every office accumulates pamphlets, booklets, periodicals, and the like that contain information likely to be needed in the future.

Numerical System of Filing Applied to Clients' Files

What is the numerical system of filing? Under the numerical system of filing, each file is given a number, and the folders are arranged in numerical sequence. This is an indirect filing system since it must be used in connection with a cross-index. The subject and number of each file are put on an index card, and the cards are arranged alphabetically. The advantages of the numerical system are the rapidity and accuracy of refiling and the opportunity for unlimited expansion. The disadvantages are the maintenance of the auxiliary card index and the necessity of making two searches, one of the index and one of the files, whenever papers or folders are withdrawn.

How to use the numerical system in a law office. A method of numerical filing used successfully in law offices is to give a key number to a client instead of to a case. Each case for that client is given the client's key number plus an identifying number or letter. An explanation of how to set up and maintain a filing system of this kind follows. There are variations in the details, but to point them out here would only cause confusion.

1. Assign a key number to the client in numerical sequence. His general file has this number. Then assign an identifying *number* to each matter that is litigation and an identifying *letter* to each matter that is not litigation. For example, Client Brown & Rogers, Inc. has a file of general correspondence, a profit-sharing plan for employees, and a suit against Ellis & Lewis Co. You give the general file the number 85, the profit-sharing file the number 85-A, and the suit the number 85-1. The next suit will be 85-2. (If you prefer, you might identify all files by number or letter instead of using numbers for the suits and letters for the non-suit files, but the number and letter system segregates the client's court matters from his non-litigation matters in the file cabinet and in the card index.)

2. Make index cards under each name that appears in connection with the matter. In some instances, for example estate matters, your client's name does not appear in the subject of the file; nevertheless a card should be made in the client's name.

Type on the card the title of the case, the number assigned to it, and the client's name if it does not appear in the title. In a matter of litigation the card under the defendant's name will read *defendant ads. plaintiff,* instead of plaintiff vs. defendant. If the matter is not a suit or claim, type on the card, in addition to the client's name, an identifying description of the subject matter. For example:

Brown & Rogers, Inc.
Profit-sharing Plan

It is not necessary but you might also make a card under the subject, which would read:

Profit-sharing Plan
Brown & Rogers, Inc.

Make index cards and cross-index cards freely, and be liberal

in the information that you type on them. They are the key to
your filing system and eventually justify the time consumed in
typing them. Figures 14a, b and c illustrate three types of index
cards. Figures 14a and b are printed especially for law offices.
See page 63 for an explanation of the entries on 14c.

Doe, John ads Thomas Green (Client)			
Document File	**Correspondence File**	**Printed Papers**	**Storage**
152-1	152-1		

Figure 14a. File Index Card.

3. File the index cards alphabetically. When there is more than
one card under a client's name, place them in this order: general
card, non-litigation cards arranged alphabetically according to
subject, litigation cards arranged alphabetically according to

Jones, John v. Smith, Allen				81-5
Correspondence	DOCUMENTS	PRINTED PAPERS	GENERAL SAFE	
81-5	81-5	Cabinet 2		
Cabinet #2 - Extra copies of Briefs, case on appeal, etc.				

Figure 14b. File Index Card—Another Form.

Brown, John A.	395-1
vs Acme Printing Company Blue Book Paper File Duplicates	

Figure 14c. File Index Card—Another Form.

opposing party. Suppose a client has a general file and five other files. The cards will be arranged as follows:

Brown & Rogers, Inc	52
Brown & Rogers, Inc.—Arbitration	52-B
Brown & Rogers, Inc.—Legislation	52-C
Brown & Rogers, Inc.—Profit-sharing Plan	52-A
Brown & Rogers, Inc. vs. Jones	52-2
Brown & Rogers, Inc. ads. Matthews	52-1

If the client's cases are numerous, you might put a guide card between the litigation and non-litigation to facilitate locating the desired card.

4. File the folders in numercial sequence according to key number. If there is more than one file for a client, arrange those bearing identifying letters in alphabetical sequence; follow with those bearing identifying numbers in numerical sequence. Thus, in the cabinet, all files pertaining to one client are together; all of his non-litigation matters are together, and all suits and claims are together.

5. Keep a card showing the key number to be assigned to the next client in front of the index box.

6. When a client brings a case to the office, give the client a

key number and assign the case an identifying letter or number. Reserve the key number, without identifying letters or numbers, for the client's general correspondence should it become desirable to have a file of that nature for him.

7. Reserve a key number for miscellaneous clients, who might want a letter written for them or have some small matter involving only one or two papers. These matters can be filed under the same key number, but all necessary index cards should be made.

Assigning numbers according to type of case. When files are separated according to type of case, a group of numbers is set aside for each category. For example, cases involving litigation will be numbered 1 through 199; probate cases, 200 through 399, and so on. The client does not have a key number. A list of available numbers is kept for each category, and the number of a closed file is placed on the appropriate list and used again.

Another method of numbering when files are separated according to type of case is for each category to have a separate sequence of numbers. There might be, for example, a Claim 485 and a Probate 485. Different colored labels or folders should be used for each category.

How to transfer numerical files. Apparently it is against the lawyer's conscience to destroy a file. Consequently all available space in the office is used for retired files, and the overflow is sent to a warehouse, or to the attic, or to any place where space is available. The procedure followed by many firms is to retain in the office as many closed files as space permits; and from time to time to send the oldest closed files to outside storage, replacing them in the office with more recently closed files. When there are retired files in the office, the active files might be kept in the top drawers of the filing cabinets and the retired files in the lower drawers. The retired files are referred to only occasionally, and by using the top drawers for active files, stooping and bending are eliminated. We use the words *closed* and *retired* interchangeably here.

Law files are not retired periodically but are closed when the matter is presumably completed. A file opened in 1950 might be completed and ready for retirement in 1951, whereas a case opened in 1945 might remain active until 1955, or longer.

Ideally you should process a file for retirement as soon as you are informed that the matter has been completed, without permitting an accumulation. But this is a job that secretaries are inclined to postpone until there is a lull in the work. As soon as you are informed that the matter has been completed, stamp the file jacket "closed." Then when time permits, you can go through your filing cabinets and withdraw all closed cases and process them for retirement. Use old jackets for storage files.

Here are the steps in processing a file for retirement or storage.

1. Withdraw from the active index all cards relating to the closed case. Stamp the cards "Closed" with a small rubber stamp. If you wish you might also stamp the date on the card. You will notice that the index card illustrated in Figure 14a has a column for this purpose, and the card shown in Figure 14b has a column that can be designated *storage*.

2. Withdraw from the active files all jackets or folders holding papers that relate to the completed case. Your index card will indicate whether there are extra copies or printed papers that have been removed from the regular filing cabinet. (See Figure 14b.) The documents in the safe will not be sent to storage. They will be returned to the client, or other appropriate disposition will be made of them.

3. Keep your index of closed files separate from your index of active files.

4. File the index cards in the closed card index, alphabetically, just as they were filed in the current index.

5. File the closed files in the transfer cabinets numerically just as they were filed in the active files.

Alphabetical System of Filing Applied to Clients' Files

What is the alphabetical system of filing? Under the alphabetical system of filing, the folders are filed alphabetically according to name or subject. A cross-index is not necessary with this system of filing but is frequently desirable. The principal advantage of the alphabetical system of filing is that it is not necessary to look up a file number in a cross-index when papers or folders are filed or withdrawn. The disadvantages are that the system does not lend itself to expansion as readily as the numerical system and requires more shifting of folders. The alphabetical system is also widely used in law offices.

How to use the alphabetical system. Each client has a general folder and each of his matters has a separate folder. All matters of a specific client are filed under his name. The order of arrangement of the various folders is similar to that of the index cards in a numerical system: The general folder comes first and is followed by the non-suit files arranged alphabetically according to subject. These are followed by the litigation files arranged alphabetically according to opposing party. The various matters of Client Desmond & Lake, Inc. might be labeled and filed as follows:

Desmond & Lake, Inc.—General
Desmond & Lake, Inc.—Arbitration—R. E. Brown
Desmond & Lake, Inc.—Arbitration—L. F. Jones
Desmond & Lake, Inc.—Profit-sharing Plan
Desmond & Lake, Inc. ads. Bates & Co.
Desmond & Lake, Inc. vs. Cordell Lighting Effects Co.

If the active files of a client are very numerous, they might be numbered and a card index made of that client's files.

Another method of using the alphabetical system in a law office is to file under the name of the plaintiff, whether the plaintiff is the client or not. Lawyers have a tendency to think of suits and claims in terms of plaintiff vs. defendant. Non-litigation matters are filed under the name of the client. When this method of filing is followed, cross-index cards are desirable. Make the index cards in the name of the client and others connected with the case, and show on the card under which name the folder is filed.

How to transfer alphabetical files. When alphabetical files are closed or transferred to storage, cross-index cards *must* be made. The simplest method of transferring them is to assign the file a transfer number and make cross-index cards for each party connected with the matter. The files are then placed in the storage files in numerical order. This avoids shifting of files.

Some offices transfer alphabetically. The file drawers are then

numbered and the drawer number in which the file is placed is
indicated on the cross-index cards. Each year's transferred files
may be filed together alphabetically. However, this entails shifting of files from drawer to drawer unless ample space under each
letter is kept open for files to be stored under that letter in the
future.

Other Files

Personal file. The personal file is a combination name and subject file, and the alphabetical system of filing is used for it. A
twenty-five division alphabetical guide will probably be sufficient; no cross-index is needed.

Make a folder for each letter of the alphabet. File the correspondence under the first letter of the correspondent's last name,
according to date. Thus, correspondence with Mr. Moss and with
Mr. Matthews will be in the same folder. If the lawyer has
prolific correspondence with a certain person, make a separate
folder for that correspondent. Also make a separate folder for
each separate business matter and outside activity. Thus, if the
lawyer is on the Grievance Committee of the American Bar
Association, there will be a folder labeled: "American Bar Association—Grievance Committee," and the folder will be filed
under the letter *A*. Should the material for any particular subject
become voluminous withdraw it from the alphabetical file and file
it under a guide of its own.

Close these files periodically by moving them to another drawer
in the office where they will be available for reference if necessary. The correspondence folders can probably be transferred in-
tact, or several letters of the alphabet combined in one folder
to save space. However, it will probably be necessary to go
through the subject folders, such as the "American Bar Association—Grievance Committee" folder, and extract material that is
pertinent to the forthcoming year. Transfer the closed files from
the office to storage when they are several years old, to make room
in the office for the more recent personal files.

General correspondence file. The alphabetical system should
be used for this file. It is operated in the same manner as the
personal files. File according to the name of the correspondent.
The division of the alphabetical guide needed will depend upon

the volume of miscellaneous material. No card index is necessary.

Close and transfer these files periodically by the same method that you close and transfer the lawyer's personal files.

Periodicals, bulletins, etc. File these alphabetically according to subject. The filing cabinet used for them need not be fireproof, and a twenty-five division alphabetical guide will be sufficient. This material will consist of government bulletins, advertisements, catalogues, announcements of changes in law firms, announcements from law schools, and any other material of this nature that the lawyer wishes to keep. Periodically you should go through the file and discard material that is out of date.

Physical Setup of Files

Preparation of material for filing. To prepare material for filing, do the following:

1. Segregate papers belonging in different files: clients' matters; personal; general correspondence.

2. Check to see if the lawyer has initialed the paper for filing. (In offices with more than one attorney, there should be a hard and fast rule that no paper is to be filed until the responsible attorney has initialed it.)

3. Check through all papers that are clipped or stapled together to see whether they should be filed together.

4. Remove all paper clips.

5. Mend torn papers with Scotch tape.

6. See that all legal documents have been conformed.

7. Mark on all court papers the date they were filed with the clerk of the court or served upon opposing counsel. (This information is stamped by the clerk of the court on the back of the paper and is not evident when the paper is fastened to the folder unless noted on the face of the paper.)

8. Note on the paper where it is to be filed. For numerical files, write the key and identification numbers in the upper right-hand corner; for a name file, underline the name in colored pencil; for a subject file, write the subject in colored pencil in the upper right-hand corner, or underline it in colored pencil if it appears on the paper.

9. Punch a hole or holes in the *exact* place where the paper should be fastened to the folder. An electric gadget that punches

holes in the paper is a valuable time-saver when thick documents must be stapled into folders.

10. When fastening the paper in the folder, check the number and name on the paper being filed with the number and name on the folder.

How to type index tabs and labels. For best results in typing tabs, guides, and folder labels, observe the following rules:

Use the briefest possible designations. Abbreviate, omitting punctuation whenever possible. Index tabs need to be legible only at normal reading distance. Guide labels should be legible at two or three feet. File drawer labels should be legible at six feet.

Use initials caps whenever needed. Full caps, especially in elite and pica type, do not increase the legibility of label designations; they decrease the amount of light background around the letters and make reading more difficult. Do not underline.

Folder labels. The most important part of a folder label is the eighth of an inch immediately below the scoring (the place at which the label is folded when it is pasted on the folder tab). Frequently this space is the only part visible in the file. Therefore, start at the first typing space below the scoring. Typing should begin in the first or second typing space from the left edge of the label, except for one or two character designations. If this is done, all folder labels in the file drawer will present an even left margin.

Use initial caps and indent the second and third lines so that the first word of the first line will stand out.

In typing labels for a numbered subject or name file, leave space between the number and first word; type the subject in block form. Avoid exceptionally long file numbers if possible.

Guide labels. For file guide labels, use the largest type available. Begin the typing as high on the label as the guide tabs will permit. Center one- and two-character designations. Start all other designations in the second typing space from the left edge. Use abbreviations or shortened forms and omit punctuation, except for large numbers such as 10,000.

File drawer labels. In preparing labels for file drawers, use the largest type available. Center the typing on the label and leave a double space above and below detailed reference information. It is better to print file drawer labels because type is not legible at a distance.

How to arrange the papers in the file folders. A file in a law matter consists of at least two parts: correspondence and formal documents, whether they be court papers or legal instruments such as agreements, leases, and the like. Each file must have a correspondence folder and a document folder, both of which are kept together in the file jacket. It does not matter what kind of "folder" is used, as long as it has enough firmness to serve as a backing sheet to which the papers may be fastened with a brad or other fastener that permits removal when desired. Correspondence and papers are both filed in their respective folders according to date, usually with the latest on top, although some lawyers prefer the reverse order. Always keep the correspondence folder on top of the document folder in the jacket.

A file might consist of more than two parts. Separate folders are required for briefs and law memoranda; drafts; extra copies; miscellaneous memoranda, such as interoffice memos, notes made by the lawyer, etc. If a file contains both legal instruments (agreements, contracts, and the like) and court papers, a separate folder is made for each. If a case has papers filed in more than one court, a separate folder is made for each court. A law file might also contain a folder for "hold papers," that is, papers belonging to the client other than those kept in the safe. The "hold papers" should not be fastened in the folder. Always indicate on the index card the folders that are made up in each case. For example, the index card illustrated in Figure 14c indicates that a blue book, a file for duplicates, and a paper file have been made in the case. (*Blue book* denotes, in the office whose card is illustrated, the folder in which important papers, such as wills and agreements, are filed; *paper file* denotes the folder for miscellaneous memoranda.)

As a file grows, it is broken down into volumes, with all letters together in one or two folders, all court papers together, and so on. Law files frequently become so voluminous that two or more jackets are required. All of the jackets in a particular case have the same number. On each jacket, write the classification of the contents of that jacket—that is, the folders that are in the jacket—so that you will not have to open more than one jacket to find the desired papers. Some offices make a separate index card for each jacket.

If you do not think a matter will become sufficiently voluminous to warrant separate folders and a jacket, use a legal size folder and fasten the documents to the right side, and the correspondence to the left. Either an Acco or a Kompact fastener is useful for this purpose. Some offices do not put the file folders in a jacket, but simply file them together. This eliminates having to open a jacket in order to get out the folder that is needed.

Write the title of the case, the client's name, and the number of the file on each folder and on the jacket. Figure 15 illustrates a properly labeled jacket.

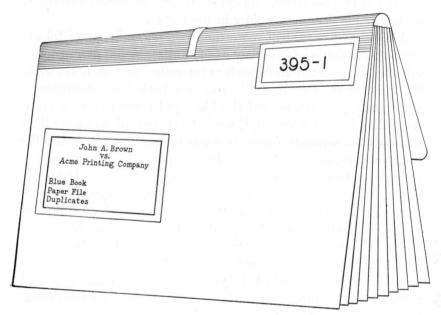

Figure 15. File Jacket Properly Labeled.

Preparation for closing a file. When closing a file, go through it carefully and remove all paper clips, pins, and the like. This procedure eliminates the possibility of storing papers that do not belong in that particular file. Quite often a misplaced paper is found, and removal of the clips reduces the size of the file. If a file has several jackets, you might be able to combine the contents into one jacket. Papers and folders in a closed file may be packed more tightly than those in an active file.

Extra copies and printed papers, drafts. A legal file usually contains extra copies and drafts of various documents. These should have separate folders. Extra copies, especially of printed papers, quickly become voluminous and impede the process of filing. Whether you have 5 or 50 cases with voluminous extra copies, try to set aside an extra filing cabinet or drawer for them. You may file them in the same order as the regular file. Notice that the index cards illustrated in Figures 14a and b have a column headed "Printed Papers." Indicate in this column (or elsewhere on the index card if you use another kind), that extra copies have been removed from the regular file. The same procedure may be followed with voluminous drafts.

Control of material taken from the files. To control folders taken from your files, use guides the same height as the file folders but of different-colored stock, with the word *out* printed on the tab. The *out* guide provides space on which to make an entry of the date, the material taken, who has it, and date it should be returned. Place the guide in the files where the removed material was located.

A secretary in a private office does not put an *out* guide in her file every time she withdraws material for the lawyer. She uses the guide under these circumstances: (1) Someone outside her immediate office wants the material. (2) The lawyer expects to take the material out of the office, say, when he goes on a trip. (3) She expects her employer to keep the material a week or so, say, to prepare a brief.

When a paper is removed from a folder, make a note of the removal and insert in the folder. Many law offices have a rule (and it is a good one) that no one may remove a paper from a folder except the person responsible for the filing.

5

Correspondence and Telegrams in the Law Office

A LETTER is one of the few forms of "advertising" permitted to the legal profession. It represents the combined efforts of the lawyer and his secretary. The lawyer's contribution is the text; the secretary is responsible for its appearance. If the mechanical presentation of the lawyer's work is careless, inaccurate, or unpleasing to the eye, the lawyer's good work is apt to suffer and perhaps be lost altogether. On the other hand, the secretary can greatly enhance the effectiveness of the lawyer's work by setting the letter up attractively and typing it accurately and neatly.

Styles of letter setups. The styles in which letters are usually set up in the law office are the semi-block style (Figure 16) and the indented style (Figure 17). Law offices have been slow to adopt the more modern styles used extensively in business offices. The official style (Figure 18) is used frequently for informal letters written to personal acquaintances.

Semi-block style. The distinguishing feature of the semi-block style of letter is that all structural parts of the letter begin flush with the left-hand margin, but the first line of each paragraph is indented ten spaces. Carry-over lines in the address are indented three spaces. All lines of the typed signature are aligned with the complimentary close. The date is typed in the conventional position.

Indented style. The distinguishing feature of the indented style of letter is that each line of address is indented five spaces more than the preceding line. The first line of each paragraph is indented ten spaces, which aligns the paragraphs with the third

CONNELLY, KARTER & MARTIN

627 Ingraham Building

Miami, Florida

Charles E. Connelly
Theodore B. Karter
Christopher A. Martin
Walter W. Ott
Louis T. Kobbe
Walter R. Behnke

March 25, 19--

Messrs. Smith Jones Nelson
35 Fifth Avenue
New York 11, New York

Dear Sirs:

Re: Semi-Block Style of Letter

This is an example of the semi-block style of letter. Many law firms prefer it to the indented style because it combines utility with an attractive appearance.

As you can see, the inside address is blocked. The first line of each paragraph is indented ten spaces. As in all letters, there is a double space between paragraphs.

The date line is flush with the right margin, two or four spaces below the letterhead. The subject line is two spaces below the salutation and is centered. The complimentary close begins slightly to the right of the center of the page. All lines of the signature are aligned with the complimentary close. Open punctuation is used in the address.

No identification line is used in this example. As the dictator's name is typed in the signature, his initials are not necessary. The typist's initials are shown on the carbon copy.

Very truly yours,

Robert E. Adams

Figure 16. Semi-Block Style of Letter.

(The distinguishing feature of a Semi-Block Style of letter is that all structural parts of the letter begin flush with the left-hand margin, but the first line of each paragraph is indented five or ten spaces. All lines of the typed signature are aligned with the complimentary close. The date is typed in the conventional position. Open punctuation is used.)

CONNELLY, KARTER & MARTIN

627 Ingraham Building

Charles E. Connelly
Theodore B. Karter
Christopher A. Martin
Walter W. Ott
Louis T. Kobbe
Walter R. Behnke

Miami, Florida

March 25, 19--

Mr. N. E. Edwards, Office Manager,
　　Elwood & Adams,
　　　　35 Fifth Avenue,
　　　　　　New York 11, New York

Dear Mr. Edwards:

　　　　　　In re: Indented Style of Letter

　　　　　This is an example of the indented style of letter.
I am enclosing three sheets from our Correspondence Manual
that describe the other forms in which you are interested.

　　　　　Many conservative law firms still use the indented
style as they prefer it to new forms. The indented style is
correct, however, for any type of organization.

　　　　　Each line of the address is indented five spaces
more than the preceding line. The beginning of each paragraph is indented the same as the third line of the address,
which is ten spaces. The complimentary close begins a few
spaces to the right of the center of the page. Each line
of the signature is indented three spaces from the beginning of the complimentary close. Close punctuation is used
in the address but not in the signature.

　　　　　　　　　　Sincerely yours,

　　　　　　　　　　John E. Marsh

jmh
Enclosures 3

Figure 17. Indented Style of Letter.

(*The distinguishing feature of the Indented Style of letter is that each line of address is indented five spaces more than the preceding line. The first line of each paragraph is indented ten spaces. If the name is typed in the signature, it is typed flush with the complimentary close, but each additional line is indented three spaces.*)

CONNELLY, KARTER & MARTIN

627 Ingraham Building

Miami, Florida

Charles E. Connelly
Theodore B. Karter
Christopher A. Martin
Walter W. Ott
Louis T. Kobbe
Walter R. Behnke

March 25, 19--

Dear Mr. Edwards:

This letter is an example of the official style. It is used in many personal letters written by executives and professional men, and looks unusually well on the executive-size letterhead.

The structural parts of the letter differ from the standard arrangement only in the position of the inside address. The salutation is placed two to five spaces below the date line, depending upon the length of the letter. It establishes the left margin of the letter. The inside address is written in block form, flush with the left margin, from two to five spaces below the final line of the signature. Open punctuation is used in the address.

Letters written in this style do not usually have a subject line. The identification line, if used, should be placed two spaces below the last line of the address, and the enclosure mark two spaces below that. As the dictator's name is typed in the signature, it is not necessary for the letter to carry an identification line. The typist's initials are on the carbon copy of the letter, but not on the original.

Very truly yours,

Thomas E. Richards

Mr. N. E. Edwards, Office Manager
Elwood & Adams
35 Fifth Avenue
New York 11, New York

Figure 18. Official Style of Letter.

(The distinguishing feature of the Official Style of letter is that the inside address is placed below the signature, flush with the left-hand margin, instead of before the salutation. The identification line and enclosure notations, if any, are typed two spaces below the last line of the address. Open punctuation is used. The style is especially appropriate for the lawyer's personal letters.)

line of address. Each line of the typed signature is indented three or four spaces from the beginning of the complimentary close.

Official style. The distinguishing feature of the official style of letter is that the inside address is placed below the signature, flush with the left-hand margin, instead of before the salutation. The address may be blocked or indented. The identification line and enclosure notations, if any, are typed two spaces below the last line of the address.

Opinion letters. Opinion letters are formal letters giving a professional opinion to a client on some legal question. Each law firm has its own method of setting them up, usually in the style that is used for ordinary letters. These letters are generally signed manually by a partner with the firm name, because they represent advice from the firm, not merely from the lawyer who dictated the letter. Usually the dictator's initials do not show on the original but do show on the office copies.

Punctuation. Either close or open punctuation may be used in the structural parts of a letter. Close punctuation means punctuation marks after the date line, each line of the address, the complimentary close, and each line of the signature. *Open punctuation* means the omission of punctuation marks after each of these parts, unless a line ends in an abbreviation.

The generally approved practice is to use close punctuation in an indented style of address and to use open punctuation in a block style of address. Whether open or close punctuation is used in the address, (1) the period after the date line is omitted, (2) a comma is usually placed after the complimentary close, and (3) the comma is omitted after each line of the signature.

Subject line. In any letter, a subject line makes it unnecessary for the writer to devote the first paragraph of the letter to a routine explanation of its subject. In correspondence about law matters the subject line is a necessity as well as a convenience. The correspondence is filed according to the subject and not according to the name of the correspondent, and, frequently, it is difficult to deduce from the letter the matter to which it refers. Since the subject is actually part of the body of the letter, it should follow the salutation. Preferably, it is centered two spaces below the salutation, and is preceded by *Re* or *In re* (see definitions in Chapter 26), which may be followed by a colon, or not, as desired.

How to type the date line. 1. Date the letter the day it is dictated, not the day it is typed, unless instructed otherwise. If you date the letter the day it is transcribed, adjust references to time made in the dictation, such as "today" or "yesterday."

2. Type the date conventionally, all on one line.

3. Do not use *d, nd, rd, st,* or *th* following the day of the month.

4. Do not abbreviate or use figures for the month.

5. Do not spell out the day of the month or the year, except in very formal letters.

Right	*Wrong*
November 15, 19..	November 15th, 19..
	9/15/..
	Nov. 15, 19..
	November fifteenth, Nineteen hundred and ....

The Address

The addressee's name. A man's name is dear to him. If it begins with *Mac,* he wants it written that way, not *Mc.* The same is true of firms and companies. Some law firms omit the comma between names of the members of the firm (for example, *Bell Wilson Nelson Adams*); others insert the ampersand between each name (*Bell & Wilson & Nelson & Adams*). Some companies include *Company, Co., The, Inc.,* or *&* as part of the official name. It is your duty to write a name the way the owner writes it. Never take a chance and write it the way you think it should be written —verify it from incoming correspondence, the file, or some other source. (See reference facilities in Chapter 25.)

Titles. For the correct forms of addressing men in official or honorary positions, see Chapter 6. Generally, the following forms apply:

1. Always precede a name by a title, unless initials indicating degrees or *Esquire* follow the name. The use of a business title or position or of *Sr.* or *Jr.* after a name does not take the place of a title.

Right	*Wrong*
Mr. Ralph P. Edwards, President	Ralph P. Edwards, President

2. *Esquire,* or *Esq.* never precedes a name and is never used with any other title, not even with *Mr.* In business correspondence *Esquire* or *Esq.* is used only to address high ranking professional men who have no other title, but the practice is different in law offices. Many law offices always address a lawyer as *Esquire.* Some firms also address their clients as *Esquire.* You, of course, must be guided by the instructions of the dictator. Clerks of courts and justices of the peace are properly addressed as *Esquire.* There is no feminine of *esquire;* therefore, the word is never used in addressing women.

Right	*Wrong*
Dr. Richard W. Nelson	Dr. Richard W. Nelson, Esq.
William S. Richey, Esquire	Mr. William S. Richey, Esquire
Robert Wilson, Jr., Esq.	Mr. Robert Wilson, Jr., Esq.

The title *Esq.* is commonly used in England and in her colonies. There it is the proper title to use in addressing the heads of business firms, banking executives, doctors, and the like.

Correct in England

Robert E. Meade, Esq., President

Laurence D. Goode, Esq., M.D.

3. *Messrs.* is used for addressing a firm of attorneys, as *Messrs. Jackson, Bell & Hunt.* It may be used in addressing a business firm of men, or men and women, when the names denote individuals, but not in addressing corporations or other business organizations that bear impersonal names.

Right	*Wrong*
Messrs. Marvin Tobin Smart Attorneys at Law	
James Marshall & Sons	Messrs. James Marshall & Sons

4. Initials or abbreviations indicating degrees and other honors

are sometimes placed after the name of the person addressed. Use only the initials of the highest degree; more than one degree may be used, however, if the degrees are in different fields. A scholastic title is not used in combination with the abbreviation indicating that degree, but another title may be used in combination with abbreviations indicating degrees.

Right	*Wrong*
Robert E. Saunders, Ph.D.	Robert E. Saunders, A.B., A.M., Ph.D.
Dr. Ralph Jones (*preferred*)	
or	Dr. Ralph Jones, M.D
Ralph Jones, M.D.	Professor Robert E. Saunders, Ph.D.
The Reverend Perry E. Moore, D.D., LL.D.	

To a professor

Professor Robert E. Saunders

Business titles or position. 1. The designation of a business position follows the name. It does not take the place of a title.

Right	*Wrong*
Mr. Ralph E. Edwards, President	Ralph E. Edwards, President
	President Ralph E. Edwards

2. Do not abbreviate business titles or positions, such as President, Secretary, and Sales Manager. *Mr.* (or *Mrs.* or *Miss*) precedes the individual's name, even when the business title is used. If a person's business title is short, place it on the first line; if it is long, place it on the second line.

Mr. James E. Lambert, President	Mr. George F. Moore
Lambert & Woolf Company	Advertising Manager
1005 Tower Street	Price & Patterson
Cleveland 3, Ohio	234 Seventh Avenue
	New York 5, New York

The modern trend is to omit the business title, particularly if it makes the address run over four lines.

3. Do not hyphenate a title unless it represents two or more offices.

Right	*Wrong*
Secretary-Treasurer	Secretary Treasurer
Vice President	Vice-President

4. If a letter is addressed to a particular department in a company, place the name of the company on the first line and the name of the department on the second line.

5. In addressing an individual in a firm, corporation, or group, place the individual's name on the first line, and the company's name on the second line.

Forms for addressing women. 1. *Firm composed of women.* In addressing a firm composed of women either married or unmarried, use *Mesdames* or *Mmes.*

2. *Unmarried woman.* Use *Miss* when you are addressing an unmarried woman or when you do not know whether she is married or unmarried.

3. *Married woman.* Socially a married woman is addressed by her husband's full name preceded by *Mrs.* In business, she may be addressed either by her husband's name or by her given name and her married name, preceded by *Mrs.* Use the form she prefers if you know it.

4. *Widow.* Socially a widow is addressed by her husband's full name preceded by *Mrs.* In business either her husband's full name or her given name and her married name, preceded by *Mrs.,* is correct. Use the form that she prefers if you know it.

5. *Divorcee.* If a divorcee retains her married name, the title *Mrs.* is preferable to *Miss.* If she uses her maiden name, she may use either *Miss* or *Mrs.* In business she may be addressed by her given name combined with her married name or by both her maiden and married names. Follow the form she prefers if you know it. Socially she is addressed by her maiden name combined with her married name.

6. *Wife of a titled man.* Do not address a married woman by her husband's title. Address her as *Mrs. Robert E. Adams* or *Mrs. R. E. Adams.* If she is addressed jointly with her husband, the

correct form is *Dr. and Mrs. Robert E. Adams, Judge and Mrs. Irving Levey.*

7. *Professional women.* Address a woman with a professional title by her title, followed by her given and last names. A married woman sometimes uses her maiden name and, if so, should be addressed by it. In social correspondence her title is sometimes dropped in addressing her and her husband.

When you do not know whether an addressee is a man or a woman, use the form of address appropriate for a man. *Women in official or honorary positions are addressed just as men in similar positions, except that Madam, Mrs., or Miss replace Sir or Mr. See the chart in Chapter 6.*

How to type the street address. The inside address and the address on the envelope are the same. The following instructions for writing it are standard, although various authorities give different rules for writing addresses.

1. Do not precede the street number with a word or a sign.

Right	*Wrong*
70 Fifth Avenue	No. 70 Fifth Avenue
	# 70 Fifth Avenue

2. Spell out the numerical names of streets and avenues if they are numbers of 12 or under. When figures are used, do not follow with *d, st,* or *th.* Use figures for all house numbers except *One.* Separate the house number from a numerical name of a thoroughfare with a space, a hyphen, and a space.

> 23 East Twelfth Street
> 23 East 13 Street
> One Fifth Avenue
> 2 Fifth Avenue
> 234 - 72 Street

3. If a room, suite, or apartment number is part of the address, it should follow the street address. This position facilitates mail delivery. If the address is an office building instead of a street, the suite number may precede the name of the building.

Right	*Wrong*
700 Baylor Drive, Room 289	Room 289, 700 Baylor Drive
1010 First National Bank Building	

4. Never abbreviate the name of a city. States, territories, and possessions may be abbreviated, but the better practice is not to abbreviate them.

5. The zone number follows the city and is separated from the state by a comma.

6. If there is no street address, put the city and state on separate lines.

7. Use post-office box number if you have it instead of street address.

Salutations

How to type the salutation. 1. Capitalize the first word, the title, and the name. Do not capitalize *dear* unless it is used as the first word of the salutation.

2. Use a colon following the salutation. A comma is used only in social letters, particularly in those written in longhand.

3. *Mr., Mrs.,* and *Dr.* are the only titles that are abbreviated.

Forms of salutation. See the chart in Chapter 6 for the correct salutation to use in letters to people in official or honorary positions. The form of salutation varies with the tone of the letter and the degree of acquaintanceship between the lawyer and the client. The trend today is toward the less formal salutation.

1. If the letter is addressed to an individual, make the salutation singular, for example, *Dear Sir.* If the letter is addressed to a company or group, make it plural, for example, *Gentlemen* or *Dear Sirs.* The latter is preferable when addressing a firm of lawyers.

2. Never use a designation of any kind after a salutation.

| *Right* | *Wrong* |
| Dear Mr. Roberts: | Dear Mr. Roberts. C.P.A.: |

3. The salutation in a letter addressed to an organization composed of men and women is *Gentlemen* or *Ladies and Gentle-*

men; to a man and woman, *Dear Sir and Madam;* to a married couple, *Dear Mr. and Mrs. Marsh.*

4. Never use a *business* title or designation of position in a salutation. (Honorary and official titles are frequently used in salutations. See the chart in Chapter 6.)

Right	*Wrong*
Dear Mr. Adams:	Dear Secretary:
	Dear Secretary Ames:

5. If a letter addressed to a firm of lawyers is to the attention of an individual lawyer, the salutation is to the firm, not to the individual.

6. Follow a title with the surname.

Right	*Wrong*
Dear Professor Ames:	Dear Professor:

Forms of salutation in letters addressed to women. 1. Do not use *Miss* as a salutation unless it is followed by a name.

Right	*Wrong*
Dear Miss Brown: (*preferred*)	Dear Miss:
Dear Madam:	

2. If the letter is addressed to a firm of women, the salutation is *Ladies* or *Mesdames.* Do not use "Dear" or "My dear" with either of these salutations.

3. The salutation to two women with the same name is:

My dear Mesdames Smith (if married)

My dear Misses Smith (if unmarried)

When in doubt as to whether the addressee is a man or woman, use the salutation appropriate for a man. *For the correct form of salutation in letters addressed to women holding official or honorary positions, see the chart in Chapter 6.*

The Complimentary Close

See Chapter 6 for the correct complimentary close to use in letters to people in official or honorary positions.

The form of complimentary close varies with the tone of the letter and the degree of acquaintanceship between the lawyer and the client. In the interchange of letters between lawyer and client, observe how the client closes the letter and be guided by his taste.

Signature

Firms of attorneys frequently sign letters manually with the firm name, particularly if the letter expresses a professional opinion or gives professional advice. In some offices the firm name is typed on the letter and the lawyer who dictated it signs his name, thus:

BLACK, WILLIAMS & LOWE

By *Edgar R. Black*

A letter signed in the firm name, whether manually or typed, is written in the first person plural, not the singular.

Many letters are signed by the dictating attorney or by a partner without having the firm name appear in the signature. The purpose of typing a signature is to enable the recipient of the letter to decipher a difficult signature. There is no need, therefore, for the lawyer's name to be typed in the signature if it appears on the letterhead.

If a firm has alternate forms of signature, the dictator will indicate his preference.

How to type the signature. 1. Type the firm name in capitals exactly as it appears on the letterhead.

2. If the signature of the dictator is typed, type it exactly as he signs his name.

Right	*Wrong*
Richard P. Miller	*Richard P. Miller*
Richard P. Miller	R. P. Miller

3. The typed signature should never extend beyond the right margin of the letter.

4. No title except *Miss* or *Mrs.* precedes either the written or typed signature.

Miscellaneous Suggestions About Correspondence

Envelopes. The items in the address on the envelope are the same as those on the inside address (see page 71 *et seq.*). Figures 19 and 20 show acceptable and commonly used styles of address. They also show the correct placement of the attention line and mailing notations. The Post Office Department prefers the indented style.

If there is no street address, put the name of the state on a separate line from the name of the city. Do not abbreviate the name of the state. Write the name of a foreign country in capitals on the envelope; use initial capitals in the inside address.

```
CONNELLY, KARTER & MARTIN
    627 Ingraham Building
       Miami, Florida

                                              SPECIAL DELIVERY

             Mr. R. S. Jackson, President

                Northern Manufacturing Company

                   25 West 79 Street

                      Milwaukee, Wisconsin
```

Figure 19. Indented Style of Address with Correct Placement of Special Delivery Notation.

```
CONNELLY, KARTER & MARTIN
    627 Ingraham Building
       Miami, Florida



                    Northern Manufacturing Company

                    25 West 79 Street

                    Milwaukee, Wisconsin



    Attention Mr. R. S. Jackson
```

Figure 20. Block Style of Address with Correct Placement of Attention Line.

Attention line. Strictly business letters addressed to a firm are often directed to the attention of an individual by the use of an *attention line,* in preference to addressing the letter to the individual. This practice marks the letter as a business rather than a personal letter and insures that it will be opened in the absence of the individual to whom it is directed.

Type the attention line two spaces below the address. The word *of* is not necessary. The attention line has no punctuation and is not underscored. When a letter addressed to a firm has an attention line, the salutation is *Gentlemen* because the salutation is to the firm, not the individual. It is permissible to direct the letter to the attention of an individual without including his given name or initials, if they are unknown.

Preferable   Attention Mr. Walter R. Richardson

Permissible   Attention Mr. Richardson

Responsibility, or identification line. The responsibility line shows who dictated the letter and who typed it. The only purpose of the identification is for reference by the firm *writing* the letter. It does not belong on the original of a letter, but many firms have the line typed on the original because it saves time.

The usual position of responsibility marks is on a line with the last line of the signature, flush with the left margin. If the dictator's name is typed on the letter, there is no need for his initials to appear in the responsibility marks.

Personal notation. A letter or envelope should not be marked "Personal" or "Confidential" as a device to insure its delivery to a busy man. These words should be used only when no one but the addressee is supposed to see the letter. Type the word *Personal* or *Confidential* four spaces above the address. (In the official style of letter place the personal notation at the top of the letter.) You may underline the notation to catch the eye. The notation is also typed, in solid caps underlined, on the envelope, two spaces above the address.

Mailing notation. When a letter is sent by any method other than regular mail, type a notation of the exact method on the envelope, in the space below the stamps and above the address. Make a similar notation on the carbon copy of the letter.

Enclosure mark. When a letter contains enclosures, type the word *Enclosure* or the abbreviation *Enc.* flush with the left-hand margin one or two spaces beneath the identification line. If there is more than one enclosure, indicate the number. If the enclosures are of special importance, identify them. If an enclosure is to be returned, make a notation to that effect.

RPE:es   RPE:es   RPE:es
Enclosure   Enc. 2   Enc. Cert. ck. $2,350
                                         Mtge.—Nelson to Jones
RPE:es
Enc. Policy 35 4698-M (to be returned)

The secretaries in a well-known law firm in the East follow the practice of placing an asterisk in the margin of the letter opposite the line that refers to the enclosure. This eliminates the possibility of forgetting to indicate at the bottom of the letter that there are enclosures.

Carbon copy distribution notation. When a carbon copy is to be sent to another person, type the distribution notation flush with the left-hand margin, below all other notations. If space permits, separate it from the other notations by two spaces.

SRE:NG
Enclosure
Copy to Mr. S. A. Williams

The abbreviaton *c.c.* may be used instead of *Copy to.* In the simplified form of letter neither is used.

Blind copy notation. Type the carbon copy notation in the upper left-hand portion of the letter *on the carbons only.* This indicates that the addressee of the letter does not know that a copy was sent to anyone.

Postscript. When it is necessary to add a postscript to a letter, type it two spaces below the identification line or the last notation that is on the letter. The left margin of the postscript should be indented five spaces from the left margin of the letter itself. You may include or omit the abbreviation "P.S." Type the dictator's initials after the postscript.

Heading on succeeding pages. Law firms generally have continuation sheets, loosely called second sheets, with the firm name, but no address, engraved on them for use when a letter runs more than one page. If your office does not have engraved continuation sheets, use a plain sheet of the same size and quality as the letterhead. Type enough descriptive matter at the top of succeeding pages to make them recognizable if they should become separated from the first page. The name of the addressee, the number of the page, and the date should be sufficient.

Enclosures. When it is necessary to fasten enclosures together or to a letter, use staples. The Post Office Department objects to pins or metal clips because the pins injure the hands of postal employees and the clips tend to damage post office canceling machines.

1. *Enclosures the size of the letter.* These are easily folded and inserted, with their accompanying letters, into commercial envelopes of the ordinary size. If the enclosure consists of two or more sheets, staple them together but do not fasten the enclosed material to the letter. Fold the enclosure, then fold the letter, and slip the enclosure inside the last fold of the letter. Thus when the letter is removed from the envelope, the enclosure comes out with it.

2. *Enclosures larger than the letter.* These include briefs, abstracts, and other legal documents too large to fit into a commercial envelope of ordinary size. These are generally mailed in large manila envelopes. Enclosures of this kind may be handled in one of three ways.

(*a*) The letter is inserted with the enclosure in the large envelope, which is sealed. In this case first-class postage is charged for both the letter and the enclosure.

(*b*) A combination envelope is used. This is a large envelope with a flap that is fastened by a patent fastener of some kind, *but not sealed.* A smaller envelope of commercial size is affixed on the front of this envelope in the process of manufacture. The letter is inserted into the small envelope and the flap is sealed. Postage is affixed to the large envelope at third-class rate and to the small envelope at first-class rate.

(*c*) The enclosure may be sent, *unsealed,* in one envelope and the letter, *sealed,* in another. In this case, of course, the letter should not refer to an enclosure but should state that the material is being sent by third-class mail.

3. *Enclosures smaller than the letter.* When enclosures are considerably smaller than the letter, staple them to the letter in the upper left-hand corner, on top of the letter. If two or more such enclosures are sent, put the smaller one on top.

Some Concrete Aids in Letter Writing

We do not all have the talent that makes an outstanding letter writer, but we can improve the style and effectiveness of our own letters by studying those written by experts. Careful planning and highly developed techniques make those letters outstanding. This section will help you develop techniques that will improve the quality and persuasiveness of your letters.

Suggested techniques. The language of a letter should be natural, just as though the writer were talking to the reader. Unfortunately, lawyers are frequent offenders against this basic requirement of letter writing, and their secretaries are inclined to follow their style.

Here are six suggestions that will help you write letters in simple, straightforward language. When you draft a letter for the lawyer's signature, if you will follow these suggestions he will probably be favorably impressed by the clarity and effectiveness of your letter.

1. Never use stilted or trite phrases.
2. Avoid unnecessary words or phrases.
3. Do not use two words with the same meaning for emphasis.
4. Avoid favorite words or expressions.
5. Do not use big words.
6. Use short sentences.

Trite terms to be avoided.[1] Here is a list of expressions that are stilted or trite and hence not good usage.

Advise. Used with too little discrimination and best reserved to indicate actual advice. Often *say* or *tell* is better.

> BAD: We wish to *advise* that your case has been set for trial on November 15.

---

[1] Adapted from Charles C. Parkhurst, *Modern Business Communication,* pp. 468–474, Englewood Cliffs, N. J.: Prentice-Hall, Inc., 1955.

BETTER: We are pleased to *tell* you that your case has been set for trial on November 15.

As per; per. Correctly used with Latin words: *per annum* and *per diem.*

> ALLOWABLE: 1 dollar *per* page.
> BETTER: 1 dollar *a* page.
> BAD: As *per* our telephone conversation.
> BETTER: *In accordance with* our telephone conversation.
> BAD: *Per* our agreement.
> BETTER: *According to* our agreement.

At all times. Often used with little meaning. Better to use *always.*

> POOR: We shall be pleased to talk with you *at all times.*
> BETTER: We shall *always* be pleased to welcome you at our office.

At this time. Also unnecessary in most cases. Try *at present* or *now.*

> POOR: We wish to advise that we have no further information *at this time.*
> BETTER: We are sorry to tell you that we have no further information *at present.*

At your convenience; at an early date. Trite, vague, and unnecessary in most cases. Be specific.

> INDEFINITE: Please notify us *at an early date.*
> BETTER: Please let us know *within ten days* (or *by the first of next month*).
> VAGUE: We should appreciate hearing from you *at your convenience.*
> BETTER: We should appreciate hearing from you *by the tenth of ——.*

Beg. Avoid such expressions as *beg to state, beg to advise, beg to acknowledge,* and so on.

> POOR: In answer to yours of the 10th inst., *beg to state. . . .*
> BETTER: In answer (or response; or reply) to your letter of May 10, *we are pleased. . . .*

Contents carefully noted. Contributes little to a letter.

> POOR: Yours of the 5th received and *contents carefully noted.*
> BETTER: The instructions outlined in your letter of June 5 have been followed in every detail.

Duly. Needless and unnecessary.

> POOR: Your request has been *duly* forwarded to our offices in Washington.
> BETTER: Your request has been forwarded to our offices in Washington.

Enclosed please find. Needless and faulty phraseology. The word *please* has little meaning in this instance. And the word *find* is improperly used.

> POOR: *Enclosed please find* draft of the contract.
> BETTER: *We are enclosing* (or *we enclose*) draft of the contract.

Esteemed. Too flowery and effusive.

> Poor: We welcomed your *esteemed* favor of the 9th.
> Better: Thank you for your letter of April 9.

Favor. Do not use the word *favor* in the sense of letter, order, or check.

> "Thank you for your *letter* (not *favor*) of October 5."

Handing you. Out of place in correspondence today.

> Poor: We are *handing you* herewith affidavit made by Mr. R. M. Davis.
> Better: We *enclose* affidavit made by Mr. R. M. Davis.

Have before me. A "worn-out" expression.

> Poor: I *have before me* your complaint of the 10th.
> Better: *In answer* (or *response;* or *reply*) *to* your letter of November 10. . . .

Hereto. Trite.

> Poor: We are attaching *hereto* a copy of the agreement.
> Better: We are attaching *to this letter* a copy of the agreement.

Herewith. Often redundant.

> Poor: We enclose *herewith* a copy of the charter.
> Better: We are pleased to enclose a copy of the charter.

In re. Avoid except in subject line. Use *regarding* or *concerning.*

> Poor: *In re* our telephone conversation of this morning. . . .
> Better: *Supplementing* (or *confirming;* or *regarding*) our telephone conversation of this morning. . . .

Inst. Avoid the abbreviation of the word *instant,* and the word *instant* itself.

> Poor: Your favor of the 6th *inst.* (or *instant*). . . .
> Better: Your letter of *June 6.* . . .

Our Mr. Becker. Say, *our associate, Mr. Becker,* or just *Mr. Becker.*

> Poor: *Our Mr. Becker* will call on you next Tuesday, May 10.
> Better: *Our associate, Mr. Becker,* will call on you next Tuesday, May 10.

Proximo. A Latin word meaning *on the next.* Better to give the exact name of the month.

> Poor: The meeting will be held on the 10th *prox.* (or *proximo*).
> Better: The meeting will be held *December 10.*

Recent date. Vague and unbusinesslike. Better to give the exact date.

> Vague: Your letter of *recent date.*
> Definite: Your letter of *June 2.*

Same. A poor substitute for one of the pronouns *it, they,* or *them.*

POOR: Your letter of the 5th received. We will give *same* our immediate attention.

BETTER: Thank you for your letter of March 5. We will make the requested arrangements immediately.

State. Often too formal. Better to use *say* or *tell.*

POOR: We wish to *state.* . . .

BETTER: We are pleased to *tell* you. . . .

Take pleasure. A trite expression. Better to say, *are pleased, are happy,* or *are glad.*

POOR: We *take pleasure* in arranging reservations for you.

BETTER: We *are pleased* to make arrangements for you.

Thanking you in advance. Discourteous and implies that your request will be granted.

POOR: Kindly mail me any information you may have concerning the ARS bill. *Thanking you in advance* for the favor, I remain

Yours truly,

BETTER: I shall appreciate any information you may have concerning the ARS bill.

Very truly yours,

Ultimo. A Latin word meaning *the preceding month.* No longer used in modern correspondence.

POOR: Yours of the 9th *ultimo* (or *ult.*) received.

BETTER: We have received your letter of *June 9.*

Under separate cover. Rather meaningless. Better to be specific and give the method of shipping.

POOR: We are sending you *under separate cover* a copy of the record.

BETTER: We are pleased to send you *by insured parcel post* a copy of the record.

Valued. Too effusive and suggestive of flattery. Better to omit.

POOR: We appreciate your *valued* suggestion given to Mr. McCall.

BETTER: We appreciate your suggestion given to Mr. McCall.

Wish to say; wish to state; would say. All are examples of needless, wordy phraseology. Simply omit.

POOR: Referring to your letter of the 10th, *wish to say* that we cannot make the necessary arrangements before the first of December.

BETTER: In response to your letter of March 10, we regret we cannot make the necessary arrangements before December 1.

Unnecessary words and phrases. Many letter writers add unnecessary words to their phrases because of an erroneous idea that the padding gives emphasis or rounds out a sentence. For example, letter writers frequently speak of *"final* completion," *"month* of January," or *"close* proximity." The completion must be final or it is not complete; January must be a month; incidents in proximity must be close. Here is a list[2] of some padded phrases frequently used in business letters. The italicized words are *totally* unnecessary.

It came *at a time* when we were busy.
Leather depreciates *in value* slowly.
During *the year of* 19...
It will cost *the sum of* one hundred dollars.
At a meeting *held* in Chicago.
We will mail the abstract *at a* later *date.*
In about two weeks' *time.*
The mistake *first* began owing to a misunderstanding.
A *certain* person by the name of Bill Jones.
The *close* proximity of these two incidents.
It happened at *the hour of* noon.
We see some good in both *of them.*
In *the city of* Columbus.
The body is made *out* of steel.
During the *course of the* campaign.
Perhaps it may be that you are reluctant.
Our uniform *and invariable* rule is.
We are now *engaged in* moving to new offices.
By *means of* this device we are able.
The property sold sells for *a price of* $20,000.

Two words with the same meaning. Some letter writers think that if one word does a job, two words add emphasis. Actually, the second word makes the thought less effective. Here are a few examples of "doubling."

sincere and good wishes
the first and foremost
appraise and determine the worth-while things
our experience together and contacts in a civic association
deeds and actions
feeling of optimism and encouragement

[2] Acknowledgment is made to L. E. Frailey, *Handbook of Business Letters,* Englewood Cliffs, N. J.: Prentice-Hall, Inc., 1948, p. 57.

we refuse and decline
unjust and unfair manner
advised and informed
at once and by return mail
immediately and at once
we demand and insist
right and proper consideration
assume obligation or responsibility

Favorite words and expressions. Avoid acquiring favorite words or expressions. They become habitual, and your letters sound cut and dried. For example, a lawyer might easily overwork the word "records." One letter might say, "According to our records, the grace period will expire next Monday," and the next, "The enclosed is for your records." A skillful letter writer would simply say, "The grace period will expire next Monday," and "The enclosed copy is for you."

Big words versus one syllable words. Some people think that a large vocabulary of big words marks them as learned; but simple, short words do the best job. This statement does not mean a large vocabulary is not an asset. The more words a writer has, the more clearly and forcibly he can express himself, but he never uses words of many syllables unless there is a reason for it. Why say "propertied interests" when you mean "rich people," or "annihilate" when you mean "wipe out," or "transcend" when you mean "go beyond."

Sentence length. Since the aim of a letter is to transfer a thought to the reader in the simplest manner with the greatest clarity, avoid long, complicated sentences. Lawyers probably disregard this technique of good letter writing more than any other. Break up overlong, stuffy sentences by making short sentences out of dependent clauses. Here is an example (101 words):

Believing the physical union of the two businesses to be desirable and in the best interests of the stockholders of each corporation, the Boards of Directors have given further consideration to the matter and have agreed in principle upon a new plan that would contemplate the transfer of the business and substantially all of the assets of the A Company to B in exchange for shares of common stock of B on a basis that would permit the distribution to the A Company stockholders of one and one-half shares of B common stock for each share of A Company common stock.

Rewritten in four sentences and reduced to 70 words, this becomes:

The Boards of Directors of both companies thought a merger desirable and in the best interests of the stockholders. They finally agreed on a new plan. The business and substantially all assets of the *A* Company will be transferred to *B* in exchange for *B* common stock. *A* Company stockholders will get one and one-half shares of *B* common stock for each share of *A* Company common stock.

Telegrams

How to send a telegram. Law offices generally have a call box connected with the telegraph office; a twist of the button brings a messenger. If the telegraphic business does not warrant the installation of a call box, a messenger is summoned by calling "Western Union" on the phone. Many large law offices have their own Western Union teleprinter, over which messages are sent directly to the Western Union office.

How to type a telegram. 1. The number of copies depends upon the requirements of your office. Four is the usual number.

a. The original for pickup by the telegraph messenger.

b. A carbon copy for confirmation by mail.

c. A carbon copy for your file.

d. A carbon copy for the telegraph account file against which the charges may be checked.

2. Check the class of service—whether straight telegram, day letter, or night letter—in the form provided on the telegraph blank. Also type the class of service two spaces above the address.

3. Type the date and hour in the upper right corner.

4. Omit the salutation and complimentary close.

5. Double space the message.

6. Do not divide a word at the end of a line.

7. Use caps and small letters and punctuate just as you would any other material.

8. In the lower left-hand corner type:

a. The dictator's initials and yours.

b. Whether the message is to be sent "Charge," "Paid," or "Collect."

c. Address and telephone number of your firm, unless printed on the blank.

9. If the telegram is to be charged, type the name of the charge account in the space provided on the blank.

How to send the same message to multiple addresses. If you want to send the same message to a number of people, type the telegram only once. List the names and addresses on a special sheet obtainable from Western Union (or on a plain sheet). Above the list type "Please send the attached message to the following 12 (whatever the number is) addresses."

How to send a telegram to a person on a train. If you want to reach someone who is on a train, send the telegram in care of the conductor. Give the name of the passenger, the train name or number and the direction in which it is traveling, car and reservation number, station and arrival time, city and state.

> Mr. Robert E. Jones
> Care of Conductor
> The Congressional, Northbound
> Car 156, Roomette 12
> Due Broad Street Station, January 10, 7:18 P.M.
> Philadelphia, Pennsylvania

The telegram may be sent to any point en route where the train makes a stop.

How to send a telegram to a person on a plane. You may send a message to an airport to be delivered to a plane passenger. Give the name of the passenger, the name of the airline, the flight number and direction in which it is traveling, airport and arrival time, city and state.

> Edgar Patterson, Passenger
> Eastern Air Lines
> Flight 56, Westbound
> Due La Guardia Field, May 12, 10:23 A.M.
> Flushing, New York

It is not possible to send a message to a passenger on a plane when it is in transit.

Punctuation. There is no charge for punctuation marks in telegrams between points in the United States: The words *Stop, Comma,* and the like are charged for.

Paragraphing. Telegrams written in paragraphs are transmitted in paragraphs at no extra cost.

Mixed groups of letters and figures. Mixed groups of letters, figures, affixes, and the characters $, /, &, %, #, ' (indicating feet or minutes) and " (indicating inches or seconds) are counted at the rate of five characters, or fraction thereof, to the word in messages between points in the United States. Thus, "one hundred" is counted as two words, but 100 is counted as one word; $34.50, as one word (the decimal is not counted); but 1000th (six characters) is counted as two words.

How to type a telegram when work is in the machine. Always transcribe a telegram as soon as it is dictated. Often a rush telegram will be given to you when you have other work in the typewriter, but it is not necessary to remove the work to type the telegram. Follow this procedure:

1. Back feed the paper and carbons that are in the machine until the paper shows a top margin of about two inches.

2. Insert the first sheet of the telegram behind the material you are typing, against the paper table, just as if nothing were in the typewriter.

3. To make carbons of the telegram, insert the second sheet of the telegram against the coated side of the carbon paper that is already in the machine. Thus, the second sheet of the telegram is between the carbon and the second sheet of your letter. Do the same for each carbon that you have in the typewriter. (You must insert a sheet for each carbon in your machine to prevent the typing from showing on the carbon copies of your work.) For additional copies add carbon sheets in the usual manner.

4. Turn the platen knob until the telegram blanks are in position for typing.

5. After typing the message, back feed until you can remove the telegram from the machine.

6. Forward feed to the point at which you stopped writing your letter or other work and continue with your typing.

6

How to *Address Persons Holding Honorary or Official Positions*

A SECRETARY in a law office is frequently asked to write a letter to a person who holds an official or honorary position. The question then arises as to the proper form to use. The following chart gives the correct forms of written address, salutation, and complimentary close in letters to persons holding official or honorary titles, whether of high or low rank. It also gives the correct form for referring to those persons in a letter and the correct form to use in speaking to or informally introducing them.

The forms of informal introduction and of reference are generally the same.

You should make every effort to learn the name of the person addressed, as well as his title. Use the name in writing, except in those few instances where the name is omitted in the chart. If you know the person's title only, address him by the title prefaced by *The*. For example, *The Lieutenant Governor of Iowa*. The salutation would be *Sir* or *My dear Governor*.

In many cases the name in the address is followed by the abbreviation of a scholastic degree. If you do not know whether the addressee has the degree, you should not use the initials. Nor should a person be addressed by a scholastic title unless he actually possesses the degree that the title indicates.

Women in official or honorary positions are addressed just as men in similar positions, except that Madam, Mrs., or Miss replaces Sir or Mr.

UNITED STATES GOVERNMENT OFFICIALS

PERSONAGE	ENVELOPE AND INSIDE ADDRESS	FORMAL SALUTATION	INFORMAL SALUTATION	FORMAL CLOSE	INFORMAL CLOSE	1. SPOKEN ADDRESS 2. INFORMAL INTRODUCTION OR REFERENCE [1]
The President	The President The White House Washington 25, D. C.[2]	Mr. President	My dear Mr. President:	Respectfully yours,	Faithfully yours, (official) Very respectfully yours (private individual)	1. Mr. President 2. NOT INTRODUCED (The President)
Vice President of the United States	The Vice President United States Senate Washington, D. C. *or* The Honorable John R. Blank Vice President of the United States Washington, D. C.	Sir:	My dear Mr. Vice President:	Very truly yours,	Sincerely yours,	1. Mr. Vice President *or* Mr. Blank 2. The Vice President
Chief Justice of the United States	The Chief Justice The Supreme Court Washington, D. C.	Sir:	My dear Mr. Chief Justice:	Very truly yours,	Sincerely yours,	1. Mr. Chief Justice 2. The Chief Justice
Associate Justice of the United States Supreme Court	Mr. Justice Blank The Supreme Court Washington, D. C.	Sir:	My dear Mr. Justice:	Very truly yours,	Sincerely yours,	1. Mr. Justice *or* Mr. Justice Blank 2. Mr. Justice Blank
Speaker of the House of Representatives	The Honorable John R. Blank Speaker of the House of Representatives Washington, D. C.	Sir:	My dear Mr. Speaker:	Very truly yours,	Sincerely yours,	1. Mr. Speaker *or* Mr. Blank 2. The Speaker, Mr. Blank (The Speaker *or* Mr. Blank)

93

[1] The form of introduction and the form of reference to a person are usually similar. When they differ, the form of reference is shown here in parentheses.
[2] On the inside address it is permissible to omit "Washington 25, D. C."

UNITED STATES GOVERNMENT OFFICIALS (Continued)

PERSONAGE	ENVELOPE AND INSIDE ADDRESS	FORMAL SALUTATION	INFORMAL SALUTATION	FORMAL CLOSE	INFORMAL CLOSE	1. SPOKEN ADDRESS 2. INFORMAL INTRODUCTION OR REFERENCE
Cabinet Officer (man)	*Formal* The Honorable the Secretary of State Washington, D. C. *Informal* The Honorable John R. Blank Secretary of State Washington, D. C. *If written from abroad* The Honorable John R. Blank Secretary of State of the United States of America Washington, D. C.	Sir:	My dear Mr. Secretary:	Very truly yours,	Sincerely yours,	1. Mr. Secretary *or* Mr. Blank 2. The Secretary of State, Mr. Blank (The Secretary *or* Mr. Blank)
Cabinet Officer (woman)	*Formal* The Honorable the Secretary of Labor Washington, D. C.	Madam:	My dear Madam Secretary:	Very truly yours,	Sincerely yours,	1. Madam Secretary *or* Mrs. (Miss) Blank 2. The Secretary of Labor, Mrs. (Miss) Blank (The Secretary *or* Mrs. (Miss) Blank)
Under Secretary of a Department	The Honorable John R. Blank Under Secretary of the Treasury Washington, D. C.	My dear Mr. Blank:	My dear Mr. Blank:	Very truly yours,	Sincerely yours,	1, 2. Mr. Blank
Assistant Secretary of a Department	The Honorable John R. Blank Assistant Secretary of Agriculture Washington, D. C.	My dear Mr. Blank:	My dear Mr. Blank:	Very truly yours,	Sincerely yours,	1, 2. Mr. Blank

94

Position	Address	Formal salutation	Informal salutation	Formal close	Informal close	Reference / spoken address
Director of an Office, Chief of a Division or a Bureau	John R. Blank, Esquire Chief, Bureau of Labor Statistics Department of Labor Washington, D. C.	My dear Mr. Blank:	My dear Mr. Blank:	Very truly yours,	Sincerely yours,	1, 2. Mr. Blank
United States Senator (man)	The Honorable John R. Blank United States Senate Washington, D. C.	Sir:	My dear Senator Blank:	Very truly yours,	Sincerely yours,	1. Senator Blank *or* Senator Blank 2. Senator Blank
United States Senator (woman)	The Honorable Mary Blank United States Senate Washington, D. C.	Madam:	My dear Senator Blank: *or* My dear Mrs. (Miss) Blank:	Very truly yours,	Sincerely yours,	1. Senator Blank *or* Mrs. (Miss) Blank 2. Senator Blank
United States Representative (man)	The Honorable John R. Blank House of Representatives Washington, D. C.	Sir:	My dear Mr. Blank:	Very truly yours,	Sincerely yours,	1. Mr. Blank 2. Mr. Blank *or* Representative Blank
United States Representative (woman)	The Honorable Mary Blank House of Representatives Washington, D. C.	Madam:	My dear Mrs. (Miss) Blank:	Very truly yours,	Sincerely yours,	1, 2. Mrs. (Miss) Blank
Territorial Delegate	The Honorable John R. Blank Delegate of Hawaii House of Representatives Washington, D. C.	Sir:	My dear Mr. Blank:	Very truly yours,	Sincerely yours,	1, 2. Mr. Blank
Resident Commissioner	The Honorable John R. Blank Resident Commissioner of Puerto Rico Washington, D. C.	Sir:	My dear Mr. Blank:	Very truly yours,	Sincerely yours,	1, 2. Mr. Blank
Secretary to the President	The Honorable John R. Blank Secretary to the President The White House Washington 25, D. C.	Sir:	My dear Mr. Blank:	Very truly yours,	Sincerely yours,	1, 2. Mr. Blank
Secretary to the President with military rank	Major General John R. Blank Secretary to the President The White House Washington 25, D. C.	Sir:	My dear General Blank:	Very truly yours,	Sincerely yours,	1, 2. General Blank

UNITED STATES GOVERNMENT OFFICIALS (Continued)

Personage	Envelope and Inside Address	Formal Salutation	Informal Salutation	Formal Close	Informal Close	1. Spoken Address 2. Informal Introduction or Reference
Assistant Secretary to the President	The Honorable John R. Blank Assistant Secretary to the President The White House Washington 25, D. C.	Sir:	My dear Mr. Blank:	Very truly yours,	Sincerely yours,	1, 2. Mr. Blank
High Officials of the United States, in general: Comptroller General, Director of Bureau of the Budget, Librarian of Congress	*Formal* The Comptroller General of the United States Washington, D. C. *Informal* The Honorable John R. Blank Comptroller General of the United States Washington, D. C.	Sir:	My dear Mr. Blank:	Very truly yours,	Sincerely yours,	1, 2. Mr. Blank
Heads of Independent Federal Agencies, Boards, Commissions, Establishments, Organizations, etc.	*Formal* The Chairman of the Board ot Governors of the Federal Reserve System Washington, D. C. *Informal* The Honorable John R. Blank Director, Mutual Security Agency Washington, D. C.	Sir:	My dear Mr. Chairman (*or* Mr. Director): *or* My dear Mr. Blank:	Very truly yours,	Sincerely yours,	1, 2. Mr. Blank

STATE AND LOCAL GOVERNMENT OFFICIALS

PERSONAGE	ENVELOPE AND INSIDE ADDRESS	FORMAL SALUTATION	INFORMAL SALUTATION	FORMAL CLOSE	INFORMAL CLOSE	SPOKEN ADDRESS 1. INTRO- DUCTION OR REFERENCE 2. INFORMAL
Governor of State [a]	*Formal* The Honorable the Governor of Iowa Des Moines *Informal* The Honorable John R. Blank Governor of Iowa Des Moines	Sir:	My dear Governor:	Respectfully yours,	Sincerely yours,	1. Governor Blank *or* Governor 2. Governor Blank *or* The Governor (Outside his own state: The Governor of Iowa)
Lieutenant Governor	The Honorable John R. Blank Lieutenant Governor of Iowa Des Moines	Sir:	My dear Governor Blank:	Respectfully yours, *or* Very truly yours,	Sincerely yours,	1. Governor Blank 2. The Lieutenant Governor of Iowa, Governor Blank (The Lieutenant Governor *or* Governor Blank)
Secretary of State	The Honorable John R. Blank Secretary of State of Iowa Des Moines	Sir:	My dear Mr. Secretary:	Very truly yours,	Sincerely yours,	1, 2. Mr. Blank
Attorney General	The Honorable John R. Blank Attorney General of New York Albany, New York	Sir:	My dear Mr. Attorney General	Very truly yours,	Sincerely yours,	1, 2. Mr. Blank
State Representative or Assembly- man	The Honorable John R. Blank House of Representatives Nashville, Tennessee	Sir:	My dear Mr. Blank:	Very truly yours,	Sincerely yours,	1. Mr. Blank 2. Mr. Blank *or* Representative Blank
Mayor of a city	The Honorable John R. Blank Mayor of Memphis Tennessee	Sir:	My dear Mayor Blank:	Very truly yours,	Sincerely yours,	1. Mayor Blank *or* Mr. Mayor 2. Mayor Blank

[a] The form of addressing Governors varies in the different states. The form given here is that used by the State Department of the United States.

97

STATE AND LOCAL GOVERNMENT OFFICIALS (Continued)

Personage	Envelope and Inside Address	Formal Salutation	Informal Salutation	Formal Close	Informal Close	Spoken Address 1. Informal Introduction or Reference 2.
Commissioners of a city	*Formal* The Commissioners of the City of Buffalo New York	Sirs:	Sirs:	Very truly yours,	Very truly yours,	1. Gentlemen 2. The Commissioners
President of Board of Commissioners	*Formal or Informal* The Honorable John R. Blank President, Board of Commissioners of the City of Buffalo New York	Sir:	My dear Mr. Blank:	Very truly yours,	Sincerely yours,	1, 2. Mr. Blank
District Attorney	The Honorable John R. Blank District Attorney, Sunflower County County Courthouse Indianola, Mississippi	Dear Sir:	Dear Mr. Blank:	Very truly yours,	Sincerely yours,	1, 2. Mr. Blank
City Attorney City Counsel Corporation Counsel	The Honorable John R. Blank City Attorney (City Counsel, Corporation Counsel) Aliceville, Alabama	Dear Sir:	Dear Mr. Blank:	Very truly yours,	Sincerely yours,	1, 2. Mr. Blank
Alderman	Alderman John R. Blank City Hall Aliceville, Alabama	Dear Sir:	Dear Mr. Blank:	Very truly yours,	Sincerely yours,	1, 2. Mr. Blank

COURT OFFICIALS

Personage	Envelope and Inside Address	Formal Salutation	Informal Salutation	Formal Close	Informal Close	1. Spoken Address 2. Informal Introduction or Reference
Chief Justice[4] of a State Supreme Court	The Honorable John R. Blank Chief Justice[4] of the Supreme Court of Minnesota Minneapolis, Minnesota	Sir:	My dear Mr.[5] Chief Justice: *or* My dear Judge Blank:	Very truly yours,	Sincerely yours,	1. Mr. Chief Justice *or* Judge Blank 2. Mr. Chief Justice Blank *or* Judge Blank
Associate Justice Presiding Justice	The Honorable John R. Blank Associate (Presiding) Justice, Appellate Division Supreme Court, New York, New York	Sir:	My dear Mr. Justice:	Very truly yours,	Sincerely yours,	1, 2. Mr. Justice (*or* Judge) Blank
Judge of a Court[6]	The Honorable John R. Blank Judge of the United States District Court for the Southern District of California Los Angeles, California	Sir:	My dear Judge Blank:	Very truly yours,	Sincerely yours,	1, 2. Judge Blank
Clerk of a Court	John R. Blank, Esquire Clerk of the Superior Court Boston, Massachusetts	Sir:	My dear Mr. Blank:	Very truly yours,	Sincerely yours,	1, 2. Mr. Blank

99

[4] If his official title is *Chief Judge*, substitute *Chief Judge* for *Chief Justice*.
[5] Never use *Mr.* with *Chief Judge* or *Judge*.
[6] This does not apply to a Justice of the United States Supreme Court. See page 93.

UNITED STATES DIPLOMATIC REPRESENTATIVES[7]

Personage	Envelope and Inside Address	Formal Salutation	Informal Salutation	Formal Close	Informal Close	1. Spoken Address 2. Informal Introduction or Reference
American Ambassador (man)	The Honorable John R. Blank American Ambassador Paris	Sir:	My dear Mr. Ambassador:	Very truly yours,	Sincerely yours,	1. Mr. Ambassador or Mr. Blank 2. The American Ambassador (The Ambassador or Mr. Blank)
American Ambassador (woman)	The Honorable Mary L. Blank American Ambassador Paris	Madam:	My dear Madam Ambassador:	Very truly yours,	Sincerely yours,	1. Madam Ambassador or Mrs. (Miss) Blank 2. The American Ambassador (The Ambassador or Mrs. (Miss) Blank)
American Minister (man)	The Honorable John R. Blank American Minister Budapest	Sir:	My dear Mr. Minister:	Very truly yours,	Sincerely yours,	1. Mr. Minister or Mr. Blank 2. The American Minister, Mr. Blank (The Minister or Mr. Blank)
American Minister (woman)	The Honorable Mary Blank American Minister Rabat (Morocco)	Madam:	My dear Mrs. (Miss) Blank: or My dear Madam Minister:	Very truly yours,	Sincerely yours,	1. Madam Minister or Mrs. (Miss) Blank 2. The American Minister, Mrs. (Miss) Blank (The Minister or Mrs. (Miss) Blank)

American Chargé d'Affairs ad Interim	John R. Blank, Esquire American Chargé d'Affairs ad Interim Rome	Sir:	Very truly yours,	Sincerely yours,	1, 2. Mr. Blank
American Consul General, Consul, or Vice Consul	John R. Blank, Esquire American Consul General London, England (The same form for Consul or Vice Consul)	Sir:	Very truly yours,	Sincerely yours,	1, 2. Mr. Blank
High Commissioner	*Formal* The United States High Commissioner to Peru Lima *Informal* The Honorable John R. Blank United States High Commissioner to Peru Lima	My dear Mr. Commissioner: *or* My dear Mr. Blank:	Very truly yours,	Sincerely yours,	1, 2. Commissioner Blank *or* Mr. Blank
United States Delegate to the United Nations (with Ambassadorial rank)	The Honorable John R. Blank Chief of the United States Mission to the United Nations United Nations, New York	My dear Mr. Ambassador: *or* Sir:	Very truly yours,	Sincerely yours,	1, 2. Mr. Ambassador (The Chief of the United States Mission to the United Nations)

7 With reference to ambassadors and ministers to Central or South American countries, substitute "Ambassador of the United States" or "Minister of the United States" for "American Ambassador" or "American Minister."

When an Ambassador or Minister is not at his post, the name of the country to which he is accredited must be added, thus, "The American Ambassador to France."

FOREIGN OFFICIALS AND REPRESENTATIVES

PERSONAGE	ENVELOPE AND INSIDE ADDRESS	FORMAL SALUTATION	INFORMAL SALUTATION	FORMAL CLOSE	INFORMAL CLOSE	SPOKEN ADDRESS 1. INFORMAL INTRO- 2. DUCTION OR REFERENCE
Foreign Ambassador in the United States[8]	His Excellency, John R. Blank Ambassador of Colombia Washington, D. C.	Excellency:	My dear Mr. Ambassador:	Respectfully yours,	Sincerely yours,	1. Mr. Ambassador *or* Mr. Blank 2. The Ambassador of Colombia (The Ambassador *or* Mr. Blank)
Foreign Minister in the United States[8]	The Honorable John R. Blank Minister of Hungary Washington, D. C.	Sir:	My dear Mr. Minister:	Respectfully yours,	Sincerely yours,	1. Mr. Minister *or* Mr. Blank 2. The Minister of Hungary (The Minister *or* Mr. Blank)
Foreign Diplomatic Representative with a Personal Title	His Excellency, Count John Blank[9] Ambassador of Italy Washington, D. C.	Excellency:	My dear Mr. Ambassador:	Respectfully yours,	Sincerely yours,	1. Mr. Ambassador *or* Count Blank 2. The Italian Ambassador (The Ambassador *or* Count Blank)
Secretary General of the United Nations	Mr. John R. Blank Secretary General of the United Nations United Nations, New York	Sir: *or* My dear Mr. Secretary General:	My dear Mr. Blank:	Respectfully yours,	Sincerely yours,	1. Mr. Blank *or* Sir 2. The Secretary General of the United Nations *or* Mr. Blank

102

	Address		Salutation	Complimentary close		Reference
President of a Republic	His Excellency, John R. Blank President of the United States of Brazil Rio de Janerio	Excellency:	My dear Mr. President:	I remain, with great respect, Very truly yours,	Sincerely yours,	1. Your Excellency NOT INTRODUCED (President Blank or The President) 2. NOT INTRODUCED
British Prime Minister	The Right Honorable John R. Blank, M. P. Prime Minister London	Sir:	My dear Mr. Prime Minister: *or* My dear Mr. Blank:	Respectfully yours,	Sincerely yours,	1. Mr. Blank 2. Mr. Blank *or* The Prime Minister
Canadian Prime Minister	The Right Honorable John R. Blank, C. M. G. Prime Minister of the Dominion of Canada Ottawa	Sir:	My dear Mr. Blank:	Very truly yours,	Sincerely yours,	1. Mr. Blank 2. Mr. Blank *or* The Prime Minister
Member of the British Cabinet [10]	The Right Honorable John R. Blank, P. C. Secretary of State for Foreign Affairs London	Sir:	My dear Mr. Secretary of State: *or* My dear Mr. Blank:	Respectfully yours,	Sincerely yours,	1, 2. Mr. Blank
Lord Chief Justice	The Right Honorable The Lord Chief Justice of England [11] London [11]	Sir:	My dear Lord Chief Justice:	Respectfully yours,	Sincerely yours,	1. My Lord Chief Justice [11] *or* Sir 2. The Lord Chief Justice

103

[8] The correct title of all ambassadors and ministers of foreign countries is "Ambassador (Minister) of ...." (name of country) with the exception of Great Britain. The adjective form is used with reference to representatives from Great Britain—British Ambassador, British Minister.

[9] To avoid a long line of address, use this style.

[10] All members of the British Cabinet are members of the Privy Council and as such are entitled to the initials *P. C.* after their names.

[11] If he is a peer in his own right, he is addressed by his title of nobility.

OFFICERS OF THE ARMED FORCES[12]—ARMY

Personage	Envelope and Inside Address	Formal Salutation	Informal Salutation	Formal Close	Informal Close	1. Spoken Address 2. Informal Introduction or Reference
General of the Army	John R. Blank, U.S.A.,[13] General of the Army Department of the Army Washington, D. C.	Sir:	My dear General Blank:	Very truly yours,	Sincerely yours,	1, 2. General Blank
General, Lieutenant, Major, or Brigadier General	General (Lieutenant General, Major General, or Brigadier General) John R. Blank, U.S.A. Fort Sam Houston Texas	Sir:	My dear General Blank:	Very truly yours,	Sincerely yours,	1, 2. General Blank
Colonel, Lieutenant Colonel	Colonel (Lieutenant Colonel) John R. Blank, U.S.A. Fort Leavenworth Kansas	My dear Colonel Blank:	My dear Colonel Blank:	Very truly yours,	Sincerely yours,	1, 2. Colonel Blank
Major	Major John R. Blank, U.S.A. Fort Dix New Jersey	My dear Major Blank:	My dear Major Blank:	Very truly yours,	Sincerely yours,	1, 2. Major Blank
Captain	Captain John R. Blank, U.S.A. Fort Schuyler New York	My dear Captain Blank:	My dear Captain Blank:	Very truly yours,	Sincerely yours,	1, 2. Captain Blank
First Lieutenant, Second Lieutenant[14]	Lieutenant John R. Blank, U.S.A. Fort Shelby Mississippi	My dear Lieutenant Blank:	My dear Lieutenant Blank:	Very truly yours,	Sincerely yours,	1, 2. Lieutenant Blank
Chaplain in the United States Army	Chaplain John R. Blank Captain, U.S.A. Fort Dix New Jersey	My dear Chaplain:	My dear Chaplain:	Very truly yours,	Sincerely yours,	1. Chaplain Blank[15] 2. Captain Blank (Chaplain Blank)[15]

[12] Air Force titles are the same as the Army's, U.S.A.F. is used instead of U.S.A. and A.F.U.S. is used to indicate the Reserve.
[13] U.S.A. is changed to A.U.S. (Army of the United States) to indicate the Reserve.
[14] Modern usage sanctions the form shown here for unofficial correspondence.
[15] Roman Catholic chaplains and certain Anglican priests are spoken and referred to as "Father Blank" but are introduced as "Chaplain Blank."

OFFICERS OF THE ARMED FORCES[16]—NAVY

Personage	Envelope and Inside Address	Formal Salutation	Informal Salutation	Formal Close	Informal Close	1. Spoken Address 2. Informal Introduction or Reference
Admiral	Admiral John R. Blank, U.S.N.[17] Chief of Naval Operations Department of the Navy Washington, D. C.	Sir:	My dear Admiral Blank:	Very truly yours,	Sincerely yours,	1, 2. Admiral Blank
Fleet Admiral	Fleet Admiral John R. Blank, U.S.N.	Sir:	My dear Admiral Blank:	Very truly yours,	Sincerely yours,	1, 2. Admiral Blank
Rear Admiral	Rear Admiral John R. Blank, U.S.N. United States Naval Academy Annapolis, Maryland	Sir:	My dear Admiral Blank:	Very truly yours,	Sincerely yours,	1, 2. Admiral Blank
Vice Admiral	Vice Admiral John R. Blank, U.S.N. U.S.S. Mississippi San Diego, California	Sir:	My dear Admiral Blank:	Very truly yours,	Sincerely yours,	1, 2. Admiral Blank
Commodore, Captain, Commander	Commodore (Captain, Commander) John R. Blank U.S.S. Texas San Diego, California	My dear Commodore (Captain, Commander) Blank:	My dear Commodore (Captain, Commander) Blank:	Very truly yours,	Sincerely yours,	1, 2. Commodore (Captain, Commander) Blank
Junior Officers (Lieutenant Commander, Lieutenant, Lieutenant, Junior grade, Ensign)	Lieutenant Commander (Lieutenant, etc.) John R. Blank, U.S.N. U.S.S. Missouri Norfolk, Virginia	My dear Mr. Blank:	My dear Mr. Blank:	Very truly yours,	Sincerely yours,	1. Mr. Blank[18] 2. Lieutenant Commander or Lieutenant, etc.) Blank (Mr. Blank[18])
Chaplain	Captain John R. Blank (Ch. C.), U.S.N. Department of the Navy Washington, D. C.	Reverend Sir:	My dear Chaplain:	Very truly yours,	Sincerely yours,	1. Chaplain Blank 2. Captain Blank (Chaplain Blank)

[16] Marine Corps titles are the same as the Army, except that the top rank is *Commandant of the Marine Corps. U.S.M.C.* indicates the Reserve.

[17] *U.S.N.* indicates regular service, *U.S.N.R.* indicates the Reserve.

[18] Junior officers in the medical or dental corps are spoken to and referred to as "Dr." but are introduced by their rank.

CATHOLIC FAITH

Personage	Envelope and Inside Address	Formal Salutation	Informal Salutation	Formal Close	Informal Close	1. Spoken Address 2. Formal Introduction or Reference
Pope	His Holiness The Pope *or* His Holiness Pope Pius XII Vatican City	Your Holiness:	*Always Formal*	I have the honor to profess myself, with profound respect, the servant of your Holiness.	*Always Formal* *or* Respectfully yours, (permissible)	1. Your Holiness *or* Most Holy Father 2. NOT INTRODUCED (His Holiness *or* The Pope)
Apostolic Delegate	His Excellency, The Most Reverend John Blank The Apostolic Delegate Washington, D. C.	Your Excellency:	My dear [Archbishop]:	I have the honor to be, Excellency, Respectfully yours,	Respectfully, *or* Sincerely, yours, (permissible)	1. Your Excellency 2. NOT INTRODUCED (The Apostolic Delegate)
Cardinal in the United States	His Eminence, John Cardinal Blank Archbishop of New York New York, New York	Your Eminence:	My dear Cardinal Blank:	Respectfully yours,	Respectfully, *or* Sincerely, yours, (permissible)	1. Your Eminence 2. NOT INTRODUCED (His Eminence *or* Cardinal Blank)
Archbishop in the United States	The Most Reverend John Blank, D.D. [S.T.D.] Archbishop of Boston	Most Reverend Sir: Your Excellency:	My dear Archbishop:	Respectfully yours,	Respectfully, *or* Sincerely, yours, (permissible)	1. Your Excellency *or* Archbishop Blank 2. Archbishop Blank
Bishop in the United States	The Most Reverend John Blank Bishop of New Orleans New Orleans, Louisiana	Your Excellency: (ecclesiastical usage) Most Reverend Sir:	My dear Bishop:	Respectfully yours,	Respectfully, *or* Sincerely, yours, (permissible)	1. Your Excellency *or* Bishop Blank 2. Bishop Blank
Abbot	The Right Reverend John R. Blank Abbot of Westmoreland Abbey Washington, D. C.	Right Reverend Father Abbot:	Dear Father Abbot: *or* Right Reverend and dear Father Blank:	Respectfully yours,	Respectfully, *or* Sincerely yours, (permissible)	1. Father Abbot 2. Father Blank

Now

		Formal salutation	Informal salutation	Formal close	Informal close	Spoken address
Canon	The Very Reverend Canon John R. Blank, D.D. [LL.D.] Canon of Washington Cathedral Washington, D. C.	Very Reverend Canon:	Dear Canon Blank:	Respectfully yours,	Respectfully, *or* Sincerely yours,	1, 2. Canon Blank
Monsignor	The Right (or Very)[19] Reverend Msgr. John R. Blank Baltimore, Maryland	Monsignor:	Right (Very) Reverend and dear Monsignor Blank:	Respectfully yours,	Respectfully, *or* Sincerely yours,	1, 2. Monsignor Blank
Brother	Brother Albert Francis, F.S.C. Superior 206 Elm Street Madison, Delaware	My dear Brother:	Dear Brother Francis:	Respectfully yours,	Respectfully, *or* Sincerely yours, (permissible)	1, 2. Brother Francis
Superior of a Brotherhood[20] *and Priest*	The Very Reverend John R. Blank, M.M. Director Maryknoll, New York	Very Reverend Father Superior	Dear Father Superior:	Respectfully,	Respectfully,	1. Father Blank
Priest	*With Scholastic Degree:* The Reverend John R. Blank, Ph.D. Notre Dame University Indiana	My dear Dr. Blank:	Dear Dr. Blank:	Very truly yours,	Sincerely yours,	1, 2. Doctor Blank
	Without Scholastic Degree: The Reverend John R. Blank St. Patrick's Church Mobile, Alabama	Reverend Sir:	Reverend and dear Father Blank:	Very truly yours,	Sincerely yours,	1, 2. Father Blank

[19] Dependent upon rank. See the *Official* (Roman) *Catholic Directory.*
[20] The address for the superior of a Brotherhood depends upon whether or not he is a priest or has a title other than Superior. Consult the *Official Catholic Directory.*

107

CATHOLIC FAITH (Continued)

Personage	Envelope and Inside Address	Formal Salutation	Informal Salutation	Formal Close	Informal Close	Spoken Address or Informal Introduction or Reference
Sister Superior	The Reverend Sister Superior[21] (order, if used) Convent of the Angels New Orleans, Louisiana	My dear Sister Superior: or My dear Reverend Sister:	My dear Sister Superior:	Respectfully,	Respectfully,	1. Sister Blank or Sister St. Mary 2. The Sister Superior or Sister Blank (Sister St. Mary)
Sister[22]	Sister Mary Pia, O.P. St. Thomas High School Bayswater, New York	Dear Sister:	My dear Sister Mary Pia:	Respectfully,	Respectfully,	1, 2. Sister Mary Pia
Mother Superior of a Sisterhood (Catholic or Protestant)	The Reverend Mother Superior, O.C.A.[21] Sacred Heart Convent New Orleans, Louisiana or Mother Superior, O.C.A. Sacred Heart Convent New Orleans	My dear Reverend Mother or My dear Mother Superior:	My dear Reverend Mother: or My dear Mother Superior:	Respectfully,	Respectfully, Respectfully,	1, 2. Reverend Mother
Member of Community	Mother Mary Jones, R.S.C.J. Convent of the Sacred Heart	Dear Mother Jones:	My dear Mother Jones:	Respectfully,	Respectfully,	1, 2. Mother Jones

[21] The address of the superior of a Sisterhood depends upon the order to which she belongs. The abbreviation of the order is not always used. Consult the *Official Catholic Directory*.
[22] A special classification for a *nun* is not given here because the exact sense of the word implies a strictly cloistered Religious.

JEWISH FAITH

Personage	Envelope and Inside Address	Formal Salutation	Informal Salutation	Formal Close	Informal Close	1. Spoken Address 2. Informal Introduction or Reference
Rabbi	*With scholastic degree:* Rabbi John R. Blank, Ph.D. *or* Dr. John R. Blank	Sir:	My dear Dr. Blank: *or* My dear Rabbi Blank:	Very truly yours,	Sincerely yours,	1, 2. Dr. Blank
	Without scholastic degree: Rabbi John R. Blank	Sir:	My dear Rabbi Blank:	Very truly yours,	Sincerely yours,	1, 2. Rabbi Blank

109

PROTESTANT FAITH

Personage	Envelope and Inside Address	Formal Salutation	Informal Salutation	Formal Close	Informal Close	1. Spoken Address 2. Informal Introduction or Reference
Archbishop (Anglican)	To His Grace The Lord Archbishop of Canterbury Canterbury England	Your Grace: *or* My Lord Archbishop:	My dear Archbishop:	Respectfully yours,	Sincerely yours,	1. Your Grace NOT INTRODUCED (His Grace *or* The Archbishop)
Presiding Bishop of the Protestant Episcopal Church in America	The Most Reverend John R. Blank, D.D., LL.D. Presiding Bishop of the Protestant Episcopal Church in America Seabury House Greenwich, Conn.	Most Reverend Sir:	My dear Bishop Blank: *or* My dear Bishop:	Respectfully yours,	Sincerely yours,	1, 2. Bishop Blank
Anglican Bishop	The Right Reverend The Lord Bishop of London London, England	My Lord Bishop:	My dear Bishop:	Respectfully yours,	Sincerely yours,	1. My Lord 2. The Lord Bishop of London
Methodist Bishop	The Reverend Bishop Blank Methodist Bishop Memphis, Tennessee	Reverend Sir:	My dear Bishop Blank:	Respectfully yours,	Sincerely yours,	1, 2. Bishop Blank
Protestant Episcopal Bishop	The Right Reverend the Bishop of Jacksonville *or* The Right Reverend John R. Blank, D.D., LL.D. Bishop of Jacksonville Jacksonville, Florida	Right Reverend Sir:	My dear Bishop: *or* My dear Bishop Blank:	Respectfully yours,	Sincerely yours,	1, 2. Bishop Blank
Anglican Archdeacon	The Venerable John R. Blank The Archdeacon of San Francisco San Francisco, California	Mr. Archdeacon:	My dear Archdeacon:	Very truly yours,	Sincerely yours,	1, 2. Archdeacon Blank

Position	Address	Formal Salutation	Salutation			Reference
Protestant Episcopal Archdeacon	The Venerable John R. Blank, D.D. The Archdeacon of Baltimore Diocese of Maryland Baltimore, Maryland	Mr. Archdeacon:	My dear Archdeacon:	Very truly yours,	Sincerely yours,	1, 2. Archdeacon Blank *or* Dr. Blank
Dean[23]	The Very Reverend John R. Blank, D.D. Dean of St. Luke's Cathedral New York, New York	Very Reverend Sir: *or* My dear Mr. Dean:	My dear Dean Blank:	Very truly yours,	Sincerely yours,	1, 2. Dean Blank *or* Dr. Blank
Protestant Minister	*With Scholastic Degree:* The Reverend John R. Blank, D.D., Litt. D. Starkville, Mississippi	My dear Dr. Blank:	My dear Dr. Blank:	Very truly yours,	Sincerely yours,	1, 2. Dr. Blank
	Without Scholastic Degree: The Reverend John R. Blank Brownsville, Texas	My dear Mr. Blank:	My dear Mr. Blank:	Very truly yours,	Sincerely yours,	1, 2. Mr. Blank
Protestant Priest	*With Scholastic Degree:* The Reverend John R. Blank, D.D. St. Thomas' House Richmond, Virginia	My dear Dr. Blank:	My dear Dr. Blank:	Very truly yours,	Sincerely yours,	1, 2. Dr. Blank
	Without Scholastic Degree: The Reverend John R. Blank Richmond, Virginia	My dear Mr. Blank: *or* My dear Father Blank:	My dear Mr. Blank: *or* My dear Father Blank:			1, 2. Mr. Blank *or* Father Blank

[23] Applies only to the head of a Cathedral or of a Theological Seminary.

COLLEGE OFFICIALS

PERSONAGE	ENVELOPE AND INSIDE ADDRESS	FORMAL SALUTATION	INFORMAL SALUTATION	FORMAL CLOSE	INFORMAL CLOSE	1. SPOKEN ADDRESS 2. INFORMAL INTRODUCTION OR REFERENCE
President of a University	John R. Blank, LL.D., Ph.D. *or* Dr. John R. Blank President, Wells College Aurora, New York (Use only highest degree unless degrees are in different fields)	Sir:	My dear Dr. Blank:	Very truly yours,	Sincerely yours,	1, 2. Dr. Blank
	Catholic Priest The Very Reverend John R. Blank, S.J., D.D., Ph.D. President, Fordham University New York 10, New York	Sir:	My dear Father Blank:	Very truly yours,	Sincerely yours,	1, 2. Father Blank
University Chancellor	Dr. John R. Blank Chancellor, University of Alabama University Alabama	Sir:	My dear Dr. Blank:	Very truly yours,	Sincerely yours,	1, 2. Dr. Blank
Professor	Professor John R. Blank *or* (If he holds a doctor's degree) John R. Blank, Ph.D. George Washington University Washington 10, D. C.	My dear Sir: *or* My dear Professor (Doctor) Blank: *or* My dear Dr. Blank:	My dear Professor (Doctor) Blank	Very truly yours,	Sincerely yours,	1, 2. Professor Blank *or* Dr. Blank
Dean or Assistant Dean of a College Dean of Graduate School or Graduate School	Dean John R. Blank School of Commerce *or* (If he holds a doctor's degree) Dr. John R. Blank Dean (Assistant Dean) School of Commerce University of Mississippi Oxford, Mississippi	My dear Sir: *or* My dear Dean Blank:	My dear Dean Blank:	Very truly yours,	Sincerely yours,	1. Dean Blank 2. Dean Blank *or* Dr. Blank, the Dean (Assistant Dean) of the School of Commerce

112

7

How to Keep Account Records
in the Law Office

ALTHOUGH the practice of law is a profession and not a business, the successful lawyer today practices his profession in a businesslike way. He maintains an orderly system of accounts that shows him whether a fee is adequate for the time spent on a case, what percentage his overhead bears to his income, and the like. Of course, you will be punctilious in maintaining any system that has been established in an office in which you are a secretary. You will also have the privilege of making suggestions for the improvement of the system.

This chapter describes the fundamentals of bookkeeping in the lawyer's office. It also tells you how to keep records that will show the lawyer immediately the cost of his services.

How to Keep Books in the Law Office

System of bookkeeping in the law office. In many law offices, you will find in operation a simple "double entry" system of bookkeeping that you can maintain even though you have had little or no experience in keeping books. Although the books of account may vary in detail, the fundamental principles involved are the same. The following explanation will make it easier for you to follow the instructions of the person who describes the setup of the books to you.

Books required. In addition to checkbooks, the books usually maintained are a cash journal, a general ledger, and a subsidiary accounts receivable, or clients, ledger, all of which are usually maintained in loose-leaf post binders. The function of each is explained in this chapter.

Basic principles of double entry bookkeeping. In every double entry system, records are kept by accounts. An account is a formal record of related transactions kept in a ledger. Entries are made in a book of original entry and are posted to the appropriate accounts in the ledger. Posting merely means transferring items from a book of original entry to a ledger account. Each account has a debit column and a credit column. The debit is the left-hand column and the credit is the right-hand column.

In double entry bookkeeping every transaction must be recorded in two accounts—as a debit in one account and a credit in another.

Debits and credits. A few principles for debit and credit are all you need to learn to be able to keep the simple bookkeeping books that are ordinarily kept in a lawyer's office. Application of these rules will be explained later.

1. A debit *increases* asset accounts. Cash (bank account), accounts receivable, furniture and fixtures, and other property owned by the firm are assets.

2. A debit *increases* expense accounts, such as salaries, office supplies, taxes, and the like.

3. A debit *decreases* the capital account. The money that the lawyer puts into the bank when he opens his law office is shown in his capital account. It is decreased when he withdraws any of that money or when he incurs a loss in carrying on his practice.

4. A debit *decreases* an income account.

5. A debit *decreases* liability accounts. Accounts payable is a liability account. So is any other item that the firm owes.

6. A credit does exactly the reverse of a debit.

These principles may be expressed as a formula as follows:

> Debit —*Increases* assets and expense accounts.
>   *Decreases* capital, income, and liability accounts.
> Credit—*Decreases* assets and expense accounts.
>   *Increases* capital, income, and liability accounts.

Simple rules to remember. Since almost all transactions in a law office involve either bank deposits or bank withdrawals, or charging clients for services and receiving payment from them, you will have no difficulty in making your entries if you remember the four rules on the following page.

1. Cash received (bank deposits) is always debited to the bank account in which it is deposited and therefore must be credited to another account.

2. Cash payments (bank withdrawals) are always credited to the bank account on which the check is drawn and therefore must be debited to another account.

3. Accounts Receivable is always debited when bills for services are sent to a client, and the amount charged must be credited to the Services Charged account.

4. Accounts Receivable is always credited when a client pays for services, and the payment must be debited to the Services Charged account.

Cash journal. In a law office the book of original entry commonly used is referred to as a *cash journal*. It is a chronological record of every cash or other transaction that passes through the office. It is, of course, supplemented by a record of the lawyer's time, referred to on page 133, from which billings are made. The usual journal sheet consists of from 16 to 18 columns, spread across two facing pages (see the illustrations on pages 122-125). Appropriate headings, which will vary with the office, are written in the columns. An acceptable form of journal sheet has the lines numbered at each side to facilitate following the line across the sheet. In addition to space for date, description of item, and check number, the cash journal sheet in a law office will usually include the following columns, for the purposes indicated:

Cash (Firm Bank Account), debit. All deposits of moneys belonging to the firm are entered here.

Cash (Firm Bank Account), credit. All checks drawn on the firm bank account are entered here.

Trust Bank Account, debit. All receipts of moneys belonging to clients are entered here. Large advances by clients for expenses are also usually deposited in the trust account and, therefore, are entered in this column. Collections of commercial items for clients (Chapter 24) are deposited to the trust account.

Trust Bank Account, credit. All checks drawn on the trust bank account are entered here.

Accounts Receivable, debit. All charges made to clients are entered here.

Accounts Receivable, credit. All payments made by clients are entered here.

Accounts Payable, debit. All payments made on accounts owed are entered here. Law firms have few outstanding accounts payable. Therefore this column is frequently omitted, and the payments on accounts owed are entered in the General Ledger (debit) column, from which the detail entry is posted to the debit column of the control account in the general ledger.

Accounts Payable, credit. All accounts owed are entered here. As indicated above, this column may be omitted and entries made instead in the General Ledger (credit) column, from which the detail entry is posted to the credit column of the control account in the general ledger.

Services Charged, debit. All payments made by clients for services are entered here.

Services Charged, credit. All charges made to clients for services are entered here.

General Ledger, debit, and General Ledger, credit. These columns are for accounts that do not have separate columns of their own, such as Furniture and Fixtures, Library, and Accounts Payable. Expenses that occur only occasionally, such as rent, insurance, and entertainment, are entered in the General Ledger column. The entries are posted in detail to the respective accounts in the general ledger.

Income from Fees. All income from fees is entered here. Only one journal column is necessary because all entries are credits.

Tax Expense. Taxes that the firm pays are entered here. They include the firm's share of the social security tax, unemployment tax, use and occupancy tax, and others. All entries are debit entries.

Overhead expenses. There may be any number of columns for overhead expenses, such as Office Supplies, Utilities, Telephone and Telegraph, and the like. The breakdown depends upon the need and the number of columns. All entries are debits.

Miscellaneous Expense. Expenses that cannot be readily classified and have no account of their own in the ledger, are entered here. All entries are debits.

General ledger. The general ledger is a loose-leaf book containing all the accounts, including the control account for the individual clients' accounts. The entries in the journal are posted to the accounts affected. The cash journal shows what transactions took place on a certain date, whereas the ledger shows the recorded status of each specific account at any time.

The accounts in the ledger may be arranged alphabetically, but they are usually classified by kind and grouped in the following order in the ledger to facilitate the preparation of statements.

Assets (Bank Accounts, Furniture and Fixtures, Accounts Receivable, etc.)
Liabilities (Accounts Payable, Loans Payable, etc.)
Capital (Proprietorship)
Income
Expense

The general ledger will have accounts for the following columns shown in the cash journal (pages 122-125): Cash (Firm Bank Account), Trust Bank Account, Accounts Receivable, Services Charged, Accrued Withholding Tax, Accrued Federal Insurance Contributions, Income from Fees, Tax Expense, Telephone and Telegraph, Office Supplies, Salaries, and Miscellaneous Expense in which any miscellaneous expense may be entered in detail. The general ledger will also have accounts for items that are entered in the General Ledger column, such as Rent, Insurance, Petty Cash, Accounts Payable, and others.

In addition, it will have some accounts that are not immediately affected by the journal. They will have been opened when the books were set up. Entries are usually made in them only once a year, when the books are closed. They generally include a Capital (proprietorship) account, Profit and Loss, Reserve for Depreciation, Depreciation, Bad Debts, and others. The closing entries, which are posted to these accounts, are usually made by the accountant.

Subsidiary ledger. The subsidiary accounts receivable ledger is the most important record in the law office—the accounts receivable are the lawyer's largest asset. The Accounts Receivable account in the general ledger is a "control" account; it summarizes the individual accounts in the subsidiary ledger. Its balance equals the sum of the balances of the individual accounts in the subsidiary accounts receivable ledger. The control account simplifies getting a trial balance and, especially, detecting any error that might be made in posting to the wrong side of the individual accounts that it controls. When the client's ledger sheets are the same size and shape as the sheets in the general ledger, the accounts receivable may be kept in a separate part of the general ledger. The accounts are kept in alphabetical order according to the client's name.

Unless a separate record is kept of the hours worked on a case (see page 136), it is desirable that the client's ledger sheet should have columns for this information. It should also have separate columns for disbursements and charges for services and a column for payments. Figure 21 shows a form of client's ledger sheet suitable for a law office. There are, of course, other forms.

		Hours			Debits			
Date	Lawyer	Partner	Staff	Description	Disburse-ments	Service	Credits	Balance
Mar. 8	R.S.E.	1.25		Conference with client				
9				Abstract of title	20.			
12	L.E.T.		2.50	Examination of Abstacts				
13	R.S.E.	1.00		Conference with Smith Attorney				
14				Deposit for Trust			1,000.	980.
18	L.E.T.		2.50	Draft Agreement				
19	R.S.E.	1.25		Conference with Smith Attorney				
21	L.E.T.		1.00	Drawing deed				
23	R.S.E.	.50		Conference with client				
24	R.S.E.	1.25						
	L.E.T.		1.25	Closing				
24				Ch. R.D. Smith settlement	780.			200.
25				Services		200.		

Nature of Case: (3) Escrow Agreement, Real Estate

Name of Client S. M. Jones
Address 215 East 18 Street, Jamestown, Michigan

Figure 21. Client's Ledger Sheet.

As soon as a new case is received, open a ledger sheet for it and fill in all of the data shown in the heading of the account illustrated in Figure 21. Because of the manner in which lawyers bill their clients, a separate sheet is opened for each case. Thus, a client with three cases pending would have three sheets in the ledger. When a case is disposed of, the sheet is removed from the active ledger. You can get the information necessary to open the account from the New Matter Report (see page 16, *et seq.*).

The column for disbursements and the column for services

charged are debit items. Postings are made to these columns from the cash journal.

Posting to the general ledger. Recording the items from the cash journal to the affected accounts in the ledger is called *posting*. The items in the Accounts Receivable column should be posted daily to the client's subsidiary ledger account, so that charges for disbursements are apparent when the lawyer decides to bill the client. (See page 138 for billing the client.) The other items may be posted monthly. The items in the General Ledger column must be posted individually to the accounts affected. Only the totals of the other columns are posted to the corresponding accounts.

Here is the procedure for posting from the cash journal to the accounts in the general ledger:

1. Total each column in the journal. Then total the debit columns and the credit columns. The totals of the debit and credit columns must equal each other. If they do not, you have made an error in the entries or in addition.

2. Post the totals from all columns except General Ledger to the corresponding accounts in the general ledger as a debit or credit, as indicated in the column. You have previously posted the individual items in the Accounts Receivable column to the respective clients' accounts. The total of the Accounts Receivable column is posted to the control account in the general ledger.

3. Post the individual items from the General Ledger column to the respective accounts in the general ledger, as a debit or credit, as indicated in the column. Place a check mark at each item to show that it has been posted.

4. Draw a double red line under the total of each column that has been posted. Your next entries will be below these lines and new totals will not include the figures above the red lines.

Explanation of cash journal entries and posting. A cash journal sheet is illustrated on pages 122-125. Each of the entries shown and the manner in which they are posted to the general and subsidiary ledgers is explained below. The entries will not normally be in the order in which they are shown here, but this order is presented for purposes of the explanation.

Line 1. The balances are brought forward from the bottom of the preceding page of the journal.

Line 2. Check #1132 in the amount of $300, payable to the Real Estate Co. for rent is drawn on the firm bank account. It is entered in the credit column of the Firm Bank Account and in the debit column of General Ledger, because there is no column for rent expense.

At the end of the month all rent items will be posted to the debit column of the Rent account in the general ledger. The credit entry in the Firm Bank Account column will be included in the total that will be posted at the end of the month to the Firm Bank Account in the general ledger.

Line 3. Check #1133, in the amount of $6 is drawn on the firm bank account in favor of Clerk of the Court for the account of client Henry Fowler. It is entered in the credit column of the Firm Bank Account and in the debit column of Accounts Receivable.

It is posted from the journal to the debit Disbursement column in Henry Fowler's account in the subsidiary ledger. It will be included also in the total that will be posted at the end of the month to the debit column of the Accounts Receivable control account in the general ledger. The credit entry in the Firm Bank Account column will be included in the total that is posted at the end of the month to the credit column of the Firm Bank Account in the general ledger.

Line 4. Client Henry Fowler is charged $100 for services. This is not a cash transaction. The $100 for services is entered in the debit column of Accounts Receivable and in the credit column of Services Charged.

It is posted from the cash journal to the debit Services column in Henry Fowler's account in the subsidiary ledger. It will be included also in the total that will be posted at the end of the month to the debit column of the Accounts Receivable control account in the general ledger. The credit entry in the Services Charged column will be included in the total that will be posted at the end of the month to the credit column of the Services Charged account in the general ledger.

Line 5. Client Henry Fowler sends the firm a check for $106. It is entered in the debit column of the Firm Bank Account and in the credit column of Accounts Receivable.

The amount of $106 is posted in the credit column of Henry

Fowler's account in the subsidiary ledger. It will be included also in the total that will be posted at the end of the month to the credit column of the Accounts Receivable control account in the general ledger, and in the total that will be posted at the end of the month to the debit column of the Firm Bank Account.

However, $100 of the $106 is for income from fees, which was previously credited to Services Charged. Therefore, $100 is entered in the debit column of Services Charged and in the credit column, Income from Fees.

The $100 will be included in the total that will be posted at the end of the month to the debit column of the Services Charged account in the general ledger. It will be included also in the total of the Income from Fees that will be posted at the end of the month to the credit of that account in the general ledger.

Line 6. Client S. M. Jones gives the firm a check for $1,000 as advance for expenses in a real estate matter. That amount is entered in the debit column of the Trust Bank Account and in the credit column of Accounts Receivable.

It is posted to the credit column of S. M. Jones's account for that particular case in the subsidiary ledger, and will be included also in the totals that will be posted at the end of the month to the debit column of the Trust Bank Account and to the credit column of the Accounts Receivable control account in the general ledger.

Line 7. An abstract of title was ordered for Jones and received, together with an invoice for $20. The $20 is entered in the debit column of Accounts Receivable and in the credit column of General Ledger.

The law firm pays the abstract company only once a month, but it is important that Jones's account be charged with $20 immediately. It is posted, therefore, to the debit Disbursements column of S. M. Jones's subsidiary ledger account immediately. It is also posted to the credit column of the abstract company's account in the general ledger. (If transactions with the abstract company are too few to justify a separate account in the general ledger, the $20 will be posted to the Accounts Payable account in the general ledger.) It will be included also in the total posted to the debit column of the Accounts Receivable control account at the end of the month.

	19—	Description	Ck. No.	Cash (Firm Bank Act) Debit	Credit
1	Apr. 11	Forward		3195 90	1900 00
2	15	Real Estate Co.—Rent	1132		300 00
3		Clerk of Court—for Henry Fowler	1133		6 00
4	16	Henry Fowler—Services			
5	17	Ck. from Henry Fowler		106 00	
6		Ck. from S. M. Jones—Real Est. Escrow			
7	18	Title Abs Co.—abs for S. M. Jones			
8	19	R. D. Smith—Jones Escrow matter	105		
9		S. M. Jones—Services			
10	20	Ellwood & Jones (S. M. Jones acct.)	106	220 00	
11	22	Ck. A. H. Brown—retainer		100 00	
12	23	A. H. Brown—Services			
13		Bell Telephone Co.	1134		65 00
14		L. R. Ellwood—Drawing acct.	1135		833 33
15	30	Agnes Smith—salary	1136		124 25
16		Internal Revenue Service	1137		247 90
17		Petty Cash	1138		40 00
18					
19					
20					
21					
22					
29					
30					
31					
32					
33					
34					
35					
36				3621 90	3571 48

Double-page Spread Journal Sheet (Left Edge).
(Follow each numbered line through page 125.)

Line 8. Check #105 for $780 is drawn on the Trust Bank Account to the order of R. D. Smith, in the Jones escrow matter. It is entered in the credit column of the Trust Bank Account and in the debit column of Accounts Receivable.

It is posted immediately to the debit Disbursement column of Jones's account in the subsidiary ledger and will be included in the total posted to the debit column of the Accounts Receivable

	Trust Bank Account Debit	Trust Bank Account Credit	Accounts Receivable Debit	Accounts Receivable Credit	Services Charged Debit	Services Charged Credit	
	500.00	300.00	400.00	350.00	350.00	400.00	1
							2
			6.00				3
			100.00			100.00	4
				106.00	100.00		5
	1000.00			1000.00			6
			20.00				7
		780.00	780.00				8
			200.00			200.00	9
		220.00			200.00		10
				100.00			11
			400.00		100.00	400.00	12
			30.00				13
							14
							15
							16
			20.00				17
							18
							19
							20
							21
							22
							29
							30
							31
							32
							33
							34
							35
	1500.00	1300.00	5556.00	4706.00	3900.00	4700.00	36

Double-page Spread Journal Sheet (Left Center).
(Follow each numbered line from page 122 through page 125.)

control account at the end of the month, and in the total posted to the credit column of the Trust Bank Account at the end of the month.

Line 9. The Jones matter having been completed, Jones is charged $200 for services rendered. The charge is handled in the same manner as in Line 4. However, Jones has money on deposit with the firm in the Trust Bank Account, and the charge of $200

	General Ledger		Accrued Withholding Tax		Accrued F.I.C.	
	Debit	Credit	Debit	Credit	Debit	Credit
1	2500 00	1000 00		173 40		22 50
2	300 00					
3						
4						
5						
6						
7		20 00				
8						
9						
10						
11						
12						
13						
14	833 33					
15				22 00		3 75
16			195 40		26 25	
17						
18						
19						
20						
21						
22						
29						
30						
31						
32						
33						
34						
35						
36	3633 33	1020 00	195 40	195 40	26 25	26 25

Double-page Spread Journal Sheet (Right Center).
(*Follow each numbered line from page 122 through page 125.*)

will close out his account. A bill is sent to him showing no balance owing, and the ledger sheet for the case is transferred to an inactive account file.

Line 10. To obtain payment from Jones for the $200 service charge and the $20 disbursements, shown by his ledger account, check #106 for $220 is drawn on the Trust Bank Account in favor of the law firm. It is entered in the debit column of the Firm

Income from Fees	Tax Expense	Tel. & Tel.	Office Supplies	Salaries	Misc Expense Debit	
4100 00		100 00	200 00	900 00	100 00	1
						2
						3
						4
100 00						5
						6
						7
						8
						9
200 00						10
						11
100 00						12
		35 00				13
						14
				150 00		15
	26 25					16
					20 00	17
						18
						19
						20
						21
						22
						29
						30
						31
						32
						33
						34
						35
4500 00	26 25	135 00	200 00	1050 00	120 00	36

Double-page Spread Journal Sheet (Right Edge).
(Follow each numbered line through from page 122.)

Bank Account and in the credit column of the Trust Bank Account.

The $220 will be included in the totals that will be posted at the end of the month to the debit column of the Firm Bank Account and to the credit column of the Trust Bank Account in the general ledger.

However, the $200, which represents income from fees, was

previously credited to Services Charged. Therefore $200 is entered in the debit column of Services Charged and in the credit column Income from Fees.

The $200 will be included in the totals that will be posted at the end of the month to the debit column of the Services Charged account in the general ledger, and in the total of the Income from Fees that will be posted at the end of the month to the credit column of that account in the general ledger.

Line 11. Client A. H. Brown pays an advance retainer of $100 on account of services to be rendered. This money represents income from fees *when earned,* but is not to be held in trust as was the $1,000 in the Jones matter (Line 6). An advance retainer is also to be distinguished from a yearly retainer (see page 9, Chapter 1), which is considered earned income immediately. The $100 advance retainer is entered in the debit column of the Firm Bank Account and in the credit column of Accounts Receivable. It is not yet income from fees nor a debit to Services Charged, because the services have not been rendered. Later when Brown is billed for services rendered, the $100 will represent a part of the bill (see Line 12).

The $100 is posted immediately to the credit column in Brown's account in the subsidiary ledger, and is included also in the totals that will be posted to the debit column of the Firm Bank Account and to the credit column of the Accounts Receivable control account in the general ledger.

Line 12. Client Brown is charged $400 for services rendered and is billed for that amount. The $400 is debited to Accounts Receivable and credited to Services Charged. It is posted immediately to Brown's ledger account and is also included in the totals posted to the respective general ledger accounts.

But the $400 includes $100 already collected (Line 11). Therefore Services Charged is debited and Income from Fees is credited with $100. The amount is included in the totals posted to the respective general ledger accounts. (When the balance of $300 is paid, it will be handled in the same manner as any fee for services. See Line 5.)

Line 13. Check 1134 payable to the telephone company is drawn on the firm bank account for $65 and entered in the credit column of the Firm Bank Account. Clients are charged with toll calls made in their behalf. Telephone bills must therefore be broken down to determine what part of the bill is telephone expense and what part must be charged to individual clients as disbursements. In this case, the breakdown shows $30 chargeable to clients and $35 to telephone expenses. In the cash journal, $30 is entered in the debit column of Accounts Receivable and the remaining $35 is entered in the debit Telephone and Telegraph Expenses column.

These amounts will be included in the totals posted at the end of the month to the debit of the Accounts Receivable control account, the debit of the Telephone Expense account, and the credit of the Firm Bank Account in the general ledger. From the breakdown of the telephone bill, the amount chargeable to each client is posted immediately in the debit Disbursements column of his account in the subsidiary ledger.

Line 14. Check #1135 in the amount of $833.33 is drawn on the firm bank account to the order of L. R. Elwood, one of the partners. It is entered in the credit column of the Firm Bank Account and in the debit General Ledger column.

It is posted to the debit side of Mr. Elwood's drawing account in the general ledger. The credit will be included in the total posted at the end of the month to the Firm Bank Account in the general ledger.

All entries in Mr. Elwood's account are debits until the end of the year, or other accounting period, when the profits of the firm are credited in accordance with the partnership agreement. Drawing accounts of the partners are not "expenses" for the purpose of figuring profit and loss, nor for income tax purposes. No tax is withheld from checks payable to the partners.

Line 15. Agnes Smith, a stenographer with no dependents, receives a salary of $300 per month, payable semi-monthly. A total of $25.75 is taken out of her salary each payday—$22.00 for the withholding tax and $3.75 for the Social Security Tax (Federal Insurance Contribution). A check for $124.25 ($150 − $25.75) is drawn on the firm bank account. It is entered in the credit column of the Firm Bank Account; $150 is entered in the Salaries expense column; $22 and $3.75 are entered in the credit columns of the Accrued Withholding and F.I.C. accounts respectively.

The $22.00 and $3.75 will be included in the totals posted to the credit of Accrued Withholding and Accrued F.I.C. accounts in the general ledger. It is also included in the total of the Salaries column that will be posted to the debit of the Salaries account in the general ledger. This procedure is followed for salaries paid all office employees, including associate lawyers who work for a salary, but not including the partners.

All entries in the Salaries account are debits, until the end of the year when the closing entries are made. Then the Salaries account is credited with the total of salaries for the year and the Profit and Loss account is debited with the same amount.

An individual salary account for each employee should also be kept. See page 130.

Line 16. Check #1137 for $247.90, payable to Internal Revenue Service, is drawn on the firm bank account. It is entered in the credit column of the Firm Bank Account. The $195.40 and $26.25 previously withheld from employees, are entered in the debit columns of Accrued Withholding and Accrued F.I.C. accounts. The remainder, $26.25 represents the firm's share of the Social Security Tax (Federal Insurance Contribution) and is entered in the Tax Expense column.

The $247.90 will be included in the total that is posted to the credit of the Firm Bank Account in the general ledger; $195.40 and $26.25 will be included in the totals posted to the debit of the Accrued Withholding and Accrued F.I.C. accounts; $26.25 will be posted as a debit to the Tax Expense account in the ledger.

Line 17. Check #1138 for $40 is drawn on the firm bank account to replenish the petty cash fund (see page 139) and is entered in the credit column of the Firm Bank Account. Petty cash payments are analyzed to determine what part of the expenditures is miscellaneous expense and what part must be charged to individual clients as disbursements. In this instance, the analysis shows that $20 was spent for items chargeable to clients and $20 for items chargeable to miscellaneous expense. In the cash journal, $20 is entered in the debit column of Accounts Receivable and $20 is entered in the debit Miscellaneous Expenses column.

These amounts will be included in the totals posted to the debit of the Accounts Receivable control account, the debit of the Miscellaneous Expenses account, and the credit of the Firm

Bank Account in the general ledger. From the analysis of the petty cash disbursements, the amount chargeable to each client is posted in the debit Disbursements column of his account in the subsidiary ledger.

Trial balance. The process of listing the titles of the accounts in the ledger and showing the balance of each, whether debit or credit, is known as *taking a trial balance*. The purpose is to determine whether the total debits equal the total credits and to establish a basic summary for financial statements.

Here are the steps in taking a trial balance:

1. Get the balance of each account in the general ledger by subtracting the total of the debits from the total of the credits, or vice versa if the debit total is larger than the credit total.

2. Enter the balance on the ledger sheet, in the explanation column on the debit side if the balance is a debit; in the explanation column on the credit side if the balance is a credit. You may keep a running record of the account by bringing down the totals in pencil in small figures at the end of each month.

3. Type at the top of a legal-size sheet, "Trial Balance as of (date)."

4. Type a list of the accounts, placing balances in two parallel columns, debit balances in the left column and credit balances in the right.

5. Total the columns. They will equal one another unless you have made an error.

Taking a trial balance of accounts receivable. Whenever a trial balance is taken, the accuracy of the accounts in the clients' subsidiary ledger should also be proved. This is done by adding the debit balances and the credit balances, if any, and subtracting the credits from the debits. The result should be the same as the balance shown in the Accounts Receivable control account in the general ledger. If it is not, you have made an error in your posting or in your calculations.

In taking the balance of accounts receivable, remember that both the disbursement entries and the charges for services are debits, whereas the payments received are credits.

Services Charged account is in reality a reserve set aside for the collection of accounts receivable for services and should be in balance with the amounts that are receivable for services.

In taking off your trial balance of the accounts receivable, a separate listing should be made of the accounts receivable for advances made by the attorney for clients' expenses, indicated on the client's ledger sheet as Disbursements. After deducting from the total listing of all receivables the amount of receivables for expense, the balance should equal the credit balance in the Services Charged account, unless there are certain prepayments in the accounts receivable balances in the form of advance retainers or trust deposits. A glance at the illustrated cash journal will show that every debit to Accounts Receivable *for services rendered* is reflected in the credits to Services Charged.

Profit and loss statement. A profit and loss statement shows the lawyer whether he made a profit or lost money over a given period of time.

It also shows him the amount of each type of expense. The accountant usually prepares this statement after he has closed the books for the period. However, you can at any time prepare a profit and loss statement as follows:

1. Take a trial balance as explained on page 129.

2. Take a sheet of paper and rule the right of the page with two columns for the insertion of figures. Entitle the sheet "Profit and loss statement for the period beginning (insert the date) and ending (insert the date)."

3. List the income accounts shown in the trial balance, carrying the figure for each account to the right column. Draw a line under the figures and show the total of the income accounts.

4. List the expense accounts shown in the trial balance, carrying the figure to the left column. Draw a line under the figures and show the total of the expense accounts.

5. Subtract. The balance shows the law firm's net profit or loss.

Drawing account. Each member of the firm has a drawing account. All of the entries are on the debit side. These accounts are closed out at the end of the accounting period, usually by the accountant.

Payroll record. An individual account for each employee should also be kept, to facilitate reports to the Government and the preparation of the withholding receipt that must be given to each employee. Figure 22 is a form suggested for this purpose when employees are paid weekly. The form provides space for recording and accumulating taxes withheld for remittance to the Internal Revenue Service and for the annual withholding statement. These entries are posted from the cash journal.

PAYROLL

NAME							SOCIAL SEC. NO.						
ADDRESS						PHONE					NO. OF EXEMPTIONS		
DATE 19	PERIOD PAID FOR	RATE	EARNINGS				DEDUCTIONS					NET PAID	CHECK NUMBER
			REGULAR	OTHER		TOTAL	W. H. TAX	O. A. B.			TOTAL		
JAN.													
TOTAL JANUARY													
FEB.													
TOTAL FEBRUARY													
MAR.													
TOTAL MARCH													
TOTAL 1ST QUARTER													
APR.													
TOTAL APRIL													
MAY													
TOTAL MAY													
JUNE													
TOTAL JUNE													
TOTAL 2ND QUARTER													
TOTAL HALF YEAR													

FORM A-36, COLWELL PUBLISHING COMPANY, CHAMPAIGN, ILLINOIS

From Daily Log for Lawyers. *Courtesy Colwell Publishing Company.*

Figure 22. Payroll Record.

Capital account. It takes money to open a law office and operate it before the fees are received. The money that the lawyer puts up for this purpose is known as *capital*. It is entered in the debit column of the Firm Bank Account and in the credit column of the Capital account. At the end of each year when the books are closed and the lawyer finds out whether he has made a profit or has lost money on the operation of his office, an entry is made to show the change in Capital account. A profit is posted to the credit of the Capital account and a loss to the debit. As previously mentioned, the accountant usually makes the closing entries.

Time and Cost of Professional Services

Records required to find time and cost of service. The records required to ascertain the cost of the lawyer's service on a specific case are the following:

Daily time sheet

Clients ledger (kept in connection with bookkeeping)

Finding the cost of a lawyer's time. In figuring the profit and loss in a law office for accounting purposes, the lawyer's time is not counted, but the lawyer who practices his profession in a businesslike manner wants to know the cost of the time spent on a case. The fee charged may be more than the cost, giving the lawyer a profit; or it may be less, resulting in a loss. But at least the cost of his time is a basis for a fair fee. Even when a client is on a yearly retainer or when the lawyer accepts a case on a contingent basis, he wants to know the cost to him.

The cost per hour of a lawyer's time is arrived at by adding the lawyer's drawing account to the overhead and dividing by the number of hours he expects to be working during the year. If there is more than one attorney practicing for the firm, the overhead is proportioned among them, including the associates, on the basis of their drawing accounts. The senior member of the firm, who has the largest drawing account, is thus charged with a larger proportion of the overhead than a junior member. This is as it should be since he has a better office, a higher paid secretary, and the like. Salaries paid associate attorneys are not included in overhead for the purpose of calculating the cost of services; the associate's cost to the firm is figured in the same manner as the cost of a partner's service.

Example: The firm of Elwood & Adams is composed of two partners and a salaried associate. Senior Partner Elwood draws $10,000 per year, Junior Partner Adams draws $9,000, and Associate Tucker is paid a salary of $5,200. The overhead is $18,000, or approximately 75 per cent of $24,200, the total paid the three lawyers. (The overhead figure is taken from the books, but Tucker's salary is deducted from that figure.) The overhead each lawyer is expected to carry bears the same relation to the total overhead that the amount paid him by the firm bears to the total paid all the lawyers. The overhead of each lawyer is, therefore, 75 per cent of his earnings, or $7,500, $6,750, and $3,900 respectively. Each lawyer works 1,600 hours per year. Senior Partner's cost is approximately $10.93 per hour [($10,000 + $7,500) ÷ 1600]; Junior Partner's cost is approximately $9.85 per hour [($9,000 + $6,750) ÷ 1600]; and the associate's is approximately $5.70 per hour [($5,200 + $3,900) ÷ 1600].

Daily time sheet. To arrive at the cost of a job, each lawyer in the office must keep a daily time sheet. The diary illustrated in Figure 10, Chapter 3, can be used as a time record. Figure 23 illustrates another form. These forms do not provide for an estimated fee, but this is covered by the new matter reports illustrated in Figures 5 and 6, Chapter 1. In some offices the secretaries and stenographers also keep time sheets. The time spent on each matter is posted to the client's ledger account and is considered in calculating the fee.

Figure 24 is a combination time sheet and diary form. Appointments, trial dates, deadlines, and the like are scheduled at the top of each daily page. Either you or the lawyer may make these entries. Then follows a chronological record of the day's work.

The "case number" heading is used when your office handles more than one item for a client. In order to keep careful cost records on each of several matters for one client, it is advisable to assign a serial number to each item and to use this number throughout the records.

Next is a column provided to check off items as they are posted to the time columns of the client's account (see Figure 21). Then follows the name of the client and the nature of the work done for him. If this is a new item, it is checked in the column headed "New."

HALL and DOBB

Daily Service Report of		Date		
CLIENT	CASE	Key CHARACTER OF SERVICES T T, telephone to T F, telephone from L T, letter to L F, letter from S L, study of law P F, preparation of facts M T, memorandum to M F, memorandum from Ct. T, court trial Ct. M, court motion Ct. A, court argument C W, conference with Ex, examination of title P P, passing papers R P, recording papers R T, reviewing title	TIME HOURS	 TENTHS

Figure 23. Daily Time Sheet.

Monday
March 8

HOUR	CASE NUMBER	✓	CLIENT	NATURE AND CLASSIFICATION	NEW	ESTIMATED FEE	TIME	EXPENSE	FEE
8 00	·								
8 30									
9 00	3		C. L. Schum	Drafting lease			1		
9 30									
10 00			Williams Estate	Hearing					
10 30									
11 00									
11 30	4		Rogers	Conference re income tax			.50		
12 00			Hugh Bailey	Auto accident	X	50	.75		
12 30									
12:45 1 00			Luncheon	Clemens – Biltmore					
1 30									
2 00									
2 30									
3 00				Community Chest					
3 30	3	✓	Henry Fowler	Conference	2	200	1.25		
4 00									
4 30									
5 00									
5 30									
EVENING	9:00			Churchill Dinner - Waldorf					

FORM A 11 COLWELL PUBLISHING COMPANY CHAMPAIGN ILLINOIS

From Daily Log for Lawyers. *Courtesy Colwell Publishing Company.*

Figure 24. Daily Time Sheet Combined with Diary.

The lawyer then enters the *estimated* fee for the new case.
Next is a column for the amount of time with which the client

is being charged. Use decimals instead of fractions of hours for recording time, because it is easier to add decimals. Thus, ¼ hour is posted as ¼ of 100, or .25; ½ hour is posted as .50; ¾ hour is .75.

Under "Expenses," enter only expenses that are paid out of petty cash. The last column is for the fee to be charged, but this column is not filled in unless the lawyer disposes of the case in one conference. The fee is not fixed until a matter is completed, or until considerable work has been done on it.

Collect the lawyer's time sheet each night for posting to the client's ledger account and other records.

Posting the time charges. Post the time charges to the client's ledger account (Figure 21) from the daily time sheet, showing which lawyer did the work. When the lawyer is ready to fix the fee, he will ask for the time spent on the case by each attorney. He knows the cost per hour and can thus calculate the cost to the firm of the services rendered. The fee may be more or less than that cost.

Some law firms do not post the time to the client's ledger account but keep it on a service ledger sheet similar to those illustrated in Figures 25 and 26. In that case, the lawyer calls for the

	CHARGE RECORDS NO. 325

City Bank #56
    Lester Trust

DATE	LAWYER	PARTNER HOURS	STAFF HOURS	
195-				
3-6	S.E.T.		7:15	Preparation of Draft
3-8	R.L.A.	2:30		Examination of Draft

Figure 25. Service Ledger Sheet.

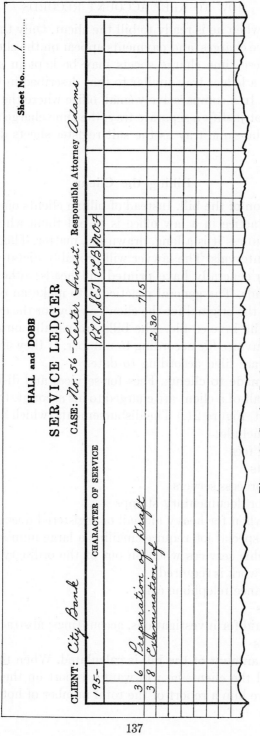

Figure 26. Service Ledger Sheet—Another Form.

137

time record when he is ready to bill the client. Only the disbursements, service charges, and payments appear on the client's ledger account. These time charge sheets may be kept in a loose-leaf ledger, or in a ledger tray similar to that described in Chapter 15 (Figure 80). In a comparatively small office where the number of cases does not justify a separate tray, the time charge sheets may be kept in the same tray as the suit register sheets described in Chapter 15.

Billing the Client

Preparation of the bill. Instead of billing clients once a month, the usual practice in a law office is to bill them when a case is completed, unless it is a long, drawn-out matter. Then the client is billed at intervals. The lawyer will probably dictate the bill.

Law firms generally have printed bill heads; otherwise, they use letterheads. The general practice is to make an original and two copies—the original for the client, a copy for the case file, and a copy for the invoice file. The bills are usually numbered and filed in the invoice file according to number. If they are not numbered, they are filed according to date.

Charges made to clients. Fees for services and disbursements made in behalf of a client are charged to his account. (See Client's Ledger Sheet, Figure 21.) The disbursements, which are itemized in the bill, include:

Recording fees

Court costs

Fee paid process servers

Revenue or documentary stamps

Postage, when for heavy airmail or registered documents; also when a special job requires mailing a large number of letters

Stenographic services when an out of the ordinary amount of clerical work is required

Long distance telephone calls

Telegrams

All fees paid for investigations, accountings, abstracts, etc.

Photostats

How the amount of the bill is calculated. When the lawyer is ready to bill the client, he will want a report on the time costs. You will give him a report of the total number of hours spent on the case by each lawyer from the time the case was opened, or from the date of the last bill. Each lawyer's time is listed separately, because the cost per hour varies with the lawyer. You can get this information from the client's service ledger sheet (Figures 25 and 26), or from his account ledger sheet if the account shows the time record (Figure 21). The lawyer knows the cost per hour of each member of the firm and of each associate lawyer (you might not), and calculates the cost accordingly.

He will also want a record of the advances made for the client, and the status of the account as a whole. He will get this from the client's account ledger sheet, or you will give him a record of the disbursements. Whenever a client is billed, examine the current petty cash record to see if any expenditures have been made in his behalf; also examine records of toll telephone costs. After a client is billed, the lawyer cannot very well send him a bill for 50 cents for a photostat that you paid out of petty cash, but numerous small advances add up to sizable sums.

Petty cash fund. Keep a petty cash fund in the office to pay for any incidental expenses that may arise, such as recording fees and collect messages. The size of the fund will vary according to the demands made upon it, but it should be large enough to last about a month. Keep the money in a safe place because you are responsible for it. Never mix this money with your own funds; never make change from it unless you can make the exact change; and *never* borrow from it.

Keep a running record of expenditures made from the fund. As each expenditure is made, no matter how small, enter the date, the amount, purpose for which spent, and the client and case to which it is chargeable. When the petty cash fund gets low, add up the expenditures and write a check, payable to yourself, for the total—that is, the amount necessary to bring the petty cash fund up to its original figure. Attach the record to the check when you give it to your employer for his signature. Mark the record, "Paid —(date)—, Ck. No. ———," initial, and file it. Then start a new running account for future expenditures from the fund.

Part II

Preparing Legal Instruments and Documents

8. Distinctive Features of Dictation and Typing   143
9. Basic Information about Legal Instruments   168
10. Specific Instruments: Affidavits; Powers of Attorney;
    Wills   193

8

Distinctive Features of Dictation and Typing

MATERIAL dictated in the law office has certain characteristics peculiar to the legal field. This chapter points out some of those peculiarities and makes practical suggestions (1) for overcoming difficult features connected with the work and (2) for saving time.

Common practice requires that legal documents (and we use the term to mean legal instruments and court papers) be set up in a style all their own. The directions in this chapter will enable the secretary to produce a legal document that is professional in format and style even if she does not have a model in front of her. These directions are general and apply to all legal papers. Directions that are peculiar to a specific document are given when that document is discussed. The directions, although necessarily arbitrary in many respects, are based upon standards adopted by many leading law firms.

The secretary's loose-leaf notebook. Every secretary in a law office should have a loose-leaf binder to hold copies of each kind of instrument used frequently in her office. The copy will show not only the style in which the instrument should be typed, but also the wording used by the lawyer for whom she works. Reference to your own loose-leaf book is much quicker than reference to a practice manual or to the file of a case that contains a similar instrument. Arrange the papers alphabetically according to the name of the instrument, or, if you prefer, break them down into litigation and non-litigation papers. The binder should be legal size. It may be made out of heavy Manila stock.

Dictation in the Law Office

Importance of understanding dictated material. A well-trained legal stenographer could take the dictation and transcribe it accurately without a notion of the meaning of the sentences, but she would consider her job boring and arduous. The dictated material is rarely monotonous and is intensely interesting to the secretary who understands what is being dictated. One of the objects of this book is to clarify what would otherwise be jargon to you.

Another difficult feature of dictation in a law office is the length of the material dictated. Frequently, dictation on one matter lasts three or four hours. Here, again, an understanding of what is being dictated changes the arduous task into a pleasant one. Being able to follow the lawyer's thought also enables you to take dictation more rapidly and to transcribe more accurately, thus saving time and eliminating rewrites.

Errors in the dictation. As a rule lawyers are excellent dictators. They think clearly and express themselves fluently, thus enabling the secretary to follow their trend of thought. However, sentences in legal work are long and involved and the best of dictators sometimes makes errors in grammar and sentence structure. Some of the responsibility for the English in the document is yours, and it is up to you to catch obvious errors. One of the most common errors is the omission of a main verb or a conjunction when a parenthetic clause intervenes. To detect an inaccuracy in sentence structure, read the independent clause in the sentence without the intervening subordinate clauses or parenthetic material. If you are following the dictator's thought, you will immediately realize that something is wrong with the sentence. At the first break in the dictation, you should call the sentence to the dictator's attention, because you cannot supply the omission.

As an example, let us analyze the following sentence.

The courts below have decided, [although this plaintiff failed to bring her action within the time limit because an alternative remedy, which as against the employer was exclusive, was apparently granted to her by a statute] yet the courts are powerless to afford her any relief if under the express terms of the statute the action is now barred.

The words in brackets are parenthetic. During dictation the

stenographer places a comma after *decided* and mentally awaits the objective clause that should follow. Without the intervening parenthetic clause, the sentence reads: "The courts below have decided, yet the courts are powerless" etc. In this instance, the dictator evidently intended to follow the material in brackets with the conjunction *that;* but, intent on the point he was making, he lost sight of his sentence structure. The secretary immediately realizes that the sentence is incomplete, but she cannot supply the word, because the dictator might have intended to say ". . . decided . . . against the plaintiff, yet the court . . . ," instead of simply ". . . decided that. . . ." Call the omission to the lawyer's attention.

Another common error, and one that you can easily detect and correct, is the repetition of the conjunction *that* in introducing a single clause when a phrase or clause intervenes between *that* and the clause it introduces. For example, in the sentence cited above, the dictator might easily have preceded and followed the bracketed material with *that,* instead of omitting it altogether.

Another common slip on the part of the dictator that you must guard against is calling the plaintiff "defendant" and vice versa. You are more likely to detect this slip when transcribing your notes than when taking the dictation. If you have any doubt about which is accurate, check with the dictator.

Pairs of words that cause confusion. Many words used frequently in legal dictation sound alike and look alike when written in shorthand. Some of them have similar but not exact meanings and it is difficult to judge from the sense which is the correct word. A list of pairs of words that are confusing follows. It is limited to words used frequently in legal work and does not include words that the secretary should have become thoroughly familiar with in school or in other fields of work. For example, it does not include *affect, effect.* Definitions of the words in this list that have a special legal significance are included in the definitions of legal terms in Chapter 27. Do the following with reference to the pairs of words given on page 146:

1. Fix firmly in your mind the meaning of each, particularly differences between meanings that are similar.

2. If the shorthand outlines for a pair of words are similar, make up a variation for one and become familiar with it.

3. When you are taking dictation, be particularly careful about the formation of the outlines for these words.

abjure, adjure
act, action
adverse, averse
apperception, perception
arraign, arrange
atonement, attornment
avoid, void
avoidable, voidable
case, cause
casual, causal
casualty, causality
cite, site
collision, collusion
comity, committee
cost, costs
corporal, corporeal
descent, dissent
defer, differ
depositary, depository
devisable, divisible
devisor, devisee
disburse, disperse
dower, dowry

drawer, drawee
estop, stop
in re, in rem
interpellate, interpolate
judicial, judicious
jura, jurat
malfeasance, misfeasance,
    nonfeasance
mandatary, mandatory
payor, payee
persecute, prosecute
precedence, precedents
prescribe, proscribe
presence, presents
return, writ
situate, situated
status quo, in statu quo
thereon, therein
therefor, therefore
tortious, tortuous
transferor, transferee
vendor, vendee

Recurring phrases, clauses, and paragraphs. Many phrases, clauses, and short paragraphs are used over and over again in legal work. The lawyer's familiarity with them causes him to dictate them at a high rate of speed. Often, he will not dictate the entire clause or paragraph but will dictate only the first few words and the secretary completes it when transcribing her notes. These phrases, clauses, and paragraphs vary with the field of practice and the wording varies with the state and, to a lesser extent, with the office. As soon as you recognize one that is used in your office, make up an abbreviated shorthand outline for it. Also, you should memorize the wording so that you will not have to refer to a form when transcribing your notes. Throughout this book attention is called to phrases, clauses, and paragraphs that recur in legal work.

Special outlines for unusual words. In legal dictation, an unusual word that is difficult to write in shorthand might be repeated many times in the dictation of one matter. It might be a proper name or a scientific term. The first time the word is dictated make up an abbreviated outline and use that outline throughout the dictation. For example, the dictation might be about *thaumaturgy,* involving a *Mr. Kopooshian.* If you make a note that your shorthand symbol for "thau" stands for thaumaturgy, and your symbol for K stands for Kopooshian, your speed will not be reduced by writing these difficult words.

Take-ins. Frequently in legal work a dictator will tell the stenographer to "take in" certain material, meaning for her to copy it. The take-in might be quoted material from a text or testimony, in which case the take-in is indented and quoted. (See Quotations, page 158.) Or the take-in might be a portion of a printed form or other document, the wording of which is applicable to the document that is being dictated. When the take-in is material of this kind, it follows the rest of the dictation just as if it were original dictation instead of a take-in.

The lawyer's instructions. Every office has a system of marking books, documents, drafts, and the like to indicate to the typist what is to be copied. The marks are made very lightly in pencil and should be erased with an art gum eraser after the material has been proofread. The following system of marking material to be copied is arbitrary, but practical.

1. The signs $<$ $>$ indicate that the matter within them is to be omitted.

2. A number in a circle indicates that the matter to be copied begins or ends at that point. Odd numbers indicate the beginning; even numbers the end. Thus ①—② would mean copy from the point marked ① to the point marked ②.

3. Crosses (XX) indicate that the matter between them is to be underscored.

4. To signify that something once erased, or marked for omission, is to remain, the word *stet* is written in the margin and dots are placed under the word or words to be retained. (Printers use this method of marking.)

Figure 27 illustrates a page marked for copying.

the sink and suddenly became dizzy and after reaching his room he vomited for about two hours. He reported that Dr. Smith was called who only talked with his daughter-in-law and did not examine him but pronounced with a grin "indigestion." Mr. Jorn called another doctor, a Dr. Palmer, who made a thorough examination and said it was not indigestion. Mr. Jorn also related that when he became dizzy at the sink that his daughter-in-law in a sassy fashion told him to get away as though his sickness was not altogether unexpected. He also reported that she had tampered with a bottle of his medicine. Was Mr. Jorn's process of thinking on the subject of his being poisoned by his son's wife so fantastic that it could reasonably be denominated as insane delusion? A complete answer to this inquiry can be found in the case of Owen v. Crumbaugh, 228 Ill. 380, at page 401, 81 N.E. 1044, at page 1051, 119 Am. St.Rep. 442, 10 Ann.Cas. 606, where the court used this language: "Whatever form of words is chosen to express the legal meaning of an insane delusion, it is clear, under all of the authorities, that it must be such an aberration as indicates an unsound or deranged condition of the mental faculties, as distinguished from a mere belief in the existence or nonexistence of certain supposed facts or phenomena based upon some sort of evidence. A belief which results from a process of reasoning from evidence, however imperfect the process may be or illogical the conclusion, is not an insane delusion. An insane delusion is not established when the court is able to understand how a person situated as the testator was might have believed all that the evidence shows that he did believe and still have been in full possession of his senses. Thus, where the testator has actual grounds for the suspicion of the existence of something in which he believes, though in fact not well founded and disbelieved by others, the misapprehension of the fact is not a matter of delusion which will invalidate his will. Stackhouse v. Horton, 15 N.J.Eq. 202; Potter v. Jones, supra [20 Or. 239, 25 P. 769, 12 L.R.A. 161]; Martin v. Thayer, 37 W.Va. 38, 16 S.E. 489; Mullins v. Cottrell, supra [41 Miss. 291]."

[2, 3] The trial judge wrote a short memorandum opinion giving his reasons for sustaining the validity of testator's will. It was his observation that the lay witnesses who testified for the defendant had a better opportunity to observe the testator than the doctors who appeared for the plaintiff, and accordingly their opinions were entitled to greater weight. The chancellor's findings should not be disturbed unless they are palpably wrong. A careful reading of the record convinces us we cannot so hold. The trial judge who sees and hears witnesses is in a much superior position to find the truth than the reviewing court who has before it only the printed page. Well worth repeating in this connection is the language of the Judge of the Supreme Court of Missouri in the case of Creamer v. Bivert, 214 Mo. 473, 113 S.W. 1118, 1120. "He (Trial Court) sees and hears much we cannot see and hear. We well know there are things of pith that cannot be preserved in or shown by the written page of a bill of exceptions. Truth does not always stalk boldly forth naked, but modest withal, in a printed abstract in a court of last resort. She oft hides in nooks and crannies visible only to the mind's eye of the judge who tries the case. To him appears the furtive glance, the blush of conscious shame, the hesitation, the sincere or the flippant or sneering tone, the heat, the calmness, the yawn, the sigh, the candor or lack of it, the scant or full realization of the solemnity of an oath, the carriage and mien. The brazen face of the liar, the glibness of the schooled witness in reciting a lesson, or the itching overeagerness of the swift witness, as well as honest face of the truthful one, are alone seen by him. In short, one witness may give testimony that reads in print, here, as if falling from the lips of an angel of light, and yet not a soul who heard it, nisi, believed a word of it; and another witness may testify so that it reads brokenly and obscurely in print, and yet there was that about the witness that carried conviction of truth to every soul who heard him testify."

We are of the opinion that the decree entered herein should be affirmed.

· Decree affirmed.

Figure 27. Page from Law Book Marked for Copying.

Testimony. Many occasions arise when the secretary in a law office is required to take the testimony of a person under oath. The testimony is usually in question and answer form and is referred to as a *deposition*. Counsel for both sides are present at the examination. You must take the testimony verbatim and transcribe it verbatim, without editing even glaring grammatical errors. If the exchange of questions and answers is too rapid and you fall behind in your notes, raise your left hand as a signal to the attorney conducting the examination to slow down. This might be embarrassing to you, but it is essential that every word of the testimony be reported accurately.

Use a notebook that has a vertical line down the center of the page. Divide each half of the page into three columns by lightly pencilled vertical lines in the positions shown in Figure 28. (It is assumed that you customarily write only to the dividing line, treating each column as a separate page.)

Notes of the questions by the examining attorney are placed

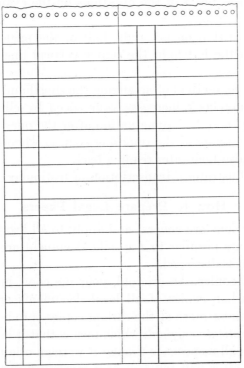

Figure 28. Notebook Ruled for Question and Answer Testimony.

on the page in the same position as notes are ordinarily placed. Each question begins at the extreme left of the page, extends to the center line, and, if it takes more than one line, continues at the extreme left of the next horizontal line.

Notes of the witness' answers begin at the right of the first vertical line and extend to the center line. If more than one line is necessary, the answer continues on the next horizontal line at the right of the first vertical line. The witness' answers never extend to the left of that line.

Notes of the interpolations by opposing counsel begin at the right of the second vertical line and extend to the center line. If more than one line is necessary, the interpolation continues on the next horizontal line at the right of the second vertical line. Remarks by opposing counsel never extend to the left of that line.

Notes of actions that must be indicated, such as marking exhibits for identification, are enclosed in brackets, thus distinguishing them from notes of the testimony. They are written in the same position as notes of the questions by the examining attorney.

Notes are written on the right half of the page in the same manner as on the left half, the center vertical line representing the left edge.

The preceding method of arranging the shorthand notes on the page of the notebook increases your speed by eliminating the writing of "Q" and "A," punctuation after the questions and answers, and the name of the opposing counsel when he makes an objection. It also facilitates reading back.

Figure 29 illustrates a transcription of testimony.

How to Prepare Legal Papers

These directions are general and apply to all legal papers. Directions that are peculiar to a specific document are given when that document is discussed.

Number of copies. An original, your file copy, and a varying number of carbon copies of all legal documents are necessary. Frequently, one or more of the carbon copies is to be a *duplicate original,* or *triplicate original,* which means that it is to be signed and treated in all respects as though it were an original or ribbon copy. The dictator will tell you how many copies to make. In-

DIRECT EXAMINATION BY MR. SMITH:

Q. Mr. Jones, what is your full name?

A. Richard C. Jones.

Q. What is your address? A. 226 Clinton Avenue, Mamaroneck, New York.

Q. Where are you employed, sir? A. Robert S. Still, Inc., 607 Tenth Avenue, New York, N. Y.

Q. How long have you been employed there? A. Since 1943.

Q. What is your position at Still's? A. Salesman.

Q. Do you know Mrs. Mary Jackson, the plaintiff in this action? A. Not too well; I know her as a customer.

Q. In April, 19——, did you see her when she brought in the necklace to Still's? A. No.

Q. What officer or employee did see her? A. Another salesman.

Q. What is his name? A. William A. Nelson.

Q. You don't know what he said to her concerning

(*Continued on following page*)

151

the work to be done?

MR. HOWARD: I object to the form of that question.

A. No, only from our records.

Q. What records do you have with you that show the delivery of the necklace to Still's?

[Mr. Jones produces record and Mr. Smith studies it.]

MR. SMITH: I offer that in evidence.

MR. HOWARD: Can I see that?

MR. SMITH: Certainly, I thought you had already seen it.

MR. HOWARD: It should not be admitted in evidence but should be marked for identification.

[Marked Plaintiff's Exhibit 1 for Identification.]

Q. Mr. Jones, with reference to plaintiff's exhibit marked Exhibit 1 for identification on your examination, do you recognize the handwriting in pencil on the notations on that exhibit? A. Yes, sir, that's Mr. Nelson's.

MR. SMITH: I have no further questions at this time. Mr. Benjamin, would you like to cross-examine?

Figure 29. Transcription of Question and Answer Testimony.

structions are usually given in this manner: "Two and four," meaning an original, a duplicate original, and four copies; or, "One and five," meaning an original and five copies, no duplicate original being necessary.

Paper. Use heavyweight paper for the original or ribbon copy, and light weight for the carbons, the weight depending on the number of copies. Duplicate and triplicate originals are usually typed on paper of the same substance as the ribbon copy. Some offices follow the practice of making the last carbon copy, which is the office copy, on heavy paper because it is more durable.

The kind of paper used depends upon the document that is being typed and also varies with the office. See the discussion of the specific document; also the list of stationery supplies in Chapter 1.

How to align paper in typewriter. Every legal stenographer experiences difficulty in inserting numerous sheets of paper in the typewriter. Here is how you can make a device that will enable you to feed a large pack of paper to the typewriter and obtain perfect alignment of the sheets, without jogging. (Figure 30 illustrates the process of making the device; Figure 31 shows it after completion, with paper inserted.)

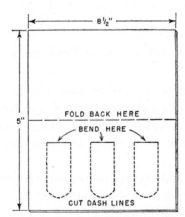

Figure 30. Device for Feeding Paper to Typewriter—Process of Making Device.

1. Fold a 5″ by 8½″ strip of flimsy Manila tag (a cheap file folder will do) across the center, lengthwise.

2. Cut three U-shaped slots across the upper half of the folded strip, about one-half inch from the crease.

3. Lift up and bend backward the tongues formed by the slots.

4. Insert the assembled sheets of paper in the folded strip.

5. Feed the tongues from the U-slots into the typewriter. The platen grasps them more readily than it does a thick pack of paper.

6. Remove the folded strip before beginning to type.

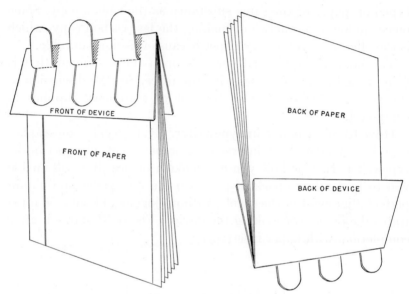

Figure 31. Device for Feeding Paper to Typewriter, with Papers Inserted.

Several sheets of paper and carbon may be inserted easily in the typewriter by placing them beneath the flap of an envelope. The platen, however, does not grasp a large pack as readily, and the alignment is not as perfect, as when the device described above is used.

Margins. Documents typed on legal-size paper are bound at the top; those on letter-size or short paper, at the left. Leave a margin of at least 1½″ for binding.

Top margin. Begin typing either five or six double spaces from the top of the paper, but make a habit of always allowing the same number of spaces. By following this practice, you know that every page of a document starts at the same place on the paper and has the same number of typed lines.

Bottom margin. Leave a margin of approximately one inch at the bottom. With a margin of five double spaces at the top and an inch at the bottom, each legal-size page of typing will have 32 lines double spaced; each letter-size page (8½″ by 11″), 24 lines.

In a neatly typed legal document, the typing on every page of manuscript ends exactly the same number of spaces from the bottom of the page. Carbon paper with a numbered margin, or a backing sheet with a numbered margin, will insure an even bottom margin. If you do not have carbon paper with a numbered margin, or if you are making too many copies to use a backing sheet, mark lightly the place where the typing should end, before inserting the paper in the typewriter.

Left margin. Leave a margin on the left of approximately 1¼″, or 1½″ if the paper is to be bound on the left. On legal cap, begin typing one space to the right of the colored line that indicates the left margin.

Right margin. Leave a right margin of approximately one inch. On legal cap, this will place the margin approximately ⅝″ to the left of the colored line that indicates the right margin. This allows a leeway of seven spaces between the right margin and the line. Avoid excessive hyphenation and also a ragged right margin.

Under no circumstances should the typing extend beyond the colored lines that indicate the margins.

Paragraphs. Indent paragraphs 10 spaces.

Numbering pages. Number pages of legal documents one-half inch from the bottom of the page, in the center of the line. The number should be preceded and followed by a hyphen, thus: -4-. If the first page is not numbered, the numbering begins with -2-. Be exact in placing the number; when the pages are collated the numbers should overlie one another.

Marginal and tabular stops. On a typewriter with pica type, and pica type is most frequently used in law offices, set your marginal and tabular stops as follows:

Paper guide	0
Left marginal stop	15
Right marginal stop	75
First tabular stop	25
Second tabular stop	30
Third tabular stop	35

With the stops set at these points, practically no adjustment of the typewriter will be necessary for margins, paragraph indentations, proper placement of quotations, and the like.

Tabulated material. When portions of a paper or letter are tabulated or itemized, the items are usually preceded by a number or letter in parentheses or followed by a period. Begin each line of the tabulated text two spaces to the right of the number. Preferably, the punctuation and capitalization should be the same as if the tabulated material were written without breaks, in regular lines (see Figure 32), but this style is not followed in all law offices.

```
                I have revised the affidavit that you returned,
    I hope in accordance with your recommendations.  If you
    find it satisfactory as now drawn, may I ask you

        (1)  to swear to it before a notary and have him affix
             his seal and notarial stamp;

        (2)  to fill in the last column of Schedule B as to  the
             months for which payments are in default on each
             vehicle; and

        (3)  to return the affidavit with five forms of the
             conditional sale contract.
```

Figure 32. Tabulated Items.

Responsibility and distribution line. In the upper left-hand corner, type a notation of the number of copies made, the date, the dictator's initials and your initials.

Example: 2-3
                              7/23/..
                              ERJ:sm

This indicates that an original and a duplicate original and three copies, one of which is for the files, were typed on July 23, 19.., and that the document was dictated by ERJ to sm. The binding covers the notation. It is not necessary to put the notation on any page except the first one. If a page of the document is retyped subsequent to the date shown, put a new responsibility line on that page. The identification data should appear on the file copy *only* of wills, minutes, proxies, and statistical statements.

In the upper right-hand corner of your file copy, indicate the distribution, thus:

```
1 orig. to JRA     7/24/..
1 orig. to MDE        "
1 copy to SRT         "
1 copy to LRS         "
```

The third copy that was made is your file copy.

Line spacing. As a rule all legal work is double spaced. Some law firms even double space letters, regardless of length, but this practice is not generally followed. Usually quotations are single spaced.

Triple space before and after all indented material. Also triple space drafts.

It is permissible to single space an acknowledgment (page 176) in order to get it on the signature page.

Standard rules for spacing. Usage has established the following rules for spacing:

After a comma	1 space
After a semi-colon	1 space
After every sentence	2 spaces
After a colon	2 spaces
Before or after a dash, which is two hyphens	No space
Before or after a hyphen	No space
Between quotation marks and the matter enclosed	No space
Between parentheses and the matter enclosed	No space
Between any word and the punctuation following it	No space
After an exclamation mark used in the body of a sentence	1 space
After a period following an abbreviation or an initial	1 space
After a period following a figure or letter at the beginning of a line in a list of items	2 spaces
Between dots used to show an ellipsis	No space
Between asterisks used to show an ellipsis	1 space
Before and after x meaning *by*, for example, 3″ x 5″ card	1 space
Before or after an apostrophe in the body of a word	No space
Between the initials that make a single abbreviation, for example, C.O.D. (but see "Citations," in Chapter 16)	No space

Space for fill-ins. When a date is to be filled in later, leave a space instead of typing a line for the fill-in.

June	, 19..	3 spaces
This	day of June, 19..	6 spaces

Do not leave the blank for a subsequent fill-in at the end of a line, because it will not be noticeable.

Underscoring. Underscoring, or underlining, in typed material is equivalent to italics in printed material but is used less freely, probably for appearance' sake. For example, the title of a book is italicized in print but, preferably, is enclosed in quotations in typed material. The underlining is continuous and not broken at the spacing between words. The following uses of underscoring in legal work is recommended.

1. Underscore for emphasis. The dictator indicates when underscoring is to be used for emphasis.

2. Underscore material that is in italics in the original.

3. Underscore to indicate Latin words and phrases, or abbreviations of them. Words of other foreign languages are also underlined, but Latin is used most frequently in legal work.

Exceptions. Do not underscore foreign words that have become a part of the English speech through continuous use. If in doubt, consult Webster. You will note that parallel bars (||) precede foreign words that occur frequently in speech and print in English but that are not yet completely Anglicized, as is shown by their being printed generally in italic type. In the list of Latin words and phrases in Chapter 26, those that should not be underlined are in Roman type, whereas those that should be underlined are in italic type. You will notice that some words are in Roman when standing alone but are in italics when used in certain phrases. For example, the word *caveat* is not italicized, but the phrase *caveat emptor* is.

Quotations and other indented material. *Margins and paragraphs.* The left margin of quotations and other indented material should be five spaces to the right of the principal left margin; the beginning of a paragraph within the material should be indented an additional five spaces. If a quotation begins in the middle of a paragraph, the paragraph indentation is omitted.

The right margin of indented material may be even with the principal right margin or about five spaces to the left of it.

Short lines of indented material should be indented about fifteen spaces, thus:

>The American Bar
>The Bar Register
>The Lawyer's List

Line spacing. Quotations are usually single spaced, but this does not apply to all indented material. Triple space before and after each quotation or other indented material; double space between paragraphs of single-spaced indented material.

Quotation marks. Place double quotation marks at the beginning and end of the quotation and at the beginning of each new paragraph within the quoted material. Change double quotation marks in material that you quote to single quotation marks, thus conforming to the rule that quotations within quotations should be enclosed in single quotation marks. Change single quotation marks in quoted material to double quotation marks.

Errors. Copy quotations exactly, even obvious errors. Indicate errors in the same way that you do in making an exact copy of any material (page 162).

Italics. If words in the original are in italics, underscore them. If words that are not in italics in the original are underscored at the direction of the dictator, the words "Italics ours" in parentheses are added at the end of the quotation. It frequently happens that part of a quoted passage is italicized and that the dictator wishes to emphasize another part of it. In that case, put "italics theirs" in parentheses immediately following the italicized matter, and add the words "Emphasis ours" in parentheses at the end of the quotation. In Figure 33, the word *records* was italicized in the original. The rest of the underscoring was added by the dictator for emphasis.

How to show omissions. Omissions of part of a quotation are indicated by the use of ellipses. They may be points (dots) or asterisks (stars) and are usually in groups of three. Preferably, there is a space between asterisks, but not between points. Some law offices that formerly used asterisks now use points, probably because they eliminate the necessity of using the shift key and, also, they look neater if the material contains many omissions. You will be guided by the practice in your office.

In using either points or asterisks, simply remember that they take the place of words, and place them accordingly. Thus, if a quotation begins in the middle of a sentence, there is no space between the quotation mark and the first ellipsis, but there is a space between the final ellipsis and the following word. If an entire sentence is omitted, two spaces precede and follow the ellipses, just as they would the sentence. Punctuation is placed in the same relation to the ellipses as if they were words.

Indicate omission of one or more entire paragraphs by a line of ellipses, five spaces apart. Some law offices use a single group of three asterisks in the center of the line instead of a full line.

Figure 33 illustrates a quotation with points showing omissions. (It also shows errors that were in the material being copied. See page 162.) Note that the first paragraph begins in the middle; that there are one or more paragraphs omitted; the next

---

The pertinent part of the opinion rendered by the Copyright Office at our request reads as follows:

"The Copyright Office does not undertake to pass upon his [the author's] rights, leaving the question to the courts in case of dispute. It simply records (italics theirs) his claims, and by this recording gives him certain rights provided his claims can be substantiated.

. . . .

"... this [copyright] is taken out in the name of the publisher rather than of the author, as the contract itself is really a license to sell from the publisher to the author [sic]. It is also the duty of the publisher to take all necessary steps to effect renewals... .

"An auther should be 'guided' by his publisher in all questions of copyright." (Emphasis ours.)

We contend that this opinion strongly supports the contention of the petitioner.

Figure 33. Exact (Chinese) Copy of Quoted Material.

paragraph begins and ends in the middle of a sentence; the last paragraph is quoted in full. Note also in Figure 33 that there are four points at the end of the second paragraph. The fourth one is a period, indicating the end of the sentence.

Drafts. Type drafts on an inexpensive grade of legal-size paper. Usually law offices provide a cheap yellow paper for this purpose. Use legal-size paper even though the document in final form will be typed on short paper. Make no carbon copies unless otherwise instructed. Lawyers expect to make changes in drafts; therefore, triple space all dictated material. Extracts copied from books or other documents may be single spaced in the draft, because it is not necessary to make corrections in them. Leave wide margins. Type the date, the initials of the dictator and your initials, and the word DRAFT in capital letters in the upper left-hand corner of the first page. If there is a second or a third draft, indicate this fact. Follow the usual practices for form and style except with reference to line spacing and margins.

Crossing-out is permissible in typing a draft—in fact, it is preferable to erasing because it takes less time. Speed is more desirable than neatness, but accuracy must not be sacrificed. Although a lawyer expects to make changes in a draft, careless transcription of his dictation is annoying and is not tolerated any more than it would be in a final copy.

Before retyping a corrected draft, study the corrected page, noting:

1. Portions marked for omission
2. Additional material to be inserted
3. Transpositions
4. Corrections in spelling, punctuation, and the like

Note carefully the changes in each sentence before typing. Difficult handwriting between lines of typing and in the margins may often be deciphered quickly by referring to the scratched out typewriting, of which the handwritten matter is usually a revision.

Correction of errors. If an insertion or deletion does not jibe with the other material, then you are misinterpreting it, or the lawyer has overlooked something. When you detect an error of this kind, or any error other than typographical, in a draft that you are retyping, check with the lawyer. If you cannot locate him and you cannot get a clarification, use your judgment in making the change and call it to his attention when you return the work to him.

Copying. In *retyping* an unsigned draft, type it in correct form in accordance with the practices recommended in this book. But the practice is different when *copying* an executed document, signed letter, extracts from books, and in any case where an exact copy is required. The following instructions apply when you are typing an exact copy, sometimes called a *Chinese* copy (see Figure 33, page 160).

1. Type the word COPY in the upper left-hand corner, under your initials and the date.

2. Copy exactly, even obvious errors, because the copy purports to be a "true and exact" copy.

3. Indicate obvious errors copied from the original as follows: (a) Underline an incorrect letter or figure. (b) Put "sic" in parentheses or brackets after apparently or obviously incorrect words or phrases. (c) Show an omission by a caret. If your typewriter does not have a caret, use the slanting bar and underscore key (∠).

agreement entered into the 31th day of April. . . .

upon reciept. . . .

I give, devise and bequest [sic] unto. . . .

meeting of the United ∧ Assembly in Paris. . . .

4. Copy page for page and line for line as far as practicable.

5. When the document is completed, proofread (see Chapter 17) it with some other person. That person reads aloud from the original copy while the typist checks the copy. The reader should indicate paragraphs, punctuation, underlining, full capitals, hyphens, and so on.

See page 147 for the method by which the lawyer gives instructions for copying certain material.

Test-writing. When retyping a page of a document that has had matter added to or taken from it, and the paragraph does not end at the bottom of the page, it may be necessary to make a test-write of the revised portion so that the last line of the page will be full length.

Letterheads. When only part of a letterhead is copied, type across the top of the page, in solid caps, enclosed in brackets, the name of the firm [LETTERHEAD OF ....]. This is in addition to your initials, the date, and COPY in the upper lefthand corner.

Collating. Every legal paper of two or more pages should be collated. *Collating* is the process of checking a set of pages for correct sequence. The task is facilitated by the use of a rubber finger or a pencil eraser.

Conforming. After the original of a document is signed, conform the copies—that is, make them like the original. This includes writing in, or typing in signatures, dates, recording data, and notarial data inked or stamped on the original. In typing the signature, there is no need to type *Signed* in front of the typed copy. Do not be afraid to copy the signature of a judge or anybody else; you are not forging but only making a true copy. You should not try to imitate the signature.

When conforming an executed document bearing an official or a corporate seal, write in brackets at the left of the official or corporate signature the words [CORPORATE SEAL] if the seal is a corporate seal; [NOTARIAL SEAL] if the seal is that of a notary public; or [OFFICIAL SEAL] if the seal is that of any officer other than a notary public. Seals of individuals are indicated by SEAL unless written otherwise on the original.

When a county clerk's certificate is attached to an original document, it is advisable for you to find out from the lawyer whether a notation, such as:

$$\left\{\begin{array}{l}\text{County Clerk's Certificate} \\ \text{for _____ County, State} \\ \text{of _____ attached to} \\ \text{original.}\end{array}\right.$$

is sufficient, or whether the entire certificate must be copied and annexed to the conformed copies of the document. It is sometimes important to have a copy of the entire certificate, especially in cases where a certified copy of an original instrument is required.

Ditto marks. Ditto marks are not permissible in a legal document. They are used in exhibits and schedules but not in the document to which the exhibits and schedules are annexed. Ditto marks may sometimes be used in drafts to save time, but repeat the language in full when typing in final form.

Legal backs. Typed legal instruments and court papers are usually backed with a manuscript cover, called a *legal back*, of

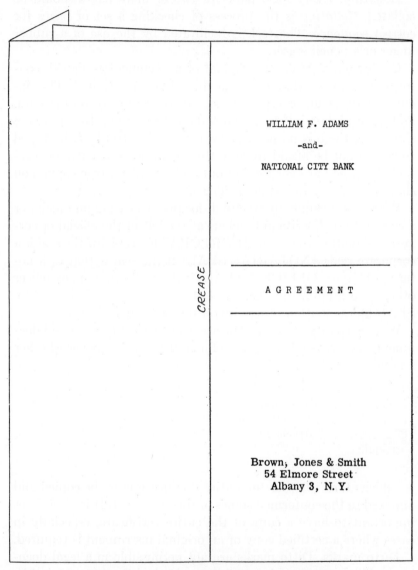

CREASE

WILLIAM F. ADAMS

-and-

NATIONAL CITY BANK

A G R E E M E N T

Brown, Jones & Smith
54 Elmore Street
Albany 3, N. Y.

Figure 34. Endorsed Legal Back for Agreement.

thick paper 8½″ or 9″ by 15″. Certain data, referred to as the *endorsement,* are typed on the back of the cover. An endorsed back of an agreement is illustrated in Figure 34. The contents of the endorsement vary with the instrument, but usually include a brief description of the instrument and the names of the parties to it. The endorsement is typed in a definite position on the backing sheet. Court papers (see Figure 55, Chapter 12) usually have a printed panel in which the endorsement is typed; some backs have the name and address of the law firm engraved on them; others are plain.

To type the endorsement:

1. Lay the backing sheet on the desk as though for reading.

2. Bring the bottom edge up to approximately one inch from the top and crease.

3. Bring the creased end (which is now at the bottom) up to approximately one inch from the top. (You now have a fold with about one inch of the top edge of the backing sheet protruding beyond the fold.)

4. The surface of the folded sheet that is uppermost is the surface on which the endorsement is to be typed. (If the backing sheet has a printed panel or the firm's name on it, that portion of the sheet will be the uppermost surface.) Put a small pencil check in the upper *left*-hand corner of that surface.

5. Partially unfold and insert in typewriter so that the pencil mark is on the upper *right*-hand corner of the surface when you type on it.

6. Do not type to the left of the crease (see Figure 34). After typing the endorsement, turn down the top edge of the backing sheet about an inch (see step 3), crease, insert document in the crease, and staple. Fold the document and the backing sheet, creasing the document to fit the creases in the backing sheet.

How to make corrections on bound pages. Frequently after a legal document is neatly bound, it is necessary to make a minor change on one of the pages. Corrections can be made on pages that are bound at the top without unstapling them. Insert a blank sheet of paper in the typewriter, as though for typing. When it protrudes about an inch above the platen, insert between it and the platen the unbound edge of the sheet to be corrected. Turn the platen toward you until the typewriter grips the sheet to be corrected. You can then adjust the bound sheet to the proper position for making the correction.

Corrections cannot be made on pages that are bound at the side without unstapling them.

Printed law blanks. Printed law blanks are widely used in drawing up legal instruments and some court papers. Law blank printers publish a catalogue showing the numbers and titles of the blanks that they print. Each law blank has its title and, usually, the printer's catalogue number, printed in small letters in the upper left-hand corner. The blanks are obtainable at almost any stationery store. Frequently the secretary can fill in these blanks without any dictated instructions from the lawyer. When it is necessary to dictate the material to be inserted in the blanks, the usual manner of giving instructions is as follows:

The lawyer numbers in pencil the spaces to be filled in, 1, 2, 3, etc. He then dictates the material that should be typed in each numbered blank, thus eliminating any confusion about where each dictated insertion should be typed.

Observe the following suggestions about filling in law blanks, so that the completed form will be neat and accurate:

Typing on ruled lines. Make certain that the typing is adjusted so that the bases of letters with tails that extend below the line of type (g, p, and y) just touch the ruled line.

Date of printing. Printed forms bear a printer's mark showing the number of copies printed and the date of the printing. When filling in more than one copy, use forms that were printed at the same time, because a change might have been made in the form.

Registration of printing. Before attempting to fill in more than one blank form at a time by using carbon paper, make sure that the printing on all copies registers exactly. To do this, place the edges of the forms together and hold to the light. You can then see whether the printed matter in one copy lies exactly over corresponding material in the other copy. If you use the device suggested at page 153 for inserting assembled paper and carbons, the forms should be perfectly aligned without jogging. Otherwise, after inserting the forms and carbon in the typewriter, loosen your typewriter platen and adjust the edges of the forms. They must be exactly even or the typing will not be properly spaced on the copies.

Fill-ins on both sides of sheet. When making carbon copies of a form that has fill-ins on both sides of the sheet, take particular care to avoid having one side the ribbon copy and the other side the carbon copy, thus rendering the form unfit for execution. Double sheet forms are particularly apt to cause trouble in this respect.

Small blanks. When the blanks on the form are small, fill in each form individually; do not use carbons. Be careful not to overlook any of the small blanks. In many forms they are not indicated by underlining, but only by a small space. Many of them call only for letters identifying the person or persons signing the document. For example, a printed mortgage form might include the following: "Said mortgagee ___, ___h___ heirs or assigns." If there is more than one mortgagee, *s* is added to *mortgagee* and ___h___ becomes *their*. If there is only one mortgagee, the first blank is not filled in, and ___h___ becomes *her* or *his*.

"Z" ruling. Frequently the material typed on a printed form does not fill the space provided. To protect the instrument from alteration, draw a "Z" ruling, as illustrated below, with pen and ink in the unused space.

9

Basic Information about Legal Instruments

O VER three-fourths of a lawyer's practice relates to matters that are not litigated. This practice involves, among other things, the preparation of numerous legal instruments. In this chapter we give basic information about legal documents generally. And because you, as secretary in a law office, will probably have to notarize many of these legal instruments, we describe the duties of a notary.

What is a legal instrument? A legal instrument is a formal written document, such as a deed, bill of sale, lease, or will. It gives formal expression to a legal act or agreement. Although both legal instruments and court papers are referred to as legal documents, a legal instrument is not to be confused with a court paper. A court paper, or pleading as it is called professionally (see Chapter 12), constitutes a step in bringing or defending a law suit and is prepared and filed for the information of the court, whereas a legal instrument is designed for the use of the parties who sign it and constitutes evidence of the agreement between them. A legal instrument is not a step in a court action, but it is frequently the basis of one. If one of the parties to a legal instrument does not abide by its provisions, the other party may sue to enforce the provisions of the instrument. Copies of a legal instrument are used frequently as exhibits in court actions.

Parties to an instrument. Those who acquire a right or give up a right, as evidenced by a written instrument, are the parties to the instrument. A party may be an individual, a partnership, or a corporation. Almost all instruments have two or more parties; but there are some, for example, assignments and powers of attorney, which have only one party. All parties who have a common interest in the subject matter of the document are grouped together and are usually referred to throughout the instrument by a descriptive identification, instead of by name. An expression frequently used is "party (parties) of the first part," "party (parties) of the second part." Or the term may be a description such as *contractor, seller,* or any term appropriate to the party's interest in the subject matter of the instrument. There may be more than one party in a group designated by a descriptive term. You will notice that the instrument illustrated in Figure 35 has two parties of the first part but only one of the second part.

How to type legal instruments. Although certain instruments, such as deeds and wills, are set up in a special style, the type-written style of agreements or contracts generally varies only slightly, no matter what the subject matter is. Many specific instruments are illustrated throughout this book (see the index). Figure 36 illustrates a skeleton of a form of agreement used by many law offices. It is easily adaptable to any general agreement or contract. Always make duplicate originals for the parties to the contract and a copy for your file. If the lawyer wants an extra copy, he will tell you. Agreements may be typed on long or short paper, with or without the ruled margin. If the lawyer has a preference, he will specify it.

Execution of an Instrument

What is "execution" of an instrument? Technically, execution of an instrument is doing that which is required to give effect or validity to the instrument and, therefore, includes signing and delivery. In law office parlance, *execution* more frequently refers merely to the signing of an instrument by the party or parties described in it. Legal instruments must be executed with a certain formality. Some or all of the following formalities attach to the execution of various instruments: sealing, attestation, acknowledgment and notarization, each of which is discussed below.

Testimonium clause. The testimonium clause is the clause with which an instrument closes. It immediately precedes the signature. It is a declaration by the parties to the instrument that their signatures are attached in testimony of the preceding part of the instrument. The testimonium clause is not to be confused with the *witness* or *attestation* clause (see below). The testimonium clause relates to the parties themselves, whereas the witness or attestation clause relates to those who sign the paper as witnesses, not as parties to the instrument.

Quite often, the testimonium clause will guide you in setting up the signature lines. It will indicate (1) what parties are to sign the instrument; (2) what officer of a corporation is to sign; (3) whether the instrument is to be sealed; and (4) whether a corporate seal is to be attested. For example, from the following clause, which is a form commonly used, you know that the president of the corporation is to sign, that the seal is to be affixed, and that the secretary of the corporation is to attest the seal.

IN WITNESS WHEREOF, Alvin Corporation has caused its corporate seal to be hereto affixed, and attested by its secretary, and these presents to be signed by its president, this 26th day of October, 19...

On the other hand, from the following clause, also commonly used, you know that the instrument is not to be sealed.

IN TESTIMONY WHEREOF, the parties hereto have hereunto set their hands the day and year first above written.

The introductory words to the testimonium clause, *in witness whereof, in testimony whereof,* and the like, are usually typed in solid caps. The word following begins with lower case unless it is a proper name. A comma usually follows the introductory words.

Signatures. An instrument recites who will sign it. As a general practice, lines are typed for signatures. Type the first line of signature four spaces below the body of the instrument, beginning it slightly to the right of the center of the page. Type a line for the signature of each person who must sign the instrument. There are no special requirements for the spacing of signature lines, except that sufficient space should be allowed for the average-size handwriting and the lines should be evenly spaced. Three or four spaces between lines are practical.

Frequently the descriptive identification of the parties signing is placed under the signature lines, for example, "First Party," "Parties of the First Part," or whatever identification was used in the instrument. The lawyer will probably instruct you as follows: "Two signature lines for parties of the first part, and one for the party of the second part," but you will know from the content of the instrument what signature lines are necessary. Figure 35 illustrates signature lines and identification of the parties.

```
      IN WITNESS WHEREOF, the parties hereto have here-

unto set their hands and seals, the day and year first above

written.

In the Presence of:
                          _____L.S.

_____

                          _____L.S.
                              Parties of the First Part

_____

                          _____L.S.
                              Party of the Second Part
```

Figure 35. Testimonium Clause, Signature and Seal for Individuals, Witnessed.

When a corporation is a party to an instrument, the instrument is signed in the name of the corporation by the officer or officers authorized to execute it. Type the name of the corporation in solid caps, leave sufficient space beneath it for a signature, and type "By" and a line for signature. Under the signature line, type the title of the corporate officer who is going to sign the instrument. The testimonium clause usually recites the title of the officer who is supposed to sign the instrument. The corporate seal is placed at the left margin, parallel to the signature (see Figure 36).

When a partnership is a party, type the name of the partnership in solid caps, leave sufficient space beneath it for signature, and type "By" and a line for signature. Since partnerships do not have officers, there will be no title under the signature line.

How to fit the signatures on the page. Arrange the body, or text, of the instrument so that at least two lines appear on the page with the signatures. The signatures must all be on the same page unless there are so many that they require more than a full page. To comply with these requirements you must gauge carefully the length of the material to be typed. This is not difficult if you are copying from a draft; otherwise, you might have to make a test copy and adjust your spacing accordingly. Here are methods by which you may lengthen or shorten the available typing space in order to fit the signatures on the page.

1. Leave wider or narrower top and bottom margins.

2. If you are using paper without ruled margins, leave wider or narrower left and right margins.

3. If the last line of a paragraph is full-length, adjust the right margin of that paragraph so that at least one word carries over to another line, thereby taking up an extra line. Or, if a paragraph ends with one word on a line, adjust the margin so that it is not necessary to carry over the one word, thereby saving a line of space.

4. Triple space between paragraphs.

5. Leave less space between the text of the instrument and the signatures.

6. Leave less space between the signatures.

Sealing an instrument. Figure 36 illustrates signatures to a sealed corporate instrument. The practice of affixing a seal to an instrument originated in the days when only a few people could write their names. Written instruments were marked with sealing wax, which was impressed with a ring or other device. This seal was the mark of the person making the instrument and took the place of his signature. The process of affixing the seal is referred to as *sealing* the instrument, and the instrument then becomes a *sealed* instrument. Today, the sealed instrument has a twofold significance: (1) Under the statutes of limitations, the time during which suit may be brought on a sealed instrument is longer than on an unsealed instrument. (2) Suit on a contract cannot be defended on the basis that it was without consideration, because the consideration of a sealed instrument cannot be questioned. If an instrument is to be sealed, the testimonium clause will so indicate.

A corporation's seal. Almost all corporations adopt a formal seal. It is engraved on a metal plate and impressed by this means upon the paper. The seal usually recites the name of the corpora-

tion and the year and state of incorporation. As a practical
matter, a corporation's by-laws usually provide that any instru-

THIS AGREEMENT, entered into on the ___ day of

_____, 19--, by and between _____ CORPORATION,

a corporation organized and existing under and by virtue of

the laws of the State of _____, and having its office

at _____, _____, hereinafter referred to as

"_____," and THE _____ COMPANY, a corporation organ-

ized and existing under and by virtue of the laws of the

State of _____, and having its office at _____,

_____, hereinafter referred to as "_____,"

W I T N E S S E T H :

WHEREAS _____

_____; and

WHEREAS _____

_____

_____.

NOW, THEREFORE, in consideration of the premises

_____

_____,

IT IS AGREED:

1. _____

_____

(*Continued on following page*)

(Continued from preceding page)

```
_____  .

        2.  _____

_____  .

        IN WITNESS WHEREOF the parties hereto have on the
day and year first above written caused these presents to be
executed in their behalf and in their corporate names re-
spectively by their proper officers hereunto duly authorized
and their respective corporate seals to be hereto attached
by like authority.


(Corporate Seal)                    _____CORPORATION

                                    By _____
ATTEST:                                         President

_____
            Secretary               THE _____COMPANY

(Corporate Seal)                    By _____
                                               Vice President
ATTEST:

_____
            Secretary
```

Figure 36. Agreement Between Two Corporations with Seals Attested.

(Number page in center, one-half inch from bottom.)

ment signed on behalf of the corporation shall be impressed with the corporate seal. An officer of the corporation impresses the seal on the instrument when it is signed. In many cases the corporate secretary must bear witness, or "attest." to the fact that the imprint on the paper is the seal of the corporation. Whenever the testimonium clause recites that the seal is to be *attested*, type the following on the left side of the page, opposite the signature lines:

ATTEST

_____

Secretary

The attest by the officer of a corporation to its seal is not to be confused with the attestation or "witness" clause, which relates to the subscribing witnesses (see Figure 37).

```
     IN WITNESS WHEREOF, we, the lessors and the
lessee, have hereunto set our hands and seals to the fore-
going lease, consisting of twenty-two pages, on this day
of April 19——.
Signed, sealed, and delivered )
                              )
by lessors in the presence of:)
                              )
                              )
                              )
_____)
                              )         _____ L. S.
                              )
_____)
                                        _____ L. S.
                                               Lessors

Signed, sealed, and delivered )
by lessee in the presence of: )
                              )         _____ L. S.
                              )               Lessee
_____)
                              )
                              )
_____)
```

Figure 37. Legend and Signature Lines for Two Groups of Witnesses.

An individual's seal. The wax seal formerly used by individuals has been replaced by the word *seal* or *L.S.* (abbreviation for *locus sigilli,* meaning "place of the seal"), or any other scroll or mark. At the end of the signature lines on an instrument that must be sealed, type SEAL or L.S. in solid caps.

Attestation clause. Frequently the signatures to an instrument must be witnessed in order to make the instrument legal. The act of witnessing the signature to a written instrument, at the request of the party signing the instrument, is *attestation.* The witness is called a subscribing witness, because he signs his name as a witness. A legend or clause that recites the circumstances surrounding the signing of the instrument often precedes the signature of the attesting witnesses and is called the *attestation clause.* The wording of the attestation clause varies from a simple "In the presence of" to the rather lengthy clause used in wills (see Figure 46 on page 206).

The legend and the lines on which witnesses sign are written opposite the lines for the signatures of persons who will execute the instrument. When parties to an instrument do not sign at the same time, different people witness the signature. The instrument then carries signature lines for each of the witnesses, with an identification of the parties whose signatures each group is witnessing (see Figure 37).

Acknowledgments

Importance of acknowledgments in the law office. An acknowledgment is a familiar tool in the law office, and the secretary should acquire an intimate knowledge of it. Technically, an *acknowledgment* is the act by which a person who executes a legal instrument declares to an officer, designated by statute, that he is the person who executed the instrument. In law office terminology, the term signifies both the declaration of execution and the officer's written certificate of the declaration. It is common practice for a legal instrument to carry a certificate of acknowledgment, because almost all states require the acknowledgment of an instrument before it can be recorded or filed. Furthermore, when an instrument is introduced in court as evidence, the certificate of acknowledgment is usually sufficient proof of the authenticity of the instrument.

Laws governing acknowledgments. Many states have adopted the Uniform Acknowledgment Act, and in these states the law governing the use of acknowledgments and the form of the certificate are similar. Otherwise, the law varies with the state. Some of the statutes are very precise in their requirements and they must be adhered to strictly. The acknowledgments illustrated in Figures 38 through 42 are for the purpose of showing

```
STATE OF WISCONSIN)
                  : ss.
COUNTY OF CHIPPEWA)


          On this the      day of        , 19—, before me,
               , the undersigned officer, personally ap-
peared ALBERT JONES, known to me to be the person whose
name is subscribed to the within instrument and acknowledged
that he executed the same for the purpose therein contained.
          IN WITNESS WHEREOF, I have hereunto set my hand
and official seal.


                    _____
                              Notary Public
               My commission expires                .
```

Figure 38. Certificate of Acknowledgment of Individual.

you how acknowledgments are set up when typed and to give you a general idea of the wording of various forms of acknowledgment. They are not supposed to be copied word for word. At first the lawyer will either dictate or make available to you a form of the acknowledgment he wants you to use. Make an extra copy for your looseleaf book of forms for future reference when you are expected to type an acknowledgment without detailed instructions.

A principle of law governing acknowledgments that you should remember is this: The law of the state where the instrument is to be recorded or used, not the law of the state where the instrument is executed, governs. Thus, if your office is in New York and you prepare an instrument that is to be recorded in Florida, the form and wording follow the Florida statutes, although the certificate will show that the acknowledgment was made in New York. But if you send an instrument to Florida to be signed and

```
STATE OF GEORGIA)
               : ss.
COUNTY OF BAKER )


        I, ELAINE BAKER, a notary public in and for the
said state and county, duly commissioned and sworn, hereby
certify that HENRY R. DAVIS and NANCY R. DAVIS, his wife,
who are to me personally known, this day appeared before me
personally, and severally acknowledged that they signed,
sealed, and delivered the foregoing deed for the purposes
therein stated. The said NANCY R. DAVIS, wife of said HENRY
R. DAVIS, being duly examined by me, separate and apart from
her said husband, did declare that she signed, sealed, and
delivered the said deed freely and voluntarily, and without
compulsion by her said husband, with intention to renounce
and convey all dower or other right, title, and interest in
the property thereby conveyed, for the uses and purposes
therein stated.
        IN WITNESS WHEREOF, I have hereunto set my hand and
official seal this 30th day of April, 19—.



                         _____
                                    Notary Public
```

Figure 39. Certificate of Acknowledgment by Husband and Wife—Separate Examination.

returned for recording in New York, the certificate of acknowledgment will follow the New York law, although it will show that
the acknowledgment was made in Florida.

Essentials of an acknowledgment. Although acknowledgments
vary with the state, they all have certain basic essentials. You
will observe that the following basic essentials are apparent in
the acknowledgments illustrated in Figures 38 through 42.

```
STATE OF FLORIDA)
                : SS.:
COUNTY OF DUVAL )


        I hereby certify that on this day before me, an

officer duly authorized in the state aforesaid and in the

county aforesaid to take acknowledgments, personally ap-

peared ALFRED JONES and LESTER S. SMITH, to me known and

known to be the persons described in and who executed the

foregoing instrument as president and secretary, respec-

tively, of National Company, Inc., a corporation named

therein, and severally acknowledged before me that they

executed the same as such officers, in the name of and for

and on behalf of the said corporation.

        IN WITNESS WHEREOF, I have hereunto set my hand

and affixed my official seal this      day of September,

19--.


                        Notary Public

        My commission expires
```

Figure 40. Certificate of Acknowledgment by Corporation—Two Officers.

Venue. An acknowledgment always begins with a recital of the venue, that is, the name of the state and county in which the acknowledgment is made. In Kentucky, Massachusetts, Pennsylvania, and Virginia, the venue recites the name of the commonwealth instead of the state; in Louisiana, the parish instead of

```
STATE OF CALIFORNIA )
                    : ss.
COUNTY OF EL DORADO )


         On this          day of          , 19—, before me,

Nancy Jones, notary public in and for said county and state,

personally appeared FRED C. BELL, known to me to be one of

the partners of the partnership that executed the within

instrument, and acknowledged to me that such partnership

executed the same.



                         _____
                         Notary Public in and for said
                               County and State
```

Figure 41. Certificate of Acknowledgment by Partnership.

the county. Type the statement of the venue in solid caps, bracket it, and follow with *ss.*, the abbreviation for *scilicet* (*sc*, though correct, is not used in legal papers). The abbreviation may be caps or small letters. Like all abbreviations, it is followed by a period. Technically, a colon should also follow because scilicet means "to wit," but few law offices observe this technicality.

Date of acknowledgment. An acknowledgment always recites the date on which the acknowledgment is made. When you type the certificate of acknowledgment, leave blank spaces for the day of the month, and also for the name of the month if you are preparing the instrument near the end of the month. Although a client is supposed to sign and acknowledge an instrument on the 30th of April, he might not get into the office until the 1st day of May. The date of the acknowledgment does not necessarily coincide with the date of the instrument, but the date of an acknowledgment must *never* precede the date the instrument was signed.

```
STATE OF NEW HAMPSHIRE)
                      : SS.
COUNTY OF MERRIMACK   )


        On this the      day of        , 19—, before

me,                    , the undersigned officer, per-

sonally appeared ROGER L. HUNT, known to me to be the person

whose name is subscribed as attorney-in-fact for EDWARD R.

STEVENS, and acknowledged that he executed the same as the

act of his principal for the purposes therein contained.

        IN WITNESS WHEREOF I hereunto set my hand and

official seal.


                    _____
                         Notary Public
```

Figure 42. Certificate of Acknowledgment by Attorney-in-Fact.

Designation of person making acknowledgment. The name of the person making the acknowledgment always appears in the certificate. Type it in solid caps. If the person making the acknowledgment is making it in a capacity other than that of an individual, that capacity is also stated, but not in solid caps. For example, when a person makes an acknowledgment as secretary of a corporation, the designation is written, ". . . EDWARD WILLIAMS, secretary of Royal Matches, Inc., . . ." The person who makes the acknowledgment does not sign the certificate.

Signature and designation of officer taking acknowledgment. The officer who takes an acknowledgment signs the certificate. In typing the certificate, type a blank line for his signature four spaces beneath the body of the certificate. Type his title underneath the line. (In Indiana, the name of the notary must also be typed, or printed.) In many states the certificate also recites the name and full title of the officer taking the acknowledgment. If you do not know who is to take the acknowledgment, leave a blank space long enough for the average name to be inserted in handwriting.

Date of expiration of commission. Many states require that an acknowledgment taken by a notary public show the date of the expiration of his commission. On acknowledgments to be used in those states, which are listed in Table II, page 186, *et seq.,* type "My commission expires   , 19   ." two spaces below the signature. Notaries usually have a rubber stamp showing the expiration date of their commission, and the typed line is not necessary except as a reminder that the date of expiration must appear on the certificate.

Notary's seal. In almost all cases the certificate of acknowledgment must also bear the notary's seal, especially if the instrument is acknowledged outside the state where it is to be recorded. (See Table II for those states that require a notary's seal.)

How and where to type the acknowledgment. Acknowledgments are usually double spaced. They follow the signatures. Although there is no rule of law governing the placement of an acknowledgment on the page, it is desirable that the entire acknowledgment be placed on the signature page of the instrument, even if single spacing is necessary to accomplish this. If the entire acknowledgment cannot be placed on the signature page it is preferable to type part of it on that page. In the case of some instruments, for example a power of attorney that authorizes the conveyance of any interest in real estate, it is practically mandatory to type the acknowledgment on the same page as the signatures. The suggestions given on page 171 for fitting signatures on the page are applicable to fitting the acknowledgment on the page.

Who may make an acknowledgment. Any person who signs an instrument is qualified to acknowledge it, and he acknowledges it in the same capacity that he signed. A person who signs an instrument in his own behalf acknowledges it as his act in his individual capacity (Figure 38). If husband and wife sign, each makes an acknowledgment, but in almost all states only one certificate of acknowledgment is necessary (Figure 39). See also page 188.

The officer of a corporation acknowledges that the corporation executed the instrument, and the acknowledgment associates the acknowledger with the corporation. In those states that require a corporate instrument to be signed by two officers, each officer acknowledges the instrument but both acknowledgments are included in the same certificate (Figure 40).

A partner acknowledges that an instrument was executed by the partnership (Figure 41).

An attorney-in-fact acknowledges that he signed the principal's name and his own as attorney-in-fact (Figure 42).

A subscribing witness may also acknowledge an instrument. The wording of an acknowledgment by a subscribing witness differs considerably from an acknowledgment made by a party to the instrument. The lawyer will dictate the acknowledgment, or give you a form to follow.

Who may take an acknowledgment. The statutes in the various states designate the officers before whom an acknowledgment may be made, or who may "take acknowledgments." These officers include, among others, judges, clerks of courts, and notaries public. Usually the secretary in a law office is appointed notary public, so that she may take acknowledgments of clients to instruments prepared in the office. (See page 185 for the qualifications and duties of a notary public.)

Authentication. As previously pointed out, instruments are frequently acknowledged in one state and recorded in another. Some states require that instruments acknowledged outside the state must have the notary's certificate of acknowledgment authenticated by a designated official, usually the clerk of the county court in which the notary public is registered. The clerk's authentication is a certification to the effect that the notary is authorized to take acknowledgments and that the signature on the certificate of acknowledgment is his. The statutes usually prescribe the wording of the certificate of authentication. If your office is in a state that requires authentication of the notary's certificate, prepare the certificate of authentication in accordance with the statute in your state. (The lawyer will dictate it or give you a form to follow. Make a copy for your loose-leaf notebook.) Your letter forwarding the instrument for acknowledgment should point out that the authentication, as well as the certificate of acknowledgment, should be signed. (See Table I.)

TABLE I

AUTHENTICATION OF INSTRUMENTS

State	When an instrument is notarized outside the state for recording within the state, must it be authenticated if notary affixes his seal?	Who authenticates acknowledgments taken by notary public in state for use in another state?
Alabama	No	Clerk of Circuit Court
Alaska	No	Clerk of District Court
Arizona	Yes	Clerk of Superior Court
Arkansas	Yes	Secretary of State or Clerk of Court of Record
California	Yes	County Clerk
Colorado	No	Clerk of County Court
Connecticut	Customary	Clerk of Superior Court
Delaware	No	Prothonotary
District of Columbia	No	Secretary of Board of Commissioners
Florida	No	Clerk of Circuit Court
Georgia	No	Clerk of Superior Court
Hawaii	No	Clerk of Circuit Court
Idaho	No	Clerk of District Court
Illinois	No	County Clerk (Secretary of State may grant certificates of magistracy to notaries)
Indiana	No	Clerk of Circuit Court
Iowa	Yes	Clerk of District Court
Kansas	No	Clerk of District Court
Kentucky	No	Clerk of County Court
Louisiana	No	Clerk of District Court
Maine	No	Clerk of Court
Maryland	No	Clerk of Circuit Court (Clerk of Superior Court of Baltimore City)
Massachusetts	Yes	State Secretary; Clerk of Superior Court
Michigan	Yes	Clerk of County
Minnesota	No	Clerk of District Court
Mississippi	No	Chancery Clerk
Missouri	No	Clerk of County Court (Clerk of Circuit Court for City of St. Louis)
Montana	No	Secretary of State or County Clerk
Nebraska	No	County Clerk
Nevada	No	County Clerk
New Hampshire	Yes	Secretary of State or Clerk of Courts of Record
New Jersey	Yes	County Clerk
New Mexico	Not required but customary	County Clerk
New York	Yes	County Clerk
North Carolina	No	Clerk of County
North Dakota	No	Clerk of District Court
Ohio	No	Clerk of Common Pleas Court

TABLE I (Continued)

State	When an instrument is notarized outside the state for recording within the state, must it be authenticated if notary affixes his seal?	Who authenticates acknowledgments taken by notary public in state for use in another state?
Oklahoma	No	Secretary of State
Oregon	No	County Clerk
Pennsylvania	No	Prothonotary of Common Pleas Court
Rhode Island	No	Superior and Supreme Court Clerks
South Carolina	No	Clerk of Court
South Dakota	No	Clerk of Circuit Court
Tennessee	No	Clerk of County
Texas	No	County Clerk
Utah	No	Secretary of State
Vermont	No (banks usually request authentication)	County Clerk
Virginia	No	Clerk of Court
Washington	No	Secretary of State or County Clerk
West Virginia	No	Clerk of County Court
Wisconsin	No	Clerk of Circuit Court
Wyoming	No	County Clerk

Notaries Public

What is a notary public? A notary public is a commissioned officer of the state, whose powers and duties consist, among others, in administering oaths, certifying to the genuineness of documents, and taking acknowledgments. In some states a notary is authorized to act only in the county in which he is commissioned; in others, he is qualified to act throughout the state. Almost all law offices have a notary public, and frequently the secretary is the notary. Lawyers in New Jersey and New York have *de facto* notarial authority, but they must qualify, register, and have a notarial seal or stamp. The eligibility requirements are not stringent, relating primarily to age and residence. If your office wants you to be commissioned as a notary, write to the official in your state who appoints notaries for an application blank. Table II shows the official to whom to write in each state and whether a bond is required. The table also indicates those states that require a notary public to keep a record of his official acts. In some states, as will appear from the

TABLE II

NOTARIES PUBLIC

State	Appoint-ments made by	Length of term	Notary must affix		Record of acts required	Bond required
			Seal	Date commis-sion expires		
Alabama	Governor	4	No	No	Yes	Yes
Alaska	Secretary of State	4	Yes	Yes	Yes	Yes
Arizona	Secretary of State	4	Yes	Yes	Yes	Yes
Arkansas	Governor	4	Yes	Yes	Yes	Yes
California	Governor	4	Yes	No	Yes	Yes
Colorado	Secretary of State	4	Yes	Yes	Yes	Yes
Connecticut ...	Governor	5	Yes	No	No	No
Delaware	Governor	2	Yes	No	No	No
District of Columbia	D.C. Com-missioners	5	Yes	No	Yes	Yes
Florida	Governor	4	Yes	Yes	No	Yes
Georgia	Clerks of Superior Court	4	Yes	No	No	No
Hawaii	Atty. Gen.	4	Yes	No	Yes	Yes
Idaho	Governor	4	Yes	No	No[1]	Yes
Illinois	Governor	4	Yes	No	No[2]	Yes
Indiana	Governor	4	Yes	Yes	No	Yes
Iowa	Governor	3	Yes	No	Yes	Yes
Kansas	Governor	4	Yes	Yes	No	Yes
Kentucky	Secretary of State	4	No	Yes	No[1]	Yes
Louisiana	Governor	Indefinite	No	No	Yes	Yes
Maine	Governor	7	Yes	No	No[3]	No
Maryland	Governor	2	Yes	No	Yes	No
Massachusetts ..	Governor	7	No	Yes	No	No
Michigan	Governor	4	No	Yes	No	Yes
Minnesota	Governor	7	Yes	Yes	No[1]	Yes
Mississippi	Governor	4	Yes	Yes	Yes	Yes
Missouri	Governor	4	Yes	Yes	Yes	Yes
Montana	Governor	3	Yes	Yes	No[1]	Yes
Nebraska	Governor	6	Yes	Yes	No	Yes
Nevada	Governor	4	Yes	Yes[4]	Yes	Yes
New Hampshire.	Governor	5	Yes[4]	No	No	No
New Jersey	Secretary of State	5	No	No	No	No
New Mexico ...	Governor	4	Yes	Yes	Yes	Yes
New York	Secretary of State	2	No	Yes	No	No
North Carolina .	Governor	2	Yes	Yes	No	No
North Dakota ..	Governor	6	Yes	Yes	No[1]	Yes
Ohio	Governor	3	Yes[4]	No	No[1]	Yes
Oklahoma	Secretary of State	4	Yes	Yes	Yes	Yes

TABLE II (Continued)

State	Appointments made by	Length of term	Notary must affix			Record of acts required	Bond required
			Seal	Date commission expires			
Oregon	Governor	4	Yes	Yes		No[1]	Yes
Pennsylvania ..	Governor	4	Yes	Yes		Yes	Yes
Rhode Island ..	Governor	5	No	No		No	No
South Carolina .	Governor	"pleasure of Governor"	No	No		No	No
South Dakota ..	Governor	8	Yes	Yes		No	Yes
Tennessee	Governor	4	Yes	Yes		Yes	Yes
Texas	Secretary of State	June 1 of odd numbered years	Yes	No		Yes	Yes
Utah	Governor	4	Yes	Yes		No	Yes
Vermont	Judges of the County Court	2	No[2]	No		No	No
Virginia	Governor	4	No	Yes		No	Yes
Washington	Governor	4	Yes	No		No	Yes
West Virginia ..	Governor	10	No	Yes		No	Yes
Wisconsin	Governor	4	Yes	Yes		No	Yes
Wyoming	Governor	4	Yes	Yes		Yes[5]	Yes

[1] Except with reference to commercial papers.
[2] Except with reference to negotiable instruments.
[3] Except with reference to mercantile and marine protests.
[4] In practice, but not by statute.
[5] For official acts required by law to be recorded.

application blank, the application must be endorsed by a member of the legislature, a judge, or some other designated official.

After the commission is received, order a notary's seal and stamp. Then register your commission with the clerk of the court (or other designated official) in your county, so that the officer can authenticate your certificate of acknowledgment on papers that are to be recorded in another state.

Following the letter of the law when you notarize a paper. A commission as a notary public is a trust; it confers certain powers upon you as well as requiring that you perform certain duties. In exercising those powers and duties, you should observe punctiliously the "letter of the law." In a law office your principal duty as a notary public will be taking acknowledgments.

Notice that all of the certificates of acknowledgments previously illustrated (Figures 38 through 42) recite that the person making the acknowledgment "personally appeared" before the notary. This is true of all forms of acknowledgments in every state. You, therefore, should never take an acknowledgment without the actual appearance of the individual making the acknowledgment. In fact, it is illegal to do so. If a client's wife signs an instrument at home and wants to acknowledge it over the telephone, politely but firmly decline to take the acknowledgment, and state the reason for your refusal.

Acknowledgments also recite that the individual "acknowledged" that he signed the instrument. You do not administer an oath to a person making an acknowledgment, but ask him: "Do you acknowledge that you signed this instrument?" or, "Do you acknowledge that you executed this instrument as attorney-in-fact for Edward R. Stevens?" or a similar question, depending upon whether the acknowledgment is being made by an individual in his own behalf, an officer of a corporation, a partnership, or an attorney-in-fact.

Acknowledgments also recite that the notary knows, or has satisfactory evidence, that the person making it is the person "described in and who executed" the instrument. You must have satisfactory evidence of the identity of a person whose acknowledgment you take. Of course, in taking acknowledgments made by clients, you are not likely to have difficulty in this respect. A notary who willfully makes a false certificate that an instrument was acknowledged by a party to the instrument is guilty of forgery.

A certificate of acknowledgment also shows the date it is signed by the notary. You should never post-date or ante-date a certificate. To do so constitutes fraud and deceit in the exercise of your powers.

The following states require that the wife be examined by the notary "separate and apart" from her husband: Delaware, Georgia, New Jersey, North Carolina, South Carolina, Texas. This is especially true with reference to instruments relating to real estate. If the state in which an instrument is to be recorded has this requirement, you should follow the statutory procedure strictly. Do not take the wife's acknowledgment in the presence of her husband. Figure 39 illustrates a certificate in a state requiring a separate acknowledgment by the wife.

Details to observe when you notarize a paper. You should exercise special care to see that documents that you notarize are executed correctly. If the papers are not in conformity with the requirements of the office where they are to be recorded, they will be rejected. You do not read an instrument that you notarize, but you should read the acknowledgment and also glance over the instrument. Observe the following details when taking an acknowledgment:

1. If the instrument recites that it is "under seal," be sure that the signature to the instrument is followed by "L.S." or "Seal."

2. When a corporation is a party to an instrument, be sure the corporate seal is impressed on the instrument if required; seals are usually required on corporate instruments.

3. Fill in all blanks in the instrument and in the certificate of acknowledgment.

4. Be sure to show the date of the expiration of your commission, when required.

5. Be sure to impress your notarial seal on the certificate, when required. Table II shows which states require a notary's seal on papers acknowledged within the state. All states require a seal on papers acknowledged in another state.

6. Be sure that rubber stamps used by you make legible imprints. A black stamp pad is preferable because the black ink photostats more distinctly than other inks.

7. Be sure to have the clerk of the court (or other designated official) authenticate your certificate of acknowledgment if authentication is required.

Recording Legal Instruments

Purpose in recording instruments. Legal instruments are frequently *recorded* in a public office, and the record is available to anyone who is interested. The purpose of recording the instruments is to protect the interests of all persons. For example, *A* wants to purchase some property from *B*. He learns from the public record that *C* holds a mortgage on the property. *A* purchases the property, but he makes legal arrangements that will protect not only his own interests but those of *C* as well.

Distinction between recording and filing. The terms *record* and *file* are used loosely. They are not synonymous and should not be used interchangeably. If an instrument is to be *recorded*, it is given to an official designated by the state statute. The official copies the instrument in a book, thereby preserving it perpetually. This record furnishes authentic evidence of the existence of the instrument. After the official records the instrument, he stamps upon it the date and the number and page of his record book in which it is recorded and returns it to the person who gave it to him, usually the lawyer. When a paper is *filed*, it is placed in the custody of a designated official, who enters upon the paper the date of its receipt and keeps it in his office, where it is available for inspection. Legal instruments are generally recorded, whereas court papers are always filed. However, in some states certain legal instruments are filed and recorded in the abstract; that is, only a summary of the essential parts is recorded. The official designated to record legal instruments varies with the locality. He might be the county clerk, the town clerk, a register or recorder of deeds, or some other official.

Instruments that are recorded or filed are also appropriately indexed so that the record or file can be easily located.

In many places the photostat method of copying records is used. Therefore, it is necessary that all instruments submitted for recording be typed with heavily inked ribbon, preferably black.

What the secretary does. When the lawyer asks you to have an instrument recorded, be sure you know not only what official is to record it, but also *where* it is to be recorded. For example, although your office is located in Adams County and the client signs the paper there, if the instrument relates to property located in Brown County, the instrument will be recorded in Brown County, not in Adams County.

Your firm's name and address will probably appear on the legal back in which the instrument is bound. Before having the instrument recorded, write immediately above it, "Please record and return to:" If the firm's name and address are not printed on the legal back, type them on it.

If the instrument is to be recorded in a place located near your office, take it in person to the office of the proper official. He will give you a receipt for it and return it to your office when he has recorded it. You will have to pay a recording fee, which is fixed by the state statutes. Unless the photostat method of recording is used, the fee is usually based on the number of folios (groups of 100 words) in the instrument. Pay the fee out of petty cash, or take a blank check to the recording office and fill in the amount when you are told what the recording fee will be.

When it is necessary to mail the instrument to the recording office, send it by registered mail, return receipt requested, with a covering letter. The letter should be addressed to the designated official and should describe the instrument sufficiently to identify it. You will also have to enclose a check for the fee or request that a bill be forwarded. The official will not record the instrument until the fee is received. A model letter for this purpose follows.

REGISTERED

RETURN RECEIPT REQUESTED   November 14, 19. .

John R. Blank, Esquire
Clerk of the County Court
Starkville, Mississippi

Sir:

    We are enclosing for recording lease, dated November 14, 19. ., between Edgar S. Norris and Robert T. Ellis.

    If you will tell us the correct amount of your fee for recording this instrument, we shall forward a check to you promptly.

            Very truly yours,

            ELDWOOD & SMITH

            By

                S. R. Elwood

Enclosure

Place the receipt from the recording official, or a copy of your covering letter to him, in your follow-up file so that you may trace him if the instrument is not returned promptly. Allow about two weeks for the return of the instrument. When it is returned, send it to the client with a covering letter (unless, for some reason, the instrument is to be kept by the lawyer). After an instrument has been recorded, there is no necessity to forward it by registered mail.

10

Specific Instruments: Affidavits; Powers of Attorney; Wills

IN THE preceding chapter we gave basic information about legal instruments generally. In this chapter we discuss specifically three representative instruments that are a part of the work in every law office.

Affidavits

What is an affidavit? An affidavit is a written statement of facts sworn to by the person making the statement in the presence of an officer authorized to administer the oath. A person whose religion forbids him to take an oath, *affirms* the facts instead of swearing to them. The person making the affidavit is called the *affiant* or the *deponent*. The purpose of an affidavit is to help establish or prove a fact. Affidavits are used to prove, among other things, identity, age, residence, marital status, and possession of property. They are also an essential part of court motions (see Chapter 14).

Distinction between affidavit and acknowledgment. An affidavit is a complete instrument within itself, but an acknowledgment is always part of, or rather an appendage to, another instrument. The purpose of an affidavit is to prove a fact, whereas the purpose of an acknowledgment is the declaration by the person making it that he signed the instrument to which the certificate of acknowledgment is attached. An affidavit is sworn to, but an acknowledgment is not. Both the person making an affidavit and officer administering the oath sign an affidavit; only the officer taking an acknowledgment signs it. An affidavit has a jurat, but an acknowledgment does not.

Essentials of an affidavit. Some affidavits are written in the first person and some in the third person, but they all have the following basic essentials.

Venue. When an affidavit is used in a court case, it is always preceded by the caption of the case (see page 314). The affidavit itself begins with a recital of the venue.

Name of affiant. The name of the person making the affidavit is written in solid caps.

Averment of oath. The introduction to the affidavit avers that the affiant was sworn, or made the statement under oath.

Statement of facts. The body of the affidavit is a narrative of the facts that the affiant wishes to state.

Signature of affiant. The affiant always signs the affidavit, even those that are written in the third person.

Jurat. A jurat is a clause in an official certificate attesting that the affidavit or deposition was sworn to at a stated time before an authorized officer. It is often referred to as the "sworn to" clause. The form of jurat varies slightly in the different states. In a few states, the jurat recites the title of the officer and the state, or state and county, in which he is authorized to act. In a few other states, the name of the affiant is repeated in the jurat. The most common form of jurat is:

Subscribed and sworn to before me
this _____ day of _____, 19___.

_____

Notary Public

Signature of notary. The notary signs immediately beneath the jurat. He also affixes his seal and the expiration date of his commission. In some states the expiration date precedes the signature.

Authentication. If the affidavit is to be used in a state other than that in which it is made, an authentication of the officer's signature and authority is sometimes necessary. The procedure is the same as when an acknowledgment is authenticated. (See Chapter 9.)

Preparation of affidavit. Directions for the preparation of an affidavit for use in a court case are given at page 313. The directions given here apply to affidavits that are not to be used in a court case. Usually affidavits are typed on legal-size paper, but they may be typed on letter-size paper. Inquire as to the number of copies to make.

1. The venue is typed like the venue on an acknowledgment (Chapter 9).

2. Double space.

3. Type the affiant's name in solid caps.

4. Make a signature line at the right for the affiant to sign.

5. Usually the jurat is typed on the left half of the page (see Figure 43), but in a few jurisdictions, the practice is to type it across the entire page.

```
STATE OF SOUTH CAROLINA   )
                          : ss.
COUNTY OF FLORENCE        )



        ROBERT T. SMITH, being duly sworn, deposes and
says:

        He is the Secretary of National Corporation, and

that no stockholder of said Corporation has filed with the

Secretary thereof a written request (other than such written

request or requests as may have heretofore expired or been

withdrawn) that notices intended for him shall be mailed to

some address other than his address as it appears on the

stock book of the said Corporation.



                    _____
                            Secretary

Sworn to before me this

    day of          , 19—

_____
    Notary Public
```

Figure 43. An Affidavit.

6. Type a signature line for the notary public (or other officer who is to administer the oath) immediately beneath the jurat,

at the left margin of the page. If the jurat is typed across the page, type the signature line on the right half of the page.

7. Beneath the signature line type the officer's title. In some states the officer's authority to act in the particular political subdivision is required. For example: Notary Public in and for the County of *Los Angeles,* State of California."

8. Type "My commission expires　　　　." (when required) two spaces beneath the officer's title if the jurat is typed on the left half of the page. If the jurat is typed across the page, the expiration date line is typed at the left margin, parallel to the officer's signature and title.

Powers of Attorney

What is a power of attorney? A power of attorney is a written instrument giving authority to the agent appointed to act in the name and on behalf of the person signing it. Authority may be given to another to borrow money; collect debts; manage, lease, sell, or mortgage real estate; prosecute a suit at law, and for almost any other purpose. Frequently, a lawyer gives his secretary a power of attorney to sign his name to checks.

Parties to a power of attorney. The person who gives the authority to another to act for him is called the *principal.* The principal may be an individual, a corporation, or a partnership, but a principal must be capable of performing the act that he authorizes another to perform for him.

The person to whom authority is given is the *agent,* or *attorney-in-fact.* The latter designation does not imply that the agent is a lawyer. An attorney-at-law may be an attorney-in-fact, but an attorney-in-fact is not necessarily an attorney-at-law.

Forms of powers of attorney. A power of attorney is either general or limited. A general power of attorney is broad in scope and enables the agent to transact almost any business for the principal, whereas under a limited power of attorney, the agent's power is limited to a specified act or acts.

Statements and clauses. Except with respect to the powers granted by the instrument, all powers of attorney are similar. No state requires a specific form. A power of attorney begins with the words *Know all men by these presents,* or simply *Know all men,* typed in solid caps. After a recital of the parties and their residence, the powers granted by the instrument are set forth. This portion of the instrument is most important and requires careful and expert phrasing so that powers granted may be clearly and precisely defined. The lawyer dictates the recital of powers or gives you a special form to follow.

A power of attorney ends with a testimonium clause, which is similar to the testimonium clause in any instrument (see page 169). Those relating to real estate are always acknowledged.

Directions for the preparation of a power of attorney. Unless otherwise instructed, follow these directions when typing a power of attorney.

1. Make an original for the attorney-in-fact, a copy for the principal, and a copy for your files.

2. Use legal cap.

3. Place the responsibility marks on the office copy only.

4. Double space.

5. Don't forget to have at least two lines of typing on the signature page.

6. Prepare signature line for the principal or principals only.

7. If the powers granted relate to the conveyance of real estate, the instrument must be prepared with the formalities required for a deed. Follow directions 7, 9, 11, 12, 13, 16, and 19, on page 464, *et seq.*, in Chapter 20.

8. If the powers granted do not relate to real estate, ask the lawyer if the power of attorney is to be witnessed and acknowledged. If so, follow instructions in Chapter 9.

9. Collate.

10. Endorse legal back (Chapter 8) as illustrated in Figure 44.

11. Check to see that the principal's signature agrees with the name typed in the instrument.

12. After the instrument is signed, and acknowledged if necessary, conform copies to original (see Chapter 8).

13. If a power of attorney relates to real property, it is recorded like any conveyance. However, sometimes it is not recorded until the attorney-in-fact exercises the power granted. Ask the lawyer for instructions as to recording.

14. The lawyer will tell you whether the original of the power of attorney is to be delivered directly to the attorney-in-fact, or to the principal.

15. Make a notation on your office copy of the distribution of the original and copy.

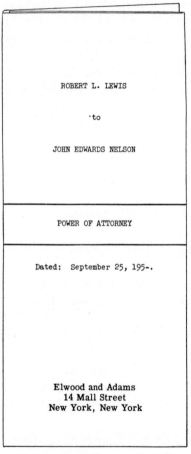

ROBERT L. LEWIS

·to

JOHN EDWARDS NELSON

POWER OF ATTORNEY

Dated: September 25, 195-.

Elwood and Adams
14 Mall Street
New York, New York

Figure 44. Endorsed Back for Power of Attorney.

Wills

What is a will? A *will* is the disposal of one's property to take effect after death. At one time only real estate was disposed of by *will*, personalty being disposed of by testament. The distinction between the terms will and testament is no longer of legal significance, and the terms are frequently used interchangeably.

Who are the parties to a will? *Testator*. Actually the only party to a will is the *testator*, or *testatrix* if a woman. The testator is the person who makes the will—who disposes of the property and issues the instructions that are to be carried out after his death. A testator must be of sound mind and of the age required by the state statutes. In the majority of states, the age requirement is 21. In many states the age requirement for the testator of personal property is lower than for the testator of real property; also, many states lower the age requirement of a testatrix. The table on page 203 shows the age requirements in the various states.

The law of the state where the testator resides (his domicile) controls with respect to personalty, but with respect to real estate, the law of the state where the property is situated controls. Thus, although a resident of Florida only 18 years of age can make a will, it will not operate as to his real property situated in New York.

Frequently a man and his wife make a joint will in which case both sign the will as *joint testators.*

Beneficiaries. Beneficiaries are not actually parties to the will, but are the ones who benefit from it. Strictly speaking, a devisee is one to whom real estate is willed, whereas a legatee is one to whom personalty is bequeathed. Like the terms *will* and *testament,* devisee and legatee are frequently used interchangeably, but you will notice that the careful lawyer does not use the terms loosely in the wills that he drafts.

Forms and kinds of wills. None of the states requires that a will and testament shall follow any specific wording, but the statutes do provide for certain formalities in its execution.

Oral wills, known as *nuncupative* wills, are recognized in almost all of the states, but written wills are far more common. A will may be written entirely in the testator's handwriting; such a will is called a *holographic* (sometimes spelled *olographic*) will. The lawyer's secretary is concerned principally with the formal written will, typed and executed in the lawyer's office.

Reciprocal wills. Wills made by two or more persons with reciprocal testamentary provisions in favor of each other are called *reciprocal wills.* The term is used whether the testators make a joint will or separate wills. Husbands and wives quite often make reciprocal wills.

Printed forms of wills. Although it is possible to buy printed forms of wills, they are seldom, if ever, used in a law office. In the first place, clients regard the making of a will as a very serious matter and would not be favorably impressed by the use of a printed form. Then, too, the detailed contents of wills vary so greatly that the use of a printed form saves little time and effort on the part of the lawyer and his secretary.

Pattern of the contents of wills. Although no two wills are alike in detail, they are all drafted from similar patterns. The outline given below generally is followed in properly drawn wills. The explanation in the succeeding paragraphs will enable you to recognize each part and clause.

Title
Introductory paragraph
   Revocation clause
Body or text
   Payment of debts and funeral expenses
   Dispositive clauses
      Devises
      Bequests
      Trust provisions
      Residuary clause
   Appointment of executor
   Appointment of guardian
   Precatory provisions
Testimonium clause
Signature and seal
Attestation clause
Witnesses' signatures

Title. The title merely identifies the document, as "Last Will and Testament of Robert Brown," or "First Codicil to the Last Will and Testament of Robert Brown." It is typed in solid caps, underscored, and arranged symmetrically, beginning about six double spaces from the top of the page. See page 205.

Introductory paragraph. In the introductory paragraph, the testator sets forth his name and residence and recites that he does "hereby publish and declare this my Last Will and Testament." Introductory clauses also frequently recite the mental capacity of the testator to make a will, that is, "of sound mind and disposing memory."

Revocation clause. The revocation clause specifically revokes all former wills. All wills do not include this clause, even though the testator has made other wills, because the act of executing a new will normally has the effect of revoking prior wills. The revocation clause is either a part of the introductory paragraph or is a separate paragraph, usually near the end of the will.

Text, or body. The text, or body, of the will disposes of the testator's property, appoints his executor, and expresses wishes of the testator that are not necessarily mandatory. The provisions in the body of the will are often referred to as *articles,* or *items,* and are numbered. There are no fast rules as to numbering schemes, but the following are among those commonly used.

In the center of the page: ARTICLE I, ARTICLE II, etc.; ITEM I, ITEM II, etc.; or I, II, etc.

At the side of the page: FIRST:, SECOND:, etc.; First:, Second:, etc.; or, in a short will, 1., 2., etc.

The various articles might have subparagraphs that are also numbered (1), (2), etc., or (a), (b), etc., and these in turn might be subdivided. If you use numbers for subparagraphs, use letters for sub-subparagraphs. The left margin of sub-subparagraphs is usually indented about 10 spaces.

You must be consistent throughout the will in the numbering system that you use, and, also, on the lookout for inconsistencies in the lawyer's dictation in this respect. He might dictate, "Article I," and "Item 20." If a certain article contains more than 26 bequests, you should choose numbers, rather than letters, for the subparagraphs in all of the articles.

Payment of debts and funeral expenses. The first paragraph in the body of a will usually directs an executor to pay debts, expenses of last illness, and funeral expenses. This provision is normally not necessary, because the law requires the executor to pay these debts, but it is customarily included.

Dispositive clauses. The dispositive clauses are the provisions that express the testator's will as to what shall be done with his property—the provisions that *dispose* of his property. Disposal of real property is a *devise;* disposal of personal property, a *bequest* or *legacy.* In a carefully drawn will, the testator will "give and devise" real property; "give and bequeath" personal property; and "give, devise, and bequeath" both real and personal property.

Trust provisions. Many wills set up trusts, which are known as testamentary trusts. The testator wills property to an institution, or an individual, "in trust for the following purposes. . . ." A testamentary trust is usually created when the testator wants the beneficiary to receive the income from it during his life, or until he reaches a certain age, or until the happening of some other contingency. Wealthy testators frequently set up endowment funds in trust for charitable and educational purposes. The trust provisions of many wills are very explicit and, therefore, quite lengthy. They constitute part of the dispositive provisions of the will.

Residuary clause. The residuary clause is that part of the will that disposes of all of the testator's property not otherwise devised or bequeathed, ". . . all the rest, residue, and remainder. . . ." A residuary clause is an essential part of the will. Specific or general devises and bequests have priority over the residuary clause, and it is therefore the last dispositive provision of a properly constructed will. No set form of words is necessary.

Appointment of executor. Someone must see that the provisions of the testator's will are carried out after his death. He appoints an *executor* in his will for this purpose. The executor may be an individual or an institution, such as a bank. If the individual is a woman, she is the *executrix* (plural, *executrices*). Frequently, the testator appoints more than one executor, or he may appoint an alternate, in the event of the incapacity or refusal of his first choice to act. Usually the paragraph naming the executor follows the dispositive provisions (bequests) of the will.

Appointment of guardian. If a testator is the surviving parent he will probably appoint a guardian of the "person and property" of his minor children. Or he might choose to appoint one guardian for the person of the children and another for their property. The paragraph appointing a guardian normally follows the paragraph appointing an executor.

Testimonium, or signature, clause. The testimonium, or signature, clause to a will is similar to the testimonium clause in any written instrument (see page 169). Triple space between the text of the will and the testimonium clause, and *do not number it*.

Attestation clause and witnesses' signatures. All of the states require that a will be witnessed, but the required number of witnesses varies (see Table III). The attestation clause (see page 176) to a will recites that the will was witnessed at the request of the testator and that it was signed by him in the presence of the witnesses, who subscribed their names in the presence of the testator and in the presence of each other. The clause is not usually typed in full measure, but extends only about three-quarters across the page. However, it may be typed in full measure when necessary to conserve space. Holographic wills are seldom witnessed.

TABLE III

STATE REQUIREMENTS FOR AGE OF TESTATOR
AND NUMBER OF WITNESSES TO WILL
(*Not applicable to holographic wills*)

State	Real property		Personal property		Witnesses
	Male	*Female*	*Male*	*Female*	
Alabama	21	21[9]	18	18	2
Alaska	21	21	21	21	2
Arizona[1]	21	21	21	21	2
Arkansas	18	18	18	18	2
California	18	18	18	18	2
Colorado	18	18	18	18	2
Connecticut	18	18	18	18	3
Delaware	18	18	18	18	2
District of Columbia ...	21	18	21	18	2
Florida	18	18	18	18	2
Georgia	14	14	14	14	2
Hawaii	20	20	20	20	2
Idaho	18	18	18	18	2
Illinois	18	18	18	18	2
Indiana[2]	21	21	21	21	2
Iowa	21	21	21	21	2
Kansas[8]	21	21	21	21	2
Kentucky	21	21	21	21	2
Louisiana	16	16	16	16	3[10]
Maine[3]	21	21	21	21	3
Maryland	18	18	14	12	2
Massachusetts	21	21	21	21	3
Michigan	21	21	21	21	2
Minnesota	21	21	21	21	2
Mississippi	21	21	21	21	2
Missouri[2]	18	18	18	18	2
Montana	18	18	18	18	2
Nebraska	21	21	21	21	2
Nevada	18	18	18	18	2
New Hampshire[4]	18	18	18	18	3
New Jersey[11]	21	21	21	21	2
New Mexico	21	21	21	21	2
New York	21	21	18	18	2
North Carolina	21	21	21	21	2
North Dakota	18	18	18	18	2
Ohio	21	21	21	21	2
Oklahoma	18	18	18	18	2
Oregon[4]	21	21	21	21	2

TABLE III (Continued)

State	Real property		Personal property		Witnesses
	Male	Female	Male	Female	
Pennsylvania	21[2]	21	21[2]	21	2
Rhode Island	21	21	18	18	2
South Carolina[8]	21	21	21	21	3
South Dakota	18	18	18	18	2
Tennessee	18	18	18	18	2
Texas[6]	19	19	19	19	2
Utah	18	18	18	18	2
Vermont	21	21	21	21	3
Virginia	21	18	18	18	2
Washington[7]	21	21	21	21	2
West Virginia	18	18	18	18	2
Wisconsin[2]	21	21[8]	21	21[8]	2
Wyoming	21	21	21	21	2

[1] 18 if in the armed forces. No age requirement if ever married.
[2] No age requirement if in the armed forces.
[3] No age requirement if married or a widow or a widower.
[4] No age requirement if married.
[5] Not required but usual.
[6] No age requirement if in the armed forces or ever married.
[7] 18, if in the armed forces or every legally married.
[8] 18, if married.
[9] 18, if married or a widow.
[10] One of which is a notary.
[11] 18, if in active military service in time of war.

Typing a will. Figures 45 and 46 illustrate the first and last pages, respectively, of a will. The typing of a will offers a greater challenge to the typist than possibly any other typing that she does. Many wills are short, but many of them are very long and involved, ranging from 10 to 50 or more pages, all of which is dictated. The lawyer chooses his words very carefully and the dictation, therefore, is not rapid. The transcription should cause no difficulty; the challenge lies in the typing of the final copy. There should be no erasures in names or amounts, and no discernible erasures in other parts. Probate of wills has been refused when material provisions have been erased, because the courts could not tell whether the alteration was made before or after execution. The typing should begin and end at the same point on every page, except the last, and yet there must be continuity from page to page, which means that no page should end with a paragraph or with a sentence. The purpose of the continuity is to avoid the omission, or the possible insertion, of a page. Some lawyers go so far as to require that the last word on each page be hyphenated. The placement of the signature with reference to the

THE LAST WILL AND TESTAMENT OF
THOMAS I. DEAN

I, THOMAS I. DEAN of Centerville, Center County,
State of Florida, being of sound mind and disposing memory,
do make, publish and declare this to be my Last Will and
Testament, and hereby revoke any and all former wills and
codicils by me made.

ARTICLE I.

I hereby direct my executors hereinafter named,
to pay all my just debts and funeral expenses as soon after
my demise as can be lawfully done.

ARTICLE II.

I give and devise my farm located just outside and
to the West of Centerville, to my son Richard and his heirs
and assigns forever.

ARTICLE III.

I give and bequeath to my daughter Anne fifty (50)
shares of common stock of United States Steel, Inc.

ARTICLE IV.

I give and bequeath the following sums of money to
the following persons, to-wit:

(a) The sum of Seven Hundred Fifty Dollars ($750.)
to Robert Jones of Allentown, Georgia.

(b) The sum of One Thousand Dollars ($1,000.) to
Edna Jones of Ellisville, Florida.

ARTICLE V.

I give and bequeath to the Merchants' Loan and
Trust Company, a corporation, organized under the laws of

-1-

Figure 45. First Page of Will.

requesting him to appropriate it or so much of it as he
shall think proper for presents to servants in our employ
at the time of my death.

       <u>IN WITNESS WHEREOF</u>, I have signed my name at the
foot and end of this my Last Will and Testament and affixed
my seal this   day of May, 19—.

_____ [L.S.]

    The foregoing instrument, consisting of
ten pages, including this page, each page being typewritten only on one side, was at the
date thereof by the said THOMAS I. DEAN signed,
sealed, published and declared to be his Last
Will and Testament in the presence of us, who,
at his request, in his presence and in the
presence of each other, have subscribed our
names as attesting witnesses thereto.

_____ residing at _____

_____ residing at _____

_____ residing at _____

Figure 46. Last Page of Will.

(Number page in center, one-half inch from bottom.)

testimonium and attestation clauses is of prime importance in a
will.

Frequently the lawyer will tell you to copy a certain paragraph
from another will, or from a skeleton form. Be on the lookout
for differences between the will you are typing and the form you
are following, such as a change from singular to plural, or from
his to *her*, and the like.

Signature page and preceding page of a will. The placement
of the signature often presents a problem. Good practice makes

the solution obligatory in some respects, permissible in others.

It is obligatory that at least one line of the testimonium clause be on the same page as part of the will (see Figure 47). In other words, a new page cannot begin with the testimonium clause, because this arrangement would increase the possibility of the loss of a page, or permit the insertion of a page without detection.

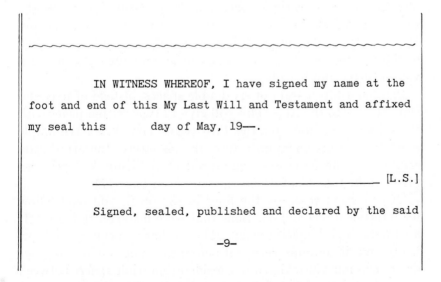

Figure 47. One Line of Testimonium Clause on Page with Part of Text of Will.

Figure 48. One Line of Attestation Clause on Page with Signature.

It is obligatory that at least one line of the attestation clause be on the page with the signature (see Figure 48). The purpose of this requirement is to tie in the witnesses' signatures with that of the testator.

The most desirable setup of the signature page is to have at least three lines of text on the page with the testimonium clause, the signature, and the attestation clause and witnesses' signatures (see Figure 46).

It is permissible, though not desirable, to have the signature and attestation clause on a page containing only one line of the testimonium clause.

How to gauge and test the page length. Unless a will is very short and simple, a draft, triple spaced, is always typed.

1. Count the lines, exclusive of the testimonium clause, signature line, attestation clause, and witnesses' signatures.

2. Assume the draft is 15 pages, 25 lines to the page (drafts are triple-spaced), or a total of 375 lines.

3. Plan on a top margin of five double spaces and an inch margin at the bottom, on 13-inch paper; this will leave room for 32 lines of typing.

4. Divide the total number of lines by the lines per page. You will have 11 typewritten pages with 23 lines left over for the 12th page. A triple space between the text and a three-line testimonium clause, plus three spaces for the signature line places the signature line at the bottom of the page without room for any of the attestation clause. But it is obligatory that at least one line of the attestation clause be on the page with the signature. So, you must try another plan.

Plan on a top margin of six double spaces, instead of five, and type 31 lines to the page. This will give 12 typewritten pages with three lines remaining for the 13th page. You then have ample room for the testimonium clause, the signature, the attestation clause, and the witnesses' signatures. (See Figure 46.) See also "How to fit the signature on the page," on page 171.

Of course, in counting the lines in the draft, you must allow for interlineations and deletions that were made on the draft. If a paragraph is changed considerably, so that you cannot tell how many lines it contains, retype it before counting the lines of your draft. You must also take into consideration triple spaces between articles or items, if you plan to use them. In the illustration in Figure 45, there is a triple space between the title and the introductory paragraph; also, each article is separated from the preceding one by a triple space, making a total of six extra spaces, which is equivalent to 3 double spaces, on that page. Although the page length is 32 lines, that page actually has only 28 lines of typing. The extra spaces throughout the will must be added to the total number of lines.

Witnessing a will. When a will is drawn up and executed in your office, you will probably be asked to witness it. The procedure of witnessing a will is rather formal. The general practice is for the testator to "publish" the will in the presence of the witnesses by declaring that the document is his will. He also asks the witnesses to witness the signing of it. The testator not only signs the will but initials the left margin of the other pages. Each witness signs in the presence of the testator and of each other, and no one leaves the room while the will is being signed, witnessed, and sealed.[1] You will notice from Figure 46 that space for the address of the witness is provided. The address is important because the witness will be called upon to prove the will after the testator's death.

Certifying copies of wills. It is customary in many law offices for the secretary to certify the copies of a will. This certification is not for the purpose of the formal affidavit required when the will is probated (see Chapter 23) but is for authentication of the carbon copies made when the will was typed. Type the form of certification on the copies and, after the copies have been conformed to the original, sign the certification. The following is a form of certification to be used when the typist conforms the copies.

I certify that this carbon copy is one that I typed simultaneously with the original will and that after the execution of the original, I

---

[1] The procedure in Louisiana is different. Generally, the will is not witnessed until after it is placed in an envelope, or other cover, that is closed and sealed. The testator presents the closed and sealed envelope to a notary public and three witnesses, declares that the envelope contains his testament, signed by him. The notary then superscribes the envelope, and he, the testator, and the witnesses sign the superscription. The superscription must state that the testator declared, in the presence of witnesses, that the testament was signed by him, and written by him or another at his direction.

conformed this copy to the original by adding the initials, date, signatures, and the addresses of the witnesses.

If someone other than the typist of the will conforms it, the form of certification to be signed by the typist should be changed to read:

I certify that this carbon copy is one that I typed simultaneously with the original will and that after the execution of the original, this copy was conformed to the original by the addition of the initials, date, signatures, and the addresses of the witnesses.

Some large law firms use the following form of certification:

We, the undersigned, hereby certify that we have compared the foregoing copy with the original will of .... dated .... and find it to be a true and accurate copy thereof.

This last form of certification requires the reading of the will by three persons, or more if more than two copies are made. One person reads the original will aloud and signs the top line of the certification on each of the copies. Each person who follows a copy signs the second line of the certification on the copy that she has followed.

Capitalization and punctuation. You will notice from Figure 45 that the testator's name is written in solid caps, whereas all other names are underscored (preferably with red ink). The words *last will and testament* are written with initial caps in the will and in the attestation clause. In the phrases *make, publish and declare* and *give, devise and bequeath,* no comma precedes the conjunction *and.* Many lawyers prefer that *executor* and *trustee* be capitalized. You will notice from Figure 46 that the words *in witness whereof* are written in solid caps and are followed by a comma. These arrangements are arbitrary but are followed extensively in law offices that give considerable attention to these details.

"Do's and don'ts" in preparing a will. Unless otherwise instructed follow these directions when preparing a will.

1. Type first in draft form unless the will is only a few pages in length.

2. In the final typing, make an original and two copies, the original and one copy for the testator and the other copy for your files. (If a bank or other institution is named executor, ask if an extra copy is to be made for it.)

3. Use the best legal cap available. See Chapter 1.

4. Place the responsibility line at the top of the office copy *only*. (See Chapter 8.)

5. Double space, except the attestation clause.

6. Type the same number of lines on each page, calculating the number of lines as suggested on page 208.

7. Number each page no more than one double space below the last line, except the last page, which should be numbered one-half inch from the bottom of the page.

8. Don't forget to precede and follow the page number with a hyphen. Type the hyphen preceding the number at 42 on the typewriter scale, if a pica type machine is used.

9. Triple space between the text of the will and the testimonium clause.

10. Start the signature line at point 30 on the typewriter scale, if a pica, and continue the line to 67, writing the first bracket in [L.S.] or [SEAL] at point 68. These two scale points are important: the first to accommodate a long signature, and the second to permit a neat application of the seal. (It is customary to seal a will whether or not the statute requires it.)

11. If a wax seal is used, omit the typed seal. Have wax and ribbon available.

12. Single space the attestation clause. Start it at the regular left margin, indenting the first line five spaces. Set the right margin stop at 55 on the typewriter scale. (If necessary to conserve space at the end of the will, type the attestation clause all the way over to the right ruled margin of the paper.)

13. Start the first witness line three spaces below the attestation clause, at the left margin, and underscore for 25 spaces; then type "residing at" and underscore for another 25 spaces.

14. Triple space between the witness lines.

15. Collate.

16. Check and double check spelling of names.

17. Endorse the back as shown in Figure 49, using back engraved with firm's name. Back the original and first carbon.

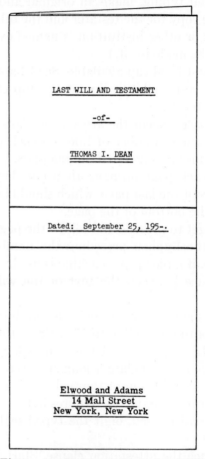

LAST WILL AND TESTAMENT

-of-

THOMAS I. DEAN

Dated: September 25, 195-.

Elwood and Adams
14 Mall Street
New York, New York

Figure 49. Endorsed Back for Will.

18. If real estate devised by the will is described, have someone compare the description with you.

19. Bind firmly and securely.

After the will is signed and witnessed:

20. Conform copies to original. (See Chapter 8.)

21. Certify the copies as described on page 209.

22. If your office is to retain the original of the will for safe-

keeping, give the testator a receipt, signed in the firm's name by one of the lawyers or yourself, reading as follows: "The will of . . . . , dated . . . ., is in our possession for safe-keeping."

23. Enclose the original in an envelope, marked "Last Will and Testament of . . . . , dated . . . ."

24. If an institution is named executor, forward conformed copy with covering letter.

25. If a copy of a former will by the testator is in your file, note on it that a later will, of a certain date, has been executed.

Codicil. After making a will, a testator might decide to change, delete, or add certain provisions. He does this by means of a *codicil,* which is a supplement to the will. A codicil is written and executed with the same formality as the will. It is not attached to the will, but should be placed in a separate envelope on which is typed, "Codicil to Last Will and Testament of . . . ., dated . . . ." A testator may make more than one codicil.

Suggestions for red-inking a will. The usual method of red-inking a will is as follows:

Draw *double* red lines:

    Under the name of the testator in the introductory para-graph and on the cover

    Under each Article number

    Under "IN WITNESS WHEREOF"

Draw *single* red lines:

    Under each name appearing in the will

    Under "Executor" and "Trustee"

    Under everything appearing on the cover, including the en-graved name of the law firm but excepting the name of the testator, which has double lines under it.

Part III

Courts and Litigation

11. Courts and Their Functions 217
12. Basic Information about Litigation Papers 239
13. Specific Court Papers—What They Are and How to
    Prepare Them 267
14. Specific Court Papers—What They Are and How to
    Prepare Them (Cont'd) 303
15. How to Keep a Progress Record of Court Matters 326
16. When a Case Is Appealed 335
17. Handling Material for Printing 367

11

Courts and Their Functions

ALTHOUGH a secretary might never go into a courtroom, a large part of her work revolves around the courts or is dependent upon functions of the court. Therefore, an understanding by the secretary of the organization of courts and their functions that touch upon her work is not only desirable but necessary. This chapter shows the relation between the courts and the secretary's work. It also includes a table giving (1) the names of the various Federal and state courts of record and (2) the membership of those courts.

The word "court." The word *court,* as it relates to the practice of law, is commonly used in these senses:

1. *Court* refers to the *persons* assembled under authority of law, at a designated place, for the administration of justice. These persons are the judge or judges, clerk, marshal, bailiff, reporter, jurors, and attorneys, and they constitute a body of the government. Thus, the lawyer's secretary says that her employer "is in court this morning," meaning that he is appearing before this duly assembled body in the interest of a client. It is not necessary that all of these persons be present to constitute a court—court is frequently held without a jury.

2. The word refers to the authorized *assembly* of the persons who make up the court. Thus, we say, "Court will be held . . ." meaning that the judge, clerk, attorneys, etc. will gather together to administer justice. Or we say, "Judge Smith's court . . . ," meaning the clerk, attorneys, jurors, etc. over which Judge Smith presides.

3. *Court* refers to the judge or judges themselves, as distinguished from the counsel or jury. Thus, we have the expression,

"In the opinion of the Court . . . ," "May it please the Court, . . . ," "The Court stated. . . ." In this sense, the word is written with a capital, because it is personified when it stands for the judge.

4. The word *court* is used occasionally to refer to the chamber, hall, or place where court is being held. Thus, a spectator is present "at court," in the courtroom, but the defendant is "in court" because he is part of the assembly.

5. The name of a specific court always includes the word *court,* which is capitalized; for example, Probate Court, Essex County. Neither probate nor court is capitalized if reference is made to probate courts generally; for example, "Petitions for letters of administration are filed in probate courts."

Court procedure. All court proceedings are conducted for and in behalf of the litigants by attorneys-at-law. It is permissible for a party to a law suit to represent himself in court, but a layman seldom has the required technical knowledge. Court actions consist of a series of written statements of the claims and defenses of the parties to a court action. These written statements are known professionally as *pleadings.*

In almost all states a legal proceeding is commenced when the first pleading is filed with the clerk of the court by the person bringing the suit. The plaintiff—the person bringing the suit—makes a written statement in clear and concise language of the facts that caused him to bring the suit. The designation of this first pleading varies with the court; it might be called a complaint, a declaration, a libel, or a petition. In some states the first pleading in an equity action is designated as a *bill in equity* or a *bill of complaint.* A summons, or its equivalent, is then issued and served upon the person against whom the action is brought —usually called the defendant. The defendant answers the summons and complaint, defending himself by raising legal arguments or by denying the facts stated by the plaintiff in the complaint. When the case is finally submitted to the court for a decision, the judge decides controversies about legal points; a jury, or a judge acting in place of a jury, decides questions of fact. See Chapter 13 for pleadings that might be filed in a civil action.

American court system. The American court system consists of Federal courts plus the various systems of all of the states. The courts of the District of Columbia and Puerto Rico are part of the Federal court system. The Supreme Court of the United States is the highest tribunal in our land—it is the apex in the hierarchy of courts, both Federal and state. There is no appeal from its decisions. The power of this court *demands* respect from every member of the legal profession; the manner in which the learned judges of this court have exercised their power has fostered and developed this respect to the point of reverence in some instances.

State courts. The system of state courts follows a fairly consistent pattern, indicated in Table IV-B, page 222. Each system consists of the state's highest appellate court and of courts of original jurisdiction, that is, courts where suits are instigated. States with a large volume of cases also have intermediary appellate courts to relieve the congestion of cases in the highest court. A case is brought and tried in a lower court and may be appealed to a higher court having appellate jurisdiction until it reaches the state's highest appellate court, or, in some cases, the United States Supreme Court.

Under some of the state systems, the state is divided into circuits or districts with a court for each. Usually court is held in each county seat and the judges travel the "circuit" to the county seats to hold court. Other states have only one superior, or trial court, which is composed of geographical divisions. The distinction is reflected in the wording of the captions on court papers. For example, Mississippi is divided into 17 judicial circuits, with a separate court for each. The captions on the court papers read:

IN THE CIRCUIT COURT OF THE FIRST JUDICIAL DISTRICT
OF HINDS COUNTY, MISSISSIPPI

On the other hand, there is only one superior court of Massachusetts, which is composed of divisions according to counties. The captions on the court papers read:

COMMONWEALTH OF MASSACHUSETTS
ESSEX, ss   SUPERIOR COURT

In many jurisdictions the courts are also divided into Parts, for the purpose of facilitating the court's work. There is no standard principle upon which the division is based. For example, the Chancery Court of Davidson County, Tennessee, is divided into Part One and Part Two, and members of the Nashville Bar can bring their suits in either part. The caption designates the part. In Kings County, New York, Part One of the Supreme Court is the part in which all cases are called when they appear on the ready day calendar (see page 237). The judge presiding in Part I sends cases to the different trial parts. After a case is assigned to a certain part, that part is designated in the caption.

The courts in one state have no control over, or relation to, the courts in another state—the hierarchy in each state is complete. Nor do the Federal courts, with the exception of the Supreme Court of the United States, have any relation to the state courts.

Federal courts. When our country first adopted its Constitution, a rivalry and jealousy existed among the states that made up the Union, and between the Federal Government and the respective state governments. The citizens of one state were fearful that they would not receive a fair verdict from judge or jury in another state. The Federal Government feared that the state courts would not interpret and enforce the national laws to the best of their ability. To avoid any miscarriage of justice that might result from interstate antagonism, the Congress provided for a Federal system of courts for the trial of cases involving Federal laws and interstate commerce and, also, cases involving diversity of citizenship—cases brought by a citizen of one state against a citizen of another state.

The Federal system of courts consists of the Supreme Court of the United States, 11 courts of appeal, district courts, a court of claims, a customs court, an emergency court of appeals, and a tax court. (See Table IV.) The United States is divided into 11 judicial circuits—ten are comprised of several states each, and there is in addition the District of Columbia Circuit. Table V gives a list of the states in each circuit; Table VI lists the states alphabetically and shows the circuit each state is in.

Each state has at least one district court. Twenty-six of the states are divided into two, three, or four districts with a court for each district. For example, in Alabama we have the United States District Court for the Northern District of Alabama; the United States District Court for the Middle District of Alabama;

and the United States District Court for the Southern District of Alabama. The states that have only one Federal district court are indicated by an asterisk in Table VI (page 228).

Many of the district courts are divided into divisions. For example, we have the United States District Court for the Western District of Arkansas, El Dorado Division. It is important to know whether or not a district court is divided into divisions because the division must appear in the caption on papers filed in that court. In the following examples, the words in italics change according to the state, district, and division:

EXAMPLE 1.   IN THE UNITED STATES DISTRICT COURT
                    FOR THE DISTRICT OF *IDAHO*
                    (*SOUTHERN* DIVISION)

EXAMPLE 2.   IN THE UNITED STATES DISTRICT COURT
                    FOR THE *SOUTHERN* DISTRICT OF
                    MISSISSIPPI (*JACKSON* DIVISION)

TABLE IV-A

FEDERAL COURTS OF RECORD IN THE UNITED STATES AND THEIR MEMBERS

Court	Members
Supreme Court of the United States	Chief Justice Justices
United States Court of Appeals for the District of Columbia	Circuit Justice Chief Judge Circuit Judges
United States Court of Appeals for the (First) Circuit	Circuit Justice Chief Judge Circuit Judges
United States District Court for the (Southern) District of (New York) *Or where the state is all in one district* United States District Court for the District of (Maryland)	Chief Judge District Judges
United States Court of Claims	Chief Judge Judges
United States Court of Customs and Patent Appeals	Chief Judge Judges
United States Customs Court	Chief Judge Judges
United States Emergency Court of Appeals	Chief Judge Judges
The Tax Court of the United States	Chief Judge Judges

TABLE IV-B

State Courts of Record in the United States[1] and Their Members

(Asterisks indicate intermediate appellate courts.
Municipal courts are not included.)

State	Court	Members of Court
Alabama	Supreme Court	Chief Justice
		Associate Justices
	*Court of Appeals	Presiding Judge
		Associate Judges
	Circuit Courts	Judges
	Probate Courts	Judge
Alaska	Supreme Court	Chief Justice
		Associate Justices
	Superior Court	Judges
Arizona	Supreme Court	Chief Justice, Justices
	Superior Courts	Judges
Arkansas	Supreme Court	Chief Justice
		Associate Justices
	Circuit Courts	Judges
	Chancery Courts	Chancellors
	Probate Courts	Judges
California	Supreme Court	Chief Justice
		Associate Justices
	*District Courts of Appeal	Presiding Justice
		Justices
	Superior Courts	Judges
Colorado	Supreme Court	Chief Justice, Justices
	District Courts	Judges
	County Courts	Judges
Connecticut	Supreme Court of Errors	Chief Justice
		Associate Justices
	Superior Court	Judges
	Courts of Common Pleas	Judges
	Probate Courts	Judges
Delaware	Supreme Court	Chief Justice
		Associate Justices
	Court of Chancery	Chancellor
		Vice Chancellor
	Superior Court	President Judge
		Associate Judges
	Registers' Courts	Register of Wills
Florida	Supreme Court	Chief Justice, Justices
	District Courts of Appeal	Chief Judge, Judges
	Circuit Courts	Judges
	Civil Court of Record	Judges
	Probate Courts	Judges

[1] State judicial system of Hawaii not yet organized by the legislature.

TABLE IV-B (Continued)

State	Court	Members of Court
Georgia	Supreme Court	Chief Justice Presiding Justice Associate Justices
	*Court of Appeals	Chief Judge Presiding Judge Judges
	Superior Courts	Judges
	Courts of Ordinary	Ordinaries
Idaho	Supreme Court	Chief Justice Justices
	District Courts	Judges
	Probate Courts	Judges
Illinois	Supreme Court	Chief Justice Justices
	*Appellate Courts	Judges
	Circuit Courts	Judges
	Court of Claims	Chief Justice Judges
	County Courts	Judges
	Probate Courts	Judges
Indiana	Supreme Court	Chief Justice Associate Judges
	*Appellate Court	Chief Judge Presiding Judge Associate Judges
	Circuit Court	Judges
	Superior Courts	Judges
	Probate Courts	Judges
Iowa	Supreme Court	Chief Justice Justices
	District Courts	Judges
Kansas	Supreme Court	Chief Justice Justices
	District Courts	Judges
	Probate Courts	Judges
Kentucky	Court of Appeals	Chief Justice Associate Justices Commissioners of Appeals Special Commissioners
	Circuit Courts	Judges
	County Courts	Judges
Louisiana	Supreme Court	Chief Justice Associate Justices
	*Court of Appeal	Judges
	District Courts	Judges

TABLE IV-B (Continued)

State	Court	Members of Court
Maine	Supreme Judicial Court	Chief Justice
		Associate Justices
	Superior Court	Justices
	Probate Courts	Judges, Registers
Maryland	Court of Appeals	Chief Judge
		Associate Judges
	Circuit Courts	Chief Judges, Judges
	Orphans' Courts	Judges
		Register of Wills
Massachusetts	Supreme Judicial Court	Chief Justice
		Associate Justices
	Superior Court	Chief Justice
		Associate Justices
	Probate Courts	Judges
	Land Court	Judge, Associate Judges
	District Courts	Justice, Special Justices
	*Appellate Divisions of District Courts	Presiding Justice
		Associate Justices
Michigan	Supreme Court	Chief Justice
		Associate Justices
	Circuit Courts	State Presiding Circuit Judge
		Judges
	Court of Claims	Judge
	Probate Courts	Judges
Minnesota	Supreme Court	Chief Justice
		Associate Justices
	District Courts	Judges
	Probate Courts	Judges
Mississippi	Supreme Court	Chief Justice, Associate Justices
	Circuit Courts	Judges
	Chancery Courts	Chancellors
	County Courts	Judges
Missouri	Supreme Court	Chief Justice
		Presiding Judge
		Associate Judges
	*Courts of Appeals	Presiding Judge
		Associate Judges
	Circuit Courts	Judges
	Probate Courts	Judges
Montana	Supreme Court	Chief Justice
		Associate Justices
	District Courts	Judges

TABLE IV-B (Continued)

State	Court	Members of Court
Nebraska	Supreme Court	Chief Justice
		Associate Justices
	District Court	Judges
	County Courts	Judges
Nevada	Supreme Court	Chief Justice
		Associate Justices
	District Courts	Judges
New Hampshire	Supreme Court	Chief Justice
		Associate Justices
	Superior Court	Chief Justice
		Justices
	Probate Courts	Presiding Judges
		Registers
New Jersey	Supreme Court	Chief Justice
		Justices
	*Superior Court,	Senior Judge
	Appellate Division	Judges
	Superior Court,	Judges
	Chancery Division	
	Superior Court,	Judges
	Law Division	
	County Courts	Judges
	Surrogate's Courts	Surrogates
New Mexico	Supreme Court	Chief Justice
		Justices
	District Courts	Presiding Judge
		Judges
	Probate Courts	Judges
New York	Court of Appeals	Chief Judge
		Associate Judges
	*Supreme Court,	Presiding Justice
	Appellate Division	Justices
	Supreme Court	Justices
	County Courts	Judges
	Surrogates' Courts	Surrogates
North Carolina	Supreme Court	Chief Justice
		Associate Justices
	Superior Courts	Judges
	County Courts	Judges
North Dakota	Supreme Court	Chief Justice
		Judges
	District Courts	Judges
	County Courts	Judges

TABLE IV-B (Continued)

State	Court	Members of Court
Ohio	Supreme Court	Chief Justice
		Judges
	*Courts of Appeals	Judges
	Courts of Common Pleas	Judges
	Probate Courts	Judges
Oklahoma	Supreme Court	Chief Justice
		Vice Chief Justice
		Justices
	Criminal Court of Appeals	Presiding Judge
		Judges
	District Courts	Judges
	Superior Courts	Judges
	County Courts	County Judges
Oregon	Supreme Court	Chief Justice
		Acting Chief Justice
		Associate Justices
	Circuit Courts	Judges
	County Courts	County Judges
Pennsylvania	Supreme Court	Chief Justice
		Justices
	Superior Court	Presiding Judge
		Judges
	Courts of Common Pleas	Judges
	Orphans' Courts	Judges
Rhode Island	Supreme Court	Chief Justice
		Associate Justices
	Superior Court	Presiding Justice
		Justices
	District Courts	Judges
	Probate Courts	Judges
South Carolina	Supreme Court	Chief Justice
		Associate Justice
	Circuit Courts	Judges
	County Courts	Judges
	Probate Courts	Judges
South Dakota	Supreme Court	Presiding Judge
		Judges
	Circuit Courts	Judges
	County Courts	Judges
Tennessee	Supreme Court	Chief Justice
		Associate Justices
	*Court of Appeals	Presiding Judge
		Associate Judges

TABLE IV-B (Continued)

State	Court	Members of Court
Tennessee (Continued)	Chancery Courts	Chancellors
	Circuit Courts	Judges
	County Courts	Judges
	Probate Court of Shelby County	Judge
Texas	Supreme Court	Chief Justice
		Associate Justices
	*Court of Civil Appeals	Chief Justice
		Associate Justices
	Court of Criminal Appeals	Presiding Judge, Judges
		Commissioners
	District Courts	Judges
	County Courts	Judges
Utah	Supreme Court	Chief Justice
		Justices
	District Court	Judges
Vermont	Supreme Court	Chief Justice
		Associate Justices
	County Courts	Superior Judge, Judges
	Chancery Court	Chancellors
	Probate Courts	Judges
Virginia	Supreme Court of Appeals	Chief Justice
		Justices
	Circuit Courts	Judges
Washington	Supreme Court	Chief Justice
		Associate Judges
	Superior Courts	Judges
West Virginia	Supreme Court of Appeals	President
		Judges
	Circuit Courts	Judges
	County Courts	Commissioners
Wisconsin	Supreme Court	Chief Justice
		Associate Justices
	Circuit Courts	Judges
	County Courts	Judges
Wyoming	Supreme Court	Chief Justice
		Associate Justice
	District Courts	Judges

TABLE V

Judicial Circuits and the States in Each Circuit

District of Columbia Circuit	District of Columbia
First Circuit—	Maine, New Hampshire, Massachusetts, Rhode Island, and Puerto Rico
Second Circuit—	New York, Connecticut, and Vermont
Third Circuit—	New Jersey, Pennsylvania, Delaware, and Virgin Islands
Fourth Circuit—	Maryland, Virginia, West Virginia, North Carolina, and South Carolina
Fifth Circuit—	Texas, Louisiana, Mississippi, Alabama, Georgia, Florida, and Canal Zone
Sixth Circuit—	Tennessee, Kentucky, Ohio, and Michigan
Seventh Circuit—	Indiana, Illinois, and Wisconsin
Eighth Circuit—	Arkansas, Iowa, Minnesota, Missouri, Nebraska, North Dakota, and South Dakota
Ninth Circuit—	California, Arizona, Nevada, Oregon, Washington, Idaho, Montana, Alaska, and Hawaii
Tenth Circuit—	Colorado, Kansas, New Mexico, Oklahoma, Utah, and Wyoming.

TABLE VI

States and Judicial Circuit in Which Each Is Located

State	Circuit	State	Circuit
Alabama	Fifth Circuit	Nebraska*	Eighth Circuit
Alaska	Ninth Circuit	Nevada*	Ninth Circuit
Arizona*	Ninth Circuit	New Hampshire*	First Circuit
Arkansas	Eighth Circuit	New Jersey*	Third Circuit
California	Ninth Circuit	New Mexico*	Tenth Circuit
Colorado*	Tenth Circuit	New York	Second Circuit
Connecticut*	Second Circuit	North Carolina	Fourth Circuit
Delaware*	Third Circuit	North Dakota*	Eighth Circuit
Florida	Fifth Circuit	Ohio	Sixth Circuit
Georgia	Fifth Circuit	Oklahoma	Tenth Circuit
Hawaii	Ninth Circuit	Oregon*	Ninth Circuit
Idaho*	Ninth Circuit	Pennsylvania	Third Circuit
Illinois	Seventh Circuit	Puerto Rico	First Circuit
Indiana	Seventh Circuit	Rhode Island*	First Circuit
Iowa	Eighth Circuit	South Carolina	Fourth Circuit
Kansas*	Tenth Circuit	South Dakota*	Eighth Circuit
Kentucky	Sixth Circuit	Tennessee	Sixth Circuit
Louisiana	Fifth Circuit	Texas	Fifth Circuit
Maine*	First Circuit	Utah*	Tenth Circuit
Maryland*	Fourth Circuit	Vermont*	Second Circuit
Massachusetts*	First Circuit	Virginia	Fourth Circuit
Michigan	Sixth Circuit	Washington	Ninth Circuit
Minnesota*	Eighth Circuit	West Virginia	Fourth Circuit
Mississippi	Fifth Circuit	Wisconsin	Seventh Circuit
Missouri	Eighth Circuit	Wyoming*	Tenth Circuit
Montana*	Ninth Circuit		

* Only one district court.

Jurisdiction. The laws of our country provide that certain causes of action (law suits, cases) must be brought in one court, others in another. The authority of a court to hear a particular cause of action and to render a binding decision in it is called *jurisdiction.* It is the lawyer's problem to determine in which court his client's case should be brought—which court has jurisdiction over it. In order to hear a case, a court must have jurisdiction *in personam* (of the person) and *in rem* (of the matter).

In personam jurisdiction. This means that a court must have jurisdiction over the litigants (the person or persons bringing the suit and those defending it). For example, if the litigants live in different cities in the same county, the county court, rather than a city or municipal court, has jurisdiction. A New York court does not have jurisdiction over a citizen of Mississippi in a suit brought by a New York citizen.

In rem jurisdiction. This means that the court must have jurisdiction over the subject matter in controversy. *In rem* jurisdiction depends upon several factors: nature of the case, amount involved, location of the property. For example, a magistrate's court has jurisdiction over a traffic violation but cannot try a person for murder. A suit for damages caused by an automobile collision cannot be brought in a probate court. Foreclosure actions can be brought only in the county where the property is located.

Some courts have original jurisdiction, whereas others have appellate jurisdiction. Suits are commenced and tried only in courts of original jurisdiction, which are usually the lower courts. After a case has been decided in a court of original jurisdiction, it may be brought into a higher court having appellate jurisdiction for another decision. Appellate courts have original jurisdiction over some matters.

The term *jurisdiction* is also used to refer to the *sphere* of a court's authority, as distinguished from the authority itself. Thus, we might say that the jurisdiction of a district court is limited to that particular district; of a state supreme court, to that particular state. The decisions of a particular court prevail within that court's jurisdiction, although they might be in conflict with the decisions of a court in another jurisdiction—another sphere of authority.

Limitations on the jurisdiction of each court vary too much to attempt to give more than a general resume here. Furthermore, it is the lawyer's job, not the secretary's, to know in which court a particular action should be brought. But the secretary should have a general understanding of jurisdictional limitations so that she will understand why a case is brought in a certain court. Any classification of courts is necessarily incomplete and, also, overlapping, but for our purpose we arbitrarily classify courts as (1) inferior, (2) superior, (3) courts of special jurisdiction, (4) courts of intermediate review, and (5) supreme appellate courts. The general jurisdiction of each class is given below.

Inferior courts. The most common inferior courts are justice of the peace courts, small claims courts, and a class of courts whose jurisdiction is confined to violations of city ordinances. Courts of this class are variously called police, magistrate's, municipal, or recorder's courts. All inferior courts have a very narrow jurisdiction. In criminal matters, they are restricted to preliminary hearings or inquiries except in minor matters. In civil actions, they have jurisdiction over actions involving small amounts only, the amount varying with the state. For example, in Alabama justice of the peace courts have jurisdiction over claims of $100 or less; in Illinois, of $500 or less. Inferior courts are usually courts not of record, that is, their proceedings are not recorded. Frequently the judge of an inferior court is not a lawyer. The decisions of these courts are subject to review or correction by higher courts. Actually, circuit and district courts are "inferior" to appellate or supreme courts, but the term is usually applied to the courts not of record described here.

Superior courts. These are the highest state courts of original jurisdiction. They are usually designated as circuit, district, or superior courts. (In New York the highest court of original jurisdiction is called the Supreme Court.) They have original jurisdiction in the first instance and are the courts where cases without the jurisdiction of inferior courts are tried originally. They also have appellate jurisdiction over matters arising in inferior courts and, in many states, over probate matters. They control or supervise the lower courts by writs of error, appeal, or certiorari.

In some states, superior courts have one or more departments or divisions that have jurisdiction over special matters. For example, the Superior Court of New Jersey has a law division for the trial of actions at law and a chancery division for hearing equity matters; in California, a department of each superior court acts as a probate court. Other states have courts of special jurisdiction to probate matters.

Courts of special jurisdiction. These are courts of original jurisdiction over certain restricted matters. Some states have courts of special jurisdiction in some fields; other states, in other fields. The most common courts of special jurisdiction are probate courts, criminal courts, chancery courts, juvenile courts, county courts, and municipal courts in large cities.

Probate courts have jurisdiction over the probate of wills, administration of a decedent's estate, and guardianship of minors and insane people.

Criminal courts have original jurisdiction over criminal cases. Criminal trial courts may be called *oyer & terminer* (hear and determine).

Chancery courts have jurisdiction over equity or chancery matters and apply rules of chancery law. See page 232 for the distinction between equity and law.

Juvenile courts usually have exclusive original jurisdiction over all neglected, dependent, or delinquent children under eighteen.

County courts have widely diverse jurisdictions in the different states. For example, in Alabama they are courts of criminal jurisdiction; in Colorado, they have jurisdiction over probate matters, over delinquent children in some counties, and in civil actions if the amount involved is not over $2,000; in Mississippi, they have concurrent jurisdiction with circuit and chancery courts if the amount involved does not exceed $2,000.

Municipal courts in large cities are frequently courts of record and have concurrent jurisdiction with superior courts, if the amount involved does not exceed a stated sum, usually not more than $3,000.

Courts of intermediate review. As previously indicated, courts of intermediate review are established to relieve congestion in a state's highest appellate court. They are indicated in Table IV by an asterisk. Some states have more than one court of intermediate review. These courts exercise appellate jurisdiction only, except that in some states they have original jurisdiction to issue writs of mandamus, certiorari, habeas corpus, and the like. They have jurisdiction of matters of appeal from the final judgments, orders, or decrees of superior courts, usually in both law and chancery matters. The appellate jurisdiction of intermediate courts is frequently restricted. For example, the Georgia Court of Appeals, which is a court of intermediate review, does not have jurisdiction over appeals involving the Constitution of Georgia or of the United States. The appellate courts of Illinois do not have jurisdiction over criminal appeals other than misdemeanors. In New Jersey and New York, divisions of the superior court (New York's equivalent of superior courts is called Supreme Court) exercise intermediate jurisdiction.

Supreme appellate courts. There is only one supreme appellate court in each state. These courts are courts of last resort in their respective states. (In Oklahoma, the Criminal Court of Appeals, and in Texas, the Court of Criminal Appeals, are courts of last resort in criminal cases.) The jurisdiction of these courts is appellate, their original jurisdiction, if any, being limited to the issuance of writs of mandamus, certiorari, habeas corpus, and the like.

The highest court in 40 states is designated as the *Supreme Court*. The designations in the eight other states are as follows:

Connecticut	Supreme Court of Errors
Kentucky	Court of Appeals
Maine	Supreme Judicial Court
Maryland	Court of Appeals
Massachusetts	Supreme Judicial Court
New York	Court of Appeals
Virginia	Supreme Court of Appeals
West Virginia	Supreme Court of Appeals

Distinction between equity and law. The word *equity* means "fair dealing," and that is the purpose of the system of legal rules and procedures known as equity. Remedies at the common law in England were frequently inadequate to give the wronged party a fair deal. He would then take his case to the King's Chancellor, who tempered the strict letter of the law with fairness. As a result of this practice, chancery courts, in which equity is practiced, were established, presided over by a chancellor instead of a judge. A few states still have courts of chancery, as indicated in Table

IV. Other states do not separate cases in equity from cases at law, but apply equity principles when appropriate. In the majority of states, equity and law are organized under a single court, which has two dockets—one in equity and one in law.

Ordinarily, law actions have for their object the assessment of damages, but a court of equity goes further and attempts to prevent the wrong itself or to give the complainant what he bargained for. Among the more common equity actions are injunction suits, specific performance, partition suit, rescission of a contract, reformation of a contract, and all matters relating to trusts and trustees.

In the course of its development, equity has established certain fundamental principles or maxims, which the lawyer frequently uses in dictating briefs. Among these are the following:

1. *He who seeks equity must do equity.* If I seek the return of property that I was induced to sell through fraud, I must offer to return the purchase price.

2. *He who comes into equity must come with clean hands.* If I induce you to breach a contract and to make one with me instead, and then you breach the contract with me, a court of equity will not compel specific performance of your contract with me.

3. *Equity will presume that to be done which should have been done.* If I unlawfully take possession of your cow, a calf from that cow will belong to you, because a court of equity will presume that I was holding the cow for you.

4. *Equity aids the vigilant, not those who slumber on their rights.* Where the statute of limitations (page 614) has not run, but a claimant has delayed unreasonably in bringing suit, a court of equity may bar the claim by reason of such delay.

5. *Equity follows the law.* Except where the common law is clearly inadequate, equity follows the precedents of the common law and the provisions of the statutes. Thus, if a deed is void by common law or statute, the mere fact that a holder has given valuable consideration for it will not make the deed valid in equity.

6. *Equity regards substance rather than form.* Common law is normally governed by legal form. Corporations, for example, are regarded in law as artificial beings, separate from their stockholders, directors, and officers. To accomplish justice, equity may dis-

regard the corporate fiction and examine the substance of the dispute. For example, several men sold out a fish business and agreed not to go into the fish business in the same locality. They immediately formed a corporation to carry on a fish business in competition with the purchaser. The Court ignored the corporate entity and granted an injunction against this violation of the agreement not to compete.

Judges and justices. In so far as power, authority, and duty are concerned, there is no distinction between a judge and a justice. The law in each state specifies whether the members of each court in that state shall be designated as judges or justices. In the majority of states the members of the highest appellate courts are called justices, whereas the members of the trial courts are judges. Tables IV-A and IV-B, page 221, show the technical designation of the members of each court listed there.

The lawyer prepares orders and decrees for the court's approval. It is important, therefore, for you to know whether the technically correct designation of the Court is judge or justice, because these papers always contain the Court's title, either in the heading or in the signature. Almost all of them commence with a heading similar to the following:

EXAMPLE 1.

> Present:
> HONORABLE JOHN E. SMITH,
> > Justice.

EXAMPLE 2.

> Present:
> HONORABLE JOHN E. SMITH
> United States District Judge.

See page 315, *et seq.* for an explanation of orders and decrees; see Figures 76, 77, and 78, Chapter 14, for approved styles of setting them up.

It is also important for you to know whether a member of a court is a judge or a justice when writing and speaking to or about him. The chart in Chapter 6 gives the correct forms of address, salutation, and complimentary close in letters to judges, justices, and clerks of courts, and also the correct form for refer-

ring to them in a letter and the correct form to use in speaking to
or informally introducing them.

Clerk of the Court. The secretary's contact with the court is
chiefly through the clerk. Almost all correspondence is addressed
to him (see the chart in Chapter 6 for the correct form of addressing clerks of courts); he answers inquiries, written or telephonic,
about pending court cases, court rules, the calendar, and any
other matters pertaining to his office. The clerk of a court and the
personnel in his office can be of considerable help to the lawyer's
secretary. It is frequently necessary for her to look up something
in the records of his office or to telephone for information regarding a case. It behooves the secretary to maintain cordial relations
with the personnel in the clerk's office at all times.

Although the systems of keeping records in clerks' offices vary
in detail because of statutory requirements and custom, they are
fundamentally the same. A brief explanation of how these records
are kept will clarify the secretary's duties in so far as her contact
with the clerk's office is concerned.

Clerk's index system. The clerk receives all court papers—
complaints, answers, amendments, motions, appearances, and the
like. As soon as the summons and complaint, or other first pleading, is filed, the clerk assigns an index number, also called a docket
number and an action number, to the case. The numbers are consecutive. In some courts, an initial is used to indicate the court
in which the case is filed. For example, S for Superior, C for Circuit, P for Probate. In courts that have separate law and equity
divisions, the letter L or the letter E will be a part of the index
number. In some courts, the successive numbering of cases starts
over at the beginning of each year, and the number includes the
year. Thus, the index number might read 51S-1328, or 1328/51,
or 1328-1951, indicating that the case was filed in 1951. When a
clerk uses this system of numbering, the year is as important as
any part of the number. The clerk keeps a cross-index of the
cases, arranged alphabetically according to the name of the plaintiff, and, also, in some courts, a cross-index arranged according to
the name of the defendant.

How the secretary uses the index number. 1. If you file the first
pleading, get the index number from the clerk of the court or
from his records so that you may enter it in your office file. If an

attorney in your office files the paper, he should get the number and give it to you. Ask him for it. To find an index number in the clerk's records, look in the plaintiff's index under his name. You should procure the index number as soon as possible after it is assigned to a case.

2. After an index number is assigned to a case, you *must* type that number on all papers thereafter prepared in the case in that court. Before filing a paper or giving it to an attorney to file, check to see that the proper index number is endorsed on it, both on the paper itself and on the backing.

3. You must have the index number in order to get information about the status of a case.

Clerk's permanent record book. The permanent record book kept by the clerk of the court is usually called the *docket* or the *register*. It contains a record of all legal papers filed in the suit. The cases are entered consecutively according to index number, a case to a page. The clerk enters on the docket sheet the index number, the title of the case, the names and addresses of the attorneys, and the date the summons was served. He also enters on the docket sheet all subsequent proceedings.

How the secretary uses the register. Although the lawyer keeps his own record of the information in the clerk's register (Chapter 15), it is sometimes necessary to consult the register for the purpose of checking on dates that papers were filed by opposing counsel. Besides, an attorney is frequently interested, for one reason or another, in the developments in a case in which he is not representing any of the litigants. He is usually interested in knowing the status of cases immediately preceding his on the court calendar, so that he can judge when his case will be reached.

If you want information on any case in court, look in the alphabetical index under the plaintiff's name and get the index number, unless you already have the number. Then turn to that page number in the docket and read the entries made there. If you want to read the original papers on file, give the clerk the index number and ask him to get them for you. Sometimes he will let you get them yourself; if he does, be sure to put the papers back exactly where you found them.

Clerk's minute books. The clerk enters abstracts of all court orders in a minute book, numerically according to index number.

He might have separate books for law, chancery, divorce, and the like.

How the secretary uses the minute book. If you want any information about the court's orders in a case, you can get it by consulting the minute book. You must have the index number. Usually the clerk's office will give you the information over the telephone.

Court calendar and calendar number. The court calendar is a list of cases that are ready to be brought to the attention of the court. When Notice of Trial, or Note of Issue, is filed (see page 284), the Clerk of the Court assigns the case a *calendar number* and places it on the general court calendar. Successive numbers are given to successive cases. The purpose of the calendar number is to have the case come up for trial in its turn. Do not confuse it with the index number, which will continue to appear on papers prepared for the case. After the clerk gives a case a calendar number, it must await its turn to be called for trial in numerical order. From the cases on the general calendar, the clerk prepares a list of cases for the judge to try each day, or as fast as he can get to them. The cases on the list are "called" before the court on a certain date.

Calendar call. The list of cases to be called before the court is referred to as the *daily call* in courts where cases are called daily, and as the *weekly call* in courts where cases are called weekly. The lists are published in the local law journal, so that the lawyers will know when their cases are to be called before the court. Both sides are supposed to be in court when the case is called. If the plaintiff responds and the defendant does not appear, there will be a judgment or decree by default. If the defendant is ready and the plaintiff does not appear, the case will be dismissed for want of prosecution (DWP).

Answering the calendar call. In some offices the secretary answers the calendar call to save the lawyer's time. The cases will be called by calendar number and by title. When your case is called, answer, "Ready"; or, when the lawyer is trying a case in another court, "Ready subject to engagement." Then explain to the court that the lawyer is trying a case in another court but will be available at a later hour. The lawyer will not send you to answer the calendar call if he is not ready and must ask for an adjournment. If the case has been settled out of court, you will answer, "Settled."

After all the cases on the list are called, they are called for trial, in turn. There is no need for the lawyer to sit through the trial of other cases. You, or whoever is answering the call for him, will wait in the courtroom until a reasonable time before his case is about to be reached for trial, and then telephone him to come to court to try the case.

Term of court. The designated period of time prescribed by law during which a court may sit to transact business is known as a *term of court* or *term time*. The periods during the term when the court actually sits are known as *sessions*. The terms are usually designated by the time they commence, for example, *November term*. A term of court is also referred to in various jurisdictions as *general term* or *trial term,* meaning the term during which cases are tried.

12

Basic Information about Litigation Papers

Pleadings and supporting papers, such as affidavits and bills of particulars, are commonly called court papers or litigation papers, as distinguished from the legal documents or instruments described in Chapter 9. Court rules require that they be set up in a particular style.

An understanding of the various parties that may become factors in a legal action, and their designations, is essential to the preparation of a court paper. An explanation concerning the parties, therefore, is given first in this chapter. General instructions applicable to the preparation of all court papers follow. Detailed instructions for the preparation of specific papers are given in subsequent chapters when the use of that paper is explained.

Parties to an Action

Party bringing a law suit. The party who brings a law suit—the one who has a cause of action—is the *plaintiff*. He is the one who complains. In Alabama, Mississippi, Rhode Island, Tennessee, and Virginia, the party bringing the action is called the *complainant* when the suit is an action in equity. In Massachusetts, the practice is not uniform; it varies with the court and with local custom. In all the other states, the party who brings an action in equity is no longer called the complainant, but is known as the plaintiff, just as in actions at law.

Party defending a law suit. The party against whom suit is brought is the *defendant*. In Alabama and Rhode Island, the person defending an equity action is known as the *respondent*. In Massachusetts and Virginia, he is referred to as either defendant or respondent. In all other states, the party defending an equity action is no longer called the respondent but is referred to as the defendant, just as in actions at law.

Parties to a cross action. In some cases, defendant's interests cannot be defended properly by answering the plaintiff's complaint or by a counterclaim (page 587). For example, an airline and an airplane manufacturer were co-defendants in a death action. The complaint alleged that the plane was improperly designed and was not safe for its intended use. The airline claimed that if defective and hazardous conditions existed in the plane, they were caused by the failure of the airplane manufacturer to keep his guarantee that the plane would be free from defect in design.[1]

Under these circumstances, in almost all states the defendant (airline here) files a cross-complaint and is called the *defendant and cross-complainant,* or *cross-claimant,* or *cross-plaintiff,* or *cross-petitioner,* the designation varying with the state. The party against whom a cross-complaint is brought (airplane manufacturer here) is the *cross-defendant.* The plaintiff or a co-defendant in the initial action may be the cross-defendant and is then referred to as the *plaintiff and cross-defendant,* and *defendant and cross-defendant,* respectively. A party who was not a party to the original action may be brought into the case, also, as a cross-defendant.

Party intervening. A law suit sometimes affects adversely a third party who is not a party to the litigation. If the Court permits, that person may become a party to the action by filing a *complaint in intervention,* and is called an *intervenor,* or in some states, the third-party plaintiff. For example, while negotiations for a contract were in progress, the employee who was negotiating the contract as agent for his employer suddenly quit the employer and closed the contract in his own behalf. The former employee later sued to enforce the contract. His former employer claimed that the former employee was his agent, and was permitted to intervene to assert his interest in the contract. He became a party to the action as an *intervenor.*[2]

---

[1] Blue et al. v. United Air Lines, Inc., et al., 98 N.Y.S. (2d) 272.
[2] Patterson v. Pollock, et al., 84 N.E. (2d) 606.

Parties on appeal. The party who loses a law suit or is dissatisfied with a judgment or court order may appeal to a higher court. See Chapter 16 for the designation of parties on appeal.

Amicus curiae. An *amicus curiae* (Latin for "friend of the court") is not strictly speaking a party to the law suit. He is a person who has no inherent right to appear in the suit but is allowed to participate to protect his own interests. Leave to file a brief as *amicus curiae* is frequently granted to a lawyer when he has another case that will be affected by the decision of the Court in the pending case. An *amicus curiae* might also volunteer information for the benefit of the judge. For example, in adoption proceedings the guardian of a child might seek permission to appear as *amicus* for the purpose of presenting evidence about which the Court should be informed and which might lead the Court to refuse the order of adoption.

Who may be parties to a law suit. A party to a law suit may be an individual, a partnership, a corporation, or an association.

Minors and incompetents. An individual ordinarily sues on his own behalf, but minors (frequently referred to as infants) and incompetents (persons of unsound mind or habitual drunkards) are legally incapable of bringing a legal action. If the minor or incompetent has a legally appointed guardian, the suit is often brought by him. Otherwise, depending upon the state, a suit is brought on behalf of a minor or incompetent by his "next friend," or by a guardian *ad litem* appointed by the Court for the special purpose of the litigation. The fact that the plaintiff sues by his guardian or next friend is indicated in the caption of the case and is alleged in the pleadings. If a minor or an incompetent is defendant in a suit, he answers by a guardian *ad litem* or next friend. In Louisiana a minor is represented by a *Tutor,* and a mentally incompetent person, by a *Curator.*

The expressions commonly used follow:

JAMES JONES, a minor, suing by his
father and next friend, TOM JONES

JOHN JONES, guardian ad litem of
JAMES JONES, an incompetent

MARY ANN JONES by her next friend,
GEORGE G. JONES

JOHN BROWN by ROBERT BROWN,
guardian by appointment of Orphans' Court of
Baltimore City

Executors, administrators, trustees. Often a plaintiff has a
cause of action, not for a wrong against him in his individual
capacity, but for a wrong against him in his representative capacity as executor, administrator, or trustee. The action is then
brought by the plaintiff in that capacity. The capacity in which
the action is brought is indicated in the caption and is stated in
the introductory sentence of the pleadings. An executor (executrix, if a woman) sues "as executor of the last will and testament
of Mary Jones, deceased." An administrator (administratrix, if a
woman) sues "as trustee under will of Mary Jones," or "as trustee
under trust created by Mary Jones." Actions are also brought
against, and defended by, executors, administrators, and trustees
of estates and trusts.

Husband and wife. In some actions if a married person sues, the
spouse joins in the complaint. The caption indicates, and the first
paragraph of the pleading declares, the relationship. If the husband has the cause of action, the suit is brought by Thomas W.
Jones and Mary R. Jones, his wife; if the wife has the cause of
action, the suit is brought by Mary R. Jones and Thomas W.
Jones, her husband. The same practice is followed when a married
person is sued. In the caption of all pleadings, except the complaint, and in the endorsements on the back of a court paper
(page 259), the Latin phrase *et uxor,* or *et ux.,* may be substituted
for "and Mary R. Jones, his wife"; *et vir* may be substituted for
"and Thomas W. Jones, her husband."

Partnerships. When a party to an action is a partnership, that
fact is indicated in the caption and declared in the first paragraph
of the pleading.

Expressions similar to the following are used in the caption.

JOHN JONES and HENRY A. BROWN,
doing business as a partnership
under the name of JONES and BROWN.

JOHN JONES and RICHARD ROE d/b/a
JONES & ROE, a partnership

JOHN DOE and RICHARD ROE, individually
and as co-partners doing business under
the firm name and style of ROE'S

The stock statement in the pleading is: ". . . John Brown and
Thomas Smith are now, and at all times mentioned were, co-
partners, doing business under the fictitious firm name and style
of Brown-Smith Company, a co-partnership, and have filed the
certificate and published the notice as required by . . . (*insert
code or statute section*). . . ."

Corporations. When a litigant is a corporation, its corporate
existence is alleged in the first paragraph of the complaint. The
wording of the allegation depends upon whether the corporation
is a domestic corporation, that is, incorporated in the state where
suit is brought, or a foreign corporation, that is, incorporated in
a state other than that in which suit is brought.

In some states, a party's corporate existence is also indicated in
the caption, as follows:

Domestic corporation

AMERICAN TICKET COMPANY, INC., a domestic
corporation,

Foreign corporation

AMERICAN TICKET COMPANY, a corporation organized
and existing under and by virtue of the laws of the State
of _____.

Verifications

What is a verification? A verification is a sworn statement by
a qualified person that the allegations contained in a pleading are
true. The statutes require that many pleadings and supporting
papers be verified, and some law firms follow the practice of verifying all pleadings whether the statute requires it or not. The
litigation papers commonly verified are:

Complaints
Answers
Petitions
Bills of particulars

If the complaint is verified, the answer *must* be verified.

A verification always recites the venue and always has a jurat, or "sworn to" clause. One of the duties of a notary public is to administer the oath to a person verifying a pleading. (See page 246, for directions about administering the oath.) The verification is usually written on a separate page, but you may type it on the last page of the pleading, or at least begin it on the last page, if you wish. No rule of law or court governs. Some legal backs have verifications printed on the inside, but the verifications are generally typed.

Who may verify a pleading? Generally the verification is by a party to the action, but under some conditions an agent or the attorney for a party to an action may verify a pleading. The attorney will tell you who is going to verify the pleading.

Forms of verification. There is a special form of verification appropriate for each capacity in which the person verifying the pleading (called the deponent or the affiant) might make a verification. Figures 50, 51, 52, and 53 illustrate verifications by an individual, an officer of a domestic corporation, an officer of a foreign corporation, and an attorney for a party to the action. They are included here to give you an understanding of the general content of a verification and to show you how one should be set up. Use them as a pattern for making forms of verifications for your loose-leaf notebook of forms, but get a lawyer in your office to approve the wording of them or to dictate the forms he wants you to use. You will notice that if an agent or attorney verifies, he states, in addition to the allegation ordinarily used:

1. The grounds of his belief as to all matters not stated upon his knowledge.

2. Why the verification is not made by the party to the action.

The last two paragraphs of a verification by an attorney or an agent change with the facts, but otherwise the wording of the verifications as indicated in these illustrations remains practically the same in every action.

The venue of the verification depends, of course, on where the verification is made.

How to type a verification. Observe the following points with reference to the typing of verifications:

1. There is no space between the longest line of typing and the bracketing of the venue.

2. The abbreviation for scilicet (SS) may be in lower case or in caps, followed by a period or by a period and a colon.

3. There are three single spaces between the venue and the body of the verification.

4. The name of the deponent is in solid caps.

5. There are three spaces between lines of signature and the jurat, which is at the left of the page.

In Figure 52, the month in the jurat, as well as the day of the month is filled in by the notary. Whenever you prepare a paper for signature near the end of the month and are not certain that it will be signed before that month expires, leave the month blank, so that it will not have to be changed if the verification is not sworn to until the following month.

```
STATE OF NEW HAMPSHIRE)
                       : ss.
COUNTY OF COOS         )


        EDGAR R. WILSON, being duly sworn, deposes and

says: That he is one of the defendants herein; that he has

read the foregoing answer and knows the contents thereof,

and that the same is true of his own knowledge, except as to

the matters therein stated to be alleged upon information

and belief, and as to those matters he believes it to be

true.


                              _____



Sworn to before me this
   21st day of June, 19—.



_____
```

Figure 50. Verification of Answer by Individual.

How to administer the oath to person verifying a pleading. Unlike an acknowledgment of the execution of a legal instrument (Chapter 9), the verification of a pleading must be sworn to. If you are a notary in a law office, it will be your duty to administer the oath to the person verifying the pleading. The proper procedure is to stand and raise your right hand and ask the verifier to do the same. Then administer the oath in the following, or similar, words: "Do you solemnly swear that the contents of the foregoing instrument subscribed by you are the truth, the whole truth, and nothing but the truth, so help you God?" The verifier should answer, "Yes" or "I do."

```
COMMONWEALTH OF VIRGINIA)
                         : SS.
COUNTY OF HENRICO        )


          AUSTIN L. NELSON, being duly sworn, deposes and

says: That he is the treasurer of Southwestern Pine, Inc.,

the plaintiff in the above entitled action; that he has read

the foregoing complaint and knows the contents thereof; that

the same is true of his own knowledge, except as to matters

therein stated to be alleged upon information and belief,

and as to those matters he believes it to be true.




                           _____


Given under my hand and seal this

      day of September, 19--.



      _____
             Notary Public
My commission expires             .
```

Figure 51. Verification of Complaint by Officer of Domestic Corporation.

STATE OF NEW YORK)
               : SS.
COUNTY OF NEW YORK)

       ALEXANDER N. ROGERS, being duly sworn, deposes and says: That he is a vice president of Bentley—Jones Manufacturing Company, Inc., the defendant in the above entitled action; that he has read the foregoing answer and knows the contents thereof; that the same is true to his own knowledge, except as to the matters therein stated to be alleged on information and belief, and that as to those matters he believes it to be true.

       That the reason why this verification is made by deponent and not by defendant is that defendant is a foreign corporation organized under the laws of the State of Delaware and deponent is an officer thereof, to wit: a vice president; that the sources of deponent's knowledge and the grounds of his belief as to all matters therein alleged upon information and belief consist of _____

_____

_____ .

                                   _____

Sworn to before me this
       day of   , 19—.

_____

My commission expires   .

Figure 52. Verification of Complaint by Officer of Foreign Corporation.
247

STATE OF OHIO   )
: ss.
COUNTY OF HAMILTON)

        ROBERT N. EDWARDS, being duly sworn, deposes and says: I am an attorney at law and a member of the firm of Smith and Jones, attorneys for the plaintiff in the above entitled action. I have read the foregoing complaint and know the contents thereof and the same is true of my own knowledge except as to the matters therein alleged to be upon information and belief, and as to those matters I believe it to be true.

        The reason why this verification is made by deponent and not by plaintiff is that plaintiff is a foreign corporation and none of its officers are within the City of Cincinnati and County of Hamilton where I reside and have my offices for the transaction of business.

        The sources of my information and the grounds of my belief as to all matters in said complaint stated to be alleged upon information and belief are correspondence with persons representing plaintiff and an examination of a file with reference to this account.

_____

Subscribed and sworn to before me this   day of
, 19—.

_____
Notary Public

My commission expires

Figure 53. Verification of Complaint by Attorney for Plaintiff.

If the verifier's religion forbids him to swear, use the word *affirm* instead of swear. The word *affirmed* should also be substituted for *sworn to* in the jurat.

You will notice from the preceding illustrations of verifications that, again unlike acknowledgments (Chapter 9), the verifier signs the verification as well as the instrument that precedes it. The jurat follows the verifier's signature. You, as notary public, will sign the jurat and affix your notary seal and show date your commission expires, if required in your state. (See Table II.)

How to Type Court Papers

Paper. All pleadings and supporting papers, except those for which printed law blanks are used, are typed on legal-size paper except in Massachusetts. In some states *legal cap* (legal-size paper with ruled margins) is used for court papers; in others, plain legal-size paper, without ruled margins, is used; in some states, either may be used. In a few states, the legal cap has numbers in the left margin. See Table VII, at the end of this chapter.

Heading or caption. All court papers have a heading, or caption, which is written on every separate document, although several documents might be bound together. The caption consists of the following parts:

1. *Jurisdiction and venue.* Usually the jurisdiction, that is, the name of the court in which the case is brought, and the venue are recited together in phraseology similar to this:

IN THE DISTRICT COURT WITHIN AND FOR
OKLAHOMA COUNTY, STATE OF OKLAHOMA

or

IN THE DISTRICT COURT OF SEDGWICK COUNTY
KANSAS

In a few states the venue is recited separately from the jurisdiction, thus:

STATE OF ILLINOIS)
                   : SS.   IN THE CIRCUIT COURT
COUNTY OF COOK   )   THEREOF

2. *The title of the case.* This gives the names and designation of the various parties to the action (page 239). The heading that appears on the summons and complaint is used throughout the action until it is appealed, unless (1) there should be a change of parties by amendment, or (2) there is more than one plaintiff or defendant. In the latter case, it is necessary to show only the first-named plaintiff and the first-named defendant, followed by appropriate words indicating that there are others, such as *et al., et ux., et vir.*

3. *The index number.* The index, docket, or action number is assigned by the clerk of the court (see page 235). Although it is not known at the time the first paper is filed in court, it must be included on all future papers.

4. *Title of the pleading.* Each litigation paper has a designation or title, such as Petition, Complaint, Notice of Trial, and the like. The common practice is to include the title in the heading or just beneath it. All offices do not follow this practice.

How to type the caption. Court rules specify the information that goes into the caption, but only a few courts regulate the style in which the caption shall be typed. Twenty styles of captions are given below. One of them, perhaps with a slight variation, is appropriate for your office. Ask the lawyer to designate the one he wants you to follow. After the appropriate style has been indicated:

1. Note carefully the capitalization, punctuation, alignment, and spacing.

2. Notice the placement of each part of the caption with reference to the other parts. For example, in Style 5, the title of the document follows the caption, whereas in Style 2, the title of the document is typed at the right of the title of the case.

3. Set your margins and tabular stops at the appropriate places on the typewriter scale and try to keep them there, so that you will not have to change them each time you type a paper.

4. If in the style appropriate for your office the title of the case is set off by a box or other outline, form the habit of making all boxes the same width, or making all outlines at the same point on the typewriter scale. This habit facilitates typing the captions.

IN THE DISTRICT COURT IN AND FOR THE CITY AND COUNTY

OF DENVER AND STATE OF COLORADO

CIVIL ACTION NO. 3-504, DIV. 7

RICHARD R. ROBERTSON,

               Plaintiff,

      -vs.-   ANSWER

EDGAR L. EDWARDS,

               Defendant.

Style 1.

IN THE SUPERIOR COURT OF THE STATE OF WASHINGTON
FOR KING COUNTY

RICHARD B. ROBERTSON,

               Plaintiff,

         vs.   No. 5786

EDGAR L. EDWARDS,

                            DEMURRER TO COMPLAINT

               Defendant.

Style 2.

IN THE DISTRICT COURT OF THE STATE OF IOWA
IN AND FOR POLK COUNTY

RICHARD R. ROBERTSON,

               Plaintiff,   No. _____

vs.

                              PETITION

EDGAR L. EDWARDS,

               Defendant.

Style 3.

251

IN THE CIRCUIT COURT OF THE FIRST JUDICIAL DISTRICT

OF HINDS COUNTY, MISSISSIPPI

RICHARD R. ROBERTSON   PLAINTIFF)
)
)
VS.   )   NO. _____
)
)
)
EDGAR L. EDWARDS   DEFENDANT)

Style 4.

6

                                   W. E. Roe
                                   Carson City, Nevada

7   Attorney for Plaintiff

8   No. 19856

9   IN THE FIRST JUDICIAL DISTRICT COURT OF THE STATE OF NEVADA,

10   IN AND FOR THE COUNTY OF ORMSBY

11   ——oOo——

12   RICHARD R. ROBERTSON,   )
)
13   Plaintiff,   )
)
14   vs.   )
)
15   EDGAR L. EDWARDS,   )
)
16   Defendant.)

17   ——oOo——

18   **C O M P L A I N T**

19   ——oOo——

Style 5.
252

IN THE DISTRICT COURT OF SEDGWICK COUNTY,
KANSAS

RICHARD J. JONES,)
           Plaintiff)
)
vs.) No. _____
)
ESTELLA JONES,) Div. No. _____
         Defendant)

Style 6.

NO. 3456

RICHARD R. ROBERTSON   :   SUPERIOR COURT
:
      v.   :   COUNTY OF HARTFORD
:
EDGAR L. EDWARDS   :   APRIL   19—
:

Style 7.

STATE OF WISCONSIN : CIRCUIT COURT : MILWAUKEE COUNTY

RICHARD R. ROBERTSON,

           Plaintiff

      vs.   COMPLAINT

EDGAR L. EDWARDS,

           Defendant

Style 8.
253

IN THE CIRCUIT COURT, FOURTH
JUDICIAL CIRCUIT OF FLORIDA,
IN AND FOR DUVAL COUNTY.

----------------------------------x
RICHARD R. ROBERTSON,   :

                                :   NO. 3456
                Plaintiff, :
                                :   ANSWER
           vs.   :

EDGAR L. EDWARDS,   :

                                :
              Defendant. :
----------------------------------x

Style 9.

IN THE DISTRICT COURT OF THE THIRD JUDICIAL DISTRICT OF THE
STATE OF IDAHO, IN AND FOR THE COUNTY OF ADA

----------------------------------x
RICHARD R. ROBERTSON,   :

                                :
                Plaintiff, :   No. _____
                                :
           –vs.–   :   COMPLAINT

EDGAR L. EDWARDS,   :

                                :
              Defendant. :
----------------------------------x

Style 10.

254

CIVIL DISTRICT COURT FOR THE PARISH OF ORLEANS

STATE OF LOUISIANA

NO. ....   DIVISION ....   DOCKET.........

RICHARD W. ROE

VS.

JOHN H. DOE COMPANY

TO THE HONORABLE, THE JUDGES OF THE CIVIL DISTRICT COURT FOR
THE PARISH OF ORLEANS, STATE OF LOUISIANA:

FILED: _____

                                    _____
                                         DEPUTY CLERK

Style 11.

THE STATE OF NEW HAMPSHIRE

Hillsborough, SS.   Superior Court

_____

NATIONAL BANK AND TRUST   v.   COMMERCIAL BANK, LYDIA
COMPANY, EDGAR S. JONES,   ROBERTSON, and NELSON
and RICHARD R. ROBERTSON,   ROBERTSON
Executors of the Estate
of Edward Robertson,
deceased

_____

MOTION TO AMEND DECLARATION

Style 12.

255

PULASKI CIRCUIT COURT

JOHN DOE, ... Plaintiff,

   – vs. –   No. _____

RICHARD ROE, ...Defendant.

COMPLAINT AT LAW

Style 13.

FRANKLIN CIRCUIT COURT

RICHARD R. ROBERTSON   PLAINTIFF

VS.   PETITION

EDGAR L. EDWARDS   DEFENDANT

Style 14.

SUPREME COURT OF THE STATE OF NEW YORK

COUNTY OF NEW YORK

————————————————————x

RICHARD R. ROBERTSON,   :   NO. . . . .

              Plaintiff, :   COMPLAINT

          vs.   :

EDGAR L. EDWARDS,   :

            Defendant. :

————————————————————x

Style 15.

256

STATE OF ILLINOIS)
) SS.   IN THE CIRCUIT COURT THEREOF
COUNTY OF SANGAMON)

RICHARD R. ROBERTSON,   )
)
                  Plaintiff,   )
)   IN EQUITY
       –against–   )   NO. 111/—
)
EDGAR L. EDWARDS,   )
)
                  Defendant.   )
                    Style 16.

VIRGINIA:

IN THE LAW AND EQUITY COURT OF THE CITY OF RICHMOND

JOHN DOE,   Plaintiff,

v.

EDGAR L. EDWARDS,   Defendant.

                 MOTION FOR JUDGMENT

                     Style 17.

STATE OF SOUTH DAKOTA)   IN CIRCUIT COURT
) SS
COUNTY OF HUGHES   )   SIXTH JUDICIAL CIRCUIT
Richard R. Robertson,   PLAINTIFF)
)
         –vs–   )   SUMMONS
)
Edgar L. Edwards,   DEFENDANT)
                    Style 18.

                       257

```
RICHARD R. ROBERTSON,           *           IN THE
                                *
                                *
                    Plaintiff   *        CIRCUIT COURT
                                *
        vs.                     *      OF BALTIMORE COUNTY
                                *
EDGAR L. EDWARDS,               *          IN EQUITY
                                *
                                *
                    Defendant   *   Docket No. 85, Folio 196


                       * * * * * * *
                          ANSWER
```

Style 19.

Captions on papers filed in Federal district courts. It is mandatory that the caption on all papers filed in Federal district courts set forth the name of the court, the title of the case, the

```
                UNITED STATES DISTRICT COURT
                EASTERN DISTRICT OF LOUISIANA
                   NEW ORLEANS DIVISION


ROBERT L. SMITH                 :

                    Plaintiff   :   NO._____

        vs.                     :   CIVIL ACTION

THOMAS J. JONES                 :

                    Defendant   :
: : : : : : : : : : : : : : : : :

            MOTION FOR EXTENSION OF TIME
```

Figure 54. Caption of Paper Filed in a Federal District Court.

file number, and the designation of the paper being filed. Usually the title of the case is boxed, although it is not mandatory that the caption be typed in any particular style. Figure 54 illustrates a caption on a Motion for Extension of Time filed in a Federal District Court.

Indentations. Indent 10 spaces for paragraphs. Never block paragraph a court paper.

The left margin of quotations and other indented material should be five spaces to the right of the principal left margin; the beginning of a paragraph of indented material should be indented an additional five spaces.

The right margin of indented material should be approximately five spaces to the left of the principal right margin.

Spacing. Double space the body of all court papers. Quotations and descriptions may be single spaced, but many courts prefer that this material also be double spaced.

Single space names of parties in the caption.

Single space the line of signature and address and, also, the name and address of opposing counsel, which appear on many court papers.

Number of copies. When typing court papers, always make an original for the court, a copy for each opposing party or his attorney, and a copy for your file. Some courts require an extra copy. It is frequently necessary to make additional copies and also duplicate originals. When this is the case, the dictator will tell you how many copies to make. If you are in doubt as to the number of copies needed, inquire. (See also specific paper in the following chapters and Table VII on page 264, *et seq.*)

Numbering pages. Number pages of court papers about one-half inch from the bottom in the center of the page.

Conforming copies. After the original and duplicate originals are signed, conform the copies (see page 163).

Legal backs for court papers. All papers that are filed in, or submitted to, a court, are stapled in legal backs, similar to the backs on legal instruments (page 164). The copy, or copies, that are served on opposing counsel are also bound, but the office copy that you keep in your file is not. Before binding, collate the original and the copies.

It is preferable that all copies of backs be ribbon copies; certainly no more than one carbon copy should be made at a time. Some law firms follow the practice of using backs of one color for the original and backs of another color for the copy to be served on the counsel. This avoids the possibility of filing the copy of the paper instead of the original in court.

Endorsement. The endorsement on the back of a court paper (see Figure 55) includes:

1. *Index number.* Leave blank space for this until the number is ascertained.

2. *Name of the court.* Get this from the heading of the paper itself.

3. *Style of the case.* This is the same as the caption in the box. It is sometimes difficult to get a long title into the limited typing space provided on the back. This can be overcome in three ways:

    (1) Type only the name of the first plaintiff, or defendant, if there are more than one, and follow by *et al.,* the abbreviation for *et alius* and *et alii* meaning "and another," and "and others." It is inaccurate to use *et als.*

    (2) Substitute "etc." for a lengthy description of the parties. For example, ". . . constituting the Legal Committee, etc." would be substituted for ". . . constituting the Legal Committee of the Parent and Teachers Association of Henry County." Usually a title is shortened in this manner only at the direction of the attorney.

    (3) Loosen the platen and use variable spacing, thus gaining a line or two. This mars the appearance of the back but is sometimes necessary.

4. *Name of paper or papers stapled in the back.* When two or more papers are bound together, they must be bound in a certain order, but the back is not necessarily endorsed in that order. For example, an order and notice of entry are bound together, with the notice first, or on top, but the back is endorsed "Order and Notice of Entry." This is because the order is more important than the notice. The wording of endorsements for specific papers, as well as the order in which they are bound, will be given in the detailed instructions relating to each paper in subsequent chapters.

5. *Name and address of attorney filing the paper.* This is usu-

ally printed on the back. If it is not printed, type it. Some courts, especially in large cities, require that the telephone number also be included.

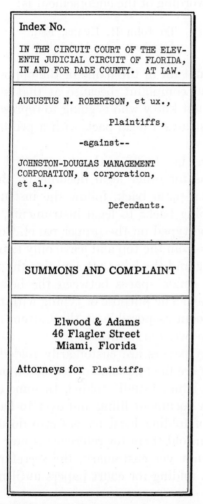

Index No.

IN THE CIRCUIT COURT OF THE ELEV-
ENTH JUDICIAL CIRCUIT OF FLORIDA,
IN AND FOR DADE COUNTY.   AT LAW.

AUGUSTUS N. ROBERTSON, et ux.,

                    Plaintiffs,

           -against--

JOHNSTON-DOUGLAS MANAGEMENT
CORPORATION, a corporation,
et al.,

                    Defendants.

SUMMONS AND COMPLAINT

**Elwood & Adams
46 Flagler Street
Miami, Florida**

Attorneys for Plaintiffs

Figure 55. Endorsed Back on Summons and Complaint.

6. *Party represented.* The name and address of the attorney is followed by the designation of the party in whose behalf the paper is filed. For example, Attorneys for Defendant. However, if there is more than one defendant, and the paper is filed on

behalf of only one of them, the name of the defendant must be given.

7. *Name of opposing counsel and designation of the party he represents.* The wording of the endorsement is:

> To John R. Evans, Esq.
> Attorney for Defendant

Usually you cannot fill in the name of the opposing attorney on the summons and complaint, because at that stage of the proceedings you do not know who is going to represent a defendant.

Figure 55 illustrates a legal back with a printed panel for the endorsement.

Some law firms use backs without a printed panel for court papers as well as for other legal documents. Before typing an endorsement on a plain back, follow the instructions given on page 164 for typing backs to legal instruments, so that the endorsement will be typed on the proper panel. Commence typing two single spaces from the top and leave only two spaces between the court heading and the box that contains the title of the case. Leave only two single spaces between the box and name and address of attorney. The purpose of typing with this spacing is to leave as much room as possible at the bottom of the panel for stamped and handwritten notations.

Folding. Court papers are customarily folded into document form before they are filed in court or served on opposing counsel. Your office copy is not usually folded. In some courts there is a trend away from document filing and over to flat filing, because the uselessness of folding legal papers into document form and then having to unfold them for reference is now widely realized. As flat filing is not yet customary, the secretary will continue to use document folding for court papers until instructed to the contrary.

Printed litigation blanks. Printed forms for some court papers are available and, in many cases, it is preferable to use them. When they are used, the same care should be taken in filling them in that is taken with all printed forms (page 166). When detailed instructions are given about specific pleadings and supporting papers in the subsequent chapters, you will be told if printed blanks are generally used.

Practice and Procedure

The secretary's responsibility. The procedure in a civil action is highly technical and is the lawyer's responsibility. He will also dictate many of the pleadings in their entirety because their wording must be precise to meet statutory requirements. The secretary's responsibilities might consist in (1) keeping an accurate calendar and record of the proceedings; (2) preparing the pleadings in a workmanlike manner; and (3) relieving the lawyer of details.

Variations in practice and procedure. The rules of civil practice and procedure vary in detail not only in the various states but, to a lesser extent, in various jurisdictions within a state. A fundamental variation of interest to the secretary is the requirement with respect to the service and filing of pleadings. For the purpose of this chapter the jurisdictions may be grouped in respect to service and filing as follows:

A. In the majority of jurisdictions, a copy of every pleading and supporting paper must be served on opposing counsel, and the original filed in court. When copy of the initial pleading is served with the summons, as is often the case, it is served on the defendant, because there is no counsel of record at that time.

B. In a few jurisdictions copies of pleadings and supporting papers do not have to be served on opposing counsel, but *a copy as well as the original must be filed in court.* Counsel withdraws the duplicate from court in order to learn the contents of the papers filed by opposing counsel. (All jurisdictions require service of the summons on the defendant.)

C. In a few jurisdictions, for example in New York Supreme Court, copies of pleadings are served on opposing counsel, but the originals are not filed in court until the case is at issue. The court has no indication that a law suit is pending until the case is ready to be set for trial. This does not apply to municipal courts.

D. In some jurisdictions a copy must be served on opposing counsel, and an original and a copy filed in court.

The directions in this chapter are based on the practice in jurisdictions that fall within Group A. If a jurisdiction in which suit is filed falls within group B, C, or D, you can easily adapt the directions. Suppose the directions tell you to serve copy on opposing counsel and file the original in court, but your action is pending in a jurisdiction that falls within group B. You know that you need not serve a copy on opposing counsel but that you must file an original and copy in court. Or suppose the directions say to make three copies—an original for the court, a copy for opposing counsel, and a copy for your office file, but the jurisdiction is within group D. You know that you will have to make four copies, because a copy as well as the original must be filed in court. Table VII shows (1) the number of copies to be filed in

TABLE VII

Pleadings in Courts of Original Jurisdiction

(Copies of initial pleading for service on each defendant are filed with the clerk of the court.)

State	Copies filed in court	Is copy served on adverse party or opposing counsel?	Kind of paper used—Legal Cap or Plain Legal Size
Alabama	Original	Yes[2]	Either
Alaska	Original	Yes	Plain Legal Size
Arizona	Original	Yes	Legal Cap
Arkansas	Original and one copy	No[5]	Legal Cap
California	Original[3]	Yes	Legal Cap with numbered margin
Colorado	Original	Yes	Plain Legal Size
Connecticut	Original[10]		Either Legal Cap
Delaware	Original	Yes	
D.C.	Original	Yes	
Florida	Original	Yes	Either
Hawaii	Original and one	Yes	
Georgia	Original	Yes	Either
Idaho	Original	Yes	Either
Illinois	Original and one copy	No[4]	Legal Size
Indiana	Original	Yes[1]	Plain Legal Size
Iowa	Original and one copy for each opposing counsel	Yes[2]	Plain Legal Size
Kansas	Original and one copy	Yes	Legal Cap
Kentucky	Original and one copy	No	Either
Louisiana	Original	Yes	Either
Maine	Original	Yes[2]	Either
Maryland	Original	Yes	Legal Cap
Massachusetts	Original	Yes	Legal Size or 8½ x 11
Michigan	Original	Yes	Either
Minnesota	Original	Yes	Plain Legal Size
Mississippi	Original[5]	Yes[2]	Plain Legal Size
Missouri	Original	Yes	Either
Montana	Original	Yes	Legal Cap
Nebraska	Original and copy for each adverse party[8]	Yes[2]	Either

TABLE VII (Continued)

State	Copies filed in court	Is copy served on adverse party or opposing counsel?	Kind of paper used—Legal Cap or Plain Legal Size
Nevada	Original	Yes	Legal Cap with numbered margin
New Hampshire ..	Original	Yes	Either
New Jersey	Original and one in Superior Court— only an original in other Courts	Yes	Plain Legal Size
New Mexico	Original	Yes	Plain Legal Size
New York	Original	Yes	Legal Cap[9]
North Carolina ..	Original and copy for each adverse party	No	Plain Legal Size
North Dakota ...	Original	Yes	Plain Legal Size
Ohio	Original and one copy for each adverse party	Yes	Plain Legal Size
Oklahoma	Original	Yes[2]	Either
Oregon	Original	Yes	Legal Cap
Pennsylvania	Original	Yes	Plain Legal Size
Rhode Island	Original and one copy of initial pleading, thereafterwards original only	Yes[11]	Either
South Carolina ..	Original	Yes	Plain Legal Size
South Dakota ...	Original	Yes	Plain Legal Size
Tennessee	Original and one copy for each opposing counsel	Yes	Legal Cap
Texas	Original	Yes[6]	Plain Legal Size
Utah	Original	Yes	Either
Vermont	Original and one copy for each opposing counsel	No	Plain Legal Size
Virginia	Original	Yes	Either
Washington	Original	Yes	Plain Legal Size
West Virginia ...	Original and one copy	No[12]	Plain Legal Size
Wisconsin	Original	Yes	Either
Wyoming	Original and one copy for each opposing counsel	No[7]	Either

[1] Some counties do not require service on opposing counsel. In those counties it is customary to file in court copy for each opposing counsel.
[2] Not required, but customary through courtesy. Affidavit of service, or receipt for copy, is not necessary unless service is required by court rules.
[3] In courts where branch sessions are held in places other than county seat, signed duplicate as well as original is filed in court.
[4] Copy must be served under the rules of the local courts in some counties.
[5] If no copy is given opposing counsel, it is customary to file in court copy for each opposing counsel of record.
[6] If there are more than four opposing counsel, four copies are filed with clerk of the court instead of being served on counsel.
[7] If acknowledgment of service is desired, it is customary to deliver copy of pleading to opposing counsel and ask him to acknowledge service on the original before filing it in court, but copy for each opposing counsel must also be filed in court.
[8] Only one copy is required, but it is customary to file additional copies.
[9] Letter size is permissible, but the prevalent practice is to use legal cap.
[10] Copies must be mailed to all parties who have entered appearance and original certified to that effect is filed in court.
[11] Except original pleading filed with copy in court.
[12] Copies of only certain papers must be served on adverse party.

court and (2) whether a copy is served on opposing counsel. *Opposing counsel* refers to the counsel for each adverse party. Thus, if the rules require service on opposing counsel and there is more than one adverse party, sufficient copies of the paper are prepared to permit service of a copy on counsel for each party.

13

Specific Court Papers: What They Are and How to Prepare Them

WE HAVE selected for discussion and illustration in this chapter, and the following one, pleadings and supporting papers that will demonstrate to the secretary how all court papers are prepared, and her responsibilities in connection with them. The secretary can adapt the demonstrations to other pleadings and supporting papers. Keep in mind the variations in practice and procedure discussed on page 263, *et seq.* Refer to Table VII at the end of the preceding chapter for variations in number of copies, filing requirements, service requirements, and the like. Remember, also, that local courts in some jurisdictions have requirements that are not state-wide.

Summons and Complaint

Plaintiff's first pleading. The first pleading by the plaintiff is a formal and methodical specification of the facts and circumstances surrounding the cause of action. It sets forth in detail the grounds upon which the plaintiff is suing the defendant, and asks the court for damages or other relief. The lawyer will usually dictate complaints, except very simple ones, because the facts and circumstances differ, although the phraseology is standard.

The plaintiff's first pleading is called the *complaint* in the majority of states; the *petition* or the *declaration* in a few states. In those states where a distinction still exists between actions at law and in equity, the first pleading in equity actions is called the *bill of complaint* or *bill in equity.* (We shall use the term *complaint* to refer to the first pleading regardless of the terminology in the various states.)

267

Analysis of a complaint. Although complaints necessarily differ in detail, they follow a standard pattern. A complaint consists of the following parts:

1. *Caption.* (See Chapter 12.) The caption to the complaint designates the court in which the action is brought and lists the full names of all plaintiffs and defendants. It does not show the clerk's index number because that is not available at the time the complaint is prepared.

2. *Introduction.* The opening paragraph of the complaint simply states, "The plaintiff, by his attorney, John Jones, complaining of the defendant, alleges as follows:" or words to that effect.

3. *Body.* The body of the complaint states the facts and circumstances that are the basis for the action. The complaint may contain one or more causes of action, each of which is a separate and complete division within itself. These divisions are referred to as *counts* in some jurisdictions. A cause of action, or count, is composed of one or more *allegations*. These are statements that the plaintiff expects to prove. Complaints in certain actions must contain standard allegations, which the lawyer dictates from memory or from a practice manual. For example, when a domestic corporation is the plaintiff, the allegation will allege the corporate status in a form similar to the following:

That at all times hereinafter mentioned, the plaintiff was and still is a domestic corporation, organized and existing under and by virtue of the laws of the State of . . . .

When a corporation is the defendant, the allegation is introduced by the words, "Upon information and belief . . ."

4. *Prayer.* The prayer, or "wherefore" clause, is the final paragraph of the complaint and "demands" judgment against the defendant for a specified sum, or, in equity actions, "prays" for other relief to which the plaintiff believes he is entitled. The language used in equity gives the prayer its name. The complaint will also demand interest if the action is for a definite amount of money owed by the defendant, as when the action is on a stated account or a promissory note.

5. *Signature.* Either the plaintiff or his attorney must sign the complaint. The original must be signed manually in every state

except New York, where a typed signature is sufficient. In Federal courts, pleadings must be signed by an attorney in his individual name, not in the firm name.

6. *Verification.* The law in the various states specifies which complaints shall be verified, but many lawyers follow the practice of having all complaints verified. The verification is signed before a notary public. (See "Verifications," page 243, *et seq.*)

How to prepare the complaint. Simple forms of complaint, such as complaints in actions for goods sold or in actions on promissory notes, are often left to the secretary to draw, without dictation. At first the lawyer will give you a form to follow, but you will soon memorize the wording, especially if your office handles many cases of a particular kind of litigation. Make an extra copy of the complaint in each kind of action for your loose-leaf form book.

Figure 56 illustrates a complaint. Follow the general directions for the preparation of litigation papers (page 249, *et seq.*). The following directions relate specifically to the preparation of a complaint:

1. Make an original for the court, a copy for each defendant, and a copy for your files. (See Table VII for variations in number of copies.)

2. Number the counts or causes of action.

3. Number the allegations.

4. Type a line for signature and "Attorneys for Plaintiff" underneath it. (In New York, do not type the signature line; instead, type the firm name, followed by "Attorneys for Plaintiff" and the firm's address.)

5. The verification, when required, is typed preferably on the last page of the document or at least is started on the last page, but it may be typed entirely on a separate sheet. There is no rule of law about this. If the verification is printed on the inside of the legal back, the office copy will not have a verification. The lawyer will tell you who is to verify the complaint.

6. In large cities it is customary to follow the verification (or the signature if there is no verification) with the name, address, and telephone number of the firm representing the plaintiff.

7. Endorse legal backs (see the directions on page 259) for each copy of the complaint, except your office copy. In the space pro-

IN THE CIRCUIT COURT OF THE ELEVENTH
JUDICIAL CIRCUIT OF FLORIDA, IN AND
FOR DADE COUNTY.   AT LAW.

---------------------------------------x
                      :

AUGUSTUS N. ROBERTSON and ELIZABETH
R. ROBERTSON,   :

             Plaintiffs, :

      -against-   :   COMPLAINT

JOHNSTON–DOUGLAS MANAGEMENT CORPORA-
TION, a corporation, and FREDERICK
FASHIONS, INC., a corporation, :

            Defendants. :

---------------------------------------x

       Plaintiffs by their attorneys, Elwood & Adams,
complaining of the defendants above named, allege:

FOR A FIRST CAUSE OF ACTION:

       FIRST: That the plaintiffs_____

_____

_____.

       SECOND: Upon information and belief, that _____

_____.

FOR A SECOND CAUSE OF ACTION:

       THIRD: Plaintiffs repeat, reiterate_____

(Continued on following page)

(Continued from preceding page)

_____

_____

_____.

     WHEREFORE, plaintiffs demand judgment against de-

fendants for the sum of Five thousand three hundred twenty-

five and 36/100 dollars ($5,325.36), with interest thereon

from the 20th day of December, 19——, together with the costs

and disbursements of this action.

                          _____

                             Elwood & Adams
                       Attorneys for Plaintiffs

Figure 56. Complaint.

(If verification required, type on this page or on separate sheet.)

vided for the title of the document, type "Summons and Complaint." Staple after the summons is prepared.

    8. Collate.

The summons. Strictly speaking, a summons is not a pleading,
but it is an essential part of every law suit. It is the first paper
that is served on the defendant, sometimes being served before
the preparation of the complaint. It notifies the person named in
the summons that suit has been brought against him and commands him to appear in court or answer the complaint by a certain date. Although the secretary to the plaintiff's attorney prepares the summons, it is generally issued and signed by the clerk
of the court.

A summons consists of the following parts:

    1. Caption.

    2. Body. This commands the defendant to answer the com-
plaint within the time specified.

    3. Signature and seal of the clerk of the court. (In New York
the plaintiff's attorney signs the summons.)

How to prepare the summons. A printed form of summons
(see Figure 57) is used, unless there are numerous parties plaintiff or parties defendant.

In The Circuit Court of Duval County, Florida At Law

RICHARD JONES AND MARY JONES, his wife,
          Plaintiff.s....

Civil Action -
Damages $ 5,000

vs.

SMITH & DOUGLAS, INC., a corporation,
          Defendant.......

No................................I

Summons at Law

The State of Florida -

  To ....SMITH & DOUGLAS, INC. ....

  You are hereby summoned and required to serve upon ...... Allen S. Brown ......

plaintiff's attorney, whose address is ... 321 Main Street, Jacksonville, Florida,

an answer to the complaint which is herewith served upon you within 20 days after service of this summons upon you, exclusive of the day of service. If you fail to do so, judgment by default will be taken against you for the relief demanded in the complaint.

   Witness *my hand and the seal of said Court, at Jacksonville, Florida, this*
      Sixth   *.....day of* November *.....A. D. 19 ....*

          Clerk Circuit Court

   By...
          Deputy Clerk

Sheriff's Return of Service

Figure 57. Printed Form of Summons.

1. If the name of a court is printed on the form, make certain that it is the court in which the action is being filed.

2. Make an original for the court, a copy for each defendant, and a copy for your file. An extra copy of the summons must be filed in court in those jurisdictions that require an extra copy of pleadings to be filed (see Table VII).

3. The caption is exactly like that of the complaint. List names of all parties in full.

4. If there are numerous parties, type on legal-size paper instead of using a printed form. Copy the printed form exactly, making sure that all punctuation is included, because usually the statutes direct the form of a summons.

5. Put a legal back on a typed summons, so that the affidavit of service can be filled in.

6. Endorse the back of the original summons and of each copy, unless the summons is stapled to the complaint. The endorsements need not list all the parties. It is sufficient to show the name of the first plaintiff and the name of the first defendant, with appropriate words indicating that there are others (see page 250).

Return day of summons. The civil practice and procedure codes and statutes provide the date by which, or the time within which, a defendant shall answer a summons, or at least file a notice of appearance. The final day for the defendant's appearance is designated as the *return day* of the summons. Thus, if the defendant is required to answer "within 20 days" from the service of the summons, the 20th day is the return day. In some jurisdictions certain days, designated as *return days* or *rule days,* are set aside for filing papers in court. In these jurisdictions the rules provide that the defendant shall appear "by the next rule day," if the summons is served on him a certain number of days before rule day; otherwise, he shall appear on the following rule day. Thus, the return date is always a rule day.

These return dates are very important and should always be *entered in your diary,* whether your office is serving the summons or has received a summons for a client.

How to compute the time. The statutes and codes also provide how the time shall be computed. The usual method is to *exclude* the date from which the period of time begins to run, but to *in-*

clude the last day of the period of time. If it falls on Sunday or a legal holiday, the next business day is the return date. Intermediate Sundays or holidays are included in the computation, unless the period of time allowed is less than seven days. The period of time begins to run the day the summons is served, not the day it is dated. This method of computation of time applies to the time for filing all pleadings as well as to the return day of the summons.

Alias summons; pluries summons. If the original summons is not served on all of the defendants for any reason, the clerk will issue another summons, designated as an *alias summons*. It is prepared like the original summons, except that *alias* precedes *summons*. If the alias summons is not served, and it is necessary to issue a following summons, the third one is designated as a *pluries summons*.

What the secretary does about the summons and complaint. (See page 263 and Table VII for variations in filing and service in different states.)

1. Prepare the complaint, and verification when required.

2. Have original complaint signed and verified, after approval by the lawyer.

3. Conform the copies.

4. Prepare summons.

5. Attach copy of summons to each copy of complaint. Place the complaint against the inside of the cover so that the verification printed on the inside cover shall read as a continuation of the complaint. Put the summons on top of the complaint. Do not attach original summons to original complaint.

6. Open case in suit register (Chapter 15) and make appropriate entry.

7. File original complaint in court, have clerk of court issue (sign, seal, and date) original summons, and pay required fee.

8. Conform copies of summons, by filling in date, name of clerk, and seal of court.

9. Make a note of the index number assigned by the clerk and put it on all subsequent papers prepared by you in that particular case.

10. Give original of summons, together with copy of summons and copy of complaint for each defendant, to process server for

service on defendants. (In some jurisdictions, the copies are given to the clerk of the court at the time the original summons is issued, and he, in turn, delivers them to the sheriff for service.)

11. The summons illustrated in Figure 57 has a space for the sheriff's return, which the sheriff fills in after he serves the summons. If a process server is employed to make service, instruct him to get in touch with you as soon as he serves the summons and complaint, for the purpose of making affidavit of service. The affidavit should be made on the same day that service is made. If affidavit of service is on a separate sheet, it should have a regular caption, like that on the complaint, but if the affidavit is made on the back of the summons, no caption is necessary.

12. File original summons and proof of service in court. If the summons is not filed within the time permitted by the practice rules, a new summons must be served.

13. Mark on office copy date service is made, and by whom.

14. *Enter in diary* return date of summons. Remember that the period of time begins to run the date the summons is served, not the date it is prepared.

15. If you are secretary to the lawyer for defendant, *enter in diary* return day of summons. This is very important. Failure to answer by that date might mean a default judgment.

The Answer

Defendant's first pleading. The modern summons contains a notice to the defendant to appear in court or to file and serve an answer to plaintiff's complaint within a specified time. If the summons directs the defendant to appear only, he may do so by filing an appearance with the clerk of the court (see page 281). If a copy of the complaint is served with the summons, the defendant is directed to file and serve his answer. The filing and service of an answer by the defendant constitute his appearance in court. Failure to obey the summons subjects the defendant to a judgment by default in favor of the plaintiff.

As soon as a client brings a summons to your office, *enter in your diary* the time by which he must appear or answer. It is your responsibility to see that no default judgment is taken against a client of your office because of your negligence.

Analysis of an answer. The answer is the defendant's formal written statement of his defense, signed by his attorney. It denies some, or all, of the allegations of the complaint and sets forth the grounds of his defense. It may also set up claims that the defendant has against the plaintiff, as *counterclaims*.

The answer consists of the following parts:

1. Caption
2. Introduction
3. Denials of allegations of the complaint
4. Counterclaims, if any
5. "Wherefore" clause; prayer, if answer contains a counterclaim
6. Signature of attorney for defendant
7. Verification if the complaint is verified

How to prepare the answer. The lawyer will dictate the answer to you, but it is your responsibility to set it up in a workmanlike manner. Unless the lawyer indicates his preference, follow the style illustrated in Figure 58.

1. Type on legal-size paper.

2. Make an original for the court, a copy to serve on each plaintiff's attorney, and a copy for your file. (See Table VII for variations in number of copies.)

3. The caption is the same as that on the complaint, but if there are numerous parties the title of the case may be shortened.

4. The index number must appear on the answer, at the right of the box.

5. The title of the document is "Answer."

6. Number the paragraphs consecutively throughout, except the last paragraph, which is the "wherefore" clause. Do not start new series of numbers for the paragraphs in each separate defense.

7. Type a line for signature of attorney.

8. The answer must be verified if the complaint is.

9. In some large cities, the attorney's name, address, and telephone number must appear after the verification, but usually this is not necessary. The attorney's address is on the legal back.

10. Endorse a legal back for each copy except your office copy. See Figure 59. Notice that the endorsement differs from the endorsement on the complaint in that it shows the court's index number and the name of the attorney for the plaintiff, on whom

BMM:r 4/22/— 1-2-1

IN THE CIRCUIT COURT OF THE ELEVENTH
JUDICIAL CIRCUIT OF FLORIDA, IN AND
FOR DADE COUNTY. AT LAW.

```
------------------------------------------x
                                          :
AUGUSTUS N. ROBERTSON and ELIZABETH
R. ROBERTSON,                             : Index No. 11660-19—

               Plaintiffs,   :

          -against-          :        ANSWER

JOHNSTON—DOUGLAS MANAGEMENT CORPORA-  :
TION, a corporation, and FREDERICK
FASHIONS, INC., a corporation,

               Defendants.   :
                                          :
------------------------------------------x
```

The defendant Johnston—Douglas Management Corporation, answering the amended complaint herein by his attorneys, Jones & Smith:

1. Admits_____

_____

_____.

2. Denies that he has knowledge or information
sufficient to form a belief as to the allegations contained
in the paragraph of the complaint designated "SECOND."

(Continued on following page)

(Continued from preceding page)

FOR A FIRST SEPARATE AND COMPLETE
DEFENSE, DEFENDANT ALLEGES:

3. On information and belief_____

_____.

FOR A SECOND SEPARATE AND PARTIAL
DEFENSE, DEFENDANT ALLEGES:

4. _____

_____.

FOR A DISTINCT SEPARATE AND AFFIRM—
ATIVE DEFENSE AND BY WAY OF A
COUNTERCLAIM, DEFENSE ALLEGES:

5. _____

_____.

WHEREFORE, defendant demands that the complaint be
dismissed with costs and asks judgment in the amount _____

_____.

_____
Attorneys for Defendant
Johnston—Douglas Manage-
ment Corporation

Figure 58. Answer.

(If verification required, type on this page or on separate sheet.)

a copy of the answer is served. When the complaint was prepared, the secretary for the plaintiff did not know the index number or who would represent the defendant.

11. Collate and staple in backs.

12. After signature and verification, conform exactly.

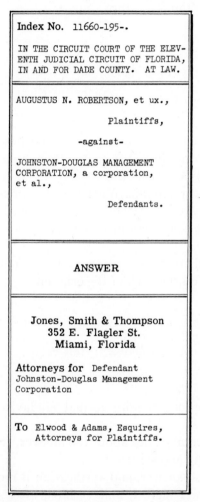

Figure 59. Endorsed Back of Answer.

Methods of service of answer on plaintiff's attorney. Although
practice may vary with the jurisdiction, the answer is generally
served on the plaintiff's attorney by (1) handing him a copy, or
leaving it at his office with his clerk or other person in charge of

the office; or (2) by mailing it to the attorney. No regular process server is necessary in the majority of jurisdictions. You, or a clerk in your office, may serve the papers.

Proof of service. The attorney on whom the answer is served, or you if you are authorized, writes on the back of the original a receipt similar to the following:

(date)
Copy received . . . .
      (Firm name)
. . . .
          (name of client)
Attorneys for . . . .

Many offices have rubber stamps for this purpose.

Printed legal backs have printed on them an admission of service, which usually contains the words "due and proper" service, "timely" service, or the like. When you accept service, be sure to strike out these words. Although you are authorized to accept service, it is not your responsibility to admit that it was due, proper, or timely.

In some jurisdictions, the attorney whose office is serving the answer endorses on the back of the original:

I do hereby certify that copy hereof has
been furnished to . . . .
by mail (or delivery), this . . . . day
of . . . ., 19 . . .

Many jurisdictions require formal affidavit when service is made by mail.

What the secretary does about the answer. (See Table VII for variations in filing and service.)

1. Prepare the answer, and verification if required.

2. Have answer signed, and verified, after approval by the attorney.

3. Notarize verification.

4. See that copy is served on plaintiff's attorney.

5. Be sure that receipt of service is endorsed on back of original, or that affidavit of service is attached.

6. Conform your office copy.

7. File original, with admission of service in court, with fee if required.

8. Make entry in suit register of service and filing.

9. If you are secretary to the attorney on whom the answer is served, make a notation on the back of your copy of the date and hour it was served; also make entry in suit register.

10. *Enter in diary* date by which next action must be taken.

Notice of Appearance

Analysis of a notice of appearance. In jurisdictions where a summons may be served on the defendant without a copy of the complaint, the defendant appears by filing a *notice of appearance* with the clerk of the court and serving a copy of it on the plaintiff's attorney. It is a statement that the defendant appears by his attorney. Thereafter, copies of all pleadings are served on the attorney appearing for the defendant, if service is required (see Table VII). In some jurisdictions, the notice of appearance is addressed to the attorney for the plaintiff; in others, to the clerk of the court. Figure 60 illustrates a typed notice of appearance in a common law case; Figure 61, in an equity case.

How to prepare a notice of appearance. A printed form of the notice of appearance is available, but the notice may be typed on legal-size paper.

1. Prepare an original for the court, a copy to be served on opposing counsel, and a copy for your office file.

2. The caption is identical with that on the summons. If the title of the case is long, you may shorten it as described on page 260.

3. Type signature line for the attorney, with his address underneath. When a printed form is used, it is advisable to type the attorney's name in parentheses underneath the line for signature so that the opposing counsel will have no difficulty in deciphering the signature.

4. Endorse the back. If you type the notice, put a properly endorsed legal back on it.

What the secretary does about the notice of appearance. A notice of appearance is never verified, because it contains no statements of fact. Otherwise, your responsibilities with respect

SUPREME COURT OF THE STATE OF NEW YORK

COUNTY OF NEW YORK

———————————————————————————————————————x

JOHN ROBERTS,   :

                                    Plaintiff,   :

                    —against—   :

THOMAS SMITH,   :

                                    Defendant.   :

———————————————————————————————————————x

S I R:

          PLEASE TAKE NOTICE that the defendant Thomas Smith
hereby appears in the above entitled action and that we are
retained as attorneys for him therein, and hereby demand
that a copy of the complaint and of all other papers in this
action be served on us at the office below designated.

Dated, New York, July 25, 19——.

                              Yours, etc.,

                                   RANDOLPH & PETERS,
                                      Attorneys for Defendant,
                                      80 Towers Avenue
                                      New York, N. Y.

To:

          HAROLD B. WRIGHT, ESQ.,
             Attorney for Plaintiff,
             14 Hale Street,
             New York, N. Y.

Figure 60. Notice of Appearance in Common Law Case.
282

UNITED STATES DISTRICT COURT

EASTERN DISTRICT OF NEW YORK

————————————————————————————————————x

RAY SMITH,   :

                              Plaintiff, :

                —against—   :   E 87–20

JACKSON & COMPANY,   :

                              Defendant. :
————————————————————————————————————x

TO THE CLERK OF THE ABOVE COURT:

        We hereby enter our appearance as attorneys and
solicitors for the defendant JACKSON & COMPANY in the above
entitled suit.

Dated, New York, July 5, 19—.

                                Yours, etc.,

                                ELWOOD & ADAMS
                                    Attorneys for Defendant
                                    Jackson & Company,
                                    36 Mall Street,
                                    New York, N. Y.

To:

        JOHN ELLIS, ESQ.,
            Attorney for Plaintiff,
            150 Brown Avenue
            New York, N. Y.

THE CLERK OF THE UNITED STATES DISTRICT COURT,
    Eastern District of New York,
        Post Office Building,
            Brooklyn, N. Y.

Figure 61. Notice of Appearance in Equity Case (Federal Court).

to the notice of appearance are the same as with respect to the answer. In some jurisdictions the notice of appearance is not served on opposing counsel; he learns from the court record that the appearance has been filed.

Notice of Trial; Note of Issue

Noticing a case for trial. A material point, raised by the pleadings, about which there is a controversy between the parties is an *issue.* The issue may be an *issue of fact* or an *issue of law.* When an issue is raised, it is said to be *joined,* and the case is *at issue.* Issue is deemed joined the date the last pleading is served.

At any time after issue is joined, either party may have the case noticed for trial. (In the New York Supreme Court no papers are filed in court until issue is joined—the court does not even know a law suit is pending.) In some jurisdictions a case is noticed for trial by the filing of a *note of issue* or *memorandum setting for trial;* in others, by the filing of a *notice of trial.* Some jurisdictions require both. In still other jurisdictions, a case is set for trial on motion of counsel. Whatever procedure, or by whatever name the notice is called, the purpose is to place the case on the trial calendar.

Noticing a case for trial does not mean that it will be brought up for trial on that date or even at that term of court, but that it will be placed on the trial calendar to await its turn.

When the notice must be served. Note of issue or notice of trial must be served on opposing counsel a designated number of days before the term of court at which the case will be placed on the trial calendar. The requirement varies with the jurisdiction. Suppose a new term of court (see page 238) commences on the first Monday of the following month, which, let us say, is May 5. Practice rules require that the note of issue or notice of trial shall be served 12 days, for example, before the commencement of the term. Therefore, the notice must be served by April 23. Service after that date will not give counsel 12 days' notice. Thus, if on April 25 the lawyer tells you to prepare a notice of trial, you know that it will have to be for the June, not the May, term of court.

It is important for you to become familiar with this particular practice requirement; otherwise, you will not be able to prepare the note of issue or the notice of trial.

Note of issue—preparation. Note of issue is a printed form that you can easily complete without directions from the lawyer. Figure 62 illustrates a completed form.

166X—Note of Issue (Rule 150)

JULIUS BLUMBERG, INC., LAW BLANK PUBLISHERS
71 BROADWAY AND 1 RECTOR ST., NEW YORK

STATE OF NEW YORK

File No. 11660-19--

SUPREME COURT,   COUNTY OF KINGS

JOHN E. THOMPSON,

                 Plaintiff

against

SMITH-ROGER, INC.,

                 Defendant

Action (Proceeding) Commenced February 4 , 19--.
Issue Joined April 23 , 19--. *Last Pleading Served* April 20 , 19--
Issue of law and fact *Trial by* Court
Nature and Object of Action (Proceeding) Breach of contract.

Note of Issue filed by plaintiff.
NOTE OF ISSUE for next TERM of this Court, to be held November 8 , 19--.

ELWOOD & ADAMS
Attorneys for Plaintiff
Office and Post Office Address
45 Main Street ·
Brooklyn, N.Y.
Main 7-3400

JONES SMITH AND EDWARDS
Attorneys for Defendant
Office and Post Office Address
14 Congress Street
Brooklyn, N.Y.
TRiangle 5-0007

Courtesy Julius Blumberg, Inc.

Figure 62. Note of Issue.

1. Make an original for the court, a copy to serve on each opposing counsel, and a copy for your file.

2. Telephone numbers of attorneys should be included in the note of issue and *must* be included in some jurisdictions.

3. Each sentence is a separate paragraph.

4. Do not staple in legal back, but endorse on printed form.

5. The back of the printed note of issue has forms for affidavit of personal service and of service by mail. After service is made, fill in the appropriate form. Figure 63 illustrates the back of a note of issue with affidavit of service by mail completed.

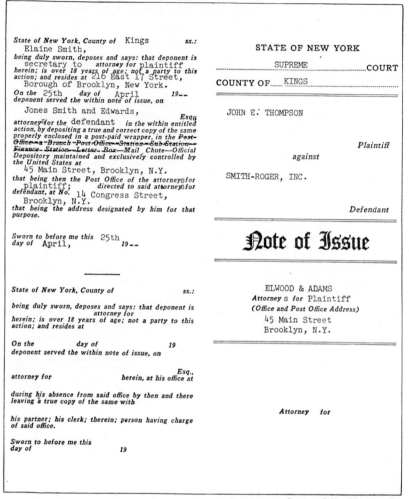

State of New York, County of Kings   ss.:
  Elaine Smith,
being duly sworn, deposes and says: that deponent is
  secretary to   attorney for plaintiff
herein; is over 18 years of age; not a party to this
action; and resides at 216 East 17 Street,
  Borough of Brooklyn, New York.
On the 25th   day of   April   19--
deponent served the within note of issue, on

  Jones Smith and Edwards,
                                    Esq.
attorney for the defendant in the within entitled
action, by depositing a true and correct copy of the same
properly enclosed in a post-paid wrapper, in the Post-
Office—a—Branch—Post-Office—Station—Sub-Station—
Finance-Station—Letter-Box—Mail Chute—Official
Depository maintained and exclusively controlled by
the United States at
  45 Main Street, Brooklyn, N.Y.
that being then the Post Office of the attorneys for
  plaintiff;   directed to said attorneys for
defendant, at No. 14 Congress Street,
  Brooklyn, N.Y.
that being the address designated by him for that
purpose.

Sworn to before me this 25th
day of April,   19--

State of New York, County of   ss.:

being duly sworn, deposes and says: that deponent is
                          attorney for
herein; is over 18 years of age; not a party to this
action; and resides at

On the   day of   19
deponent served the within note of issue, on

                              Esq.,
attorney for   herein, at his office at

during his absence from said office by then and there
leaving a true copy of the same with

his partner; his clerk; therein; person having charge
of said office.

Sworn to before me this
day of   19

STATE OF NEW YORK

............SUPREME............COURT

COUNTY OF.....KINGS

JOHN E. THOMPSON

                                        Plaintiff
                against

SMITH-ROGER, INC.

                                        Defendant

Note of Issue

ELWOOD & ADAMS
Attorney s for Plaintiff
(Office and Post Office Address)
45 Main Street
Brooklyn, N.Y.

Attorney   for

Figure 63. Back of Note of Issue.

Notice of trial—preparation. The lawyer does not usually dictate a notice of trial. You can get the wording from a practice manual in your office. The wording varies slightly with the jurisdiction, and, in some jurisdictions, notice given by the plaintiff differs from notice given by the defendant. Notice of trial given by the plaintiff recites an intention to take an "inquest," whereas notice by the defendant recites that a motion to dismiss the complaint will be made. Memorize the wording in your jurisdiction to save time in the preparation of notices. Figure 64 illustrates a notice of trial.

MUNICIPAL COURT OF THE CITY OF NEW YORK

BOROUGH OF MANHATTAN: FIRST DISTRICT

```
-------------------------------------------x
                                           :
LAWRENCE ADAMS,                            :    No. 7834/--
                                           :
                           Plaintiff,      :
                                           :    NOTICE OF TRIAL
            -against-                      :
                                           :
LUCIUS WEBB and ABC COMPANY, INC.,         :
                                           :
                           Defendants.     :
                                           :
-------------------------------------------x
```

S I R S:

PLEASE TAKE NOTICE that the issues in this action will be brought to trial and an inquest taken therein at Part II of this Court, to be held at the Court House situated at No. 8 Reade Street, Borough of Manhattan, City of New York on the 24th day of November, 19--, at 10 o'clock in the forenoon of that day or as soon thereafter as counsel can be heard.

Dated, New York, November 8, 19--.

Yours, etc.,

ELWOOD & ADAMS
Attorneys for Plaintiff,
48 Mall Street,
New York, N. Y.

To:

JONATHAN EDWARDS, ESQ.,
Attorney for Defendant,
120 Dew Street,
New York, N. Y.

CLERK OF THE MUNICIPAL COURT OF
THE CITY OF NEW YORK-
Borough of Manhattan,
First District.

Figure 64. Notice of Trial Given by Plaintiff.

1. Make an original for the court, copy to serve on each opposing counsel, and a copy for your office file.

2. Endorse legal backs.

3. Have attorney sign it.

What the secretary does about the notice of trial or note of issue. 1. Prepare the note of issue or notice of trial, as the case may be.

2. After the lawyer approves it, see that it is served on opposing counsel by the required date.

3. Be sure that receipt of service is endorsed on back or that the printed form provided is properly completed.

4. Conform your office copy.

5. File original in court.

6. *Make diary entry.*

7. Make appropriate entry in suit register.

8. If you are secretary to the counsel on whom notice is served, note on your copy date and hour of service; *make appropriate diary entry;* enter in suit register.

Stipulations

Analysis of a stipulation. Attorneys for opposing parties frequently make agreements respecting certain phases of a law suit. The agreement might be an accommodation to opposing counsel, such as an extension of the time in which to file a pleading; or it might be an agreement that will save time in court, such as an agreement admitting certain facts. These agreements between counsel are called stipulations. A stipulation is usually an agreement among the attorneys for all the parties to an action. However, it may be simply an agreement between the attorney for the plaintiff and the attorney for *a* defendant, the other parties defendant not being interested in the particular stipulation. Although stipulations are filed in court (except in those few jurisdictions where no papers are filed until note of issue), approval of the court to the stipulation is not usually required.

A stipulation consists of the following parts:

1. Caption
2. Body
3. Date line

4. Signatures of attorneys for all interested parties

How to prepare a stipulation. The wording of all stipulations about a particular step in the litigation is substantially the same. The lawyer does not usually dictate the simple stipulations. He will say, "Draw up a stipulation in the Jones case extending our time to answer until March 10"; or, "Draw up a stipulation in the Smith case to set for trial on March 18." You can get the wording from a practice manual. Whenever you prepare a stipulation of a different kind, make an extra copy for your form file. Memorize the short forms to save time in preparing them. The lawyer will dictate some stipulations, such as those admitting certain facts.

It is customary for the attorney seeking the stipulation to prepare it. When typing it, follow the style shown in Figure 65.

1. Type on legal-size paper.

2. Make an original for the court and a copy for all interested attorneys.

3. The caption is the same as that on the complaint, except that the style of the case may be shortened.

4. Type "IT IS HEREBY STIPULATED AND AGREED" in solid caps.

5. When there is more than one stipulation in the same document, type each in a separate paragraph.

6. Type a signature line for each attorney or firm of attorneys who are stipulating. Indicate the party represented by the stipulating attorney, thus: "Attorney for Defendant Richard Brown."

8. Endorse legal back for each copy of stipulation, including the copy for your office, unless you are instructed to back only the court copy, for purposes of economy.

What the secretary does about stipulations. Your responsibilities about the stipulation are the following:

1. Prepare the stipulation.

2. Staple original and all copies in endorsed legal backs.

3. Ask the attorney to sign the original and all copies.

4. Deliver them to opposing counsel who is stipulating and ask for his signature on the original and your office copy, giving him a copy that was signed at your office.

5. If the stipulation sets a date for future action, *make an entry in your diary.*

IN THE COURT OF COMMON PLEAS OF ALLEGHENY COUNTY,
PENNSYLVANIA

AUGUSTUS N. ROBERTSON and   :
ELIZABETH R. ROBERTSON,   :
                        :

        Plaintiffs, :

                       :

        vs.   : No. 223 October Term, 19——

                       :

JOHNSTON-DOUGLAS MANAGEMENT :
CORPORATION and FREDERICK   :
FASHIONS, INC.,   :

                       :

        Defendants. :

S T I P U L A T I O N

     IT IS HEREBY STIPULATED AND AGREED by and be-
tween the undersigned attorneys that the time for defendant
Frederick Fashions, Inc. to answer or otherwise plead to the
Second Amended Complaint herein, filed the 22nd day of September, 19——, be and the same hereby is extended to and
including the 13th day of October, 19——.

                                  ———————————————————
                                   (Elwood & Adams)
                              Attorneys for Plaintiff

                                  ———————————————————
                                   (Jones & Smith)
                              Attorneys for Defendant
                              Frederick Fashions, Inc.

Dated: September 25, 19——.

          Figure 65. Stipulation Extending Time to Answer.

6. Make entry in suit register (see Chapter 15).

7. If you are secretary to the attorney who did not prepare the stipulation, *make an entry in your diary* and your suit register when you receive a copy of it.

Demurrers

Analysis of a demurrer. Many states have abolished demurrers, but they are still permitted as a pleading in some states. A demurrer is a pleading that raises an issue of law, not of fact. It objects to defects that are apparent from the pleading itself. Instead of denying facts alleged in the complaint, as an answer does, a demurrer to a complaint takes exception to the complaint because it is insufficient on some legal ground. For example, a defendant may demur to a complaint on the ground that the plaintiff does not have legal capacity to sue. The defendant may also demur to the plaintiff's reply. But a demurrer is not a pleading to be used by the defendant only. A plaintiff may demur to the defendant's answer, or to a cross-complaint. Each cause of action (count), or each defense, is demurred to separately.

A demurrer consists of the following parts:

1. Caption
2. Introduction
3. Grounds of demurrer, each stated separately
4. Signature of attorney
5. Attorney's certificate of good faith when required
6. Points and authorities

The statutes name the grounds for demurrer. These grounds usually include, among others, the following: (1) that the court has no jurisdiction; (2) that the plaintiff has no legal capacity to sue; (3) that the complaint (or answer) is ambiguous, unintelligible, uncertain. A demurrer is supported by legal points and authorities sustaining the grounds of demurrer.

How to prepare the demurrer. The statement of a specific ground for demurrer usually follows a standard form, with which you will quickly become familiar. Although the lawyer ordinarily will dictate the demurrer, he might ask you to follow a form. Unless otherwise instructed, follow Figure 66 for style when typing a demurrer. Figure 67 illustrates the points and authorities supporting a demurrer.

IN THE SUPERIOR COURT OF THE STATE OF CALIFORNIA

9   IN AND FOR THE COUNTY OF LOS ANGELES

10

11   MARY JANE DOE,   )
)   No. 14788
12   Plaintiff,   )
)
13   vs.   )   DEMURRER
)   TO
14   JOHN W. DOE   )   COMPLAINT
)
15   Defendant.   )
)
16   _____

17   Comes now the above named defendant, JOHN W.

18   DOE, and demurs to Count One of the Complaint on file herein

19   upon the following grounds and each of them:

20   I

21   That Count One of said complaint fails to state

22   facts sufficient to constitute a cause of action against

23   this defendant.

24   II

25   That Count One of said complaint fails to state

26   facts sufficient to constitute a cause of action against

27   this defendant in this, that it affirmatively appears there-

28   from that the purported cause or causes of action therein

29   set forth are barred by the provisions of §§ 339(1), 343

Figure 66. Demurrer (First Page).

IV

That Count One of said complaint is ambiguous for each of the reasons heretofore set forth for its uncertainty.

V

That Count One of said complaint is unintelligible for each of the reasons heretofore set forth for its uncertainty.

DEMURRER TO COUNT TWO

Defendant demurs to Count Two of said complaint upon the following grounds and each of them:

I

(Continue as in the demurrer to Count One.)

WHEREFORE, this demurring defendant prays that this demurrer be sustained without leave to amend and that he be dismissed with his costs.

EMMETT BROWN
Attorney for Defendant

I hereby certify that this demurrer is filed in good faith; that it is not filed for the purpose of delay, and in my opinion the grounds are well taken.

EMMETT BROWN
Attorney for Defendant

Figure 66. Demurrer (Last Page).

1

POINTS AND AUTHORITIES

2

3   POINT ONE

4

5   A PARENT IS NOT BOUND TO COMPENSATE THE OTHER

6 PARENT FOR THE VOLUNTARY SUPPORT OF HIS CHILD WITHOUT AN

7 AGREEMENT FOR COMPENSATION.

8   Civil Code § 208

9   POINT TWO

10   AS BETWEEN THE PARENTS OF MINOR CHILDREN, THEIR

11 RESPECTIVE OBLIGATIONS OF SUPPORT OF EACH OTHER AND TO THE

12 MINOR CHILDREN MUST BE DETERMINED IN THE PROCEEDING FOR

13 DIVORCE, AND IN THE ABSENCE OF SOME SPECIFIC PROVISION TO

14 THAT EFFECT, THE FATHER WHO HAS BEEN DEPRIVED OF THE

15 CUSTODY OF THE MINOR CHILDREN IS NOT OBLIGATED FOR THEIR

16 SUPPORT.

17   Calegaris v. Calegaris, 4 Cal. App. 264, 87 Pac. 561;

18   Ex Parte Miller, 109 Cal. 643, 42 Pac. 428;

19   Lewis v. Lewis, 174 Cal. 336, 163 Pac. 42.

20

21   Respectfully submitted,

22   _____
                                 EMMETT BROWN
                              Attorney for Defendant

Figure 67. Points and Authorities Supporting Demurrer.

294

1. Type on legal-size paper.

2. Make an original for the court, a copy for the opposing party's counsel, and a copy for your file. (See Table VII for variations in number of copies.)

3. The caption is the same as that on the complaint, but you may shorten the title of the case.

4. The index number must appear on the demurrer, at the right of the box.

5. The title of the document is "Demurrer to Complaint," or "Demurrer to Answer," as the case may be.

6. Number the grounds of demurrer to each cause of action or count (or each defense) consecutively, beginning with "I."

7. Type a line for the attorney's signature.

8. There is no verification because a demurrer does not allege or aver facts.

9. Type the attorney's certificate of good faith in jurisdictions where it is required by the court rules. The certificate reads:

I hereby certify that this demurrer is filed in good faith and not for the purpose of delay. In my opinion the grounds are well taken.

_____

Attorney for . . . .

10. Begin the points and authorities on a separate page.

11. Endorse a legal back for each copy except your file copy. The endorsement is similar to the endorsement on the back of the answer in that it shows the index number and the name of opposing counsel on whom a copy of the demurrer is served.

What the secretary does about a demurrer. (See Table VII for variation in filing and service of pleadings.)

1. Prepare the demurrer and points and authorities.

2. Staple original and copies in endorsed legal backs.

3. Get attorney to sign original and copies, and also certificate of good faith if required.

4. Serve copy on attorney for opposing party.

5. See that admission of service is endorsed on back of original.

6. Conform your office copy.

7. File original in court, with fee if required.

8. Make entry in suit register of service and filing.

9. If you are secretary to the counsel on whom the demurrer is served, make a notation on the back of your copy of the date and hour the demurrer was served, and an entry in the suit register.

Demand for Bill of Particulars, Bill of Particulars, Interrogatories, and Motion to Make Pleading More Definite

A complaint does not contain all the minute details or particulars of the plaintiff's claim against the defendant. The defendant is entitled to those details so that he may interpose the proper answer and prepare to defend himself in the trial of the case. Likewise, the plaintiff may need more definite information from the defendant before he can adequately defend the case. The methods by which this information is obtained vary with the state and also with the kind of action.

Demand for bill of particulars. A method commonly used to obtain the specific details of a claim made by one party against another, especially when the claim is based on an account, is by a *demand for bill of particulars.* A party demands that the adverse party furnish him with a statement of the details, called a *bill of particulars,* within a specified time (or within the time provided by statute). He may request the court for an order for the bill of particulars, in which case the procedure is like that in any other motion (Chapter 14). The demand for bill of particulars is addressed to opposing counsel.

Parts of demand for bill of particulars. The demand for bill of particulars consists of the following parts:
1. Caption
2. Salutation
3. Introduction
4. Details demanded
5. Date line
6. Signature of attorney demanding the bill
7. Name and address of attorney on whom the demand is made

How to prepare the demand for bill of particulars. Usually the lawyer dictates the demand for bill of particulars. Unless otherwise instructed, follow Figure 68 for style.

1. Make an original for the court (some courts require an

JMH:p 8/23/— 1-2

SUPREME COURT OF THE STATE OF NEW YORK

COUNTY OF RICHMOND

```
----------------------------------------x
                                         :
AUGUSTUS N. ROBERTSON and ELIZABETH      :
R. ROBERTSON,                            :
                                         :
                         Plaintiffs,     :   DEMAND FOR BILL
                                         :   OF PARTICULARS
                                         :
               —against—                 :
                                         :
JOHNSTON—DOUGLAS MANAGEMENT CORPORATION, :
and FREDERICK FASHIONS, INC.,            :
                                         :
                         Defendants.     :
                                         :
----------------------------------------x
```

SIRS:

PLEASE TAKE NOTICE that the above named defendants hereby demand that the plaintiffs serve upon the attorneys for the defendants within ten days a Bill of Particulars showing in detail the following:

(1) The date and the time of day of the occurrence as closely as the plaintiffs can fix it.

(2) Its location, identifying as closely as possible the display counters and the place on the floor between them as described in paragraph FIFTH of the complaint.

(*Continued on following page*)

(Continued from preceding page)

> (3)   A statement of the injuries and a description
> of those claimed to be permanent.
>
>
> Dated, New York, August 23, 19— ,
>
>   Yours, etc.,
>
>   JONES & SMITH,
>   Attorneys for Defendants,
>   14 Mall Street,
>   New York, N. Y.
>
> TO:
>
>
> ELWOOD & ADAMS,
>   Attorneys for Plaintiffs,
>   18 Broad Street,
>   New York, N. Y.

Figure 68. Demand for Bill of Particulars.

extra copy), copy to serve on each opposing counsel, and a copy
for your file.

2. The caption is the same as that on the complaint; the title
of the case may be shortened.

3. The salutation is to opposing counsel. It is typed in solid
caps, and reads:

    SIRS: (if to a law firm)
    SIR: (if to one lawyer)
or TO.................., ATTORNEY FOR..................:

In some jurisdictions the demand for bill of particulars is addressed to the party *and* his attorney.

4. Number consecutively and indent the details demanded.

5. Type the date line at the left margin, three spaces beneath
the last numbered paragraph.

6. Type a line for signature of attorney demanding the bill.
Beneath the signature line, indicate the party he represents.

7. Type name and address of counsel to whom the demand is addressed at the left margin, several spaces beneath the signature. If the attorney's name is given in the salutation, this is not necessary.

8. There is no verification to a demand for bill of particulars.

9. Endorse legal back for original and all copies except your office copy.

10. Collate and staple in backs.

What the secretary does about the demand for bill of particulars. 1. Prepare the demand for bill of particulars.

2. Ask attorney to sign.

3. See that copy is served on opposing counsel.

4. Be sure that receipt or certificate of service is endorsed on back of original.

5. Conform your office copy.

6. *Make diary entry* of date bill of particulars must be served.

7. File original in court.

8. Make entry in suit register of service and filing.

9. If you are secretary to the attorney on whom the demand is served, make notation on back of your copy of date and hour of service. *Enter in diary date by which bill of particulars must be served.* Also make entry in suit register.

Parts of bill of particulars. The bill of particulars (bill of discovery in equity proceedings) consists of the following parts:

1. Caption
2. Salutation
3. Introduction
4. Statements of particular details required by the demand for bill
5. Date line
6. Signature of attorney
7. Name and address of attorney to whom the bill is addressed
8. Verification in some jurisdictions

How to prepare the bill of particulars. Usually the lawyer dictates the bill of particulars. Follow Figure 69 for style unless otherwise instructed. The bill of particulars is prepared like the demand for the bill, except that in almost all jurisdictions it *must* have a verification. The lawyer will tell you who is to verify the bill.

AUGUSTUS N. ROBERTSON and   *   IN THE
ELIZABETH R. ROBERTSON,
         Plaintiffs   *   CIRCUIT COURT

                       *   OF BALTIMORE COUNTY

             vs.   *

JOHNSTON—DOUGLAS MANAGEMENT   *
CORPORATION and
FREDERICK FASHIONS, INC.,   *
         Defendants

                       *

     *   *   *   *   *   *

BILL OF PARTICULARS

       The following is a bill of the particulars of the
plaintiffs' claim against the defendants, that is to say:

       (a) The accident occurred on February 23, 19—,
at approximately 9:30 o'clock A.M.

       (b) The accident occurred in the aisle between
the second and third counters from the entrance to defendants' store about midway between the ends of said counters
and nearer to the third counter.

       (c) The following amounts are claimed as special
damages:

    1. Hospital bills $ 1,758.03

    2. Physicians' services and
       medical supplies   1,023.50

    3. Nurses   1,160.00

    4. Household Assistance   904.60

    5. Transportation to hospital and
       doctor's office   43.10

       (d) Plaintiffs reside at 162 Westchester Avenue,
Baltimore, Maryland.

                                ELWOOD & ADAMS
                           Attorneys for Plaintiffs

Figure 69. Bill of Particulars.

(If verification is required, type on separate sheet.)

STATE OF SOUTH CAROLINA)   IN THE COURT OF COMMON PLEAS

COUNTY OF RICHLAND)

Perry N. Wilson,

           Plaintiff   MOTION TO MAKE COMPLAINT MORE

    vs.   DEFINITE AND CERTAIN

Lucius R. Cox,

           Defendant.

TO: Elwood & Adams, Attorneys for the Plaintiff:

      You will please take notice that the undersigned as attorneys for the defendant will move before the Honorable Richard Rogers, Judge of the Court of Common Pleas, at chambers on September 24, 19—, or as soon thereafter as counsel can be heard, for an Order directing that the complaint herein be made more definite and certain in the following particulars, by alleging:

      A. The date and time of day of the accident alleged in paragraph four (4) of the complaint.

      B. The location of the accident as alleged in paragraph four (4) of the complaint.

      C. The length of time confined to a hospital, to a bed at home and to the house as alleged in paragraph seven (7) of the complaint.

                    Jones and Smith
                    Attorneys for the defendant.

Dated at Columbia, S.C. this

10th day of September, 19—.

Figure 70. Motion to Make Pleading More Definite and Certain.

What the secretary does about the bill of particulars. A secretary's responsibilities with respect to the bill of particulars are the same as with respect to the demand for the bill. In addition, have the bill verified and notarize it before serving on opposing counsel.

Interrogatories. In some jurisdictions specific testimony may be obtained from either party by means of *interrogatories,* or written questions. Either party may file with the clerk interrogatories to be propounded to the adverse party, with an affidavit that the answers will be material testimony in the cause. The clerk then issues a copy of the interrogatories to be served upon the person to whom they are addressed, or upon his attorney. The answers to the interrogatories must be verified.

How to prepare interrogatories. 1. Make an original, a copy for the person to whom they are addressed, and a copy for your files.

2. The caption is the same as on the complaint.

3. Number the interrogatories and begin each one on a new line.

4. As the name implies, interrogatories are usually in the form of questions and each interrogatory is followed by a question mark.

5. Preferably the affidavit is typed on the last page of the interrogatories, but it may be on a separate page.

Motion to make the pleading more definite. In some jurisdiction, a party to an action obtains more specific information by filing a motion "to make the pleading more definite and certain." (See Figure 70.) The procedure is like that in any other motion. The adverse party, if the court so orders, amends his pleading in accordance with the order.

14

Specific Court Papers: What They Are and How to Prepare Them (Cont'd)

Notices

Discussion. "Notice" has more than one meaning in the field of law, but we are concerned here with the notices that play an important part in the conduct of a law suit. In this sense, a notice is a formal written advice of an act to be done or required to be done. The notice is intended to apprise opposing counsel of some proceeding in which his interests are involved. Court rules require that opposing counsel be given this notice. (Sometimes notice is given to the party to the litigation, but more frequently to his counsel.) For example, if an attorney expects to move the court for an order, notice of motion must be given opposing counsel. When the court enters an order, judgment, or decree, the prevailing counsel must give notice of entry to other interested counsel. Notice of a contemplated proceeding is not given to opposing counsel when such notice would defeat the purpose of the proceeding. For example, when a judgment creditor in an attempt to collect a judgment moves the court for an order attaching the debtor's bank account, obviously he will not give notice to the debtor or his attorney.

How to prepare a notice. Printed forms are sometimes used for notices, but more frequently they are typed on legal-size paper. The lawyer will dictate some notices, and parts of others, but you will be expected to draw many of them without dictation. Whenever you prepare a different kind, make a copy for your form book.

The kinds of notices on page 304 are illustrated in this and other chapters.

Notice of Filing and Entry (Figure 71, this chapter)

Notice of Settlement (Figure 72, this chapter)

Notice to Take Deposition upon Oral Examination (Figure 73, this chapter)

Notice of Motion (Figure 74, this chapter)

Notice of Appearance in Common Law Case (Figure 60, Chapter 13)

Notice of Appearance in Equity Case (Figure 61, Chapter 13)

Follow these figures for style; the wording might vary slightly with the jurisdiction.

1. Make an original for the court, copy for opposing counsel and a copy for your files.

2. The caption is the same as that on the complaint, but you may shorten the title of the case. Be sure to include the index number.

3. The notice is addressed usually to opposing counsel. The salutation is generally in one of the following forms:

(a) S I R: (*or* S I R S: if opposing counsel is a firm)

(b) PLAINTIFF and ELWOOD & ADAMS,
      HIS ATTORNEYS:

(c) TO:
      ELWOOD & ADAMS, ESQS.
      Attorneys for Richard Roe
      15 Albert Street
      Chicago, Illinois

4. Type the date line three spaces below the last line of the notice, at the left margin.

5. The attorney signs the notice.

6. The name and address of the attorney to whom notice is given should appear on the notice, either in the salutation or after the signature.

Backing and binding of notices. The original and copies of notices, except the office copy, are stapled in appropriately endorsed legal backs, like any other court paper. You will observe that many notices refer to an "annexed" or "attached" paper. When this is the case, the notice and the other paper are stapled together, with the notice on top, unless the other paper is to be signed by the judge. Whenever a group of papers are given to the

SRM:t 7/20/— 1-4-1

SUPREME COURT OF THE STATE OF NEW YORK

COUNTY OF NEW YORK

————————————————————————————x
                                              :
            In the Matter of
                                              :
         the Application of the   :   FILE NO.
                                                  11,422-19—
    PEOPLE OF THE STATE OF NEW YORK, by   :
    GEORGE S. VAN SCHAICK, as Superintend-
    ent of Insurance of the State of New   :
    York, for an order to take possession
    of the property and rehabilitate the   :

         EASTON FIRE INSURANCE COMPANY   :

————————————————————————————x

S I R S :
            PLEASE TAKE NOTICE that an order of which the
within is a copy was duly filed and entered in the office of
the Clerk of the County of New York on the 17th day of
July, 19—.

Dated, New York, July 20, 19—.

                              Yours, etc.,

                         Higgins & Gless
                         Attorneys for Petitioner,
                         28 Laurel Street,
                         New York, N. Y.

To:

    HENRY WHITE, ESQ.,
        Attorney for Superintendent of Insurance,
        120 Hue Street,
        New York, N. Y.

(Continued on following page)

(Continued from preceding page)

ROBERT KELLY, ESQ.,
   Attorney for Easton Fire Insurance Company
    and the Reorganization Committee,
     217 Hue Street
     New York, N. Y.

MARTIN GRAY, ESQ.,
   Attorney for certain Creditors of Easton
    Fire Insurance Company,
     39 Hue Street
     New York, N. Y.

MESSRS. GREEN & OLSON,
   Attorneys for Harris National Bank,
    15 Carrie Place,
    New York, N. Y.

Figure 71. Notice of Filing and Entry.

(To be typed on one page.)

judge for signature, any paper that he is supposed to sign is placed on top, so that he will not have to search for the appropriate paper. In the endorsement on the back, the name of the annexed paper is placed first because it is the more important paper. Thus, we have a legal back endorsed, "Undertaking and Notice of Motion"; "Order and Notice of Entry"; "Affidavit and Notice of Motion"; "Proposed Order and Notice of Settlement."

Service of notice. Since the purpose of the notice is to give information to opposing counsel, the notice must be served on him (except where service would defeat the purpose) and proof of that service filed in court. Generally notice may be served and receipt of copy or proof of service made in the same manner as service of an answer (see page 279). Enter the service and filing of notices in your suit register. If the notice refers to a date by which some action must be taken, *enter that date in your diary.* Be most meticulous about this entry, because the attorney's failure to take the required action might result in the loss of the law suit for his client. Remind the attorney of the entry in the same manner that you remind him of all diary entries (Chapter 3).

STATE OF MICHIGAN

THE CIRCUIT COURT FOR THE COUNTY OF ALGER

------------------------------------x
                                    :
MUNISING COAL CORPORATION,   :   Index No. 3548-L
                                    :
                    Plaintiff,   :
                                    :
           -against-   :   NOTICE OF SETTLEMENT
                                    :
FREDERICK MILBANK,   :
                                    :
                    Defendant.   :
------------------------------------x

To: BROWN & SMITH, ESQ.,
      Attorneys for Defendant,
        30 Avenue K,
          Munising, Michigan

S I R S :

        PLEASE TAKE NOTICE that a proposed order, of which
the annexed is a true copy, will be submitted for signature
and settlement to Honorable Edward Davis, Justice, at the
office of the Clerk of Special Term, Part II, at the Alger
County Court House, Munising, Michigan, on the 11th day of
July, 19—, at ten o'clock in the forenoon of that day.

Dated, Michigan, July 7, 19—.

                            Yours, etc.,

                                MULLIGAN & THOMPSON,
                                    Attorneys for Plaintiff,
                                      120 Hue Street,
                                        Munising, Michigan

Figure 72. Notice of Settlement.
307

JMH: 7-1—— 1-1-1

UNITED STATES DISTRICT COURT

SOUTHERN DISTRICT OF NEW YORK

——————————————————————————————————————x
                                       :
WILLIAM B. SWEET & CO., INC.,
                                       :
                          Plaintiff,   : Index No. L 69-218

                                       :

          -against-   NOTICE TO TAKE
                                       : DEPOSITION UPON
                                         ORAL EXAMINATION
ROWE STORES CORPORATION,   :

                                       :
                          Defendant.
                                       :

——————————————————————————————————————x

S I R S :

          PLEASE TAKE NOTICE that at 10:00 o'clock in the
forenoon on the 7th day of July, 19—, at the offices of
Brown & Wood, the plaintiff in the above entitled action
will take the deposition of B. Earl Rice, President of defendant Rowe Stores Corporation, who resides at 15 Shore
Road, Douglaston Manor, Long Island, New York, upon oral
examination pursuant to the Federal Rules of Civil Procedure, before an officer authorized by law to take depositions. The examination will continue from day to day until

(Continued on following page)

(Continued from preceding page)

completed. You are invited to attend and cross-examine. The

address of said offices is 15 Carrie Place, New York, N. Y.

Dated New York, July 1, 19—.

                              Yours, etc.,

                         BROWN & WOOD,
                            Attorneys for Plaintiff,
                            15 Carrie Place,
                            New York, N. Y.

To:

        ELWOOD & ADAMS
            Attorneys for Defendant
            48 Mall Street,
            New York, N. Y.

Figure 73. Notice to Take Deposition Upon Oral Examination.

(To be typed on one page.)

Motion and Notice of Motion

What is a motion? A motion is an application for an order addressed to the court or to a judge in his chambers by a party to a law suit. Whenever an attorney wants the court to take any action in a pending case, he "moves" the court to take that action. Motions are numerous and varied. They include:

Motion for Change of Venue

Motion to Strike

Motion for New Trial

Motion for Leave to Amend

Motion to Set Cause for Trial

Unless a motion is made during a hearing or trial, it is in writing. Notice of the motion is given to opposing counsel so that he will have a chance to contest it, unless notice to him would defeat the purpose of the motion.

In Federal courts and also in many other jurisdictions, the written notice to the attorney constitutes compliance with the requirement that a motion shall be in writing. Thus, we will have the written notice of motion, but no written motion, the motion being made orally at the hearing. The notice of motion states the papers and proceedings upon which the motion will be brought and also the grounds of the motion. The supporting papers usually include an affidavit that is attached to the notice of motion.

Some jurisdictions have special terms of court at which all motions are heard. In crowded jurisdictions, the contested motions are heard in one part, and *ex parte* motions (see page 592), of which opposing counsel has no notice, are heard in another part. You should acquaint yourself with the part in which they are heard, if there is a distinction in any of the courts in your locality.

Return day of motion. All notices of motion give the date the attorney will move the court for entry of the desired order. This date is the *return day* of the motion; the motion is *returnable* on that day. The practice rules provide that the notice shall be served on opposing counsel a specified number of days, or a reasonable time, before the return day of the motion. Some jurisdictions that do not have special terms of courts for motions set aside certain days in the month as motion day, on which days all motions are returnable. You will become familiar with (1) the motion days in the various courts and (2) how many days of notice are required.

Information you need to prepare a notice of motion. Figure 74 illustrates a notice of motion. They are prepared like other notices (page 303). The lawyer will dictate some notices of motions, but you should be able to prepare many of them upon instructions from him without dictation. You will need the following information:

1. Style of case. You can get this from the complaint or other papers in the file.

2. Papers and proceedings upon which the motion will be based. The lawyer usually dictates this.

3. Grounds upon which the motion will be made. The lawyer will dictate these, except when they are standard. For example, a motion to strike is always on the ground that portions of the pleadings are "sham, irrelevant and redundant." (The standard wording of the clause varies with the court.)

```
STATE OF ILLINOIS  )
                   ) SS.            IN THE CIRCUIT COURT
COUNTY OF SANGAMON )                      THEREOF



SAMUEL T. BOWEN,                )
                                )
              Plaintiff         )
                                )
                                )
        vs.                     )        NO. 431/--
                                )
ARNOLD HARRINGTON,              )
                                )
                                )
              DEFENDANT         )
```

N O T I C E

TO:
    Robert N. Carter, Esq.
    Illinois Building
    Springfield, Illinois
        Attorney for Defendant

PLEASE TAKE NOTICE that on 7th day of October, A.D. 19--, at 10:00 A.M., or as soon thereafter as counsel may be heard, we shall appear before the Honorable Roy N. Snyder, Judge of the Circuit Court, at Springfield, Illinois, and shall present the motion, true copy of which is attached hereto.

Dated this 18th day of September, A.D. 19--.

Swann and Swann
First National Bank Building
Springfield, Illinois
    Attorneys for Plaintiff

Received a true copy of the above notice, together with a copy of motion attached thereto, this ____ day of September, A.D. 19--.

_____
Attorney for Defendant

Figure 74. Notice of Motion.

311

4. Return day of motion (page 310). If you do not know how to calculate the return day, ask the lawyer.

5. Time motion will be heard. Usually court practice rules set aside a certain hour at which motions will be called. If you are not familiar with this time in the various courts, ask the lawyer or consult the rules. The notice will read "at .... o'clock in the ...... noon, or as soon thereafter as counsel can be heard."

6. Where the motion will be heard. Motions are usually heard in the court where the case is pending. In some jurisdictions specific terms, parts, departments, or divisions are set aside for motions.

7. Name of affiant and date of supporting affidavit, if the motion is based on an affidavit, as it usually is. The lawyer will give you this information. Very probably he will dictate the affidavit before he instructs you about the notice.

What the secretary does about the notice of motion and affidavit. A motion is frequently based upon an affidavit (see below), as appears from the wording of the notice. When this is the case, your responsibilities, after preparation of the notice and affidavit, are the following:

1. Endorse a legal back "Affidavit and Notice of Motion" and staple the papers together, placing the notice on top.

2. After approval by the lawyer, see that copy is served on opposing counsel.

3. See that receipt of service is on back of original. If the papers are served by mail, prepare certificate of service by mail.

4. *Enter return day of motion in your diary.*

5. Conform your office copy.

6. File original, with proof of service, in court.

7. Make entries in suit register of service and filing.

8. If you are secretary to the attorney on whom the papers are served, make notation on back of your copy of date and hour of service. *Enter in diary return day of motion.* Also make entry in suit register.

Affidavit for Use in Court

Discussion. Affidavits, other than those for use in court cases, were discussed in Chapter 10. That discussion is applicable to all affidavits. The content of an affidavit for use in court cases always relates to the case. It differs from a verification in that the affiant swears that facts stated in the affidavit are true, whereas the verifier swears to the truth of statements made in a pleading to which the verification is attached.

An affidavit for use in court cases consists of the following parts:

1. Caption
2. Title
3. Venue
4. Body
5. Signature of affiant
6. Jurat
7. Signature and seal, or stamp, of notary public

How to prepare an affidavit for court use. Figure 75 illustrates an affidavit for use in court. It is prepared like any affidavit, with this important exception: It is preceded by a caption like the one on the complaint. It differs from a verification in form in that it is complete, with caption and legal back, whereas the verification is actually a part of the pleading that it verifies.

1. Use legal-size paper.

2. Make an original for court, copy for opposing counsel, and copy for your file.

3. The caption is the same as that on the complaint, and includes the index number. The title of the case may be shortened.

4. The box is followed by recital of the venue.

5. Type a line for signature.

6. The jurat is typed at the left of the page.

7. Type a line for the notary's signature.

8. Endorse a legal back for all copies except the office copy. The endorsement will depend on what the affidavit is about. It might be "Affidavit in Opposition," or "Affidavit of Service by Mail," or any one of a number of other subjects. If another paper is bound in the back with the affidavit, the endorsement will also include the title of that paper.

9. After approval by the lawyer, have affiant sign original affidavit.

10. Notarize original and conform copies.

IN THE CIRCUIT COURT OF THE FIRST JUDICIAL DISTRICT

OF HINDS COUNTY, MISSISSIPPI

JOHN DOE,   PLAINTIFF)
)
)
)
          VS.   ) NO._____
)
)
)
RICHARD ROE,   DEFENDANT)

AFFIDAVIT OPPOSING MOTION

STATE OF MISSISSIPPI
COUNTY OF HINDS

      ROBERT HALL THOMPSON, being duly sworn, deposes
and says: He is an attorney and counsellor at law, associated with the firm of Messrs. Elwood & Adams, attorneys for
the defendant herein, and that he has knowledge of all of
the facts hereinafter set forth.

                [Set forth facts here.]

      WHEREFORE, your deponent prays that plaintiff's
motion be denied, with the costs of this motion.

_____

      SWORN TO AND SUBSCRIBED before me, this the 15th
day of December, 19——.

_____

Figure 75. Affidavit in Opposition.

Orders

Discussion. Every direction of a court, judge, or justice, made or entered in writing and not included in a judgment or decree, is called an *order*. Orders are made upon motion of counsel. A judge who decides a motion may say to counsel, "Submit order," or, "Settle order on notice." If the judge directs prevailing counsel to "submit order," counsel will prepare the order and submit it to the court without service of a copy on opposing counsel. After the order is entered, prevailing counsel serves a copy on opposing counsel with a notice that it was filed and entered in the office of the county clerk (see Figure 71).

If the judge tells counsel to "settle order on notice," the prevailing counsel is obliged to serve a copy of the proposed order on opposing counsel. Opposing counsel, in turn, is permitted to serve a "counter-order," which is his version of the judge's decision. On the date named in the order, the order and the counter-order are submitted to the judge, who will sign the order that he thinks embodies the terms of his decision. He might make changes in the order that he signs, or decide to rewrite it entirely.

If an order is entered while the court is sitting, it is called a *court order*. If it is signed by a judge, or justice, in his chambers or elsewhere while the court is not in session, it is called a *judge's order*. Both have the same legal efficacy, but in many jurisdictions there is a distinction in the form and wording.

How to prepare an order. The caption of an order entered *while the court is sitting* usually differs from the caption on the pleadings in two respects (see Figure 76):

1. It shows the term and name of the court, where the court is sitting, and the date, in a single-spaced legend at the right of the page.

2. The name of the presiding judge precedes the box. The order also has a space for the judge's signature and the initials of his title. Thus, U. S. D. J. (United States District Judge); J. S. C. (Justice of Supreme Court); J. C. C. (Justice of City Court); J. M. C. (Justice of Municipal Court), etc. In some courts the word *enter* precedes the signature, thus:

Enter,

_____

J. S. C.

At a Special Term, Part II,
of the Supreme Court of the
State of New York, held in
and for the County of Kings,
at the Courthouse thereof,
Fulton and Joralemon Streets,
in the Borough of Brooklyn,
City of New York, on the 18th
day of July, 19—.

PRESENT:

        HON. FELIX C. BENVENGA,

                    Justice.

– – – – – – – – – – – – – – – – – –x

PATRICK O'MALLEY

                  Plaintiff

     –against–

JOHN BROWN

                Defendant

– – – – – – – – – – – – – – – – –x

On reading and filing the annexed stipulation and
consent of the attorney for the plaintiff, and the attorneys
for the defendant, dated the 16th day of July, 19—, and
on motion of GEORGE RIDGEWAY, attorney for the plaintiff,
it is

ORDERED, that the testimony of the plaintiff, PATRICK
O'MALLEY, be taken as a witness in his own behalf, without
the state, pursuant to the terms of the said stipulation,
by JOHN KING, ESQ., Solicitor, residing in Downport, County
Down, Ireland, upon the interrogatories and cross-interrog-
atories annexed to the said stipulation, and it is further

(Continued on following page)

316

(*Continued from preceding page*)

```
        ORDERED, that after the taking of the said deposition
    the said JOHN KING return the same in a single packet
    securely sealed, by registered mail, postage prepaid, to
    the County Clerk of Kings County, at the courthouse, Fulton
    and Joralemon Streets, Borough of Brooklyn, City of New
    York, U.S.A., and it is further


        ORDERED, that the trial of the action be stayed until
    the return of the said deposition.
                                    E N T E R


                                    J.S.C.
```

Figure 76. Court Order.

When an order is signed by a judge *while the court is not sitting,* the caption is similar to that on the complaint. "Enter" does not precede the signature as is the case with court orders in many courts. Type the judge's title in full instead of the initials. Figure 77 illustrates a judge's order.

Although an order to show cause is a court order, it is prepared like a judge's order.

In all other respects an order is set up and typed like the pleadings.

Endorse legal backs for all copies except your office copy. If a notice is attached to the order, as is frequently the case, endorse the back "Order and Notice of Entry" (or "Notice of Settlement," or whatever the notice is called). Place the copy of the order that the judge is to sign on top of the set of papers, but in the other sets place the notice on top.

What the secretary does about an order. *When the judge instructs counsel to settle order on notice.*

1. Prepare the following three papers:
    a. Proposed order. Make an original for the court; two

IN THE CIRCUIT COURT FOR JEFFERSON COUNTY, ALABAMA

ADA REDFIELD,

                Plaintiff,

      v.

EDGAR THOMPSON,

               Defendant.

IN EQUITY

NO. 5487-X

O R D E R

The plaintiff above named having duly moved for an order_____

_____

_____;

NOW, after reading and filing the_____

_____,

on motion of Elwood & Adams, Esqs., attorneys for the plaintiff, and no one appearing in opposition thereto, it is hereby

ORDERED by the Court that_____

_____.

Dated this 6th day of July, 19__.

_____
Circuit Judge

Figure 77. Judge's Order.

copies for each opposing counsel, one to be served with notice of settlement and one to be served after the order is entered.

b. Notice of settlement. Make a copy for each opposing counsel and an office copy. The notice is not filed in court.

c. Notice of entry. If the legal back has this notice printed on the inside, you will not have to type it. If you do type it, make a copy for each opposing counsel, and an office copy.

2. Staple notice of settlement (Figure 72) on top of proposed order, a copy for each opposing counsel. The legal back will be endorsed "Proposed Order and Notice of Settlement."

3. See that service is made on opposing counsel and that receipt of service is acknowledged on the original of the order.

4. *Enter in diary* the date the proposed order will be submitted to the court.

5. Make entry in suit register of service of notice of settlement.

6. Staple notice of entry (Figure 71) on top of order, a copy for each opposing counsel. The legal back will be endorsed "Order and Notice of Entry."

7. The lawyer will take to court the original of the proposed order and the copies that are stapled with the notice of entry. The judge will "settle" the order and will make any necessary changes in pen and ink on the original of the order as submitted. If he signs and enters the order immediately, the lawyer will conform the copies to the order as entered.

8. If the judge does not sign the order immediately, make a follow-up *entry in your diary* and follow the law journal closely to see when the order is entered.

9. As soon as the order is signed, see that conformed copies with notice of entry are served on opposing counsel *immediately*. Prompt service of the settlement of order is very important, because opposing counsel's time to take an appeal begins to run when service is made, not when the order is settled.

10. Make entry in suit register of order and of service.

11. *Make entry in diary* of last day to appeal from order.

12. If you are secretary to the attorney on whom notice of

entry is served, make entries in the suit register *and in the diary*.

When the judge instructs counsel to submit order. It is not necessary to serve a copy of the order on opposing counsel before submitting it to the court or judge. No notice of settlement is necessary.

1. Make an original of the order for the court, a copy for opposing counsel, and an office copy.

2. Make copy of notice of entry for each opposing counsel and an office copy.

3. Proceed as in steps 6 through 12, above.

Findings of Fact and Conclusions of Law

What the "findings of fact and conclusions of law" are. At the trial of a case, certain facts are determined from the pleadings and evidence. Certain rules of law are applicable to those facts. After the trial of a case by the court without the jury, the court directs the attorneys to prepare a statement of the facts and applicable rules of law. This statement is designated *findings of fact and conclusions of law*. In other jurisdictions, the court directs counsel for both sides to prepare findings of fact and conclusions of law. In some jurisdictions, the court directs counsel for only one party to prepare the statement; opposing counsel then has a specified time within which to file objections and submit his proposed findings. The secretary's duties are the same in either situation.

How to prepare findings of fact and conclusions of law. The lawyer dictates the findings of fact and conclusions of law.

1. Make an original for the court, a copy for each counsel, and a copy for your file.

2. The caption is the same as on the complaint.

3. The document is entitled "Findings of Fact and Conclusions of Law."

4. The findings of fact are enumerated, beginning with FIRST, or I.

5. The conclusions of law are enumerated, beginning with FIRST, or I.

6. The date line is typed below the last conclusion of law, at the left margin.

7. Type a line for the judge's signature.

8. Endorse legal backs and all copies except your office copy.

What the secretary does about findings of fact and conclusions of law. 1. As soon as the court directs counsel to prepare findings of fact and conclusions of law, *enter in diary* the date by which the statement must be prepared.

2. See that copy is served on opposing counsel. ("Judgment," page 322, is sometimes prepared and served at the same time.)

3. See that receipt of copy is acknowledged, or make an affidavit of service by mail.

4. *Enter in diary* date by which opposing counsel must file objections and submit his proposed findings.

5. The original, with proof of service on opposing counsel, is submitted to the judge who tried the case.

6. Make entry in suit register of service, submission to judge, signing, and filing.

Instructions to the Jury

What an instruction to the jury is. When a case is tried by a jury, the court instructs or "charges" it regarding the law applicable to the action. Counsel for both sides submit to the court instructions that they want the court to give the jury. The court may give an instruction as proposed by counsel, may modify it, or may refuse to give it. Counsel may take exception to instructions given to the jury at the request of opposing counsel, or to a modification of, or refusal to give, an instruction that he proposed.

How to prepare an instruction to the jury. Many offices keep printed forms of stock instructions, but the lawyer will dictate others.

1. Make an original for the judge, a copy for opposing counsel, and an office copy.

2. Type each instruction on a separate sheet of legal paper.

3. Number each instruction for identification purposes.

4. Identify the party submitting the instructions, thus, "Plaintiff's Instruction No. ...." (This may be placed at the top or bottom of the charge; numbers are inserted later in order in which the charge is given.

5. There is no caption.

6. Instructions are not stapled in a legal back and are not endorsed.

Judgments and Decrees

What judgments and decrees are. A decision by a court, after a trial or hearing, of the rights of the parties is a *judgment*. Broadly speaking, any adjudication by a court of law or of equity is considered a judgment, but technically an adjudication by a court of equity is a *decree*. The words *judgment* and *decree* are often used synonymously by the statutes, especially now that the codes have abolished the distinction between Law and Equity. A decree usually directs the defendant to do or not to do some specific thing, as opposed to a judgment for damages in a court of law. The sentence in a criminal case is the judgment.

A decree or judgment is *interlocutory* when it leaves unsettled some question to be determined in the future; for example, a temporary injunction is an interlocutory decree. A decree or judgment is *final* when it disposes of the case, leaving no question to be decided in the future. The parties, however, may appeal to a higher court from a final judgment or decree. The execution of the judgment is *stayed* pending the higher court's decision.

A judgment is sometimes entered "on the pleadings" upon motion of counsel, before a trial of the cause is reached. For example, the plaintiff moves the court to strike the answer of the defendant and direct judgment for the plaintiff. More frequently, judgment is not entered until the case has been tried and findings of fact have been made (page 320).

How to prepare a judgment or decree. In a few jurisdictions, the clerk of the court prepares the judgments, but usually the prevailing lawyer does. The lawyer will dictate the judgment or decree. A judgment is similar in style to a court order (Figure 76). Follow Figure 78 for the style of a decree.

Number of copies. It might be necessary to prepare extra copies, in addition to the usual original for the court, copy for each opposing counsel, and your office copy. The number of copies will depend upon the following factors:

1. Number of copies to be certified for delivery to the parties.

2. Whether service of copy is made on opposing counsel with notice of entry (see page 319) after judgment is entered as well as before the judgment is submitted to the court.

3. Kind of action.

IN THE DISTRICT COURT IN AND FOR THE CITY AND COUNTY

OF DENVER AND STATE OF COLORADO

CIVIL ACTION NO. 3-504, Div. 7

ARY FRANCES HINES,

                        Plaintiff,

           –vs–   INTERLOCUTORY DECREE IN
                                                DIVORCE.

CHARLES WILLIAM HINES,

                        Defendant.

THIS CAUSE, coming on to be heard on this 9th day of
January, 19—, upon its merits, the plaintiff being represented by Elwood & Adams, attorneys of record, and the de-
dendant appearing by Ames & Thomas, attorneys of record,
and the Court having examined the full record herein, finds
that it has jurisdiction herein; and having heard the evidence and the statements of counsel, the Court now being
fully advised

DOTH FIND that a divorce should be granted to the
plaintiff herein upon the statutory grounds of_____

_____.

IT IS ORDERED, ADJUDGED and DECREED by the Court, that
an absolute divorce should be granted to the plaintiff, and
an Interlocutory Decree of Divorce is hereby entered, dis-
solving the marriage of plaintiff and defendant six months
after the date of this Interlocutory Decree.

IT IS EXPRESSLY DECREED by the Court that during such
six months period after the signing of this Interlocutory

(*Continued on following page*)

Decree the parties hereto shall not be divorced; shall still be husband and wife, and neither party shall be competent to contract another marriage anywhere during such period, and the Court during all of said period does hereby retain jurisdiction of the parties and the subject matter of this cause and upon motion of either party, or upon its motion, for good cause shown, after a hearing, may set aside this Interlocutory Decree.

It is further ORDERED, ADJUDGED and DECREED by the Court that defendant shall pay into the Registry of the District Court on the_____

_____.

It is further ORDERED, ADJUDGED and DECREED by the Court that the sole care, custody and control of the minor children, Steven Robert Hines and Marion Linda Hines, is hereby awarded to the plaintiff as a suitable person to have such care and custody until the further order of the Court, with the defendant to have reasonable visitation rights.

The Court FURTHER DECREES that after six months from the date hereof this Interlocutory Decree shall be and become a Final Decree of Divorce and the parties shall then be divorced, unless this Interlocutory Decree shall have been set aside, or an appeal has been taken, or a writ of error has been issued.

Done in open Court this 9th day of January, 19—.

BY THE COURT,

Judge.

APPROVED AS TO FORM:

Ames & Thomas
Attorneys for Defendant.

Figure 78. Interlocutory Decree of Divorce.

You will have to ask the lawyer about the number of copies, or you might get the information from a practice manual. When you prepare a judgment in the various types of actions, you should familiarize yourself with the number of copies required.

What the secretary does about a judgment or decree. 1. See that copy is served on opposing counsel. Notice is not usually attached, but findings of fact and conclusions of law (page 320) frequently accompany the judgment.

2. See that receipt of copy is acknowledged, or make affidavit of service by mail.

3. The lawyer will submit the original, with proof of service, to the judge who tried the case. If it is not signed immediately, *enter in diary* reminder to follow up.

4. When judgment has been signed and filed, the clerk of the court enters it. Check legal newspaper for book and page of entry, and note on office copy and in suit register. If entry is not made within a few days after the judgment was signed, check with the clerk of the court.

5. Serve notice of entry of judgment (see Figure 71) on opposing counsel immediately after entry. In some actions it is necessary to serve another copy of the judgment with notice of entry. This extra copy was made at the time the original was typed.

6. *Enter in diary* last day that opposing counsel may take an appeal.

7. File original notice of entry with proof of service with court. Make entry in suit register.

15

How to Keep a Progress Record
of Court Matters

IN EVERY law office a record is kept of the progress of all matters pending in court, whether the matter is a litigated case, a foreclosure, an estate administration proceeding, or a special proceeding. This record saves time that would be required to examine all of the papers in the file. A quick examination of the record shows the status of the matter. Also, just before term time the lawyer can examine quickly the records of all pending cases as a double check on things to be done. The record is variously called a suit register, a register of actions, or a docket, but the objectives and procedure are the same. This chapter explains the procedure for keeping this record and refers to it, for convenience, as the suit register.

Physical features of a suit register. The progress record of an action is typed or written on forms designed for the purpose, or on plain paper. The form or sheet used depends on where the records are kept. The records are commonly kept in (1) a loose-leaf binder, (2) the file folder, or (3) a portable tray or cabinet.

Loose-leaf binder for the suit register. Either an ordinary three-ring, letter-size binder or a post binder may be used for keeping the suit register. If the record is typed, the former is probably more expedient because the sheets are more easily removed for the purpose of typing the entries. Numerous types of forms for keeping the record are printed by various office supply houses and are on sale at local stationers. These forms are usually designed to fit a special loose-leaf binder, also manufactured by the supply house. Printed forms are not necessary, unless a special binder is used. In an ordinary loose-leaf binder, punched paper of durable quality, with reinforced edges is adequate.

File folder used for progress record. Some offices keep progress records in the file folder, either by writing the entries on the folder itself or by typing them on a sheet that is placed in the front of the folder. If the record is kept on a loose sheet, a colored sheet is desirable because it is more easily distinguished from the other papers in the folder. Figure 79 illustrates a sheet appropriate for this purpose.

COURT	HALL and DOBB	OFFICE NAME
	10 SLATE STREET	
DOCKET NO.	BOSTON, MASS.	OUR FILE NO.
SERVICES		ATTACHMENTS
	VS.	
		DATE OF WRIT
RESPONSIBLE ATTY.		RETURN DAY
ATTY. TO BE NOTIFIED		FORM OF ACTION
PLAINTIFFS ATTY.		AD DAMNUM
DEFENDENT ATTY.		NATURE OF CASE
TRUSTEE ATTY.		

COPY WITHIN	DATE FILED	DESCRIPTION	TRIAL LIST

Figure 79. Progress Record Sheet.

Portable tray or cabinet for the suit register. A portable cabinet or tray with a visible index is probably the most advantageous facility for keeping the record. The cabinet shown in Figure 80 is fireproof and has a lid that may be locked when the record is not being used. The visible index shows the name of the case, the attorney handling it, and the court index number. Celluloid tabs may be used to flag specific cases. The manufacturer of

Courtesy Remington Rand, Inc.

Figure 80. Cabinet for Action Progress Records, with Visible Index.

the cabinet or tray also manufactures strips for the index and sheets for typing the record. The sheets are designed for numerous uses and have no printing on them except a ruled space at the left for the dates. They are of heavy stock paper and come in various sizes. Unless a wide carriage machine is available for typing the record, the sheets should be small enough to fit the carriage of a standard machine. The sheets are loose in the pocket provided for them and thus are easily removed for typing entries or for reference. The portable cabinets hold a large number of cases and, therefore, are not appropriate for offices with a light docket unless they are also used to house other records, as suggested on page 138.

How to file the record sheets. The preferable method of filing the record sheets is alphabetically according to the first-named plaintiff, or the decedent in the case of an estate, or the principal corporation or individual named in a special proceeding. In offices with a heavy docket, the estates and special proceedings might be segregated from the litigated cases. Some offices with extremely heavy dockets separate the records according to the court in which the case is pending. When a visible index is used, celluloid tabs of various colors can designate specific courts, if it is desirable to be able to select quickly the cases pending in a particular court.

When and how to open a case in the suit register. A suit register sheet is not opened on every matter in the office—it is opened only on court matters. Therefore, the record is opened when the first paper is filed in court, or when a paper is served on your office, indicating that the case is pending in court. In opening the record, enter on the sheet (1) the court in which the action is pending; (2) the full title of the case, as it appears on the summons and complaint or other first paper filed; (3) nature of the proceeding, that is, "Suit on note," "Divorce," "Petition for letters of administration," and the like, as indicated by the new matter slip (page 16); (4) amount, if any, sued for; (5) names, addresses, and telephone numbers of all opposing counsel; (6) name of the attorney in your office who is handling the matter; (7) court index number as soon as available; (8) calendar number, as soon as available.

All of the above information is put at the top of the record sheet. The entries follow, and each entry is dated at the left side of the sheet. Figure 81 illustrates a suit register record.

What to enter. Some offices record only court papers and orders in the suit register. The office record is then actually a duplicate of the court docket kept by the clerk of the court; hence, the name "office docket." Many offices enter all written, formal steps in connection with an action. It is often a matter of practice and judgment as to what to enter. Obviously, you would not enter, "Received phone call from plaintiff's attorney asking when we thought case would be reached; told him we had no definite esti-

SUPREME COURT—NEW YORK COUNTY   INDEX NO. 19000-19—

```
JOHN DOE CORPORATION,                    : ACTION FOR $250,000 FOR BREACH OF CONTRACT FOR FAILURE
                                         : TO COMPLETE DELIVERY OF JEEPS AND TRUCKS PURSUANT TO
                    Plaintiff,           : TERMS OF WRITTEN AGREEMENT DATED MAY 26, 19—.
                                         :
          -against-                      : John Doe, Esq.;      Elwood & Adams,
                                         : Attorney for Plaintiff, Attorneys for Defendant,
                                         : 237 Broadway,          Partner in Charge:   Mr. Dee
RICHARD ROE CORPORATION,                 : New York, N.Y.        Principal Assistant: Mr. Blank
                    Defendant.           :
```

19—

July   13   Summons and verified complaint served on defendant.
August   1   Obtained stipulation extending defendant's time to answer or move with respect to complaint
             to and including August 21, 19—.
        21   Served verified answer to complaint on attorney for plaintiff and obtained "copy received."
        21   Served demand for a verified bill of particulars.
        31   Signed stipulation extending plaintiff's time to serve a verified bill of particulars to
             and including September 20, 19—.
Sept.   19   Gave "copy received" on plaintiff's verified bill of particulars.
        20   Served note of issue noticing this case for trial for the October 19— Term to be tried by
             Court with a jury on attorney for plaintiff and obtained "copy received"; filed original
             with County Clerk of New York County and obtained Index No. 19000-19—; filed copy with
             Trial Term Calendar Clerk, and obtained Jury Contract Calendar No. 17000.
Oct.   6   Mr. Blank attended on call of Contract Jury Reserve Calendar and this case was adjourned
             by consent to the Reserve Calendar of the Contract Jury Calendar for the November 19—
             Term.
Nov.   10   Mr. Blank attended on call of Contract Jury Reserve Calendar and this case was adjourned by
             consent to the Reserve Calendar of the Contract Jury Calendar for the February 19— Term.

19—		
Feb.	9	Mr. Dee attended on call of Contract Jury Reserve Calendar and requested the Court to set this case down for a day certain because two important witnesses must come from Japan; the Court marked this case for the head of the Ready Day Calendar for trial on March 5, 19—.
March	5	Mr. Dee attended on call of Day Calendar and this case was assigned to Mr. Justice Carter, at Trial Term, Part X.
	5	Mr. Dee reports that a jury was picked and the trial commenced at 2:00 P.M. and is to continue on March 6, 19— at 10:00 A.M.
	6	Mr. Dee reports that the trial went on all day and is to continue on March 7, 19—.
	7	Mr. Dee reports that plaintiff rested, Court reserved decision on motions to dismiss and defendant's case was commenced to be continued on March 8, 19—.
	8	Mr. Dee reports that defendant rested, the usual motions for a directed verdict were made and decision reserved, both sides summed up to the jury and the Court is to charge the jury on March 9, 19— at 10:00 A.M.
	9	Mr. Dee reports that after the Court's charge, the jury retired, and after four hours deliberation returned a verdict in favor of defendant, the Court denied plaintiff's motions to set the verdict aside and for a new trial, etc.
	12	Entered judgment dismissing plaintiff's complaint with costs as taxed in the sum of $145.00.
	12	Served judgment with notice of entry and copy of bill of costs as taxed on attorney for plaintiff and obtained "copy received."
April	17	Plaintiff paid judgment for costs as taxed amounting to $145.00 and we filed a satisfaction of said judgment.

Figure 81. Suit Register Record.

331

mate." That does not affect the progress of the case. But, also obviously, you would enter, "Served notice of trial for October 19. . Term," just as soon as the notice of trial was served on the opposing counsel. The best rule is to use your own judgment as to what actually affects the progress of the action and to enter too much rather than too little. If you are in doubt as to the advisability of making an entry, ask the lawyer in charge.

Form and sufficiency of record. In making entries in the suit register give complete information. Describe the matter entered with particularity, but not in great detail. Observance of the following directions will help you make complete and accurate entries:

1. Date all entries.

2. Avoid abbreviations.

3. When an action is commenced by the service of a summons only, open the record sheet immediately but you cannot enter the nature and substance of the action until the complaint is received. Enter this information opposite the title as soon as the complaint is received.

4. When an answer or notice of appearance is served on your office, enter the name of the attorney, his address and telephone number, and the party he represents.

5. As soon as you know the court index number, enter it opposite the title. Also enter it on the index tab if you keep a record that has a visible index (page 328).

As a condition precedent to proper filing, the court index or docket number must be placed on every paper that is filed. The individual who files the paper on behalf of your office must get the index number from the clerk of the court or from his docket and give it to you so that you can enter it on the record. Make a practice of checking the suit register weekly for any missing index numbers.

6. Keep the entries opposite the title up to date, including index number, substitutions of attorneys, changes of addresses, office file number, and the like.

7. In describing petitions, orders, and stipulations, enter a notation as to when they are verified, signed, entered, or dated, respectively, and by whom.

8. When entering stipulations, enter, "Obtained stipulation

. . ." if your office is granted something by it; enter "Signed stipulation . . ." if your office gives a right. For example, if your office represented the plaintiff, the entry of the stipulation illustrated in Figure 65, Chapter 13, would be:

Signed stipulation with Jones & Smith, dated September 25, 19.. extending time of Frederick Fashions, Inc. to answer to October 13, 19...

If your office represented the Frederick Fashions, Inc., the entry would read:

Obtained stipulation from Elwood & Adams, dated September 23, 19.., extending time to answer to October 13, 19...

Some stipulations, for example a stipulation of discontinuance, are both "obtained" and "signed."

9. Enter the name of the attorney from your office who attends motions, calls of calendar at trials, hearings, arguments of appeals, and the like, and the disposition of the respective matters.

10. Enclose in quotation marks any entry from a law journal or similar publication with a reference to the date and page of the publication, because the date of the event is often different from the date upon which the event is announced in the publication.

11. When cases are settled out of court, enter the amounts paid, dates of payment, data concerning exchange of general releases, if any, and the like.

12. When judgment is entered, enter the amount of the judgment, the amount of costs, and payment received, if any.

13. Examine the diary (Chapter 3) each day for the day just past, to be certain that a report and entry has been made for everything listed there.

Closing the record of a case. Do not close the record of a case in the suit register until you are reasonably certain that no further steps, such as appeal, collecting on a judgment, moving to vacate a judgment, recording a satisfaction, levying execution, and the like, are to be taken by either party. The time to appeal should always have elapsed before the case is closed.

As soon as a case is closed, remove the sheet on that case from the record file and place it in the designated place. This might be another loose-leaf book, or a file cabinet. File the sheets alphabetically according to the first-named plaintiff, or the decedent in the case of an estate, or the principal corporation or individual named in a special proceeding. The closed sheets are kept indefinitely; some law offices have them bound from time to time.

16

When a Case Is Appealed: Records, Briefs, Citations

T HE PARTY who loses a law suit, or who is dissatisfied with a judgment or court order or decree, may ask a higher court to review the decision of the lower court with the hope that the higher court will reverse or modify the lower court's decision. When a case is appealed, the lawyers for each party file a *brief* with the appellate court in support of their contentions. This chapter tells about procedure for review by a higher court. It also gives the fundamentals that affect your part in the preparation of a brief. Illustrations show the appearance of typed and printed briefs.

Rules of the reviewing court. The procedure for taking a case to a higher court is governed by the rules of the highest state tribunal. These rules are based upon the civil practice acts or codes of civil procedure and are usually found in an appendix to the act or code. They may also be obtained in pamphlet form from the clerk of the appellate court or from the state judicial council. The United States Supreme Court makes the rules for appeals to it and, also, for appeals from Federal district courts to Federal courts of appeal.

You can easily find in these rules the information you should have in order to do your part of the appellate work in accordance with the court's requirements. The rules provide, among other things, for the following:

1. Methods for review
2. Content of the record on appeal
3. Form of testimony (question and answer, narrative, or abstract)

335

4. Preparation and format of record
5. Preparation and format of brief
6. Time allowed for filing and service of papers
7. Method of service on opposing counsel
8. Costs

Methods for review by a higher court. The method for review by the higher tribunal is by *appeal* from the lower court to the higher court, in the majority of states. In a few states, the method is by a petition to the higher court for a *writ of error*. At one time chancery cases were reviewed by means of an appeal and law cases by means of a writ of error. This distinction in appellate procedure no longer exists except in a few states. Regardless of the method for review, the procedure is loosely referred to as *taking an appeal, appealing a case*. The use of the term *appeal* here embraces both appeals and writs of error.

A case may also be referred to a higher court, under special circumstances, by means of extraordinary writs, such as *certiori, mandamus, habeas corpus, prohibition, quo warranto,* and *stay writs*. These writs eliminate the necessity of hearings and trials in the lower court.

In some states the appeal is to an intermediate appellate court (see page 230) and thence to the highest state court. In states that do not have intermediary appellate courts (and in certain cases even if they do), the appeal is direct from the trial court to the highest court. The procedure for taking an appeal to an intermediate appellate court is similar to, but not exactly the same as, taking an appeal to the highest state tribunal. The main variations are in the details, such as the time allowed for the various steps taken, disbursements to be paid, whether the papers are to be typewritten or printed, and the size and quality of paper that is to be used. Check the rules of the intermediate appellate court.

Diary entries. The reviewing court's rules require that an appeal shall be perfected according to a strict time table. It is your duty to make diary entries of the schedule so that there will be no slip-up on the part of your office. You should also note the progress of the appeal in the suit register (see Chapter 15). The rules of some courts provide for return days of appeals, just as they do for pleadings (see page 273). Other courts consider the date upon which the record on appeal is filed as the date from

which the time for filing motions and briefs shall run. You can
get the appropriate time table from the reviewing court's rules,
or the lawyer will give it to you. Dates by which the following
steps must be taken should be entered in the diary:

1. Filing notice of appeal by appellant
2. Assignment of errors and instructions by appellant for making up transcript of record
3. Filing of additional instructions by appellee
4. Filing of record on appeal in reviewing court
5. Appellee's motion to quash or dismiss an appeal
6. Hearing of motions
7. Filing of appellant's brief
8. Filing of appellee's brief
9. Filing of appellant's reply brief

Change in caption of case. From the time that the record is
filed with the appellate court, the caption of the case changes.
The caption on all motions and briefs thereafter filed shows the
name of the appellate court, and the designation of the parties
shows their appellate status. The lower court's index number of
the case is no longer indicated.

Designation of parties to an appeal. In almost all of the states
the party appealing is referred to as the *appellant,* and the party
opposing the appeal is referred to as the *appellee* or the *respondent.* When the defendant in the lower case is the appellant, the
title of the case is reversed in the majority of the states. Thus,
John Smith v. Alfred Jones becomes *Alfred Jones v. John Smith.*
But this is not the practice in all of the states. Eight methods of
designating parties on appeal in the caption are on page 338.
Table VIII, following these examples, lists the states and indicates the style followed in each state, assuming that the title of
the case in the lower court was *John Jones v. Albert Smith* and
the defendant brings the appeal to the highest state court. In
cases where review is by petition for a writ, the party appealing is
designated as the petitioner, and the other party as the *respondent.*

Although the designation of the parties changes in the title of
the case, the briefs sometime refer to the parties by their designation in the lower court. (Some rules require this designation.)
Or the brief might refer to a party by the lower court designation

on one page and by the appellate court designation on the other. The change in designation is very confusing, and the lawyer might inadvertently refer to the defendant-appellant when he means plaintiff-appellant, or to the plaintiff when he means plaintiff-in-error. Before the lawyer commences to dictate a brief to you, fix firmly in your mind the designation of the parties in both the trial and appellate courts so that you will observe any error in designation of parties.

STYLES OF DESIGNATION OF PARTIES ON APPEAL BY DEFENDANT TO HIGHEST STATE COURT WHEN TITLE OF CASE IN LOWER COURT WAS

John Jones, Plaintiff, vs. Albert Smith, Defendant

Style 1 (Names reversed)

Albert Smith,
    Appellant,
    vs.
John Jones,
    Appellee.

Style 2 (Names not reversed)

John Jones,
    Plaintiff and Respondent,
    vs.
Albert Smith,
    Defendant and Appellant.

Style 3 (Names not reversed)

John Jones,
    Plaintiff and Appellee,
    vs.
Albert Smith,
    Defendant and Appellant.

Style 4 (Names reversed)

Albert Smith,
    Plaintiff-in-Error
    vs.
John Jones,
    Defendant-in-Error.

Style 5 (Names not reversed)

John Jones,
    Appellee,
    vs.
Albert Smith,
    Appellant

Style 6 (Names not reversed)

John Jones,
    Respondent,
    vs.
Albert Smith,
    Appellant.

Style 7 (Names reversed)

Albert Smith,
    Appellant and Defendant,
    vs.
John Jones,
    Respondent and Plaintiff.

Style 8 (Names reversed)

Albert Smith,
    Defendant Below, Appellant,
    vs.
John Jones,
    Plaintiff Below, Appellee

TABLE VIII

DESIGNATION OF PARTIES ON APPEAL TO HIGHEST STATE COURT

State	Designation	State	Designation
Alabama	Style 1	Nevada	Style 7
Alaska	Style 1	New Hampshire[1]	
Arizona	Style 1	New Jersey	Style 2
Arkansas	Style 1	New Mexico	Style 3
California	Style 2	New York	Style 2
Colorado	Style 4	North Carolina[2]	
Connecticut	Style 3	North Dakota	Style 2
Delaware	Style 8	Ohio	Style 3
Florida	Style 1	Oklahoma	Style 4
Georgia	Style 4	Oregon	Style 6
Hawaii	Style 1	Pennsylvania	Style 5
Idaho	Style 2	Rhode Island[1]	
Illinois	Style 3	South Carolina	Style 2
Indiana	Style 1	South Dakota	Style 6
Iowa	Style 1	Tennessee	Style 1
Kansas	Style 5	Texas	Style 1[3]
Kentucky	Style 1	Utah	Style 2
Louisiana	Style 3	Vermont[1]	
Maine	Style 5	Virginia	Style 1
Maryland	Style 1	Washington	Style 6
Massachusetts[2]		West Virginia	Style 1
Michigan	Style 3		(Equity)
Minnesota	Style 2		Style 4
Mississippi	Style 1		(Law)
Missouri	Style 6	Wisconsin	Style 7
Montana	Style 2	Wyoming	Style 2
Nebraska	Style 3		

[1] Title in both trial court and appellate court: John Jones vs. Albert Smith. There is no designation.
[2] Not reversed. Designation the same as in the trial court.
[3] Except that in the Supreme Court the person seeking relief is called the "Petitioner" and the other party is the "Respondent."

Notice of appeal. Under the rules of a typical state, the filing of a *notice of appeal* with the clerk of the court whose order is appealed from gives the appellate court jurisdiction, and an appeal is deemed to have commenced. The time usually allowed for filing a notice of appeal is 30 days (see the rules) after receipt of a copy of the judgment with notice of entry.

You can get the wording of the notice of appeal from the court rules or from a form book, or the lawyer will dictate it or give you a form to follow. Set it up in the same manner and use the same kind of paper as for other court papers.

1. Make an original, a copy for each appellee, and a copy for your files (but see 5 below).

2. The caption is the same as that on the pleadings.

3. Bind in a legal back, properly endorsed.

4. The attorney for the party who appeals signs the notice of appeal.

5. Serve a copy on counsel for appellee, and file the original, with proof of service, with the clerk of the court. In some states the rules do not require service of notice of appeal on opposing counsel, but a copy is usually given to him for his file. In other states the rules require that the notice be filed in duplicate, one containing the proof of service.

Service on opposing counsel. Service of all papers and notices required by the rules of the appellate court may be made by leaving the same in the office of the opposing counsel during regular office hours with a person in charge of the office, or by depositing it, securely sealed and post paid, in the post office directed to such attorney at his usual post office address. Proof of service is made by affidavit. You, as the lawyer's secretary, probably will be the one who mails the document and, therefore, the one who makes the affidavit, when service is had by mail. Placing the properly sealed and addressed document in an "outgoing basket" to be dispatched by the mail clerk in your office is not compliance with the statute. You must actually do what the affidavit of service says. Figure 82 illustrates an affidavit of service by mail. If the wording of the affidavit used in your office differs, make an extra copy for your form book.

Notice that the affidavit is preceded by the caption of the case. When this affidavit is copied into the record on appeal, the caption will be omitted, but the recital of venue will be included.

Contents and Preparation of the Record on Appeal

What is a record on appeal? A record on appeal is a copy of the pleadings, exhibits, orders or decrees filed in a case in the lower court, and a transcript of the testimony taken in the case. The purpose of the record is to inform the appellate court of what transpired in the lower court. The rules specify that the record shall be abbreviated as much as possible, so that the judges will not have to wade through a mass of extraneous material. The appellate court does not need to be informed about matters that are not pertinent to the decision of the questions before it. Furthermore, the larger the record, the more expensive it is.

IN THE CIRCUIT COURT OF THE ELEVENTH
JUDICIAL CIRCUIT OF FLORIDA, IN AND
FOR DADE COUNTY. IN CHANCERY.

```
----------------------------------------x
JOHN JONES,                    :        No. 13,670-C

              Plaintiff,       :

      vs.                      : AFFIDAVIT OF SERVICE

ALBERT SMITH,                  :

              Defendant.       :
----------------------------------------x
```

STATE OF FLORIDA,)
              : SS.
DADE COUNTY.   )

    Before the subscriber personally appeared MARY ED-
WARDS, who, being first duly sworn, deposes and says that
she is employed by Elwood and Adams and was so employed on
January 8, 19—; that on said date she personally placed in
an envelope addressed to J. W. Brown, Jr., Esq., a true
copy of the foregoing Notice of Appeal; that said envelope,
having been properly addressed and sealed, with sufficient
postage affixed thereto, was deposited by her on said date
in the United States Mails at Miami, Florida.

                                             _____

Subscribed and Sworn to Before Me
This 8th day of January, 19—.

_____
Notary Public, State of Florida
at Large.
My commission expires: 5/8/—.
(SEAL)

Figure 82. Affidavit of Service by Mail.

341

Assignment of errors and instructions to the clerk. Within a certain number of days after the notice of an appeal is filed, the number being specified by the rules, the appellant files assignments of error and directions to the clerk for making up the transcript of record on appeal. The assignments of error and directions to the clerk may be combined in one document.

The purposes of an assignment of errors are to apprise the appellate court of the specific questions presented by the appellant for consideration, and to inform the opposite party of the matters of error relied on, so that discussion may be limited and concentrated on those points.

The directions to the clerk designate the portion of the proceedings and evidence to be included in the transcript of record —those portions pertinent to the questions before the appellate court. The appellee might consider that other portions of the record will throw light on the questions to be reviewed by the court. If so, the appellee files additional directions and cross-assignments.

In lieu of directions to the clerk the parties may file written stipulations with the clerk designating the contents of the record.

Preparation. The directions for preparing the notice of appeal apply also to assignments of error and instructions to the clerk (see page 339). The originals are filed with the clerk of the court, and copies are served on counsel for the appellee. Proof of service of these documents on opposing counsel is filed with the clerk and included in the transcript of record.

Who prepares the record. The clerk of the court or the appellant prepares the record from the directions to the clerk filed by the parties. The common practice is to employ a court reporter to make up the transcript, but as secretary to the attorney for the appellant, it will sometimes be your task to prepare the record.

How to prepare the record. The instructions to the clerk will indicate to you the documents and evidence that are to be included in the record. You will copy them from the papers in the court file, which you may obtain from the clerk of the court. The following directions are applicable to the preparation of records in any state:

1. Omit formal parts of documents.

2. Copy pleadings in the order of filing.

3. In the center of the page, just above the pleading, put in solid caps the nature or kind of document, such as "Demurrer to Amended Complaint" (not simply "Demurrer").

4. Do not copy the caption of the pleadings.

5. Indicate the filing date of each pleading by typing "Filed" and the date at the end of the pleading. This information is usually stamped on the back of the document.

6. The first page in the record is a complete index that gives in chronological order the date of the filing of each instrument in the court below, the name or character of the instrument, and the page of the record where the same may be found. The index is prepared last.

Format and make-up of record. *Consult the rules.* They provide whether the record shall be printed or typewritten, or either. They also specify the kind of paper, size of type, folio size, and the like. Here are the requirements in a typical state that permits a record to be either printed or typewritten. If directions refer to printed records, see Chapter 17, "Preparing Material for the Printer." The following requirements also apply to briefs.

1. Black and distinct lettering
2. Type no smaller than small pica
3. Double spaced (this requirement is stated in terms of leading for a printed brief)
4. Margin no less than one inch
5. Quoted material indented and singled spaced (for a printed record this requirement is stated in terms of ems)
6. Opaque, white, unglossed paper
7. Legal cap if typewritten; 6 by 9 inch folio if printed

Binding, volumes, and title. The record is bound in pamphlets. If typewritten, the pamphlets are securely fastened; if printed, they are stitched. If the record consists of more than 200 pages, it should be bound in two or more volumes. The cover of each volume contains the style of the cause, the title of the appellate court, the title of the court from which the cause is appealed, and the names and addresses of counsel, and, if more than one volume, the number of the volume.

Certification, filing, and service. The record is certified by the clerk of the lower court, and also verified by him if he does not prepare it. A copy (or copies) is served on opposing counsel, and the original and required number of copies (see the rules) filed with the clerk of the appellate court, together with proof of service. The record must be filed within the time specified by the rules. A filing fee is required at the time the record is filed.

The Brief

Nature of a brief. Black's Law Dictionary gives the following complete, yet concise, definition of a brief: "A written or printed document, prepared by counsel to serve as the basis of an argument upon a cause in an appellate court, and usually filed for the information of the court. It embodies the law which the counsel desires to establish, together with the arguments and authorities upon which he rests his contention." *Brief* is short for *brief of argument*.

The brief must contain a history of the appealed case, a statement of the questions or points involved, and the argument. The history is a concise statement of the essential facts without argument. It states the purpose of the litigation, contains a chronological enumeration of the pleadings, the issues, and the judgment of the trial court, giving references to applicable pages of the transcript. The questions or points should be stated as concisely as possible. Each one is numbered and set forth in a separate paragraph and is usually followed by a statement of whether it was answered in the negative or the affirmative by the trial court. The section of the brief entitled *Argument* contains a division for each of the questions involved, with discussion and citation of authorities.

Preliminaries to preparing the brief. Before the lawyer dictates the brief, he *briefs* cases to be used in support of his position. This means that he makes a summary, digest, or abstract of a case, quoting pertinent parts from the court's opinion. Although the lawyer will dictate notes of these abstracts to you, the dictation will consist principally of instructions to take-in (see page 147) excerpts of the court's opinion. Type each summary on a separate sheet of paper. Put the name of the case and the citation at the top of the sheet, double space the lawyer's language and indent and single space the take-ins. No copy is necessary.

Check carefully the spelling of names and the volume and page number of citations. After typing the notes, have someone read back the take-ins, if possible. This is especially important if the book quoted from is a borrowed book that must be returned before the final brief is written.

Time element. The court rules provide that the appellant must file his brief within a specified number of days after the record is filed, and that the appellee has a specified number of days thereafter to file his brief. The appellant then has an additional time in which to file a reply brief. The timing is close. If the brief is to be printed, there is a deadline by which the manuscript must reach the printer. Unfortunately, many lawyers are inclined to put off the preparation of a brief until the last minute, and there is nothing you can do about it except remind the lawyer of the date the brief must be filed.

Preparation of the brief. *Draft.* Type a rough draft of the dictated brief. Occasionally the lawyer will dictate part of a brief and then, because of the press of other matters, be unable to complete the dictation for a day or two. In the meantime, you should transcribe your notes and place a copy on his desk for reference when he is able to work again on the brief.

Number of copies. After the lawyer revises the draft, retype it, making the number of copies required by the rules, unless the lawyer asks for a second draft. If the brief is to be printed, make an original and two copies—the original for the printer, one copy for the lawyer, and one for your files.

Format. Figure 83 illustrates a page from a typed brief, Figure 84 from a printed brief. The rules governing the format of the record (see page 343) apply to briefs. Notice also the following points about the make-up of a brief:

1. The questions or points are typed in solid caps or printed in bold face.

2. When several cases are cited in support of the same proposition, they are placed one under the other unless they are in a quotation.

Index and list of authorities cited. A brief of more than 12 pages (consult the rules) must be indexed and prefaced by an alphabetical list of the authorities cited. These pages are numbered with small roman numerals. The index is actually a table of contents. Figure 85 illustrates an index; Figure 86, the list

I

THE BROAD POWERS GIVEN UNDER THE WILL CLEARLY IN-
DICATE AN INTENTION TO PERMIT THE EXECUTORS AND
TRUSTEES TO MAKE THE PROPOSED TEN-YEAR LEASE AND
OTHER LONG-TERM LEASES

By the terms of Article EIGHT of the Last Will and
Testament of_____

_____

Article EIGHT reads in part as follows:

"I hereby give to my Executors or Executor and
to my Trustees or Trustee, as the case may be, and
to such of them and their successors or successor as
shall qualify or may be acting for the time being,
full power, authority and discretion to manage and
operate any property which I may leave; * * * and
in general to do and perform all acts which seem to
them wise and necessary for the proper management,
investment and reinvestment of my estate, it being
my intention and direction that they should have the
widest possible powers, authority and discretion in
relation thereto." (Italics ours.)

Among the powers expressly conferred upon the Trustees
by the testator_____

_____

In Corse v. Corse, 144 N. Y. 569, 572, power to grant
leases for a term not limited_____

_____

See cases in point.

Goddard v. Brown, 12 R. I. 31, 46, 47 (1821);
Holland v. Bogardus-Hill Drug Co., 314 Mo. 214;
        284 S. W. 121;
Lord v. Roberts, 84 N. H. 517; 153 Atl. Rep. 1, 3;
Matter of Jones, 122 F. 2d 853.

Figure 83. Page from Typed Brief.

of cases. In this list, the titles of the cases cited are not necessarily underscored or in italics. Underscoring of a long list of
authorities takes considerable time.

Notice in the illustration (Figure 86) that there is no volume
and page number cited for the case of *City of Miami Beach v.
Perrell*. It sometimes happens that a case is cited before the

9

ARGUMENT.

PART I.

An Answer to the Spurious Questions Posed by the Appellants.

The Court can dispose of this case either on narrow technical grounds which will result in its being tried over again and appealed again, or on broad equitable principles. We hope it will choose the latter and thus effectively put an end to this controversy that has already gone on too long and caused too much ill feeling in the Village.[2] The whole trend of modern judicial thought is away from decisions on pin points. This case was fully and fairly submitted to the Chancellor who gave the parties almost unlimited opportunity to present everything they had. The appellants failed miserably to establish any defense and are asking this Court to reverse the case on the sheerest technicalities.

The City's Brief.

The first, second and fifth questions posed by the appellant, Miami Shores Village, can be treated together. They are:

"FIRST QUESTION.

May a property owner resort to the courts for relief from alleged oppressive zoning without first having exhausted the administrative remedies?

---

[2]See Plaintiff's Exhibits Nos. 10 and 11 in Appendix.

Figure 84. Page from Printed Brief.

INDEX

History of the Case _____ 1

Appellants' Statement of the Questions Involved _____ 4

Appellee's Statement of the Questions Involved—

    Question No. 1 _____ 4

    Question No. 2 _____ 5

Foreword _____ 6

Argument—

    Part I. An Answer to the Spurious Questions
    Posed by the Appellants _____ 9

        The City's Brief _____ 9

        A Planning Board or Adjustment Board Would
        Have Had No Authority to Change the
        Zoning _____ 12

    Question No. 1 _____ 23

    Part II. An Outline of the Position of the Prop-
    erty Owner and an Over-all Discussion of the
    Case _____ 25

        Estoppel _____ 34

    Question No. 2 _____ 37

    Part III. A Detailed Discussion of the Evidence
    Containing References to the Transcript of Rec-
    ord _____ 41

    The Testimony for the Plaintiff—

        Walter _____ 42

        D. _____ 49

        Leonard A. _____ 55

        Adrian _____ 58

        Lon _____ 61

Figure 85. Index to Brief.

INDEX III

.AUTHORITIES CITED

Allen v. *Avondale Co.* (1938), 135 Fla. 6, 185 So. 137 28

Barton v. *Moline Properties* (1935), 121 Fla. 683, 164 So.
551, 103 A. L. R. 725 30

City of Coral Gables v. *State ex rel. Worley* (1950), 44
So. 2d 298 18

City of Fort Lauderdale v. *Smith* (1950), 44 So. 2d
302 107

City of Miami Beach v. *Daoud* (1942), 149 Fla. 514, 6
So. 2d 847 ....50, 110

City of Miami Beach v. *First Trust Co.* (1950), 45 So.
2d 681 ....31, 42, 50, 108

City of Miami Beach v. *Gulf Oil Corp.* (1940), 141 Fla.
642, 194 So. 236 100

City of Miami Beach v. *Perrell* (1951), ... So. 2d
....11, 109

City of Miami Beach v. *Sun Oil Company* (1940), 141
Fla. 645, 194 So. 237 100

City of Miami Beach v. *Texas Company* (1940), 141 Fla.
616, 194 So. 368 98

Dade County v. *Thompson* (1941), 146 Fla. 66, 200 So.
212 29

De Carlo v. *Town of West Miami* (1950), 49 So. 2d
596 ....12, 110

Downs v. *Kroeger* (1927), 200 Cal. 743, 254 P. 1101 29

Ehinger v. *State* (1941), 147 Fla. 129, 2 So.. 2d 357 103

Forde v. *City of Miami Beach* (1941), 146 Fla. 676, 1 So.
2d 642 ....32, 36, 37, 101

Glogger v. *Bell* (1941), 146 Fla. 1, 200 So. 100 100

Green Point Savings Bank v. *Board of Zoning Appeals*
(1939), 281 N. Y. 534, 24 N. E. 2d 319 11

Harrington v. *Board of Adjustment, City of Alamo
Heights* (Tex. 1939), 124 S. W. 2d 401 ....11, 16

Figure 86. List of Authorities Cited in Brief.

court's opinion is published in the reporter, or even in the advance sheets. The page and volume numbers are then left blank. Should the opinion be published before the brief is filed, the reference may be inserted.

Cover and binding. The cover of the brief contains the name of the court, the style of the case, identification of the brief

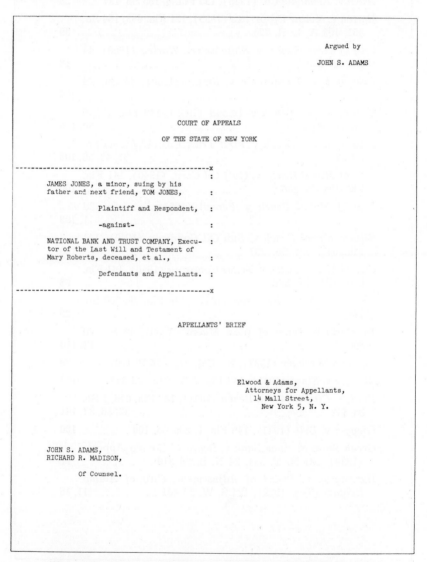

Figure 87. Cover for Brief on Letter-Size, or Smaller, Paper.

IN THE SUPREME COURT OF FLORIDA

MIAMI SHORES VILLAGE,
Appellant,

vs.

BESSEMER PROPERTIES, INCORPORATED,
Appellee.

BRIEF OF APPELLEE.

Connelly Karter Behnke Ott & Martin
627 Ingraham Building,
Miami, Florida,
Attorneys for Appellee.

Figure 88. Cover for Printed Brief (6 x 9 inches).

(the party filing it), and the name and address of the attorneys representing the party filing the brief. When the brief is typed on legal-size paper, use a legal back, endorsed with these items, and staple at the top. When the brief is typed on letter-size paper, use double covers and staple at the side. Some rules specify different colors for the backs of the appellant's brief, the appellee's brief, and the appellant's reply brief. Figures 87 and 88 illustrate brief covers.

Filing and service. The rules specify the number of copies of the brief that must be filed with the clerk of the appellate court and the number of copies that must be served on opposing counsel. Service on opposing counsel may be by mail or in person. Proof of service must be made to the appellate court.

Application for oral argument. Although witnesses do not appear before appellate courts, the lawyers are permitted to argue the case before the court. In many cases the lawyer feels that the brief is sufficient and does not choose to argue the case. If he wishes to appear before the appellate court, he makes application for oral argument at the time the brief is filed. Copy of the application is served on opposing counsel in the same manner that the brief is served.

Procedure when having a brief printed. "Handling Material for Printing," Chapter 17, tells the secretary in detail how to prepare material for the printer and how to follow through until the material is in printed form. It also gives her the information she needs about printing in order to be able to assume this responsibility efficiently. Figure 89 is a page of typed manuscript from a brief, marked for the printer in accordance with the directions given in Chapter 17. (Figure 84 illustrates the same page after it is printed.) Printers who specialize in court work are usually familiar with the requirements of the court rules.

Upon receipt of the galley proofs, the lawyer will read the brief again and make any changes he desires. You have the following responsibilities:

1. Proofread for typographical errors (see Chapter 17).

2. Check the make-up, that is, see that material that should be in boldface type is in boldface; quotations are indented, etc.

3. Compare the quotations with the source from which taken, or, if this is impractical, with your manuscript.

4. Check the citations, preferably by reference to the cited case in the reporter; otherwise, against your manuscript.

5. Check the record references against the record itself.

6. Return the corrected proof to the printer with instructions as to number of copies to be printed, stock and color of cover, and the like.

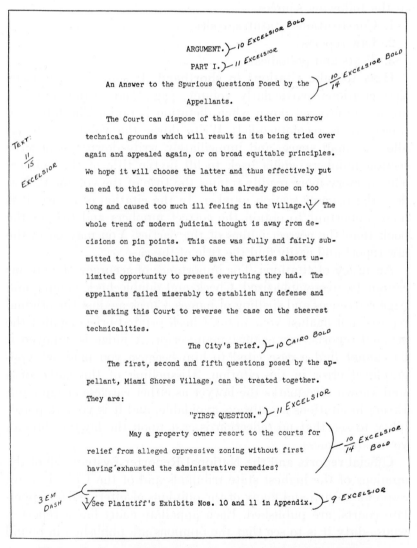

Figure 89. Page of Manuscript from Brief, Marked for Printer.

Citations

What is a citation? A citation[1] is a reference to an authority that supports a statement of law or from which a quotation is taken. Citations occur most frequently in briefs, law memoranda, and opinion letters. The lawyer speaks of *citing a case,* a *cited case, citing a report,* and the like. The references are principally to the following sources:

1. Constitutions, statutes, codes
2. Law reports
3. Texts and periodicals

How to take citations in shorthand. It sometimes happens that citations, particularly volume, page, and section number, are incorrectly set down when dictation is rapid. The following procedure is recommended: Write down the volume number, allow a small space, and immediately write down the page or section numbers, going back to fill in the title of the volume. The memory more readily retains the title of the volume than it does the page or section number. In the citation of a case, it is more important to obtain the correct numbers and title of the book than the correct names of the parties. You may go to the law report and easily find the title of the case.

Accuracy of citations. The importance of accuracy of citations cannot be overemphasized. Check and doublecheck volume and page references and spelling of names. Check against the original reports, not against your notes. Check printed briefs against the original reports, not against manuscript. A judge is annoyed if he cannot find a case cited to him because you made a typographical error in the citation. Misspelling of the name of a well-known case marks the lawyer as either careless or ignorant. Errors in citations are always avoidable, and it is your responsibility to see that no reflection is cast upon the lawyer through your carelessness.

Official reports and the National Reporter System. All of the opinions of the highest state tribunals and of the United States Supreme Court, and many of the opinions of intermediary appellate courts, are published. Each appellate court has a reporter, whose duty it is to see that the opinions are published in bound

---

[1] Certain writs and summonses issued by courts are also known as citations.

form at intervals. The publication under the direction of the state reporter is considered the *official* report of the court's opinion.

TABLE IX

OFFICIAL REPORTS AND HOW THEY ARE CITED

Official report	Cite as
Alabama Reports	Ala.
Alabama Appellate Reports	Ala. App.
Alaska Reports	A.
Arizona Reports	Ariz.
Arkansas Reports	Ark.
California Appellate Reports	Cal. App.
California Appellate Reports, Second Series	Cal. App. 2d
California Reports	Cal.
California Reports, Second Series	Cal. 2d
Colorado Reports	Colo.
Connecticut	Conn.
Delaware Reports	By name of Rep.
Delaware Chancery Reports	Del. Ch.
Florida Reports[1]	Fla.
Georgia Reports	Ga.
Hawaii Reports	H.
Idaho Reports	Idaho
Illinois Reports	Ill.
Illinois Appellate Court Reports	Ill. App.
Indiana Reports	Ind.
Indiana Appellate Reports	Ind. App.
Iowa Reports	Iowa
Kansas Reports	Kan.
Kentucky Reports[2]	Ky.
Louisiana Reports	La.
Maine Reports	Me.
Maryland Reports	Md.
Massachusetts Reports	Mass.
Michigan Reports	Mich.
Minnesota Reports	Minn.
Mississippi Reports	Miss.
Missouri Reports	Mo.
Missouri Appeal Reports	Mo. App.
Montana Reports	Mont.
Nebraska Reports	Neb.
Nevada Reports	Nev.
New Hampshire Reports	N. H.
New Jersey Equity Reports	N. J. Eq.
New Jersey Reports	N. J.
New Jersey Superior Court Reports	N. J. Super.
New Mexico Reports	N. M.
New York Appellate Division Reports	N. Y. App. Div.
New York Miscellaneous Reports	N. Y. Misc.
New York Reports	N. Y.
North Carolina Reports	N. C.

[1] Up to Vol. 160 only. Now the Southern Reporter is official.
[2] Up to Vol. 314 only. Now the Southwestern Reporter is official.

TABLE IX (Continued)

Official report	Cite as
North Dakota Reports...............................	N. D.
Ohio Appellate Reports..............................	Ohio App.
Ohio State Reports..................................	Ohio St.
Oklahoma Reports...................................	Okl.
Oklahoma Criminal Reports..........................	Okl. Cr.
Oregon Reports.....................................	Or.
Pennsylvania Reports...............................	Pa.
Pennsylvania Superior Court Reports..................	Pa. Sup.
Rhode Island Reports...............................	R. I.
South Carolina Reports..............................	S. C.
South Dakota Reports...............................	S. D.
Tennessee Reports..................................	Tenn.
Tennessee Appeals Reports...........................	Tenn. App.
Texas Reports......................................	Tex.
United States Reports...............................	U. S.
United States Court of Apeals, District of Columbia......	U. S. App. D. C.
Utah Reports.......................................	Utah
Vermont Reports...................................	Vt.
Virginia Reports...................................	Va.
Washington Reports................................	Wash.
Washington Reports, Second Series....................	Wash. 2d
West Virginia Reports..............................	W. Va.
Wisconsin Reports..................................	Wis.
Wyoming Reports...................................	Wyo.

West Publishing Company publishes the opinions of the Federal courts and the courts of every state, those of several states being published in the same bound volume. This system of reports, covering the entire country, is called the *National Reporter System.* Table X shows the names of the reporters, how they are cited, and the courts covered by each. You will notice some of the reporters are designated "Second Series." The designation is for numbering purposes and indicates that the numbers of the volumes have started over with 1.

These reporters, which are "unofficial" reports of the courts' opinions, are published much sooner than the official reports, especially those in some states. Some states have discontinued the publication of state reports and use the appropriate reporter of the *National Reporter System* as the official report.

Before the opinions are published in bound volumes of the *National Reporter System,* they are published in weekly pamphlets known as *Advance Sheets.* (Some official reports also have advance sheets.) Thus, the lawyer is informed immediately of the decisions of courts in which he is interested. The page numbers in the advance sheets correspond with the page numbers that will appear in the bound volumes.

TABLE X

REPORTERS OF NATIONAL REPORTER SYSTEM

Name of reporter	Cite as	Courts covered
Supreme Court Reporter	S. Ct.	United States Supreme Court
Federal Reporter	F.	United States Circuit Courts of Appeals and the District Courts
Federal Reporter, Second Series	F. 2d	United States Courts of Appeals, United States Court of Customs and Patent Appeals, United States Emergency Court of Appeals
Federal Supplement	F. Supp.	United States District Courts, United States Court of Claims
Atlantic Reporter Atlantic Reporter, Second Series	A. A. 2d	Connecticut Delaware Maine Maryland New Hampshire New Jersey Pennsylvania Rhode Island Vermont District of Columbia
New York Supplement New York Supplement, Second Series	N. Y. Supp. N. Y. S. 2d	New York Court of Appeals Appellate Division of the Supreme Court Miscellaneous Courts
Northeastern Reporter Northeastern Reporter, Second Series	N. E. N. E. 2d	Illinois Indiana New York Massachusetts Ohio
Northwestern Reporter Northwestern Reporter, Second Series	N. W. N. W. 2d	Iowa Michigan Minnesota Nebraska North Dakota South Dakota Wisconsin

TABLE X (Continued)

Name of reporter	Cite as	Courts covered
Pacific Reporter Pacific Reporter, Second Series	P. P. 2d	Arizona California Colorado Idaho Kansas Montana Nevada New Mexico Oklahoma Oregon Utah Washington Wyoming
Southeastern Reporter Southeastern Reporter, Second Series	S. E. S. E. 2d	Georgia North Carolina South Carolina Virginia West Virginia
Southern Reporter Southern Reporter, Second Series	So. So. 2d	Alabama Florida Louisiana Mississippi
Southwestern Reporter Southwestern Reporter, Second Series	S. W. S. W. 2d	Arkansas Kentucky Missouri Tennessee Texas

How to cite a constitution. Show the number of the article, or amendment, in roman numerals; the section number in arabic numerals. Give date if the constitution cited is not in force.

U. S. Const.	Art. IV, §2
U. S. Const.	Amend. VI, §2
Ga. Const.	Art. XI, §3
Ga. Const.	Art. II, §1 (1875)

How to cite statutes and codes. Whenever full reference to a Federal statute is necessary, cite date, chapter number, statute citation, and United States Code citation, thus: Section 1 of the Act of June 13, 1934, c. 482, 48 Stat. 948, 40 U.S.C. 276b. Compilations of state statutes and codes are cited by chapter, title, or section number. Table XI gives the approved form of citing the

TABLE XI

APPROVED METHOD OF CITING COMPILATIONS OF STATUTES AND CODES

State	Title of compilation	How cited
Ala.	Code of Alabama, 1940	Code of Alabama, 1940, Tit. 10, § 101
Alaska	Alaska Compiled Laws Annotated 1949	Sec. 10-11-10 ACLA 1949
Ariz.	Arizona Revised Statutes Annotated	ARS § 10-101
Ark.	Arkansas Statutes Annotated 1947	Ark. Stats. (1947) Sec. 10-101
Calif.	Deering's California Codes (Code of Civil Procedure)	CCP § 101
Colo.	Colorado Revised Statutes, 1953	101-10-1, C.R.S. '53
Conn.	General Statutes, Revision of 1958	Conn. G. S. 1958 Sec. 101
Del.	Delaware Code Annotated, 1953	10 Del. C. § 110
D.C.	District of Columbia Code Annotated, 1951	D.C. Code 1951, Title 26, § 703
Fla.	Florida Statutes, 1957	Florida Statutes, 1957, § 101.01
Ga.	Code of Georgia, Annotated	Ga. Code Ann. § 10-1010
Hawaii	Revised Laws of Hawaii, 1955	R.L.H. 1955 § 172-1
Idaho	Idaho Code	Idaho Code, Sec. 101-101
Ill.	Illinois Revised Statutes 1951 Smith-Hurd Illinois Annotated Statutes	Ill. Rev. Stat. 1951 Ch. 10, § 101 Smith-Hurd Ann. St. Ch. 10, § 101
	Jones Illinois Statutes Annotated	Jones Ill. Stat. Ann. Ch. 10, § 101
Ind.	Annotated Indiana Statutes	Burns Ann. St. § 3-2201
Iowa	Code of Iowa, 1958	Code of Iowa, 1958, § 110.10
Kan.	General Statutes of Kansas (Annotated) 1949 1957 Supplement to General Statutes 1949	G.S. 1949, § 10-101 G.S. 1957 Supp., § 10-101
Ky.	Kentucky Revised Statutes of 1953 Kentucky Civil Code	KRS 101.010(1) Civil Code, Sec. 101
La.	Louisiana Revised Statutes of 1950	R.S. 10:101
Maine	Revised Statutes of Maine, 1954	R.S. of Maine 1954, C. 10, § 11
Md.	Annotated Code of Maryland, 1957	Md. Code (1957), Art. 10, Sec. 101
Mass.	General Laws of Massachusetts, Tercentenary Edition, 1932	G.L. (Tr. Ed.) C. 10 § 101
Mich.	1948 Compiled Laws of Michigan Michigan Statutes Annotated	C.L. 1948, § 10.101 Stat. Ann. § 10.101
Minn.	Minnesota Statutes 1957	Minn. Stat. 1957, Sec. 101.10
Miss.	Mississippi Code, 1942, Annotated	Miss. Code. 1942, Ann., § 101

TABLE XI (Continued)

State	Title of compilation	How cited
Mo.	Missouri Revised Statutes, 1949	R.S. Mo. 1949, § 101.010
Mont.	Revised Codes of Montana, 1947, Annotated	RCM 1947, § 10-101
Nebr.	Nebraska Revised Statutes, 1943	Sec. 1-101, R.S. Nebr., 1943
	Reissue Revised Statutes of Nebraska, 1943	Sec. 1-101, R.R.S. Nebr., 1943
Nev.	Nevada Revised Statutes	NRS § 19.010
N.H.	1955 New Hampshire Revised Statutes Annotated	RSA 101:1
N.J.	Revised Statutes of New Jersey, 1937	N.J.R.S., 10:101-10
	New Jersey Statutes Title 2A and 3A	N.J.S.
N.M.	New Mexico Statutes Annotated, 1953	NMSA Comp., 3-7-16
N.Y.	McKinney's Consolidated Laws of New York	(Corporation) Law, § 101
N.C.	General Statutes of North Carolina, 1943	G.S. 10-101
N.D.	North Dakota Revised Code of 1943	§ 10-1010 of NDRC 1943
Ohio	Baldwin's Ohio Revised Code, Annotated	R.C. § 1110.10
Okla.	Oklahoma Statutes, 1951	10 O.S. 1951 § 101
Ore.	Oregon Revised Statutes	ORS 11.010
Penn.	Purdon's Pennsylvania Statutes Annotated	10 P.S. § 101
R.I.	General Laws of Rhode Island of 1956	Gen. Laws 1956, 1-1-10
S.C.	Code of Laws of S.C. 1952	1952 Code, § 10-101
S.D.	South Dakota Code of 1939	SDC 10.1010(10)
	South Dakota Code Supplement of 1952	SDC Supp. 11.0111
Tenn.	Tennessee Code Annotated	T.C.A., § 10-101
Tex.	Vernon's Texas Statutes, 1948	Vernon's Texas St. 1948, Art. 101
Utah	Utah Code Annotated, 1953	UCA 1953, 10-10-1
Vt.	Vermont Statutes Annotated	VSA, Title I, § 51
Va.	Code of Virginia, 1950	Code, § 10-101
Wash.	Revised Code of Washington 1951	RCW 10.11.101
W. Va.	West Virginia Code of 1955	Michie's § 1010(1)
Wis.	Wisconsin Statutes 1957	101.01(1) Stats.
Wyo.	Wyoming Statutes 1957	WCS 1945, § 10-1010

latest compilation in each state. The list is not exclusive—some
states have more than one approved compilation.

When citing statutes and codes, observe these directions:

1. If a compilation in its preface gives the method of citing
it, use that citation.

2. Where the date is incorporated in the title of the compilation, show it.

3. When statutes or codes of one state are cited outside of that
state, the name of the state is always indicated for identification
purposes. For example, lawyers in Kansas cite the Kansas
General Statutes as "G.S." but outside of Kansas the citation is
Kan. G. S.

4. When citing an act or law that has been repealed and no
longer appears in the latest compilation, give the date of the
compilation cited.

Ill. Rev. Stat. c. 114, §88 (1889)

How to cite cases in official reports and reporters. Cases in
official reports and reporters are cited alike. Directions for citing
cases must be considered in the light of applicable court rules.
Some courts lay considerable emphasis on how cases should be
cited and whether citation to the National Reporter System
should be included. The following directions are the rules of
thumb used in many law offices. Examples of citations are on
pages 365 and 366.

Names of parties. 1. Cite the name of the case as it appears
in the running head of the report, not as it appears at the beginning of the opinion. Do not abbreviate the first word.

2. When the United States is a party, do not abbreviate to
U. S. unless it is part of the name of a Government vessel. (See
Example 1.)

3. Do not substitute the initials of a Government agency or a
labor union for its full name in briefs. You may in other legal
writings. (See Example 2.)

4. Use the first name of railways, but abbreviate the balance.
(See Example 3.)

5. When *Co.* and *Inc.* are both part of a name omit the *Inc.*

6. When the names of parties change completely on appeal

indicate that fact by the use of *sub nom.* (See Example 4.) This direction does not apply when the names of the parties are merely reversed.

Volume and page. Cite the volume and page number of the report or reporter in which the opinion is published. The reference is to the entire opinion and gives the page at which the opinion begins. A *spot page reference* follows when it is desired to call attention to a particular page, such as one from which a quotation is taken. (See Example 5.)

The designation "2d" *must* be included in the citation of a volume in a second series. A reference to 58 N. E. is not the same as a reference to 58 N. E. 2d.

Date. Show in parentheses the year the decision is handed down by the court. It appears at the beginning of the court's opinion. Both *A Uniform System of Citation* and *Practical Manual of Standard Legal Citations* place the date at the end of the citation (Example 1), but lawyers, when writing briefs, frequently place it between the title of the case and the volume reference (Example 5). Many lawyers do not show the date of the decision unless it is relevant to the argument.

Jurisdiction and court. When the name of the reporter does not indicate the jurisdiction, show the jurisdiction in parentheses preceding the date. (See Example 6.) Also show the name of the court deciding the case if it is not the highest court in the state. (See Example 7.) This is always necessary when only the unofficial reporter is cited.

Parallel citations. Both the official and unofficial reports should be cited if available. (See the use of the Blue Books on page 557.) Cite the official report first. (See Example 8.) When the case has not been published in the official reports, but will be in the future, cite the name of the official report, preceded and followed by blanks, thus, ___ Miss. ___, 55 So. 2d 477. (See Example 9.)

Federal courts. When citing cases decided by the Federal courts of appeals, show the circuit in parentheses. (See Example 10.) The District of Columbia circuit is indicated by *D. C.* (See Example 11.) When citing cases decided in the Federal district court, show the district, but not the division, in parentheses. (See Example 12.)

Selective case series. In some law report series, such as *American Law Reports* and *Law Reports Annotated,* only certain cases are published. These series are cited by the year of publication, the *letter* of the volume (A, B, C, or D), and page. (See Example 13). In parallel citations, they follow the National Reporter citation. It is customary to cite selective case series in briefs for state courts but not in those for Federal courts.

Named reporters. Old court reports carry the name of the reporter. When citing cases in the U. S. reports prior to volume 91, always cite by the volume number and name of the reporter, not by the subsequently assigned consecutive U. S. number. To cite these volumes by the U. S. number is considered bad form. The following are the names of the old court reports and the number of volumes they reported.

> 4 of Dallas (cited as 1 Dall. 10)
> 9 of Cranch (cited as 1 Cranch 10)
> 12 of Wheaton (cited as 1 Wheat. 10)
> 16 of Peters (cited as 1 Pet. 10)
> 24 of Howard (cited as 1 How. 10)
> 2 of Black (cited as 1 Black 10)
> 23 of Wallace (cited as 1 Wall. 10)

When citing state cases, follow the local practice. For example, in Massachusetts the early reports are invariably cited by the name of the reporter, whereas in North Carolina a rule of court requires that they be cited by the consecutive number. When the named reporter is used, indicate the jurisdiction and date in parentheses. (See Example 14.)

String citations. When several cases are cited one after the other instead of on separate lines, the citation is referred to as a *string citation.* Separate the cases with a semi-colon. (See Example 15.)

How to cite an unpublished case. When citing a case that has not been reported, cite by name, court, the full date, and the docket number if known. (See Example 16.)

How to cite slip decisions. Each opinion of the United States Supreme Court is published separately as soon as it is handed down. This form of publication is called a *slip decision.* Slip decisions are printed by the Government Printing Office and also by two unofficial publishers, Commerce Clearing House and U. S. Law Week. They are widely circulated and are frequently cited in briefs. Cite by number, court, date of decision, and source if unofficial. (See Example 17.)

How to cite treatises. Cite by volume number (if more than one volume), author, title of the publication, page or section number, and the edition in parentheses. If the editor is well known, his name follows the edition. Underscore or italicize the title of the publication. (See Example 18.)

Star Page. In a few well-known works, the paging of the original edition is indicated by stars in differently paginated editions. Cite by the star page. (See Example 19.)

How to cite law reviews. Cite the volume and page number and the year. Underscore or italicize the title of the review. If an article is referred to, place it in quotation marks. Abbreviate *Law* (L.), *Review* (Rev.), and *Journal* (J.). (See Example 20.)

How to cite legal newspapers. When citing a case that has not been published in either the official or unofficial reports but has been published in a legal newspaper, give the name of the newspaper, the volume and page number, the column, the court, and the exact date of the decision. (See Example 21.)

Underscoring and italicizing. Underscoring and italicizing vary with the law office, but the following directions, some of which are arbitrary, are based upon the practices followed by many lawyers:

1. Underscore the names of the parties.

2. In a printed brief, the underscoring of *v.* or *vs.* is optional. Continuous underscoring gives a more even appearance on the typed page and requires less care than breaking the underscoring at the desired points. Printers usually set the *v.* or *vs.* in roman.

3. When a previously cited case is referred to in the text of the brief by part of the title used as an adjective, italicize it.

Under the authority of the *Daoud* case the Court held . . .

When the reference is repeated under the same point of the brief, do not italicize it.

4. Italicize *case* or *cases* only when it is part of the usual name of the case.

5. It is preferable not to underscore words and expressions between citations of the same case that relate to its history, such as *affirmed, certiorari denied,* and the like. (See Example 22.)

Spacing of abbreviations. In briefs the parts of an abbreviation are separated by a space, thus *N. E. 2d.* In other legal writings, the general practice is to close up the citation, thus *N.E.2d.*

Placement of citations. Unless a citation is part of a quotation, it is indented and placed on the line following the quotation. If it runs over one line, the carry-over line is indented.

". . . should be denied, as proposed allegations would add nothing to the equity of the bill."
> *Volunteer Security Co. v. Dowl* (1947), 159 Fla. 767, 33 So. 2d 150, 152

When several citations are given in support of a point, list them one under the other (see Figure 84).

Illustrations of citations. The following examples of citations illustrate the foregoing directions. Parts appearing in italics would be underscored on the typewriter. Apparent inconsistencies in the italics and in the placement of the dates in the examples demonstrate the variations in accepted practices. However, you should be consistent throughout a brief.

Example   *Citation*

1. *United States v. Texas & Pacific Motor Transport Co.,* 340 U. S. 450, 71 S. Ct. 422 (1951)
2. *United States v. Congress of Industrial Organization,* 335 U. S. 106, 68 S. Ct. 1349, 48 A. L. C. 1164, aff'g 77 F. Supp. 355, 48 A. L. C. 559 (D. C. Cir. 1948)
3. *Nashville, C. & St. L. Ry.* vs. *Walters,* (1934) 294 U. S. 405, 55 S. Ct. 486
4. *Blaustein v. United States,* 44 F. 2d 163 (C.C.A. 3), certiorari denied *sub nom. Sokol v. United States,* 283 U. S. 838, 51 S. Ct. 486
5. *Green Point Savings Bank* v. *Board of Zoning Appeals,* (1939) 281 N. Y. 534, 24 N. E. 2d 319, 321
6. *Harrington v. Board of Adjustment, City of Alamo Heights,* (Tex. 1939) 124 S. W. 2d 401, 404
7. *Rayl v. General Motors Corp.,* (Ind. App. 1951) 101 N. E. 2d 433 *Janice* v. *State,* 107 N. Y. S. 2d 674 (Ct. Cl. 1951)

8. *People v. Davis,* 303 N. Y. 235, 101 N. E. 2d 479
9. *In re Fortune,* (1951) _____ Ohio St. _____, 101 N. E. 2d 174
10. *American Fruit Machinery Co.* v. *Robinson Match Co.,* 191 Fed. 723 (3rd Cir. 1911)
11. *Barbee v. Capital Airlines, Inc.,* (D. C. Cir. 1951) 191 F. 2d 507
12. *Standard Oil Co.* v. *Atlantic Coast Line R. Co.,* (W. D. Ky. 1926) 13 F. 2d 633
13. *Hanover Star Milling Co.* v. *Allen & Wheeler Co.,* 208 Fed. 513, 1916D L. R. A. 136 (7th Cir. 1913)
14. *Forward* v. *Adams,* 7 Wend. 204 (N. Y. 1831)
15. *Rubin* v. *Board of Directors of City of Pasadena,* (1940) 16 Cal. 2d 119, 104 P. 2d 1041; *Harrington* v. *Board of Adjustment, City of Alamo Heights,* (Tex. 1939) 124 S. W. 2d 401; *Green Point Savings Bank* v. *Board of Zoning Appeals,* (1939) 281 N. Y. 534, 24 N. E. 2d 319
16. *Roe* v. *Doe,* No. 152 U. S. Sup. Ct., Jan. 10, 1952
17. *Jones* v. *Smith,* No. 40, U. S. Sup. Ct., No. 21, 1945 (15 U. S. Law Week)
18. 2 Pomeroy, *Equity Jurisprudence* §428 (5th ed., Symonds, 1941)
19. 2 Bl. Comm. *358
20. 42 *Yale L. J.* 419 (1933)
21. *Garden Park Apts., Inc. vs. Fletcher,* 127 N. Y. L. J. 703, col. 7 (Sup. Ct. Spec. Term Feb. 20, 1952)
22. *In re Morse,* (1928) 220 App. Div. 830, 220 N. Y. Supp. 858, rev'd on other grounds, 247 N. Y. 290, 160 N. E. 374

17

Handling Material for Printing

THE LAWYER's secretary assists in the preparation of a wide variety of printed material. Briefs, forms of deeds, mortgages, and other instruments used extensively for a special client, booklets and pamphlets, as well as office forms, pass through the secretary's hands at some of, if not all, their stages of production. The following pages explain what you should know about printing if you are to help produce a good printing job economically.

Preparing the Manuscript for the Printer

Typing rules for manuscript. A piece of writing that is to be sent to a printer is called "manuscript" or "copy." Copy should be typewritten, neatly and legibly, on sheets of paper of uniform size. Make carbon copies for reference purposes, but always send the original to the printer.

In typing the manuscript, observe the following rules:

1. Keep the typewritten line down to six inches.

2. Use double spacing, even for material that would be single spaced in a typed copy.

3. Keep the right-hand margin as even as possible, to help you later in estimating the length of the copy.

4. Indicate paragraph indentions clearly.

5. Type headings and subheadings in the position they are to occupy on the final printed page, and be uniform in your capitalization of them.

5. Use one side only of the sheet.

7. Leave a margin of at least one and a quarter inches on all four sides.

8. Keep the pages as nearly uniform in length as possible, to help you later in estimating the length of the copy.

9. Set off extracted or quoted material from the rest of the text by indenting it from the left margin or from both the left and the right margins.

10. Type any footnotes (which must always have corresponding references in the main text) either (*a*) at the foot of the page on which they occur; or (*b*) on a separate sheet immediately following the text where the corresponding reference appears; or (*c*) in a separate line immediately following the text where the reference appears, separating the footnote from the preceding and following text by lines typed across the manuscript page. Footnotes are set off in this way because they are usually printed in smaller type.

11. If references are made to material appearing in other parts of the manuscript, instruct the printer (on the manuscript) to carry a query on each successive proof, so that you will be reminded to put in the correct page reference numbers when you receive the final page proofs.

Checking the manuscript. Every piece of copy should be checked carefully for errors before it is sent to the printer. Checking saves time and money and contributes to a better finished product. *Read your manuscript over several times,* looking for errors. Remember that each error corrected on the typed manuscript will save the expense of resetting a line or even a whole paragraph. Here are some guides to follow as you read over the copy:

1. *Be consistent.* If a word can be spelled or abbreviated in more than one correct form, choose the one you prefer and use it consistently. On the first reading, make a list of your selections of optional spellings to guide you toward consistency.

2. Make *short corrections* by crossing out the incorrect word and writing the correction over it, not in the margin. The margin is used for instructions to the printer. To make *lengthy corrections,* cross out the incorrect matter and type the correct matter on a separate sheet of paper. Mark the correction as an insert and show clearly where it is to be inserted.

3. Use *proofreader's marks* (see page 374) in correcting the manuscript. For example:

(*a*) To lower a capital letter, draw a diagonal line through it;

to capitalize a lower-case letter, draw three lines under it.

(*b*) To start a new paragraph, insert a ¶ sign; to run in material typed as a new paragraph, draw a line from the word starting the new paragraph to the last word of the preceding paragraph.

(*c*) To separate two words typed as one, draw a vertical line between them.

(*d*) To make deletions, use a heavy pencil and a ruler and neatly and heavily cross out what you do not want.

(*e*) To retain material already crossed out, insert a row of dots beneath it and write the word "stet" in the margin beside it in a circle. Be sure, however, that the crossed-out material you wish to retain is legible; if there is any doubt, retype it as an insert.

4. *Number the pages* of your manuscript consecutively after all corrections and insertions have been made.

5. In checking the manuscript, do not indicate corrections to be made in the margins; make all changes within the lines of typing on the manuscript. (Correcting manuscript differs in this respect from correcting proof.)

Marking copy. Marking copy simply means telling the printer, clearly and concisely, what you want—you must never assume that the printer will know. Of course, to instruct the printer you must first know what you want yourself. This necessity entails planning.

Planning. In your planning, follow these steps:

1. Plan the size of the type area in relation to the size of the page. If you are to have page numbers and a running head—that is, a line heading on each page—include them in your estimated type area. One rule of thumb in planning a booklet, leaflet, or book is to make the inside margin (the one in the center of the book) the smallest margin, the top margin larger, the outside margin (the one at the outer edge of the page) larger than that, and the bottom margin the largest.

2. Decide what kind and size of type you want, and whether you want to use more than one kind and size of type (a different kind of type for headings, a different size for quotes, for example). Your printer will supply you with a specimen sheet or booklet showing the kinds and sizes of type he has. Type is measured

by points. Each kind is available in different sizes. The same type faces appear in several styles, such as **boldface,** *italics,* and SMALL CAPS. The printer can advise you.

3. Determine the pica width and depth of the type area. A pica is an arbitrary printer's measure. There are approximately six picas to an inch. Type and space between lines (leading) are measured in points. There are 12 points to the pica.

4. Settle all other points of style. For example: (*a*) Will you center all headings or make them flush with the left-hand margin? (*b*) Do you want to use italics? (*c*) Do you want to use boldface type? (*d*) How do you want your quotations and citations set? Plan a consistent style and *stick to it.* Then mark your copy *consistently.*

How to mark copy. When you mark copy, remember that you get what you ask for and that you must mark clearly and accurately. Instruct the printer about the following points, all of which are illustrated in Figure 90:

1. Underline all words or sections to be set in italics.

2. Draw a wavy line under the words or sections to be set in boldface, or type them in red.

3. Indicate what is to be set in capital letters and what in small capitals or a combination of capitals and small capitals.

4. Mark all headings in the desired size and style of type.

5. In the left-hand margin, mark the size and name of the body type and the pica width of the type area, thus: $\dfrac{11 \text{ on } 13}{18}$ Caslon, which calls for 11 point Caslon type, leaded 2 points, set 18 picas wide. Your printer may use a numerical code instead of names for his types. If the code number for Caslon were 97, you could write your instructions thus:

$$11 \ / \ 13$$
$$18 \ / \ 97$$

In marking copy, use proofreader's marks, shown on page 374, whenever possible. These marks are a shorthand system that will save you time and that will be perfectly clear to your printer.

How to estimate length of copy. You may estimate the length of copy by a count of (*a*) words or (*b*) characters. Both methods are described below, the character method first because it is the more accurate.

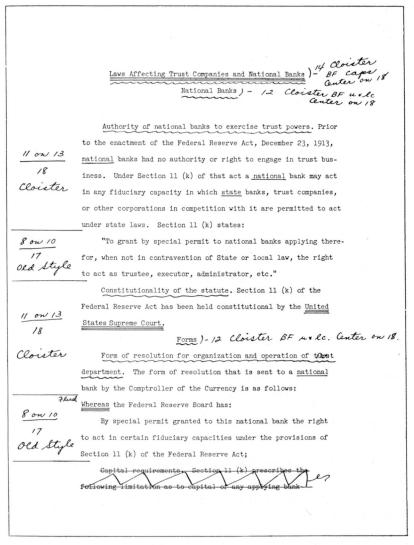

Laws Affecting Trust Companies and National Banks) – *14 Cloister BF caps Center on 18*

National Banks) – *12 Cloister BF u & lc Center on 18*

11 on 13
18
Cloister

Authority of national banks to exercise trust powers. Prior to the enactment of the Federal Reserve Act, December 23, 1913, national banks had no authority or right to engage in trust business. Under Section 11 (k) of that act a national bank may act in any fiduciary capacity in which state banks, trust companies, or other corporations in competition with it are permitted to act under state laws. Section 11 (k) states:

8 on 10
17
Old Style

"To grant by special permit to national banks applying therefor, when not in contravention of State or local law, the right to act as trustee, executor, administrator, etc."

11 on 13
18
Cloister

Constitutionality of the statute. Section 11 (k) of the Federal Reserve Act has been held constitutional by the United States Supreme Court.

Forms) – *12 Cloister BF u & lc. Center on 18.*

Form of resolution for organization and operation of trust department. The form of resolution that is sent to a national bank by the Comptroller of the Currency is as follows:

8 on 10
17
Old Style

Flush Whereas the Federal Reserve Board has:

By special permit granted to this national bank the right to act in certain fiduciary capacities under the provisions of Section 11 (k) of the Federal Reserve Act;

Capital requirements. Section 11 (k) prescribes the following limitation as to capital of any applying bank.

Figure 90. Marked Copy.

If you have followed the typing rules of keeping the right-hand margin fairly even and of writing the same number of lines on each page, you will find it easy to apply the following methods of estimating length of copy.

1. *Estimating by character count:*

(a) Measure the length of a typewritten line in inches.

(*b*) Multiply the result in step (*a*) by 10, if your typewriter type is pica; by 12, if it is elite. (Pica type has 10 characters, elite type 12 characters, to the inch.) This step gives you the number of characters to the line.

(*c*) Multiply the number of characters in a line, step (*b*), by the number of lines on a page of typewritten copy.

(*d*) Multiply the number of characters to a page, step (*c*), by the number of pages of typewritten copy.

Apply the following rules in counting characters: consider spaces between words and quotation marks and other punctuation as characters; count a short line at the end of a paragraph as a full line.

EXAMPLE: Suppose that each line of typewritten copy measures 6 inches. If your typewriter has pica type, the number of characters in a line will thus be 6 × 10, or 60. If each page contains 27 lines of type, there will be 1,620 characters on the page (27 × 60). If your manuscript has 5 pages, there will be 1,620 × 5, or 8,100, characters in the manuscript.

2. *Estimating by word count:*

(*a*) Find the average number of words to a line by counting the number of words in several lines and dividing this total by the number of lines counted.

(*b*) Multiply the average number of words to a line, step (*a*), by the number of lines to a page to get the average number of words per page.

(*c*) Multiply the average number of words to a page, step (*b*), by the number of pages.

Apply the following rules in counting words: count two short words as one word; count a long word as two words.

EXAMPLE: Suppose that in 5 typewritten lines you have counted 60 words, or 12 words to a line (60 ÷ 5). If each page contains 27 lines of type, there are an estimated 324 (27 × 12) words to a page. If your manuscript has 5 full pages, there are an estimated 1,620 (324 × 5) words in the manuscript.

Correcting Galley and Page Proofs

Procedure. The printer returns your original manuscript with at least two sets of the material set in type. You may ask for more than two sets of *galley proofs,* as they are called, but if you ask for many there may be an extra charge. Read the proofs that have been marked by the printer carefully against the original manuscript, make all corrections on them and, after the lawyer has made any desired changes, return them to the printer.

If the manuscript has illustrations, tables, and the like, you should prepare a dummy for the printer to be returned with the corrected galleys, in order to be sure that these breaks in the text fall where you want them. (A dummy consists of blank sheets of paper cut and folded to the size of a proposed leaflet, folder, booklet, or book, to indicate shape, size, and general appearance. The galley proofs are cut to size and pasted on the sheets.) In preparing this dummy, you must make allowance for changes in lines resulting from your corrections on the galleys.

When the printer receives the corrected galleys, and the dummy if any, he makes the desired changes and sends you *page proofs.* If major changes are necessary in the page proofs, ask the printer for corrected page proofs. When you are satisfied that the proofs are perfect in so far as your work is concerned (see page 352), give them to the lawyer for his approval. He will mark them "O.K. to print" and initial them.

Importance of correcting galley and page proofs. The checking and reading of galley proofs is the second major step in the successful preparation of the printed work. As much care should go into the reading of proofs as went into the preparation of copy. The importance of this step is stressed because it is on the galley or page proofs that you get your last chance to make corrections.

Any corrections on galley or page proofs that deviate from the original manuscript sent to the printer are called author's alterations. These corrections are charged for at a penalty time rate. That is, the cost of setting a line at this stage is many times greater than the original cost. It can easily be seen, then, that excessive author's alterations make the job needlessly expensive. Also, there is the possibility that the printer will commit serious typographical errors in making trivial changes. Where time is an important factor, numerous corrections can slow up the job considerably.

Proofreader's marks. Before you begin to read the proof, fa-

PROOFREADERS' MARKS

∧	Make correction indicated in margin.	⌐⌐	Raise to proper position.
Stet	Retain crossed-out word or letter; let it stand.	⌐⌐	Lower to proper position.
		////	Hair space letters.
. . . .	Retain words under which dots appear; write "Stet" in margin.	*w.f.*	Wrong font; change to proper font.
Stet		*Qu?*	Is this right?
		l.c.	Put in lower case (small letters).
✕	Appears battered; examine.	*s.c.*	Put in small capitals.
☰	Straighten lines.	*Caps*	Put in capitals.
√√√	Unevenly spaced; correct spacing.	*C+s.c.*	Put in caps and small caps.
//	Line up; i.e., make lines even with other matter.	*rom.*	Change to Roman.
		ital.	Change to Italic.
run in	Make no break in the reading; no ¶	☰	Under letter or word means caps.
no ¶	No paragraph; sometimes written "run in."	=	Under letter or word, small caps.
		—	Under letter or word means Italic.
out see copy	Here is an omission; see copy.	∿	Under letter or word, bold face.
¶	Make a paragraph here.	,/	Insert comma.
tr	Transpose words or letters as indicated.	;/	Insert semicolon.
		:/	Insert colon.
ℐ	Take out matter indicated; dele.	⊙	Insert period.
ℨ	Take out character indicated and close up.	/?/	Insert interrogation mark.
		(!)	Insert exclamation mark.
¢	Line drawn through a cap means lower case.	/=/	Insert hyphen.
		✓	Insert apostrophe.
℮	Upside down; reverse.	''/''	Insert quotation marks.
⊂	Close up; no space.	*v*	Insert superior letter or figure.
#	Insert a space here.	⊓	Insert inferior letter or figure.
⊥	Push down this space.	[/]	Insert brackets.
⊡	Indent line one em.	(/)	Insert parenthesis.
⎣	Move this to the left.	—/m	One-em dash.
⎤	Move this to the right.	≞/m	Two-em parallel dash.

Figure 91. Standard Proofreading Marks.

miliarize yourself with proofreader's marks, which are standard and are understood by all printers. Figure 91 is an illustration of these marks, and Figure 92 shows how they are used.

HOW TO CORRECT PROOF

It does not appear that the earliest printers had any method of correcting errors before the form was on the press. The learned correctors of the first two centuries of printing were not proofreaders in our sense; they were rather what we should term office editors. Their labors were chiefly to see that the proof corresponded to the copy, but that the printed page was correct in its latinity, and that the sense was right. They cared little about orthography, bad letters or purely printers' errors, and when the text seemed to them wrong they consulted fresh authorities or altered it on their own responsibility. Good proofs in the modern sense, were impossible until professional readers were employed, men who had first a printer's education, and then spent many years in the correction of proof. The orthography of English, which for the past century has undergone little change, was very fluctuating until after the publication of Johnson's Dictionary, and capitals, which have been used with considerable regularity for the past 80 years, were previously used on the miss or hit plan. The approach to regularity, so far as we have may be attributed to the growth of a class of professional proof readers, and it is to them that we owe the correctness of modern printing. More errors have been found in the Bible than in any other one work. For many generations it was frequently the case that Bibles were brought out stealthily, from fear of governmental interference. They were frequently printed from imperfect texts, and were often modified to meet the views of those who published them. The story is related that a certain woman in Germany, who was the wife of a printer, and had become disgusted with the continual assertion of the superiority of man over woman which she had heard, hurried into the composing room while her husband was at supper and altered a sentence in the Bible, which he was printing, so that it read Narr instead of Herr, thus making the verse read "And he shall be thy fool" instead of "And he shall be thy lord." The word not was omitted by Barker, the king's printer in England in 1632, in printing the seventh commandment. He was fined £3,000 on this account.

Figure 92. Corrected Galley.

Reading the proof. On the proof you may find the printer's proofreading marks. They call for corrections of errors the typesetter has made. These corrections are made at the printer's own expense.

Here is a checklist of errors to look for:

1. Spelling
2. Punctuation
3. Inconsistencies in spelling, punctuation, use of italics, boldface, capitals, and in paragraph indentions and spacing
4. Transpositions of lines
5. Page numbers
6. Continuity from page to page

If the material to be proofread is technical or lengthy, have someone read aloud the original manuscript to you (including punctuation marks, capitalization, italics, and so on) slowly enough so that you can follow the proof. Make all corrections in a neat, legible hand. Should the correction consist of more than several words, type it directly on the proof. If it is quite lengthy, type it on a separate sheet, label it "Insert 1," and mark the proof with the same words ("Insert 1") at the proper place of insertion. Attach the insert to the proof on which the insert is noted.

Part IV

Assisting in Specialized Practice

---

18. Organizing a Corporation 379
19. Acting As Corporate Secretary 419
20. Real Estate Practice: Deeds; Mortgages; Leases 450
21. Real Estate Practice (Cont'd): Contracts of Sale and
    Closings 483
22. Foreclosure Actions 500
23. Probate and Estate Administration 511
24. Handling Commercial Collections 540

18

Organizing a Corporation

THE WORK of forming a corporation and qualifying it to do business in more than one state is highly technical, requiring strict observance of specific state laws, and of Federal laws if public issues of stock are involved.

In the case of a complicated corporation, the lawyers may engage the services of a firm, such as The Prentice-Hall Corporation System, Inc., which specializes in incorporating, qualifying, and maintaining corporations. In that case the secretary has no part in the incorporating work. If the lawyer undertakes to incorporate a complicated company without the aid of an outside agency, the secretary's work consists principally in typing from dictation. The organization of a simple corporation with no public issues of stock is not particularly complicated and is a frequent assignment in every law office. The task offers the secretary a chance to assume considerable responsibility, thereby relieving the busy lawyer.

This chapter is limited to telling the secretary how she can work with the lawyer on simple corporate organizations, and gives directions for doing her part of the task. Forms are included wherever practicable.

What is a corporation? A corporation is a device for carrying on an enterprise. It is a legal entity separate and apart from the persons who are interested in and control it. The state authorizes its existence and gives it certain powers. It also has certain powers that it gives itself, within the limits prescribed by the state, when it goes through the formalities of organization. A corporation has fundamental characteristics that make it the most popular form of business organization. Probably the most favorable aspect of the corporate form is the assurance of limited liability to the persons who put capital into the business.

Corporations may be classified as public corporations, corporations not for profit, and corporations for profit, each class being organized under different statutes.

Public corporations include all the subdivisions of the state, such as cities, tax districts, and irrigation districts. They also include Government-owned corporations, such as the Reconstruction Finance Corporation and the Commodity Credit Corporation.

Corporations not for profit are those organized for purposes other than the pecuniary gain of their members. Non-profit corporations do not have capital stock or pay dividends. Those who are interested in and control the corporation are referred to as its members, rather than its stockholders or shareholders as in a corporation for profit. These corporations include religious, civil, social, educational, fraternal, charitable, and cemetery associations.

Corporations for profit, or *business corporations,* are corporations with capital stock that carry on an enterprise for profit. Business corporations fall into three groups: (1) banks and insurance companies, which are known as moneyed corporations; (2) corporations that furnish public utility services to the public, such as transportation and electricity, which are known as *public service corporations;* and (3) corporations engaged in ordinary business pursuits, such as manufacturing, which are known as *private corporations.* The first two classes are subject to stricter governmental control than the private corporation.

The organization procedure described in this chapter relates to a private business corporation, but it is adaptable to other corporations.

Steps in the organization of a corporation. To organize a corporation means to bring it into existence. Each state designates a specific department and official through which the lawyer must work. (The table at the end of this chapter shows the official or department in each state.) Certain steps are necessary. These involve routine procedure that you can follow at the lawyer's direction without detailed instruction.

The usual steps in the organization of a corporation, each of which is described in detail here, are shown on the next page.

1. Reservation of name
2. Preparation of incorporating papers
3. Execution of papers
4. Filing of papers
5. First meeting of incorporators
6. First meeting of directors

Who may form a corporation? Those who unite for the purpose of forming a corporation are *incorporators*. They tell the lawyer the kind of business the corporation will engage in and the other details that are necessary for the lawyer to know before he commences the legal organization procedure. They also put up the capital for the corporation. Only natural persons may incorporate, although they may actually be representing a corporation or a partnership.

A large majority of the states require three or more incorporators. Many states also require that one or more of the incorporators shall be a resident of that state, or that the organization meeting of the corporation shall be held in that state. For these reasons, and for convenience, the incorporators are frequently *dummies*. They are not the principals who are actually interested in the organization of the corporation, but merely act for them until the organization meeting. Secretaries frequently act as dummy incorporators.

State of incorporation. A state in which a corporation is organized is the *state of incorporation*. A corporation is not necessarily incorporated under the laws of the state in which its executive office is located, especially if it is to carry on business in more than one state. Each state has a corporation law (see Table XII at the end of this chapter for the name of the corporation law in each state) under which private business corporations for profit are organized. The laws of some states are more favorable to corporations generally than those of other states. The lawyer recommends the state whose laws are most favorable to the proposed corporation. The cost of incorporating and the tax laws in each state are also taken into consideration. Therefore, the lawyer for whom you work might organize a corporation under the laws of a state far removed from your office. Delaware is the leading incorporating state.

In the state of incorporation, a corporation is known as a *domestic* corporation; in all other states, as a *foreign* corporation.

(Corporations organized outside the United States are referred to as *alien* corporations.) Thus, a corporation incorporated in Delaware is a domestic corporation there, but in New York and California it is a foreign corporation. A corporation is sometimes incorporated in more than one state, but generally if it wants to carry on its business in another state, it qualifies to do business in that state as a foreign corporation.

Memorandum preliminary to preparation of incorporating papers. Each lawyer has his own method of giving instructions to his secretary about the preparation of incorporating papers. A method commonly followed, and a very workable one, is the dictation of a preliminary memorandum. After the lawyer has a conference with the principals interested in forming a corporation, he dictates a memorandum of the conference. This memorandum covers all information necessary to the preparation of the charter. It will include:

1. State of incorporation.

2. The corporate name selected by the principals, usually first and second choice.

3. Nature of business in which the corporation proposes to engage. This clause is known as the *purpose clause*. The lawyer might direct you to a form in the form file or in a form book instead of dictating the clause.

4. Names and addresses of incorporators.

5. Names and addresses of directors.

6. Number of shares of stock each incorporator and director will hold, if any.

7. Designation of resident agent.

8. Location of principal office within the state of incorporation.

9. Fiscal year of the corporation.

10. Date for annual stockholders' meeting.

11. Amount of capital with which the corporation will commence business (the corporation law in each state fixes a minimum amount).

12. Authorized capital stock and its breakdown (number of shares of common stock and of preferred stock; number of shares with par value, and the par value of each; number of shares of no par stock).

13. Designations, rights, preferences, and all other details relating to preferred stock. This clause in the charter is known as the *stock clause*. It is frequently quite complicated, and sometimes several drafts of it are written before its provisions satisfy the principals.

This memorandum will serve as the basis for the organization of the corporation. With the help of the memorandum and appropriate forms, you will be able to complete the organization of a simple corporation without detailed instructions from the lawyer.

Reservation of name. Deciding on a corporation's name is a serious matter, to which the incorporators and the lawyer give careful consideration. All of the states require that a corporation's name should indicate that it is a corporation by the use of *company, association, incorporated,* or similar words or abbreviations of them. Also, the majority of the states will not permit the use of the word *bank* or *trust* in the name of a corporation unless it is a banking institution. The chief importance of a name to the incorporators is that, as a business develops, its name acquires a value in itself, representing to a great extent the good-will of the company. The state laws and the courts generally protect the corporation's exclusive right to the use of its name. The state official will not accept for filing a charter or articles of incorporation, if the name of the proposed corporation so closely resembles that of a corporation existing in the state that deception or confusion might result. Therefore, as soon as the lawyer dictates the memorandum described in the preceding paragraph, he will tell you to find out if the choice of name is available, and, if so, to reserve it.

What the secretary does to clear the name. Write to the designated state official (see Table XII) and ask if the chosen name is available.[1] You have to ascertain if the proposed name is available not only in the state of incorporation, but also in any states in which the corporation expects to qualify. If the organization of the corporation must be completed quickly, you might wire, or at least ask the state official to answer by wire collect.

In some states the state official will reserve a name for a speci-

---

[1] Illinois publishes annually a two-volume list of the names of existing corporations in Illinois, which may be obtained from the Secretary of State.

fied period of time for the payment of a fee or as a courtesy. (See Table XII at the end of this chapter.) In the states that require a fee enclose a check when you ask to have the name reserved. When you wire, send the check to the designated official as soon as you have a reply to your wire.

Your letter might read as follows:

The Honorable John R. Blank
Secretary of State of Delaware
Dover, Delaware

Sir:

<u>Johnson E. Jones, Inc.</u>

Will you please advise us whether the above styled name is available for a domestic corporation, which we are about to organize under the laws of your state.

If so, will you be good enough to reserve it for us for a statutory period. Enclosed is check for $3.00 in payment of reservation fee.

Please reply by wire, collect.

Very truly yours,

Elwood & Adams

If the incorporators expect to qualify as a foreign corporation in another state, the first paragraph will be changed to read: ". . . foreign corporation, which we are about to qualify to transact business in your state."

If you wire, your telegram might read: "Wire collect if Johnson E. Jones, Inc. is available for corporation."

Charter. The next step in the organization of a corporation is the preparation of the proposed charter, to be submitted to the designated public official for approval. The charter determines what the corporation is authorized to do, and the corporation cannot function until it has been granted, that is, approved by the proper official. Charters are variously called articles of incorporation, certificate of incorporation, or articles of association, depending upon the terminology used in the state of incorporation. (See "Organization records" in Table XII.) Some states provide a printed form (see Table XII) that may be used; otherwise, the charter is drawn from models that have been approved by the public official with whom the papers must be filed. Your office will have, or you will accumulate, a form file from charters prepared for previous clients. These forms will serve as models in the preparation of the charter for a corporation in the process of organization.

The states have different requirements for the provisions of the charter, but all of the states require that they shall contain special information with reference to the items set forth in the memorandum dictated to you by the lawyer.

Preparation of charter. The preparation of the average charter is largely routine, and you should be able to prepare it from the memorandum previously dictated, by using a form from your files as a model.

1. Consult Table XII at the end of this chapter for the number of copies that the law requires. *Make three extra copies*—one to be kept at the principal office of the corporation, one for your file, and one for the minute book. (In some states, including California, New Jersey, and Pennsylvania, an extra copy is required as an exhibit to the application for a permit to sell securities to the public. A copy of the charter must also be filed with the application to the Securities Exchange Commission.) The table gives the minimum number required by the corporation law. Some states also require that a certified copy be filed in each county where the corporation owns real estate. You will also have to make an extra copy for each state in which the proposed corporation expects to qualify. Two typings are necessary, the second being on minute paper.

2. Use either 8½" by 11" good quality bond paper, or legal cap. The trend is toward the use of the letter-size paper, except in those states where printed forms prepared by the state are used. When letter-size paper is used, the ribbon copy of the second typing is made on minute paper, thus saving the time required to copy the charter in the minute book.

3. If printed blank forms are used, as in Illinois, be sure they are of the same date of printing; otherwise, they might not be exact copies. When filling in the blanks, follow the instructions in Chapter 8 for filling in any printed form.

4. When typing the charter, always use pica type and a very black ribbon, and double space it. These requirements are mandatory in nearly every state. Otherwise, there is no specific form

in which the charter must be typed. Figures 93, 94, and 95 illustrate the first, second, and last pages of a charter and will serve as a model for style. The following details are customary, though not mandatory:

(a) The title of the document and name of the corporation are written in solid caps.

(b) The following words are written with initial caps when-

CERTIFICATE OF INCORPORATION

OF

JOHNSON E. JONES, INC.

———

We, the undersigned, for the purpose of associating to establish a corporation for the transaction of the business and the promotion and conduct of the objects and purposes hereinafter stated, under the provisions and subject to the requirements of the laws of the State of Delaware (particularly an act entitled "An Act Providing a General Corporation Law", approved March 10, 1899, and the acts amendatory thereof and supplemental thereto, and known as the "General Corporation Law of the State of Delaware"), do make and file this Certificate of Incorporation in writing and do hereby certify as follows, to wit:

FIRST: The name of the corporation (hereinafter called the Corporation) is

JOHNSON E. JONES, INC.

SECOND: The respective names of the County and of the City within the County in which the principal office of the Corporation is to be located in the State of Delaware are the County of Kent and the City of Dover. The name of the resident agent of the Corporation is The Prentice-Hall Corporation System, Inc. The street and number of said principal office and the address by street and number of said resident agent is 317-325 South State Street, Dover, Delaware.

Figure 93. First Page of Charter.

ever they refer to the corporation that is being organized: corporation, certificate of incorporation (or any other name by which the charter is known), board of directors, by-laws.

(c) The left margin of indented material is indented five spaces from the principal left margin, and the first line of an indented paragraph is indented five additional spaces. The right margin is also indented.

THIRD: The nature of the business of the Corporation and the objects or purposes to be transacted, promoted or carried on by it are as follows:

To ____

____

____.

To ____

____

________________________:

(a) ______________________________

____

______;

(b) ______________________________

______________________.

To ____

__________.

FOURTH: The name and place of residence of each of the incorporators are as follows:

NAME	PLACE OF RESIDENCE
E. G. Smith	Dover, Delaware
R. S. Lacey	Dover, Delaware
L. M. Stark	Dover, Delaware

FIFTH: The Corporation is to have perpetual existence.

SIXTH: ____

____.

-2-

Figure 94. Second Page of Charter.

(d) Subindentations are indented an additional five spaces.

(e) Numbered or lettered items are indented.

(f) Purpose clauses are indented.

(g) Pages are numbered.

(h) Numbers are written out, followed by figures in parentheses.

IN WITNESS WHEREOF, we, the undersigned, being all of the incorporators hereinabove named, do hereby further certify that the facts hereinabove stated are truly set forth and accordingly have hereunto set our respective hands and seals.

Dated at Dover, Delaware

October 31, 19--

_____ (L.S.)

_____ (L.S.)

_____ (L.S.)

STATE OF DELAWARE)
) SS.:
COUNTY OF KENT)

   BE IT REMEMBERED that personally appeared before me, Robert R. Steele, a Notary Public in and for the County and State aforesaid, E. G. Smith, R. S. Lacey, and L. M. Stark, all the incorporators who signed the foregoing Certificate of Incorporation, known to me personally to be such, and I having made known to them and each of them the contents of said Certificate of Incorporation, they did severally acknowledge the same to be the act and deed of the signers, respectively, and that the facts therein stated are truly set forth.

   Given under my hand and seal of office this 31st day of October, A. D. 19--.

             _____
                Notary Public

-10-

Figure 95. Last Page of Charter.

5. Type a signature line for each signer.

6. In almost all states the charter is a sealed instrument (see page 172). Consult Table XII and if the state of incorporation requires the seals of the signers, type (L.S.) or (SEAL) after each signature line.

7. If an acknowledgment (see Table XII) is required, type the certificate of acknowledgment in the form required by the state of incorporation. The venue will recite the state and county where the incorporators sign, not the state of incorporation. The rules that govern the acknowledgment of any instrument govern the acknowledgment of a charter. Remember that some states require acknowledgments taken outside the state to be authenticated. Therefore, if the acknowledgment is to be taken in a state other than the state of incorporation, consult Table I in Chapter 9 to see if authentication is necessary. If all incorporators sign at the same time, one certificate of acknowledgment is sufficient, but if they sign at different times, there must be a separate acknowledgment for each. Some states do not require that all incorporators who sign shall acknowledge the instrument.

8. Prepare a cover for each copy except the one that is on minute paper. The only typing on the cover is, "Certificate of Incorporation (or articles, or charter, as the case may be) of (name of corporation)."

Execution of the charter. In a few states all copies of the charter required to be filed with the designated public official must be ribbon copies, carbons not being acceptable. In others, an original and duplicate originals or triplicate originals (see page 150) are acceptable. Some states will accept an original and conformed copies. The table at the end of this chapter indicates the requirements in each state.

If the papers are to be executed in your office, notify the incorporators that the papers are ready for signature and arrange a time for them to come in to sign. (It is advisable to do this as soon as you know when the papers will be ready, in order to avoid delay.) If some or all of the incorporators are to sign outside your office, forward the document with a covering letter.

Each original, duplicate original, and triplicate original must be signed, but the copies that are to be conformed need not be signed. The signature must be the same on each copy, and must be written exactly as in the document. Thus, if an incorporator signs his name *R. P. Edwards,* his name should not be written *Richard P. Edwards* in the document.

When acknowledgments are required, take the acknowledgment of the incorporators who sign in your office, and notarize all signed copies of the charter. Conform the unsigned copies.

Filing the charter and payment of fees. After the charter has been executed, send the required number of copies (see Table XII) to the proper state official, with a letter of transmittal and a check in payment of the organization tax and fees. Your letter of transmittal might read as follows:

Secretary of State
State of Delaware
Dover, Delaware

Gentlemen: Re: Johnson E. Jones, Inc.

     We are enclosing an original and two conformed copies of Certificate of Incorporation of Johnson E. Jones, Inc. Please record the original of the Certificate in your offices and certify and return to us the conformed copies.

     We are also enclosing our check in the amount of $40, covering (1) the organization tax, $10; (2) filing and indexing fee, $5; (3) recording fee, $15; (4) certification of copy for recording, $6; and (5) certification of one extra copy, $4.

                            Very truly yours,

                            Elwood & Adams

Enclosures   (4)

If the charter is acceptable, the public official will retain the original. He will mark the copy, or copies, to show that the charter has been filed with him and endorse his approval upon it, or attach a certificate of approval to it, and return it, together with receipt for tax and fees, to your office. You will then do the following:

1. Conform your office copy, noting particularly the date of the official's filing marks. This date, rather than the date on which the charter was executed, is the date of incorporation.

2. Draw check for the local filing fee and file the certified copy of the charter in the appropriate local office if required (see Table XII).

3. Note on your office copy the date the charter was filed locally.

4. Paste the tax receipt in the minute book.

Organization Meetings

Necessity and purpose of organization meeting. From a practical, as well as legal, standpoint, a corporation cannot transact its business until details of its organization are completed. Therefore, as soon as the charter is approved and filed with the proper authorities, and other mandatory requirements of the law are complied with, an organization meeting is held. The states do not all use the same terminology as to the participants in the organization meeting. There are at least four variations: (1) *incorporators;* (2) *incorporators and subscribers* (to the stock); (3) *shareholders* or *stockholders;* (4) *subscribers* (signers of the charter). In some states the organization meeting is a meeting of the directors named in the charter. The column headed "Organization records" in Table XII will indicate the terminology for each state. The actions taken at organization meetings are routine and are usually agreed upon in advance by the principals organizing the corporation. Frequently, therefore, the meeting is not actually held but the minutes are prepared as though the meeting had been held.

The secretary's preparation for the organization meeting. As the lawyer's secretary you will have to make certain preparations for the organization meeting. These preparations include:

1. Obtaining a corporate outfit

2. Preparation of waiver of notice of meeting, and obtaining signatures to it

3. Preparation of by-laws

4. Preparation of minutes of first meeting of incorporators

5. Preparation of minutes of first meeting of directors

6. Preparation of bank account resolution

7. Preparation of stock certificates

Corporate outfit. Simultaneously with the preparation of the charter, order a *corporate outfit.* This consists of a seal, minute book, stock certificate book, and a stock ledger, and may be obtained from any stationer who handles legal supplies. Some minute books contain printed forms for minutes and by-laws, but many lawyers object to the use of them. When you order the outfit, your letter should give all data necessary to the preparation of the seal and stock certificates. The following model letter indicates the necessary data.

Smith Stationery Company
103 Broadway
New York 7, New York

Gentlemen: Re: Johnson E. Jones, Inc.

Please forward to us at your earliest convenience the following corporate supplies:

1. Hand Seal (JOHNSON E. JONES, INC., a Delaware corporation, Incorporated 19..).
2. Minute Book with Filler.
3. Stock Certificate Book (minimum number of certificates).
4. Stock Ledger.

For your convenience in preparing the stock certificates, we submit the following information: There are authorized to be issued 150 shares of capital stock (only one class authorized) having no par value, fully paid and non-assessable. JOHNSON E. JONES, INC. is a corporation of the State of Delaware and was incorporated in the year 19...

Please send your invoice when the supplies are mailed to us, and we will immediately forward our check in payment.

Very truly yours,

p   Elwood & Adams

If there are two classes of stock, it is advisable to send a copy of the charter with the order. The stationer can then get the preferred stock clause, which is printed on the back of the stock certificate, directly from the charter. The certificate of common stock will be one color; preferred stock, another.

Waiver of notice of organization meeting. The statutes require that the incorporators, directors, shareholders, or subscribers, as the case may be, shall be given notice of the organization meeting, just as of any other meeting (see page 422), unless they waive notice. It is customary for them to waive notice of the organization meeting. It is your responsibility to prepare the waiver and obtain the signatures of the interested parties. Forms 2 and 3, on page 442, illustrate waivers of notice of first meeting of incorporators, and of first meeting of directors, respectively. Waivers are usually typed on legal cap.

Preparation of by-laws. The by-laws of a corporation are the rules adopted to govern the corporation, its officers, directors, and stockholders. Like the charter, the by-laws usually follow a more or less routine pattern. The lawyer will dictate special clauses or paragraphs peculiar to the corporation being organized, and will dictate a memorandum that includes the following information:

1. Place of stockholders' meeting.

2. Day and hour of annual meeting of stockholders.

3. Time when notice of annual meeting of stockholders must be given (usually 10 days before meeting).

4. Who may call special meetings of stockholders (usually president, vice president, or upon request two directors or holders of 25 per cent of the outstanding stock).

5. Time when notice of special meeting of stockholders must be given (usually 10 days before meeting).

6. Percentage of stock that constitutes a quorum (usually a majority).

7. Place of directors' meetings.

8. When regular directors' meetings are to be held.

9. Time when notice of regular meetings of directors must be given (usually three or five days before the meeting).

10. Who may call special meetings of directors (usually president, vice president, or upon request two directors).

11. Time when notice of special meetings of directors must be given (usually three or five days before the meeting).

12. Number of directors to constitute quorum.

13. Officers who are to sign and countersign checks.

14. Officers who are to sign and countersign stock certificates.

15. When the fiscal year of the company ends.

With the help of this memorandum and the charter you will be able to follow a form and prepare the by-laws. By-laws are too lengthy to be included here, but you may refer to any book of incorporating forms,[2] or you may obtain a printed copy of the by-laws of corporations that are listed on a stock exchange. Fig-

---

[1] See *Encyclopedia of Incorporating Forms*. Englewood Cliffs, N. J.: Prentice-Hall, Inc., 1950.

ure 96 shows how the by-laws should be set up. Letter-size paper is preferable.

```
                    JOHNSON E. JONES, INC.

                         B Y  L A W S

                         ARTICLE I.

                           Office.

            The principal office of the Corporation shall be
        located in the Borough of Manhattan, City of New York,
        _____

        _____

                         ARTICLE II.

                    Meetings of Stockholders.

                Section 1.  Annual Meeting.  The annual meeting
        of the stockholders of the Corporation after the year 19
        _____

        _____

                Section 2.  Inspectors of Election.  The annual
        election of Directors shall be conducted by two inspectors
        _____

        _____

                         ARTICLE III.

                          Directors.

                Section 1.  Management.  The property, business
        and affairs of the Corporation shall be managed by a
        _____

        _____
```

Figure 96. First Page of By-Laws.

Minutes of first meeting of incorporators. You can prepare minutes of the first meeting of incorporators without instructions from the attorney, by following a form. The purpose of the minutes is to place on record the filing date of the original of the charter; the filing date of a certified copy in the appropriate county office, where required (see Table XII); the election of directors; the presentation and adoption of the by-laws; and the authorization of the board of directors to issue capital stock of the corporation. Form 1 on page 440 is a form of minutes of the first meeting of a Delaware corporation. Detailed directions for the typing of minutes in final form are given on page 429. California, Maryland, and Utah corporations do not hold an incorporators' meeting but transact this business at the first meeting of directors, who are named in the charter.

Minutes of first meeting of directors. The purposes of the first, or organization, meeting of the board of directors are to elect officers, approve and ratify the acts of the incorporators, adopt a seal, approve the form of stock certificate, open a bank account, designate a resident agent, and to transact any other business that may properly come before the meeting. The lawyer usually dictates the minutes of the organization meeting of the board of directors. See page 429 for typing directions.

Resolution opening a bank account. The resolution of the board of directors authorizing the opening of a bank account must conform to the requirements of the bank in which the account is to be carried. Banks usually have printed forms of these resolutions. Therefore, obtain the forms and signature cards and fill them in prior to the meeting. The necessary information is available from the memoranda dictated by the lawyer immediately after his original conference with the principals (pages 382 and 393). The signature cards and resolutions must be signed by the proper individuals. See page 425 for procedure in handling resolutions prepared by outside organizations.

Preparation of stock certificates. The lawyer will tell you to whom stock certificates shall be issued and the number of shares each stockholder shall receive, or the preliminary memorandum dictated by him will give you this information. See page 433, *et seq.* for directions about issuance of stock. The certificate must be signed and sealed as required by the by-laws. In some instances when the incorporators are dummies, stock is issued to them and they, in turn, assign it to the actual incorporators. This procedure is not generally necessary, but if it is followed, prepare assignments of certificates in blank of any stock the dummies hold.

Table XII

ALABAMA. Department of State is in charge. General Corporation Law governs. Name reserved 60 days, by Secretary of State, through courtesy.

Execution and Filing

Original Certificate of Incorporation signed by each subscriber, without seal or acknowledgment, filed with Probate Judge of county in which principal office is located. Original subscription agreement executed at pre-incorporation meeting and affidavit of subscription officer or agent also filed with Probate Judge. He files statement with Secretary of State.

Organization Records

Certificate of Incorporation.
Affidavit of Subscription Officer or Agent.
By-laws.
Notice or Waiver of Notice of First Meeting of Stockholders.

Minutes of First Meeting of Stockholders.
Waiver of Notice of First Meeting of Directors.
Minutes of First Meeting of Directors.

ALASKA. Office of Director of Finance is in charge. Alaska Business Corporation Act governs. Name reserved 120 days, by Director of Finance, $5 fee.

Execution and Filing

Duplicate originals of Articles of Incorporation, signed and verified by incorporators, sent to Office of Director of Finance, which endorses both, files one and returns other with Certificate of Incorporation attached.

Organization Records

Articles of Incorporation.*

* *Official forms may be obtained by applying to the department in charge of corporations.*

By-laws.
Notice of First Meeting of Directors.
Minutes of First Meeting of Directors.

ARIZONA. Corporation Commission is in charge. General Corporation Law governs. Name reserved 60 days, by Corporation Commission, $5 fee.

Execution and Filing

Original of Articles of Incorporation filed and acknowledged by incorporators. Executed original and conformed copies sent to Corporation Commission, which certifies and returns copies. Certified copies filed and recorded in office of county recorder in each county where corporation proposes to do business. Articles published in newspaper **6** times. Affidavit of publication and appointment of agent filed with Corporation Commission, which then issues Certificate of Incorporation.

Organization Records

Articles of Incorporation.
By-laws.
Appointment of Agent.
Notice or Waiver of Notice of First Meeting of Incorporators.
Minutes of First Meeting of Incorporators.
Waiver of Notice of First Meeting of Directors.
Minutes of First Meeting of Directors.

Affidavit of Publication of Articles of Incorporation.

ARKANSAS. Department of State is in charge. General Corporation Act governs. No reservation of name. Write Secretary of State for availability of name chosen.

Execution and Filing

Duplicate originals of Articles of Incorporation signed and acknowledged by incorporators. Sent to Secretary of State, who files one and returns the other, which is filed and recorded by county clerk of county in which principal office is located.

Organization Records

Certificate of Incorporation.
Agent's Statement.
Code of By-laws.
Notice or Waiver of Notice of First Meeting of Stockholders.
Minutes of First Meeting of Stockholders.
Waiver of Notice of First Meeting of Directors.
Minutes of First Meeting of Directors.

CALIFORNIA. Department of State is in charge. Corporations Code governs. Name reserved 30 days, by Secretary of State, $2 fee.

* *Official forms may be obtained by applying to the department in charge of corporations.*

Execution and Filing

Original of Articles of Incorporation signed and acknowledged by directors named therein. Executed and conformed copies sent to Secretary of State, who files original and certifies and returns conformed copies. Certified copies filed with county clerk of county in which principal office is located and with county clerk of each county in which corporation owns real property.

Organization Records

Articles of Incorporation.
By-laws.
Notice or Waiver of Notice of First Meeting of Directors.
Minutes of First Meeting of Directors.
Application for Permit to Issue Shares.
Statement by Corporation of Principal Office, Names of Officers and Designation of Agent.*

COLORADO. Department of State is in charge. Colorado Corporation Act governs. Name reserved 120 days, by Secretary of State, $5 fee.

Execution and Filing

Duplicate originals of Articles of Incorporation, signed and acknowledged by each incorporator, sent to Secretary of State, who endorses both, files one and returns other with Certificate of Incorporation attached.

Organization Records

Certificate of Incorporation.*
By-laws.
Waiver of Notice of First Meeting of Directors.
Minutes of First Meeting of Directors.

CONNECTICUT. Department of State is in charge. General Corporation Law governs. No reservation. Write Secretary of State for availability of name chosen.

Execution and Filing

Original Certificate of Incorporation subscribed and sworn to by each incorporator. Executed original and conformed copy sent to Secretary of State, who files original and certifies and returns conformed copy to be filed with clerk of town where corporation is to be located.

Organization Records

Certificate of Incorporation.*
By-laws.
Notice or Waiver of Notice of First Meeting of Incorporators and Subscribers.
Minutes of First Meeting of Incorporators and Subscribers.
Waiver of Notice of First Meeting of Directors.
Minutes of First Meeting of Directors.
Certificate of Organization.*
Directors' Certificate of Shares to be Issued Without Par Value.*

* Official forms may be obtained by applying to the department in charge of corporations.

DELAWARE. Department of State is in charge. General Corporation Law governs. Name reserved 30 days, by Secretary of State, through courtesy.

Execution and Filing

Original of Certificate of Incorporation signed, sealed, and acknowledged by each incorporator. Executed original and conformed copy sent to Secretary of State, who files executed copy and certifies and returns conformed copy, to be recorded with county recorder of county where principal office is located.

Organization Records

Certificate of Incorporation.
By-laws.
Notice or Waiver of Notice of First Meeting of Incorporators.
Minutes of First Meeting of Incorporators.
Waiver of Notice of First Meeting of Directors.
Minutes of First Meeting of Directors.

DISTRICT OF COLUMBIA. Office of Commissioners of District of Columbia is in charge. District of Columbia Business Corporation Act governs. Name reserved 60 days, by Commissioners, $5 fee.

Execution and Filing

Duplicate originals of Articles of Incorporation signed and verified by in-corporators, sent to Commissioners, who endorse both, file one and return other with Certificate of Incorporation attached.

Organization Records

Articles of Incorporation.*
By-laws.
Waiver of Notice of First Meeting of Directors.
Minutes of First Meeting of Directors.

FLORIDA. Department of State is in charge. General Corporation Law governs. No reservation. Write Secretary of State for availability of name chosen.

Execution and Filing

Original of Articles of Incorporation subscribed and acknowledged by each incorporator and filed with Secretary of State. Within 30 days certificate of designation of domicile and of agent filed with Secretary of State.

Organization Records

Certificate of Incorporation.
By-laws.
Notice or Waiver of Notice of First Meeting of Stockholders.
Minutes of First Meeting of Stockholders.
Waiver of Notice of First Meeting of Directors.
Minutes of First Meeting of Directors.

* *Official forms may be obtained by applying to the department in charge of corporations.*

Certificate of Designation of Domicile for Service of Process.*

Directors.
Minutes of First Meeting of Directors.

GEORGIA. Department of State is in charge. General Corporation Law governs. Name reserved 90 days, by Secretary of State, $1 fee.

Execution and Filing

Original Application for Charter, signed by incorporators or by Georgia counsel, presented to Judge of Superior Court, who issues Order. Within 1 week of filing application, publish Application and Order once a week for 4 weeks in newspaper. File Application, Order, and publisher's affidavit with court clerk. Have clerk certify two copies of Application and Order, which are sent to Secretary of State. He retains one set; attaches certificate and returns other set.

Organization Records

Application for Charter.*
Charter of Incorporation (Order).
Publisher's Affidavit.
By-laws.
Notice or Waiver of Notice of First Meeting of Incorporators.
Minutes of First Meeting of Incorporators.
Notice or Waiver of Notice of First Meeting of Stockholders.
Minutes of First Meeting of Stockholders.
Waiver of Notice of First Meeting of

HAWAII. Office of the Treasurer is in charge. General Corporation Law governs. Name reserved 30 days, by Treasurer, $1 fee.

Execution and Filing

Original of Articles of Association, signed and acknowledged by subscribers together with affidavit and supplemental affidavit, if any, with regard to capital stock, signed by President, Secretary and Treasurer, and filed with Treasurer.

Organization Records

Articles of Association.
By-laws.
Notice of First Meeting of Subscribers.
Minutes of First Meeting of Subscribers.
Notice of First Meeting of Directors.
Minutes of First Meeting of Directors.
Officers' affidavit as to Capital Stock.

IDAHO. Department of State is in charge. Business Corporation Act governs. Name reserved 60 days, by Secretary of State, no fee; beyond that to one year, $1 fee.

Execution and Filing

Triplicate originals of Articles of In-

Official forms may be obtained by applying to the department in charge of corporations.

corporation, signed by each incorporator and acknowledged by at least 3 of them, sent to Secretary of State, who files and records one triplicate original, endorses his approval upon the other two, and issues a Certificate of Incorporation. He returns the two endorsed triplicate originals, together with Certificate. One triplicate original is then filed for record with clerk of county court in county where registered office is located. Certified copy is also filed with county clerk of each county in which corporation owns real estate.

Organization Records

Articles of Incorporation.
By-laws.
Notice or Waiver of Notice of First Meeting of Incorporators.
Minutes of First Meeting of Incorporators.
Waiver of Notice of First Meeting of Directors.
Minutes of First Meeting of Directors.

ILLINOIS. Department of State is in charge. Business Corporation Act governs. Name reserved 60 days, by Secretary of State, $5 fee.

Execution and Filing

Duplicate originals of Articles of Incorporation signed and verified by incorporators, sent to Secretary of State, who endorses both, files one, and returns other with Certificate of Incorpo-

ration attached. Record within 15 days with Recorder of Deeds in county in which initial registered office is located

Organization Records

Initial Subscription Agreement.
Articles of Incorporation.*
By-laws.
Call or Waiver of Notice of First Meeting of Shareholders.
Minutes of First Meeting of Shareholders.
Call and Waiver of Notice of First Meeting of Directors.
Minutes of First Meeting of Directors.

INDIANA. Department of State is in charge. General Corporation Act governs. Name reserved 30 days, by Secretary of State; no fee.

Execution and Filing

Triplicate originals of Articles of Incorporation, signed and acknowledged by at least three incorporators, sent to Secretary of State, who files one and issues Certificate of Incorporation. Returns two triplicate originals of Articles with his stamp of approval thereon, one of which must be filed with recorder of county in which principal office is located.

Organization Records

Subscription Agreement.
Articles of Incorporation.*
By-laws.

* *Official forms may be obtained by applying to the department in charge of corporations.*

Affidavit of Paid-in Capital.*

Notice or Waiver of Notice of Meeting of Subscribers.

Minutes of First Meeting of Subscribers.

Waiver of Notice of First Meeting of Directors.

Minutes of First Meeting of Directors.

IOWA. Department of State is in charge. Iowa Business Corporation Act governs. Name reserved 90 days by Secretary of State, $5 fee.

Execution and Filing

Original of Articles of Incorporation, signed and acknowledged by incorporators, sent to Secretary of State, who issues Certificate of Incorporation, records Articles, and forwards original of Articles to Recorder of Deeds in county where principal place of business is located. Within 3 months after Secretary of State issues Certificate, publish notice of incorporation in newspaper once a week for four weeks. Thereafter file publisher's affidavit with Secretary. If corporation maintains no office in county of organization, file with secretary certified copy of directors' resolution appointing process agent. Within 30 days after issuance of stock, file with Secretary certificate as to issue of capital stock.

Organization Records

Articles of Incorporation.
By-laws.

Waiver of Notice of First Meeting of Directors.

Minutes of First Meeting of Directors.

Published Notice of Incorporation.

Affidavit of Publication of Notice of Incorporation.

Certificate as to Issue of Capital Stock.*

KANSAS. Department of State is in charge. General Corporation Code governs. Reasonable time, by Secretary of State, through courtesy.

Execution and Filing

Original of Articles of Incorporation, signed and acknowledged by incorporators, and copy sent to Secretary of State, who files original and certifies and returns copy. Certified copy filed for record with Register of Deeds of county in which principal office is located.

Organization Records

Articles of Incorporation.*
By-laws.
Notice or Waiver of Notice of First Meeting of Incorporators.
Minutes of First Meeting of Incorporators.
Waiver of Notice of First Meeting of Directors.
Minutes of First Meeting of Directors.
Affidavit of Paid-in Capital.

* *Official forms may be obtained by applying to the department in charge of corporations.*

KENTUCKY. Department of State is in charge. General corporation law governs. No reservation. Write Secretary of State for availability of name chosen.

Execution and Filing

Triplicate originals of Articles of Incorporation, signed and acknowledged by incorporators, sent to Secretary of State, who files and records one triplicate original, endorses his approval upon other two, and issues Certificate of Incorporation. He returns Certificate and two endorsed triplicate originals, one of which is filed for record with clerk of county court in county where registered office is located.

Organization Records

Articles of Incorporation.
By-laws.
Notice or Waiver of Notice of First Meeting of Stockholders.
Minutes of First Meeting of Stockholders.
Waiver of Notice of First Meeting of Directors.
Minutes of First Meeting of Directors.

LOUISIANA. Department of State is in charge. Business corporations law governs. Name reserved 30 days, by Secretary of State, through courtesy.

Execution and Filing

Duplicate originals of Articles of In-

corporation signed by each incorporator as an authentic act (before notary and two witnesses). One duplicate original filed for record in office of recorder of mortgages in parish in which registered office is located. Recorder attaches certificate of recording to other duplicate original (or to certified copy of Articles), which is then filed with Secretary of State, who issues certificate of incorporation. Within 90 days after incorporation, file with Recorder of mortgages and with Secretary of State, Verified Report of Consideration for Shares. File with Clerk of District Court in parish in which registered office is located Notice of Registered Office and Registered Agents.

Organization Records

Articles of Incorporation.
By-laws.
Notice or Waiver of Notice of First Meeting of Incorporators and Subscribers.
Minutes of First Meeting of Incorporators and Subscribers.
Waiver of Notice of First Meeting of Directors.
Minutes of First Meeting of Directors.
Report and Affidavit as to Consideration for Shares.
Notice of Registered Office and Registered Agents.

MAINE. Department of State is in charge. General corporation law governs. No reservation. Write Secretary of State for availability of name chosen

* Official forms may be obtained by applying to the department in charge of corporations.

Execution and Filing

Original Certificate of Organization signed and sworn to by president, treasurer, and majority of directors. Executed original and one conformed copy submitted to Attorney General, who retains copy and returns original with certificate that it is properly drawn. Certified original and second conformed copy filed with register of deeds in county where corporation is located. Original and copy certified by register then filed with Secretary of State, who enters date of filing on original Certificate, which is kept by incorporators. Secretary of State also enters date of filing on copy and records it.

Organization Records

Articles of Association (Pre-organization Agreement).
By-laws.
Notice or Waiver of Notice of First Meeting of Incorporators.
Minutes of First Meeting of Incorporators.
Waiver of Notice of First Meeting of Directors.
Minutes of First Meeting of Directors.
Certificate of Organization.*

MARYLAND. State Tax Commission is in charge. General corporation law governs. Name reserved 30 days, by State Tax Commission, $2 fee.

Execution and Filing

Original of Articles of Incorporation signed and acknowledged by incorporators sent to State Tax Commission, which endorses thereon date and time of acceptance, records Articles and transmits to clerk of court of county in which principal office is located. Clerk records Articles and returns to incorporators.

Organization Records

Articles of Incorporation.
By-laws.
Call and Waiver of Notice of First Meeting of Directors.
Minutes of First Meeting of Directors.
Stock Issuance Statement.

MASSACHUSETTS. Commissioner of Corporations and Taxation is in charge. General corporation law governs. Name reserved 10 days, by Commissioner of Corporations and Taxation, through courtesy.

Execution and Filing

Original of Agreement of Association signed by incorporators, Record of first meeting of incorporators including by-laws, and original of Articles of Organization signed and sworn to by majority of directors, sent to Commissioner of Corporations and Taxation. He returns the Agreement and Record and endorses his approval on Articles, which

* *Official forms may be obtained by applying to the department in charge of corporations.*

are filed with Secretary of State, who issues Certificate of Incorporation.

Organization Records

Agreement of Association.*
Articles of Organization.*
By-laws.
Notice or Waiver of Notice of First Meeting of Incorporators.
Minutes of First Meeting of Incorporators.
Waiver of Notice of First Meeting of Directors.
Minutes of First Meeting of Directors.

MICHIGAN. Corporation and Securities Commission is in charge. General Corporation Act governs. Name reserved 30 days, by Corporation and Securities Commission, through courtesy.

Execution and Filing

Triplicate originals, signed by incorporators and acknowledged by at least one of them, sent to Michigan Corporation and Securities Commission, which files one triplicate original, returns one certified triplicate original, and forwards other triplicate original to county clerk of county in which registered office is located.

Organization Records

Articles of Incorporation.*
Appointment of Resident Agent.*

By-laws.
Notice or Waiver of Notice of First Meeting of Incorporators.
Minutes of First Meeting of Incorporators.
Waiver of Notice of First Meeting of Directors.
Minutes of First Meeting of Directors.

MINNESOTA. Department of State is in charge. Business Corporation Act governs. Name reserved 12 months, by Secretary of State, $3 fee.

Execution and Filing

Original of Articles of Incorporation, signed by all incorporators and acknowledged by at least 3 of them, and conformed copy, sent to Secretary of State, who files Articles and issues and records Certificate of Incorporation. He certifies copy of Articles and Certificate and transmits them, together with required fee, to Register of Deeds in county in which registered office of corporation is located. Within 21 days after Secretary of State issues Certificate, publish notice of incorporation in newspaper in county in which registered office is located, filing proof of publication with Secretary of State within 21 days after publication.

Organization Records

Articles of Incorporation.
By-laws.
Notice or Waiver of Notice of First

---

* *Official forms may be obtained by applying to the department in charge of corporations.*

Meeting of Incorporators.

Minutes of First Meeting of Incorporators.

Waiver of Notice of First Meeting of Directors.

Minutes of First Meeting of Directors.

Notice of Incorporation.

Affidavit of Publication of Notice of Incorporation.

MISSISSIPPI. Department of State is in charge. General corporation law governs. No reservation of name. Write to Secretary of State for availability of name chosen.

Execution and Filing

Original of Charter of Incorporation signed and acknowledged by each incorporator and filed with Secretary of State. If approved by Governor and Attorney General, Secretary of State records and certifies it and returns to applicants. Copy of charter published once in newspaper, within 30 days after it is granted.

Organization Records

Charter of Incorporation.*

By-laws.

Call or Waiver of Notice of First Meeting of Incorporators, Subscribers, and Stockholders.

Minutes of First Meeting of Incorporators, Subscribers, and Stockholders.

Waiver of Notice of First Meeting of Directors.

Minutes of First Meeting of Directors.

Designation of Agent.*

Acceptance of Agency by Agent.

Report of Organization.*

Publication of charter.

MISSOURI. Department of State is in charge. General and Business Corporation Law governs. Name reserved 60 days, by Secretary of State, $5 fee.

Execution and Filing

Duplicate originals of Articles of Incorporation, signed, acknowledged, and sworn to by all incorporators, sent to Secretary of State, who files one duplicate original and issues a Certificate of Incorporation. Returns certified copy of Certificate and second duplicate original, which are filed and recorded in office of Recorder of Deeds of city or county in which registered office is located.

Organization Records

Articles of Incorporation.

By-laws.

Notice or Waiver of Notice of First Meeting of Shareholders.

Minutes of First Meeting of Shareholders.

Waiver of Notice of First Meeting of Directors.

Minutes of First Meeting of Directors.

Directors' Affidavit.*

* *Official forms may be obtained by applying to the department in charge of corporations.*

MONTANA. Department of State is in charge. General corporation law governs. Name reserved a reasonable time by Secretary of State, through courtesy.

Execution and Filing

Original of Articles of Incorporation signed and acknowledged by incorporators. Executed original and conformed copy filed in office of county clerk of county in which principal business of corporation is to be transacted. Copy certified by clerk filed with Secretary of State who issues certificate that Articles have been filed in his office. Conformed copy authenticated by clerk or certified by Secretary of State must be filed in office of county clerk of each county in which corporation owns real estate.

Organization Records

Articles of Incorporation.
By-laws.
Waiver of Notice of First Meeting of Directors.
Minutes of First Meeting of Directors.

NEBRASKA. Department of State is in charge. General Corporation Law governs. Name may be reserved a few weeks through courtesy.

Execution and Filing

Original of Articles of Incorporation signed and acknowledged by each of incorporators, and filed with Secretary of State who furnishes a certified copy, which is recorded in office of county clerk of county where principal office is located. Notice of incorporating published three successive weeks in legal newspaper. Proof of publication filed with Secretary of State and in office of county clerk.

Organization Records

Articles of Incorporation.
By-laws.
Notice or Waiver of Notice of First Meeting of Incorporators.
Minutes of First Meeting of Incorporators.
Waiver of Notice of First Meeting of Directors.
Minutes of First Meeting of Directors.
Published Notice of Incorporation.
Proof of Publication.

NEVADA. Department of State is in charge. General corporation law governs. Name reserved 10 days, by Secretary of State, $2 fee.

Execution and Filing

Original of Certificate of Incorporation, signed and acknowledged by incorporators, and one conformed copy sent to Secretary of State, who files original and certifies and returns copy. Certified copy filed with county clerk of county in which principal office is to be located. Within 60 days after fil-

* Official forms may be obtained by applying to the department in charge of corporations.

ing Articles of Incorporation, file with Secretary of State list of Officers and Directors, Designation of Agent and Certificate of Acceptance by Agent.

Organization Records

Articles of Incorporation.*
By-laws.
Waiver of Notice of First Meeting of Directors.
Minutes of First Meeting of Directors.
List of Officers, Directors and Agent.*

NEW HAMPSHIRE. Secretary of State and Attorney General are in charge. General Corporation Law governs. No reservation of name. Write Secretary of State for availability of name chosen.

Execution and Filing

Original Articles of Agreement signed by incorporators, who then hold organization meeting. Affidavit of Record of Organization signed and sworn to by treasurer and majority of directors. Organization Record consists of executed original of Articles of Organization (or a true copy), names and addresses of officers and directors, and original or true copy of record of organization meeting attested by clerk. Record of Organization and Affidavit sent to Attorney General, who endorses his approval on it. Record and endorsement then sent to Secretary of State, who records it and issues certificate of incorporation.

Organization Records

Affidavit of Record of Organization.
Articles of Agreement.
By-laws.
Notice or Waiver of Notice of Organization Meeting of Incorporators.
Minutes of Organization Meeting of Incorporators.
Waiver of Notice of First Meeting of Directors.
Minutes of First Meeting of Directors.

NEW JERSEY. Department of State is in charge. General corporation law governs. No reservation. Write Secretary of State for availability of name chosen.

Execution and Filing

Original of Certificate of Incorporation, signed and acknowledged by incorporators, and one conformed copy sent to Secretary of State, who files and records original and certifies and returns copy. Certified copy recorded in office of county clerk of county in which principal office of corporation is located. Within 30 days after first election of directors and within 10 days after payment of each installment, file with Secretary of State, First Annual Report and Certificate of Payment of Capital Stock respectively.

Organization Records

Certificate of Incorporation.*
By-laws.

---

* Official forms may be obtained by applying to the department in charge of corporations.

Notice or Waiver of Notice of First Meeting of Incorporators and Subscribers.

Minutes of First Meeting of Incorporators and Subscribers.

Waiver of Notice of First Meeting of Directors.

Minutes of First Meeting of Directors.

Certificate of Payment of Stock.*

First Annual Report.*

NEW MEXICO. State Corporation Commission is in charge. General corporation law governs. Name reserved 30 days, by State Corporation Commissioner, $5 fee.

Execution and Filing

Original Certificate of Incorporation, signed and acknowledged by each incorporator, and conformed copy sent to State Corporation Commission, which certifies and returns copy. Certified copy recorded in office of county clerk of county where principal office is located. Within 30 days of filing, synopsis of incorporation published in newspaper once, and affidavit of publication filed with State Corporation Commission. Within 30 days after first election of directors or, if they are named in Certificate of Incorporation, within 30 days of filing such certificate, file First Annual Report. Also file, with State Corporation Commission, Certificate of Payment of Capital Stock within 10 days after payment.

Organization Records

Certificate of Incorporation.

By-laws.

Notice or Waiver of Notice of First Meeting of Incorporators and Subscribers.

Minutes of First Meeting of Incorporators and Subscribers.

Waiver of Notice of First Meeting of Directors.

Minutes of First Meeting of Directors.

Certificate as to Payment of Capital Stock.*

Notice of Publication of Certificate of Incorporation.

Affidavit of Publication of Certificate of Incorporation.

First Annual Report.*

NEW YORK. Department of State is in charge. General Corporation Law and Stock Corporation Law govern. No reservation of name. Write Secretary of State for availability of name chosen.

Execution and Filing

Original of Certificate of Incorporation, signed and acknowledged by each subscriber, filed with Secretary of State, who prepares photostatic copy of Certificate, certifies and files same with county clerk of county in which principal office is located.

Organization Records

Certificate of Incorporation.

* *Official forms may be obtained by applying to the department in charge of corporations.*

By-laws.

Notice or Waiver of Notice of First Meeting of Incorporators and Subscribers.

Minutes of First Meeting of Incorporators and Subscribers.

Waiver of Notice of First Meeting of Directors.

Minutes of First Meeting of Directors.

Certificate Required to Be Filed under Section 275A of the Tax Law.

NORTH CAROLINA. Department of State is in charge. Business Corporation Act governs. Name reserved 90 days, by Secretary of State, $5 fee.

Execution and Filing

Original of Articles of Incorporation, signed, sealed, and acknowledged by the incorporators, and one copy sent to Secretary of State, who files original and certifies and returns copy. Certified copy recorded in office of clerk of superior court of county in which principal office is to be located.

Organization Records

Articles of Incorporation.*

By-laws.

Notice or Waiver of Notice of First Meeting of Incorporators.

Minutes of First Meeting of Incorporators.

Waiver of Notice of First Meeting of Directors.

Minutes of First Meeting of Directors.

NORTH DAKOTA. Department of State is in charge. Business Corporation Act governs. Name reserved 120 days, by Secretary of State, $5 fee.

Execution and Filing

Duplicate originals of Articles of Incorporation, signed and verified by incorporators, sent to Secretary of State. who files one and issues Certificate of Incorporation. The other original with Certificate attached is returned to incorporators.

Organization Records

Articles of Incorporation.*

By-laws.

Notice or Waiver of Notice of First Meeting of Subscribers.

Minutes of First Meeting of Subscribers.

Waiver of Notice of First Meeting of Directors.

Minutes of First Meeting of Directors.

OHIO. Department of State is in charge. General Corporation Law governs. Name reserved 60 days, by Secretary of State, $5 fee.

Execution and Filing

Original of Articles of Incorporation, signed and acknowledged by incorporators, together with Appointment of Agent, signed by all or majority of in-

* *Official forms may be obtained by applying to the department in charge of corporations.*

corporators, filed and recorded by Secretary of State.

Organization Records

Articles of Incorporation.
Original Appointment of Agent.*
Code of Regulations.
Subscription to Shares.
Notice or Waiver of Notice of First Meeting of Shareholders.
Minutes of First Meeting of Shareholders.
Waiver of Notice of First Meeting of Directors.
Minutes of First Meeting of Directors.

OKLAHOMA. Secretary of State is in charge. Business Corporation Act governs. Name reserved 60 days, by Secretary of State, $2 fee.

Execution and Filing

Triplicate originals of Articles of Incorporation, signed by incorporators and acknowledged by at least 3 of them, sent to Secretary of State, together with certificate of Appointment of Agent. Notice of Appointment must also be filed with county clerk of county in which principal office is located. Secretary of State files one duplicate original and returns other endorsed duplicate original, together with his Certificate of Incorporation.

Organization Records

Articles of Incorporation.*

By-laws.
Notice or Waiver of Notice of First Meeting of Stockholders.
Minutes of First Meeting of Stockholders.
Waiver of Notice of First Meeting of Directors.
Minutes of First Meeting of Directors.
Incorporators' Affidavit of Paid-in Capital.*

OREGON. Corporation Department is in charge. Business Corporation Act governs. Name reserved 120 days, by Corporation Commissioner, $5 fee.

Execution and Filing

Duplicate originals of Articles of Incorporation, signed and verified by incorporators, sent to Corporation Commissioner, who endorses both, files one, and returns other with Certificate of Incorporation attached.

Organization Records

Articles of Incorporation.*
By-laws.
Notice or Waiver of Notice of First Meeting of Incorporators.
Minutes of First Meeting of Incorporators.
Waiver of Notice of First Meeting of Directors.
Minutes of First Meeting of Directors.

Official forms may be obtained by applying to the department in charge of corporations.

PENNSYLVANIA. Department of State is in charge. Business Corporation Law governs. Name reserved 60 days, by Department of State, $5 fee.

Execution and Filing

Original of Articles of Incorporation, signed by each incorporator and acknowledged by at least 2 of them. Notice of intention to file, or notice of filing of, Articles of Incorporation must be published once in two newspapers, one being a legal paper, either before or after the day Articles are filed. Present executed original of Articles to Department of State for filing. Department makes and retains a copy and issues Certificate of Incorporation, to which it attaches original. Also file with Department of Revenue Registry Report.

Organization Records

Notice of Application for Charter.
Proof of Publication of Notice.
Articles of Incorporation.*
By-laws.
Notice or Waiver of Notice of First Meeting of Shareholders.
Minutes of First Meeting of Shareholders.
Waiver of Notice of First Meeting of Directors.
Minutes of First Meeting of Directors.
Domestic Registry Report.*

RHODE ISLAND. Department of State is in charge. General corporation law governs. No reservation. Write to Secretary of State for availability of name chosen.

Execution and Filing

Duplicate originals, signed and acknowledged by incorporators, sent to Secretary of State, together with certificate of state treasurer that corporation fee has been paid. Secretary of State certifies and returns one duplicate original. Also file with Secretary of State power of attorney appointing resident agent.

Organization Reports

Articles of Association.*
By-laws.
Notice or Waiver of Notice of First Meeting of Incorporators.
Minutes of First Meeting of Incorporators.
Waiver of Notice of First Meeting of Directors.
Minutes of First Meeting of Directors.
Power of Attorney.*

SOUTH CAROLINA. Department of State is in charge. General corporation law governs. No reservation. Write to Secretary of State for availability of name chosen.

Execution and Filing

Original Declaration for Charter signed by incorporators after three days

* Official forms may be obtained by applying to the department in charge of corporations.

notice in newspaper of their intention to file. Signed original sent to Secretary of State, who issues a certified copy of Declaration, which constitutes Charter. Within 30 days after issuance of Charter, it must be recorded in office of register of mesne conveyance or clerk of court of each county where corporation has an office or place of business.

Organization Records

Declaration for Charter.*
By-laws.
Notice of Application for Issuance of Charter and of First Meeting of Subscribers.
Minutes of First Meeting of Subscribers.
Waiver of Notice of First Meeting of Directors.
Minutes of First Meeting of Directors.

SOUTH DAKOTA. Secretary of State is in charge. General Corporation Law governs. Name reserved 60 days, by Secretary of State, $2 fee.

Execution and Filing

Original Articles of Incorporation signed and acknowledged by incorporators and filed with Secretary of State, who issues certificate to corporation.

Organization Records

Articles of Incorporation.*
By-laws.

Notice or Waiver of Notice of First Meeting of Incorporators.
Minutes of First Meeting of Incorporators.
Waiver of Notice of First Meeting of Directors.
Minutes of First Meeting of Directors.

TENNESSEE. Department of State is in charge. General Corporation Law governs. No reservation. Write to Secretary of State for availability of name chosen.

Execution and Filing

Original of Certificate of Incorporation, signed and acknowledged by incorporators, and formal application for charter, signed by incorporators, to Secretary of State, who records Certificate and attaches his certificate to that effect to original, and returns it. Certified original then recorded in office of Register of Deeds in county in which principal office is to be located.

Organization Records

Certificate of Incorporation.*
By-laws.
Notice or Waiver of Notice of First Meeting of Stockholders.
Minutes of First Meeting of Stockholders.
Waiver of Notice of First Meeting of Directors (Incorporators).
Minutes of First Meeting of Directors (Incorporators).

* Official forms may be obtained by applying to the department in charge of corporations.

TEXAS. Department of State is in charge. Business Corporation Act governs. Name reserved 120 days, by Secretary of State, $5 fee.

Execution and Filing

Duplicate originals of Articles of Incorporation, signed and verified by incorporators, together with subscription list, are sent to Secretary of State, who files one and returns the other with Certificate of Incorporation attached.

Organization Records

Articles of Incorporation.
Subscription List.
By-laws.
Waiver of Notice of First Meeting of Directors.
Minutes of First Meeting of Directors.

and Oath, together with Report of Property verified by two officers named in the Articles, and Oath of Office by officer, filed with county clerk of the county in which the principal place of business is to be situated. Clerk issues certificate of filing, which is attached to copy of Articles of Incorporation, Oath, and Report of Property (but not Oath of Office), and filed in office of Secretary of State, who issues his certificate of filing.

Organization Records

Articles of Incorporation.
Oath of Incorporators.
Officers' Oath.
By-laws.
Report of Property.
Waiver of Notice of Organization Meeting of Directors.
Minutes of Organization Meeting of Directors.

UTAH. Department of State is in charge. General Corporation Law governs. No reservation. Write Secretary of State for availability of name chosen.

Execution and Filing

Original of Articles of Incorporation is signed by each incorporator and sworn to by at least three of them, to which is added prescribed Oath of three or more of incorporators taken before notary or other officer. Executed original and conformed copy of Articles

VERMONT. Department of State is in charge. General Corporation Law governs. No reservation of name. Write to Secretary of State for availability of name chosen.

Execution and Filing

Original Articles of Association, signed by the incorporators, and copies sent to Secretary of State, who records Articles, and returns certified copies, one of which is filed with town clerk where principal office is located.

* Official forms may be obtained by applying to the department in charge of corporations.

Organization Records

Articles of Association.*

By-laws.

Notice or Waiver of Notice of First Meeting of Incorporators.

Minutes of First Meeting of Incorporators.

Waiver of Notice of First Meeting of Directors.

Minutes of First Meeting of Directors.

Affidavit of Proposed Issue of Capital Stock.*

Certificate of Paid-in Capital.*

VIRGINIA. State Corporation Commission is in charge. Stock Corporation Act governs. Name reserved 4 months, by State Corporation Commission, $5 fee.

Execution and Filing

Original Articles of Incorporation, signed and acknowledged by incorporators, filed with State Corporation Commission, which issues certificate of incorporation and records in its office. Certificate is forwarded to office of recorder in city or county where registered office of corporation is located. (Not required, if registered office is in city of Richmond or county of Henrico.) After further recording, certificate is returned to Commission.

Organization Records

Articles of Incorporation.

By-laws.

Waiver of Notice of First Meeting of Directors.

Minutes of First Meeting of Directors.

Statement to Be Filed before Issuing Stock (or Bonds).*

WASHINGTON. Department of State is in charge. Business Corporation Act governs. Name reserved one year, by Secretary of State, $5 fee.

Execution and Filing

Triplicate originals of Articles of Incorporation signed and acknowledged by at least 3 incorporators, sent to Secretary of State, who files and records one and issues Certificate of Incorporation. The two remaining triplicate originals, with endorsement of Secretary of State, are returned, one of which must be filed with County Auditor of county in which registered office is located. Directors' affidavit regarding payment of capital also filed with auditor. Within 30 days after incorporation, file with County Auditor and Secretary of State First Report and Statement as to Shares and First List of Directors and Officers.

Organization Records

Articles of Incorporation.

By-laws.

Waiver of Notice of First Meeting of Directors.

Minutes of First Meeting of Directors.

Affidavit of Initial Payment of Capital Stock.

* *Official forms may be obtained by applying to the department in charge of corporations.*

First Report and Statement as to Shares.

First List of Directors and Officers.

WEST VIRGINIA. Department of State is in charge General Corporation Law governs. Name reserved 30 days, by Secretary of State, through courtesy.

Execution and Filing

Original of Agreement of Incorporation, signed and acknowledged by incorporators, filed with Secertary of State, who issues certificate, or charter. Charter must be filed in office of county clerk where principal office is located; if not in state, in county where principal business is done.

Organization Records

Agreement of Incorporation.*

By-laws.

Notice or Waiver of Notice of First and General Stockholders' Meeting.*

Minutes of First Stockholders' Meeting.

Waiver of Notice of First Meeting of Directors.

Minutes of First Meeting of Directors.

WISCONSIN. Department of State is in charge. Wisconsin Business Corporation Law governs. Name reserved 60 days, by Secretary of State, $5 fee.

Execution and Filing

Duplicate originals of Articles of Incorporation are signed and acknowledged by incorporators. One is filed in office of Secretary of State; the other is recorded in office of Register of Deeds of county in which registered office is located. Register of Deeds issues certificate of recording; Secretary of State issues Certificate of Incorporation.

Organization Records

Articles of Incorporation.*

By-laws.

Subscription Agreement.

Notice or Waiver of Notice of First Meeting of Subscribers.

Minutes of First Meeting of Subscribers.

Waiver of Notice of First Meeting of Directors.

Minutes of First Meeting of Directors.

Certificate of Newly Elected Officers.*

WYOMING. Department of State is in charge. General Corporation Law governs. No reservation. Write Secretary of State for availability of name chosen.

Execution and Filing

Duplicate originals of Certificate of Incorporation, signed and acknowledged by incorporators. One duplicate original filed with Secretary of State and one with county clerk of county in which principal part of business is to be

* *Official forms may be obtained by applying to the department in charge of corporations.*

transacted. Within 30 days, notice of incorporation is published 3 times in newspaper, and proof of publication accompanied by written consent of agent named in notice of incorporation filed with Secretary of State.

Organization Records

Certificate of Incorporation.
By-laws.

Waiver of Notice of First Meeting of Directors.

Minutes of First Meeting of Directors.

Notice of Incorporation.

Affidavit of Publication of Notice of Incorporation.

Certificate of Appointment of Agent and Location of Office.*

Consent of Agent.

Acceptance of Constitution.*

---

* *Official forms may be obtained by applying to the department in charge of corporations.*

19

Acting as Corporate Secretary

THE LAWYER works closely with the corporate secretary. He is frequently a director and officer of the corporation, and many responsibilities that are ordinarily those of the corporate secretary are delegated to him. He drafts resolutions and makes the preparations for holding directors' and stockholders' meetings. He prepares the minutes of meeting and submits them to the corporate secretary for his signature. He is also responsible for seeing that certain matters, such as a lease renewal, are attended to at certain times.

As his secretary, you might have the following duties and responsibilities pertaining to the affairs of a corporate client:

1. Making all preparations for corporate meetings
2. Recording the minutes of the meetings
3. Issuing certificates of stock and handling ordinary stock transfers, if the corporation is small
4. Making a record of important documents and safekeeping them
5. Keeping the corporation calendar
6. Looking after details if corporation changes its name

You will perform some of these duties on your own initiative without instructions from the lawyer; others you will undertake only under instructions from the lawyer and, at first, under his close supervision. If you are to be successful in the performance of these duties, you must be *thoroughly familiar with the by-laws* of the corporation.

Information folder. When the lawyer has the responsibilities listed in the preceding paragraph, it is advisable to keep an information folder (or loose-leaf notebook) pertaining to the corporation. The material in the folder makes available information needed at a moment's notice, without the necessity of removing a document from the safe or looking at the minute book or other records. The material will vary with the need, but ordinarily includes:

1. Schedule of stockholders' meetings (showing when annual meetings are to be held; how special meetings are called; notice required; what constitutes a quorum)
2. Schedule of directors' meetings (showing how called; notice required; what constitutes a quorum)
3. Dividends (chronological record of dividends paid)
4. Number of stockholders
5. Record of incorporation
6. By-laws
7. States in which the corporation is doing business
8. List of bank accounts (showing where located; who may sign checks)
9. Abstracts of indentures (including abstracts of special agreements such as option to purchase property)

Corporate Meetings

Kinds of meetings. In addition to the organization meetings described in the preceding chapter, the kinds of corporate meetings are (1) annual stockholders' meetings, (2) special stockholders' meetings, (3) regular meetings of directors, (4) special meetings of directors, and (5) committee meetings.

Preparations for meetings. Preparations for meetings include the following activities:

1. Keeping a current meeting file
2. Sending notices of the meeting
3. Preparing the agenda
4. Reserving the meeting room and getting it ready
5. Arranging for payment of directors' fees
6. Preparing to record minutes

Meeting folder. Keep a current folder for each forthcoming meeting, with the name and date of the meeting noted on the cover or tab. Keep in the folder all papers and documents pertaining to matters to be discussed at the meeting. As matters to be taken up at the meeting come before the lawyer, he examines them, makes whatever notes are necessary, arranges the material for presentation at the meeting, and gives you the material. Shortly before the meeting, the corporate secretary might submit a list of items for the agenda. File this material, together with the material given you by the lawyer, in the current meeting folder and make up the agenda for the meeting from it (see page 423).

Also place in the meeting folder all copies of calls, notices of meetings, a list of those to whom the notice must be sent, drafts of resolutions to be taken up at the meeting, and possibly a skeleton of the minutes (see page 425). On the list of stockholders, show the number of shares owned by each.

In addition to the current material, keep in the folders on stockholders' and directors' meetings (1) a pamphlet copy of the corporation laws of the state in which the corporation is organized, (2) a copy of the corporation's charter and by-laws, with amendments, and (3) other papers of a similar nature that may be needed at any stockholders' or directors' meetings. After the meeting has taken place, remove the current papers and file them in their respective folders, leaving in the current file only the documents necessary for all meetings. The folder is then ready to receive papers for the next meeting.

Notice of stockholders' meeting. The by-laws tell how and when notices of stockholders' meetings, both annual and special, shall be sent. The secretary must follow those provisions closely. The notices are usually in writing, and the secretary mails them to the stockholders a certain number of days before the meeting, *as specified in the by-laws.*

Form and content of notice. The notice of a stockholders' meeting may be in the form of a postcard or of an announcement sent in a sealed envelope. The notice should specify the date, the place, the hour at which the meeting is to be held, and the purpose of the meeting.

An example of a notice of the stockholders' annual meeting and an example of a special meeting notice are given on page 443.

Waiver of notice of stockholders' meeting. Notices of meetings are sent to all stockholders who have the right to vote. However, in small corporations, the stockholders frequently "waive" notice. In that case prepare a waiver for the stockholders to sign either before or at the meeting. You can easily adapt Form No. 2 on page 442 as a waiver of notice of stockholders' meeting.

When a stockholder waives notice, indicate that fact on the list of stockholders that is kept in the current meeting folder.

Quorum at a stockholders' meeting. In a small corporation, the secretary has the responsibility of making sure that a quorum will attend the meeting; without a quorum the meeting cannot be held. If you have this responsibility, consult the by-laws to see what representation is required. In business corporations the "majority" representation that is normally required is based upon shares of stock and not upon number of individual stockholders. For example, if a company has a total of 20 stockholders, 5 of whom own over half the stock, those 5 stockholders would constitute a majority. Thus, you see the necessity for indicating on the stockholders' list the number of shares owned by each.

Proxies and proxy statement. As it is impossible for all stockholders of a large corporation to attend meetings, it is customary for a stockholder who cannot attend to give some other person, or a committee, authority to vote his stock. This authority is known as a *proxy*. The word is also used to denote the person to whom the authority is given, and the form on which the authority is given. The proxy form is sent to each stockholder with the notice of meeting.

The Securities Exchange Commission requires a corporation whose stock is listed on a stock exchange to furnish a written proxy statement to each person whose proxy is being solicited. The proxy statement must set forth the nature of the matters to be voted on under the proxy, whether the person giving the proxy has power to revoke it, and other information relating to the proxy. Proxy statements are technical legal documents. The lawyer will dictate the statement to you and ask for a draft. After the draft has been corrected, you will retype it for the printer.

What the secretary does. Usually the secretary of a small corporation does not send proxies with the notice of meeting. However, if for any reason you anticipate that there will not be a quorum present, get proxies from stockholders who cannot attend, representing a sufficient number of shares to make up a quorum. As small corporations do not list their stock, a proxy statement is not required.

Although large corporations use printed proxy forms, proxies may be reproduced by any mechanical process. If only a few are required, type them on letter-size paper, either plain or with the corporation's letterhead, but not on the lawyer's letterhead. See page 444 for form.

The proxy need not be witnessed or notarized. The signature should agree with the name in the stock certificate. The signature lines of a proxy to be executed by a corporation should be prepared in the same manner as the signature to any instrument signed on behalf of a corporation (see page 171).

As each proxy is received, check the stockholders' list in the current meeting file to show that the proxy has been received.

Notice of directors' meeting. Follow the provisions of the by-laws in sending notices of meetings to directors. Even if notice of a regular meeting is not required by the by-laws, it is advisable to notify the directors of the meeting. If a special meeting is to be called, telephone or telegraph the directors to determine whether the time is convenient for all of them. Send a written notice after the time of the meeting is definitely fixed.

The list of the directors that is kept in the current meeting folder should be tabulated, with columns showing the date each was notified, the date a follow-up notice, if any, was sent, and the replies.

Form and content of notice. Notices of directors' meetings are usually typewritten on the corporation's letterhead. Printing or multigraphing the notice on cards or paper slips, with blanks for the date, time, and place of the meeting, is a time-saving expedient. A light stock for card notices is preferable, since heavy stock is not suitable for insertion in the typewriter to fill in necessary information.

The notice is sent in the name of the corporate secretary. It should specify the date, the place, and the hour at which the meeting is to be held. It is advisable, though not obligatory unless required by statute or by-law, for the notice of a special meeting to state the purpose for which it is held.

An example of a notice of a directors' special meeting specifying the purpose of the meeting is on page 445.

Quorum at directors' meeting. A directors' meeting cannot be held unless a quorum is present. Consult the by-laws for the number of directors necessary to constitute a quorum. A quorum at a directors' meeting differs from a quorum at a stockholders' meeting in that the representation is based upon the number of directors and not upon the amount of stock owned by them.

If you learn that a quorum will not be present, telephone those directors who expect to attend and arrange, with approval of the person calling the meeting, to have the meeting postponed. This is particularly important if the directors are coming from a distance.

A director cannot give a proxy for a directors' meeting.

Preservation of notice. Keep a copy of every notice of meeting, with the date of mailing noted on it, in the current meeting folder. If the notice has been published in the newspapers, keep a clipping of the published notice and the name of the publication and dates of publication.

The agenda. The agenda consists of an itemized list of matters to be brought up at a meeting. The secretary lists them from the accumulated material in the current meeting folder. The agenda should follow the order of business as set forth in the by-laws.

Here is a typical agenda prepared for a directors' meeting:

1. Read minutes of last meeting. (Attach a typewritten copy of the minutes of the previous meeting to the corporate secretary's copy of the agenda.)

2. Submit the following statements: (Here enumerate the reports of officers and committees to be presented to the meeting. Copies of the reports may be attached to the agenda.)

3. Adopt resolution approving minutes of executive committee meetings. (If minutes are long, copies may be made and attached to the agenda.)

4. Business of the meeting. (Here enumerate business to be acted upon indicating each item by a summary of the resolution that is required.)

Begin preparation of the agenda several days before the meeting. Have it completely in order the evening before the meeting. Prepare a copy for each director. Attach to the agenda the exhibits, supporting papers, reports, and the like that contain the information necessary to supply the groundwork for discussion.

Reservation and preparation of the meeting room. If a meeting is to be held in a room that is used for other purposes, notify the person who is responsible for the room to have it available at the time of the meeting. When you enter the date of the meeting in the corporation's calendar (see page 438), also enter at an earlier date a reminder to reserve the room. This should be done in ample time to avoid conflict, the time of the advance notice depending upon the demand for the room.

In preparing the room for the meeting, have it dusted, properly heated, and ventilated. See that sufficient costumers and coat hangers are available. Provide stationery, memorandum pads, pen and ink, and pencils for each person who is expected to attend the meeting. Have a supply of clips, pins, rubber bands on the table, and put an ash tray and matches at each place.

Directors' fees. The fee payable to directors for attendance at a meeting is usually fixed by resolution adopted by the board of directors. When preparation for the meeting is the lawyer's responsibility, payment of the fees might be his responsibility also. In this case, arrange with the treasurer of the corporation to have the money at the meeting. If any money is left over because of non-attendance, return it to the treasurer. Give the money to the directors after the meeting, preferably enclosed in an envelope.

Material to take to meetings. Take the following material to directors' and stockholders' meetings:

1. Pamphlet copy of the corporation laws of the state in which the corporation is organized

2. Copy of the certificate of incorporation, with marginal notations of amendments and copies of them

3. Copy of the by-laws, with marginal notations of amendments and copies of them

4. Separate sheet for order of business

5. Rules and regulations of the corporation, if any, governing the conduct of meetings

6. Proof of the mailing of notices of the meeting and, where necessary, of publication

7. The original call for the meeting and, if there has been a demand for a call, the original of the demand

8. The minute book.

9. The corporate seal

10. Current papers pertaining to the meeting (see page 419)

11. Blank affidavits, oaths, and the like

Drafting resolutions before meetings. The lawyer will dictate all resolutions involving legal technicalities, but there are many simple resolutions that you can draft yourself. The forms on page 447, *et seq.* are examples of resolutions that almost all corporations adopt. Draft all simple resolutions that are indicated by the agenda and submit them to the lawyer before typing in final form. Frequently the lawyer submits drafts of resolutions to the office or department of the corporation that originated the proposition, to ensure that the resolution expresses the correct view. Every secretary who has any of the duties of a corporate secretary should have as part of her equipment a book of resolutions[1] as a guide to the form that the resolution should take.

Resolutions to satisfy outside person or organization. Certain actions may require the passage of a resolution in a form satisfactory to some outside person or organization. For example, the opening of a bank account by a corporation generally calls for passage of a resolution in the form required by the bank. If such a resolution is to come before the meeting, get the required form before the meeting. After the board passes the resolution, fill in the blanks. To avoid copying the resolution into the minutes, get two blank forms of the resolutions and fill in both forms, pasting one copy into the minute book and making it a part of the minutes by reference. The original of the resolution, signed by the proper officers of the corporation, is filed with the bank. Of course, if you make extra copies of the minutes you will need extra copies of the blanks.

Preparations for taking notes at meetings. In advance of the meeting prepare either a skeleton of the minutes or a memorandum form for entering notes. The skeleton, or outline, is a rough draft of the minutes with the spaces to be filled in with details as they develop at the meeting. A skeleton is particularly useful when the program of a meeting is prearranged. Use the forms of minutes on pages 440 to 442 as a guide in preparing the skeleton.

Figure 97 is a memorandum form for entering notes. The memorandum includes the nature of the meeting (regular or special) and how notice was given (regular or personal) or whether waiver was secured, so that a check mark is all that is necessary to show

---

[1] See Doris and Friedman, *Encyclopedia of Corporate Meetings, Minutes, and Resolutions,* Englewood Cliffs, N. J.: Prentice-Hall, Inc., 1958.

the facts. The resolutions that are submitted to the meeting are numbered to correspond with the numbers of the resolutions on the memorandum. The notes on this memorandum supply the secretary with all the information necessary for writing minutes of the meeting.

```
┌──────────────────┬─────────────────────────────────────────────────┐
│                  │             SECRETARY'S MEMORANDUM              │
│                  │                                                 │
│                  │         MEETING OF BOARD OF DIRECTORS           │
│                  │                                                 │
│                  │                    Stated      Reg. Notice      │
│                  │                    Annual      Personal         │
│  ORGANIZATION    │                    Special     Waiver           │
│                  │                                                 │
│  DATE            │    19—             Hour        Standard         │
│                  │                                                 │
│  PRESENT         │  No. present       Necessary for quorum         │
│  CHAIRMAN        │                                                 │
│  SECRETARY       │                                                 │
│  MINUTES         │                                                 │
│  STATEMENTS      │                                                 │
│  RESOLUTIONS     │                                                 │
│         #1       │  Proposed by       Seconded by                  │
│                  │                    For                          │
│                  │  Votes             Against                      │
│                  │                                                 │
│         #2       │  Proposed by       Seconded by                  │
│                  │                    For                          │
│                  │  Votes             Against                      │
│                  │                                                 │
│         #3       │  Proposed by       Seconded by                  │
│                  │                    For                          │
│                  │  Votes             Against                      │
└──────────────────┴─────────────────────────────────────────────────┘
```

Figure 97. Secretary's Memorandum for Entering Notes of Minutes at Meeting (Page 1).

Taking notes at meetings. Verbatim notes of a meeting are not generally necessary except at stockholders' meetings of large corporations and at board meetings when there is dissension among the directors. Expert stenographers are sometimes brought to stockholders' meetings to take the notes.

In taking notes at a meeting, make no attempt to put everything down in full, but do take important statements verbatim.

Also make a verbatim record of resolutions that are framed at the meeting. When someone at the meeting asks that his views be made a part of the record, the secretary should record his remarks in full. Do not hesitate to record in the minutes full details of what transpires at the meeting.

RESOLUTIONS CONTINUED		
#4	Proposed by	Seconded by
		For
	Votes	Against
#5	Proposed by	Seconded by
		For
	Votes	Against
#6	Proposed by	Seconded by
		For
	Votes	Against
#7	Proposed by	Seconded by
		For
	Votes	Against
NOTES		
ADJOURNMENT		
DISBURSEMENT	Fees Per member present	
	Expenses " " present Sundries Total	
	(Signed)......................	
	Secretary	

Figure 97 (Cont.). Secretary's Memorandum for Entering Notes of Minutes at Meeting (Page 2).

Do not permit the meeting to proceed to the next subject unless you have a clear understanding of what has been done. By prearranged signal let the chairman know that you do not have a clear understanding of an action that was taken or a statement that was made.

Make a separate notation of any action that is to be taken immediately after the meeting.

Minutes

The minute book. Minutes of stockholders' meetings, directors' meetings, and committee meetings are often kept in separate books. For a small company, however, it is feasible to use one book, dividing it into distinct parts. Minute books are usually loose-leaf. After a sufficient number of pages have accumulated, they may be bound. The pages of a minute book may be numbered for convenience. Both sides of the sheet are written on. Standard paper for minute books is of a special quality—smooth, heavy, and durable, usually with an outside ruled margin. Manufacturers and stationers who specialize in corporate forms can supply it.

Arrangement of contents of combined minute book. The contents of a minute book should be arranged as follows:

1. Bind or paste a certified copy of the corporation's charter in the first pages of the book, or merely copy the charter into the book.

2. Beginning at the top of a right-hand page, copy the by-laws of the corporation.

3. After the by-laws, insert the minutes of the meeting of incorporators or of other organization meetings.

4. Continue with the minutes of the stockholders' meetings, beginning each set of minutes at the top of a new page.

5. After the minutes of stockholders' meetings, begin the section on minutes of directors' meetings.

Content of minutes. The content and form of minutes are fairly well standardized (see Form 1 on page 440). The order of the contents follows:

1. Begin with the time and place of the meeting.

2. Establish that the meeting was properly called and that notice was given or waived. When the by-laws do not require notice of regular directors' meetings, omit this item from the minutes.

3. Give the names of the chairman and secretary of the meeting.

4. List those present. Also list absentees at directors' meetings. In minutes of stockholders' meetings, list those represented by proxy as well as those present in person and, also, the amount of stock represented.

5. State that the minutes of the previous meeting were read and unanimously approved, or that reading was dispensed with.

6. Follow with a clear, accurate, and complete report of all business transacted, arranged in accordance with the order of business established in the by-laws.

Preparation of draft of minutes. Write the minutes immediately after the meeting while events are still fresh in your mind.

If you do not attend the meeting, write the minutes by expanding the lawyer's notes. For example, the notes will show that a certain resolution was unanimously adopted. The minutes will be expanded to read:

On motion duly made and seconded, the following resolution was unanimously adopted:
RESOLVED, That ....

To write minutes from notes made by another, you must have before you all papers, documents, and reports that were discussed at the meeting. If the lawyer takes notes on the memorandum form described on page 425 (Figure 97), the task of expanding the notes is simple.

Submit a draft of the minutes to the lawyer for review and correction. Never write minutes in the minute book without first writing a draft.

How to prepare minutes in final form. Some of the larger corporations have strict rules about the uniformity of arrangement of minutes. Independently of rules, a secretary should take particular pains with details about the typing, arrangement, spacing, and general appearance of the minute book. The following is a suggested list of rules relating to the form to be followed in typing the minutes into the minute book:

1. Capitalize and center the heading designating the meeting.

2. Indent paragraphs ten spaces.

3. Indent names of those present or absent 15 spaces.

4. Double space the text, including preambles to resolutions.

5. Single space and indent, but do not quote, take-ins, such as letters, waivers of notice of meetings, oaths of inspectors of election, and the like. Leave at least four spaces before and after the take-in. When the take-in is a printed paper, the text following the printed take-in should start on a new page.

6. Double space between each paragraph, and triple space between each item in the order of business.

7. Indent resolutions 15 spaces and single space them.

8. Capitalize the words "Board of Directors" and the word "Corporation" when reference is made to the corporation whose minutes are being written. References to specific officers of the corporation may be capitalized or in lower case, but the capitalization should be consistent.

9. Leave an inch and a half outside margin if the paper does not have a ruled margin.

10. Put captions in the margin in capitals or in red type.

11. Capitalize all letters in the words *Whereas* and *Resolved,* follow by a comma, and begin the word *that* with a capital.

12. When sums of money are mentioned in a resolution, write them first in words and then in figures in parentheses.

Correction of errors in minutes. As previously noted, the minutes of a meeting are usually approved at the next meeting. The chairman informally directs correction of simple errors. If the error can be corrected immediately, make the correction at the meeting and offer the minutes, as changed, for approval. If the error involves a revision of the minutes, report the corrections of the minutes of the previous meeting in the minutes of the current meeting. A form of resolution correcting the minutes of a previous meeting is shown on page 448.

Inserting corrections in the minute book. Strike out the erroneous material by drawing a red line through each line of the incorrect material. Write the correct minutes in between the red lines. Make a reference in the margin of the corrected minutes to the minutes of the following meeting, to show where the correction was ordered.

When it is impractical to make the correction this way, strike out the erroneous material in red and make a note in the margin showing where the revised minutes appear. Insert the corrected minutes at the end of the original minutes. Do not throw away the pages that were incorrectly written. Retain the original pages and indicate that they are obsolete by reference to the minutes of the meeting at which the errors were corrected.

Certified extract of minutes. Directors authorize by resolution the transaction of various items of business on behalf of the corporation, and the resolutions passed by the directors are embodied in the minutes of the meetings. It is frequently necessary to produce evidence of the authority granted in the form of a *certified extract* of the minutes, or copy of the resolution. The certification is usually by the secretary of the corporation.

CERTIFIED EXTRACT OF MINUTES

I, the undersigned, Secretary of A. B. CORPORATION,

a corporation duly organized and existing under the laws of

the State of New York, and having its principal place of

business in the City of New York, hereby CERTIFY that the

following is a true copy of a certain resolution duly adopted

by the Board of Directors of the said corporation in accord-

ance with the By-Laws at, and recorded in the minutes of,

a meeting of the said Board duly held on   , 19   ,

and not subsequently rescinded or modified:

R E S O L V E D :

That an account be opened in the name of
the A. B. Corporation with the EAST RIVER
SAVINGS BANK at 41 Rockefeller Plaza, in the
Borough of Manhattan, City of New York, and
that the funds of the said A. B. Corporation
may be deposited therein and that all drafts
and other instruments for the payment of money
shall be signed by the following officers:-

John Smith   President
William Doe   Secretary & Treasurer
George Roe   Asst. Secretary &
                    Asst. Treasurer
Mary Stone   Vice-President
Alice Mead   Asst. Treasurer of
                    Committee of Managers

And the Bank is hereby authorized to pay such
drafts and instruments when so signed (including those drawn to cash or bearer or to the
individual order of the officer or officers
signing the same) and also to receive the same

Figure 98. Certified Extract of Minutes (Page 1).

Figure 98 illustrates a certified extract of minutes. It may be typed on plain letter-size paper or on the corporation's letterhead.

```
                 for deposit to the credit of any holder when
                 endorsed, without inquiry of any kind.

             I FURTHER CERTIFY that the following now occupy

        the respective offices designated in the above quoted

        resolution and that the same are duly qualified as such

        officers:


                 NAMES            TITLES OF OFFICES HELD:

                 John Smith       President
                 William Doe      Secretary & Treasurer
                 George Roe       Asst. Secretary &
                                  Asst. Treasurer
                 Mary Stone       Vice-President
                 Alice Mead       Asst. Treasurer of
                                  Committee of Managers

             IN WITNESS WHEREOF, I have hereunto subscribed my

        name and affixed the seal of the said Corporation

        this         day of              , 19


                         A. B. CORPORATION

                         By_____
                                        Secretary
```

Figure 98 (Cont.). Certified Extract of Minutes (Page 2).

Indexing of minutes. If minutes of meetings are voluminous, keep a card index so that any business that has been passed upon may be referred to easily and quickly. The making of the index is facilitated by marginal captions in the minutes. The index card contains the subject matter taken from the captions and a reference to the page on which the caption appears.

Issuance and Transfer of Stock of a Small Corporation

Authority to issue certificate. A large corporation has a transfer agent, usually a bank, which issues and transfers shares of stock. The lawyer frequently has this responsibility for a small corporation. He issues an original certificate of stock for a definite number of shares to a certain person when authorized to do so by resolution of the directors or of the stockholders.

Stock certificate book. A bound book of blank stock certificates is kept for each class of stock. The certificates and corresponding stubs are numbered consecutively. The number of shares is usually left blank so that certificates may be issued for various amounts. Figure 99 is a reproduction of a certificate and its stub. In a small corporation with only a few stockholders, the stock certificate book usually serves as a transfer record and as a stock ledger.

Original issue and transfer of stock. An original issue of stock refers to a share of stock that has never before been issued. The certificate of incorporation authorizes the corporation to issue a stated number of shares. All of these shares need not be issued immediately, but as each is issued it is considered an *original issue.* When the person to whom it is issued sells or gives it to someone else, it becomes a *transferred share.*

Taxes on stock. *Federal stamp tax.* The Federal Government imposes a tax, known as a stamp tax on all original issues and all transfers of stock. These *documentary* stamps may be purchased at the Post Office. On an original issue, the stamp is affixed to the stub in the stock certificate book. On a transfer it is attached to the certificate that is transferred and cancelled (see page 436). The stub of the certificate will not have a stamp on it. Thus, some stubs in the stock certificate book will have stamps and others will not.

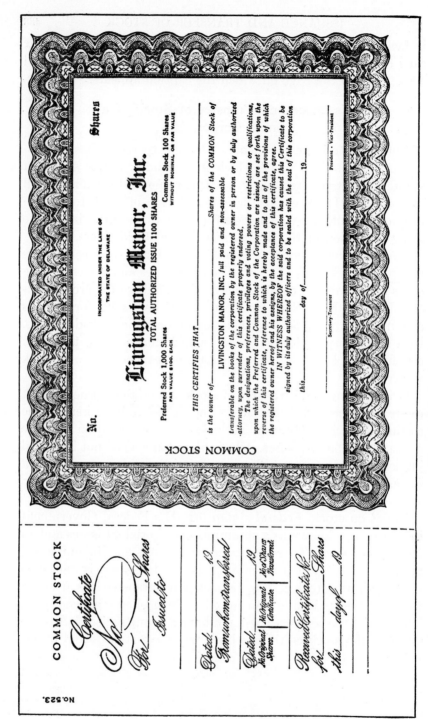

Figure 99. Stock Certificate and Stub.

The Federal stamp tax rates, effective as of January 1, 1959, are as follows:

Stock issuance tax

Ten cents for each $100 of actual values (or major fraction thereof) in *any one day* by a corporation.

Stock transfer tax

Four cents per $100 of actual value with an 8 cent per share ceiling and a 4 cent minimum tax for any single transfer of one or more shares.

Note: Previously stamp tax rates were based upon par value for par value stock and upon actual value for no-par stock.

There is also a Federal registration fee, but this is imposed only on sales that are transacted through the stock exchanges and does not affect transfers that you make in the lawyer's office.

State transfer tax. The following states have a transfer tax on stock: Florida, Massachusetts, New York, Pennsylvania, South Carolina, and Texas.

Whether or not the state tax is payable depends upon the state in which the transfer is made. Thus, a transfer in New York of a Delaware corporation's stock is subject to the New York transfer tax, although Delaware does not have a tax. It is impractical to give the rate of taxation for each state here, but you can get the information from the state statutes.

Almost every law imposing these taxes gives some official the right to call for books and documents on a moment's notice. For example, state inspectors may call on New York transfer agents and ask to see the stock transfer books to ascertain whether the proper stamps have been affixed to meet stock transfer requirements. If you are the custodian of a corporation's books, it is your duty (1) to be most punctilious in seeing that the proper documentary stamps are affixed and (2) to present the books for inspection upon presentation of the proper credentials.

Issuance of certificate of stock. Here are the steps necessary to issue a stock certificate:

1. Enter the name and address of the person to whom the certificate is issued, and the number of shares for which it is issued, on the stub.

2. Tear the certificate out of the stock book.

3. Type on the face of the certificate the name of the person to whom it is issued, the number of shares it represents, and the date.

4. Have the certificate signed by the officers whose signatures are required.

5. Impress the corporate seal in the space provided.

6. If possible, have the receipt on the stub of the certificate signed. If the person in whose name the certificate is issued is not present to sign the stub, type the receipt on a slip of paper the size and shape of the receipt printed on the stub. Be certain that the information on the receipt corresponds with the stub. Enclose the receipt with the certificate and request the person in whose name the certificate is issued to sign and return it. When it is received, paste it over the receipt portion of the stub.

7. Affix to the stub and cancel documentary stamps. (See page 464 for cancellation of stamps)

8. Send certificates *by registered mail.*

Transfer of certificate. The back of the certificate has a form for an assignment or transfer of stock from one holder to another (Figure 100). When shares of stock are transferred, the corporation issues a new certificate. The holder of a 100-share certificate might want to transfer, say, 50 shares and keep the other 50. In that case, two new certificates of 50 shares each are issued—one to the transferee and one to the original owner.

When a certificate is transferred, follow the procedure outlined on the preceding pages for the original issuance of a certificate. Notice that the stub to a transferred certificate calls for more information than the stub to an original issue. In addition, take the following steps:

1. Write "Canceled" in ink across the face of the old certificate.

2. Date and initial the canceled certificate.

3. Paste the canceled certificate to its stub in the bound stock certificate book, as nearly in the certificate's original position in the book as possible.

4. Affix the documentary stamp to the canceled certificate and cancel the stamp. The stamp tax will apply *only to the shares that are transferred,* not to the certificate for the new shares that the original owner might keep. (See page 464 for cancellation of stamps.)

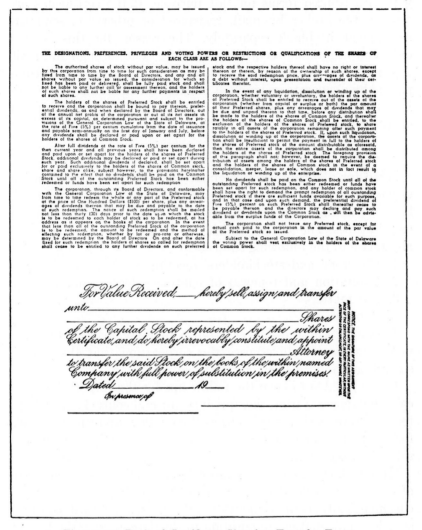

Figure 100. Back of Certificate Showing Transfer Form.

Separate form of assignment. When you handle the lawyer's personal securities, you will probably deal with a broker. Securities transferred through a broker are transferred in blank because the transferor does not know to whom they will be delivered. A transfer in blank might be made on a form of assignment separate from the stock certificate, instead of on the assignment that is printed on the back of the certificate. The broker will supply you with printed forms for this purpose. If the certificates are sent to the broker by mail, registered or otherwise, send the assignment in blank separately. The reason for this is that only non-negotiable securities should be sent through the mail. A security endorsed on the back in blank, or a security accompanied by a separate assignment in blank is negotiable. The wording of a separate assignment is similar to that of the assignment on the back of a certificate.

The Corporation Calendar

Need for a corporation calendar. The need for a corporation calendar is evident to any secretary whose office has the responsibility of seeing that certain acts of a corporation are done at certain times. The acts for which the lawyer is responsible generally relate to the following subjects:

1. Directors' and stockholders' meetings
2. Expiration and renewal of contracts, leases, and the like
3. Tax matters
4. Reports

In some cases the lawyer attends to these matters himself; in others, he merely advises the corporation that the matter should be attended to by a certain date.

It is advisable to keep the follow-ups for the corporation on a calendar separate from the appointment and court diary (Chapter 3). However, if the lawyer has these follow-up responsibilities for more than one corporation, one calendar will serve for the several corporations.

How to keep the corporation calendar. The most usual form of corporation calendar is a card index, 3 by 5 inches, arranged chronologically behind monthly tab cards. The card contains sufficient information, in addition to the date, to give the lawyer a correct idea of what he is to do, or what you are to do for him. The cards are made up as a transaction occurs or as the need for the card arises. Thus, if the lawyer is custodian of the corporate documents and you are given a lease to put in the safe, you will note the expiration date of the lease and make up a card for that particular day.

Acts that are to be done at certain times but for which no definite day is specified may be entered on a monthly reminder card. For example, suppose that in a certain state the corporation is required to file a statement with the secretary of state each time a change in officers occurs. You will make a note of the requirement on a card without a date and at the beginning of each month move it along to the next month. If you prefer, you might make a note on 12 separate cards and file one for each month.

At the beginning of each month, examine all of the items in the calendar for the succeeding two months to allow ample time for taking action on the reminders furnished by the cards. Time-consuming tasks that must be done by a certain date should be entered sufficiently in advance to permit the work to be finished on time.

Where to get dates for the corporation calendar. You will have to ask the lawyer to give you the date for many of the calendar entries, but you can get some of them from the material in the information folder (see page 418) and from the sources indicated below. In any event, the lawyer should verify the dates, because severe penalties result from failure to perform some of these acts at the required time.

Annual stockholders' meeting. See the by-laws.

Regular directors' meeting. See minutes of first meeting of directors or stockholders.

Expiration and renewal dates. See the documents or abstracts of them in the information folder.

Annual report to stockholders. The annual report is published as soon after the end of the fiscal year as possible. Work on it commences considerably in advance of the close of the fiscal year, the length of time depending upon the elaborateness of the report.

Annual report to state authority. Check the general corporation law for the state of incorporation, pamphlet copy of which should be in the information folder.

Tax matters and reports to Federal and state governments. For accurate, up-to-date information, a loose-leaf tax service, such as those published by Prentice-Hall, Inc., would probably serve your purpose best. These services cover all taxes imposed by Federal, state, and local governments and contain tax calendars. If your office maintains a corporation, its library will probably contain a service of this kind. If not, and if the service is not available in a nearby law library, write to the particular tax authority for the information desired.

Change of Corporate Name

Details when corporate name is changed. The states provide by statute the manner in which a corporation may change its name and indicate the procedure to be followed. The attorney will give you detailed instructions about the legal procedure because the directions outlined by the statute must be strictly followed. Numerous other changes are made necessary by the adoption of a new name. The corporation personnel looks after many of them, such as changes in bank accounts, stationery, and the like, but some of the changes are handled in the law office. Matters to which you should attend include:

1. Change in corporate seal
2. Change in contracts
3. Change in leases
4. Change in deeds to real property

If your office keeps the stock certificate book

5. Order new stock certificate book
6. Write to stockholders to send in certificates

Specimen Corporate Forms

No. 1

Minutes of first meeting of incorporators of a Delaware Corporation.

[*Note.* The headings in brackets may appear as marginal notes in the minute book.]

[Time and place of meeting]

The first meeting of incorporators of the .... was held at ...., in the City of ...., State of ...., at ...... o'clock in the ...... noon of the .. day of ...., 19.., pursuant to a written waiver of notice, signed by all of the incorporators, fixing said place and time.

The following incorporators were present in person or by proxy:

Name of Incorporator	*Name of Proxy**
. . . .	. . . .
. . . .	. . . .
. . . .	. . . .

being all of the incorporators named in the Certificate of Incorporation.

[Temporary officers]

On motion unanimously carried, Mr. . . . . was elected Chairman, and Mr. . . . . Secretary of the meeting.

[Waiver of notice]

The Secretary presented the waiver of notice of the meeting signed by all of the incorporators, and it was filed as part of the minutes. The Secretary was ordered to file as a part of the minutes any proxies which had been accepted.

[Certificate of incorporation reported filed]

The Chairman reported that the Certificate of Incorporation of the Corporation was filed in the office of the Secretary of State of the State of Delaware on the . . day of . . . ., 19. ., and a certified copy thereof was filed for record in the office of the recorder of Deeds in the County of . . . . . ., on the . . day of . . . ., 19. ., and a copy of said Certificate of Incorporation was ordered to be inserted in the minute book as a part of the records of the meeting.

[Adoption of By-laws]

The Secretary presented a proposed form of By-laws for the regulation and management of the affairs of the Corporation, which was read, section by section, and unanimously adopted and ordered to be made a part of the permanent records to follow the Certificate of Incorporation in the minute book.

[Election of directors]

Motions were then declared by the Chairman to be in order for the nomination of directors of the Corporation to hold office for the ensuing year and until their successors are elected and qualify, and the following persons were nominated: (*insert names of nominees*).

No further nominations having been made, a ballot was taken and all of the incorporators having voted, and the ballots having been duly canvassed, the Chairman declared that the above-named persons were elected directors of the Corporation by the unanimous vote of all the incorporators.

Upon motion duly made, seconded, and unanimously carried, it was

---

* If the incorporator was present in person, write "In person" in this column. If not, write the name of the person who represented him as proxy.

[Issuance of capital stock]

Resolved, That the Board of Directors be and it hereby is authorized in its discretion to issue the capital stock of this Corporation to the full amount or number of shares authorized by the Certificate of Incorporation, in such amounts and for such considerations as from time to time shall be determined by the Board of Directors and as may be permitted by law.

[Adjournment]

There being no other business to be transacted, the meeting was, upon motion duly made, seconded, and carried, adjourned.

....
                                                    Secretary of the Meeting

No. 2

Waiver of notice of first meeting of incorporators.

We, the undersigned, being all of the incorporators of the ...., a corporation organized under the laws of the State of ...., do hereby severally waive all the statutory requirements as to notice of the time, place, and purpose of the first meeting of incorporators of the said corporation and the publication thereof, and consent that the meeting shall be held at ...., in the City of ...., State of ...., on the .. day of ......, 19.., at .... o'clock in the ...... noon; and we consent to the transaction of any and all business that may properly come before this meeting.

Dated ...., 19...

....
....
....

No. 3

Waiver of notice of first meeting of directors.

We, the undersigned, duly elected directors of ...., do hereby severally waive notice of time, place, and purpose of the first meeting of directors of said corporation, and consent that the meeting be held at ...., in the City of ...., State of ...., on the .... day of ...., 19.., at .... o'clock in the .... noon; and we do further consent to the transaction of any business requisite to complete the organization of the company, and to any and all business which may properly come before the meeting.

Dated ...., 19...

....
....
....

No. 4

Notice of annual meeting of stockholders.

.........., ..., 19...

The annual meeting of the stockholders of the .... Company, for the election of directors and the transaction of such other business as may properly come before the meeting, will be held at the office of the Company on (*day of week*), ..., 19.., at ...... o'clock in the .... noon.

If you cannot be present at the meeting, please sign and return the accompanying proxy in the enclosed envelope.

....

Secretary

No. 5

Notice of special meeting of stockholders, indicating purpose of meeting.

NOTICE IS HEREBY GIVEN that a special meeting of the stockholders of the .... Company, a corporation of the State of ...., has been called and will be held on ...., 19.., at .... o'clock ...... M., at the registered office of the Company, (*address*) ...., City of ...., State of ...., for the following purposes:

1. (*Here insert purpose of meeting.*)
2. To transact any other business that may come before the said meeting.

If you are unable to be present in person, please sign the enclosed form of proxy and return it in the enclosed stamped envelope.

By order of the Board of Directors.

....

Secretary

Dated ...., 19...

No. 6

Affidavit of secretary that notice of annual meeting of stockholders was mailed.

STATE OF ....
COUNTY OF .... } ss.:

.............., being duly sworn, on oath deposes and says: that he is the Secretary of the .... Corporation, a corporation organized and existing under the laws of the State of ...., having its principal office in the State of ....; that on the .. day of ...., 19.., he caused notice of the annual meeting of the stockholders of the said Corporation, a copy of which is hereto attached and is hereby made a part of this affidavit, to be deposited in the United States Post Office at .... City, in a sealed envelope, postage prepaid, duly addressed to each stockholder of record of the said Corporation at his last-known post office address as the same appeared on the books of the Corporation.

....

Subscribed and sworn to before me this .. day of ...., 19...

....
Notary Public

No. 7

Affidavit of secretary of publication of notice of stockholders' meeting.

STATE OF .... ⎫ ss.:
COUNTY OF .... ⎭

................, being duly sworn, on his oath says that he is the Secretary of .... Corporation, a corporation organized and existing under the laws of the State of ....; that pursuant to the order of the Board of Directors of said Corporation, he caused the notice of the .... (*insert annual or special*) meeting of stockholders, a copy of which is hereto annexed and made a part of this affidavit, to be published in the ...., a newspaper published in the City of ...., and circulating in the County of ...., being the county in which said Corporation is located, for a period of ...., beginning the .. day of ...., 19.., as required by .... (*insert words "the laws of the State of ....," or, "the By-laws of the Corporation"*).

Sworn to before me this ....
.. day of ...., 19.. Secretary

....
Notary Public

No. 8

Proxy for special meeting of stockholders; purposes of meeting not indicated.

KNOW ALL MEN BY THESE PRESENTS, That ...., the undersigned, stockholder in the .... Company, does hereby appoint .... and ...., or either of them, true and lawful attorneys, with power of substitution for .... and in .... name to vote, as .... proxy, at the Special Meeting of the Stockholders in said Company, to be held at the City of ...., State of ...., on the .. day of ......

........, **19**.., or at any adjournment thereof, with all the powers which .... should possess if personally present.

Dated this .. day of ...., **19**...

....

No. 9

Notice of special meeting of directors, specifying purposes.

.... (*City*) .... (*State*)

To ...., ..., and ...., Directors of .... Corporation:

NOTICE IS HEREBY GIVEN That, in accordance with the provisions of Article ...., Section .... of the By-laws of the .... Corporation, and in accordance with the requirements of the laws of the State of ...., a special meeting of the Board of Directors of the said Corporation will be held at its office and principal place of business, ... (*Street*), ... (*City*), ... (*State*), on the .. day of ...., **19**.., at .... o'clock in the .... noon, for the purpose of:

1. (*Here insert particular purposes of meeting.*)

2. To transact such other business as may lawfully come before said meeting.

....

Secretary

No. 10

Minutes of annual meeting of directors.

[*Note:* The headings in brackets ordinarily appear in the minute book as marginal captions.]

[Time and place of meeting] The .... annual meeting of the Board of Directors of the .... Corporation was held at the office of the Corporation, ..., in the City of ...., State of ...., on the .. day of ...., **19**.., at .... o'clock in the .... noon, immediately following the adjournment of the annual meeting of the stockholders.

[Quorum] The following directors, being all the directors of the said Corporation, were present:

....
....
....
....
....

[Chairman; Secretary] Mr. ...., President of the Corporation, presided, and Mr. .... acted as Secretary of the meeting.

[Notice of meeting] The Secretary presented the notice of the meeting pursuant to which the meeting was held. The same was ordered to be entered in the minutes and is as follows:

(Insert notice here.)

The Chairman laid before the meeting the minutes of the annual meeting of the stockholders of the corporation, held on the .. day of ...., 19.., showing the election of the following persons as directors of the Corporation, to hold office for the term of ...... year(s), and until their successors shall be elected and shall qualify.

. . . .

. . . .

. . . .

. . . .

. . . .

[Election of officers] On motion duly made, seconded, and unanimously carried, the Board of Directors thereupon proceeded to elect the following officers of the Corporation, to wit: President, Vice President, Secretary, and Treasurer.

Mr. .... was nominated for the office of President of the Corporation. No other nominations being made, upon motion duly made, seconded, and unanimously carried, Mr. .... was elected President of the Corporation, and was declared duly elected to the said office.

(Repeat the minutes given above for each officer.)

Each of the officers so elected was present and thereupon accepted the office to which he was elected.

Upon motion duly made, seconded, and unanimously carried, the Board of Directors proceeded to fix the salaries to be paid to the President, Vice President, Secretary, and Treasurer for the year 19...

[Compensation of officers] The Chairman announced that the salary of each officer would be voted upon separately, and that the officer whose salary was under consideration would not participate in the vote.

Mr. ...., President, thereupon left the room.

On motion duly made, seconded, and affirmatively voted upon by all the directors then present, it was

[Salary of President] RESOLVED, That the salary of Mr. ...., President of the Corporation, be fixed at $...... for the year beginning ...., 19.., and ending ...., 19.., payable in semi-monthly installments on the fifteenth day and the last day of each calendar month.

The vote having been taken, Mr. .... was recalled to the meeting.

The Vice President then left the room.

(Repeat the minutes given above for each officer.)

[Adjournment] There being no further business to come before the meeting, the same was, upon motion, adjourned.

. . . .
President

. . . .
Secretary

No. 11

Resolution of directors authorizing sale and issue of stock to persons determined by executive committee.

RESOLVED, That this Corporation sell and issue . . . . (. . . . . . .) shares of the Preferred Stock of this corporation at par, and . . . . (. . . . . .) shares of Common Stock having no par value at . . . . . . dollars ($. . . . . .) per share, payable in cash at the time of purchase, to such persons, firms, or corporations as the Executive Committee shall determine, and the President and the Secretary of this Corporation are hereby authorized to execute and deliver certificates of stock to purchasers upon receipt of full payment for shares purchased.

No. 12

Resolution of directors amending a particular by-law upon authorization of stockholders.

WHEREAS, The holders of more than two-thirds of the subscribed capital stock of the corporation have, by a resolution adopted at a meeting duly called upon notice, authorized and directed the Board of Directors of this corporation to amend Section . . . . of Article . . . . of the By-laws, it is

RESOLVED, That the aforesaid Section . . . . of Article . . . . of the By-laws be amended in accordance with the said resolution of the stockholders, to read as follows:

(Here insert new by-law.)

IT IS FURTHER RESOLVED, That the Secretary of the corporation be and he hereby is authorized and directed to copy the said Section . . . . of Article . . . . of the By-laws, as amended, in the book of By-laws of the corporation, and properly to certify the same.

No. 13

Directors' resolution accepting resignation of a member of board.

RESOLVED, That the resignation of . . . . as a member of the Board of Directors of the . . . . Corporation, as evidenced by his letter to the said Corporation, dated the . . day of . . . . , 19. . , be and it hereby is accepted, and the Secretary of this Corporation is hereby instructed to notify the said .... of the acceptance of his aforesaid resignation.

No. 14

Directors' resolution accepting resignation of officer.

RESOLVED, That the resignation of Mr. .... as .... (*insert office*) be and it hereby is accepted to take effect on the .. day of ...., 19...

No. 15

Directors' resolution expressing gratitude for services of resigning officer.

WHEREAS, ... has, for the past ...... (......) years, been President of the Company, and whereas the said .... declines to be a candidate for re-election, this Board of Directors desires to spread the following resolution upon the minutes:

RESOLVED, That we recognize the excellent, energetic, and intelligent service that .... has rendered the Company during his incumbency. We feel that the high position which the Company has attained has been in large measure due to his earnest efforts and untiring devotion.

RESOLVED FURTHER, That in recognition of his services to the Company, the aforesaid .... be elected Chairman to preside at the meetings of the Board for the ensuing year.

No. 16

Blanket resolution of directors authorizing issuance of duplicate certificate in event of loss.

RESOLVED, That, in the event of the loss, mutilation, or destruction of any certificate of stock of .... Corporation, a duplicate thereof may be issued, provided the owner makes a sufficient affidavit setting forth the loss, mutilation, or destruction of the original certificate, and gives a surety bond to the Corporation to such amount as may be determined by the .... (*indicate officer*).

No. 17

Excerpt of minutes showing adoption of minutes of previous meeting as corrected.

RESOLVED, That the minutes of the meeting of ...., held on the .. day of ...., 19.., be and they are hereby adopted and approved in their entirety, except that the words "................"

be eliminated from the resolution ...... (*specify subject matter of resolution for identification*) contained therein.

No. 18

Resolution of directors (or stockholders) extending sympathy upon death of associate.

WHEREAS, The directors of the .... Corporation desire to record their deep sorrow at the death on ...., 19.., of their esteemed associate ...., who since ...., 19.., served as director of this Corporation, be it

RESOLVED, That the Board of Directors of this Corporation hereby gives formal expression of its grievous loss in the death of ...., and does hereby note in its records the passing from this life of a man who was esteemed by his associates, loved by his friends, and respected by all.

RESOLVED FURTHER, That a copy of this resolution be tendered to his family as a humble expression of the Board's heartfelt sympathy in its bereavement.

Real Estate Practice: Deeds;
Mortgages; Leases

A CAPABLE legal secretary is very valuable to a lawyer engaged in real estate practice. By becoming familiar with the various legal documents involved in real estate transactions, and the procedure necessary to consummate the transaction, she can relieve the lawyer of practically all routine work, with very little guidance from him.

In Chapter 9, we gave basic information about legal instruments generally. In this chapter we describe specific real estate instruments, with information and suggestions that will help you assume part of the responsibility for their preparation. Regardless of how capable you are, observe this rule: *Always get the lawyer's approval of an instrument both before it is signed and after it is executed, before placing it of record.*

Pattern followed for each instrument. The following pattern is followed for each instrument:

Definition: The short, precise definition given for each instrument enables you to understand more thoroughly the purpose of it.

Parties: An understanding of the parties affected by an instrument—their connection with it—assists you in preparing the testimonium clause, signature, and certificate of acknowledgment, and enables you to fill in printed forms with accuracy.

Forms and kinds: The lawyer frequently will instruct you to prepare a specific instrument in a certain form.

Checklist of information needed to fill in printed forms: In order to complete the printed form of a specific instrument, you will need the information listed in the checklists. You can probably obtain it from the lawyer's notes and other papers in the file; otherwise, you will have to ask the lawyer, or, at his direction, the client.

Statements and clauses that the instrument contains: When a lawyer dictates an instrument, he will probably instruct you to substitute certain dictated material for a particular clause or statement in a printed form; or he might tell you to pick up a certain clause from a printed form. For example, if he is dictating a mortgage, he might say, "Substitute this for the priority privilege clause in this form"; or, "Pick up the partial release clause from Sunnyside Subdivision mortgage." The explanation and examples of statements and clauses under each instrument will assist you.

Do's and don'ts: These summarize the procedure you should follow in the preparation of a specific instrument. To avoid repetition, references are made to prior chapters where detailed instructions about each item may be found, should you need to refer to them.

Illustrations: Illustrations show how instruments should look when typed and, also, how printed forms should look when completed.

Real Property Descriptions

How land is described. A description of real property appears in many legal instruments that the law secretary prepares, and constitutes an important part of the instrument. The descriptions are often complicated and difficult to follow when typing. Usually they are copies from some other document or from an abstract of title. An understanding of how these descriptions are evolved will make it easier for you to copy them and will lessen the possibility of an error. *Accuracy is essential.*

Land is identified according to section and township or by metes and bounds. In towns and subdivisions, lot and block identification is also used. Property is never identified solely by street and number because the names and numbers of streets might change.

Section and township description. In the 18th century, when the United States began to sell public lands, it was necessary to adopt some conventional method of describing the tracts that were sold. A rectangular system of surveys was devised. The survey divided the public lands into rectangular tracts, located with reference to base lines running east and west, and *prime* or *principal meridians* running north and south. The prime meridians are numbered, as Third Prime Meridian, or named, as San Bernardino Meridian. The rectangular tracts are divided into six-mile squares, known as *townships*. A row of townships running north and south is called a *range,* and the ranges are numbered east and west from the prime meridians. The townships are divided into 36 sections, each one mile square or 640 acres. The sections are numbered from 1 to 36, beginning with the section in the northeast corner of the township, proceeding west to boundary of the township; the next row is numbered from west to east, and so on. (See Figure 101.) The sections in turn are divided into half and quarter sections, and the quarters into quarter-quarter sections, designated by their direction from the center as northwest, southwest, northeast, and southeast.

The description of a given five acres of land identified by the section and township (Government Survey) description might read:

The East Half of the Northeast Quarter of the Northeast Quarter of the Northeast Quarter of Section One, Township 39 North, Range 12 East of the Third Prime Meridian.

The shaded portion of the diagram in Figure 101 represents the parcel described above, assuming that the diagram is Township 39 North, Range 12 East.

Land identification in the 29 public land states in which Government Survey description is used is thus precise and orderly; it is possible to designate any plot of land as small as five acres with perfect accuracy; no two parcels are described in exactly the same terms because they are identified with reference to a specific prime meridian. The public land states are Alabama, Arizona, Arkansas, California, Colorado, Florida, Idaho, Illinois, Indiana, Iowa, Kansas, Louisiana, Michigan, Minnesota, Mississippi, Missouri, Montana, Nebraska, Nevada, New Mexico, North Dakota, Ohio, Oklahoma, Oregon, South Dakota, Utah, Washington, Wisconsin, and Wyoming.

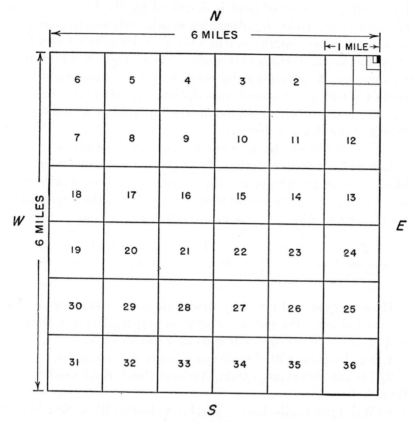

Figure 101. Diagram of Township Divided into Sections.

Metes and bounds description. Prior to the Government Survey the land in the area comprising the thirteen colonies (18 states) was held under original grants from the Crown to the Colonists. In these states—Connecticut, Delaware, Georgia, Kentucky, Maine, Maryland, Massachusetts, New Hampshire, New Jersey, New York, North Carolina, Pennsylvania, Rhode Island, South Carolina, Tennessee, Vermont, Virginia, and West Virginia—and in Texas,[1] each parcel of land is different in size and shape and is described by metes and bounds. A metes and bounds description is not correlated to any system of meridians and base

---

[1] The United States never had original title to the land in Texas because it was annexed as an independent republic.

lines, but each tract of land is described by the lines that constitute its boundaries. A natural landmark, such as a tree or river, or an artificial landmark, such as a fence, stake, railroad, or street, often marks the corners and angles. These marks are known as *monuments*. A description by courses and distances constitutes part of a metes and bounds description. The direction from the starting point in which the boundary line runs is a *course;* the length of the line is a *distance.*

Figure 102 illustrates a metes and bounds description.

Lot and block description. Property is described by lot and block number when land has been surveyed and subdivided into parcels. A map of the subdivision is recorded in the appropriate county office. A lot and block description might read:

Lot Ten (10), Block Eight (8), Bay Shore Subdivision, as recorded in Volume 5 of Plats, Page 39, records of Blank County, State of . . . .

How to type real property descriptions. Unless otherwise instructed observe the following style in preparing descriptions of real property for use in deeds and other instruments:

1. Single space, with double space between paragraphs.

2. Do not abbreviate Street, Avenue, Road, Boulevard, in the text.

3. Write the words *North, Northeast, South, West, Southwest,* and the like, with initial capitals, but do not capitalize the words *northerly, northeasterly,* and the like.

4. Capitalize quarter, township, section, and range, and the name or number of a prime meridian.

5. Write courses as follows: "South twenty (20) degrees, thirty-three (33) minutes, forty-five (45) seconds West." The single quotation mark stands for minutes, the double quotation mark for seconds.

6. Write distances as follows: "One hundred thirty-three and twenty-nine one hundredths (133.29) feet."

7. When several courses and distances are given in succession, introduced by a phrase such as ". . . the following several courses and distances . . ." each of the courses and distances is written separately, indented and single spaced, separated one from the other by a double space, and each course and distance

ALL that lot or parcel of land, situate, lying and being in the Town of Oyster Bay, County of Nassau, State of New York, bounded and described as follows:

BEGINNING at a point in the center line of Buena Vista Avenue distant two hundred sixty-one and thirty hundredths (261.30) feet southerly from the point of intersection of said line with the center line of Jones Road; running thence along the center line of Buena Vista Avenue South twenty-five (25) degrees thirty-three (33) minutes East four hundred fifty-two and seventy-eight hundredths (452.78) feet to a point; running thence North sixty-eight (68) degrees thirty-two (32) minutes East three hundred ten and eleven hundredths (310.11) feet to a point in the center line of a driveway; running thence generally along the center line of said driveway the following courses and distances:

A. North forty-five (45) degrees forty-two (42) minutes West, 50 feet;

B. North thirty-nine (39) degrees two (02) minutes West, 50 feet;

C. North thirty-four (34) degrees sixteen (16) minutes West, 50 feet;

D. North twenty-eight (28) degrees fifty-eight (58) minutes West, 50 feet;

E. North twenty-six (26) degrees seventeen (17) minutes West, 100 feet;

F. North thirty-two (32) degrees six (06) minutes West, 50 feet;

G. North fifty-five (55) degrees thirty-four (34) minutes West, 50 feet;

H. North sixty-one (61) degrees thirty-two (32) minutes West, 50 feet;

I. North eighty (80) degrees thirty-three (33) minutes West, 50 feet;

J. South seventy-nine (79) degrees eleven (11) minutes West, 50 feet;

K. South sixty-five (65) degrees thirty-two (32) minutes West, 50 feet; and

L. South sixty-four (64) degrees forty-seven (47) minutes West, 77 feet, to a point in the center line of Buena Vista Avenue, the point or place of beginning;

Containing, in area, approximately two and seven hundred seventy-four thousandths (2.774) acres;

Being and intended to be all of Plot No. 5, as shown on a map entitled "Plot Plan, Property of John Doe Estate, Town of Oyster Bay, Nassau County, New York, made by James Brown, Surveyor, November 1, 1940, as revised January 13, 1942, and December 31, 1945.

Figure 102. Metes and Bounds Description.

is ended with a semi-colon. The sentence after the last course and distance is flush with the left-hand margin of the text preceding the itemized courses and distances. (See Figure 102.)

8. It is preferable not to use figures, symbols, and abbreviations, but many law offices use them because of the limited space on a printed form. A description would then be written: "South

20° 33′ 45″ West, 50 ft." In law offices with considerable real estate practice, a special key is placed on the typewriter for the symbol of the word *degrees;* otherwise, the symbol is made by turning the platen back a half space and striking the small *o*.

How to check land descriptions. A typographical error in the description of land can cause considerable trouble and even result in a law suit. The importance of checking the description cannot be overemphasized. It is easy to make an error in copying that is not always discernible from merely reading the description. For example, the Government Survey description on page 452 contains the phrase "of the Northeast Quarter" three times. It would be easy to omit the phrase once, but difficult to realize the omission in reading over the description; yet the omission would double the amount of land conveyed by the deed. Nor is it advisable for one person to compare the description line by line. The safest method of checking the typographical accuracy of a land description is to have someone read aloud to you the original copy, slowly enough to permit you to follow your typed copy carefully.

If you have a plat or diagram showing the location of the parcel described, you can check the accuracy of the description from that, especially if the identification is by Government Survey. To compare a Government Survey description with the map designation, read the parts of the description in reverse order—that is, begin with the township and range and work backward to the designated plot.

Deeds

What is a deed? A *deed* is a formal written instrument by which title to real property is conveyed from one person to another. *A contract of sale* is an agreement to convey title, whereas a deed is the conveyance itself.

Parties to a deed. The parties to a deed are the *grantor,* who conveys his interest in the property, and the *grantee,* to whom the conveyance is made. The grantor is the seller, and the grantee is usually the purchaser, but not necessarily. The purchaser may buy the land for the grantee. Only the grantor signs the deed, unless the grantee makes special covenants (see page 463).

The *grantor* may be a natural person, a partnership, or a corporation. The individual must be of legal age and of sound mind. Frequently the grantor makes the deed in a representative capacity, for example, as the guardian of a minor. In such case, the first paragraph of the deed recites the capacity in which the grantor makes the deed. Whether or not the grantor's spouse must join in the deed depends upon the law of the state where the land is situated. Generally speaking, it is necessary for the spouse to join and for that reason the marital status of the grantor is stated in the deed, as *spinster, bachelor, widow, widower,* or *divorced and not remarried.*

The *grantee* may be a natural person, a partnership, or a corporation. A minor or insane person may be a grantee, although he cannot be a grantor. In some states, a deed cannot be made to a partnership in the firm name, but must be made to the individual partners. For example, the conveyance would not be made to "The Peerless Laundry," but would be made to "John Smith and Edwin Adams, doing business as The Peerless Laundry." In some states foreign corporations are not permitted to acquire title to land unless they have received authority to do business in that state.

Forms of deeds. There are two standard forms of deeds: *indenture deed* and *deed poll.* The distinction is in the phraseology. The standard indenture deed opens with, "THIS INDENTURE (or DEED) made . . . ," whereas the standard deed poll opens with, "KNOW ALL MEN BY THESE PRESENTS:" or similar words. Also, the deed indenture is written in the third person, whereas the deed poll is written in the first person. In some states only the indenture form is used; in others, only the deed poll; but in many states the indenture deed and deed poll are both used. The indenture is often signed by both parties.

To save the space required for recording deeds, many states provide by statute for a short form of deed, known as a *statutory form.* By statute, certain covenants and warranties are made part of the deed and, although not set forth in the deed, are binding on the grantor and his heirs. Since the statute is actually part of the deed and a state statute is not effective outside of the state enacting it, a statutory form of deed can be used only in the specific state that makes statutory provision for it.

Kinds of deeds. There are various kinds, as well as forms, of deeds. Those commonly used are the *warranty deed, bargain and sale deed, quit-claim deed,* and *deed of gift.*

A warranty deed is the most desirable from the standpoint of the purchaser. It not only transfers title in fee simple but covenants and warrants that the grantor has the right to transfer the title to the property and that the grantee shall enjoy the premises quietly, forever. Should anyone later make a claim against the property, the grantee can sue the grantor for breach of his warranty.

A bargain and sale deed conveys title as efficaciously as a warranty deed, but it does not warrant the title against adverse claims.

A quit-claim deed is not used to convey title but to obtain a release from a person who is believed to have some interest in or claim to the property, whether real or not. By this form of deed, the grantor "quits" any claim he might have, usually for a nominal consideration. These deeds do not obligate the grantor in any way, but if he should have full title, the quit-claim deed will operate as a full and complete conveyance of title.

A deed of gift is given in consideration of the "love and affection" that the grantor has for the grantee. A deed of gift passes title as completely as a deed for which there is a monetary consideration.

Printed forms of deeds. Printed forms of deeds are used almost exclusively. Figures 103a and b illustrate a printed form of deed executed by man and wife. Follow carefully the directions on page 166 for filling in printed forms. With the information called for by the following checklist, you will have no difficulty in filling in the printed forms without dictation. The lawyer will dictate any special clauses with reference to encumbrances and the like.

Some printed forms are drawn especially for use by corporations, other for use by individuals.

Printed forms of deeds with special provisions, such as cutting of timber, or harvesting of crops, or oil rights, are also available in localities where there is a need for them.

Checklist of information needed to fill in form. 1. Whether grantor is an individual, a partnership, or a corporation

2. Full name and residence of grantor, including street address in large cities

For and in consideration of the sum of $ 10.00 -
- - - - - - - - - - - - - - TEN AND NO/100 - - - - - - - - - - - - - -DOLLARS

cash in hand paid by the grantees herein, and other good and valuable considerations,

the receipt of which is hereby acknowledged,

We, John Albert Green and wife, Ellen Blake Green,

_____have bargained and sold, and by these presents do transfer and convey unto the said
ROBERT COLE BROWN and wife, MARY HOWARD BROWN
_____heirs and assigns, a certain tract or parcel of land in Davidson County, State of Tennessee, described as follows to wit:

Land in Davidson County, Tennessee, being Lot No. 26 on the Plan of a Resubdivision of Part of Royal Oaks Subdivision, as of record in Book 1424, page 31, Register's Office for said County.

Said Lot No. 26 fronts 165 feet on the northerly side of Sunnybrook Drive and runs back 271.3 feet on the easterly line and 262.8 feet on the westerly line, to a dead line in the rear, measuring 182.8 feet thereon.

Being the same property conveyed to John Albert Green and wife, Ellen Blake Green, by deed from Royal Highland Land Company, of record in book 2063, page 25, said Register's Office.

To have and to hold the said tract or parcel of land, with the appurtenances, estate, title and interest thereto belonging to the said Robert Cole Brown and wife, Mary Howard Brown,
their _____heirs and assigns, forever.

And we do covenant with the said Robert Cole Brown and wife, Mary Howard Brown,
_____that we are lawfully seized and possessed of said land in fee simple; have a good right to convey it. and the same is unencumbered.

And we, John Albert Green and wife, Ellen Blake Green
do further covenant and bind ourselves, our heirs and representatives, to warrant and forever defend the title to the said land to the said Robert Cole Brown and wife, Mary Howard Brown,
their _____heirs and assigns against the lawful claims of all persons, whomsoever.

Witness our hands this 15th day of December , 1952 .

John Albert Green
Ellen Blake Green

STATE OF TENNESSEE ⎱
Davidson County ⎰

Personally appeared before me, James D. White , a Notary Public in and for
said County and State, the within named John Albert Green and wife, Ellen Blake Green

the bargainor s , with whom I am personally acquainted, and who acknowledged that they
executed the within instrument for the purposes therein contained. Witness my hand and official seal at
Nashville , Tennessee, this 15th day of December , 1952

Commission expires May 1, 1954.

James D. White
Notary Public

Courtesy Tennessee Title Company

Figure 103a. Warranty Deed from Husband and Wife.

459

Courtesy Tennessee Title Company

Figure 103b. Endorsed Back of Warranty Deed by Husband and Wife.

3. Full description of the grantor's office and authority if he is conveying in a representative capacity

4. Marital status of grantor

5. Full name of spouse if spouse must join in the conveyance

6. Full name and residence of grantee

7. Date of deed

8. Description of property

9. Whether deed is to be a warranty, bargain and sale, quitclaim, or gift deed, the form for each being different

10. Consideration to be expressed in deed

11. When and where deed is to be acknowledged

12. Names and official positions of officers signing and acknowledging deed, if grantor is a corporation

Typed deeds. Sometimes a printed form is not adequate for the special clauses and conditions that a deed must contain. The lawyer will then dictate the deed to you, probably telling you to copy various parts from a printed form. When typing the deed, follow the general style of a printed form.

The lawyer might also dictate to you a deed that is to be printed after it is typed. These are for a special purpose, such as the sale of lots in a subdivision. Usually several drafts are written before the final typed copy is sent to the printer. They are set up in the same form as any deed. Chapter 17 tells how to prepare material for the printer.

Statements and clauses in deeds. *Consideration.* The consideration is the payment made by the purchaser for the property. It is usually a sum of money, but it might take some other form, such as the cancellation of a debt owed by the seller to the purchaser. A deed frequently states a nominal consideration because the parties do not want the actual consideration to be known. The consideration for a deed of gift is "love and affection."

EXAMPLES:

WITNESSETH, That the Party of the First Part, in consideration of Five Thousand (5,000) Dollars, lawful money of the United States, paid by the Party of the Second Part, does hereby grant . . .

. . . for the sum of Five Dollars ($5), to me in hand paid, and other good and valuable consideration, do hereby grant . . .

. . . That the First Party, in consideration of her natural love and affection for the Second Party, does hereby . . .

Encumbrances. Frequently there is an indebtedness against property that is being sold, or taxes or assessments are owed on it. These are *encumbrances* against the property, and the deed recites the agreement between the parties regarding them. The person who holds the encumbrance is the *encumbrancer.* The statement of encumbrances, if any, either follows the property description or is made a part of the habendum (see below). It is usually dictated by the lawyer.

EXAMPLES:

The said premises are conveyed subject to a mortgage thereof in the sum of Ten Thousand Dollars ($10,000), with interest, made by Roger L. Thompson to Edgar N. Wilson, dated the fifteenth day of January, 19.., and recorded in Book 27 of Conveyances, page 359, in the office of the Clerk of said county.

Subject to a purchase money mortgage made by the Grantee to the Grantor delivered and intended to be recorded simultaneously herewith,

Habendum clause. The habendum clause derives its name from the Latin phrase *habendum et tenendum,* and, accordingly, begins with the words *to have and to hold.* Its purpose is to define the extent of the interest conveyed. When special circumstances surround the transfer of the property, the lawyer dictates a substitute habendum.

EXAMPLE:

TO HAVE AND TO HOLD the premises herein granted unto the Party of the Second Part, his heirs and assigns, forever,

TO HAVE AND TO HOLD the granted premises, with all the rights, easements, and appurtenances thereto belonging, to the said John L. Thompson, his heirs and assigns, to his and their own use forever,

SUBJECT, HOWEVER, to all rights of the lessees, tenants and occupants of, or in said granted premises, or in any part, or parts, thereof.

Covenants. The covenants are the promises made by the grantor and grantee. The usual covenants by the grantor, which are printed in the deed, relate to the title to the property and to its quiet and peaceful enjoyment by the grantee. The grantor might make special promises not included in the usual printed form, such as agreeing to construct and maintain roadways. Covenants by the grantee are less common than covenants by the grantor. The most frequent use of covenants by the grantee is in connection with the sale of lots in subdivisions; they usually relate to the type of structure that may be erected on the premises. These covenants are not included in the usual printed form of deed, but special deeds that contain them are usually printed for the sale of lots in a specific subdivision.

And the said grantee does hereby for himself, his heirs and assigns, covenant with the said grantor, his heirs, executors, and administrators, that he will not, at any time hereafter, erect, or cause, or suffer, or permit, to be erected upon the hereby granted premises, or any part thereof, any building other than a brick or stone private dwelling house, not less than three stories in height.

Restrictions and conditions. Property is often sold subject to certain restrictions and conditions to be observed by the grantee. These usually relate to types of buildings that may be constructed, purposes for which the property may be used, and the subsequent sale of the property. The restrictions and conditions are not included in the usual printed form of deed, but are frequently included in specially printed forms.

Exceptions and reservations. Property is frequently sold subject to certain exceptions and reservations. These might relate to easements, rights of way, growing crops, timber, minerals, and the like. They are not included in the usual printed form of deed; the lawyer dictates them.

Testimonium clause. The testimonium clause to a deed is similar to the testimonium clause to any written instrument. (See page 169.)

Revenue stamps. Whenever property is sold, a Federal transfer tax, evidenced by a revenue stamp, must be paid. Deeds of gift are not taxed. The tax is based upon the *net* consideration paid for the property. For example, if the purchase price is $15,000, $10,000 of which is payable in cash, the purchaser to assume an existing $5,000 mortgage, the tax is paid on $10,000 only. If the purchaser pays $10,000 cash and gives the seller a $5,000 purchase money mortgage, the tax is payable on the entire $15,000.

These stamps, known as *documentary stamps,* may be obtained at the Post Office. They are issued in the following denominations: 1 cent, 2 cents, 3 cents, 4 cents, 5 cents, 8 cents, 10 cents, 25 cents, 40 cents, 50 cents, 80 cents, $1, $2, $3, $4, $5, $10, $20, $30, $50, $60, $100, $500, and $1,000. It is advisable to use as few stamps as possible.

The purchaser's lawyer usually buys the stamps, but the seller reimburses him and should see that they are affixed to the deed.

How to cancel the stamps. Revenue stamps that are affixed to deeds must be cancelled. To cancel a stamp, write your initials and the date on it in ink. If the stamp is of the value of 50 cents or more, also make three parallel incisions lengthwise through the stamp with some sharp instrument. This should be done after the stamp is affixed to the document. The stamps are usually affixed before the instrument is recorded.

State tax. Some states impose a tax on deeds, payable usually before the deed can be recorded.

Recording. The purchaser has the deed recorded for his own protection, and pays the recording fee. If he is your firm's client, the lawyer will probably ask you to have the deed recorded. Follow the instructions on page 190, in Chapter 9.

"Do's" and "don'ts" in the preparation of a deed. Unless otherwise instructed, follow these directions when preparing a deed. Obviously, some of them apply only to typed deeds, some to printed forms, and some to both.

1. Make 3 copies—the original for the grantee, a copy for the grantor, and a copy for your files.

2. Use legal cap.

3. Follow carefully the directions for filling in a printed form. (See Chapter 8.)

4. Don't forget the responsibility and distribution line at the top of the first page. (This goes on the office copy only of printed form.) (See Chapter 8.)

5. Double space.

6. Type the land description in accordance with directions on page 454.

7. Number all pages of typed deed.

8. If you are using a printed form, be sure and make the "Z" after the land description. (See Chapter 8.)

9. Don't forget to have at least two lines of typing on the signature page. (See Chapter 9.)

10. Prepare signature line for the grantor. (See Chapter 9.) The grantee does not sign a deed except in special circumstances.

11. Affix the seal in accordance with directions in Chapter 9, when it is required.

12. Remember that a corporation's seal is generally affixed to an instrument.

13. Type witness lines and attestation clause, when required. (See Chapter 9.)

14. Prepare certificate of acknowledgment. (See Chapter 9.)

15. Collate.

16. Check and double check spelling of names.

17. Get someone to compare the land description with you. (See page 456.)

18. Endorse the back of a printed form as illustrated by Figure 103b. If the deed is typed, prepare legal back. (See Chapter 8.)

19. Arrange for the grantor to come in and sign the deed and acknowledge it.

20. *Get the lawyer's approval of the instrument before it is signed.* Have the grantor sign the original only.

21. Does the grantor's signature agree with the name typed in the deed?

22. Have the deed notarized. If you are a notary, take the acknowledgment, following instructions in Chapter 9.

23. Affix and cancel revenue stamps. (See page 463.)

24. Prepare closing statement. (See page 492, *et seq.*)

25. After signature and acknowledgment, conform copies to original. (See Chapter 8.)

26. Get the lawyer's approval and then have the deed recorded. (See Chapter 9.) Don't forget to put a notation on the back of the deed asking that it be returned to you. (The secretary to the lawyer for the grantee attends to the recording.)

27. When the deed is returned by the recorder, send it to the grantee with a covering letter. (See Chapter 9.)

Mortgages

What is a mortgage? A mortgage is a *conditional* conveyance. It is given by a borrower or debtor to secure the payment of a debt, with a provision that the conveyance will become void on the payment of the debt by the date named. In early English times the debtor actually turned over his property to the lender, who would keep the income and profits from it. The land was "dead" to the owner and gave him no return; hence the word *mort-gage,* meaning *dead pledge.* A mortgage may be given on real estate or on personal property, but a mortgage on personal property is referred to as a *chattel mortgage*, whereas a mortgage on real estate is referred to simply as a *mortgage*. Some mortgages cover both real and personal property, for example, a mortgage on a furnished apartment building.

The word mortgage also refers to the instrument used to make the conveyance. The debt is evidenced by promissory notes; the mortgage is the security instrument that secures payment of the notes. In some states, New York for example, the debt is evidenced by a bond instead of a promissory note. The bond takes the place of the note. Frequently, the bond and mortgage are combined in one instrument, which is referred to as a *bond and mortgage*.

Parties to a mortgage. The parties to a conventional mortgage are the mortgagor, who is the debtor or borrower, and the mortgagee, who is the lender. The mortgagor owns the property that is being mortgaged and gives a mortgage to the mortgagee, usually in return for a loan; he is frequently referred to in the instrument as the party of the first part. The mortgagee is frequently referred to as the party of the second part.

The parties to a deed of trust are the mortgagor, party of the first part, and the trustee, party of the second part. Some states, Colorado for example, have designated officials, known as public trustees, to whom the estate is conveyed under a deed of trust.

Designation of the parties. Extreme care should be exercised to see that the name of the mortgagor appears exactly as it appears in the instrument under which he claims title to the land; otherwise, the mortgagee's title might be defective if it becomes necessary for him to foreclose. The mortgagor's name should be exactly the same in the body of the mortgage, in the signature, and in the acknowledgment. If the mortgage is a purchase money mortgage (see page 467), the names of both parties should be given precisely as they appear in the deed from the mortgagee to the mortgagor.

The requirements relative to the grantor and grantee in a deed apply generally to the mortgagor and mortgagee (see page 457).

Forms of mortgages. Practice has given rise to the use of forms that differ widely in detail in the various states. However, any instrument that is actually intended as security for a debt will generally be construed as a mortgage.

The forms of mortgages most commonly used are the form that might be termed the *conventional mortgage* and the form variously called a *trust deed, deed of trust, trust indenture* or *trust mortgage.*

A conventional mortgage is essentially a deed from the borrower to the lender, which contains a provision, known as the *defeasance clause,* that the mortgage shall be void on payment of the debt. The additional provisions, which appear in fine print in the printed form, vary with the state.

A deed of trust conveys the land to a third party instead of direct to the lender. The third party holds the property in trust for the lender until the debt is paid in accordance with the terms of the trust deed. In the District of Columbia and the following states, the deed of trust is more commonly used than the conventional mortgage: Alabama, California, Colorado, Illinois, Mississippi, Missouri, Montana, New Mexico, Tennessee, Texas, Virginia, West Virginia, and Wisconsin. In the other states, a deed of trust is seldom used except in connection with large transactions, such as railroad mortgages, that involve numerous creditors. It would be impracticable to convey part of the legal title to each lender or bondholder.

Some states have short statutory forms of mortgages, which save space when recorded. The brief statutory forms are amplified by statute and therefore are not used outside the state of origin. Many careful conveyancers feel that the short statutory form does not protect the mortgagee sufficiently.

Purchase money mortgage. A purchase money mortgage is one that is given in part payment of the purchase price of the property. For example, if the purchase price is $10,000, the purchaser might pay $6,000 cash and give the seller a purchase money mortgage for $4,000. The deed and the purchase money mortgage are executed simultaneously. The grantee in the deed is the mortgagor; the grantor in the deed is the mortgagee. All names and descriptions of property in the purchase money mortgage must agree with those in the deed. A purchase money mortgage has certain priorities that other mortgages do not have. For example, it has preference over the dower rights of the mortgagor's wife, and she, therefore, does not have to sign it. It also has priority over existing judgments and other debts of the mortgagor. On the other hand, as a rule, the mortgagee cannot get a deficiency decree against the mortgagor when he forecloses a purchase money mortgage, which he can usually get under other mortgages. (See Chapter 22 for foreclosure actions.) A purchase money mortgage contains a statement similar to the following example, which distinguishes it from a mortgage given for an existing debt.

EXAMPLE:

This mortgage is a purchase money mortgage, which is given and intended to be recorded simultaneously with a deed this day executed and delivered by the mortgagee to the mortgagor, covering the property above described; this mortgage being given to secure a portion of the purchase price expressed in said deed.

Printed mortgages. Printed forms of conventional mortgages and deeds of trust are used extensively. Follow carefully the directions given on page 166 for filling in printed forms.

Upon instructions from the lawyer, you can complete the printed forms of the ordinary mortgage and deed of trust without dictation. The lawyer will dictate any special clauses that he wants to include in the instrument.

Checklist of information needed to fill in mortgage or deed of trust. In order to complete the printed form of mortgage or deed of trust, you will need the information listed here. You can probably obtain it from the lawyer's notes and other papers in the file; otherwise, you will have to ask the lawyer, or, at his direction, the client.

1. Full name of mortgagor and mortgagee; also of trustee in the case of a trust deed
2. County and state of residence of mortgagor and mortgagee; in a large city, their street address; also residence of trustee in the case of a trust deed
3. Full description of the mortgagor's office and authority if he is conveying in a representative capacity
4. Marital status of mortgagor
5. Full name of spouse if spouse must join in the conveyance
6. If purchase money mortgage, is wife to join
7. Date of mortgage
8. Amount of mortgage

9. Period of time mortgage is to run; maturity date

10. Rate of interest and when payable

11. Description of property

12. Date and place mortgage is to be acknowledged

13. If mortgagor is corporation, name and title of officers signing and acknowledging

14. If mortgage contains power of sale, number of days notice to be given in newspaper (this is determined by statute) and where newspaper is published

15. If there is to be an affidavit of title, who is to make it

Typed mortgages and deeds of trust. Printed forms of mortgages and trust deeds are frequently inadequate for the special conditions of the transaction. The lawyer will then dictate the instrument to you. The dictation is usually lengthy and requires special care in transcription. Instead of dictating certain parts of the mortgage, the lawyer will probably tell you to copy from a printed form. For example, he might say, "Copy the defeasance clause from this form." Generally a dictated mortgage is typed in draft form before it is finally typed. When typing the instrument, follow the general style of a printed form.

Deeds of trust that are given to secure a bond issue are long and involved and are printed especially for a specific bond issue. The lawyer dictates the draft and revises it, usually several times. You can assist him in this laborious task by an especially careful and accurate transcription of your notes, thus enabling him to devote his attention entirely to the content of the draft without the distraction of typographical errors.

Statements and clauses in mortgages. *Description of debt.* A mortgage is given to secure a debt, and the mortgage instrument must describe and identify the debt with preciseness. The description includes the rate and time of payment of interest and clearly states the time of payment of the debt. Some forms call for a copy of the note secured by the mortgage to be copied in the body of the instrument.

EXAMPLE:

. . . an indebtedness in the sum of twenty thousand (20,000) dollars, lawful money of the United States, to be paid on the first day of November, 19. ., with interest thereon to be computed from November

1, 19. ., at the rate of six (6) per centum per annum, and to be paid semi-annually thereafter, according to a certain note bearing even date herewith, . . .

Defeasance clause. The provision in the mortgage that it shall become void upon payment of the debt is known as the *defeasance clause*—the mortgage will be defeated upon payment of the debt. Printed forms usually contain an adequate defeasance clause.

EXAMPLE:

Provided always, that if said mortgagor, . . . shall pay . . . a certain promissory note, a copy of which is on the reverse side hereof, and shall perform and comply with each and every stipulation, agreement and covenant of said note and of this mortgage, the estate hereby created shall be void, otherwise the same shall remain in full force and virtue.

. . . provided that if I shall punctually pay said notes according to the tenor thereof, then this mortgage shall be void.

Consideration. A mortgage recites the consideration for which it was given. Statement of the consideration might name the amount of the indebtedness, or it might recite a nominal consideration.

EXAMPLES:

. . . for and in consideration of the aforesaid debt of five thousand dollars ($5,000), and the better securing the payment of the same with interest . . .

. . . for the better securing the payment of the sum of money mentioned in the said bond, or obligation, with the interest thereon, and, also, in consideration of One Dollar ($1.) paid by the Second Party, the receipt whereof is hereby acknowledged . . .

Acceleration clause. Mortgages contain a clause providing that if principal or interest payments are not made when due, or if any obligation on the part of the mortgagor is not fulfilled, then the entire amount of the mortgage becomes payable immediately. The maturity date of the mortgage is *accelerated,* if the mortgagor defaults. This clause is the *acceleration clause.* It is usually printed in the instrument.

That the whole of said principal sum shall become due after default in the payment of any installment of principal or of interest for .... days, or after default in the payment of any tax, water rate or assessment for .... days, after notice and demand.

Description of property. See page 451 for an explanation of land descriptions and how to type them. Accuracy in the description or mortgaged property cannot be overemphasized. It is even more important in a mortgage than in a deed, because a purchaser takes possession of the premises purchased, thus giving notice to all the world of his rights; but a mortgagee must depend upon the recording of the instrument to give notice of his rights. If a mortgage describes land as being in the NE Quarter, when it is in the NW Quarter, a purchaser who buys a tract in the NW Quarter gets a good title, free and clear of the mortgage.

Prepayment privilege. The mortgagor sometimes likes to pay off the mortgage, or part of it, before maturity, but he does not have this right unless the terms of the mortgage specifically give it to him. Mortgages and mortgage notes frequently provide that the debt shall be payable *on or before* the maturity date, or they contain a specific clause giving the mortgagor this right. This clause is the prepayment privilege. A comparable provision in trust deeds securing issues of bonds permits *redemption* of the bonds prior to maturity dates. The privilege enables a mortgagor to refinance his debt when money is cheaper, or to sell the property free and clear of any mortgage. Printed forms do not usually include the prepayment privilege.

EXAMPLE:

The mortgagor is hereby authorized and permitted to pay the debt hereby secured, or any part of it, not less than .... dollars at any one time, whenever and at such time and times as he may choose, and the mortgagee hereby agrees to accept such payment or payments, and thereupon the interest shall cease upon such part of the debt as may be so paid; and upon the full payment of said debt, with all interest up to the date of actual payment, he will discharge this mortgage.

Partial release. The mortgagor, in the course of his business, frequently wishes to sell part of the mortgaged land. For example, the owner of a subdivision sells lots that are part of a subdivision covered by a blanket mortgage. The prepayment privilege (see above) does not release any of the mortgaged land from the mortgage until the entire mortgage is paid. Therefore, to permit the mortgagor to sell part of the land, some mortgages contain a *partial release* clause. The clause permits the release of a specified portion of the premises covered by the mortgage upon payment of a specified sum.

EXAMPLE:

Said mortgagor reserves the right to release all or any part of the said land from the operation of this mortgage, in case said land is subdivided, upon payment to mortgagee of a sum of money to be agreed upon for each lot, the sum to be determined according to the size and location of the lot as soon as the said land is subdivided.

Said mortgagee has agreed to sign a plat of said premises prepared by mortgagor.

Other statements and clauses. A mortgage might contain, also, some or all of the clauses in a deed, such as the habendum, or the covenants, or the testimonium clause (see page 461, *et seq.*)

State tax. In some states, a mortgage registration tax is in effect. It is payable by the mortgagee at the time the mortgage is recorded. Some states do not permit the mortgagee to collect the tax from the mortgagor.

"Do's" and "don'ts" in the preparation of a mortgage. Unless otherwise instructed, follow these directions when preparing a mortgage. Obviously, some of the directions apply only to typed mortgages, some to printed forms, and some to both.

1. Make an original for the mortgagee, a copy for the mortgagor, and a copy for your files.

2. Use legal cap.

3. Follow carefully the directions for filling in a printed form. (See Chapter 8.)

4. Don't forget the responsibilty and distribution line at the top of the first page. This goes on the office copy only of printed form. (See Chapter 8.)

5. Double space.

6. Type the land description in accordance with directions on page 454.

7. If using a printed form be sure to make the "Z" after the land description. (See Chapter 8.)

8. Number all pages of a typed mortgage.

9. Don't forget to have at least two lines of typing on the signature page. (See Chapter 9.)

10. Prepare signature line for the mortgagor. (See Chapter 9.) If the mortgagor is an individual, his wife will probably have to sign, unless the mortgage is a purchase money mortgage. The mortgagee does not sign a mortgage.

11. Affix the seal in accordance with directions in Chapter 9, when required.

12. Remember that a corporation's seal is generally affixed to an instrument.

13. Type witness lines and attestation clause, when required (Chapter 9).

14. Prepare certificate of acknowledgment. (See Chapter 9.)

15. Collate.

16. Check and double check spelling of names. If the mortgage is a purchase money mortgage, compare names of mortgagor and mortgagee with names of grantor and grantee.

17. Endorse the back as illustrated in Figure 104. If the mortgage is typed, prepare legal back (Chapter 9).

18. Get someone to compare the land description with you. See page 456.

19. Arrange for the mortgagor to sign the mortgage.

20. *Get the lawyer's approval of the instrument before it is signed.*

21. Have the mortgagor sign the original only.

22. Does the mortgagor's signature agree with the name as typed in the mortgage?

23. Have the mortgage notarized. If you are a notary take the acknowledgment, following instructions in Chapter 9.

24. After signature and acknowledgment, conform copies to original (Chapter 8).

25. *Get the lawyer's approval of the executed mortgage* and then have it recorded. (See Chapter 9.) Don't forget to put a notation on the back of the mortgage asking that it be returned to you. (The secretary to the lawyer for the mortgagee attends to the recording.)

26. When the mortgage is returned by the recorder, send it to the mortgagee. (See Chapter 9.)

No. _____

ROGER S. NELSON and MARY L.
NELSON, his wife,

TO

SUNNYSIDE ESTATES, INC., a
Delaware Corporation.

𝔅ond and 𝔐ortgage

Dated, ...August 6, ..., *19* ----
Amount, $......10,000.00. ....
Due, ...August 6, ..., *19* 60
Int. Payable.......Semi-annually ....

*The land affected by the within instrument
lies in*   Nassau County, State of
New York.

Record and return to

Smith, Jones & Roberts,
31 Broad Street,
New York, N. Y.

Courtesy Julius Blumberg, Inc.

Figure 104. Endorsed Back of Printed Form of Bond and Mortgage.

Leases

What is a lease? A lease is a binding contract, written or oral, for the possession of lands and improvements on the one side, and the recompense by rent or other compensation on the other side. When the lease is evidenced by a written instrument binding the parties to fulfill certain covenants or agreements, that instrument is known as a *lease*. It is with the preparation of the written lease that the secretary is concerned. Leases range from the letting of an apartment for one year to a 99-year lease on vacant property. They may cover real property, personal property, or both, but a lease of real property is most common. Leases of realty give the lessee a *leasehold estate in the premises*.

Parties to a lease. The parties to a lease are the *lessor,* who owns the property, and the *lessee,* who rents it. The lessor, or owner, leases the property *to* the lessee, or tenant; the lessee leases the property *from* the lessor.

A party to a lease may be a natural person, a partnership, or a corporation. Leases on behalf of minors or insane persons should be made by a guardian. The officers of a corporation enter into a lease on its behalf pursuant to authorization of the board of directors or stockholders. An administrator cannot make a lease because his function is to wind up the estate, not to lease real property. An executor or testamentary trustee must have specific authority given to him by the will in order to make a lease.

Classification of leases. *Duration.* Leases may be classified according to their duration as short-term or long-term leases. Although there is no definite duration that takes a lease out of the short-term class into the long-term class, a lease of 10 or more years is generally considered a long-term lease. The fundamental distinctions are in the responsibilities assumed by the lessee, and in the bond and security requirements. Under a short-term lease, the lessor usually requires the lessee to deposit with him one, three, or six months' rental at the time the lease is executed, whereas under a long-term lease the lessee is required to furnish a bond or collateral in an amount equal to about three-years' rental. The most common practice is for the lessee to deposit with a bank or other financial institution negotiable securities of the required amount.

A special type of long-term lease is the 99-year lease, which has been utilized extensively for the purpose of developing business districts in large cities. These leases are made on parcels of valuable real estate strategically located for business expansion. They contemplate the erection or improvement of buildings upon the property by the lessee.

Type of property. Leases may be classified as *commercial* or *residential,* according to the type of property covered by the lease. As secretary in a law office, you are more likely to prepare commercial leases than residential leases. Short-term leases may be either commercial or residential leases, but long-term leases are almost exclusively commercial leases.

Rental. The majority of leases call for the payment of a definite amount of rental, which continues at a uniform rate throughout the term of the lease. The amount is called a *flat rental.* Other leases, especially long-term leases, provide that the rental shall start at a comparatively low figure and gradually increase. A rental provision of this type is called a *graded rental.* Another method of fixing the amount of rental is to require the tenant to pay a specified percentage of the gross income from sales made upon the premises. A lease with this requirement is called a *percentage lease.* These leases generally cover premises occupied by retail businesses, such as chain stores and department stores. Percentage leases generally run for ten or more years.

Printed forms. Printed forms of leases covering almost any kind of property are available and are frequently used for short-term leases. Many concerns print their own leases, in a form prepared by the lawyer. The lawyer's secretary is more likely to be concerned with the drafting and printing of a form than with filling in the run-of-the-mill lease, such as a lease on an apartment. (See Chapter 17 for preparation of material for the printer.)

Figures 105 and 106 illustrate the first and last page of a printed form of a commercial lease covering a loft. The back of the lease contains a proper endorsement and forms of acknowledgment for an individual and for a corporation.

Standard lease clauses. Usually the lawyer dictates both the short-term and long-term leases that are prepared in his office. Although many of the clauses are standard (see below), a variety of other clauses is necessary to express the agreement between the parties, especially in long-term leases. Ninety-nine year leases and many other long-term leases are extremely technical legal instruments, their preparation requiring a lawyer who is a specialist in the field. You will probably have to type several drafts before the lawyer and his client are satisfied.

JULIUS BLUMBERG, INC., LAW BLANK PUBLISHERS
71 BROADWAY AND 1 RECTOR ST., NEW YORK

This Indenture, made the

day of

in the year one thousand nine hundred and

Witnesseth, That

as Lessor, does grant, demise and let to

and to   legal representatives, as Lessee

Term

with the appurtenances, for the term of

beginning the   day of

and ending the   day of

The Said Lessee, for   and   legal representatives, do covenant with

the said Lessor and   legal representatives, as follows:

Rent

FIRST:—To pay the annual rent of

Dollars, in equal   payments in advance on the

day of

in each year during the continuance of the said term.

Water

SECOND:—To pay whenever called upon such proportion of all the charges of water, as the number of lofts occupied by the Lessee shall bear to the total number of tenanted lofts in the building, during the term of this lease, in accordance with the bills produced from the Department of Water Supply, Gas and Electricity, or other Municipal Authority, and if not so paid, the same shall be added to the rent due or to become due.

Alterations

THIRD:—Not to use or permit to be used the roof of said building, nor cut, drill into or otherwise disfigure, nor permit the disfigurement of the iron, marble or stone of said building, nor obstruct, nor permit any obstruction of any lights or skylights, nor injure, nor deface the premises, nor without the written consent of the Lessor, make any alterations therein, nor use, nor suffer to be used, the whole or any part thereof for any purpose other than

Repairs

FOURTH:—To make all necessary repairs on said premises, including plumbing, window chains, radiators and locks, as well as other repairs, without expense to the Lessor, except damage by fire and damage to the roof. Such repairs shall only be made to restore and keep said premises in their ordinary good condition, and to be equal to the original in class and quality.

Damage

FIFTH:—That the Lessor is exempt from any and all liability for any damage or injury to person or property caused by or resulting from steam, electricity, gas, water, rain, ice or snow, or any leak or flow from or into any part of said building, or from any damage or injury resulting or arising from any other cause or happening whatsoever, unless said damage or injury be caused by or be due to the negligence of the Lessor.

To Let

SIXTH:—To permit the Lessor and   agents at all times to enter the premises or any part thereof for the purpose of inspection and repair; and to show them to persons wishing to hire or purchase, and during six months next preceding the expiration of term, to permit the usual notice "To Let" or "For Sale" to be and remain posted upon the premises.

Assignment

SEVENTH:—This lease shall not be assigned or encumbered, and the said premises, or any part thereof, shall not be let or underlet, nor used or permitted to be used, for any purpose other than above mentioned, nor by any other person without the written consent of the said Lessor.

Determination

EIGHTH:—Upon the determination of this demise to peaceably surrender the premises in as good order and condition as at the beginning of the term, reasonable wear and damage by fire only excepted.

Rules Ordinances

NINTH:—To promptly execute and comply with all rules, orders, ordinances and regulations of the City and State Governments, and all other authorities, and of any and all their Departments and Bureaus, applicable to said premises, for the correction, prevention and abatement of nuisances or other grievances, in, upon or connected with premises during said term, and shall also promptly comply with and execute all rules, orders and regulations of the New York Board of Fire Underwriters for the prevention of Fires, at their own cost and expense; also all rules and regulations, as well as suggestions of the New York Fire Insurance Exchange and also to comply with the rules and regulations hereinafter set forth and made part hereof.

Courtesy Julius Blumberg, Inc.

Figure 105. First Page of Commercial Lease Form.

Electric Current

TWENTY-FIFTH:—The Lessee hereby agrees, that at the option of the Lessor, the Lessee will purchase from the Lessor, or from any person or corporation designated by Lessor such electric current as may be required by the Lessee at the terms, classification and rates charged to such consumers by the public utility corporation serving the part of the city where the building is located. That the current consumed by the Lessee be measured in the same manner as is current furnished direct by the public utility, and that the service, in general, shall be at least equal to that furnished direct by the public utility. Such electric current shall be paid for monthly and the amount thereof shall be added to the rent for the month next following, and the Lessor shall have the same rights and remedies upon non-payment of any such charges as upon non-payment of rent.

Security

TWENTY-SIXTH:—The Lessee has this day deposited with the Lessor the sum of
Dollars as security for the full and faithful performance by the Lessee of all of the terms, covenants and conditions upon the Lessee's part to be performed, which said sum shall be returned to the Lessee after the time fixed as the expiration of the term herein, provided the Lessee has fully and faithfully carried out all of the terms, covenants and conditions on the Lessee's part to be performed.

War

TWENTY-SEVENTH:—This lease and the obligation of Lessee to pay rent hereunder and perform all of the other covenants and agreements hereunder on part of Lessee to be performed shall in nowise be affected, impaired or excused because Lessor is unable to supply or is delayed in supplying any service expressly or impliedly to be supplied or is unable to make, or is delayed in making any repairs, additions, alterations or decorations or is unable to supply or is delayed in supplying any equipment or fixtures if Landlord is prevented or delayed from so doing by reason of governmental preemption in connection with the National Emergency declared by the President of the United States or in connection with any rule, order or regulation of any department or subdivision thereof of any governmental agency or by reason of the condition of supply and demand which have been or are affected by the war.

In Witness Whereof, the parties have inter-changeably set their hands and seals (or caused these presents to be signed by their proper corporate officers and caused their proper corporate seal to be hereto affixed) the day and year first above written.

Signed, sealed and delivered in }
the presence of

....
As to Lessor

....

....

....

....
As to Lessee

....

....

....

Figure 106. Last Page of Commercial Lease Form.

If the lawyer's practice involves drawing commercial leases, he will probably have a work folder, or loose-leaf notebook from which he dictates the lease. This folder will consist of each of the standard lease clauses in the form that the lawyer prefers. (If the lawyer does not have a work folder of this kind, you might compile one for him.) Each clause will be pasted on a separate sheet, or half-sheet, and the lawyer will probably have written comments for his guidance beneath the form. The folder, or notebook, will also contain clauses that are not standard, or that do not appear in all leases. It occasionally happens that the lawyer overlooks one of the standard clauses, even when he is using the notebook for guidance. You should become familiar with the standard clauses in commercial leases so that you will be able to call the omission to his attention. Furthermore, in dictating he might tell you to insert the usual insurance, or liability clause, or some other standard clause, and you should be able to select the proper clause without further instruction from the lawyer.

Checklist of standard clauses in commercial leases. Here is a list of the standard clauses that appear in almost all commercial leases. Although each clause might not be in a separate paragraph, in all probability the lease will contain words covering each of these subjects.

1. Term of duration
2. Rent
3. Water, electricity
4. Alterations
5. Repairs
6. Damage or liability—that is, the provision fixing the liability for injury to persons or property
7. "To let" sign prior to expiration of lease
8. Assignment of the lease
9. Surrender of the premises upon expiration of the lease
10. Rules and ordinances
11. Fire—that is, the agreement about the respective rights of the parties if the building should be destroyed by fire or "other action of the elements"
12. Elevators and heat
13. Insurance
14. Default in payment of rent

15. Bankruptcy of lessee

16. Peaceful possession or quiet enjoyment of the premises

17. No waiver—that is, the provision that the consent of the lessor to a variation of the terms in one instance is not a waiver of terms and conditions of the lease

18. Subordination to mortgages

19. Sprinkler system

20. Condemnation or eminent domain proceedings—that is, the rights of the respective parties if the city, county, state, or Federal authority should condemn or take possession of the premises

21. Security deposited by lessee

22. War—that is, the provision that the lessee is not exempt from payment of rent if lessor, because of shortages caused by war, is unable to supply services or equipment called for by the lease

Style of typed lease. When a lawyer drafts a lease, he simplifies the location of specific provisions by the order in which he groups them. In planning the style in which to type the lease, your object should be to simplify further the location of specific provisions. You can do this by indicating the subject of each provision in the margin, as in the printed form illustrated in Figures 105 and 106. Another style of typing the lease is to make side headings of the subjects and underscore them. Still another style is to center the subjects. Usually the clauses are numbered consecutively throughout the lease. The numbering may be any style that you choose: I, II; FIRST, SECOND; ONE, TWO; 1., 2.; (1), (2).

Execution, acknowledgment, and recording of lease. A lease of land or commercial property is executed with the formalities of a deed. The state statutes vary, but generally the following apply:

1. Both the lessor and lessee sign the lease.

2. A lease is sealed unless the state statute does not require a deed to be sealed.

3. A lease is witnessed unless the state statute does not require a deed to be witnessed.

4. If the duration of the lease is more than one year (longer in some states), the lessor and lessee acknowledge it, and the lessee should have it recorded.

5. A lease may be signed by an agent with written authority.

The execution of the run-of-the-mill short-term lease, such as a lease on an apartment, is not so formal. Both the lessor and lessee sign, and usually the signatures are witnessed. Otherwise there are no formal requirements. The directions about acknowledgments and recording apply only to leases that must be recorded.

"Do's" and "dont's" in the preparation of a lease. Unless otherwise instructed, follow these directions in the preparation of a lease of realty or commercial property. Obviously some of them apply to typed leases, some to printed forms, and some to both.

1. Make 4 copies—an original for the lessee, a duplicate original for the lessor, a triplicate original for the broker, and a copy for your files.

2. Use legal cap.

3. Follow carefully the directions for filling in a printed form. (See Chapter 8.)

4. Don't forget the responsibility and distribution line at the top of the first page. (This goes on the office copy only of a printed form.) (See Chapter 8.)

5. Double space.

6. Number all pages.

7. Type the land description in accordance with directions on page 454.

8. If you are using a printed form, be sure and make the "Z" after the land description. (See Chapter 8.)

9. Don't forget to have at least two lines of typing on the signature page. (See Chapter 9.)

10. Prepare signature lines for the lessor and lessee. (See Chapter 9.)

11. If the state statute requires that a deed be sealed, affix seals to the lease in accordance with directions in Chapter 9.

12. Type witness lines and attestation clause if the statute requires that a deed be witnessed. (See Chapter 9.)

13. Prepare certificate of acknowledgment for lessor and lessee. (See Chapter 9.)

14. Collate.

15. Get someone to compare the land description with you. See page 456.

16. Check and double check spelling of names.

17. Endorse legal backs (Chapter 8). (If printed forms are used, no legal back is necessary.)

18. Staple in backs.

19. Arrange for lessor and lessee to come in and sign.

20. *Get lawyer's approval of the lease before it is signed.*

21. Have lessor and lessee sign three copies, including broker's copy.

22. Do the signatures agree with the names typed in the lease?

23. Have the lease notarized if it is to be recorded. If you are a notary take the acknowledgments, following instructions in Chapter 9.

24. After signature and acknowledgment conform your office copy to original. (See Chapter 8.)

25. *Get the lawyer's approval of the executed lease,* and then have the lease recorded. (See Chapter 9.) Don't forget to put a notation on the back of the lease asking that it be returned to you. (The secretary to the lawyer for the lessee attends to the recording.)

26. Make an entry in your diary to follow the recorder within ten days or two weeks.

27. When the lease is returned, send it to the lessee. (See Chapter 9.)

21

Real Estate Practice (Cont'd): Contracts of Sale and Closings

IN REAL estate sales there is almost always an agreement to buy and sell before the actual conveyance is made. This agreement is frequently an informal memorandum, or merely a receipt for a deposit on the purchase price, which is not prepared in the lawyer's office. It is usually prepared by the real estate broker and signed by the buyer and seller. The seller's lawyer enters the picture when he is asked to draw the deed and purchase money mortgage, if any; the buyer's lawyer, when he is asked to pass upon the seller's title to the property and his right to convey it. But many times the lawyer is asked to draw a formal agreement, or contract, of sale. He usually draws the contract when the property is very valuable, if the property is income producing, or if it is to be sold on the installment plan. An agreement to enter into an important lease is also necessary, before the lease itself is entered into. Under the statute of frauds these agreements, whether formal or informal, must be in writing or they are not enforceable.

Contracts of sale fix a date—called the *closing date*—at which time title to the property is actually conveyed. You, as the lawyer's secretary, will have many preparations to make for the closing. These preparations are described in detail in this chapter. Since your preparations depend to a large extent upon the contents of the contract of sale, you should first become familiar with a contract of sale. Read carefully the form of contract used in your locality.

Contract of Sale

Necessity for a contract of sale. When an owner decides to sell and a buyer decides to purchase real estate, they agree upon the terms of sale—the purchase price, the amount of cash to be paid, how the balance shall be paid, what shall be done about mortgages on the property—and upon numerous other details. The transfer of the property cannot be effected immediately because the seller must produce evidence of his right to sell, and the buyer wants his attorney to examine this evidence; the buyer needs time in which to arrange the necessary financing; the seller must collect various data regarding insurance, taxes, rents, and the like; instruments of conveyance must be prepared. Neither party wants the other to back out of the deal in the interim. Therefore, a contract of sale, which sets forth in detail the terms under which the property will be conveyed, is prepared. Great care is exercised in the drafting and preparation of a contract of sale, because the conveyance will be made upon the terms set forth in the contract.

Types of contracts of sale of land. There are two principal types of contracts of sale of land. One type contemplates the immediate transfer of title to the buyer, the buyer to pay the entire purchase price in cash, or part in cash and part by a purchase money mortgage. The contract binds the parties while the buyer is having the title examined.

The other type of contract of sale is an installment contract. The purchase price is paid in installments, and the title remains in the seller until the entire purchase price has been paid, or until the unpaid purchase price has been reduced to an amount agreed upon in the contract of sale.

Parties to a contract. The necessary parties to a contract for the sale of land are the seller or vendor, and the buyer or purchaser or vendee. Both seller and purchaser sign the contract, because each has certain obligations to perform. Since the seller agrees to convey title, the seller must be a natural person or corporation with the power and ability to make a deed of conveyance (page 456). When a married person enters into a contract of sale, it is necessary for the spouse o sign the contract in those states where the spouse must sign the deed of conveyance.

The buyer must be an adult of sound mind, or a corporation

with power to purchase real estate. Although an infant or an incompetent may be the grantee of real property, he cannot enter into a contract of sale because he does not possess contractual powers. Trustees and executors rarely have power to buy land.

The broker who brings about the agreement of sale is naturally interested in its consummation. Although he is not a party to the contract, provision is usually made in the contract for payment of his commission.

How to prepare a contract of sale. Each locality has a contract of sale form approved by the local real estate board. Printed forms of the contracts are available from stationery stores and, also, from abstract and title companies. The forms are easy to complete and require little explanation. The lawyer will give you a memorandum of the information necessary to complete the form.

Make four copies—original and duplicate original for the seller and buyer, a copy for the broker, and a copy for your file. Both the seller and the buyer sign the contract and, usually, the seller's wife. Generally an acknowledgment is not necessary, because ordinarily the contract is not recorded. Unless you receive specific instructions from the lawyer, be guided by the form. If the form adopted in your locality has an acknowledgment printed on it, fill in the acknowledgment. The form will also indicate whether it should be witnessed.

When the lawyer dictates the contract, follow the instructions for typing deeds (page 464).

Checklist of information necessary to fill in form. 1. Date of contract

2. Name and residence of seller

3. Name of seller's spouse if spouse must join in deed that is to be delivered

4. Name and residence of the buyer

5. Description of property to be conveyed

6. Purchase price, the exact amount being named

7. Amount to be paid when contract is signed (earnest money)

8. Amount to be paid at closing, when deed is delivered

9. Whether existing mortgage, if any, is to be assumed or property purchased subject to it

10. How balance is to be paid, and when

11. Name of trustee in those states where a deed of trust is the security instrument

12. Unpaid taxes and assessments

13. Fire insurance data

14. Name of broker

15. Closing date

Earnest money. An element of all contracts of sale is a cash deposit by the buyer as an indication that he intends to go through with the purchase if the seller furnishes good title to the property. The deposit is designated *earnest money*. It is also referred to as a *binder,* although this term is more frequently applied to a deposit made under informal agreements than to deposits made in connection with formal contracts of sale drawn up by the lawyer. If the buyer fails to consummate the deal, the earnest money is retained by the seller; if he does perform his part of the contract, the earnest money is applied as part payment of the purchase price. If the seller cannot convey good title to the property, the deposit is returned to the buyer. The amount of earnest money depends upon the agreement between the parties. It is ordinarily sufficient to cover the broker's commission, expenses of the title search, and compensation to the seller for the loss he might sustain should the buyer fail to go through with the deal.

Escrow for the sale of real property. One of the most common uses of escrow (see Chapter 27 for definition) is in connection with real estate transactions. Frequently the buyer's deposit is placed in escrow so that there will be no difficulty about a refund should it prove impossible for the seller to deliver a clear title to the property. Sometimes the contract of sale is put in escrow so that it cannot be recorded until the deal is consummated, because the recorded contract might be a cloud on the title. Sometimes, especially in transactions involving very valuable property, both the seller and the buyer deposit bonds in escrow to prevent either party from being damaged by the failure of the other party to consummate the sale. The ramifications of escrows for the sale of real property are manifold, but necessary components are:

1. A valid and enforceable contract for the sale of land.

2. An escrow agreement.

3. A disinterested third party, usually a bank, to act as escrow

holder, *escrowee*. Neither buyer or seller, nor their agent or attorney can act as escrowee.

When the lawyer in your office acts as escrow holder, you should deposit funds placed with him in escrow in the trust account, not in the firm's regular account. See Chapter 7, Item 8, for the method of entering the item in the books.

Title Closings and Evidence of Title

What is a title closing? The contract of sale designates a certain day, and sometimes hour, when the deed shall be delivered, the balance of the purchase price paid, and the mortgages, if any, delivered. This transaction between the seller and purchaser, and their representatives, is known as the *title closing* or *closing of title*. All of the formalities necessary to the conveyance of property are attended to at the closing. It usually takes place at the office of the lawyer for the seller. Papers that are to be signed must be ready for signature; other papers, such as receipts and insurance policies, must be produced; and a closing statement must be prepared. The date on which the title closing takes place is known as the *closing date*. Prior to the closing, the purchaser must have proof that the seller has a good title to the land.

Evidence of title. Every purchaser insists upon satisfactory evidence that the seller has good title to the land that he is selling. Proof of good title is also just as important to a mortgagee. There are four kinds of evidence of title—*abstract and opinion, certificate of title, title insurance,* and *Torrens certificate.* To a great extent, the acceptability of a particular kind of evidence of title depends upon the local custom.

Abstract of title. The evidence of title most commonly used in the United States is the abstract of title. An abstract is a history of the title to a particular tract of land. It consists of a summary of the material parts of every recorded instrument affecting the title. It begins with a description of the land covered by the abstract, and then shows the original governmental grant and all subsequent deeds, mortgages, releases, wills, judgments, mechanics' liens, foreclosure proceedings, tax sales, and other matters affecting title.

Of course, only a summary of these items is shown. For example, a deed is summarized as shown on the following page.

WILLIAM BROWN AND MARY   WARRANTY DEED
        BROWN, HIS WIFE   Dated Sept. 15, 1860
                to   Ack. Sept. 18, 1860
        JOHN ADAMS   Rec. Sept. 20, 1860
                                         Bk. 21, page 23

Conveys a large plot of land including the premises under examination.

The abstract concludes with the abstracter's certificate. This discloses what records the abstracter has examined, and what records he has not examined. For example, if the abstracter certifies that he has made no search of Federal court proceedings affecting the property, it will be necessary to write to the Clerk of the District Court, who will supply the search for a small charge.

Abstract companies, lawyers, and public officials prepare abstracts. Abstract companies do by far the greatest portion of the abstracting, except in a few states where there are no abstract companies.

What the secretary does. Always keep the name, address, and telephone number of the abstract company, or other abstracter, used by your firm in your desk directory. As secretary to the lawyer for the purchaser or the mortgagee in communities where abstracts are acceptable evidence of title, you will frequently have to order abstracts. When you order the abstract, make a follow-up entry in your diary or an extra copy of the letter for your follow-up file. It is important to get the abstract as soon as possible because the deal cannot be closed until the purchaser's attorney has examined the abstract of title. When the abstract is received, charge the cost to the client; the lawyer will pay the abstracter. (See Entry 7, Chapter 7, for bookkeeping entry.)

You will find that contracts of sale frequently provide that the seller shall furnish an abstract of title. This usually means that he will give the purchaser an abstract of title to the date that the seller obtained the property. The purchaser will have it brought down to date. You will then be asked to order a *continuation* or an *extension*. The original abstract is sent to the abstract company and the company *recertifies* its accuracy and brings it down to date.

Your letter ordering an abstract of title, or a continuation, might read as follows:

We are enclosing an abstract of title for the west three rods of Lots 30 and 31, Jacob Beeson's Addition to Niles, Berrien County, Michigan, according to the recorded plat thereof.

Please continue this to date for the land owned by Phyllis Franz and return it to us as soon as possible.

Opinion of title. When the attorney receives the abstract, he examines it and prepares his *opinion* as to the validity of the title. If he finds any difficulty, such as a deed that was improperly acknowledged, or a discrepancy in the description of the property, he states the defects in his opinion. They constitute *clouds* upon the seller's title and must be removed by affidavits, quit-claim deeds, or court procedure to quiet title. The attorney also sets forth in his opinion any liens and mortgages on the property, because the title is subject to them. Usually the contract of sale mentions the liens and mortgages and provides for their disposition.

The lawyer dictates the opinion of title, which is usually in the form of a letter. If there are no defects in the title, you might be asked to draft a routine opinion of title letter. A sample letter follows.

June 21, 19. .

Mr. and Mrs. James Jones
R. R. #1
Niles, Michigan

Dear Mr. and Mrs. Jones:
We have examined the abstract of title continued by the Benton Harbor Abstract and Title Company of Benton Harbor, Michigan to date of June 15, 19. . at 8:00 A.M., for the following described premises:

The west three (3) rods of Lots Thirty (30) and Thirty-one (31), Jacob Beeson's Addition to Niles, Berrien County, Michigan, according to the recorded plat thereof.

From such examination, we find the title thereto to be in Phyllis Franz, subject to the following:

1. There are ancient and minor errors in this title, but we do not consider any of them sufficiently important to affect the merchantability of the title.

2. There are no liens or encumbrances against said premises.

3. The abstract shows no unpaid taxes for 19. . and prior years. The summer taxes for 19. . will be due July 1, 19. . and may be checked with the City Treasurer, as may also special assessments.

It is therefore our opinion that a merchantable title exists in said above named title holder, subject to the exceptions above noted. This opinion is based upon the abstract continued as aforesaid, and does not cover rights of persons in possession, line fences, location of buildings, or any other matter or thing not contained in said abstract.

Respectfully submitted,

JC:F

Certificate of title. In some localities, an abstract is dispensed with. The attorney examines the public records and issues his *certificate,* which is merely his opinion of title based on the public records he has examined. He does not guarantee the title, but is liable for damages caused by his negligence. For example, if his certificate failed to show a mortgage that was recorded, he would be liable to a purchaser who relied upon his certificate and purchased the property without knowledge of the mortgage. Abstract companies also issue certificates of title. A certificate of title is not to be confused with title insurance policies issued by title companies.

Title insurance policies. Title guarantee companies issue title insurance policies, which guarantee against defects in title. They are called *title guarantee policies,* or *guaranty title policies.* They are issued to owners and to mortgagees. A title policy not only guarantees against defects in the title, but the company issuing it usually undertakes to defend at its own expense any lawsuit attacking the title. Of course, a title company will not insure a defective title.

The attorney for the buyer, or the mortgagee, orders the policy of insurance from the title company, and the title company then searches their records and makes any surveys necessary to the issuance of the title insurance.

Torrens certificate. In addition to the system of transferring title under the recording acts, there is a system known as the *Torrens system,* originated by Sir Robert Torrens. A landowner who wishes to register under the Torrens system first obtains a complete abstract of title to the land. He then files in the proper public office an application for the registration of title. After certain legal procedure, the court orders the registrar of titles to register the title. The registrar makes out a certificate showing the title as found by the court. These certificates are bound in books and are public records. The registrar delivers a duplicate certificate to the owner. When land that has been registered under the Torrens system is sold, the deed itself does not pass title to the land. The deed must be taken to the registrar's office, and he issues a new certificate to the grantee. The deed is not returned to the grantee but remains in the registrar's office. Likewise, a mortgage or judgment lien is not effective until a notation has been entered on the certificate of title in the registrar's office. The Torrens system is largely confined to a few metropolitan areas.

Preparations for closing. As soon as you prepare or receive a contract of sale, the closing of which is of interest to a lawyer in your office, *enter the date of the closing in your diary.* The following checklists show some of the preparations you will have to make prior to the closing:

Checklist of preparation by secretary to seller's attorney. (The asterisks indicate items that are to be delivered to the buyer at the closing.) *1. Prepare the deed (Chapter 20).

2. Prepare the purchase money mortgage and bond or note, if any (Chapter 20).

*3. Prepare, or obtain from the seller, a list of the tenants, rents paid and unpaid, and due dates.

*4. Obtain from the mortgagee holding any mortgage that the purchaser assumes a certificate, properly acknowledged, showing payment on account or the amount actually due at the closing date.

5. Prepare memorandum of closing figures (see page 493, *et seq.*) (A copy of the memorandum might be mailed to the attorney for the purchaser, thus saving time in adjusting figures at the closing.)

*6. Prepare letter to tenants advising them to pay future rent to the purchaser.

*7. Prepare assignment of any service contracts, such as exterminator's contracts, that are to be assigned to the purchaser.

8. Notify seller of the exact time, date, and place of the closing. Tell him to bring to the closing the following papers:

    a. Receipts for last interest payment on mortgages

   *b. Insurance policies and assignments of them

   *c. Last receipts for taxes, special assessments, gas, electricity, and water *d. Leases and assignments

*e. Securities deposited by tenants as security for rent, which might be in the form of cash

9. If seller is an individual, tell him that his wife must also be present at the closing to sign the deed.

10. If seller is a corporation, indicate the two officers who are to sign the deed and who, therefore, should be present at the closing. Also, advise the officers to bring the corporation's seal.

11. Notify others who might be present in behalf of seller of closing date—broker, accountant, title closer (see item 5, on page 498).

Checklist of preparations by secretary to purchaser's attorney.

1. Order abstract of title (see page 488).

2. Type opinion of title after lawyer dictates it (page 489).

3. Prepare a memorandum of closing figures (pages 493, *et seq.*) (This might be mailed to the seller's attorney, thus saving time in adjusting figures at the closing.)

4. Notify purchaser of the exact time, date, and place of the closing. Tell him to bring to the closing the following:

   a. Certified check for approximate amount that will be due to the seller. (You can get the figure from the memorandum of closing figures.)

   b. Blank check (to be filled in at the closing for any additional amount owed the seller).

5. If purchaser is a corporation indicate the two officers who are to sign the purchase money mortgage and who, therefore, should be present at the closing. Also advise the officers to bring the corporate seal with them.

6. Notify others who might be interested in behalf of the buyer of the closing date—accountant, insurance broker, title closer (see item 5, page 498).

7. Prepare for the attorney a checklist of papers that are to be delivered to the buyer at the closing. This list will include the items marked with an asterisk in the foregoing checklist of preparations by the seller's secretary.

Preparation of Closing Statement

What is a closing statement? A contract of sale, or a contract for lease, provides that certain charges against the property and the income from it should be adjusted or prorated. For example, if the seller has paid the insurance for a year in advance, he is entitled to receive an adjustment from the buyer. If the seller has collected the rents for a month in advance, the buyer is entitled to an adjustment. This prorating or adjustment results in credits in favor of each party and charges against each party. A statement of the charges and credits is known as a *closing statement,* sometimes called a *settlement sheet.*

Forms of closing statements vary. Printed forms are available and are widely used. When the printed forms do not provide for all the items that must be entered on the closing statement, the statement is typed. This situation frequently arises in large, complicated deals. The statement cannot be prepared in final form until the closing is held, because all of the necessary information is not available. It is prepared on the basis of the figures agreed upon by all parties at the closing. However, the lawyer for each party usually calculates the adjustments and prepares a memorandum of them before the closing. You will probably have the

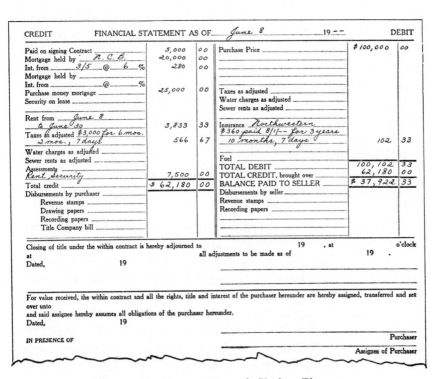

Figure 107. Memorandum of Closing Figures.

responsibility of calculating the adjustments. The lawyer will tell you what items are to be adjusted and he will check your figures. Figure 107 illustrates a printed form on the back of a contract of sale that may be used for a memorandum of the closing figures. A form of this kind is frequently used as a closing statement. (See also the closing statement illustrated in Figure 108.)

How to calculate adjustments. The practice of computing adjustments and the date of adjustment varies with the locality. In many localities, adjustments are made as of the day immediately preceding the day on which title is closed. In other words, the buyer receives the income and is charged with the expenses incurred beginning with and including the day on which title passes to him.

It is much easier to compute interest, taxes, water rates, and insurance by the 360-day method, each month representing 1/12 of the annual charge, and each day 1/30 of the monthly charge, than by the 365-day method. This is the practice adopted by many local real estate boards. Rent is usually computed on the basis of the days in the particular month in which title is closed. Although the 360-day method of computing interest, taxes, water rates, and insurance is used, where the period for which computation is made is more than one month the time is computed by full months and by the actual number of days in each partial month. For example, the period between March 15 and June 3 is 2 months (April and May) and 20 days (17 days in March, and 3 days in June).

Calculations of taxes, interest, insurance, and rents follow. Other adjustments are calculated in the same manner. For the purpose of the examples, we shall assume that title closes June 8, 1953.

Example of calculation of tax adjustment. Taxes in the locality are payable semi-annually, April 1 and October 1. The seller paid taxes on April 1 for the preceding 6-month period. During the current 6-month period, the seller is responsible for taxes from April 1 to, but not including, June 8, the closing date. He will have to allow the buyer the amount of the taxes for that period— 2 months (April and May) and 7 days. Assuming that the taxes for the 6-month period amount to $1,500, the taxes for one month are $250 ($1,500 ÷ 6); for one day, $8.33 1/3 ($250 ÷ 30). An

adjustment of $558.34 is made in favor of the purchasers [(2 ×
$250) + (7 × $8.33 1/3)].

But suppose the seller had paid taxes 6 months in advance. He
would be entitled to recover taxes from and including June 8
through September 30, or for a period of 3 months (July, August,
and September) and 23 days (June 8 through June 30). Allowance of $941.67 would be made in favor of the seller [(3 × $250)
+ (23 × $8.33 1/3)].

Example of calculation of interest adjustment. Suppose there
is a mortgage of $20,000 on the property, with interest at 6 per
cent payable quarterly on 15th of December, March, June, and
September. When title closed on June 8, interest had been paid
to but not including March 15. The purchaser is entitled to an
allowance for interest from and including March 15 through June
7, or for a period of 2 months (April and May) and 24 days (17
days in March, 7 days in June). The interest on $20,000 at 6
per cent per annum is $100 per month, $3.33 1/3 per day ($100 ÷
30). The interest for 2 months, 24 days is $280 [(2 × $100) +
(24 × $3.33 1/3)]. An adjustment of $280.00 is made in favor of
the purchaser.

Example of calculation of insurance adjustment. Suppose
there is a fire policy on the property which had been paid up for
three years. The expiration date of the policy is August 1, 1954.
The seller is therefore entitled to an adjustment of insurance for
13 months and 23 days (June 8, 1953, the date of the closing, to
August 1, 1954). The premium is $10 per month [$360 ÷ (12 ×
3)], or 33 1/3¢ per day ($10 ÷ 30). An adjustment of $137.67
[(13 × $10) + (23 × 33 1/3¢)] is made in favor of the seller.

Example of calculation of rent adjustment. The seller had
collected the rents in advance for the month of June. They
amounted to $5,000. The purchaser is entitled to an adjustment
for the period from and including June 8 through June 30, or 23
days. Since June has only 30 days, the rent per day is $5,000 ÷
30, or $166.66 2/3 per day. The purchaser is entitled to an adjust-
ment of $3,833.33 (23 × $166.66 2/3). If there is more than one
tenant, you will have to prorate the rent for each separately, unless the rents had all been collected for the same period.

Miscellaneous payments. Certain miscellaneous items are paid
by the seller and others by the purchaser. These items do not con-

stitute part of the actual closing figures because they are not charges or credits to the property itself, and they are not included in the calculation of the amount due by the buyer to the seller. However, each party must be given a memorandum of the payments for which he is responsible.

Checklist for miscellaneous payments by seller. The seller is usually responsible for the following items:

1. Broker's commission
2. Attorney's fees (attending closing, etc.)
3. Fee for drawing deed
4. Documentary stamps on deed (payable to purchaser's attorney)

Checklist of miscellaneous payments by purchaser. The purchaser is usually responsible for the following items:

1. Abstract
2. Fee for drawing purchase money mortgage (payable to seller's attorney)
3. Attorney's fees (examination of abstract, attending closing, etc.)
4. Recording tax on purchase money mortgage (payable to seller's attorney)
5. Revenue stamps on purchase money mortgage (payable to seller's attorney)

Suggested form of closing statement. Figures 108a and b illustrate the preliminary information and Part I of a closing statement, based on a form suggested by Mr. Samuel Kaplan, C. P. A., in his article "Standardization of Closing Statements for Real Estate Transactions," published in *The New York Certified Public Accountant,* Volume XVIII, No. 10. An explanation of the items will enable you to prepare a statement in any form. (The numbers appearing in the margins of the illustration do not appear on the statement but are for the purpose of this explanation.) Parts II A and II B and III of the closing statement are not illustrated here. Part II A is a list of "Adjustments in Favor of Seller"; Part II B is a list of "Adjustments in Favor of Purchaser." Part III is entitled "Supplementary Schedules and Information." It lists (1) miscellaneous payments by the seller; (2) miscellaneous payments by the purchaser (see above); (3) instruments delivered at closing, and other matters pertinent to the particular closing.

1. The description need not be the complete description given in the contract of sale and the deed. A street address is usually sufficient. A farm property might be described as "............ acres in the County of ...., State of ...., known as .... Farm."

2. Get the seller's name from the contract. If the seller is an individual and the spouse also signed the contract, both names should appear on the closing statement.

3. Sometimes the person who signs a contract of sale assigns the contract before the sale is consummated. The assignee then becomes the purchaser. This item shows the name of the purchaser signed to the contract. If he assigned it, the item shows, ".......... who conveys to ...." Printed forms of contracts frequently provide for an assignment.

4. This is the name of the party who takes title at the closing.

5. Those present at the closing vary with the size and complexity of the deal. The seller and buyer (or their representatives) and their lawyers are always present. Usually the broker attends the closing. If a mortgage loan is involved, the lender's representative usually attends. In localities where title insurance is customary, the title company's closer is present.

6. This is the purchase price indicated in the contract of sale.

7. The purchaser may purchase the property *subject* to an existing mortgage, which constitutes a lien on the property, without personal liability on the part of the purchaser, or he may *assume* the mortgage, thereby becoming personally liable for the debt.

8. This is the deposit, or earnest money, mentioned in the contract. If the contract called for additional payments between the signing of the contract and the closing, they should be listed here.

9. The contract recites the amount of the purchase money mortgage, if any.

10. Calculation of adjustments was explained on page 494, *et seq.* You can get these figures from the memorandum of closing figures (Figure 107) that you prepared, unless they were adjusted at the closing. List the adjustments in favor of the seller in one schedule; those in favor of the buyer in another.

The purchaser brings to the closing a certified check for the approximate amount and draws a check for the balance after the calculation of adjustments has been agreed upon by all parties.

CLOSING STATEMENT

1   Re: Sale of Premises located at 345 Fifth
              Avenue, New York, New York, known as
                     The Graham Building
         _____

2   Seller: Prentiss—Haley, Inc.

3   Purchaser: Lem Stewart who conveys to Lem Stewart, Inc.

4   Purchaser: Lem Stewart, Inc.

    Adjustments computed as of June 9, 19—.

    Closing held at the office of Elwood & Adams, 70 Fifth

    Avenue, New York, N.Y., at 3:00 p.m., Tuesday, June 10,

    19—.

5   PRESENT AT CLOSING

For the Seller
_____

        John J. Prentiss and Edward E. Haley, President
            and Secretary, respectively, of Prentiss—
            Haley, Inc.

        Lucius E. Elwood, Attorney.

        Robert R. Jones, C. P. A.

For the Buyer
_____

        Lem Stewart and John Jones, President and Secre-
            tary, respectively, of Lem Stuart, Inc.

        William Law, Attorney.

        Edgar Nelson, C. P. A.

        Leslie Smith, Insurance Broker.

Others Present
_____

        John E. Gibbs, the only broker on the sale.

        Alvin R. Rogers, Closer for the Title Guarantee
            Co., under their title number 14587.

        Roscoe S. Lawrence, Attorney for John Jones,
            holder of mortgage.

Figure 108. Closing Statement—Preliminary Information.

*(The numbers in the margin do not appear on the statement. See text, pages 496
and 497.)*

I REAL ESTATE AND SUMMARY

6 SALES PRICE.................................$100,000.00

7   Subject to the following mortgage:
           First mortgage, held by
           John Jones...............$20,000.00

       Mortgages assumed:
           None
                                    _____

           Total Mortgages....................$ 20,000.00

       BALANCE OF...........................$ 80,000.00

       Payable as follows:
8   Paid on contract May
               9, 19—............$10,000.00
9   Purchase Money Mort-
               gage and Notes...... 20,000.00
                                    _____
                   Total................... $30,000.00

           Balance paid at closing*..........$50,000.00

SUMMARY:

       *Payable on Real Estate at
           Closing.................$50,000.00
10   Adjustments in favor of
           Seller, per Schedule
           II A....................   102.33
                                    _____
                   Total...........$50,102.33
           Less: Adjustments in Favor
           of Purchaser, per Sched-
           ule II B................$12,180.00

BALANCE DUE SELLER...........................$37,922.33

Paid as follows:

       By certified check dated June 8, 19—,
           drawn by Lem Stewart, Inc. to the
           order of Prentiss-Haley, Inc., on
           the City Bank in the amount of........$35,000.00
       Check dated June 8, 19—, drawn by
           Lem Stewart, Inc. to the order of
           Prentiss-Haley, Inc. on the City
           Bank in the amount of.................$ 2,922.33
                                                 _____
                   Total.....................$37,922.33

SEF:r 1-2-1 5/7/—

Figure 108 (Cont.). Closing Statement—Part I.

(*The numbers in the margin do not appear on the statement. See text, pages 496
and 497.*)

22

Foreclosure Actions

T HE FORCED sale of property to satisfy the payment of a mortgage (or deed of trust) or other default under the terms of the mortgage (or deed of trust) is a *foreclosure*. In some states the foreclosure is by advertisement and sale, held in accordance with the legal technicalities prescribed by the state statutes. In the majority of states, foreclosure is by litigation. The preliminary steps in foreclosure litigation are fairly similar in all jurisdictions, but the procedure between the commencement of the action and the sale vary considerably not only with the jurisdiction but with the circumstances of the case. For that reason, emphasis here is on the preliminary procedure.

Papers necessary for institution of foreclosure action. The lawyer will need the following papers and documents before commencing a foreclosure action:

1. Bond or note
2. Mortgage or deed of trust
3. Assignment, if any
4. Abstract of title
5. Receipted bills for taxes, assessments, water rates, interest, insurance, and the like paid by the mortgagee or his assignee

These papers constitute the nucleus of your file in the case. As soon as you receive a new matter slip (Chapter 1) about the case, ask the lawyer if you should get them from the client, so that they will be on hand when he is ready to commence the action.

Information needed to prepare papers in foreclosure action. You will need the following information to prepare the preliminary papers in a foreclosure action:

1. Venue
2. Parties plaintiff
3. Parties defendant
4. Description of property
5. Description of note or bond
6. Description of mortgage
7. How the mortgage is in default

Venue. You can get the venue from the description of the property in the mortgage. An action to foreclose a mortgage is always brought in the state and county in which the property is located. A foreclosure is an equity action and in those states that have separate courts for law and equity, the action is brought in the Chancery Court.

Parties to a foreclosure action. *Parties plaintiff.* The owner of the mortgage—the mortgagee, or his beneficiary or assignee—is the plaintiff in a foreclosure action. The suit must be brought in the name of the actual owner of the mortgage. For example, if the mortgage is held by Richard Marsh as Trustee for Thomas Brown, the action is brought by Richard Marsh, Trustee for Thomas Brown, not by Richard Marsh. If the mortgage is owned jointly, say by husband and wife, the action is brought in the name of both owners.

Parties defendant. Every person who has any interest in the property covered by a mortgage is made a party defendant to the foreclosure action. These might include the mortgagor; the mortgagor's heirs, devisees, or legatees; wife of the mortgagor; *cestui que trustent;* persons in possession as tenants or occupants; the People of the State; and others. You can get the names of known defendants from the Certification of Defendants (page 503); the lawyer will give them to you if there is no certification.

Fictitious names. Since someone frequently has an interest that the plaintiff does not know about, or someone whose name is unknown has an interest in the property, several fictitious names are added as defendants. The reason for adding the fictitious names is that additional defendants can be brought into the action without the necessity of serving an amended complaint on all defendants. Perhaps an interested party's last name is known but not his first; a fictitious first name is given to that defendant, thus:

"Richard" Nelson, first name "Richard" being fictitious, defendant's real first name being unknown to the plaintiff.

Sometimes an unknown person is identified by a description, thus:

"Richard Roe," name fictitious, defendant's real name being unknown to the plaintiff, person intended conducting a stationery store at No. 35 East 18 Street.

The complaint usually alleges that the names are fictitious. The true name is substituted for the fictitious name as soon as it is learned. *In all subsequent papers filed in the case, the caption reflects the substitution.*

Description of note or bond. The foreclosure complaint contains a complete description of the note or bond secured by the mortgage. A note is usually copied verbatim. Only the gist of the bond is set forth, including the name of the person signing it, the amount, the date, rate of interest and when payable, date of maturity. You can get the wording from a good form book, but unless your office does considerable foreclosure work, the lawyer will dictate the terms of the bond. Check the names, dates, and amounts against the original bond.

Description of mortgage. A description of the mortgage sufficient to identify it is set forth in the complaint, *lis pendens,* and other papers. The description includes the name of the mortgagor, name of mortgagee, date of execution, maturity date. The description also shows when and where the mortgage was recorded—the date, the clerk's office, book (*Liber*) and page number. This information is stamped on the front of the original mortgage. In some jurisdictions a copy of the mortgage is attached to the complaint as an exhibit.

If the plaintiff is the assignee of the original mortgage, the foreclosure complaint alleges the fact of the assignment, thus showing plaintiff's right to sue.

Description of property. Get the description of the property from the mortgage. It is advisable to type it, double-spaced, on durable paper and keep the copy in your file so that you will have it handy whenever you prepare a paper in the case. Follow the directions given at page 454 for copying land descriptions. Remember, whenever you copy the description, have someone read it back to you while you follow the description in the original mortgage. This is particularly important in a foreclosure action because the action is defective if the description has an error in it.

When is a mortgage considered in default. Failure of the mortgagor to meet any obligation under a mortgage is a *default*. The default may be in payment of principal, interest, taxes, insurance, or in the observance or performance of any of the conditions of the mortgage. For example, if the mortgagor fails to pay the taxes when due, he is in default. Under the acceleration clause (page 470), the entire amount of the mortgage then becomes due, and the owner may foreclose for the entire amount, not merely for the amount that is in default.

Procedure in Foreclosure Action

Title search for foreclosures. When the mortgagor delivered the mortgage to the mortgagee, he undoubtedly turned over to the mortgagee an abstract of title to the premises. Before the lawyer commences foreclosure proceedings he will want that abstract brought down to date. Write a letter to the abstract company similar to the letter ordering a continuation of abstract when a contract of sale is entered into (page 489). In those few states where there are no abstract companies, other arrangements will have to be made for the title search.

Upon request, title companies will also furnish a *certification of defendants,* or a *foreclosure report,* as it is called in some localities. The certification lists the necessary and proper parties defendant to the foreclosure action and the interest of each in the premises. It also discloses the legal capacity of each defendant. (See "Who may be parties to a law suit" on page 241, *et seq.*) When you order the continuation of abstract, ask the lawyer if he wants a certification of defendants. The lawyer might prefer to prepare the list of parties defendant from the abstract, rather than have the title company make the certification.

Preparation of complaint. The complaint in a foreclosure action is largely standardized. The lawyer will give you a form to follow, or refer you to one in a form book, for the standard parts and will dictate any unusual parts. The complaint is typed in the same style and on the same kind of paper as a complaint in any civil action (Chapter 13).

Caption. The caption of the complaint includes the fictitious names as well as the names of the known defendants. The exact wording varies, but the following styles are typical.

ROBERT NELSON,

Plaintiff,

vs

PAUL NELSON, doing business under the trade name or style of Paul's Stores, "JOHN DOE," "RICHARD DOE," and "EARL DOE," said three last named defendants being fictitious, said defendants' true names being unknown to plaintiff, they being intended to designate tenants of portions of the premises described in the complaint,

Defendants.

ROBERT NELSON,

Plaintiff,

against

PAUL NELSON and ELSIE NELSON, husband and wife, DOE ONE, DOE TWO, DOE THREE, and DOE FOUR,

Defendants.

Number of copies. In order to know how many copies of the complaint to prepare, besides your office copy, you will have to know the answer to these practice questions:

1. How many copies are filed in court? (Table VII, page 265).

2. May we dispense with service against any group of defendants?

Table VII shows how many copies of a pleading should be filed in court and whether or not a copy is served on the adverse parties. Foreclosure actions frequently have numerous defendants, and the preparation of a copy of a long complaint for each of them works a hardship on the plaintiff. To relieve the plaintiff, some jurisdictions have adopted practice rules that make it unnecessary to serve the complaint on every defendant. For example, in Texas if there are more than four adverse parties in any action, four copies, in addition to the original, are filed in court and the adverse parties are notified of the filing. This procedure dispenses with service on each adverse party, which is required if there are less than four adverse parties. In New York, "Notice of Object of Action," which is a much shorter document than the complaint, is served on defendants against whom no personal claim is made, but who, nevertheless, are proper parties defendant. For example, in foreclosing a mortgage on an apartment house, all of the tenants are proper parties defendant, but their only interest is subordinate to the mortgage and the plaintiff has no personal claim against them. (In the course of the suit, action against them is dismissed.)

Lis pendens. *Purpose.* Whenever a law suit involving property is commenced, a notice of *lis pendens* or "pendency of action," is filed. *Lis pendens* is Latin for "pending suit." A notice of *lis pendens* gives constructive notice to the world that the property described therein is involved in a law suit. The notice is filed with the proper official, such as the county clerk, recorder, or register of titles under the Torrens system, at the time the complaint is filed.[1] The filing of the notice of *lis pendens* is a vital step in actions involving real property, such as foreclosures, actions to quiet title, condemnation proceedings, and partitions. If a defendant disposes of an interest in the property after suit is commenced but before notice is filed, the plaintiff's suit is defective. On the other hand, any claim against, or interest in, the property arising subsequent to the filing of the *lis pendens* is subordinate to the interest of the plaintiff as determined by the law suit.

Preparation of notice of lis pendens. As soon as you receive the certification of defendants, or foreclosure report, from the title company, you can prepare the notice of pendency without waiting for the lawyer to give you instructions about the complaint. He will not dictate the notice; you will be expected to follow a form. The only parts that change are the names of the defendants, the description of the mortgage, and the description of the property. Figure 109 illustrates a notice of pendency of action or *lis pendens*, but the wording varies with the state.

1. Use the same kind of paper that you use for any court paper (see Table VII, Chapter 12).

2. Make an original and a file copy. Also make an extra copy for your loose-leaf notebook. Copy of the notice is not served on the defendants.

3. The caption is the same as the caption in the complaint.

---

[1] In New York Supreme Court, notice of pendency is filed before the complaint because in that court no pleadings are filed until issue is joined.

IN THE DISTRICT COURT OF THE STATE OF IOWA

IN AND FOR POLK COUNTY

ROBERT COLE BROWN and MARY HOWARD
BROWN,

	Plaintiffs,	No. 4896
vs.		NOTICE OF LIS
		PENDENS

JOHN ALBERT GREEN and ELLEN BLAKE GREEN,
husband and wife, PAUL NELSON, DOE ONE,
DOE TWO, DOE THREE, and DOE FOUR,

Defendants

NOTICE IS HEREBY GIVEN, That an action has been
commenced and is pending in this Court upon a complaint of
the above named plaintiffs against the above named defendants for the foreclosure of a mortgage, bearing date the
twenty-first day of September, one thousand nine hundred
and ...., executed by John Albert Green and wife,
Ellen Blake Green, to Robert Cole Brown and wife, Mary
Howard Brown, to secure the sum of Five Thousand Dollars
($5,000), and recorded in Liber 2063 of Mortgages, at page
25, in the office of the Recorder of Deeds of the County of
Polk, on the twenty-second day of September, one thousand
nine hundred and .... at ten o'clock in the forenoon;

AND NOTICE IS HEREBY GIVEN, That the mortgaged premises affected by the said foreclosure action, were, at the
time of the commencement of said action, and at the time of
the filing of this notice, situate in the County of Polk

(*Continued on following page*)

(*Continued from preceding page*)

in the State of Iowa, and are described in the said mortgage
as follows, to wit:

      (Insert description that appears in mortgage)

              . . . .
                  Elwood & Adams
                  Attorneys for Plaintiffs

To THE CLERK OF THE DISTRICT COURT OF POLK COUNTY:

      You will please index the above notice to the name
of each of the following defendants: John Albert Green,
Ellen Blake Green, and Paul Nelson.

Dated: May 7, 19—.

              . . . .
                  Elwood & Adams
                  Attorneys for Plaintiffs

Figure 109. Notice of Lis Pendens.

You may shorten the title by the use of *et al.* (see page 250), unless the wording of the notice makes this inadvisable. See 6 below.

4. The title of the document is "Notice of Lis Pendens," or
"Notice of Pendency of Action."

5. Have someone compare the description with you against the
description in the original mortgage. *This is most important.*

6. The notice illustrated in Figure 109 contains a direction to
the county clerk: "You are hereby directed to index the foregoing notice of pendency against the names . . . ." Insert
the name of every *known* defendant as listed in the certification
of defendants, but do not include fictitious names. If the form of
notice that you follow refers to the defendants without listing
them, the title of the case must contain the name of every known
defendant and cannot be shortened by the use of *et al.* A *lis
pendens* is no good unless it is indexed against each defendant,
insofar as that defendant has an interest in the property.

7. Staple the original in an endorsed legal back (page 259).

8. The attorney for the plaintiff signs the notice.

Preparation of summons. The summons in a foreclosure action is prepared like the summons in any civil action. See the directions at page 271, *et seq.* As a foreclosure action usually has numerous defendants, you will probably have to type the summons instead of using a printed form.

Filing and service of summons, complaint, and lis pendens. After the summons, complaint, and *lis pendens* are prepared, proceed as in any civil action. See directions at page 274. File the notice of *lis pendens* with the proper county official (the official varies with the jurisdiction) at the time the summons is issued and the complaint is filed with the clerk of the court. The summons and complaint must be served on the defendants within a specified time after the *lis pendens* is filed.

Do not forget to make your diary and suit register entries.

Follow-up of process service. Follow-up of process service is necessary in all civil actions, but is particularly important in foreclosure actions because of the number of defendants. Numerous foreclosure actions are delayed because service of process is lax. It is your responsibility to see that the process server makes every effort to effect service expeditiously on all defendants. Request weekly reports on the progress of service. Insist that you be informed immediately when, where, and upon whom service is made, and that the process server make affidavit of service as soon as service is made. He should inform you of any difficulties that may arise, such as questions with respect to identity. In those jurisdictions where process is served by the sheriff or other county official, you cannot follow the matter as closely as when your office employs the process server.

Make appropriate diary and suit register entries.

Party sheet. Numerous parties defendant in a foreclosure action make it advisable to keep a special record, which might be called a *party sheet,* of service on and appearance by each defendant. (This record is not to be confused with the party sheet that is filed in court in some jurisdictions.) Use a wide sheet of paper for the record. Head the sheet:

PARTY SHEET

Action No. .... Plaintiffs .... Premises .. (brief description)..
Office File No. ....

Rule the sheet into vertical columns, with the following columnar headings:

Defendants (specify legal status, such as infant, corporation, trustee)
Interest in premises (owner, tenant, etc.)
Address where served
When served
How served
By whom served
Affidavit of service made before .... (*notary's name*)
Last day to answer
Appeared by .... (*name of defendant's attorney*)
Address and telephone number of attorney
Date appearance entered
Remarks

A glance at the party sheet will tell the lawyer the status of service and appearance of each defendant.

Other steps in foreclosure proceedings. After the summons, complaint, and *lis pendens* have been filed and served, the procedure in foreclosure litigation varies. The following steps are among those that will have to be taken, depending upon the jurisdiction and the circumstances of the case.

1. Application for receivership. If the property involved is income producing, the plaintiff will ask for the appointment of a receiver to collect the income and make the necessary disbursements.

2. Application for appointment of guardian ad litem. If the parent of an infant defendant will not ask for the appointment of a guardian ad litem, the plaintiff does.

3. *Ex parte* motion to obtain leave to sue "arm of court," such as a trustee in bankruptcy.

4. Entry of default judgment.

5. Reference to compute or reference to master in chancery.

6. Hearing before referee or master. The lawyer will want the following papers to take to the hearing:
   a. Referee's oath
   b. Referee's report ready for signature
   c. Bond or note

    d. Mortgage or deed of trust

    e. Assignments

    f. True or photostatic copies of (c), (d), and (e), so that the originals may be withdrawn when the hearing is over.

    g. Receipted bills for taxes, assessments, water rates, penalties or interest, if any, paid by mortgagee

    h. Receipt for payment of insurance if paid by mortgagee

    i. Summons with affidavit of service

    j. Check to order of referee

7. Judgment or decree of foreclosure and sale.

8. Publication of notice sale.

9. Sale.

Checklist of what to do in foreclosure action. Here is a checklist of what you will have to do when your office handles a foreclosure action.

    1. Make file and process as any other new matter (Chapter 1).

    2. *Keep diary entries* (Chapter 3) and progress record (Chapter 15).

    3. Order abstract of title continuation.

    4. Prepare all papers, as directed by the attorney.

    5. See that summons, complaint, and *lis pendens* are filed and served.

    6. Follow process server closely.

    7. Have copies (typed or photostatic) made of mortgage or deed, trust, bond or note, and assignments.

    8. Prepare party sheet and keep it up to date.

    9. If a receiver is appointed, keep after him for regular reports.

    10. Gather together papers for the lawyer to take to the hearing (see preceding paragraph).

    11. Make bookkeeping entries of all disbursements and receipts, just as in any case (Chapter 7).

23

Probate and Estate Administration

THE PROPERTY left by a deceased person is known as a *decedent's estate*. Whether the deceased died testate (leaving a will) or intestate (without a valid will), it is usually necessary that a competent person or corporation be charged with the duty of administering the deceased person's estate. The objects of the administration are, first, to collect the assets of an estate and pay the claims against it; and, second, to determine the persons to whom any residue of the estate belongs and deliver it to them. The administration of an estate is under the jurisdiction of the probate court (known as the Surrogate's Court in New York), and it is only through proceedings in this court that the executor or administrator can function.

Proceedings in probate courts, although similar, vary in detail not only from state to state but from county to county. The courts have printed forms for almost all of the papers that are filed in the administration of an estate. You can prepare many of these without detailed instruction from the lawyer. Those that you might find difficult to fill in are reproduced in this chapter. The procedure described here and the illustrated forms are based upon practice in New York County. They are typical, with deviations, of the procedure and forms in many states.

Distinction between executor and administrator. The general term used to describe any person appointed to administer an estate, whether testate or intestate, is *personal representative* or *legal representative*. If the decedent leaves a valid will naming the person or corporation whom the testator wanted to administer the estate, the person or corporation named in the will is an *executor* (*executrix*, if a woman). The testator may name as many

511

executors as he desires. Often a man names his wife and a bank as co-executors—his wife because he wants her to have a voice in the administration of the estate; the bank, to advise his wife and to relieve her of the considerable amount of work involved in the administration.

If the decedent died intestate, the court will appoint a person who is entitled to share in the estate as *administrator* (*administratrix*, if a woman). If the decedent left a will but did not nominate an executor, or if the person named is incompetent, or refuses to act, or dies, the court will appoint an administrator *cum testamento annexo* (with the will annexed).

There is little practical difference between the authority and duties of an executor and administrator, except that a will may confer on an executor powers in addition to those the law gives him. The executor, although nominated by the testator, receives authority to act by petitioning the probate court for *letters testamentary*. The administrator receives authority to act by petitioning for *letters of administration*. The will controls the distribution the executor (or administrator c.t.a.) makes of the property, whereas state inheritance statutes control the distribution the administrator makes.

The lawyer's part in the administration of an estate. Every lawyer is at some time the executor or administrator of one or more estates. However, the lawyer's chief participation in the administration of an estate is in his capacity as counsel to an executor or administrator. Every executor and administrator, corporate or individual, constantly requires the services of an attorney in the administration, settlement, and distribution of the estate. The attorney probates the will, files the petition for letters testamentary or letters of administration, institutes the necessary proceedings, such as tax proceedings and accounting proceedings, and advises the executor about the legality of his acts. The executor or administrator receives a commission from the estate, unless he consents to serve without compensation. If an attorney is also executor or administrator, he may perform the necessary legal services and receive proper compensation in addition to his commission.

Probate of Will

The executor's right to act. The executor named in a will cannot take over the administration of an estate without first indicating his intention to act and receiving the sanction of the court. Three documents are necessary to establish the executor's right to act: (1) the will itself, (2) the decree admitting it to probate, and (3) letters testamentary. The will is generally considered the source and measure of an executor's power, but the will must first be proved. It is proved by a legal proceeding in probate court known as *probate of will*. The proceeding culminates in a decree by the court admitting the will to probate and directing that letters testamentary issue to the executor. The letters testamentary are the evidence of the executor's authority.

Probate of will. The attorney for the estate generally prepares and submits to the executors the necessary papers in the proceeding to probate the will. The probate proceeding is initiated by the filing of the will itself, together with a copy of it, certified to be a correct and true copy. (Figure 110 shows entries made in the suit register record (Chapter 15) in a probate proceeding.) A petition for the probate of the will is also filed with the will and the copy. Simultaneously, a transfer tax affidavit is filed. The inheritance tax is not based upon the affidavit. A special proceeding must be had for that. Legal notice of the probate proceeding must be served upon all interested parties, and affidavit of service (or waiver of service) filed with the court. Sworn depositions of witnesses to the will must also be filed. If there are no objections to the admission of the will within the time specified, the will is admitted to probate by a decree of the court to that effect. The person named as executor in the will then files a bond (unless waived in the will) and an oath, and letters testamentary as executor issue to him. A corporate fiduciary named as executor does not file a bond.

Parties to a probate proceeding. The proponent of the will, that is, the person or corporation seeking to have the will probated, is the *petitioner*. The petitioner is usually the person or corporation named in the will as executor. There are three groups of interested parties who must be informed of the probate proceeding so that they may protect their interests:

1. The surviving spouse and the distributees. These are the

SURROGATE'S COURT—COUNTY OF NEW YORK

```
                                    x
In the Matter                       :
                                    :
    of                              :
                                    :
CHARLES RAY DOE,                    :
              Deceased,             :
                                    :
As a Will of Real and Personal Property.  :
                                    x
```

FILE NO. P 1277 – 19——

PROBATE PROCEEDING

Date of death: March 28, 19——
                105 East 37th Street, NYC.

Elwood & Adams, Esqs.,
Attorneys for Petitioners
    Partner in Charge: Mr. Rey
    Principal Assistant: Mr. Blank

<u>19——</u>

April 23   Mr. Blank filed original and sworn copy of will dated February 25, 19—— and petition of
           Charles T. Doe, John T. Roe and Barbara S. Roe, and their oaths and designations as execu-
           tors and trustees and filed waiver of citation executed by Beatrice S. Roe.

24   M. J. Ryan mailed 31 copies of notice of probate to legatees, etc. named therein.
25   Filed original notice of probate with proof of mailing.
25   Depositions of the subscribing witnesses Mary Roeman and Anthony J. Maurman were sworn to
     before John A. Killoran, Probate Clerk.

25   Decree signed, Collins, S., and filed, admitting will to probate and directing that letters
     testamentary and letters of trusteeship be issued to the executors and trustees who may
     qualify thereunder.

25   Letters Testamentary issued to Charles T. Doe, John T. Roe and Barbara S. Roe, Liber 633,
     Page 434.

26   Letters of Trusteeship issued to Charles T. Doe, John T. Roe and Barbara S. Roe, in Liber
     51, Page 842.

Figure 110. Progress Record in Probate of Will.

heirs-at-law of the deceased who would have inherited if the decedent had died intestate. This group of distributees includes the heirs-at-law who are also named in the will as legatees, because they might take less by the will than they would have inherited if there had been no will.

2. The executors and trustees named in the will who do not sign the petition.

3. Legatees or devisees who are not distributees. These are the legatees or devisees named in the will who would not have inherited if the decedent had died intestate. They are interested in the proceeding because they lose their legacies if the will is not admitted to probate.

Copy of will and affidavit. A copy of the will is filed in the probate court with the original will. In some jurisdictions a photographic or photostatic copy may be filed. In the administration of a large, complicated estate, where numerous copies of the will are needed, the will is sometimes mimeographed or printed.

1. Make as many legible copies as you can in one typing.

2. Copy the will exactly, typing also the signature and data that are written in ink.

3. Have two adults (you may be one of them) compare one copy with the original and make an affidavit to that effect. They must both compare the same copy. Figure 111 illustrates the affidavit.

4. Fill in the blanks on the back of the affidavit. If you do not use a printed form of affidavit, make a legal back endorsed like the printed form illustrated in Figure 112.

5. Staple the affidavit to the compared copy of the will, placing the affidavit beneath the copy.

Petition for probate of will. The petition sets forth certain factual data about the testator, his heirs, legatees, and devisees, and prays that the will be admitted to probate and that letters testamentary be issued to the executor. If trustees are named in the will, the petition also prays for letters of trusteeship. Figure 113 illustrates a printed form of petition, properly completed.

1. Make an original for the court and a copy for your office file.

2. Be especially careful about names, addresses, and values of legacies and devises.

Surrogate's Court
County of New York

In the Matter of Proving the Last Will and
Testament of

EDGAR BROWN

Deceased

Affidavit Proving a Correct Copy
of the Will Filed for Probate

P..195....

County and State of New York, ss.:

We, PAUL BELL

and MARY WILLIAMS , being duly and severally sworn,

say, each for himself, that he has carefully compared the foregoing paper S   with the original thereof

dated the   23rd   day of   November   , 19 39 ,

about to be filed for probate, and that the same   are   in all respects a true and correct copy of

said instrument   and of the whole thereof.

Paul Bell

Mary Williams

Sworn to before me this 5th day of

          June   , 195.−

Leslie Nash

(Notary Stamp)

Figure 111. Affidavit Proving a Correct Copy of Will Filed for Probate.

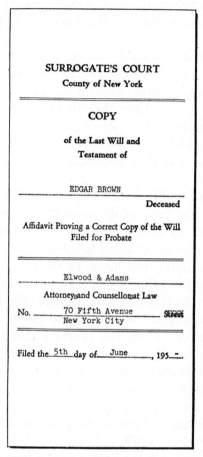

SURROGATE'S COURT

County of New York

COPY

of the Last Will and

Testament of

EDGAR BROWN

Deceased

Affidavit Proving a Correct Copy of the Will

Filed for Probate

Elwood & Adams

Attorneys and Counsellors at Law

No. _____70 Fifth Avenue_____ Street

New York City

Filed the 5th day of June, 195_.

Figure 112. Back of Affidavit Proving a Correct Copy of Will Filed for Probate.

3. The lawyer will give you a memorandum of (a) the name and address of the petitioner or petitioners; (b) the name of the testator, his residence at the time of his death, and the time and place of his death; (c) the names, addresses, ages, and degree of kinship to the decedent of the heirs-at-law and of those interested in the will; (d) the addresses of the other legatees and devisees. This memorandum and the copy of the will give you the information necessary to fill in the form, unless the will is complicated. If so, the lawyer will dictate the necessary information.

4. The executors and trustees, if any, named in the will are listed with the distributees (subdivision a. of the form illustrated in Figure 113).

5. Notice the marginal note, "Delete unnecessary allegations," at the bottom of page 2 of Figure 113. The relationship of the distributees (listed in Subdivisions a, b, c, and d of the illustration) indicates the allegations that should be deleted. A surviving spouse always shares in a decedent's estate. The distributees, other than the surviving spouse, take in the following order:

Children and issue of deceased children

Father, mother

Brothers, sisters, and issue of deceased brothers and sisters

Uncles, aunts, and issue of deceased uncles and aunts

There is no need to make an allegation concerning relatives of a deceased who are not entitled to inherit. Thus, in the illustration, surviving children are listed as distributees. There is no need to make an allegation about a surviving mother or father, or others, because in this case they cannot inherit. If there were no surviving children or issue of a predeceased child, and no surviving mother or father, the brothers and sisters would be listed as distributees. It would then be necessary to allege that there were no surviving children or issue of a deceased child, and no surviving mother or father. It would not be necessary to allege that there were no surviving aunts or uncles and no issue of a deceased aunt or uncle, because they could not inherit, unless specifically named in the will.

6. You can always get the names of the legatees and devisees from the copy of the will.

7. The petition indicates the kind of legacy, as well as its value. You can get this information from the will. Thus, the testator might leave the residue of his estate in trust for his widow, the remainder to go to his children upon the death of his widow. The petition would show that the widow was the "beneficiary of a residuary trust," and that the children were given a "remainder interest in the residuary trust."

If the testator does not place the residue of his estate in trust but leaves it outright to someone, the petition indicates that the person is the "residuary legatee."

When specific personal property, rather than a sum of money,

87697-51 (CK)

Surrogate's Court,
County of New York

| In the Matter of Proving the Last Will and Testament of | **Petition for Probate of Will.** |

EDGAR BROWN
....
deceased,
as a Will of Real and Personal Property

When all parties waive citation all papers must be filed two days before the day fixed for the hearing.

To the Surrogate's Court of the County of New York:

The petition of Thomas Nelson and The City Trust Company of New York residing at No. 52 Gramercy Park, North, and having its principal place of business at 70 Fifth Avenue, New York City, respectively,

respectfully states

That your petitioners are the executors named in the last will and testament of deceased, and is a citizen of and a corporation of New York State, respectively,

That said last will and testament, to be herewith presented and hereby offered for probate, relates to both real and personal property, and bears date November 23, 1939, and is signed at the end thereof by the said testator and by Loretta Ames and William Black as subscribing witnesses.

The petition shall describe any other wills of the same testator on file in the Surrogate's office of New York County. Section 139, S. C. A.

That petitioners does not know of any codicil to said last will and testament, nor is there any to the best of their information and belief.

That the said deceased was, at the time of his death, a resident of No. 214 East 17 Street, New York City, in the County of New York, and departed this life in said county, on the 27th day of May 19 5-, leaving personal property within the County of New York. That decedent was a citizen of United States at the time of his death.

If the testator was the donee of a Power of Appointment created by will or deed those who would take under such will or deed in the event of the denial of probate herein must be cited.

That the widow and all the other distributees of said testator , each person designated in the will herewith presented and hereby offered for probate as executor, testamentary trustee or guardian, all persons having an interest in any estate herein attempted to be disposed of by any exercise of a Power of Appointment; and their residences and post office addresses are hereinafter mentioned in subdivisions a, b, c, and d hereof, as follows:

a. The following named persons who are of full age and of sound mind:

Elizabeth R. Brown, a widow of deceased
who resides at 214 East 17 Street, New York City.

John Brown, a son of deceased
who resides at 214 East 17 Street, New York City.

Mary Brown, a daughter of deceased
who resides at 214 East 17 Street, New York City.

a of deceased
who resides at

If any person or his name, residence and post office address be unknown, the petition must substantially set forth the facts which show what efforts have been made to ascertain the same and a general description of the person, showing his connection with the decedent and his interest in the matter. Section 51, S. C. A.

Thomas Nelson, an executor of deceased
who resides at 52 Gramercy Park, North, New York City.

The City Trust Company of New York, an executor of deceased
whose resides at whose principal place of business is at 70 Fifth Avenue, New York City.

a of deceased
who resides at

a of deceased

Figure 113. Petition for Probate of Will (Page 1).

Use BLACK ink only, as this sheet will be photographed.

b. The following named persons who are infants over fourteen years of age:

Robert Brown, aged 16, _____ a son _____ of deceased

who resides at __214 East 17 Street, New York City.__

Said infant resides with his mother, Elizabeth R. Brown, at the above

address, and has no general or testamentary guardian.

c. The following named persons who are infants under fourteen years of age:

Irene Brown, aged 13, _____ a daughter _____ of deceased

who resides at __214 East 17 Street, New York City.__

Said infant resides with her mother, Elizabeth R. Brown, at the above

address, and has no general or testamentary guardian.

d. The following named persons who are of full age but of unsound mind:

_____ a _____ of deceased

who resides at _____

That the above named decedent left h im surviving no widow no child or children, no child or issue of a deceased child, no adopted child or children, no issue of any deceased adopted child or children, other than those above named.

That no petition for the probate of the will herewith presented and hereby offered for probate, or for letters of administration on said estate, has been heretofore filed in this or any other Surrogate's Court of this State.

That there is no person designated in the will herewith presented and hereby offered for probate as executor, testamentary trustee or guardian, except as hereinbefore mentioned.

That there is no person named as executor, testamentary trustee, guardian, devisee or beneficiary in any other will of the same testator filed in the Surrogate's office of the County of New York.

That the names and post office addresses of the devisees, legatees and other beneficiaries named in the will herewith presented and hereby offered for probate, are as follows:

1. The following named legatees, etc., have been hereinbefore mentioned:

Name of Legatee or Devisee.	Post Office Address.	Value of Legacy or Devise.
Elizabeth R. Brown	214 East 17 Street New York City.	Legacy of $75,000.00; beneficiary of residuary trust; specific legacy.
John Brown	214 East 17 Street New York City.	Legacy of $15,000.00; remainder interest in the residuary trust.
Mary Brown	214 East 17 Street New York City.	Legacy of $15,000.00; remainder interest in the residuary trust.
Robert Brown	214 East 17 Street New York City.	Legacy of $15,000.00; remainder interest in the residuary trust.
Irene Brown	214 East 17 Street New York City.	Legacy of $15,000.00; remainder interest in the residuary trust.

Figure 113. Petition for Probate of Will (Page 2).

2. The following named legatees, etc., have not been hereinbefore mentioned and they are the only persons who are entitled to a notice of Probate pursuant to Section 146 of the Surrogate's Court Act.

Name of Legatee or Devisee.	Post Office Address.	Value of Legacy or Devise.
Mary Jane Adams	35 West 10 Street New York City	Annuitant of $1,500.00 annually.
James Wilson	30 West 10 Street New York City	Specific legacy--25 shares of Procter & Gamble common stock.

State the age of the infant and whether or not the infant has a general or testamentary guardian, whether or not his father, or, if he be dead, his mother, is living, giving the name and post office address of such person, and the name and post office address of the person with whom such infant resides, and if such person be judicially declared incompetent, the name and post office address of his committee.

That all of said legatees are of full age and are of sound mind, except: Robert Brown, further described in paragraph b., above, and Irene Brown, further described in paragraph c., above.

Figure 113. Petition for Probate of Will (Page 3).

That the value of the entire estate of the decedent ~~is~~ exceeds Ten Thousand dollars.
That the value of the real property in this State of which the testator died seized ~~is~~ exceeds
Five Thousand dollars and that the value of
the personal property of which said testator died possessed ~~is~~ exceeds Five Thousand dollars.
That there are no persons interested in this proceeding other than those hereinbefore mentioned.

Wherefore your petitioner prays

That a citation to show cause issue herein to the persons hereinbefore named, described, and included in subdivisions a, b, c and d hereof, citing them to show cause why the last will and testament herewith presented and hereby offered for probate should not be admitted to probate;

That an order be granted directing the service of the citation personally without the State or by publication upon the persons hereinbefore named, described and included in subdivisions a, b, c and d hereof who are not residents of the State of New York, and also upon the persons hereinbefore described and included in those subdivisions who and whose names or residences and post office addresses are unknown and cannot be ascertained; and

That the last will and testament herewith presented and hereby offered for probate may be admitted to probate as a will of real and personal property and that letters testamentary/ and trustees/ may be issued to the executors /who may qualify thereunder.   *Thomas Nelson*

Dated, New York,   June 5,   , 195 - .   THE CITY TRUST COMPANY
                                                          OF NEW YORK ~~Petitioner~~
                                                          By *Fred Ball*
                                                             Trust Officer
County and State of New York, ss.:   Petitioners

____Thomas Nelson, one of_____

the petitioner_s_ named in the foregoing petition being_____duly sworn, depose_s_
and say_s_ that____h e____ha_s_____read the foregoing petition subscribed
by_____h i m_____and know_s_ the contents thereof; and that the same is true to____h i s____
own knowledge except as to the matters therein stated to be alleged on information and belief, and that
as to those matters____h e____believe_s_ it to be true.

Sworn to this___5 th____day
of____June_____, 195 - .   *Thomas Nelson*
                                                    Petitioner.
        Mary Williams
        (Notary Stamp)   N. Y. Co.

STATE OF NEW YORK)
                 SS.:
COUNTY OF NEW YORK)

Fred Ball, being duly sworn, deposes and says that he is a Trust Officer of the City Trust Company of New York, one of the petitioners herein; and that he has read the foregoing petition and knows the contents thereof; and that the same is true to his own knowledge, except as to the matters therein stated to be alleged upon information and belief, and as to those matters he believes it to be true.

Deponent further says that the reason this verification is made by deponent and not by the City Trust Company of New York, is that the said City Trust Company of New York is a domestic corporation and deponent an officer thereof, to wit: a Trust Officer.

Sworn to before me this   *Fred Ball*
5th day of *June, 195-*.
     Mary Williams
(Notary Stamp)

Figure 113. Petition for Probate of Will (Page 4).

522

is bequeathed, the bequest is indicated in the petition as a "specific legacy." Thus, in the illustration, the widow and James Wilson received specific legacies. The exact nature of the widow's specific legacy is not indicated because it consisted of numerous items—the testator's jewelry, his household effects, automobiles, wearing apparel, and the like.

8. Arrange for the petitioners to come in and sign the petition.

9. Have the petitioners verify the petition. The illustrated petition has a form of verification by an individual printed on it. When the petitioner, or one of them, is a corporation, type a verification by a corporation (see page 246) on the form if there is space. If there is no space, type it on plain paper the width of the printed form and paste on the form immediately following the individual verification (see page 4 of Figure 113).

10. Conform your office copy.

11. File the original of the petition, the original and certified copy of the will, and the transfer tax affidavit (see below) in the probate court.

12. Mark on your office copy the date the petition was filed.

13. Make entry in suit register.

Transfer tax affidavit. A transfer tax affidavit is filed with the petition. This is a sworn statement as to the totals of realty and personalty affected by the will and of the names, amounts of legacies, residences, and relationship of those who receive gifts under the will. The affidavit supplies the state taxing authorities with data to be used by them for taxing purposes. It is typed on a printed form supplied by the taxing commissioner.

Citation and waiver in probate proceeding. The Surrogate's Court Act of New York provides that the surviving spouse, distributees, and executors and trustees named in the decedent's will shall be given notice of the petition for probate by service of a *citation*. Probate acts of other states have similar provisions. The citation is a legal writ citing those to whom it is addressed to appear in court on a certain date and show cause why the will should not be admitted to probate. It does not *command* an appearance like a summons does. Those who do not wish to contest the will need not appear in court. A citation is issued by the clerk of the court, but is prepared by the petitioner's attorney.

Any person over eighteen may serve a citation. Service is

made by delivering a copy to the person upon whom it is served. If an infant is a distributee, the citation is addressed to him, but is served upon the parent with whom he resides or upon his guardian. If an infant is over fourteen, service is made upon him, as well as his parent or guardian.

Service of citation by publication and mailing. If any of the distributees live outside the state, or if there are any heirs or next of kin whose names and place of residence are unknown, service is had upon them by publication and mailing. The procedure is similar to that in a civil action (page 613).

Adults may waive the issuance and source of a citation in the matter of proving the last will and testament of the deceased, but infants may not. Thus, before the citations are prepared, waivers are secured.

How to prepare a waiver of citation. Figure 114 illustrates a properly completed form of waiver.

1. Make an original for the court and an office copy.

2. Have those who waive citation sign the original in the presence of two witnesses.

3. Take the acknowledgment of those signing the waiver.

4. Conform office copy, marking on it the date the original is filed.

5. File original in court.

6. Make entry in suit register.

How to prepare a citation. Figure 115 illustrates a properly completed form of citation in probate proceedings.

1. Make an original for the court, an office copy, and a copy for each person to be served. In the illustrated case 5 copies must be made—an original for the court; an office copy; a copy for service upon Robert Brown, an infant over fourteen; a copy for service upon his mother in his behalf; a copy for service upon the mother of Irene Brown, an infant under fourteen. The adult distributees waived citation.

2. The return date may be any date within the time allowed by the court rules.

3. Get the clerk of the court to sign the original.

4. Conform copies and give original and copies (except office copy) to person who is to serve the citation.

76446-51 (C.S.) ⟨94⟩

Surrogate's Court, County of New York

In the Matter of Proving the Last Will and
Testament of

EDGAR BROWN

Deceased,
As a Will of Real and Personal Property

Waiver of Citation in Probate
Proceeding

P 11,235 , 195–

xⅹ We, ELIZABETH R. BROWN, JOHN BROWN, and MARY BROWN,

the undersigned, being ⅹheirsat law and next of kin of

EDGAR BROWN , deceased, do hereby

appear in person and waive the issuance and service of a citation in the matter

of proving the last will and testament of said deceased, bearing date November 23, 1939,

and consent that the said instrument be admitted to probate.

Dated, New York
June 6 , 195 –

Elizabeth R. Brown
John Brown
Mary Brown

Signed in the presence of

John Blank
Susie White

State of New York
County of New York } ss.:

On the 6th day of June , 195– , before me personally came

ELIZABETH R. BROWN, JOHN BROWN, and MARY BROWN,

to me known and known to me to be the individualS described in and who executed the fore-

going instrument, and they duly acknowledged that they executed the same.

Mary Williams

(Notary Stamp)

NOTE—Outside the State of New York use the certificate printed on the reverse page.
(OVER)

Figure 114. Waiver of Citation in Probate Proceeding.

76445-51 (C. S.) ━━━94

CITATION

P 11,235 _____, 195—.   The People of the State of New York
By the Grace of God Free and Independent,

To

ROBERT BROWN, IRENE BROWN

the above   next of kin and heirs at law of   EDGAR BROWN

, deceased, send greeting:

Whereas, Thomas Nelson and The City Trust Company of New York, residing

at 52 Gramercy Park, North, New York City and having its principal , ▨▨▨▨▨▨

place of business at 70 Fifth Avenue, New York City, respectively ,▨▨▨▨▨▨

have
▨▨▨▨ lately applied to the Surrogate's Court of our County of New York to have a

certain instrument in writing bearing date November 23, 1939,

relating

to both real and personal property, duly proved as the last will and testament of EDGAR BROWN

, deceased, who was at the time of his death a resident of

214 East 17 Street, New York City   , the County of New York,

Therefore, you and each of you are cited to show cause before the Surrogate's Court of our

County of New York, at the Hall of Records in the County of New York, on the 18th

day of June   , one thousand nine hundred and -------- , at half-past ten o'clock

in the forenoon of that day, why the said will and testament should not be admitted to probate as a

will of real and personal property. and why letters of testamentary and letters of trusteeship should not be issued to the executors and trustees who may qualify there- .
under.

In testimony whereof, we have caused the seal of the Surrogate's Court of the said County of

New York to be hereunto affixed.

Witness, Honorable John Doe

Surrogate of our said County of New York, at said county, the

(L. S.)   6th   day of   June   in the

year of our Lord one thousand nine hundred and fifty —.

Richard Roe

Clerk of the Surrogate's Court

Use BLACK ink only, as this sheet will be photographed.

Figure 115. Citation in Probate Proceeding.

526

5. Prepare affidavit of service, which is usually printed on the back of the citation (Figure 116), and have the person who served the citation sign and swear to the affidavit in the presence of a notary.

6. Conform office copy, marking on it the date the original is filed in court.

7. File original in court.

8. *Enter in diary* return date of citation.

9. Make entry in suit register.

Preparations for hearing. The hearing in an uncontested probate proceeding is rather informal. The lawyer for the petitioners appears before the clerk of the court with the witnesses to the will. The date of the hearing is the return day indicated in the citation. (In some jurisdictions the clerk of the court sets the date for hearing at the time the petition is filed.) You will have to make certain preparations prior to the hearing:

1. Prepare deposition of witnesses.

2. Notify witnesses to the will.

3. Prepare and mail notice of probate.

4. Prepare oath of executor.

5. Prepare decree.

6. Prepare letters testamentary; also letters of trusteeship if the petition prays for them.

Notice of probate. The legatees and devisees who are not heirs-at-law must be given notice that the will has been offered for probate. The printed form of notice calls for the name and address of the proponents (the petitioners) and for a list of the names and addresses of the legatees, devisees, and beneficiaries who have not been cited or have not waived citation. In the illustrated case, Mary Jane Adams and James Wilson (see page 3 of Figure 113) should receive notices.

1. Make an original for the court, an office copy, and a copy for each person listed in the notice.

2. The notices may be sent by mail. The attorney for the petitioners makes affidavit of service by mail on the back of the notice.

3. Notarize the affidavit made by the attorney.

4. Conform the office copy.

5. Place the original with the papers that the lawyer will take to the hearing.

Surrogate's Court, County of New York

Note.—*Outside the State of New York* a certificate must be procured from the proper official. Such certificate must show that the officer taking the acknowledgment is an officer of the state where it is taken and is authorized by the laws thereof *to take the acknowledgment of deeds*; that said official is well acquainted with such officer's handwriting and believes the signature to the original certificate is genuine.

In the Matter of Proving the Last Will and Testament of

EDGAR BROWN

Deceased,

As a Will of Real and Personal Property

AFFIDAVIT OF SERVICE
OF CITATION

State of New York
County of...... New York .... ss.:

Mathew Davis

of.................. 33 West 10 Street, New York City ...., being duly sworn, says that he is over the age of eighteen years; that he made personal service of the within citation in the above-entitled special proceeding on the persons named below, whom deponent knew to be the persons mentioned and described in said citation, by delivering to and leaving with each of them personally a true copy of said citation, as follows:

On the...... 7th ....day of.... June,
195 --, at... 214 East 17 Street, New York City, on Robert Brown.

On the...... 7th ....day of.... June,
195 , at... 214 East 17 Street, New York City, on Elizabeth R. Brown, in behalf of Robert Brown, an infant.

On the...... 7th ....day of.... June,
195 , at... 214 East 17 Street, New York City, on Elizabeth R. Brown, in behalf of Irene Brown, an infant.

On the............day of............
195 , at...............

On the............day of............
195 , at...............

Specify clearly time and place of service of each party served.

Mathew Davis

Sworn to before me on the

8th day of June 195 -.

Mary Williams

(Notary Stamp)

Figure 116. Affidavit of Service of Citation.
528

6. Make entry in suit register that the notices were mailed.

Deposition of witnesses to the will. As soon as you know the date of the hearing, notify the witnesses to the will of the time and place of the hearing. You can get their names and addresses from the will. If the witnesses are not available, the lawyer will have to take other legal steps to prove the will. Make an entry of the notice in your suit register.

Printed forms of depositions are available.

1. Prepare an original and an office copy for each witness. Thus, if there are two witnesses, you will prepare two sets of depositions.

2. Do not date the depositions. They are signed and sworn to before an officer of the court, who dates them at that time.

3. Place the originals with the papers that the lawyer will take to the hearing.

4. Draw checks to witnesses for fee allowed by law. The lawyer will probably take the checks to the hearing and pay the witnesses at that time; otherwise mail the checks after the depositions are taken.

Oath of executor. An executor must take an oath that he will faithfully perform his duties as executor. Printed forms are available.

1. Prepare an original and an office copy for each executor. Thus, if there are two executors, you will prepare two sets of oaths.

2. Each executor signs the original of his oath in the presence of a notary.

3. Conform your office copies.

4. Place the originals with the papers that the lawyer will take to the hearing.

5. Make an entry in the suit register that the oaths have been executed.

Decree admitting will to probate. A decree in a probate proceeding serves the same purpose as an order or judgment in a civil action. A favorable decree admits the will to probate and directs that letters testamentary issue to the executor nominated in the will. The probate judge (the surrogate in New York) signs the decree, but the petitioner's attorney prepares it. Printed forms are available.

1. Make an original for the court and a copy for your office file.

2. Do not date the decree. It will be dated when the judge signs it.

3. Place the original with the papers that the lawyer will take to the hearing.

4. The decree might not be signed for several days after the hearing. *Make a follow-up entry in your diary* for a few days after the hearing and inquire of the clerk of the court if it has been signed.

5. Mark on your office copy the date the decree was signed.

6. Make entry in the suit register.

Letters testamentary. After the judge signs the decree, the clerk of the court issues letters testamentary to the executor. The attorney for the executor prepares the letters. They are the evidence of the executor's authority to act. Anyone dealing with the executor as the representative of the estate will require a certificate to the effect that letters have been issued and are still in force. Certificates are available from the clerk of the court for a small fee.

1. Prepare an original, or duplicate original, for each executor, an office copy, and a sufficient number of copies to be certified by the clerk of the court. Thus, if there are two executors, prepare three copies in addition to the copies that are to be certified. There must be a certified copy for each bank account, each security issue, each safe deposit box, and the like.

2. If there are two or more executors, all of them are named in the letters.

3. Do not date the letters. The clerk of the court will date them when he issues them.

4. Place the original and duplicate original with the papers that the lawyer will take to the hearing. The clerk will sign a copy for each executor named in the letters and return them to your office.

5. Conform your office copy.

6. Deliver a signed copy to each executor. If the lawyer is an executor, he will retain one of the signed copies.

7. Make entries in suit register.

Notice to creditors. As soon as letters testamentary are issued, notice to creditors should be published in a local newspaper.

Creditors of the decedent are given a certain length of time in which to file any claims they may have against the decedent. *Enter in your diary* the last day the creditors have to present claims.

Newspapers usually have an appropriate printed form of notice to creditors that you can fill in without any difficulty. Within a specified time after the last publication, affidavit of publication is filed with the clerk of the court. The publisher makes the affidavit of publication and delivers it to either the clerk of the court or the attorney. *Enter in your diary* the date by which the affidavit must be filed; also make entries in your suit register.

Appointment of Administrator

Application for letters of administration. When a person dies without leaving a will, a person who is over 21, of sound mind, and entitled by law to share in his estate, may ask to be appointed administrator of the estate. He does this by applying to the probate court for *letters of administration.* The procedure is governed by statute but is more or less similar in all of the states.

Parties. The person who files an application for letters of administration is known as the *petitioner.* There are no plaintiffs and defendants—the petitioner does not bring a suit against someone else—but there are other necessary and interested parties. Those nearer of kin to the deceased than the petitioner have a prior right to be appointed; those of an equal degree of kinship have an equal right to be appointed. The kin of the decedent in these two categories are, therefore, necessary parties to the proceeding and are made parties to it by the service of a citation (see page 537), unless they waive citation.

All of those who are entitled by law to share in the intestate's estate—the distributees—are interested parties to the proceeding, although they may not be entitled to letters of administration. For example, a minor child of the deceased, or a minor child of his prior deceased child, are distributees of the estate and are interested parties. They are not served with citations because they cannot serve as administrators, but they are given notice of the application for letters of administration.

Who has prior right to letters of administration. The statutes provide the order of priority by which distributees of the decedent's estate are entitled to letters of administration. The usual order is:

1. Surviving spouse
2. Children
3. Grandchildren
4. Parents
5. Brothers and sisters
6. Nephews and nieces

Necessary papers in application for letters of administration. Printed forms of papers that must be prepared by the attorney and filed in an application for letters of administration are usually available, and the courts prefer that they be used. The forms are not uniform, varying even from county to county within a state, but they are similar. In every state, there is a petition for letters of administration, an oath of administrator, and a notice in some form to interested parties. In New York County, the papers consist of the following:

1. Petition for letters of administration ⎱ Frequently combined
2. Oath of administrator ⎰ in one paper
3. Designation of the clerk of the court as a person on whom service of process may be made. (Sometimes combined with petition and oath.)
4. Renunciation, if any
5. Citation
6. Notice of application for letters of administration, if necessary

How to prepare petition; oath; designation of clerk. Figure 117 illustrates a printed form, used in New York County, which combines a petition for letters of administration, oath of administrator, and designation of clerk of the court as a person on whom service of process may be made. The form is basically similar to forms used in other states.

The lawyer will give you a memorandum of the factual information necessary to fill in the form.

1. Prepare an original and one copy of the petition.

2. Fill in the blanks not only in the petition but also in the form of verification, oath, and designation of clerk, even if they are on separate forms.

57226-51-(CK)

Surrogate's Court
County of New York

In the Matter of the Application for Letters of
Administration on the Goods, Chattels
and Credits of

EDGAR BROWN

**Petition for Letters of
Administration**

Deceased

To the Surrogate's Court of the County of New York:

The petition of........JOHN BROWN..

of ....216 East 17 Street............................, of the County of New York, respectfully shows:

That the above named decedent was at the time of h^{is} death a resident of No..214 East 17 Street

........in the County of New York, and died at....New York Hospital, New York City,............

on the....8th......day of....April..................................., 195.–....

That your petitioner is of full age and is the............................son............................of the deceased.

That your petitioner has made diligent search and inquiry for a will of said deceased
and has not found any such will, nor has your petitioner obtained any information concerning any
such will.

That a search of the records of this court made by........Thomas Jones............................
of....70 Fifth Avenue....................., on the....10th......day of....April..................., 195–.,
shows that no application has ever been made thereto for letters of administration upon the
estate of said deceased, or for the probate of a will of said deceased, or for letters testamentary
thereupon, and your petitioner is informed and verily believes that no such application has ever been
made to the surrogate's court of any other county of this state.

That the said deceased died possessed of certain personal property in the County and State of New York,
and that the value of all the personal property, wherever situated, of which the deceased died possessed, does not
exceed the sum of........One Hundred Thousand-- Dollars.

That the decedent died seized of.........................real property in this state. That said real property is
improved. A brief description of each parcel is as follows: ....
~~unimproved.~~

      214 East 17 Street, New York City   .

      216 East 17 Street, New York City

That the estimated value of such real property and improvements is.One Hundred Thousand------Dollars.

That the estimated gross rents for the period of eighteen months from the date of the death of decedent is
the sum of....Ten Thousand----------------------Dollars.

That a right of action exists granted to the administrator of the decedent by special provision of law, the
probable amount to be recovered in which cannot be ascertained, and that it is impracticable to give a bond sufficient to cover the probable amount to be recovered in said action.

Figure 117. Petition for Letters of Administration, Oath, and Designation of
Clerk (Page 1).

That said deceased left surviving the following distributees, whose names, degrees of relationship, post-office addresses and ages are as follows:

Name	Relationship	Post-office Address	Age
Elizabeth R. Brown	Widow	214 East 17 Street New York City	60
John Brown	Son	216 East 17 Street New York City	35
Mary Brown	Daughter	214 East 17 Street New York City	25
Nancy B. Smith	Daughter	60 Fifth Avenue New York City	30
* Robert Jones	Grandson	72 Riverside Drive New York City	10
* Irene Jones	Granddaughter	72 Riverside Drive New York City	8

* The grandchildren are the issue of a predeceased daughter and reside with their father, Albert Jones, at the above address.

That the above named deceased left him surviving no ~~husband~~ wife, no child or children, no child or issue of a deceased child, no adopted child or children, no issue of any deceased adopted child or children, ~~xxx~~ ~~father, mother, brother, sister, or the half or the whole blood, or descendant of a deceased brother or sister, xxx~~ ~~grandparents, uncle, aunt, or child or descendant of a deceased uncle or aunt,~~ other than those above named.

That there are no other persons than those mentioned interested in this proceeding.

That all of the above named persons are of sound mind ~~xxxxxx~~.

That all of the above named persons are of full age except Robert Jones and Irene Jones, and that none of said infants has a general or testamentary guardian.

That said deceased was in his lifetime a citizen of the United States. ~~xxxxxxxx~~

Your Petitioner Therefore Prays that a citation issue to show cause why

a decree should not be made awarding letters of administration to your petitioner.

Dated, New York April 8 , 195⁻

John Brown

Petitioner

See §118, Surrogate's Court Act.

Show that there are no persons related in a nearer or in the same degree to the deceased other than those above named.

Strike out unnecessary allegations.

Figure 117. Petition for Letters of Administration, Oath, and Designation of Clerk (Page 2).

534

Verification

State of New York
County of New York } ss.:

_____ JOHN BROWN _____, the above named petitioner

being duly sworn, doth depose and say that   he   has read the foregoing petition subscribed by___him___

_____and knows the contents thereof, and that the same is true to____his_____own

knowledge except as to the matters therein stated to be alleged on information and belief, and as to those

matters   he believes it to be true.

Sworn to this___*8th*___day of ⎫
___April_____, 195_ ⎬
    Mary Williams
   (Notary Stamp)

John Brown

Oath of Administrator

State of New York
County of New York } ss.:

  I, _____JOHN BROWN_____, a Citizen of the United States, do solemnly swear

and declare that____I_____will well, honestly and faithfully discharge the duties of administra_tor_____

of the goods, chattels and credits of_____EDGAR BROWN_____

deceased, according to law.

Sworn to this_____*8th*____day of ⎫
___April_____, 195_ ⎬
    Mary Williams
   (Notary Stamp)

John Brown

**Designation of the Clerk of the Surrogate's Court as a Person on Whom Service of Process
May Be Made Pursuant to Section 95, S. C. A.**

  I, _____JOHN BROWN_____, the petitioner herein

for letters of administration on the goods, chattels and credits of_____EDGAR BROWN_____

_____, deceased, do hereby designate the Clerk of the Surrogate's Court and his

successor in office as a person on whom service of any process issuing from the Surrogate's Court of the County

of New York may be made in like manner and with like effect as if it were served personally upon me, whenever

I cannot be found and served within the State of New York after due diligence used. I reside at No.__214__

_____East 17 Street_____, New York City.

John Brown

State of New York
County of New York } ss.:

  On this____8th____day of____April_____, 195_, before me

personally came____JOHN BROWN_____

to me known to be the individual   described in and who executed the foregoing instrument, and   he   acknowl-

edged to me that   he   executed the same.

    Mary Williams

    (Notary Stamp)

Figure 117. Petition for Letters of Administration, Oath, and Designation of
Clerk (Page 3).

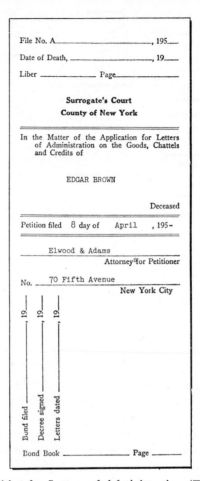

Figure 117. Petition for Letters of Administration (Endorsed Back).

3. The information called for by the lower half of the printed back is not available at the time the petition is prepared.

4. The petition must be verified.

5. Arrange for the client to come in and sign the petition when it is ready for his signature.

6. Have the petitioner sign on the line designated "Petitioner" in the presence of a notary public; also immediately beneath the verification, immediately beneath the oath, and immediately beneath the designation of the clerk for service of process. You will notice that on the illustrated form there are no lines for signature.

7. If you are a notary, ask the petitioner to swear to the petition and to the oath (see page 246 for administration of oath) and to acknowledge the designation of the clerk (see page 188 for taking an acknowledgment).

8. Notarize the instrument.

9. Conform your copy.

10. The original is filed in court.

11. Get court file number from clerk and enter on back of office copy.

12. Make entry in suit register.

13. In some states the clerk of the court sets a hearing date when the petition is filed. If this is the practice in your state, *enter hearing date in diary.*

Renunciation. The Surrogate's Court Act of New York provides that a person who is entitled to letters of administration may renounce his right. He does this by signing a simple printed form entitled, "Renunciation of Rights to Letters of Administration and Waiver of Citation." The waiver has the same caption as the petition. It reads:

I, ..., do hereby renounce all rights to letters of administration on the estate of the said deceased and hereby waive the issuance of a citation in the above-entitled proceeding.

The *I* may be changed to *We* and several distributees may sign the same waiver. It is acknowledged in the presence of a notary. The renunciation makes it unnecessary to serve a citation on those who renounced.

Citations. All interested parties must be notified of the application for letters. The method of notifying them varies. In New York State, parties who have a prior or an equal right with the petitioner to letters of administration are made parties to the proceeding by the service of a *citation,* except those who waive citation by renunciation of their right to letters of administration. The writ is signed by the clerk of the probate court (surrogate's court in New York), but is prepared by the attorney for the petitioner. It cites the person or persons upon whom it is served to appear before the court on a certain date and show cause why the letters of administration should not be granted to the petitioner. The person cited does not have to appear in court or reply in any way unless he opposes the appointment of the petitioner. Service is had in the same manner as service of citation in a proceeding to prove a will (see page 523). Printed forms of citations are available. They are similar to, but not the same as, the form used in a proceeding to prove a will.

1. The citation does not have a caption.

2. Address the citation to those distributees who have a right prior or equal to that of the petitioner to letters of administration. You can get the names and addresses of those to whom the citation is to be addressed from the petition. In the illustrated petition (Figure 117), the right of Elizabeth R. Brown, the widow, to letters is prior to her son's right; she, therefore, must be served with a citation. The other children, Mary Brown and Nancy B. Smith, have an equal right with their brother John to letters; therefore, they must be served. However, Mary Brown has renounced her right (see above) and so it is not necessary to serve her. The minor grandchildren are not entitled to letters. Even if the grandchildren were over twenty-one, it would not be necessary to serve them with a citation because grandchildren of a deceased do not have an equal right with children of the deceased to letters of administration.

3. Make an original for the court, a copy for each person to whom the citation is addressed, and an office copy. Thus, in the illustrated case, four copies are necessary—the original for the court, a copy for Elizabeth R. Brown, a copy for Nancy B. Smith, and an office copy.

4. The return date of the citation may be any date within the time allowed by the court rules. In some jurisdictions the date is set by the clerk of the court when the petition is filed.

5. Get the court clerk to sign the original.

6. Conform the copies and serve.

7. Make affidavit of service.

8. *Enter return date in diary.*

9. Make entry in suit register, and follow the court calendar just as in a contested action.

Notice of application for letters of administration. In New York State distributees who do not have a right to letters of administration equal to that of the petitioner are not served with a citation but are notified of the application. Printed forms are available.

1. Make an original for the court, a copy for each distributee entitled to the notice, and an office copy. In the illustrated case (Figure 117), four copies are necessary—the original for the court, a copy for Robert Jones, a copy for Irene Jones, and an office copy. All other distributees have a right to letters of administration equal to that of the petitioner and were served with citations (except Mary Brown who renounced citation).

2. The notice of application may be dated at any time subsequent to the filing of the petition, before the issuance of the letters.

3. Have the petitioner sign the notice.

4. Mail copies of the notice to each distributee entitled to it at the address given in the petition.

5. Make affidavit that notice was mailed.

6. Conform office copy and file original in court.

7. Enter in suit register.

Letters of administration. If there is no opposition to the appointment of the petitioner as administrator, the court enters a decree directing that letters of administration issue to the petitioner. The letters of administration serve the same purpose for the administrator as letters testamentary do for the executor. The attorney for the petitioner prepares the decree and the letters in the same manner as when a will is admitted to probate and letters testamentary are granted (see page 530).

As soon as letters of administration are granted, notice to creditors must be published. See notice to creditors after letters testamentary are granted, on page 530. Be sure and make appropriate *diary entries* and suit register entries.

24

Handling Commercial Collections

C OMMERCIAL items, that is, past due accounts, that the lawyer undertakes to collect for others are referred to in his office as *collections*. Collections may be turned over to the lawyer by local clients, or they may be forwarded to him from another town by a collection agency or by another lawyer. Unless suit is filed, collections are handled on a contingent fee basis, usually at standard Commercial Law League rates. Although some commercial items involve large amounts, the majority of them are for small sums, with a correspondingly small fee. It is, therefore, desirable in the case of small items to curtail the usual office procedure as much as is consistent with efficiency. Collections are usually segregated from the other cases and are handled in a special manner. The procedure is routine and, after it has been established, the secretary can assume responsibility for the entire operation of the collection department.

Commercial law lists. Lawyers who wish to handle the collection of commercial items obtain representation on one or more bonded commercial law lists. It is from these lists that out-of-town lawyers select an attorney in the debtor's locality to handle the claim. It is from these lists that the lawyers in your office will select attorneys to whom to forward accounts against debtors in another jurisdiction.

Usually the forwarder of an item will mention the law list from which the lawyer's name was obtained. Some lists produce better results than others. You, therefore, should keep a record of the items the lawyer receives through each list and the fees he earns by reason of his representation on that list. The lawyer can then determine whether continued representation on a special list is warranted. A simple record is sufficient. Keep a separate sheet for each law list and show on it the forwarder, the item (creditor, debtor, and amount), and, when the matter is closed, the amount of the fee. You might keep these sheets in a folder in the front of the file drawer in which the collection cases are filed.

Office procedures affecting collections. The office procedures affecting collections involve the following:

1. Files
2. Follow-up system
3. Acknowledgment of claim
4. Letters to debtor
5. Reports to forwarder
6. Records of collections
7. Remittances to forwarder
8. Forwarding collection items
9. Suit

How to file collection matters. As soon as a collection item is received, make a file folder for it. File the folders alphabetically under the debtor's name. The creditor-client is not given a number, nor is the case. In conformance with the policy of keeping office procedure at a minimum, file index cards are not made. If your office prefers that index cards should be made, use plain 3″ by 5″ cards and keep them separate from your other index cards. Show on the card the name of the creditor, the name of the debtor, and the name of the forwarder.

You will notice that the printed file folder illustrated in Figure 118 has a space for a file number. When the numbering system of filing is used for collections, cross-reference index cards are, of course, essential.

When suit is brought on a collection, the case is transferred to a legal folder and handled like any other litigated case. Since default judgment is obtained in the majority of collection cases, considerable clerical work can be saved by not transferring the file unless the suit is contested.

Follow-up system. A desirable method of following collections is to use a file folder that has the days of the month printed on the top edge of the folder. See Figure 118. The alphabet on the folder is ignored. Folders without any printed matter except the days of the month are also obtainable. A metal tab is placed on the date that the file should come up for action, and the folder is filed alphabetically under the name of the debtor. Thus, regardless of the follow-up date, the folder is always in its proper alphabetical position in the filing cabinet. Each morning you pull all folders that have the metal tab placed on the current date. After the necessary action is taken, the metal tab is moved to the date on which the file again should come up for action.

Another popular method of follow-up for collections is a follow-up file with the folders tabbed so that they can be located alphabetically. The folder illustrated in Figure 118 is also appropriate for this system; the dates on the top edge are ignored. Each file drawer, if more than one is necessary, is arranged as a follow-up file, with guides for the months and dates. Each drawer is operated as a separate follow-up file, in the same manner as the follow-up system described on page 45, Chapter 3. How can a folder be located if it is needed before the follow-up date? The letters of the alphabet printed near the top edge of the front leaf of the folder make this possible. A small gummed tab marked with the debtor's name is pasted on the back leaf of the folder, opposite the index letter printed near the top of the front leaf. Thus, the name *Jones* is on the folder opposite *J;* the name *Smith* is opposite *S,* and so on. It makes no difference under what date the folder is filed, the *J's* are always in one line in one position in the file, and so is each letter of the alphabet. By looking at the proper line, you can easily find the proper folder at any time. The folder can be returned to the correct follow-up date, because the last date in the space for follow-up dates, on the front of the folder, shows where it is to be filed. This system simplifies the task of pulling the folders each morning. because all folders to be brought up on a certain date are together. It also eliminates moving the metal tabs, which are sometimes difficult to move without tearing the folder.

Acknowledgment of claim. Simultaneously with the preparation of the folder, the claim should be acknowledged. Promptness in acknowledging the collection is very important, because the forwarder is naturally interested in knowing that the matter is receiving immediate attention. The acknowledgment might read:

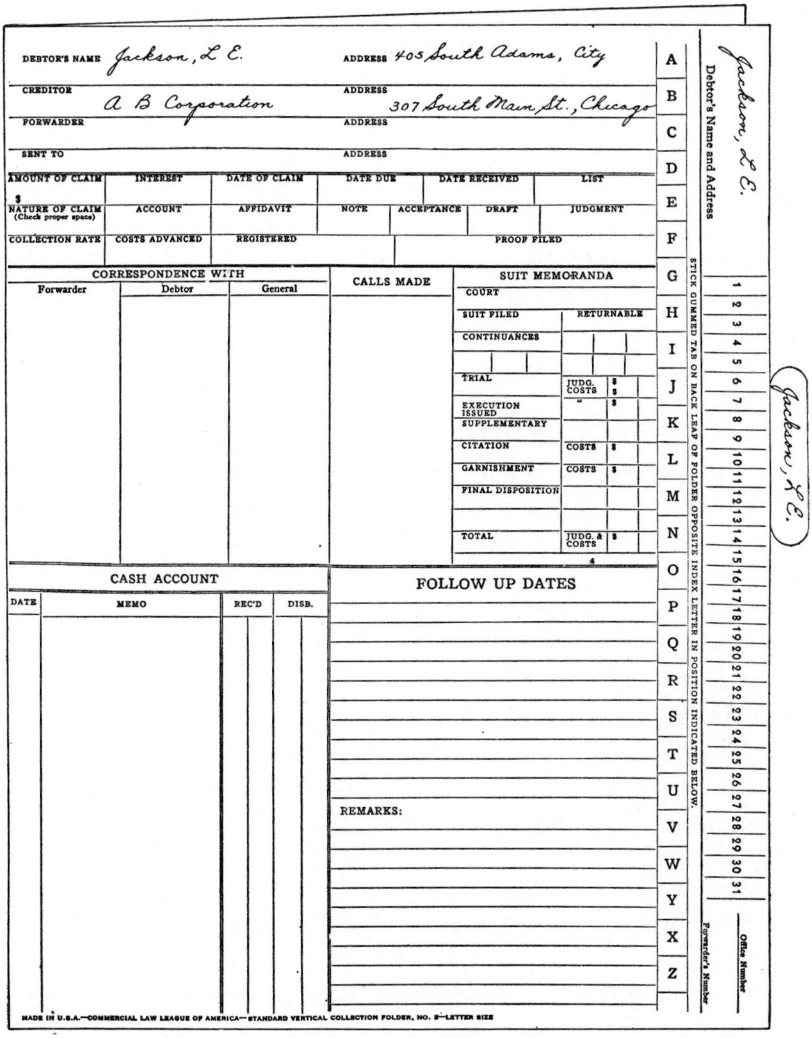

DEBTOR'S NAME Jackson, L. E. ADDRESS 405 South Adams, City

CREDITOR A B Corporation ADDRESS 307 South Main St., Chicago

FORWARDER ADDRESS

SENT TO ADDRESS

AMOUNT OF CLAIM	INTEREST	DATE OF CLAIM	DATE DUE	DATE RECEIVED	LIST
$					
NATURE OF CLAIM (Check proper space)	ACCOUNT	AFFIDAVIT	NOTE	ACCEPTANCE	DRAFT	JUDGMENT
COLLECTION RATE	COSTS ADVANCED	REGISTERED		PROOF FILED	

CORRESPONDENCE WITH: Forwarder | Debtor | General

CALLS MADE

SUIT MEMORANDA
COURT
SUIT FILED — RETURNABLE
CONTINUANCES
TRIAL — JUDG. COSTS $ $
EXECUTION ISSUED — " $
SUPPLEMENTARY
CITATION — COSTS $
GARNISHMENT — COSTS $
FINAL DISPOSITION
TOTAL — JUDG. & COSTS $

CASH ACCOUNT

DATE	MEMO	REC'D	DISB.

FOLLOW UP DATES

REMARKS:

A B C D E F G H I J K L M N O P Q R S T U V W Y X Z

STICK GUMMED TAB ON BACK LEAF OF FOLDER OPPOSITE INDEX LETTER IN POSITION INDICATED BELOW.

Debtor's Name and Address — Jackson, L. E.

1 2 3 4 5 6 7 8 9 10 11 12 13 14 15 16 17 18 19 20 21 22 23 24 25 26 27 28 29 30 31

Forwarder's Number — Office Number

Jackson, L. E.

MADE IN U.S.A.—COMMERCIAL LAW LEAGUE OF AMERICA—STANDARD VERTICAL COLLECTION FOLDER, NO. 5—LETTER SIZE

Figure 118. Collection Folder with Name Tab.

Dear Sir:

Re: Department Stores, Inc. v. J. C. Adams
Amount $345

We acknowledge receipt of the above styled claim and accept the claim for collection on the basis of the terms and regulations of the Commercial Law League of America.

You are recognized as the client's agency. We will report developments and make remittances to you.

Yours very truly,

Elwood & Adams

Collection letters. In a comparatively small community, the attorney frequently knows the debtor against whom he has a collection claim. His handling of the collection is often tempered by the personal relationship, but in normal cases he proceeds promptly and vigorously. You will probably be called upon to draft collection letters. If so, keep these premises in mind:

1. The purpose of the letter is to collect money; therefore, do not hesitate to ask for a check.

2. Do not take the attitude that the account "probably has been overlooked," because numerous demands for payment are made before the account is given to an attorney.

3. Use *dated action.* That is, tell the debtor that a certain action is expected by a given date, or within a given number of days, not in the "near future."

4. The *divided urge* is a serious fault in a collection letter. Suggest only one course of action—do not mention an alternative. For example, do not tell the debtor that you expect a check by a certain date and then suggest to him that he should telephone if payment is impossible.

5. The period between letters should be short—from 5 to 10 days.

A first letter to the debtor from the attorney on May 3 might read:

Dear Sir:

Department Stores, Inc. has retained us to collect your past due account in the amount of $345.

Since this account has been delinquent for six months, it is imperative that you give it your immediate attention. Please let us have your check in full by May 8.

Very truly yours,

After this letter is written, mark your file for follow-up for May 10. If the debtor does not reply by that date, you might send another letter that reads:

Dear Sir:

We have received no reply to our letter of May 3 concerning your past due account with Department Stores, Inc. in the amount of $345. We shall be compelled, therefore, to bring suit against you for the above amount, together with costs, disbursements, and interest, unless your check in full payment is received at this office by May 15.

Very truly yours,

Reports to the forwarder. The forwarder is interested in developments. As soon as contact is made with the debtor, write to the forwarder telling him what the prospects for collection are. It is helpful to the forwarder to send reports in duplicate, especially those in which the lawyer recommends suit or some special arrangement. The forwarder can then send a copy to the client, thus saving the time and trouble involved in copying the report.

Installment payments. Suit to collect a small sum is a last resort. It is expensive, and the judgment may be as difficult to collect as the debt. For this reason, attorneys will "play along" with a debtor and accept partial payments from him. Usually the arrangement is that the debtor shall pay a certain amount at regular intervals. As a matter of fact, an arrangement of this type is often made even after judgment is obtained against the debtor. It is your responsibility to bring up the file for attention on the dates that payments are due. If a payment is not made as promised, you should communicate with the debtor, either by telephone or mail. You will notice that the illustrated folder (Figure 118) has space for these data.

Record of collections. A payment on an account, whether in full or partial, is *noted on the file folder* as soon as it is received. The "Cash Account" on the printed folder illustrated in Figure 118 is for this purpose. If you use a plain folder, simply enter the date and the amount received. All entries should be made in ink. The payments are also entered in the journal and posted to the client's ledger account in the same manner as payments in any other kind of case. The amount of bookkeeping involved is one of the drawbacks to accepting partial payments.

When a collection is made, put it in the trust account (see Chapter 7). It is the client's money and should not be commingled with the firm's funds. The fee may be deposited to the firm account.

Remitting. As soon as any money is collected, remit promptly to the forwarder, after deducting the fee. This is a "must" in handling collections. If it is necessary to collect an account in installments, report the details to the forwarder and have an understanding as to when and how often an accumulation of small payments shall be remitted.

Fees. Suit fees are not contingent, but other collection fees are. The Commercial Law League of America recommends a sliding rate schedule, which is generally adhered to by lawyers who handle collections. The recommended schedule follows:

18% on the first $500
15% on the next $500
10% on the balance
50% on claims of $30 or less
$15 on claims of $30 to $83.33

You will have to calculate the lawyer's fee before remitting to the forwarder, because only the net is remitted. Thus, if you collect $35 on a claim, you will deduct, according to the above schedule, $15 for a fee and remit $20. The $15 fee is run through the books like any other fee (Chapter 7). The fee is calculated on the basis of the collections in each case, not on the total of collections for a certain client.

Forwarding an item for collection. The lawyer sometimes receives for collection a claim against a debtor in another locality. He then consults the law lists and selects the name of an attorney in the debtor's locality, to whom he sends the claim. You will make up a file for a claim that is forwarded, just as you do for claims that were forwarded to your office, and follow them in the same manner. Your letter forwarding the claim should give the name and address of the creditor, name and address of the debtor, amount of the claim, law list from which the attorney's name was selected, and the terms upon which the claim is forwarded. Your letter might read:

Dear Sir:

Client: Department Stores, Inc.
West Palm Beach, Florida
Debtor: John Jones
324 W. Fourth Street, Birmingham, Ala.
Amount: $284.36

We are forwarding to you for collection the above account. This claim is sent to you on the basis of two-thirds of our fee, which is the Commercial Law League rate.

Please acknowledge and keep us informed of developments. If for any reason you are not in a position to handle this account, we shall appreciate it if you will return it promptly. Please do not institute suit before informing us.

We obtained your name from the .... Law List.

Very truly yours,

The documentary evidence necessary to collect the account should be forwarded with your letter. The evidence depends upon whether the suit is upon open account or upon an instrument. In the case of suit upon open account, you should forward: (1) copies of the original written order for the merchandise, if any; (2) copies of the invoice; and (3) copies of the bills of lading. If the suit is upon an instrument, that is, upon a dishonored trade acceptance or promissory note, the necessary documents are: (1) the trade acceptance or note; (2) the bank's memorandum of nonpayment; and (3) copies of any notices of dishonor sent to the buyer and to accommodation endorsers, if any.

When your office forwards a collection to an attorney whose name is taken from a law list, check his name on the law list. If he handles the account satisfactorily, you will know to whom to forward the next claim that your office has against a debtor in that locality.

Uncontested Suit

When the lawyer recommends suit. Lawyers seldom write more than two collection letters. If the debtor does not make some arrangement for payment, the lawyer recommends suit or returns the claim to the forwarder. This decision, of course, is the lawyer's, not yours. Tell the forwarder the prospects of collection by suit. Also tell him what advanced court costs will be required and what papers will be needed. The defendant in a suit on a collection item rarely has a defense against the claim, and so he lets the suit go by default. It will save time if you get all papers that are needed in the ordinary course of a default judgment before suit is actually filed. These vary with the jurisdiction—the lawyer will tell you what papers are needed, or you can get the information from other collection files. The legal procedure is not complicated, and you should be able to draw the necessary court papers without detailed instructions from the lawyer.

Summons and complaint. A short-form complaint is usually permissible. A brief statement of the indebtedness is alleged instead of a statement of the specific facts required by code pleading (Chapter 13). The statement may be typed on the back of the printed form of summons. The causes of action, or counts, generally alleged in suits on collection items are for:

1. Goods sold and delivered
2. Account stated
3. Open book account
4. Account for services

Preparation and service of summons and short-form complaint. Use a printed form of summons and type the complaint in the space provided on the back for that purpose. When inserting the forms in the typewriter for endorsement of the back, be careful to endorse the original as the ribbon copy.

The service, affidavit of service, and filing of a short-form complaint in a collection suit is the same as in any other action (see Chapter 13). If it is the practice in your office to make a litigation file of all collection suits in which summons is served, *enter return date of summons in diary* and open a suit register sheet for the case. If your practice is not to transfer uncontested cases, *mark the file for follow-up on the return date of the summons*. Remember that the period of time to answer begins the date the summons is served, not the date it is prepared.

Keep in close touch with your process server and immediately recall the summons from him if the account is paid before service of the summons. If by any chance the summons is served on the defendant after he has paid the account, the summons and affidavit of service should not be filed in court. The lawyer will depend upon you to keep track of these matters, and if your records are not accurate and up to date, he has no way of knowing the status of an account or an action.

Checklist of information needed to draw summons and complaint in suit on a collection item. 1. *The court in which to bring the action.* This will depend on the amount of the claim and the jurisdiction of the local courts. Usually suit on a collection item may be brought in a municipal court or a justice of the peace court.

2. *The court district,* if the city is divided into districts with a municipal court in each.

3. *The amount of the debt.* A collection item is for a *liquidated amount*—that is, the amount is certain as distinguished from an indefinite amount to be determined by the court or jury, as in the case of an action for damages in an accident case. The file shows the amount of the debt.

4. *The rate of interest and the date from which it is to be charged.* The rate is the legal rate of interest in the state in which the debt was contracted, unless a lower rate had been contracted for. Interest runs from the date the debt became due.

5. *The wording of the complaint.* The wording varies with the jurisdiction and with the cause of action, but the counts are short and you will become familiar with the wording in your state very quickly. Examine the files on similar cases for the wording. You will notice that in an action on an account for merchandise, which is the most common action, the legal phraseology is "goods, wares, and merchandise," whether the merchandise is hardware, groceries, drugs or wearing apparel. Whenever you type a count for a new cause of action, make an extra copy for your loose-leaf notebook.

Judgment by default. If the defendant decides to contest the suit, a copy of his answer will probably be delivered to your office. However, in municipal court, the defendant may go to the court and make his answer orally, at any time before court closes on the return day of the summons. Therefore, you will not know until the day after the return day whether the defendant has answered or has defaulted. The day after return day, ask a law clerk to go to the court and find out if the defendant appeared. Or you can get the information yourself, by going to the court and looking at the papers in the court file under the index number of the case. If the defendant has not answered, prepare a *judgment by default.*

How to prepare a judgment by default. A printed form is generally available. You can get the necessary information from your file.

1. Make an original and two copies.

2. Calculate the interest at the legal rate, from the date indicated in the summons.

3. Itemize the cost disbursed by your office and include the total in the amount of the judgment.

4. Get the clerk of the court to sign the original and file it in court.

5. Conform the two copies.

6. Fill in the notice of entry of judgment in the space provided on the back of the judgment.

7. Mail one copy to the defendant. The other copy is for your office file.

After judgment by default is entered, the plaintiff is known as a *judgment creditor* and the defendant as a *judgment debtor.* If the judgment debtor does not pay the judgment, the attorney for the judgment creditor may ask the clerk of the court to issue execution. Should the execution be returned unsatisfied, the attorney will commence supplementary proceedings, if he believes the judgment debtor has any assets out of which the judgment may be collected.

Part V

Reference Material

---

25. The Law Library and How to Use It 553
26. Latin Words and Phrases 569
27. Law Terms and Miscellaneous Procedures Explained . . 577

25

The Law Library and How to Use It

WITHOUT law books, the lawyer could not function. Before he draws an agreement, brings a court action, undertakes to defend a law suit, advises a client—before he makes a move of any kind—he "looks up the law." The books that enable him to do his job efficiently are:

1. Statutes and codes
2. Reports of decided cases
3. Books that classify the law
4. Form books

Statutes and Codes

Compilations of laws. The laws enacted by the Congress of the United States and the various state legislatures are systematically sorted and arranged in chapters and subheads to facilitate their use. The compilations, known as statutes and codes usually contain, also, the Constitution of the United States and of the particular state. See Chapter 16, page 359, for a list of compilations.

Every lawyer has the compilation of his own state; law firms that practice in several states have the compilations for those states; nearly all lawyers have the United States Code; law association libraries and law college libraries usually have the compilations of every state.

The majority of the compilations are kept up to date by pocket parts and supplements, but in some states the session laws for all years after the date of the compilation must be used in con-

junction with the compilation. Florida and Wisconsin publish a
new compilation after every session of the legislature.

How to find a law. You should familiarize yourself with the
plan of arrangement of the compilation for your state. You will
find that the preface contains explanatory and useful material.
All of the compilations contain a general index, and some of
them also have an index in each volume. The indexes vary in
their completeness and usefulness, but with a little perseverance
you will be able to find the desired section of the law. After you
search the compilation, search the supplements and pocket parts,
if any, and all session laws since the date of the compilation
or since the date of the latest supplement. The section of the law
in which you are interested might have been amended or repealed
since the compilation, or a new law on the subject might have
been enacted.

When a law suit involves a statute, the court's judicial inter-
pretation and construction of that statute becomes as much a part
of the law as the statute itself. You will notice that the notes
in annotated compilations (see Figure 119) include references to
the published opinions that relate to the statutes. If the compilation is not annotated, you will have to look elsewhere (see "Books
that classify the law," below), to locate the judicial interpreta-
tions of the statutes.

Reports of Decided Cases

Scope and organization of reports. When a point of law has
once been settled by a judicial decision, it forms a precedent for
the guidance of the courts in similar cases. The decisions are
published in order that they may be readily accessible to the
lawyers and the courts. Every practicing attorney must have
access to the published reports of decisions in his own state,
either in the official state reports or the appropriate reporter of
the National Reporter System. See "Official reports and the
National Reporter System," Chapter 16, page 354, *et seq.*

Preceding the opinion in a case is a brief statement of each
point of law determined by the case. These statements are known
as the *syllabus,* or the *headnotes.* In the reporters, the headnotes
are numbered, and the part of the opinion that covers a particular
headnote is numbered to correspond with the headnote number.

64-2826 [14384]. Power of state board to make and enforce rules.— Whenever by the provisions of this act, any power is granted to or duty enjoined upon any board, officer or person, and there is no provision for the method or manner of executing such power or performance of such duty, the state board of tax commissioners may make and enforce all rules and regulations in relation thereto which may be necessary fully to carry out the purposes of this act. [Acts 1919, ch. 59, § 336, p. 198.]

In General.

The statutory authority given the state board of tax commissioners to make rules and regulations to carry out the purposes for which it was constituted gives such board no authority to enact a law or add to or deduct from the law as enacted, nor may it by rule extend its powers beyond those conferred upon it by law. McCreery v. Ijams, 115 App. 631, 59 N. E. (2d) 133.

Under the law as it existed prior to the 1943 amendment, prescribing the time when county boards of review should convene and the period of time during which they could legally function, the state board of tax commissioners had no authority to enlarge such period by rule or otherwise. McCreery v. Ijams, 115 App. 631, 59 N. E. (2d) 133.

The 1943 amendment of §§ 64-1201 and 64-1205 which permits the state board of tax commissioners to require sessions of the county boards of review and to fix the time for the duration of such sessions could not affect the validity of reassessment and revaluation of lands made by a county board of review at a reconvened session in 1939, which session had been held after the expiration of the time then limited by the statute in force at the date thereof. McCreery v. Ijams, 115 App. 631, 59 N. E. (2d) 133.

Where a county board of review which had convened in 1939 recessed by order of the state board of tax commissioners after it had been in session for 28 days and reconvened several months later to review the 1939 assessment of certain mineral lands, the reassessment and revaluation so made by the board after the time limited by §§ 64-1201, 64-1205, prior to the 1943 amendment, for the duration of the term of its session were void, and the amendment by the state board of tax commissioners of its rules so as to authorize it to recess and convene county boards of review did not validate the void action of such board. McCreery v. Ijams, 115 App. 631, 59 N. E. (2d) 133.

From Burns Indiana Statutes, Annotated. *Courtesy The Bobbs-Merrill Company, Inc.*

Figure 119. Excerpt from Annotated Compilation.

Thus, if you are interested only in a statement made in headnote 3, you turn to the "[3]" in the opinion.

Each series of reports or reporters is numbered consecutively. Additional volumes of the reporters in the National Reporter System are published about every three months; volumes of the official state reports, less often. In arranging the books on the library shelf, leave an empty shelf, or part of a shelf, after the last volume of a series so that you will not have to shift the books when additional volumes are received. Keep the advance sheets (see page 357) in consecutive order after the last volume of the series. When a new bound volume is received, destroy the advance sheets that are covered by it.

How to use the reports and reporters. Finding a case in a report or reporter when you have the volume and page number needs no explanation. Just be careful not to confuse the second series of a reporter with the first series. If the lawyer tells you that a case is in "76 Northeastern," he does not mean "76 North-eastern Second." Each report and reporter has a list of the cases cited in it with the cases arranged alphabetically under the name of plaintiff and defendant. For example, *Abbot v. Bralov* is also listed *Bralov; Abbot v.* Since a reporter covers more than one state, it contains a general table of all the cases reported, followed by a separate table for each state. Thus, if you know the volume and the name of either party to a case, you can easily find the page number where the opinion begins.

In the back of each reporter there is a digest of the cases reported in that volume, arranged according to subject. The lawyer might know the substance of a decision and the approximate time it was decided, but be unable to recall the name of the case. You can refer to the volume or volumes covering the approximate time of the decision and, under the appropriate subject in the digest, you will be able to locate the desired case. This might involve searching several volumes and is not a desirable method of research, but is sometimes necessary.

You can find the names of the justices of the appellate courts in the front of the reports and reporters.

The name and location of the attorneys in a case are given immediately following the syllabus, preceding the opinion.

Purpose of the blue book and the blue and white book. The lawyer may have a citation to a case in the state report, but need the citation in the unofficial reporter. You can find the reporter citation for him by reference to the appropriate blue book. There are one or more blue books for each reporter. In some cases a blue book covers more than one state report. For example, one volume of the Atlantic Blue Book covers Rhode Island, Connecticut, and Pennsylvania reports, whereas one entire volume of the Northeastern Blue Book is devoted to the Massachusetts reports.

Each blue book contains blank pages. From time to time supplemental lists of reported cases are sent to the subscriber. When you receive the supplemental reports paste them in the back of the appropriate blue book beginning at the first blank page.

The blue and white books are designed for use in a particular state. The blue pages show citations in the reporter when the parallel citation in the state report is known; the white pages show the state report citation when the reporter citation is known.

How to use the blue book. Suppose that the citation to the case of *Fowler v. Gillman* is 76 Utah 414. You need the reporter citation. Utah cases are reported in the Pacific Reporter (see Table X, in Chapter 16). From the backbones of the Pacific blue books, you see that Part 4 contains the Utah reports. The volume number of the state report appears at the top of each page, and these are pasted in the blue book in numerical sequence. Turn to the page headed, "Vol. 76 Utah Reports." The cases are listed alphabetically; the reporter citation appears in parentheses immediately following the title of the case; the page number of the state report is at the right of the column. Thus, you will find:

Fowler v. Gillman (290 P. 358) 414

On some pages of the blue book, you will find triple columns of numbers. The left column lists in numerical sequence the state report page numbers at which cases begin. The middle column lists the volume of the reporter in which the case is reported, and the right column lists the page number of the reporter. Thus, you will find:

Utah Rep.	Pac. Rep.	
Pg.	Vol.	Pg.
414	290	358

From this you can tell that *Fowler v. Gillman,* which is reported at page 414 of 76 Utah Reports, is also reported in Vol. 290 of the Pacific Reporter, on page 358.

The old pages of the blue books do not list the cases alphabetically; some pages list the cases alphabetically and also show a table of numbers; the latest pages do not have the numbers.

How to use the blue and white book. The blue pages in the blue and white book are similar to the blue book. The white pages are just the reverse—that is, the reporter volume appears at the top of the page; the reporter pages are in the left column, and the corresponding state report volume and number are in the middle and right columns respectively.

Other publications of decisions. In addition to state reports and the National Reporter System, there are several other types of publications of decisions.

Selected cases series, annotated. Selected cases series limit the cases reported to (1) decisions that deal with questions upon which there is a conflict of law; (2) decisions that deal with novel questions; and (3) decisions that are outstanding by reason of their treatment of the question involved and their review of the authorities. The decisions are reported in full, with headnotes, and are fully annotated. They thus may be used not only as a report of the decision, but as a guide to other cases in point and as a source of original research.

American Law Reports is the only current selected series of American cases. The series is the merger of, or successor to, all previous selective cases series. The following diagram shows the development that resulted in the current series. The diagram gives the abbreviations by which the publications are cited. The full titles, in the sequence in which they appear in the diagram, are:

Lawyers' Reports Annotated
Lawyers' Reports Annotated, New Series
Lawyers' Reports Annotated, Third Unit
American Decisions
American Reports
American State Reports
American and English Annotated Cases
American Annotated Cases
American Law Reports

L.R.A.—>L.R.A. (N.S.)—>L.R.A. (3rd Unit)

Am.Dec.—>Am.Rep.—>Am.State Rep.

Am. & Eng.Ann.Cas.   Ann.Cas.   A.L.R.

The volumes are identified by year of publication and by letter, thus, 1916A, 1916B, etc.

Subject reports. Some reports publish only those decisions that relate to a particular subject or topic of law. Among the series of subject reports are the American Federal Tax Report (A.F.T.R.) and American Labor Cases (A.L.C.).

Books That Classify the Law

The books that classify the law enable the lawyer to pick from among the millions of cases those that are in point with the legal problem that confronts him. These books, because of their nature, are sometimes called *books of index.* They include digests, encyclopedias, texts, loose-leaf services, citators, and tables of cases. The lawyer uses them initially to give him a lead, and also to direct him to other cases in point. Among the books of index most commonly used are the *American Digest, Corpus Juris* and *Corpus Juris Secundum, Shepard's Citations,* and loose-leaf services such as *Prentice-Hall Federal Tax Service.* Knowledge of how to use these books will enable you to use other books of index.

American Digest

Organization of American Digest system. The *American Digest,* which goes back to 1658, is tied in with the National Reporter System. It is broken down as follows:

Century Digest	1658-1896	50 Vols.
First Decennial Digest	1897-1906	19 Vols.
Second Decennial Digest	1907-1916	24 Vols.
Third Decennial Digest	1916-1926	29 Vols.
Fourth Decennial Digest	1926-1936	34 Vols.
Fifth Decennial Digest	1936-1946	49 Vols.
General Digest, Second Series	1946 to date	

The bound volumes of the General Digest, cumulated about every four months, are followed by monthly pamphlets and by the weekly advance sheets of the reporters (page 357). The Decennials, as their names imply, are cumulated every 10 years and supersede the General Digest for that period.

The digest covers approximately 500 main topics, arranged alphabetically. The Century and Decennials are broken down alphabetically, each volume containing certain main topics. Thus, Volume 19 of the Fourth Decennial Digest, "Judgment to Kidnapping," contains a reference to each case published from 1926 to 1936 on the topics of Judgment, Judicial Sales, Jury, Justices of the Peace, and Kidnapping. Each volume of the General Digest Series contains a reference to all the cases on every topic published during the period of time covered by that particular volume. Thus, each volume of the General Digest, Second Series, contains the topic *Judgment.*

A detailed fact index constitutes part of the American Digest System. The index is contained in several volumes, with a binding differing from that on the digests, entitled "Descriptive Word Index." The descriptive words are listed in black type in alphabetical order. Different situations involving the fact element are listed in lighter type and refer to the place in the digest where cases in point may be found. The reference is by means of topic and key number.

An analysis precedes each main topic. The digests of cases are grouped according to the point of law involved, and each point is given a key number. The key numbers in the First Decennial are preceded by the section symbol (§) instead of the key symbol, but the numbers correspond. The Century section numbers do not correspond to the key numbers but may be translated into key numbers (see below).

How to use the digest system. Suppose that you are interested in the priority over other claims of an allowance by the executor to a widow.

1. The first step in finding the authorities through the digest system is to get the key number. There are three methods of getting the key number:

> (a) If you already have at least one case in point, from the key numbers in the headnotes in the reporters, which correspond to the key numbers in the digests
>
> (b) From the Descriptive Word Index
>
> (c) From the analysis that precedes each topic

2. You may start your search with any of the Decennials or with the General Digest, and then work forward and backward. You will find all of the cases involving the suggested question digested under the topic Executors and Administrators, Key 182. The backbones of the volume will indicate in which volumes of the Decennials you will find the topic Executors and Administrators.

3. The topic is in every volume of the General Digest, First and

Second Series, but there probably is not a case in point in all volumes. To avoid unnecessary research, use the cumulative tables of key numbers, which are paper pamphlets published in conjunction with the General Digest. These pamphlets list the topics in alphabetical order and list the key numbers under each topic. On a line with each key number are the numbers of the volumes of the General Digest in which reference is made to cases having that key number. Thus, in the table of key numbers to General Digest, Second Series, Volumes 11-16, under the topic Executors and Administrators, you will find:

Key
182—12, 13, 15

Thus, you know that volumes 12, 13, and 15 refer to cases in point. You need not look in the other volumes of the General Digest, Second Series.

4. Continue your search for the key number through the monthly digests that are in pamphlet form, and through the digests in the reporter advance sheets published subsequent to the latest monthly digest.

5. Then search in the Century for cases decided prior to 1897. The Second Decennial refers you to the volume, topic, and section number in the Century, if there is a case in point referred to in the Century. Thus, when you search the Second Decennial under Executors and Administrators, Key 182, you will find: See 22 Cent. Dig. Ex. & Ad. §§ 651, 686-693. If there is no reference, there are no cases in point digested in Century.

6. Possibly you began your search with a reference in Century. You found that cases in point were digested at § 686 of the topic Executors and Administrators. To get subsequent authorities, you translate the section number to the key number of the Digest. In the front of Volume 21 of the First Decennial, there is a parallel table on pink sheets. The table gives under each topic, the section number in the Century and the corresponding key number in the Decennial.

Table of cases. If you know the name of a case, you can find where it is reported from the tables of cases. The last five volumes of the First Decennial (Volumes 21-25) cover the cases digested

in the Century and in the First Decennial. The last volumes of
the Second, of the Third, and of the Fourth Decennials are tables
of cases. The back of each volume of the General Digest contains
a table of cases. Since each unit of the *American Digest* covers a
period of time (page 559), your search is narrowed if you know
the decade in which the case was decided.

Shepard's Citations

Purpose of Shepard's Citations. To prove his point, the lawyer
cites a decision contained in a published opinion. Before citing
the case he wants to know something of its history and subsequent
treatment. He is interested in knowing whether the case has been
appealed to a higher court, whether it was affirmed or reversed;
whether it has been followed in many other cases; and whether
it has been overruled in a subsequent case. *Shepard's Citations* is
designed to give the lawyer this information. It is quite easy to
"shepardize" a case, and you will probably be asked to assist the
lawyer with this research. A lawyer never cites a case as authority
without first shepardizing it.

Abbreviations used. The following abbreviations are used by
Shepard for the purpose of indicating the "Judicial History of
Case."

History of Case

a	(affirmed)	Same case affirmed on appeal.
cc	(connected case)	Different case from case cited but arising out of same subject matter or intimately connected therewith.
D	(dismissed)	Appeal from same case dismissed.
m	(modified)	Same case modified on appeal.
r	(reversed)	Same case reversed on appeal.
s	(same case)	Same case as case cited.
S	(superseded)	Substitution for former opinion.

Treatment of Case

c	(criticised)	Soundness of decision or reasoning in cited case criticised for reasons given.
d	(distinguished)	Case at bar different either in law or fact from case cited, for reasons given.
e	(explained)	Statement of import of decision in cited case. Not merely a restatement of the facts.
f	(followed)	Cited as controlling.

h	(harmonized)	Apparent inconsistency explained and shown not to exist.
j	(dissenting opinion)	Citation in dissenting opinion.
L	(limited)	Refusal to extend decision of cited case beyond precise issues involved.
o	(overruled)	Ruling in cited case expressly overruled.
p	(parallel)	Citing case substantially alike or on all fours with cited case in its law and facts.
q	(questioned)	Soundness of decision or reasoning in cited case questioned.

How to use Shepard's Citations. An explanation of how to use the Shepard's Federal Reporter Citations will enable you to use the other Shepard's Citations. Figure 120 illustrates a page from the Federal Reporter Citations.

Illustrative Case

(Acknowledgment is made to Shepard's Citations, Inc., for this explanation.)

Let us assume that by reference to a digest, encyclopedia, textbook or other unit of legal research, you have located the case of *Hanover Star Milling Co.* v. *Allen & Wheeler Co.*, reported in Volume 208 of the Federal Reporter on page 513, dealing among other things with the property right which a complainant has in a trademark.

Figure 120 on the following page is a reproduction of page 1175 from the 1938 edition of Shepard's Federal Reporter Citations. Note the volume of reports to which the citations apply, "Vol. 208", in the upper right-hand corner of the page.

An examination of the heavy face type numbers within the page locates the page number "—513—" in the seventh column of citations. This is the initial page of the case under consideration. Following this page number you will find the citation "sLRA1916D 136" indicating that the same case "s" is also reported in 1916D Lawyers Reports Annotated 136.

In obtaining the history of this case you will observe that upon appeal to the United States Supreme Court, it was affirmed "a" in 240 United States Reports "US" 403, 60 Lawyers Edition of United States "LE" 713, 36 Supreme Court Reporter "SC" 357,

FEDERAL REPORTER   Vol. 208

164NW 920	s232F 318	53F2d 135	1720kl 15	243F 1630	87NJE547	s247F 421	26F2d 8
12ÆR 1382n	219F ²167	19ABn 139	43P2d1050	244F 1194	100At 608	217SW 425	12ABn237
12ÆR 1388n					**—513—**		26F2d²192

Same case reported in Lawyers Reports Annotated

f222F 145					f1048n	sIRA1916D	33F2d²666
243F 124			**—409—**	11F2d¹336	1049n	a240US 403	'30MC²283
269F 1505	**—360—**				8ÆR21546n	a 60LE 713	L 54F2d

Affirmed by United States Supreme Court

a220F 626	269				ÆR 1343n	a '16CD 265	IRA1915A
cc115F 886	271F 2327	26ABn2759	64F2d1535	39F2d1201	90AÆ51113n	f215F 1495	51ÆR 2786n

Followed to paragraph one of the syllabus

cc160F 504					**—469—**	e226F 5551	cc224F 248
cc162F 479	75LE1306	9FS 211	**—410—**	D213F 1022	232F 3682	cc34AB 697
cc168F 923	51SC 572	27ABn2124	Case 2	246F 2249	h234F 4470	cc235F 807
s 168F 927	**—373—**	264US 1437	s257US 657	15FS 376	247F 1409	cc38AB 99
245F 1869	243F 3979	68LE 1776	s 66LE 420	30PQ 115	s196F 419	**—544—**
—289—	39AB 3839	44SC 1400	s 42SC 184	119CaA 769	239F 1421	s183F 894

Citations in parallel sets of reports grouped

s210F 164					'27F 2327	52ADC¹371	**—546—**
—291—					q235F 2908	'23CD 1308	cc213US 276
s 29AB 772	48AB 3467	58SC 2271	s259US 579	**—779n**	q 37AB 2605	22F2d 278	cc 53LE 796
272F 1526	295F 3862	17ABn²275	s 66LE1072	AC'15A 48n		59F2d 115	cc 29SC 426
46AB 168	1ABn 392	229Ky 11	s 42SC 585	AC'15A 49n	**—482—**	13PQ 1298	s220US 616
289US 1170	6F2d¹102	16SW 766	s259US 579	28AÆ21385n	211F 1532	77F2d 562	s 55LE 611
77LE¹1104	6ABn¹101	14ABn738	s 66LE1073	28AÆ31388n	243F 170	25PQ 449	s 31SC 720
53SC 1553	15F2d³703	91Mt 70	s 42SC 587	**—424—**	261F 1971	1FS 1585	cc230US 84
22ABn1594	9ABn³207	5P2d 556	s261US 399	217F 1632	**—486—**	15PQ 1199	cc 57LE1400
—293—	e 45F2d1808	52SD 323	s 67LE 719	233F 1926	cc256US 698	6FS 1879	cc 33SC 997
s206F 116	17ABn1363	217NW 392	s 43SC 458	243F 1249	cc 65LE1177	22PQ¹163	s230US 98

Cited in Illinois Appellate Court Reports prior to their inclusion in National Reporter System

s 30AB 48					41SC 537	226IIA 274	s 57LE1409
—295—					72F 678	229IIA 559	s 33SC 1003
a225F 102					47AB 72	159Msc 558	s186F 705
220F 2527	6ABn593	19ABn615	cc291F 1016	'24MC 234	292F 2128	288NYS536	**—548—**
234F 243					2ABn 245	126Tex 163	s234US 716

Cited in units of the National Reporter System and cases to correspond in the State Reports

22F2d 1					5F2d¹187	86SW 723	s 58LE1579
27F2d 16					6ABn1247	182Wis 344	s 34SC 675
4BTA1038	**—378—**	s 31AB 344	26F2d1685	6FS 2304	61F2d1109	193NW 374	f 36F2d1746

Cited in case in National Reporter System not reported in State Reports

62Ut 33					4ABn1176	266SW 553	f 15ABn 197
218P 97					FS 1894	**—549—**	
88Vt 41					4ABn 121	36AÆ 2922n	70F2d 58
92At 637	**—381—**	s 35SC 201	5PQ1392	228F 7226	268US 11	36AÆ 4922n	21PQ 242
65AÆ 310n	r2				39LE 1874		

Cited in notes of Annotated Reports System

—319—	A				SC 1459	**—524—**	**—564—**
a247US 1					5ABn1745	212F 2631	s193F 69
a 62LE 939	71AÆ 2806n	229F 2135	17PQ¹267	12F2d6690	40AB 691	60Col 91	s201F 926
a 38SC 422	71AÆ 2816n	36AB 2129	9FS 1519	37F2d6519		151P 936	cc201F 930
a222F 669	**—383—**	d 21F2d1754	24PQ1243	'30MC 6975	**—488—**	65Col 135	276F 678
cc206F 562	51Lns525n	31F2d²319	29AÆ 4921n	AC'14B	e208F 1492	173P 944	20F2d 262
280US 416	AC'16A 82n	13ABn²595	29AÆ 4990n	1200n	e 30AB 1698	AC'18C634n	**—566—**
74LE 4137	AC'16A 85n	32Ida 550	**—416—**	**—441—**	215F 2703	AC'18C657n	cc242US 350
50SC 48	7AÆ 1463n	186P 914	215F 4379	IRA1918B	32AB 2455	15AÆ21392n	cc 61LE 356
263Mo 42	**—385—**	44AB 623	271F 2447	772n	221F 2732	15AÆ21398n	cc 37SC 169
172SW 905	116CaA398	236Ky 91	14F2d4967	26AÆ 4176n	34AB 2789	**—530—**	cc'17CD 388
324Mo 76	2P2d 847	32SW 719	16F2d4811	**—455—**	h252F 24	212F 1927	cc227F 93
22SW 792	88Or 316	222Mch 442	48F2d³269	a211F 288	h 41AB 2780	238F 1861	d210F 1355
289Pa 145	171P 589	192NW 665	50F2d1207	**—461—**	200Ia 58	239F 1784	212F 1452
137At 181	**—393—**	49AB 686	10FS 1881	1F2d6584	202NW 558	241F 1416	e214F 1844
AC'18D	s191F 633	21ABn504	22PQ1216	27F2d1453	82ABn1003	291F 1422	215F 1379
1060n	s208F 399	IRA1917C	260US 2165	36F2d1602	214Ia 263	q296F 2176	e217F 194
50AÆ 5121n	s 31AB 348	29n	67LE 2188	f 44F2d1118	242NW 75	13F2d1542	235F 1900
—335—	h216F 1846	**—403—**	43SC 250	50F2d2850	21ABn101	17F2d1613	f243F 1407
230F 2132	h 32AB1757	s207F 809	193Cal 113	50F2d1851	**—497—**	21F2d1446	243F 1630
227IIA 212	229F 1647	cc213F 990	222P 813	50F2d4852	231Ala 426	28F2d1290	244F 1194
110A 15	36AB1227	7F2d1594	119NJE337	249US 1382	165So 396	279US 122	c279F 1760
AC'15D	275F 1814	59F2d1380	33At 886	63LE 1658	AC'16B984n	73LE 1585	11F2d1536
1054n	4ABn 110	73F2d1172	4PQ 26	39SC 1339	AC'16B999n	49SC 1220	93Fla 917
—347—	284F 3768	e 78F2d1469	**—419—**	289US 112	**—503—**	'29MC1333	112So 840
a217F 344	49AB3478	8FS 1814	Case 1	77LE 1998	s241US 668	102Msc 448	103Fla 110
s197F 1017	9F2d1490	9FS 1232	s227F 998	53SC 1468	s 60LE1229	169NYS261	137So 131
—353—	7ABn185	118PaS 254	s '15CD 43	247Ap 63	s 36SC 552	'28MC 147	**—571—**
a223F 756	40F2d 323	180At 181	208F 1418	286NYS761	cc264US 552	AC'15C787n	208F 1576
217F 3338	41F2d1250	**—406—**	215F 1379	272Mas 32	cc 68LE 845	AC'17C 49n	31AB1433
—359—	50F2d2422	cc177F 419	217F 194	226Mch 17	cc173F 1022	**—534—**	88Col 452
s208F 361	18ABn²299	cc193F 649	235F 1899	196NW 761	s 222F 67	246F 2435	297P 994
Continued	*Continued*	*Continued*	*Continued*	*Continued*	*Continued*	247F 218	AC'16A 946n
						Continued	*Continued*

For later Citations see (1938-1953) Bound Supplement, current issue of 1175
Cumulative Supplement and intervening Advance Sheet

Courtesy—Shepard's Citations, Inc.

Figure 120. Page from Shepard's Federal Reporter Citation.

1916 Decisions of the Commissioner of Patents " '16 CD" 265. Wherever there are parallel sets of reports covering the same citing case these citations immediately follow each other.

It is also to be observed that by examining the abbreviations preceding the citations, this case has been followed "f," explained "e," and harmonized "h" in subsequent cases in the Federal Reporter.

The next citation covers the reference "215F^{1}495." The small superior figure " ^{1} " in advance of the citing page number 495, indicates that the principle of law brought out in the first paragraph of the syllabus of the cited case is also dealt with in 215 Federal Reporter 495.

Assuming that you are primarily interested in the principle covered in paragraph one of the syllabus, we find that the additional citations which contain the superior figure " ^{1} " in advance of the citing page number include numerous other cases that deal with this particular point of law and that are reported in the Federal Reporter; Federal Reporter, Second Series "F2d"; Federal Supplement "FS"; Appeal Cases District of Columbia "ADC"; Decisions of the Commission of Patents and United States Patents Quarterly "PQ."

In addition to the citations in point with paragraph one of the syllabus, there are several citations to other paragraphs of the syllabus of this case in cases reported in the Federal Reporter, Federal Reporter, Second Series, and in the notes "n" of the American Law Reports "ALR." Thus, the citations dealing with a point of law in any particular paragraph of the syllabus may be referred to instantly without examining every citation to the case.

It will be noted that this case has been cited by the courts of Illinois, New York, Texas, and Wisconsin. These citations are arranged alphabetically by the state reports with the corresponding reference in the National Reporter System. The citation 266 Southwestern Reporter (SW) 533 is a case decided in the Court of Civil Appeals of Texas and not reported elsewhere. This case has also been cited in the notes of 1914C Annotated Cases 932 (AC'14C932n).

By examining this same volume and page number in the 1938-1953 Bound Supplement, latest issue of the Cumulative Supplement, and intervening Advance Sheet, all subsequent citations to this case will be found.

Corpus Juris Secundum System

Scope and organization of system. The Corpus Juris Secundum System consists of Corpus Juris Secundum and Corpus Juris. The system is a complete statement of the body of American law in encyclopedic form, broken down into approximately 430 titles. Corpus Juris Secundum is superseding Corpus Juris. As each title of the Secundum is published, it brings down to date the same title in Corpus Juris, but all titles have not yet been published. The authorities cited in the notes in the Secundum are the cases decided since that title in Corpus Juris was written. If there are earlier cases on the point, footnote references in Corpus Juris Secundum direct the searcher to the precise page and note in Corpus Juris where they will be found. The absence of a footnote reference to Corpus Juris is conclusive evidence that there are no earlier cases. Thus, although the text of Corpus Juris is being superseded by Corpus Juris Secundum, Corpus Juris remains a vital part of the lawyer's library because of the footnotes.

The titles embraced by the system are alphabetically arranged. Judicially defined words, phrases, and maxims are alphabetically interspersed through the titles. The backbone of each volume shows the first and last words in that volume and also the volume number. Volume 72 of Corpus Juris is a complete descriptive word index to all volumes of Corpus Juris. Each volume of the Secundum has an index to the titles contained in that volume.

How to use Corpus Juris Secundum System. There are three methods of finding the discussion and supporting authorities in the Corpus Juris Secundum System.

1. *The fact, or descriptive, word index.* Find the descriptive word in the index to the title in the back of the volume. For example, if you are interested in the extent of an implied agency, your title would be *Agency*. In the index you will find "Implied agency," with the section and page number where implied agency is discussed. At the head of the section is an analysis of points covered in the section, which enables you to narrow your search.

Each volume of Corpus Juris does not contain an index. If the title in which you are interested has not been published in the

Secundum, look for the descriptive word in Volume 72, "Descriptive-word Index and Concordance," of Corpus Juris.

2. *The general analysis preceding each title.* At the beginning of each title is an analysis, or breakdown, of the contents of the title. The topics are in boldface capitals and are numbered with roman numerals. Each of the topics has a subanalysis. Judge which topic should cover the point in which you are interested, and then look at the subanalysis for the specific point. "III Creation and Extent of Relation" should cover implied agency. In the subanalysis of that topic, you will find, "§ 24. Implied Agency— p. 1045."

If you cannot judge which topic should cover your problem, you can look at each of the subtopics, but this, of course, is a slower method of research.

3. *Words and phrases alphabetically arranged throughout the set.* If an important word or words in your problem can be picked out, you can refer to those words in CJS and find cross-references to many related topics in which the words have meaning or importance.

How to cite. Cite by volume number, title, and page and section number.

> 57 C.J., Set-Off and Counterclaim, p. 376, § 22
> 24 C.J.S., Criminal Law, p. 147, § 1606

Form Books

Practice manuals. Practice manuals contain forms of pleadings, which the lawyer usually follows when dictating. Since the wording of pleadings differs with the state, a practice manual is used only in the state for which it is prepared. With the aid of a practice manual you can draft many pleadings without dictation. The forms always indicate by italics, by parentheses, or in some other manner the wording that must be changed with each case, such as names, dates, and various clauses applicable to a particular situation, and the like. In addition to the complete forms, the manuals contain many clauses applicable to various circumstances, which may be substituted for the clauses contained in the complete form.

Books of legal forms. Books of legal forms contain forms of instruments and documents as distinguished from litigation papers. Although the statutes prescribe the wording of many instruments, books of legal forms are generally useful for all states. They call attention to statutory requirements and often given forms for each state. For example, *Jones Legal Forms Annotated* published by Bobbs-Merrill, Indianapolis, one of the best known books of legal forms, gives forms of acknowledgments, deeds, mortgages, and wills, that meet the requirements of each state. Some form books cover only forms in one particular field. For example, *Encyclopedia of Incorporating Forms,* published by Prentice-Hall, Inc., contains forms covering every conceivable situation relating to the organization of a corporation. Numerous clauses, as well as complete forms, enable the user to pick out the appropriate clause to suit his purpose. In giving instructions for the preparation of a legal instrument, the lawyer will frequently tell you to copy certain forms or clauses from a form book.

Reference Facilities for Checking Names and Addresses

The following reference books are useful for confirming the spelling of names and the accuracy of addresses:

New York City Official Directory
Official Guide of the Railways
Telephone directories
Postal Guide
The American Bar
The Bar Register
Congressional Directory
Directory of Directors in the City of New York
The Law List (British)
The Lawyer's List
Martindale-Hubbell's Law Directory
Moody's Manuals
State Legislative Manuals
Official Register of the United States
Polk's (Trow's) New York Co-partnership and Corporation
    Directory (Manhattan and Bronx)
Poor's Manuals
Rand McNally's Bankers Directory
World Almanac

26

Latin Words and Phrases

EGAL dictation in every field contains many Latin words and
phrases. Those that you are most likely to hear are listed
below. The list also contains a few French terms. The list will
enable you to write the words and phrases correctly; the almost
literal translations will enable you to understand the meaning of
the dictation. Ordinarily, foreign words and phrases are italicized
in printing and underlined in typing. However, some of them
have become completely Anglicized and are not generally printed
in italic type or underlined. The words and phrases that are italicized in the list should be underlined when typed. Those in
roman type should not be underlined. You will notice that some
words are not underlined unless used in a phrase or expression.
For example, "animus" is not italicized when written alone, but
is italicized in the phrase *animus furandi.*

a fortiori. With stronger reason; much more.
a mensa et thoro. From bed and board.
a priori. From what goes before; from the cause to the effect.
a vinculo matrimonii. From the bonds of marriage.
ab initio. From the beginning.
actiones in personam. Personal actions.
ad faciendum. To do.
ad hoc. For this; (for this special purpose).
ad infinitum. Indefinitely; forever.
ad litem. For the suit; for the litigation. (A guardian *ad litem* is a person appointed to prosecute or defend a suit for a person incapacitated
by infancy or incompetency.)
ad quod damnum. To what damage; what injury. (A phrase used to
describe the plaintiff's money loss or the damages that he claims.)

ad respondendum. To answer.

ad satisfaciendum. To satisfy.

ad valorem. According to value.

aggregatio menium. Meeting of minds.

alias dictus. Otherwise called.

alibi. In another place; elsewhere.

alii. Others.

aliunde. From another place; from without (as evidence outside the document).

alius. Another.

alter ego. The other self.

alumnus. A foster child.

amicus curiae. Friend of the court.

animo. With intention, disposition. design, will.

animus. Mind; intention.

animus furandi. The intention to steal.

animus revertendi. An intention of returning.

animus revocandi. An intention to revoke.

animus testandi. An intention to make a testament or will.

anno Domini (A.D.). In the year of the Lord.

ante. Before.

ante litem motam. Before suit brought.

arguendo. In the course of the argument.

assumpsit. He undertook; he promised.

bona fide. In good faith.

bona vacantia. Vacant goods. (Personal property that no one claims, which escheats to the state.)

capias. Take; arrest. (A form of writ directing an arrest.)

capias ad satisfaciendum (ca. sa.). Arrest to satisfy. (A form of writ.)

causa mortis. By reason of death.

caveat. Let him beware; a warning.

caveat emptor. Let the buyer beware.

cepit et asportavit. He took and carried away.

certiorari. To be informed of; to be made certain in regard to. (See Chapter 27.)

cestui (*pl. cesuis*). Beneficiaries. (Pronounced "setty.")

cestui que trust. He who benefits by the trust.

cestui que use. He who benefits by the use.

cestui que vie. He whose life measures the duration of the estate.

civiliter mortuus. Civilly dead.

Consensus, non concubitus, facit nuptias vel matrimonium. Consent, not cohabitation, constitutes nuptials or marriage.

consortium (*pl. consortia*). A union of lots or chances; (a lawful marriage).

contra. Against.

contra bonos mores. Against good morals,

contra pacem. Against the peace.

coram non judice. In presence of a person not a judge. (A suit brought and determined in a court having no jurisdiction over the matter is said to be *coram non judice,* and the judgment is void.)

corpus. Body.

corpus delicti. The body of the offense; the essence of the crime.

corpus juris. A body of law.

corpus juris civilis. The body of the civil law.

Cujus est solum, ejus est usque ad coelum. Whose the soil is, his it is up to the sky.

cum testamento annexo (c.t.a.). With the will annexed. (Describes an administrator who operates under a will rather than in intestacy.)

damnum absque injuria. Damage without injury. (Damage without legal wrong.)

datum (*pl.* data). A thing given; a date.

de bonis non administratis. Of the goods not administered. Frequently abbreviated to *de bonis non.*

de bono et malo. For good and ill.

de facto. In fact; in deed; actually.

de jure. Of right; lawful.

De minimis non curat lex. The law does not concern itself with trifles.

de novo. Anew; afresh.

de son tort. Of his own wrong.

dies non. Not a day (on which the business of the courts can be carried on).

donatio mortis causa. A gift by reason of death. (A gift made by a person in sickness, under apprehension of death.)

duces tecum. You bring with you. (A term applied to a writ commanding the person upon whom it is served to bring certain evidence with him to court. Thus, we speak of a *subpoena duces tecum.*)

dum bene se gesserit. While he shall conduct himself well; during good behavior.

durante minore aetate. During minority.

durante viduitate. During widowhood.

e converso. Conversely; on the other hand.

eo instanti. Upon the instant.

erratum (*pl.* errata). Error.

et alii (et al.). And others.

et alius (et al.). And another.

et cetera (etc.). And other things.

ex cathedra. From the chair.

ex contractu. (Arising) from the contract.

ex delicto. (Arising) from a tort.

ex gratia. As a matter of favor.

ex necessitate legis. From legal necessity.

ex officio. From office; by virtue of his office.

ex parte. On one side only; by or for one party.

ex post facto. After the act.

et uxor (et ux.). And wife.

et vir. And husband.

felonice. Feloniously.

feme covert. A married woman.

feme sole. A single woman (including one who has been married but whose marriage has been dissolved by death or divorce).

ferae naturae. Of a wild nature.

fiat. Let it be done. (A short order or warrant of a judge, commanding that something shall be done.)

fieri. To be made up; to become.

fieri facias. Cause to be made. (A writ directed to the sheriff to reduce the judgment debtor's property to money in the amount of the judgment.)

filius nullius. The son of nobody; a bastard.

filius populi. A son of the people.

flagrante delicto. In the very act of committing the crime.

habeas corpus. You have the body. (See Chapter **27**.)

habere facias possessionem. That you cause to have possession. (A writ of ejectment.)

habere facias seisinam. That you cause to have seisin. (A writ to give possession.)

honorarium (*pl.* honoraria). An honorary fee or gift; compensation from gratitude.

idem sonans. Having the same sound (as names sounding alike but spelled differently).

Ignorantia legis neminem excusat. Ignorance of the law excuses no one.

illicitum collegium. An unlawful association.

Impotentia excusat legem. Impossibility is an excuse in law.

in bonis. In goods; among possessions.

in esse. In being; existence.

in extremis. In extremity (in the last illness).

in fraudem legis. In circumvention of law.

in futuro. In the future.

in loco parentis. In the place of a parent.

in pari delicto. In equal fault.

in personam. A remedy where the proceedings are *against the person,* as contradistinguished from those against a specific thing.

in praesenti. At present; at once; now.

in re. In the matter.

in rem. A remedy where the proceedings are *against the thing,* as distinguished from those against the person.

in rerum natura. In nature; in life; in existence.

in specie. In the same, or like, form. (To decree performance *in specie* is to decree specific performance.)

in statu quo. In the condition in which it was. (See *status quo.*)

in terrorem. In terror.

in toto. In the whole; completely.

in transitu. In transit; in course of transfer.

indebitatus assumpsit. Being indebted, be promised, or undertook. (An action in which plaintiff alleges defendant is indebted to him.)

indicia. Marks; signs.

infra. Below.

innuendo. Meaning.

inter. Among; between.

inter vivos. Between the living.

interim. In the meantime.

intra. Within; inside.

ipse dixit. He himself said (it). (As assertion made but not proved.)

ipso facto. By the fact itself.

ita est. So it is.

jura personarum. Rights of persons.

jura rerum. Rights of things.

jure divino. By divine right.

jure uxoris. In his wife's right.

jus (pl. jura). Law; laws collectively.

jus accrescendi. The right of survivorship.

jus ad rem. A right to a thing.

jus civile. Civil law.

jus commune. The common law; the common right.

jus gentium. The law of nations; international law.

jus habendi. The right to have a thing.

jus proprietatis. Right of property.

levari facias. Cause to be levied; a writ of execution.

lex loci. Law of the place (where the cause of action arose).

lex loci rei sitae. The law of the place where a thing is situated.

lex mercatoria. The law merchant.

lis pendens. Litigation pending; a pending suit.

locus delicti. The place of the crime or tort.

locus in quo. The place in which.

locus sigilii (L.S.). The place for the seal.

mala fides. Bad faith.

mala in se. Wrongs in themselves; (acts morally wrong).

mala praxis. Malpractice.

mala prohibita. Prohibited wrongs or offenses.

malo animo. With evil intent.

malum in se. Evil in itself.

mandamus. We command. (See Chapter 27.)

manu forti. With a strong hand; (forcible entry).

mens rea. Guilty mind.

nihil dicit. He says nothing. (Judgment against defendant who does not put in a defense to the complaint.)

nil debet. He owes nothing.

nisi prius. Unless before. (The phrase is used to denote the forum where the trial was held as distinguished from the appellate court.)

nolle prosequi. To be unwilling to follow up, or to prosecute. (A formal entry on the record by the plaintiff or the prosecutor that he will no further prosecute the case.)

nolo contendere. I will not contest it.

non compos mentis. Not of sound mind.

non est factum. It is not his deed.

non obstante. Notwithstanding.

non prosequitur (*non pros.*). He does not follow up, or pursue, or prosecute. (If the plaintiff fails to take some step that he should, the defendant may enter a judgment of *non pros.* against him.)

nudum pactum. A nude pact. (A contract without consideration.)

nul tiel record. No such record.

nul tort. No wrong done.

nulla bona. No goods. (Wording of return to a writ of *fieri facias.*)

nunc pro tunc. Now for then.

obiter dictum. Remark by the way. (See *dictum* in Chapter 27.)

onus probandi. The burden of proof.

opus (*pl.* opera). Work; labor.

ore tenus. By word of mouth; orally.

pari delicto. In equal guilt.

particeps criminis. An accomplice in the crime.

pater familias. The father (head) of a family.

peculium. Private property.

pendente lite. Pending the suit; during the litigation.

per annum. By the year.

per autre vie. For another's lifetime. (See also *pur autre vie.*)

per capita. By the head; as individuals. (In a distribution of an estate, if the descendants take per capita, they take share and share alike regardless of family lines of descent.)

per centum (per cent). By the hundred.

per contra. In opposition.

per curiam. By the court.

per diem. By the day.

per se. By itself; taken alone.

per stirpes. By stems or root; by representation. (In a distribution of an estate, if distribution is *per stirpes*, descendants take by virtue of their representation of an ancestor, not as individuals.)

post-mortem. After death.

post-obit. To take effect after death.

praecipe or *precipe*. Command. (A written order to the clerk of the court to issue a writ.)

prima facie. At first sight; on the face of it.

pro. For.

pro confesso. As confessed.

pro forma. As a matter of form.

pro hac vice. For this occasion.

pro rata. According to the rate or proportion.

pro tanto. For so much; to that extent.

pro tempore (pro tem.). For the time being; temporarily.

prochein ami. Next friend.

publici juris. Of public right.

pur autre vie. For, or during, the life of another. (See also *per autre vie.*)

quaere. Query; question; doubt. (This word indicates that a particular rule, decision, or statement that follows it is open to question.)

quantum. How much; the amount.

quantum meruit. As much as he deserved.

quantum valebant. As much as they were (reasonably) worth (in absence of agreement as to value).

quare. Wherefore.

quare clausum fregit. Wherefore he broke the close. (A form of trespass on another's land.)

quasi. As if; as it were. (Indicates that one subject resembles another, but that there are also intrinsic differences between them. Thus, we speak of quasi contracts, quasi torts, etc.)

quid pro quo. What for what; something for something. (A term denoting the consideration for a contract.)

quo warranto. By what right or authority. (See Chapter **27**.)

quoad hoc. As to this.

quod computet. That he account.

reductio ad absurdum. Reduced to the absurd.

res. A thing; an object; the subject matter.

res gestae. Things done; transactions.

res ipsa loquitur. The thing speaks for itself.

res judicata. A matter adjudicated.

scienter. Knowingly.

scilicet (SS. or ss.) To wit. (sc. is not used in legal papers)

scintilla. A spark; the least particle.

scire facias. Cause to know; give notice. (A writ used to revive a judgment that has expired.)

se defendendo. In self-defense; in defending oneself.

semper. Always.

semper paratus. Always ready. (A plea by which the defendant alleges that he has always been ready to perform what is demanded of him.)

seriatim. Severally; separately.

sigillum. A seal.

simplex obligato. A simple obligation.

sine die. Without day. (Without a specified day being assigned for a future meeting or hearing.)

situs. Situation; location.

stare decisis. To abide by decided cases.

status quo. State in which (the existing state of things at any given date.) See *in statu quo.*

sub judice. Under consideration.

sub modo. Under a qualification; in a qualified way.

sub nom. Under the name.

sui juris. Of his own right; (having legal capacity to act for himself).

supersedeas. That you supersede. (A writ commanding a stay of the proceedings.)

supra. Above.

terminus a quo. The starting point.

ultra vires. Without power; beyond the powers of. (See Chapter 27.)

venire facias. That you cause to come; (a kind of summons).

Verba fortius accipiuntur contra proferentem. Words are to be taken most strongly against the one using them.

versus (vs., v.). Against.

vi et armis. By force and arms.

via. A road; a right of way; by way of.

vice versa. On the contrary; on opposite sides.

videlicet (*viz.*) (contraction of *videre* and *licet*). It is easy to see; (that is to say; namely).

virtute officii. By virtue of his office.

viva voce. By the living voice; by word of mouth.

voir dire. To speak the truth. (Denotes a preliminary examination to determine the competency of a witness.)

27

Law Terms and Miscellaneous Procedures Explained

<hr>

THE FOLLOWING pages give clear and concise definitions and explanations of words and terms that you will hear in your daily work as a lawyer's secretary. Many of the words are not, strictly speaking, law terms, but are used in the preceding text with special legal significance. The words in the texts of the definitions that are in caps and small caps are defined in their respective alphabetical positions in this chapter.

This chapter also discusses some miscellaneous practices and procedures that are not covered elsewhere in the text.

Abrogation. The annulment or repeal of a law or obligation. The COMMON LAW, for example, is abrogated by statute.

Acceleration clause. An essential clause in contracts evidencing a debt, such as mortgages and installment contracts, which provides that if interest or an installment is not paid when due, the entire debt becomes payable at once. Without an acceleration clause, the mortgagee or seller would have to sue for the amount of each payment as it became due, or would have to wait until the entire debt matured.

Account stated. An account balance, as determined by the creditor, which has been accepted as correct by the debtor. In law, the *account stated* operates as an admission of liability by the debtor. He is barred from disputing the accuracy of the computation, the bar being raised either by the debtor's explicit approval of the account or by his failure within a reasonable time to indicate any exception to it.

Acknowledgment. The act by which a person who has signed an instrument goes before an authorized officer, such as a notary public, and acknowledges that he executed the instrument. *See also Index.*

Adjective law. See SUBSTANTIVE LAW.

Administrative law. The rules and regulations framed by an administrative body created by a state legislature or by Congress to carry out a specific statute. For example, the Federal income tax law is administered by the Bureau of Internal Revenue. The Bureau issues regulations and rules that have the weight of law as long as they keep within the scope of the income tax statute. Frequently such regulations interpret in a specific way the legislature's general intent when it enacted the statute. Thus, administrative bodies, which are primarily executive in nature, may also have powers that resemble legislative or judicial authority.

Administrator. A person appointed by the court to settle the estate of a deceased person who has left no valid will or whose named executor fails to serve. *See also Index.*

Affidavit. A written statement signed and sworn to before some person authorized to take an oath; frequently required as proof when no other evidence of a fact is available. *See also Index.*

Affirmance. See RATIFICATION.

Agency. The relationship that exists when one person authorizes another to act for him. The one granting the authority is the *principal;* the one authorized to act is the *agent.* For an agent to act, a *third party,* with whom he contracts, is necessary. An agency relationship is created when a person gives a POWER OF ATTORNEY or a PROXY, and in other situations. An agency may be *general*—the agent has broad powers to represent the principal; or the agency may be *special*—the agent represents the principal for a specific purpose or for a series of routine tasks.

Alien corporation. A business organization incorporated outside the United States and its territories. The state statutes make no distinction between an alien and a FOREIGN CORPORATION.

Allegation. A statement made by a party who claims it can be proved as fact. *See also Index.*

Allonge. (French.) A piece of paper attached to a bill of exchange or a promissory note, on which to write endorsements when there is no room on the instrument itself.

Ancillary. Auxiliary; subordinate. The term *ancillary letters* is used to apply to letters testamentary or letters of administration (see Index) that are taken out in a state other than that of the decedent's domicile, but in which he had assets or debts. Those letters are subordinate or supplementary to the letters issued in the decedent's domicile. The term *ancillary* also applies to court proceedings that are auxiliary to the main action—for example, a bill of discovery is ancillary to the principal action.

Antitrust laws. Laws designed to prevent restraint of trade, monopoly, and unfair practices in interstate commerce. The antitrust statutes are the Sherman Act (Antitrust Act of 1890); the Clayton Act; the Federal Trade Commission Act; the Robinson-Patman Act; the Miller-Tydings Act; the Wheeler-Lea Act.

Assault and battery. An assault is a threat made with the apparent intention of doing bodily harm to another. An essential element of assault is real or apparent ability on the part of the person making the threat to do bodily harm to another. Mere words do not constitute an assault. A *battery* is the wrongful touching of another's person or clothing as a result of an assault. A battery always includes an assault, but an assault may be made without a battery. A person guilty of assault and battery is liable for damage to the injured party. Assault and battery may also be a crime punishable by the state.

Assignment. The transfer of one's rights to another. Assignments are made (a) by the act of the parties, as in the case of a tenant assigning his lease to another; or (b) by operation of law, as in the case of death or bankruptcy. The party transferring his right is the *assignor;* the party to whom the rights are transferred is the *assignee.*

An assignment need not be in any particular form; it may be oral or written. It may be a formal document or an endorsement on the contract signed by the assignor. An assignment does not require any consideration, but it must effect an immediate transfer to a specific assignee.

Attestation. The act of signing a written instrument as witness to the signature of a party, at his request; for example, witnessing signatures to a contract or a will. *See also Index.*

Attorney-in-fact. One who is appointed by another, with the authority to act for him in matters specified in the term of the appointment. (See AGENCY; *also Index.*)

Bailment. A delivery of personal property for some particular purpose, upon a contract, express or implied, that the property will be returned to the person delivering it after the accomplishment of the purpose for which it was delivered. An essential of a bailment is that return of the property is contemplated. The person delivering the property is a *bailor;* the person receiving it is a *bailee.* If under the terms of the contract the bailee is obligated to pay a sum of money instead of returning the goods, the obligation is a debt and not a bailment. Thus, a conditional sale is distinguished from a bailment, even though the contract calls the transaction a bailment. The parties to a consignment of goods expect that the goods will be sold for the account of the consignor or returned to him; a consignment is therefore considered a bailment. A bailee is liable for breach of his contract to keep the property in a particular manner in a particular place for a particular purpose. The following transactions are bailments: lease of a car for hire; deposit of goods for storage or safekeeping; pledge of stocks as collateral. Title to the property remains in the bailor.

Bankruptcy. *What is bankruptcy.* Bankruptcy is a state of insolvency in which the property of a debtor is taken over by a receiver or trustee in bankruptcy for the benefit of the creditors. This action is taken under the jurisdiction of the Federal courts as prescribed by the National Bankruptcy Act.

Voluntary bankruptcy. Voluntary bankruptcy is brought about by the filing of a petition in bankruptcy by the debtor. The form of the petition is prescribed by the act. By filing a voluntary petition, the debtor seeks, first, to have his assets equally distributed among all his creditors, and, second, to free himself of his debts. He is thus able to begin his business life anew, unencumbered.

Voluntary bankruptcy is open to all individuals, firms, and corporations, except banking, building and loan, insurance, railroad, and municipal corporations. No special amount of indebtedness is required; a person owing one dollar or several millions may file a petition in voluntary bankruptcy.

Involuntary bankruptcy. Involuntary bankruptcy is brought about by the filing of a petition by the creditors against an insolvent debtor. If there are fewer than twelve creditors, one creditor may file the petition; if there are more than twelve, three creditors must join in the filing. Before creditors can throw a debtor into bankruptcy, these conditions must exist:

1. The debtor must owe at least $1,000.

2. The creditor or creditors filing the petition must have provable claims aggregating $500.

3. The debtor must have committed an act of bankruptcy within four months preceding the filing of the petition.

Involuntary bankruptcy proceedings cannot be brought against a wage earner, a farmer, or a banking, building and loan, insurance, railroad, or municipal corporation.

Steps in bankruptcy proceedings. After a petition is filed in the Federal courts, in a form prescribed by the United States Supreme Court, the basic steps are: (1) application for receiver, (2) adjudication of the bankrupt, (3) referral to referee in bankruptcy, (4) filing of schedules by the bankrupt, (5) meetings of creditors, (6) election of trustee in bankruptcy, (7) proof and allowance of claims, and (8) discharge of the bankrupt.

Referee in bankruptcy. When the court signs a decree of adjudication it refers the case to a "referee" in bankruptcy. The referee, who is a lawyer, acts in place of the bankruptcy court, conducts all the usual proceedings, and grants the final discharge of the bankrupt from further liability for his debts. He presides over all creditors' meetings.

Filing of schedules by the bankrupt. Within five days after the debtor has been adjudged bankrupt he must file, in involuntary cases, a schedule of his assets and liabilities on a form prescribed by the United States Supreme Court. If the debtor files a voluntary petition, he must accompany the petition with similar schedules.

What the secretary does. Open a file and process a bankruptcy matter just as you do any new matter. *Make diary entries* and keep a progress record sheet. The petition, application, schedules, and the like are prepared on forms prescribed by the United States Supreme Court. You will have no difficulty filling them in.

Bill of sale. A formal document issued by a seller to a buyer, as evidence of transfer to the latter of title to the goods described in the instrument. A bill of sale may be used in the case of any sale of PERSONAL PROPERTY.

Blue-sky laws. Laws that have been enacted by most of the states to protect the public from fraud in the offering of securities. Such laws are an exercise of the POLICE POWER of the states; they supplement interstate regulation of securities offerings, securities exchanges, and speculative practices, through the Securities and Exchange Commission. Actually, protection is achieved through (1) specific legislation— Blue-sky laws; and (2) through enforcement of anti-fraud statutes.

Breach of contract. The failure or refusal by one of the parties to a contract to perform some act the contract calls for. A contract may also be breached by making performance impossible, as when a person contracts to sell a car and wrecks it before delivery; or by "anticipatory" breach, as the unqualified announcement by a seller, before delivery date, that he will not deliver the goods.

Breach of a contract by one party may discharge the other from performance. Or the injured party may sue for damages representing the loss directly incurred from the breach. Damages cannot be obtained for speculative or possible losses that cannot be shown to have resulted directly from the breach.

Breach of warranty. When a WARRANTY made by a vendor proves to be false, the warranty is said to be breached. For the breach, the buyer has a choice of four remedies: (1) Accept or keep the goods and set up the breach to reduce the purchase price. (2) Keep the goods and recover damages for the breach of warranty. (3) Refuse to accept the goods if title has not passed, and bring an action for damages for breach of warranty. (4) Rescind the contract, or if the goods have been delivered, return them, and recover any part of the purchase price that had been paid. The buyer can claim only *one* of these remedies.

Business trust. See MASSACHUSETTS TRUST.

By-laws. Rules adopted by a corporation to regulate its conduct as a corporate entity and to define and determine the rights and duties of its stockholders and the rights, powers, and duties of the directors and officers. They are permanent, except in so far as they may be amended. *See also Index.*

Caveat emptor. (Latin for "let the buyer beware.") This COMMON LAW doctrine or maxim imposes on the buyer the duty of examining what he buys. If he does not observe ordinary defects at the time of purchase, he has no recourse against the seller because of those defects. Exceptions to the *caveat emptor* doctrine are made under the following circumstances: (1) A fiduciary relationship exists between the parties, as between principal and agent, attorney and client, trustee and beneficiary. (2) The defects are not obvious and the buyer has not had an opportunity for thorough inspection. (3) The sale was made by sample or by description. (4) The sale was for a specific purpose.

Certificate of incorporation. See CORPORATION; *also Index.*

Certiorari. A writ issued by a superior court to an inferior court directing it to send to the former court the record of a particular case. A writ of certiorari is an extraordinary remedy resorted to in cases obviously entitled to redress where no direct appellate proceedings are provided by law. A writ of certiorari cannot be used as a substitute for an appeal or a writ of error. It is distinguished from an appeal in that it brings up the case on the record, whereas on appeal a case is brought up on the merits. A litigant is entitled to a writ of error as a matter of right, but a writ of certiorari lies within the court's discretion.

The dissatisfied party in the lower court petitions the appellate court for a writ of certiorari. If, on the face of the record, the appellate court determines that the lower court has not proceeded in accordance with the law, it will consent to issue the writ and hear the case. If the record itself does not indicate that the petitioner has been wronged by the proceeding, the court will deny the petition for writ of certiorari. The denial is, in effect, an affirmance of the lower court's decision on the point of law before the appellate court, but the issuance of the writ does not mean that the appellate court will decide in favor of the petitioner. The court may then order the certiorari dismissed; or return it to the lower court with instructions; or render a final judgment which must finally govern the case.

Chattel. An article of tangible PERSONAL PROPERTY, as distinguished from real property (land and improvements) and intangibles (stocks, bonds, and the like).

Chose in action. PERSONAL PROPERTY that is not susceptible to physical possession and that requires some form of action to reduce it to possession. Some of the most important choses in action are contracts, promissory notes, checks, trade acceptances, stocks, bonds, bank accounts, and the right of legal action to recover money or property.

Civil law. The law of the Romans under Emperor Justinian was condensed and digested into a code known as Corpus Juris Civilis. The laws of Justinian were lost in the Western Empire during the early Dark Ages, but a complete copy was found about 1137. The laws were then revised and became the basis of jurisprudence for most of continental Europe. The present law on the Continent is therefore referred to as the Roman or civil law. See COMMON LAW for development of law in England.

Civil wrongs. Concern the relationship between individuals as such, as distinguished from wrongs against the public (see CRIMINAL LAW). Civil wrongs infringe on private rights and duties; remedy against them is sought by private action. TORT and BREACH OF CONTRACT are among the more common civil wrongs.

Close corporation. A corporation whose capital stock is held by a limited group; its shares are ordinarily not sold in the securities markets. Usually a close corporation is small. (The Ford Motor Company is an exception.)

Common law. A system of law, or body of legal rules, derived from decisions of judges based upon accepted customs and traditions. It was developed in England. It is known as the *common law* because it is believed that these rules were generally recognized and were in full force throughout England. Common law is now the basis of the laws in every state of the Union, except Louisiana, which bases its laws upon the early laws of France. Statutes have been enacted to supplement and supersede the common law in many fields; the common law, however, still governs where there is no statute dealing with a specific subject. Although the common law is written, it is called the *unwritten law* in contradistinction to STATUTORY LAW enacted by the legislatures.

Common law trust. See MASSACHUSETTS TRUST.

Community property. In some states a system exists whereby all earnings of either husband or wife constitute a common fund of the husband and wife. The property is known as *community property.* The central idea of the system is the same in all states where community property exists, but statutes and judicial decisions have directed the development of the system along different lines in the various states. For example, in some states only property that is acquired by the exertion or labor of either party is *common,* whereas in other states income from separate property is also considered community property. Generally, either husband or wife may have "separate" property, such as that belonging to either of them at the time of marriage, real estate acquired in a state that does not recognize community property, or property given to or inherited by either at any time. Property acquired in exchange for separate property is separate property; that acquired in exchange for community property is community property. In some states the husband may dispose of or encumber the community property, but the wife may not; nor may the community property be attached for the wife's debts, except for those contracted for necessities for herself and her children.

Competent parties. See CONTRACTS, 2.

Conditional sale. An installment sale. The buyer usually gives the seller a promissory note secured by a conditional sale contract or a chattel mortgage. A *conditional sale contract* is a contract for the sale of goods under which the goods are delivered to the buyer but in which the title remains in the seller until the goods are paid for in full, or until the conditions of the contract are fulfilled. When a chattel mortgage is used, the seller transfers the goods to the buyer who, in turn, executes a chattel mortgage in favor of the seller. This instrument gives the seller a lien on the goods.

The seller's choice of a security depends upon the laws in his state. He studies the laws and selects the type of instrument that provides the most protection with the least inconvenience. The instrument usually includes a provision that if an installment is not paid when due, the entire debt becomes payable at once. This clause, called the ACCELERATION CLAUSE, is essential in any installment contract. Otherwise the seller would have to sue for the amount of each installment as it became due, or would have to wait until the entire debt matured.

Constructive. The term "constructive" generally applies to that which amounts in the eyes of the law to an act, although the act itself is not necessarily performed. The law presumes an act to have been performed, and applies the term to many situations to prevent a miscarriage of justice.

Some of the circumstances under which the law will presume an act are indicated by the following: constructive abandonment, constructive delivery, constructive desertion, constructive eviction, constructive fraud, constructive gift, constructive notice, constructive possession, constructive process, constructive receipt of income, constructive service, and constructive trusts. A few of these are explained.

Constructive delivery. Arises when actual, or manual, delivery is impossible or undesirable. Constructive delivery includes those acts that are equivalent to actual delivery although they do not confer real possession. Acts that bar a lien or a right to stoppage in transit, such as marking and setting apart goods as belonging to the buyer, constitute constructive delivery.

Constructive notice. Notice that arises from a strictly legal presumption that cannot be controverted. The presumption is one of law and not of fact, as distinguished from implied notice that arises from an inference of facts. The presumption of constructive notice is conclusive against the actual facts. Thus, a mortgage recorded with the proper public authorities is constructive notice of the mortgagee's interest in the property.

Constructive receipt. Constructive receipt of income usually constitutes taxable income under the various tax laws. For example, any time during the year commissions may be credited on a firm's books to a salesman who may draw upon the firm to the amount of the credit. The commission is said to be constructively received. Whatever amount is credited to the salesman would have to be reported by him as income in the year the amount was credited on the books, even if the money was not drawn until the following year.

Contracts. An agreement, enforceable at law, by which two parties mutually promise to give some particular thing, or to do or abstain from doing a particular act. A contract may be formal or informal; it may be oral or written, sealed or unsealed, except that state statutes, usually designated as the STATUTE OF FRAUDS, require certain agreements to be in writing. A contract may be executed—one that has been fully carried out by both parties; or executory—one that is yet to be performed. It may be executed on the part of one party and executory on the part of the other. For example, the purchase of merchandise on credit, followed by delivery, is executed on the part of the seller and executory on the part of the buyer. A contract may be express—all the terms definitely expressed in the oral or written agreement; or implied—the terms not expressed but implied by the law from the actions of the parties. For example, when a person gets on a bus, his action implies a contract with the transit company.

To be enforceable at law a contract must have the following four elements:

1. *Offer and acceptance.* Before a contract can be formed, there must be an offer by one party, called the offeror, to do or to refrain from doing a certain thing, and an acceptance of the proposal by another party, called the offeree.

An offer is considered open until it is revoked, rejected, or accepted, or until after the lapse of a reasonable time. The only case in which an offeror cannot withdraw an offer before acceptance is the case in which he has entered into an OPTION contract, which is an agreement supported by the payment of a sum of money, or for some other consideration, to hold an offer open for a definite period of time.

An acceptance is an indication by the offeree of his willingness to be bound by the terms of the offer. The acceptance may take the form of an act, the signing and delivery of a written instrument, or of a promise communicated to the offeror. Silence on the part of the offeree is not an acceptance unless the previous dealings between the parties create a duty upon the part of the offeree to accept or reject the offer.

The acceptance must be unequivocal and must show an intention to accept all the terms of the offer. In the language frequently used by the courts, there must be a "meeting of the minds" of the offeror and the offeree.

2. *Competent parties.* All persons are presumed to have unlimited power to contract—except infants, insane persons, intoxicated persons, married women, and corporations.

Legally, a person is in his infancy until he reaches the age of twenty-one, although some states provide that women become of age at eighteen and other states, that marriage removes the infancy status. Contracts by infants are not void, but generally they may be disaffirmed by the infant. An infant is not bound by an executory contract unless he affirms the contract after coming of age; failure to affirm implies disaffirmance. An infant may disaffirm an executed contract during infancy or within a reasonable time after he attains his majority; failure to disaffirm within a reasonable time implies affirmance. Contracts for necessities, as food, clothing, shelter, medical care, education, and the like, may be binding upon an infant.

Like infants, insane persons are not absolutely incapable of making contracts; their contracts are voidable, not void, and they may be held liable for necessities. A person who is so drunk that he is deprived of his reason and does not understand the nature of his acts is in the same position as a mental incompetent: he may disaffirm his contracts if the disaffirmance does not injure third persons, and provided he disaffirms immediately upon restoration of his faculties.

Under the COMMON LAW a married woman has few contractual powers, but the statutes in most states have modified the common law. In general, a married woman may now contract as freely as a single woman, but in some states she cannot contract with her husband, enter into partnership with him, or act as surety for him.

A corporation's ability to contract is limited by its charter and by various statutes.

3. *Legality of subject matter.* A contract is illegal if it calls for the performance of an act forbidden by law or against public policy. Gambling and wagering contracts, and usurious contracts (see USURY), for example, are generally held to be illegal. In some states any contract entered into on Sunday is illegal. Federal and state laws make those contracts illegal that restrain trade, fix prices, or result in unfair practices.

4. *Consideration.* Something of benefit to the person making a promise must be given, or some detriment must be suffered by the person to whom a promise is made to make a contract binding. *Consideration* is the price, motive, or matter inducing the contract; it may consist of (a) doing some act that one is not obligated to perform; (b) refraining from doing something that one would otherwise be free to do; (c) giving some money or property; (d) giving a promise. The value of the consideration is generally immaterial.

5. *Contracts under seal.* The placing of a SEAL on a contract has lost the significance formerly attached to it, but it is still customary, and required in some states, on contracts of major importance. Deeds, mortgages, and other conveyances of real estate are among the contracts requiring a seal.

Conversion. A violation of the right of property by unlawfully taking or withholding possession of another's CHATTEL. When a seller has passed title but refuses to make delivery, the buyer may sue him for conversion. Conversion may also take the form of unauthorized destruction of another's property, or the unauthorized change of its nature.

Corporation. An organization formed under a state statute for the purpose of carrying on an enterprise in such a way as to make the enterprise distinct and separate from the persons who are interested in it and who control it; ". . . an artificial being, invisible, intangible, and existing only in contemplation of law." *The Trustees of Dartmouth College* v. *Woodward* (1819) 17 U.S. 518, 636.

The ownership of the corporation is represented by its capital stock, which is divided into identical units or groups of identical units called shares. These shares are represented by written instruments called certificates of stock. The owners of the shares are called the stockholders. Every stockholder has the right to transfer his shares—a right based on the inherent power of a person to dispose of his property. Since the shares of stock of a corporation can be transferred by sale or otherwise from one owner to another without affecting the corporate existence, the corporation enjoys continuous succession. The existence of the corporation is not disturbed by death, insanity, or bankruptcy of individual stockholders or by change of ownership. *See also Index.*

Counterclaim. A defendant may take advantage of a suit against him to ask the court for relief against the plaintiff, when otherwise he would be compelled to institute an action of his own. For example, the maker of a note might claim that the payee is indebted to him for certain sums in connection with a matter not related to the note. The cause of action set up by the defendant, to be tried at the same time as the cause of action alleged by the plaintiff, is a counterclaim.

Court bond. Litigants at law are required many times to file a bond or other security guaranteeing that, if unsuccessful in litigation, they will pay to the other party the monetary damages awarded by the court. These bonds are known as *court* or *judiciary* bonds. Another class of court bonds are known as *probate bonds*. They are issued to executors, administrators, and other fiduciaries to guarantee the faithful performance of their legal duties.

Criminal law. The statutes and general maxims that forbid certain actions or conduct as detrimental to the welfare of the state and that provide punishment therefor. Criminal acts are prosecuted by the state, as opposed to CIVIL WRONGS, which are prosecuted by an individual. A wrong may be both a criminal wrong and a civil wrong; for example, ASSAULT AND BATTERY. A crime may be a *treason,* a *felony,* or a *misdemeanor.* The Federal and state constitutions state that treason "shall consist only in levying war against them or in adhering to their enemies, giving them aid and comfort." Felonies are crimes punishable by death or by imprisonment in a Federal or state prison. They include murder, grand larceny, arson, and rape. Misdemeanors are crimes of lesser importance than felonies and are punishable by fine or imprisonment in the local jail. They include petty larceny, drunkenness, disorderly conduct, and vagrancy. Violation of traffic ordinances, building codes, and similar city ordinances are not crimes but are termed "petty offenses," "public torts," or *mala prohibita.*

Cumulative voting. A system of voting for directors of a corporation under which each stockholder is entitled to a number of votes equal to the number of shares he owns multiplied by the number of directors to be elected. He may cast all the votes for one candidate—cumulate them—or he may distribute his votes among the candidates in any way he sees fit. This system enables the minority stockholders to elect one or more of the directors. The right to cumulative voting cannot be claimed unless provided for (1) by statute, (2) by the corporation's charter or by-laws, or (3) by contract among all the stockholders, provided the agreement is not otherwise illegal.

Cy pres doctrine. (French for "as near as.") An ancient doctrine applicable to the construction of instruments in equity, whereby the intention of the party making the instrument is carried out as nearly as possible when it is impossible to carry out his precise intention. The doctrine, though ancient, is especially useful in modern times as a device to render charitable trusts useful. For example, if funds left to a charitable trust are insufficient to carry out the provisions of the testamentary trust, the fund does not necessarily revert to the estate, but may be used for a charitable purpose similar to that provided for in the trust. The doctrine is not accepted in all states.

Damages. The sum allowed by law as compensation for an injury or loss caused by another. The amount of damages to be recovered is usually a matter for the jury to determine.

Decree. The court's decision in EQUITY. A decree usually directs the defendant to do or not to do some specific thing, as opposed to a judgment for damages in a court of law. A decree is *final* when it disposes of the case, leaving no question to be decided in the future; for example, a decree ordering SPECIFIC PERFORMANCE of a contract. A decree is *interlocutory* when it leaves unsettled some question to be determined in the future; for example, a temporary INJUNCTION. *See also Index.*

Deed. A formal written instrument by which title to real property is conveyed from one person to another. *See also Index.*

Defamation. See LIBEL AND SLANDER.

Del credere. (Italian.) A term applied to an agent who, for a higher commission, guarantees his principal that he will pay for goods sold on credit if the buyer does not. Del credere agencies are common in businesses that employ commission merchants or agents whose relatively independent financial status enables them to guarantee their customers' accounts.

Dictum. An opinion expressed by a court which is not necessary in deciding the question before the court. When, in addition, such opinion does not relate to the question before the court, it is called *obiter dictum* (Latin for "remark by the way"). Dicta carry the legal weight in courts deciding subsequent questions but not to the extent that court decisions do. Court decisions are binding precedents; the dicta expressed in the opinion are not.

Disaffirmance. The act by which a person who has entered into a voidable contract indicates that he will not abide by the contract. (See VOID; VOIDABLE.) For example, an infant may refuse to honor a contract by disaffirmance when he reaches majority.

Discharge of contract. The release of the parties to a contract from their obligations under it. Contracts may be discharged by the following methods: (1) *Performance,* or the carrying out of the terms of the contract. (2) *Agreement.* The parties may agree to discharge one another from further liability under the contract. There must be sufficient consideration for the agreement. (3) *Impossibility of performance.* When a contract is based on an implied condition that certain factors shall continue to exist during the life of the contract, and those factors cease to exist, performance is impossible and the contract is discharged. (4) *Operation of law.* A change in the law in effect at the time the contract was made may bring about a discharge of the contract, or a law itself may operate as a discharge. Thus, a contract to build a garage on a certain site would be discharged by a zoning ordinance forbidding the erection of a garage within that zone. (5) *Breach.* If one party breaches a contract the other may be discharged. (See BREACH OF CONTRACT.)

Discovery. A procedure designed to obtain facts known by the defendant, or with reference to papers in his possession. The information is obtained by means of a bill of discovery.

Dishonor. Refusal to pay a NEGOTIABLE INSTRUMENT when due. Notice of dishonor is usually given to endorsers and drawers, who, in addition to the maker, are liable on the instrument. Notice of dishonor may be given orally or in writing. If it is not given, endorsers and drawers are discharged from liability. (See also PROTEST.)

Doing business. See INTERSTATE COMMERCE; INTRASTATE COMMERCE.

Domestic corporation. A corporation doing business in a state in which it was created or incorporated is known as a domestic corporation. (See FOREIGN CORPORATION.)

Duress. Coercion causing action or inaction against a person's will through fear. Duress may take the form of physical force, imprisonment, bodily harm, improper moral persuasion, or the threat of any of these. Threat of criminal prosecution constitutes duress, but threat of civil prosecution does not. A contract made under duress is voidable at the option of the party subjected to duress.

Earnest (earnest money). The payment of part of the purchase price to bind a sale. *See also Index.*

Eminent domain. The power of Federal, state, and local governments to appropriate property for public use or the public welfare. When such property is taken, the owner is reimbursed according to a fair appraisal, and has the right to sue for a greater amount. PUBLIC UTILITY corporations are also given the power of eminent domain.

Endorsement. (*See Index* for typed endorsement on back of legal documents.) *On negotiable instrument.* Writing one's name, either with or without additional words, on a NEGOTIABLE INSTRUMENT or on a paper (called an ALLONGE) attached to it. By an endorsement, the endorser becomes liable to all subsequent holders in due course for payment of the instrument if it is not paid by the maker when properly presented, and if he is given notice of dishonor (see DISHONOR).

Blank endorsement. The writing of one's name on an instrument, or an allonge, without any additional words, is a blank endorsement. Its effect is to make the paper payable to the bearer. Thus, a finder or thief might transfer the note to a third party for a consideration, and the third party may then enforce payment against the maker or the endorser.

Special endorsement. The designation of a certain person to whom the instrument is payable is a special endorsement. Thus, if an instrument is endorsed "Pay to John Jones," or "Pay to the order of John Jones," followed by the endorser's signature, no one but John Jones can receive payment for the instrument or transfer it.

Restrictive endorsement. An endorsement that transfers possession of the instrument for a particular purpose is a restrictive endorsement. Examples: "Pay to John Jones only. Sam Brown." "Pay to National City Bank for collection. Sam Brown." "For deposit only. Sam Brown." A restrictive endorsement terminates the negotiability of the instrument.

Qualified endorsement. An endorsement that qualifies or limits the liability of the endorser is a qualified endorsement. If an endorser endorses an instrument "without recourse," he does not assume liability in the event the maker fails to pay the instrument when due.

Conditional endorsement. A special endorsement with words added that create a condition which must happen before the special endorsee is entitled to payment is a conditional endorsement. The endorser is liable only if the condition is fulfilled. Example: "Pay to Greenwood Cotton Growers Association upon delivery of warehouse receipt for twenty-five standard bales cotton, strict to middling. John Jones."

Irregular or accommodation endorsement. An endorsement made for the purpose of lending the endorser's credit to a party to the instrument is an irregular or accommodation endorsement. It is also called an *anomalous* endorsement. A regular endorsement transfers title to the instrument, whereas an accommodation endorsement is for additional security only. An accommodation endorser is never the maker, drawer, acceptor, payee, or holder of the instrument he endorses.

Equity. 1. *Legal. See Index.*

2. *Accounting and finance.* The value of the owner's interest in property in excess of all claims and liens against it. Examples: (a) An owner's equity in his home is its present value less the amount of the mortgage. (b) The equity of the stockholders of a business is its net worth; hence, the interest of the stockholders as measured by capital and surplus, or the value of the assets of the business in excess of its liabilities. Sometimes, however, equity refers to the unlimited interest of common stockholders. (c) The equity of a person who has bought securities on margin is the present market value of the securities less the sum borrowed from the broker to make the purchase.

Escheat. The return of land to the state if the owner dies without legal heirs. Unclaimed personal property may also go to the state. Escheated personal property is called *bona vacantia.*

Escrow. A conditional delivery of something to a third person to be held until the happening of some event or the performance of some act. To place an instrument or a fund in escrow is to deliver the instrument or fund to a person charged with its custody and disposition under the terms of a specific agreement, known as the *escrow agreement.* For example, a grantor may deliver a deed in escrow to a trust company until the grantee makes certain payments on the purchase price, at which time the trust company delivers the deed to the grantee. *See also Index.*

Estate by the entirety. See TENANCY BY THE ENTIRETY.

Estoppel. A bar raised by law preventing a person from taking a position, denying a fact, or asserting a fact, in court, inconsistent with his previous conduct or statements. Example: *A* sells *B* a house that he (*A*) does not own, giving *B* a covenant and warranty deed, in which he warrants that he has title to the house. Later, *A* obtains title from the actual owner and attempts to eject *B* on the ground that *A* is now the true owner and *B* is not. *A* would be estopped from disputing what he formerly warranted, namely that he was the true owner when he sold the house.

Ex parte. (Latin for "of the one part.") Done for or on behalf of one party only. The term is applied to a proceeding, order, or injunction that is taken for the benefit of one party only. An injunction is granted *ex parte* when only one side has had a hearing. When *ex parte* appears in the title of a case, the name following is that of the party upon whose application the case was heard.

Execution. 1. *Of judgment.* A legal writ directing an officer of the law to carry out a judgment is an execution of judgment. *See also Index.*

2. *Of instrument.* The signature and delivery of a written instrument constitutes execution of the instrument. *See also Index.*

Fee simple. The absolute ownership of real property. It gives the owner and his heirs the unconditional power of disposition and other rights. (See REAL PROPERTY.)

Felony. See CRIMINAL LAW.

Force majeure. (French.) Superior or irresistible force. Corresponds in a general way to "Act of God"; for example, an earthquake, or the sudden death of a person. If a party to a contract is prevented from executing it by a *force majeure*, he may not be held liable for damages.

Foreign corporation. A corporation doing business in a state in which it was created or incorporated is known as a domestic corporation. All other corporations doing business in that state are known as foreign corporations. They must comply with certain terms and conditions imposed by the state. The state statutes make no distinction between a foreign and an alien corporation (a corporation organized outside the United States and its territories); both are regarded as foreign, except in those few states that do not recognize alien corporations.

Garnishment. The right of a judgment creditor to compel a third party owing money to, or holding money for, a judgment debtor to pay the money to the creditor instead of to the debtor. (See EXECUTION.) The third party against whom the proceedings are brought is called the garnishee. Not only wages and salaries, but trust funds, insurance disability payments, and the like, may be garnisheed. The laws that govern the right of garnishment differ considerably in the various states, but garnishment is known in one form or another in every state except South Carolina.

Guaranty. The term is used interchangeably with suretyship by courts and lawyers as well as laymen. A contract of guaranty or of suretyship is a contract whereby one person agrees to be responsible to another for the payment of a debt or the performance of a duty by a third person. It must be in writing and is not enforceable if made orally.

The term guaranty (or guarantee) is often loosely used in the sense of WARRANTY. In a strict legal and commercial sense, it is of the essence of a contract of guaranty that there should be a principal, liable directly to perform some act or duty. An agreement by a third party guaranteeing the honest and faithful performance of a contract of sale is a contract of guaranty; an agreement in a sales contract "guaranteeing" the efficient performance of a product for a certain number of years is a contract of warranty.

Habeas corpus. (Latin for "You have the body.") A writ commanding the person having custody of another to produce the person detained at a certain place and time in order that the court may determine if the detention is lawful.

Holder in due course. The transferee of a NEGOTIABLE INSTRUMENT who acquires the instrument under the following conditions: (1) The paper must be complete and regular on its face. (2) It must be purchased before maturity. (3) The purchase must be in good faith for a valuable consideration. (4) The purchase must be made without notice of defects in the title or of defenses against payment to the transferor. A holder in due course may enforce collection of the instrument against prior parties regardless of their claims, defenses, and offsets against one another. A transferee may acquire the rights of a holder in due course without being one himself. *Example: A,* the holder in due course of a note procured by the payee through fraud, endorses the note to *B,* who knew of the fraud and hence was not a holder in due course. *B,* however, acquires *A's* right as a holder in due course to collect the note regardless of the fraud, provided *B* had no part in the fraud.

Inchoate. Begun but not completed, as a contract not executed by all the parties. An instrument that the law requires to be recorded is an *inchoate instrument* until it is recorded, in that it is good only between the parties and privies (see PRIVITY). A wife's interest in her husband's lands which becomes a right of dower upon his death is an *inchoate right of dower* during his lifetime. An interest in real estate which may become a vested interest unless barred is an *inchoate interest.* Other phrases are *inchoate equity, inchoate lien, inchoate title.*

Indemnity. An undertaking, either express or implied, to compensate another for loss or damage, or for expenses or trouble incurred, either in the past or in the future. Under a contract of indemnity, the indemnity is the obligation or duty resting upon a particular person or company to make good any loss or damage another has suffered or may suffer, upon the happening of a specific event. The person giving the indemnity (agreeing to indemnify) is the *indemnitor*, corresponding to an insurer; the person who receives the indemnity or protection is the *indemnitee*, corresponding to the insured. The term *indemnity* also applies to the sum paid as compensation or remuneration in the event of loss or damage to the indemnitee. The indemnity may be payable to the indemnitee or to someone else in behalf of the indemnitee. For example, the payments that are made to an injured workman under workman's compensation insurance are indemnities. They are payable to the workman in behalf of his employer, who is the indemnitee.

Indenture. A formal written instrument between two or more parties. The ancient practice was to write two or more copies of the instrument on the same piece of parchment. The copies were then separated by tearing the parchment in irregular fashion, so that the indentations of each torn part would fit the other. Hence, the name *indenture. See also Index.*

Infant's contract. See CONTRACTS, 2.

Injunction. A writ restraining a person or corporation from doing or continuing to do something that threatens or causes injury, or requiring the defendant to do a particular act. The writ may be granted by the court in which the case is brought, or by a judge of the court. Injunctions may be classified as *prohibitory* and *mandatory*. A prohibitory injunction restrains the commission or continuance of an act. Thus, a prohibitory injunction may restrain a board of elections from placing a certain candidate's name on the ballot. A mandatory injunction commands acts to be done or undone. For example, a mandatory injunction may compel a property owner to open a road that he had closed by constructing a fence across it, thus depriving another property owner of the use of the road.

Injunctions may also be classified as (1) restraining orders, (2) temporary injunctions, and (3) permanent injunctions. A restraining order may be granted without notice to the opposite party, for the purpose of restraining the defendant until the court has heard an application for a temporary injunction. A temporary injunction is granted on the basis of the application, before the court has heard the case on its merits. It restrains the defendant during the litigation of a case, and may be either dissolved or made permanent when the rights of the parties are determined. Temporary injunctions are also called preliminary, interlocutory, or injunction *pendente lite*. Permanent injunctions are granted on the merits of the case. They are often called final or permanent injunctions.

Insurable interest. A person has an insurable interest if he might be financially injured by the occurrence of the event insured against. Under American law if an insurable interest is not present, the contract is a mere wager and is not enforceable.

In property. Insurable interest must exist at the time the loss occurs. Title to the property insured is not necessary; an owner, lessee, mortgagee, or purchaser has an insurable interest. Thus, the interest (1) may be contingent, as the interest of a purchaser under a contract of sale; (2) may be conditional, as the interest of a seller under a contract of CONDITIONAL SALE until the conditions of the sale have been met; (3) may arise from possession as in the case of a bailee (see BAILMENT).

In life. Insurable interest must exist at the time the policy is written but need not exist at the time death occurs. Every person has insurable interest in his own life and may name anyone he chooses as beneficiary. Other examples of relations giving rise to an insurable interest are those of (1) employer and valued employee; (2) several partners of a partnership; (3) creditor and debtor; (4) corporation and its officers; (5) wife and husband; (6) dependent children.

Interlocking directorates. Boards of directors of two or more corporations having one or more directors in common. Through this method of control, the will of the common dominant stockholders is executed.

Interlocutory decree. See DECREE.

Interstate commerce, intrastate commerce. The Constitution gives the Federal government power to regulate "commerce among the several states" (Art. I, Sec. 8). But it does not define either commerce or interstate commerce. The courts decided originally that commerce meant buying and selling. Hence, if the buying-and-selling is part of an interchange of commodities or intangibles between states, it is interstate commerce. Today, interstate commerce includes transportation, transmission of power, and communication—radio, television, telephone, and telegraph.

Interstate commerce also comprises general movements of commodities. For example, on different occasions, the courts have upheld the regulation of both buying and selling of livestock at the stockyards, and the buying and selling of grain futures. Both operations, even though local, are part of the general flow of commerce which supplies produce to the consumer markets.

A company is engaged in *intrastate commerce* as distinguished from interstate commerce if the bulk of its business (isolated cases of interstate commerce do not count) takes place entirely within a state, and is not part of an interchange or movement of tangible or intangible commodities.

As a general rule, a state cannot prohibit foreign corporations (corporations chartered in other states) from doing interstate business within its borders; however, it can prohibit them from doing intrastate business unless they meet certain qualifying conditions. Usually, the conditions include: (1) registration and filing of certain documents with state officials; (2) designation of an agent to accept service of summons; (3) payment of certain fees and taxes. If a corporation "does business" in a state without "qualifying," that is, meeting the state's requirements, it may become subject to certain fines or it may lose the right to sue in state courts on contracts made within the state.

What constitutes "doing business" is an important technical question that has come up in almost all of the state courts. A company that is engaged only in interstate commerce cannot be considered as "doing business" in a state even though it actually gets business in the state. For example, sending salesmen into a state to secure business, but filling the orders from outside of the state, is not considered "doing business." This is interstate commerce. But, if the orders are turned over to a local wholesaler within the state to be filled from the wholesaler's stock, the firm is "doing business" in the state and must qualify. These simple examples should not mislead one into thinking that it is easy to determine whether a company is or is not "doing business" in a state.

It is important to differentiate between intrastate and interstate commerce under most of the Federal regulatory laws as well. For example, the Fair Labor Standards Act (1938) (Wage-Hour Law) regulates labor conditions in industries not only "engaged in commerce" but also in the "production of goods for commerce," or "in any process or occupation necessary to the production." The Supreme Court held that the Act covered an owner who employed personnel to service his building in which tenants produced goods for interstate commerce. The services rendered by the employees were necessary for the production of goods for interstate commerce.

The regulatory laws are not consistent in their definition of what is interstate commerce, although the tendency is toward uniformity.

Issue of execution. When a judgment is obtained by one party against another, the successful party is known as a *judgment creditor* and the other party as a *judgment debtor*. If the judgment debtor does not pay the judgment, the attorney for the judgment creditor may get the clerk of court to issue execution to a designated officer of the law, usually the sheriff, constable, or marshal. The execution is a printed form, easily filled out upon the basis of the information in the file. If the officer to whom the execution is issued can find no property of the judgment debtor against which to levy, he returns the execution "unsatisfied." The lawyer may then commence a SUPPLEMENTARY PROCEEDING.

Joint adventure (venture). An association of two or more persons for a given, limited purpose, without the usual powers, duties, and responsibilities that go with a PARTNERSHIP. Thus, if two people buy a specific piece of real estate for resale at a profit, they become parties to a joint adventure; but if they enter into an agreement whereby each contributes money and services in establishing and carrying on a real estate business, they become members of a partnership.

Joint and several. An obligation or liability incurred, either under contract or otherwise, by two or more parties together and separately is said to be *joint and several*. The parties may be held jointly responsible or severally responsible. Thus, partners are jointly and severally liable on partnership transactions, whereas a subscriber to a charity is severally liable—the subscriber is not jointly liable with the other subscribers for their subscriptions. Or a bond may be joint and several, in which case the obligors are liable either individually or together, at the option of the obligee.

Joint estate. See JOINT TENANCY.

Joint stock company. A form of business organization created by an agreement of the parties. This agreement is commonly called articles of association. This type of company is similar to the CORPORATION in the following respects: (1) the ownership is represented by transferable certificates; (2) management is in the hands of a board of governors or directors elected by the members (shareholders); (3) the business continues for its fixed term notwithstanding the death or disability of one or more of the members. It is unlike the corporation and like the PARTNERSHIP in that each shareholder is personally liable for the company's debts.

In many states the laws affecting taxation and regulation of corporations make the definition of a corporation broad enough to include joint stock companies. These states regard a joint stock company organized in another state as a FOREIGN CORPORATION. In other states, a joint stock company may conduct business in the state without being subject to restrictions imposed upon corporations.

Joint tenancy. If two or more persons acquire the same estate at the same time, by the same title or source of ownership, each having the same degree of interest (including right of survivorship) as the others, and each having the same right of possession as the others, the estate is called a *joint estate* or *tenancy*. The distinguishing characteristic of a joint tenancy is that upon the death of one of the joint tenants, his interest automatically passes to the others by survivorship. The Courts do not favor joint tenancies, and in many jurisdictions permit joint tenants to defeat the right of survivorship by mortgage or conveyance. Some of the states have gone so far as to pass retroactive statutes making existing undivided interests TENANCY IN COMMON unless the survivorship element is expressly provided for in the deed or will that created the interest. (See also TENANCY BY THE ENTIRETY.)

Judgment. An adjudication by a court, after a trial or hearing, of the rights of the parties. Broadly speaking, an adjudication by a court of law or of EQUITY is considered a judgment, but technically an adjudication by a court of equity is a DECREE. The sentence in a criminal case is the judgment. A judgment for money becomes a lien on the judgment debtor's real estate; if EXECUTION is issued, the sheriff may seize the debtor's personal property. If the party against whom a judgment is rendered appeals to a higher court, execution of the judgment is *stayed* pending the higher court's decision. *See also Index.*

Judgment by default. After a SUMMONS has been served by the sheriff and returned to the court, the court has JURISDICTION over the defendant. If the defendant fails to defend a civil case by filing proper pleadings, or fails to appear within a definite time, a judgment is given against him in his absence. This judgment is called *judgment by default. See also Index.*

Jurisdiction. *See Index.*

Laches. Unreasonable delay in bringing suit or seeking remedy in an equity court. For a defendant to plead laches as a defense to a suit, he must show that he suffered from the plaintiff's delay in bringing suit.

Letters patent. See PATENTS, APPLICATIONS FOR.

Libel and slander. That which tends to injure the reputation of a living person or the memory of a deceased person, and to expose him to public hatred, disgrace, ridicule, or contempt, or to exclude him from society, is known as *defamation. Slander* is *oral* defamation of one person by another in the presence of a third person or persons; *libel* is *written* or *printed* defamation of one person by another, published before a third person or persons. A corporation is a person in this sense. For a slanderous statement to be actionable, it must be false and must cause injury to the person to whom the statement refers. In libel actions, no injury need be proved, although, of course, proved injury will affect the amount of damages awarded. (See also LIBELOUS LETTERS.)

Libelous letters. For a letter to be libelous (see LIBEL AND SLANDER), it must have been read by someone other than the person defamed. The reader may be a stenographer who takes the libelous writing by dictation and transcribes the notes, although some courts have taken the view that publication to a stenographer does not subject the writer to liability unless the letter was prompted by actual malice.

License, business. Federal, state, or city approval and permission are necessary to engage in certain businesses that are of sufficient concern to the public to justify regulation. Permission and approval are issued in the form of a license, for which a fee is charged.

Lien. A charge imposed on property by which the property is made security for the discharge of an obligation. Some liens, particularly those on personal property, must be accompanied by actual possession of the property: a lienor (the holder of a lien) who parts with possession loses his lien. Other liens, particularly those on real estate, need not be accompanied by possession: the lienor gives notice of the lien he claims by a public record of it. Some of the common liens are vendor's lien, MECHANIC'S LIEN, mortgage lien (see Mortgage, in *Index*), and TAX LIEN.

Life estate. An interest in property, real or personal, that lasts only for the duration of the owner's life. A life estate may also be for the duration of another's life, or may terminate with the happening of a certain contingency. For example, a life estate may terminate upon the marriage of the owner. This estate may be created by an act of the parties, as by deed, will, or gift; or by operation of law, as by dower or curtesy. The owner of a life estate (called the LIFE TENANT) has the current use of the property and is responsible for its maintenance, including taxes and carrying charges. He also gets the income from the property, but cannot ordinarily sell the property or do anything to impair its permanent value. However, the life tenant may be allowed to sell or consume property to support himself if the deed or will so provides. He cannot dispose of the property at his death. The person or persons to whom the estate passes upon termination of the life estate is determined when the life estate is created. The estate that is left at the termination of the life estate is called a *remainder;* the person to whom it passes is a *remainderman* (plural, *remaindermen*).

Life tenant. The owner of a LIFE ESTATE. Beneficiaries with life interests under trusts are sometimes called equitable life tenants.

Limited partnership. A partnership in which the liability of one or more special partners for debts of the firm is limited to the amount of his investment in the business. Special partners have no voice in the management of the partnership. They merely invest money and receive a certain share of the profits. There must be one or more general partners who manage the business and remain liable for all its debts.

A limited partnership is organized under state statutes, usually by filing a certificate in a public office and publishing a notice in a newspaper. The statutes, codified in many states as the Uniform Limited Partnership Law, must be strictly observed. A limited partnership is regarded as a general partnership in states other than the state in which it is organized; therefore, it must register and form a limited partnership with the same firm members under the laws of each state in which it wishes to do business.

As in a general partnership, the death, insanity, or bankruptcy of any one of the general partners dissolves the limited partnership. (See PARTNERSHIP.)

Liquidated damages. An amount that the parties to a contract have agreed upon shall be paid in satisfaction of a loss resulting from a

BREACH OF CONTRACT. The amount must be in proportion to the actual loss; otherwise the agreement is unenforceable.

Mandamus. (Latin for "We command.") A writ issued by a court of superior jurisdiction to a public or private corporation, or an official thereof, or an inferior court, commanding the performance of an official act, which the person or body named in the writ had failed or refused to perform. It is an extraordinary WRIT, which is issued in cases where the usual and ordinary procedures do not afford remedies to the party aggrieved. The writ of mandamus is known as a remedy for official inaction. It was introduced to prevent disorder from a failure of public officials to perform their duties and is still an important legal remedy for the protection of the public and of individuals against exploitation and abuse by official inaction. Mandamus is frequently applied for in order to control the letting of public contracts.

A mandamus may also enforce a private right. It compels the performance by a corporation of a variety of specific acts within the scope of the corporation's duties. For example, a stockholder may institute a mandamus proceeding to compel a corporation to submit to an inspection of its books and records.

The writ is either peremptory or alternate. The peremptory mandamus compels the defendant to perform the required act; the alternate mandamus compels him to perform the act or show cause on a certain day why he should not perform it. The alternate writ is usually issued first.

Massachusetts trust. A business association formed under a deed of trust, which is really a contract between the trustees and beneficiaries. It is also known as a business trust or a common-law trust. Its structure closely resembles that of a CORPORATION. The interests of the beneficiaries are represented by certificates, frequently called certificates of stock, which may be divided into several classes of common and preferred stock and may be listed on stock exchanges. The trustees correspond to the directors and the certificate holders to the stockholders. The trustees manage the property and pay dividends out of the profits. They usually appoint and remove the officers. Unlike a corporation, the management is permanent. The trustees are personally liable in dealing with outsiders unless they clearly indicate that they are acting as trustees and that the creditors shall look only to the trust property for all payments.

Massachusetts trusts are regarded as corporations under many taxing statutes and Federal acts.

The duration is limited by statute in most states, but the parties interested at the time the trust expires can agree to another trust.

Mechanic's lien. The statutory lien of a contractor, subcontractor, laborer, or materialman, who performs labor or furnishes material for the permanent improvement of real property with the consent or at the request of the owner or his authorized agent. The lien attaches to the building upon which the labor was performed or for which the material was furnished, and to as much of the land upon which the building is located as is necessary. A mechanic's lien is for the amount of the contract plus interest. Notice of the lien must be filed in the public filing place prescribed by statute. If a mechanic's lien is not discharged, it may be foreclosed subject to all prior liens.

Merger. The absorption of one or more corporations by another existing corporation, which retains its identity and takes over all the rights, privileges, franchises, and properties of the absorbed companies. The absorbing corporation continues its existence, whereas the other companies terminate their existence. For example, Companies *A*, *B*, and *C* agree to combine so that Companies *A* and *B* are absorbed by *C*. When the plan becomes effective, Companies *A* and *B* go out of existence and Company *C* remains. The remaining company takes care of the creditors of the constituent companies.

The procedure designated by statute to bring about the merger must be followed. The percentage of the stockholders fixed in the law must approve the agreement. Where the statute so provides, stockholders who dissent to the plan may obtain cash for the appraised value of their shares, instead of shares in the remaining company.

Minutes of corporate meetings. A minute is the official recording of proceedings at a meeting. Specifically, in the plural, the word means the official record of the proceedings at a meeting of an organized body, such as the stockholders or directors of a corporation. It is not essential to the validity or binding effect of acts done by an organized body that minutes be kept, but accurate minutes avoid future misunderstandings. They are particularly useful if the corporation institutes suit or is sued upon a matter recorded in the minutes. Ordinarily minutes are PRIMA FACIE EVIDENCE of what transpired at the meeting; frequently they are the best evidence. *See also Index.*

Misdemeanor. See CRIMINAL LAW.

Muniments of title. Written evidence by which title to real property may be defended. The word *muniments* is derived from the Latin verb *munio*, meaning *to fortify.* Hence, muniments of title fortify or strengthen rights in property. The expression as generally defined refers to deeds of conveyance, wills, legislative grants, and other documents relating to the title to land.

Negotiable instrument. A written instrument, signed by a maker or drawer, containing an unconditional promise or order to pay a certain sum of money, which can be passed freely from one person to another in a manner that constitutes the transferee the holder. If payable to bearer, the instrument may be negotiated simply by delivery; if payable to order, it is negotiated by endorsement of the holder, completed by delivery.

The Uniform Negotiable Instruments Law governs negotiable instruments in all the states except in a few where it has been replaced by the Uniform Commercial Code. The law states the manner in which a negotiable instrument shall be transferred, and it fixes the rights and duties of the maker, the payee, the holder, and the endorser. For example, under the law an endorser of a negotiable instrument vouches for its genuineness. If it is a forgery, the endorser is liable to a HOLDER IN DUE COURSE of the instrument after delivery.

Strictly speaking, documents of title (such as order bills of lading, warehouse receipts, and stock certificates) are not negotiable instruments because they do not contain an order to pay a sum of money. However, various statutes have given certain documents of title the quality of negotiability. These are known as quasi-negotiable instruments.

Negotiation. The transfer of a written instrument in a manner that makes the transferee the holder of the instrument. If payable to order, an instrument is negotiated by endorsement and delivery; if payable to bearer, by delivery alone. An instrument is not negotiated until it is transferred by the person to whom it is issued. Thus, *A* makes a note payable to *B* and delivers it to him. Subsequently, by negotiation, *B* transfers the note to *C*, and *C* to *D*, and so on. As opposed to transfer by ASSIGNMENT, the innocent transferee by negotiation takes the paper free of defenses that are good against the transferor.

Novation. The substitution of a new contract, or debtor or obligor, for an existing one. The substitution must be agreed to by all the parties.

Example: A sells a car to *B*, who makes a small down payment and agrees to pay the balance in installments. Finding himself unable to make the payments, *B* sells the car to *C*, who agrees to make the payments to *A*. If *A* agrees to release *B* from the contract and to look to *C* for payment, a novation is created.

Obiter dictum. See DICTUM.

Offer and acceptance. See CONTRACTS, 1.

Omnibus. A term applied to that which contains two or more independent matters. The term is applied, for example, to a legislative bill that relates to two or more subjects.

Option. An agreement, usually in consideration for the payment of a certain sum of money by the offeree, to hold an offer open for a definite period of time. The offer ceases to be an offer and becomes a contract of option; it cannot be withdrawn until the option period expires. Although an option is generally based upon a consideration, a few states require no consideration if the contract is in writing. Others recognize an option under seal as binding because a seal, at COMMON LAW, indicates consideration. The consideration for an option is not returnable to the optionee if he fails to take up the option; it is, however, usually applied to the purchase price if the offer is accepted.

Ordinance. A law or statute. The word is commonly used to apply to enactments of a municipality.

Partnership. "An association of two or more persons to carry on as co-owners a business for profit." [1] Partnerships are governed by fairly uniform laws, which are codified in many states by the Uniform Partnership Law. A partnership may carry on business in any state without paying greater taxes than residents of the state pay.

Each partner of a general partnership is fully liable personally for all partnership debts regardless of the amount of his investment. (See LIMITED PARTNERSHIP.) All types of capital produced or acquired by the partnership become partnership property. Real estate is generally acquired in the individual names of the partners or in the name of one partner who holds the property in trust for the partnership.

In the absence of a specific contract, partners share profits and losses equally. It is customary, however, to provide in the partnership agreement that profits and losses shall be distributed pro rata according to the amount of capital contributed by each, or in any other ratio to which they agree. Partners have no right to salaries unless they are agreed upon, even though one partner may devote all of his time to the business and the other may devote little or none. The agreement may provide for the division of profits after allowing each of the partners an agreed-upon salary.

Partnerships are dissolved without violation of the partnership agreement by (1) withdrawal of one of the members under some circumstances; (2) operation of law through death or bankruptcy of one of the partners or a change in the law that makes the partnership's business illegal; (3) court decree granted because of incapacity or insanity of one of the partners, gross misconduct, or neglect or breach of duty.

Patents, applications for. *What is a patent.* A *patent* is an exclusive right granted by the Federal Government for a fixed period of time, to make, use, and sell an invention. A person who perfects a new machine, process, or material, or any new and useful improvement of them, or who invents or discovers and reproduces a distinct and new variety of plant, may make application to the government for a patent for it. The person to whom a patent is granted is called the *patentee.* Patent rights are issued in the form of *letters* and run to the patentee, his heirs and assigns, generally for a period of 17 years. A *design patent,* which is an ornamental design to be placed upon an article of manufacture, runs for three and one-half, seven, or fourteen years, according to the application made by the patentee. A patent is not renewable. Anyone using a patented product without the owner's consent may be compelled to pay damages.

Procedure. When a client wishes to obtain a patent, he brings, or

---

[1] Uniform Partnership Law

sends, the details of his invention or discovery to the lawyer in the form of a *disclosure*. The disclosure may be a picture, a sketch, or a working model. An idea is not patentable; only the device for carrying out an idea can be patented.

The Patent Office will not respond to inquiries about the novelty of an alleged invention, so the patent lawyer must make a *search* to learn what patent or patents have already been issued on that idea. The copies of other patents issued on an idea are called *prior art*, and they may be inspected at the Patent Office. The patent lawyer studies the art prior to preparing the application. Copies of patents may be obtained from the Patent Office for 25 cents; copies of trade marks, for 10 cents.

There are various divisions in the United States Patent Office, each of which handles applications for certain types of patents. The patent lawyer sends the application to the Commissioner of Patents, who sends it to the appropriate division; the next step will be an *official action*. The official action may be an *allowance*, which means that the Patent Office deems the application ready to issue into a patent. In almost every case, however, the official action is a response by the Patent Office in which the Patent Office Examiner points out the items in the application he considers objectionable for one reason or another. Some of the divisions in the Patent Office are so overloaded with applications that it may take two years or more to get an official action. After receipt of the official action, the attorney has six months in which to file an amendment. In the amendment the lawyer takes each point objected to by the examiner and either deletes it from the application or argues for it. There is no definite time by which the Patent Office responds to the amendment, the time depending upon the volume of work in the particular division. If the first amendment does not make the application ready for allowance, then there must be another amendment and so on until the examiner states that the next amendment must be final. The average number of amendments is three or four. If the patent lawyer does not think the examiner has a clear view of the whole idea, he may go to Washington and interview the examiner. Sometimes this facilitates the allowance.

Parts of the application. The application consists of:

1. *Specification.* This is a written description of the invention or discovery and the manner and process of making it.

2. *Claims.* These are the assertions made for the invention. Each individual part of the invention is written up as a claim. A design patent has only one claim, but other patents may have many claims. These claims are numbered 1, 2, 3 and so on. A patent application might begin with 40 claims and have only 15 when it is finally allowed. Some claims will be "stricken" because the claim has been covered by a prior invention.

3. *Drawings of the invention.*

4. *Petition.* This gives the name, residence, and post office address of the inventor and the title of the invention sought to be patented.

5. *Oath or affirmation.* The applicant swears or affirms that he believes himself to be the first inventor or discoverer of the invention sought to be patented.

6. *Power of attorney.* The applicant usually gives his lawyers power of attorney (see Chapter 10) to transact all business in the Patent Office connected with the patent.

What the secretary does. 1. The lawyer will dictate the specification and claims. Make an original, a copy for each inventor, and a file copy on plain legal-size paper.

2. The oath, power of attorney, and petition are printed forms that you can easily fill in. They are frequently combined in one document. Make an original and the same number of copies as you made of the specification and claims.

3. The applications must be signed and verified before a notary public by the inventor, or inventors if there is more than one. When there is more than one inventor, there must be a separate verification for each if the inventors do not sign the application at the same time, or if they are at different locations when signing.

4. Have photoprints made of the drawings of the invention, send one copy to the inventor (or a copy to each inventor) and keep one for your files. The originals made by a draftsman accompany the application to the Patent Office for filing.

5. The Patent Office issues rules about how the papers are arranged, the backing, and the like.

6. As soon as the application is typed and assembled, send it to the applicant for signature and verification. If there is more than one inventor, you will have to send the application to each in turn for his signature and verification.

7. Make diary or calendar entries with reference to any action that must be taken at a future date. Although an application for a patent is not a legal action, it is advisable to keep a progress record sheet (Chapter 15). You might keep the sheet in the file folder. If litigation develops from the application, keep the same records that you do in any litigated matter.

Assignment of application for patent. Frequently an inventor agrees to assign his patent rights before he applies for the patent. When he does, he makes an *assignment of application* simultaneously with his application. A printed form is usually used. Make an original, a copy for each applicant, and a copy for your file. Send the original to the inventor (or inventors) for signature and acknowledgment before a notary public. When original has been executed by each inventor, forward it to the Patent Office to be recorded. The Patent Office will return the assignment after it has been recorded; forward it to the assignee.

Covering letters that the secretary writes. Whenever the lawyer sends papers to the client or to the Patent Office you can write the covering letters without dictation. Here are three sample letters.

Letter forwarding application to Patent Office.

The Commissioner of Patents
United States Patent Office
Washington, D. C.
Sir:

We are enclosing, for filing, the application of ....(inventor or inventors) .... for Letters Patent covering an improvement in ....(title)..., Case .... . We are also enclosing our check for $ ...... to cover the first government fee.

Very truly yours,

Letter forwarding assignment to Patent Office for recording.

The Commissioner of Patents
United States Patent Office
Washington, D. C.
Sir:

We enclose for recording assignment of ....(patentee or patentees).... transferring unto ....(assignee)..., a (an) ....(name of state).... corporation, all right title and interest in and to his (their) application for ....(title)...., Case ......, executed .... and transmitted for filing of even date herewith.

Our check for $3.00 to cover the recording fee is also enclosed.

Very truly yours,

Letter sending issued patent to patentee.

Dear Mr. ....:

We are enclosing original United States Letters Patent No. ...., issued to you on ....(date)..., covering an improvement in ....(title).... .

Please acknowledge receipt of the patent.

Yours very truly,

Perjury. The crime of wilfully giving, under oath, false testimony as to some material matter in a legal or judicial proceeding. Some state statutes do not consider materiality an essential of perjury. A statement that one does not remember certain facts when he really does is perjury; conversely, swearing one remembers something when in fact he has no recollection of it is also perjury. Honest but erroneous expression of opinion is not perjury. A statement substantially true but literally false is not necessarily perjury.

Personal property. A right or interest, protected by law, in something that is not land or anything permanently attached to land (see REAL PROPERTY). Personal property is movable. It may be tangibles (also called *chattels*), such as money, gold, merchandise, or any movable object susceptible to physical possession, or intangibles, such as contracts, stocks, and the like (see CHOSE IN ACTION). Personal property may be an interest in land: a 99-year lease is personal property. Products of the soil become personal property when severed from the land: trees and crops that are sold while attached to the land constitute real property, but when severed from the land they constitute personal property.

Title to personal property may be acquired by the following methods: (1) Appropriation or original possession: although almost all property today belongs to someone, there are still some kinds of property, such as wild game and fish, that may be appropriated. (2) Discovery: the finder of lost property acquires a title that is good against everyone except the rightful owner. (3) Creation: a person is entitled to that which he produces by his physical or mental labor, unless the product is produced during the course of his employment or under some other contract; then it belongs to his employer or the party for whom he contracted to create the property. (4) Gift. (5) Sale or exchange. (6) Will. (7) Operation of law: when a person dies without making a will, his property passes by operation of law to certain relatives. Or, if a person becomes bankrupt, his property, with certain exceptions, passes to a trustee for the benefit of creditors. A person's property may also be taken from him by legal process (see EXECUTION, 1).

Pleadings. *See Index.*

Pledge. The placement of personal property by the owner with a lender as security for a debt. Pawned articles and stocks and bonds put up as collateral for a loan are the most common pledges. Essentials of a pledge are (1) a debt or obligation to be secured; (2) the thing pledged; (3) the pledgor (the one who gives the pledge) and the pledgee (the one who receives the pledge); (4) transfer of possession of the property (if actual physical possession is practically impossible, the pledgee may acquire CONSTRUCTIVE possession); (5) retention of title in the pledgor; (6) the pledgor's right to redeem the pledge; (7) a contract, express or implied, covering the transaction.

When stock is pledged as collateral, the pledgee has the right and is bound to collect the dividends and apply them to the loan, in the absence of an agreement to the contrary between the pledgor and pledgee. This is the legal theory. As a matter of practice, the stockholder makes an assignment of the stock in blank and the stock is not transferred on the books of the corporation unless the pledgor defaults; the stockholder-pledgor therefore continues to collect the dividends.

Police power. That power which any governmental body has to protect the property, life, health, and well-being of its citizen by legislation. State minimum wage laws have been held by the United States Supreme Court to be a proper exercise of the states' police powers. Under police powers states license doctors and lawyers, barbers and beauticians, and the like, and only those who obtain a license are authorized to practice their profession or trade. City ordinances that require certain standards of cleanliness in restaurants, or that impose building restrictions, are regulations issued under police power. The extent of a governing body's police power is limited by the state constitutions and by the Fourteenth Amendment to the Constitution of the United States, which protects personal liberties and freedoms. The power of Congress to regulate and control business activities is not a police power but is a power granted by the several states and by the Constitution.

Power of attorney. A written instrument in which the principal (the person giving the power of attorney) authorizes another to act for him. The instrument may be a blanket authorization, but more commonly it authorizes the agent to represent the principal in one specific transaction, as the closing of a real estate deal; or to do a certain act continuously, as the signing of checks. The person appointed is commonly called an ATTORNEY-IN-FACT. A power of attorney may be revoked at the will of the principal, unless it was given to the agent for a consideration.

Pre-emptive right. The right of each stockholder, upon the issuance of additional shares by the corporation, to purchase his proportion of the new stock in order to maintain his relative interest in the corporation. *Example:*

If *A* owns $10,000 of the $100,000 worth of stock issued and outstanding, and the corporation increases its authorized capital stock to $200,000, *A* will have a right to purchase 1/10 of the new issue, or an additional $10,000 worth of stock, before the stock may be offered to outsiders. The stockholder has a right to purchase the stock at the price fixed by the corporation, and, if he fails to take it, it cannot be offered to anyone else upon more favorable terms. He must be given reasonable notice of his right to subscribe, and a reasonable opportunity to exercise the right. Stockholders who are not in a position to take and pay for the stock to which they are entitled may sell the rights to anyone who can. A stockholder may also waive his pre-emptive right by agreement with the corporation.

The pre-emptive right is governed by statute in many states. Frequently the certificate of incorporation regulates the pre-emptive right in accordance with the governing statute. In the absence of regulating statute and charter provisions, the court decisions determine under what circumstances the pre-emptive right exists; these decisions in many instances are conflicting.

Pre-trial. A system to expedite the progress of a case. Before the trial of a case, the judge calls counsel for both sides into conference for the purpose of settling issues that are either unnecessary or not disputed. Counsel agree on undisputed and indisputable facts common to both parties; on exhibits, as to authenticity of originals and accuracy of copies; and on various other matters that ordinarily consume considerable time in the trial of a case. For example, in an automobile accident case, the ownership of the car is admitted, without the necessity of putting a witness on the stand to testify as to the ownership.

Pre-trial is a comparatively new technique. Judge Ira W. Jayne, of Detroit originated it as a system in 1929, although individual judges had used the device previously. It has not yet been accepted officially in all of the states, but some judges use it in jurisdictions where court rules neither require nor specifically sanction it. Rule 16 of Federal Rules provides for Pre-trial, making the use of it optional with each judge. There is no set form for Pre-trial, the procedure varying from state to state, and from judge to judge.

At the end of the Pre-trial conference, the judge prepares an order embodying the results of the conference. There is no uniformity in the method of preparing it. The order is official and controls the case to the same extent as any other order.

Probate bond. See COURT BOND.

Prima facie evidence. Evidence deemed by law to be sufficient to establish a fact if the evidence is not disputed. For example, the placement of a corporate seal on an instrument is prima facie evidence that the instrument was executed by authority of the corporation.

Private law. See PUBLIC AND PRIVATE LAW.

Privity. Mutual or successive relationship to the same right of property, or the power to take advantage of and enforce a promise or warranty. Identity of interest is essential. There must be a connection or bond of union between parties as to some particular transaction. Thus, privity of contract exists between a lessor and lessee, because the parties are mutually interested in the lease. Privity of contract also exists between a lessor and an assignee of the lease, because the assignee succeeded to the rights of the lessee. Heirs, executors, and assigns succeed to the rights and liabilities of a contract whether it so states or not. They are thus *privies* to the contract.

Privity affects legal rights and duties and, in many cases, determines whether a party may sue or be sued. Thus, a privy has the same right to relief against mistake of fact as the original party to a contract. A stranger to a contract has no right to sue for fraud, but a privy does. An injunction extends to all persons in privity with the parties enjoined. Evidence may be admissible or inadmissible because of privity. Privity may be an element in an action for negligence, or in the substitution of parties in a legal action.

Proprietorship, sole. One of the three most common forms of business organization. Ownership of the business is vested in one proprietor. The other two common forms of business organization are PARTNERSHIP and CORPORATION.

Protest. A formal certificate attesting the DISHONOR of a NEGOTIABLE INSTRUMENT after NEGOTIATION. A protest is usually made by a notary public but may be made by a responsible citizen, in the presence of two witnesses. The certificate states that the instrument was duly presented for payment, at the proper time and place, that payment was refused for the reason given. and that the holder intends to hold the drawer and endorser responsible for payment. The protest is attached to the dishonored instrument or a copy of it. Notice of protest is then sent to the parties who are secondarily liable (drawer and endorser). Protest is required only when a bill of exchange or check drawn in one state (or country) and payable in another is dishonored, but as a matter of business practice domestic instruments are often "protested." The word protest is loosely applied to the process of presenting an instrument for payment, demanding payment, and giving notice to the drawer or endorser.

Example:

Buyer accepts a trade acceptance drawn by Seller. Seller endorses and discounts the acceptance at Doe Bank, which sends it to Roe Bank for collection. Roe Bank's notary public (usually an employee) presents the instrument to Buyer for payment, which is refused. The notary then *protests* (using the term loosely): he makes out the certificate, attaches it to the instrument and sends notice of protest to Seller, who is secondarily liable, through Doe Bank. In this case, Seller is the drawer and the endorser.

Public and private law. Public law is the law that relates to the public as a whole, rather than to a specific individual. It involves the authority of the Federal and state governments to make laws and of Federal and state executives to issue orders, as well as ADMINISTRATIVE LAW and CRIMINAL LAW. Private law is that body of the law that pertains to the relationship between individuals as such. It includes laws relating to contracts, sales, agency, negotiable instruments, and business organizations.

Public utility. A private corporation that renders service to an indefinite public, which has a legal right to demand and receive the service or commodities of the corporation. Public utilities are subject to special laws that do not apply to other corporations, and they are closely supervised by governmental agencies. They owe a duty to the public that they may be compelled to perform. For example, a railroad company cannot abandon part of its route without authority from the Interstate Commerce Commission. On the other hand, public utilities are given certain powers of a public nature, for example, the power of EMINENT DOMAIN. Public utilities include railroads, bus lines, airlines, gas and electric companies, hydroelectric, water, and irrigation corporations.

Quasi. (Latin.) Almost; like; resembling. Thus, we speak of certain Federal agencies, such as the Federal Trade Commission, as being "quasi-judicial" bodies because they have powers, resembling those of a judicial body, to enforce certain rules and regulations. Or we speak of certain documents of title as being "quasi-negotiable instruments" —they are invested by statute with certain characteristics of negotiability but are not NEGOTIABLE INSTRUMENTS as that term is defined by the Uniform Negotiable Instruments Law.

Quiet title, action to. An equity proceeding to establish the plaintiff's title to land by bringing into court an adverse claimant and compelling him either to establish his claim or to be estopped from asserting it. Whenever a deed or other instrument exists that may throw a cloud over the complainant's title or interest, a court of equity will clear the title by directing that the instrument be cancelled, or by making other decree required by the rights of the parties. For example, when a real estate mortgage is valid on its face but has ceased to be a lien, it may be cancelled as a cloud on the title by an action to quiet title.

Quit-claim deed. *See Index.*

Quo warranto. (Latin for "by what authority.") A WRIT of inquiry as to the warrant or authority for doing the act complained of. The writ tests the right of a person to hold an office or franchise or to exercise some right or privilege derived from the state. Quo warranto affirms an existing right to an office, or it sets aside wrongful claims of a pretender. An information in the nature of a quo warranto has replaced the old writ, but the terms *information in the nature of a quo warranto* and *quo warranto* are used interchangeably and synonymously and have substantially the same purpose. The power to file a quo warranto is incident to the office of the attorney general, but the privilege of instituting the proceeding upon the refusal of the attorney general to act has been granted to private individuals in their capacity as taxpayers and citizens.

Quorum. The number of persons who must legally be present at a meeting to transact corporate business or the business of any assembly of persons. When the membership of the assembling group or body consists of a *definite* number of persons as required by law—for example, a board of directors or the United States Senate—a majority (more than half) of the members are required to make a quorum, unless the controlling law expressly states that another number constitutes a quorum. At COMMON LAW, when the membership of the assembling body consists of an *indefinite* number of persons (that is, the law requires no definite number)—as the stockholders of a corporation—any number constitutes a quorum; however, the BY-LAWS, and frequently the statutes or charter, customarily make an express provision concerning a quorum. In the case of a stockholders' meeting, the designated quorum usually relates to the amount of stock represented at the meeting, and not to the number of stockholders.

Ratification. The approval of an act which had not been binding previously; ratification, or affirmance, reverts and becomes effective as of the date the act was performed. An infant may ratify, or affirm, his contracts after he reaches his majority; a principal may ratify, or affirm, the unauthorized acts of an agent; a corporation may ratify, or affirm, the unauthorized acts of its officers. A corporation cannot ratify or affirm the acts of its promoters before the corporation was formed because it was not in existence and could not possibly have entered into a contract at that date. It may, however, *adopt* the acts of the promoters.

Regulations. See ADMINISTRATIVE LAW.

Real property. (*See also Real estate, in Index.*) The land, APPURTENANCES, and man-made improvements that are attached to it. All other property is PERSONAL PROPERTY. Hence, in addition to the land, real property includes the buildings, natural growth, minerals, and timber, that have not been separated from the land. Apples on the tree constitute real property, whereas harvested apples become personal property.

An interest in real property is an *estate*, and runs the entire gamut of varying rights from an estate in FEE SIMPLE (absolute ownership) to a LEASEHOLD (the right to use property during a fixed term for a specific consideration). An *estate* is only a designation of a particular type of interest in property; it is not a legal entity. Other forms of estates are modifications and limitations of a fee simple estate. (See LIFE ESTATE; TENANCY BY THE ENTIRETY; JOINT TENANCY; TENANCY IN COMMON.)

Remainderman. See LIFE ESTATE.

Replevin. A court action to recover possession of property unlawfully taken or detained. Title to the property must be in the person bringing the action. Thus, if title passes to the buyer and the seller refuses to deliver the goods, the buyer may bring an action in replevin to get possession of the goods. Or, the seller under a conditional sale contract by which he retains title to the goods until payment is made, may recover the goods by an action in replevin if the buyer does not make the payments called for by the contract.

Rescission. An action in equity whereby a court is asked to annul a contract entered into through fraud, misrepresentation, or excusable error. For example, if a person enters into a contract of partnership and then discovers that material facts were misrepresented, he brings an action in rescission. Rescission may be absolute or qualified. Thus, in rescission of a contract of sale, the seller resumes title and possession of the goods as though he had never parted with them, but he has no claim for damages. In qualified rescission he resumes title and possession but does not rescind the entire contract because he reserves the right to sue for damages. A contract may also be rescinded by mutual consent.

Residuary estate. That part of a testator's estate remaining after payment of the legacies and debts. The testator usually makes certain bequests and then names the person or institution who shall receive the remainder, or residue, of his estate. That person or institution is the *residuary legatee.*

Restrictive covenant. A provision in an agreement limiting or restricting the action of one of the parties to the agreement. Thus, a seller of a business may agree not to engage in the same business within a certain numbers of years. Or a deed may contain a covenant restricting the type of building that may be placed upon the property. A restrictive covenant of this type is said to "run with the land"—subsequent purchasers are bound by the covenant whether or not it is expressly set forth in the deed to them.

Royalties. Payments or rentals made to the owner of a patent for the privilege of manufacturing or renting the patented article. The term is also applied to payments made to authors and composers for the sale of copyrighted material, and to payments under gas, oil, mining, or mineral leases.

Service of process. The law compels the giving of notice of a suit to a defendant, so as to make him a party to the suit, and compels him to appear in court or suffer JUDGMENT BY DEFAULT. The means of compelling a defendant to appear in court is called "process"; the giving of the notice is known as "service of process." (See SUMMONS and SERVICE BY PUBLICATION; also *Index.*)

Service by publication. Generally service of process or other notice is personal or upon the agent of the party to be served, but where personal service is impossible, service may be had in many cases by *publication.* The paper to be served is published in a designated newspaper a required number of times. Certain other legal formalities are also observed, such as mailing the paper to the party's last known address. Usually service by publication is permitted if the party to be served is a non-resident, or is absent from the jurisdiction, or if his address is unknown. *Proof of publication* is made in the form of an affidavit by the publisher.

Silent partner. A partner who has no voice in the management of the partnership business. Unless he is also a special partner (see LIMITED PARTNERSHIP), a silent partner is equally responsible with the other partners for the debts of the partnership.

Slander. See LIBEL AND SLANDER.

Special partner. See LIMITED PARTNERSHIP.

Specific performance. The performance of a contract according to its exact terms. A court of EQUITY will enforce specific performance, whereas a court of law awards damages to the injured party to a contract. Specific performance is never enforced in contracts for personal services. It is usually confined to sales of REAL PROPERTY and unique personal property, for instance an antique.

Star page. The line and word at which the pages of a first edition of a law book began are frequently indicated by a star in differently paginated later editions. The original page number is indicated in the margin. In citing a few well-known works, the edition is left out and the star page is referred to, thus, 1 Bl. Comm. *150.

Statute of frauds. A statute, enacted with variations in all the states, providing that certain contracts cannot be enforced unless they are in writing signed by the party against whom the contract is sought to be enforced. The writing need not be a formal document signed by both parties—a written note or memorandum of the transaction signed by the party to be bound by the agreement is sufficient. The laws in the various states are fairly uniform in requiring the following contracts to be in writing:

1. A special promise to be responsible for the debt, default, or miscarriage of a third person.

2. An agreement by an executor or administrator to become liable out of his own property for the debts of the estate.

3. A contract, the consideration for which is marriage. Engagement contracts are not included.

4. Contracts for the sale of real estate or any interest therein.

5. Contracts that cannot be performed within one year.

6. Contracts involving the sale of personal property in excess of a certain amount (which varies in the different states), when no part of the property has been delivered and no part of the purchase price has been paid.

In addition, many states require the following contracts to be in writing:

1. An agreement to bequeath property or to make any provision for someone by will.

2. An agreement to pay upon attaining legal majority a debt contracted during infancy.

3. The creation of a trust.

4. The promise to pay a debt that has been outlawed by the statute of limitations or barred by bankruptcy.

5. An assignment of wages to be earned in the future.

6. A mortgage of personal property.

Statute of limitations. A state statute that limits the time within which legal action may be brought, either upon a contract or TORT. State and Federal statutes also limit the time within which certain crimes can be prosecuted. The purpose of the time limitation is to make it impossible to bring suit many years after a cause of action originates, during which time witnesses may have died or important evidence may have been lost. When a debt is involved, it is possible to interrupt (or "toll") the running of the statute—that is, to lengthen the period in which action may be brought—by obtaining a payment on the debt or a promise to pay. A promise to pay a debt that has been barred by the statute of limitations does not require new consideration

STATUTES OF LIMITATIONS IN NUMBER OF YEARS

State	Open Accounts	Notes	Written Contracts	Contracts Under Seal
Alabama	3	6	6	10
Alaska	6	6	6	10
Arizona	3	6[1]	6[1]	6[1]
Arkansas	3	5	5	5
California	4	4[2]	4	4
Colorado	6	6	6[3]	6[3]
Connecticut	6	6[4]	6	17
Delaware	3	6	3	3
District of Columbia	3	3	3	12
Florida	3	5	5	20
Georgia	⸴	6	6	20
Hawaii	6	6	6	6
Idaho	4	5	5	5
Illinois	5	10	10	10
Indiana	6	10	20	20
Iowa	5	10	10	10
Kansas	3	5	5	5
Kentucky	5	15[5]	15	15
Louisiana	3	5	10	10
Maine	6	6	6	20
Maryland	3	3	3	12
Massachusetts	6	6[6]	6	20
Michigan	6	6	6	10
Minnesota	6	6	6	6
Mississippi	3	6	6	6
Missouri	5	10	5	10
Montana	5	8	8	8
Nebraska	4	5	5	5
Nevada	4	6	6	6
New Hampshire	6	6	6	20
New Jersey	6	6	6	16
New Mexico	4	6	6	6
New York	6	6	6	6
North Carolina	3	3	3	10
North Dakota	6	6	6[3]	6[3]
Ohio	6	15	15	15
Oklahoma	3	5	5	5
Oregon	6	6	6	10
Pennsylvania	6	6	6[7]	20
Rhode Island	6	6	6	20
South Carolina	6	6	6	20
South Dakota	6	6	6	20
Tennessee	6	6	6	6
Texas	2	4	4	4
Utah	4	6	6	6
Vermont	6	6[8]	6	8
Virginia	3	5	5	10
Washington	3	6	6	6
West Virginia	5	10	10	10
Wisconsin	6	6	6	20[9]
Wyoming	8	10	10	10

[1] Executed without the state, 4 years.
[2] Corporate notes, 6 years.
[3] Contracts affecting real property, 10 years.
[4] Non-negotiable notes, 17 years.
[5] 5 year period applies if note is placed on the footing of a bill of exchange.
[6] Witnessed notes, 20 years.
[7] Sales contracts, 4 years.
[8] Witnessed notes, 14 years.
[9] If action accrues outside state, 10 years.

(see CONTRACTS, 4) but many states require such a promise to be in writing. The statutes often differentiate between oral and written contracts.

Statutory law. Rules that have been formulated into law by legislative action. The Constitution of the United States and the constitutions of the various states are the fundamental written law. All other law must be in harmony with the constitutions, which define and limit the powers of Government. State constitutions must be in harmony with the Constitution of the United States. Congress, cities and towns, and other governmental units find in the constitutions their authority, either express or implied, to enact certain laws. These legislative enactments are called statutes and constitute the greater part of the written or statutory law. Statutory law supplements and supersedes COMMON LAW. (See also ADMINISTRATIVE LAW.)

Subornation. The crime of procuring another to commit perjury. We speak of *suborning* witnesses.

Subpoena. A writ or order commanding the person named in it to appear and testify in a legal proceeding.

Subrogation. The substitution of one person in another's place.

Example: *A*'s car is insured by an insurance company against collision. *A*'s car is negligently damaged by *B*. The insurance company pays $150 for repairs to *A*'s car. The insurance company is subrogated to *A*'s position and may prosecute the claim for damages against *B*.

Substantive law. The part of the law that creates, defines, and regulates rights and duties. Substantive law is opposed to *adjective* or *procedural* law, which provides the method of administering and protecting the rights, duties, and obligations created by substantive law. All statutes of a general nature are substantive law; those regulating administrative and court proceedings are adjective law. All case law, except the decisions interpreting administrative regulations, codes of procedure, and court rules are substantive law. For example, the right of administration of an estate is substantive; the procedures by which the estate can be administered are adjective law. The line of distinction between the two is narrow and often hard to define.

Summary proceeding. A form of legal proceedings in which the established procedure is disregarded, especially in the matter of trial by jury. The term is applied to the process by which a landlord may dispossess a tenant instead of having to resort to eviction, which is a long drawn-out proceeding.

Summons. A legal notice requiring a person to answer a complaint within a specified time. A copy of the summons must be left personally with (served upon) the person against whom it is directed. A corporation is served with process when a copy of the summons is left with an agent of the corporation found in the county. In a few jurisdictions the summons may be left with an adult member of the defendant's household or with some person at the defendant's place of business. An attorney-at-law is often authorized to accept service of a summons for a client. When the summons is served, the process server endorses the summons when, where, and upon whom served, with an affidavit to that effect. This procedure is called the "return of the summons." After return of the summons, the court has jurisdiction over the defendant. *See also Index.*

Supplementary proceeding. When an execution of judgment is returned unsatisfied, the judgment creditor has the right to force the judgment debtor to submit to an examination for the purpose of discovering any assets that may be applied to the payment of the debt. The legal procedure by which the judgment creditor exercises this right is known as a *supplementary proceeding*—it is suplementary to the execution of judgment (see ISSUE OF EXECUTION).

Suretyship. See GUARANTY.

Syndicate. An association of individuals formed to conduct and carry on some particular business transaction, usually of a financial character. A syndicate more nearly resembles a JOINT ADVENTURE than any other business organization. Syndicates in general are temporary associations or firms. They usually terminate automatically when the purpose for which they were formed has been accomplished.

Tax Court practice.[1] All papers filed with the Tax Court, including petitions, motions, briefs, and replies, should conform to the following standards (references are to "Rules of the Tax Court"):

1. PRINTED OR TYPEWRITTEN. All papers shall be either printed or typewritten (Rule 4(a)).

2. PRINTED PAPERS (Rule 4(b)).
   a. *Type.* Use 10- or 12-point type.
   b. *Paper.* Use good, unglazed paper, 5⅞ inches wide by 9 inches long.
   c. *Margin.* Inside margin not less than one inch.
   d. *Spacing.* Double-leaded text and single-leaded quotations.
   e. *Citations.* Italicize citations Rule 4(d)).

3. TYPEWRITTEN PAPERS.
   a. *Typing.* Type on one side only (Rule 4(c)).
   b. *Paper.* Use plain white paper, 8½ inches wide by 11 inches long, weighing not less than 16 pounds to the ream (Rule 4(c)), except for copies which may be on any weight paper (Rule 4(h)).
   c. *Covers.* Attach no backs or covers.
   d. *Citations.* Underscore citations (Rule 4(d)).
   e. *Copies.* Copies shall be clear and legible (Rule 4(h)).

[1] *Acknowledgment:* Roberts, Schultz, and Mayer, *Annotated Forms for Tax Practice.* Englewood Cliffs. N. J.: Prentice-Hall, Inc.

4. FASTENING. Papers shall be fastened on the left side only (Rule 4(a)).

5. CAPTIONS. All papers shall have the proper caption. In the case of an individual petitioner, the caption shall set forth the full given name and surname, without any prefix or title, such as "Mrs.," "Dr.," and so forth. In the case of a fiduciary, the caption shall set forth the name of the estate, trust, or other person for whom he acts, followed by his own name and pertinent title, for example:

THE TAX COURT OF THE UNITED STATES

Estate of John Doe, deceased, Richard
Roe, Executor,
      Petitioner,
          v.   } Docket No._____
Commissioner of Internal Revenue,
      Respondent.   (Rule 4(e)).

6. SIGNATURES.

    a. Original copy. The original of all pleadings, motions, and briefs shall be signed in writing by either the petitioner or his counsel.

    b. Firm name. The signature shall be in the individual and not in the firm name, except that in the case of a petitioner that is a corporation, its signature shall be in the name of the corporation by one of its active officers, for example:

John Doe, Inc.
By /s/ Richard Roe, President.

    c. Name and address. The name and mailing address of the signatory petitioner or counsel shall be typed or printed immediately beneath the written signature (Rule 4(f)).

7. NUMBER OF COPIES.

    a. Except in case of papers filed in more than one proceeding, the number of copies to be filed is tabulated below. Rule 4(g) provides for an original and four conformed copies, except as provided otherwise in the Rules; but the exceptions are numerous, as the following tabulation of the more common papers filed by taxpayers indicates:

Paper	Number To Be Filed	Rule No.
Petition	"original and four complete, accurately conformed, clear copies"	7(a) (1)
Reply	"original and four conformed copies"	15
Request for Place of Hearing	"original and two copies"	26(c)
Brief (Typewritten)	"original and two copies"	35(d)
Brief (Printed)	"20 copies"	35(d)

Paper	Number To Be Filed	Rule No.
Stipulation of Facts	"in duplicate"	31(b)
Computation for Entry of Decision Under Rule 50	"original and two copies"	50
Entry of Appearance	"in duplicate"	24
Application for Subpoena	"only the original"	44(b)
Application to Take Depositions	"verified application and two conformed copies"	45(a)
Interrogatories and Cross-Interrogatories	"original and five copies"	46
Motions (generally)	"four conformed copies with the signed original"	4(g)
Motion for Changing Place Designated for Hearing	"motion with four copies"	26(e)

Whenever a copy is required, it is advisable to submit conformed copies (see page 163). Of course, if the papers are to be submitted "in duplicate," both the original and duplicate should be executed.

b. Where papers are to be filed in more than one proceeding, add to the number of copies otherwise required one additional copy for each such additional proceeding. For example, in the case of a motion to consolidate two proceedings, it is necessary to file a signed original and *five* conformed copies. (Motions generally require *four* conformed copies and the original. See above.) After the proceedings have been consolidated, all papers subsequently filed in the consolidated proceedings should be filed with the signed original and five conformed copies. (Rule 4(g)).

Tax lien. A claim against REAL PROPERTY that accrues to the taxing agency (municipality, township, city) from taxes that are assessed against the property. If the lien is not paid when due, the taxing agency may sell the property at a TAX SALE.

Tax sale. A sale of property, usually at auction, for non-payment of taxes.

Tenancy in common. An estate held by two or more persons by separate and distinct title, with unity of possession only. If a deed is made to two or more persons who are not husband and wife, and nothing is said in the deed concerning the character of the estate created by the deed, the estate created is a *tenancy in common*. The co-owners are tenants in common. They need not have acquired their titles at the same time or by the same instrument. Their shares need not be equal. For example, one co-owner may have an undivided one-tenth interest and the other the remaining undivided nine-tenths interest. Tenants in common are entitled to share the possession of the property according to their shares in the property. Except for their sharing of possession and income, however, the situation is almost as if each tenant in common owned a separate piece of real estate. Each tenant in common may convey or mortgage his share, and the share of each is subject to the lien of judgments against him. Upon the death of one of the tenants in common, his interest passes to his heirs and legatees, and not to the other tenant in common.

Tenancy by the entirety. An estate held by husband and wife by virtue of title acquired by them jointly after marriage. Upon the death of either spouse, his or her interest automatically passes to the other by survivorship. A tenancy by the entirety cannot be terminated without the consent of both parties. Thus, neither spouse can defeat the right of survivorship by mortgage or conveyance without the consent of the other. The courts do not look with disfavor upon a tenancy by the entirety as they do upon a JOINT TENANCY. Not all states recognize tenancy by the entirety or "tenancy by the entireties," as it is sometimes called.

Testamentary trust. See TRUST.

Tort. A civil wrong inflicted otherwise than by a breach of contract. Elements of tort are (1) a wrongful act or omission to obey the law, and (2) an injury to some person. Tort gives the injured party the right to sue for any resulting money loss. Persons (including minors) and corporations are liable for torts. *Example of tort:* A visitor to a department store (even one having no expressed intention to make a purchase but intending merely to examine the merchandise) can recover damages from the proprietor for injuries caused by the negligent maintenance of the store premises. Action arises not from breach of contract but from breach of duty.

Treason. See CRIMINAL LAW.

Trespass. The common meaning of trespass is the unauthorized entry upon the land of another. It also means an unlawful and violent interference with the person or property of another. In the practice of law an *action in trespass* is brought to recover damages for injuries sustained by the plaintiff as the immediate result of trespass.

Trust. A holding of property subject to the duty of applying the property, the income from it, or the proceeds for the benefit of another, as directed by the person creating the trust. A trust is created when A transfers property to X, the trustee, and X undertakes to apply the property and income from it for the purposes and in the manner directed by A. The elements of an ordinary trust are (1) the trustor (also called settlor, donor, or grantor), who furnishes the property to be put in trust; (2) the subject matter or property that is put in trust (called the trust principal, corpus, or res) ; (3) the trustee, who holds the property and administers the trust; and (4) the beneficiaries, for whose benefit the trust exists. A trust may be created by will (testamentary trust) or by deed (*inter vivos* or living trust). Many men put property in trust to pay the income to their wives while they live, then to pay the principal to their children. In these situations the wives would be *income beneficiaries* (or "equitable life tenants") and the children would be remaindermen. (See LIFE ESTATE.)

Ultra vires. A term used to apply to a contract or act beyond the powers of a corporation as expressed or implied in its charter or by statute. For example, if a corporation contracts a debt in excess of the maximum allowed by statute, the contract is *ultra vires*—beyond the power of the corporation. If neither party to the contract has performed, either the corporation or the other party may declare the contract void. After both parties have performed, the courts will not rescind the contract; the weight of authority is to the effect that after one party has performed the other party cannot repudiate the contract by claiming that it was *ultra vires*. Directors may be held personally liable for loss to the corporation occasioned by an *ultra vires* act.

An *ultra vires* contract made by a municipal corporation is not binding upon the municipality, although the other party has performed.

Uniform laws. Conflicting state statutes have led to the adoption, in many fields of business and commercial interest, of similar laws by the various states. The laws are known as "uniform laws." Some of the more important uniform laws are the Uniform Negotiable Instruments Act, the Uniform Partnership Act, the Uniform Stock Transfer Act, and the Uniform Warehouse Receipt Act.

Usury. Contracting for or receiving something in excess of the amount of interest allowed by law for the loan or forbearance of money, as in the sale of goods on credit or under the installment plan. In the majority of states, a lender who charges a usurious rate of interest loses his right to collect any interest, although a few states permit him to collect the legal rate. In some states, both principal and interest are forfeited. Service charges, investigation fees, and commissions charged by an agent are not usually considered interest and may be added to the legal rate without usury. In some states the parties to a contract may agree upon a rate of interest higher than the legal rate but within a statutory limit; in a few states, they may agree on any rate. In some states loans to corporations, but not to individuals, may be made at more than the legal rate. Certain types of loans, such as small personal loans, are not covered by the usury law but are subject to special laws.

Void; voidable. That which is void is of no legal force or effect; that which is voidable may be rendered void. For example, a gambling or wagering contract is void (see CONTRACTS, 3); whereas an infant's contracts are merely voidable at his election (see CONTRACTS, 2).

Voting trust. A method devised for concentrating the control of a company in the hands of a few people. A voting trust is usually organized and operated under a *voting trust agreement*. This is a contract between the stockholders and those who manage the corporation, called the voting trustees. The stockholders transfer their stock to the trustees, giving them the right to vote the stock during the life of the agreement. The trustees, in turn, issue certificates of beneficial interest, called *voting trust certificates,* to the stockholders, who are entitled to the dividends. All stockholders may become parties to the agreement, which is generally subject to statutory regulation. The trust is usually for a definite period of time. When it is terminated, the certificate-holders are notified to exchange their trust certificates for certificates of stock.

Waiver. The surrender, either expressed or implied, of a right to which one is entitled by law. Thus, a stockholder might sign a waiver of notice of meeting, or he might impliedly waive that notice by participation in the meeting. The essence of waiver is conduct that indicates an intention not to enforce certain rights or certain provisions of an agreement. A widow may waive her right to share in the estate of her husband; a buyer may waive delivery on a certain date by accepting the goods at a subsequent date. *See also Index.*

Warranty. Affirmation of a material fact or promise by the seller, which acts as an inducement for the buyer to make a purchase. A warranty may be express (a direct statement made by the seller), or implied (one that is indicated by the nature of the contract). Warranties relate to many things: fitness of the goods sold for a special purpose; merchantability of the goods; title to real or personal property (see specific titles in Index); and quiet enjoyment of premises. All representations made by an applicant for insurance, whether material or not, are deemed warranties. The term "guaranty" is loosely used in the sense of warranty. The common guaranty of a product is, strictly, a warranty and not a guaranty. (See Guaranty.) Any warranty made by a seller which proves to be false gives the buyer a right of legal action.

Without recourse. A phrase used in an Endorsement which relieves the endorser from assuming liability in the event the maker fails to pay the instrument when due.

Writ. An order issued by a court, or judge, in the name of the state, for the purpose of compelling the defendant to do something mentioned in the order.

"Yellow-dog" contract. An oral or written contract under which either party, as a condition of the employment relationship, agrees to join or remain a member of some *specific* labor organization or some *specific* employer organization, or agrees not to join *any* labor organization or *any* employer organization. It is illegal under the Norris-LaGuardia Act and under many state anti-injunction laws.

Index

A

Abbot, forms of address, salutation, close, reference, 106
Abbreviations:
  codes, 359-360
  degrees and honors, 72-73
  in address, 76
  in citations, 365
  in salutations, 76
  law degrees, 5
  reporters, 357-358
  statutes, 359-360
Abstract:
  companies, 488
  of title, 487-489
    secretary's duties, 488
Acceleration clause, in mortgage, 470
Accounts:
  bank (see Bank account)
  capital, 114, 132
  debit and credit, 114
  defined, 114
  drawing, 130
  expense, 114
  income, 114
  in general ledger, 117
  liability, 114
  payable:
    defined, 116
    in cash journal, 116
    in general ledger, 117
  receivable:
    credits to, 115
    debits to, 115
    in cash journal, 115
    in subsidiary ledger, 117
    trial balance of, 129
  services charged, 116, 129
Acknowledgments:
  affidavits differentiated from, 193
  authentication of, 183

Acknowledgments (Cont.):
  by attorney-in-fact, 181
  by corporation, two officers, 179
  by husband and wife, separate examination, 178
  by individual, 177
  by partnership, 180
  corporate charter, 389
  date of, 180
  defined, 577
  essentials of, 179
  identification of signer, 188
  importance of, 176
  laws governing, 177
  officer taking, signature and designation, 181
  personal appearance, 188
  person making, designation of, 181
  purpose of, 193
  signature, 181
  spacing, 157
  typing, 182
  venue, 180
  verifications differentiated from, 246, 249
  who may make, 182
  who may take, 183
Address:
  abbreviations in, 76
  addressee's name, verifying, 71
  business titles, 73
  company's name, 71
  degrees, 71
  envelope, styles of, 79
  Esquire, 72
  foreign country, 79
  Messrs., 72
  persons holding honorary or official positions, 92-112
    army officers, 104
    Catholic faith, 106-108
    court officials, 99

(Cont.):
s holding honorary
r official positions (Cont.):
eign officials and representatives,
102-103
ewish faith, 109
naval officers, 105
Protestant faith, 110-111
state and local government officials,
97-98
U. S. diplomatic representatives,
100-101
U. S. government officials, 93-96
spoken, chart of, 93-112 (last column)
street, typing, 75
titles, 71-74
business, 73
honorary or official, chart, 92-112
hyphenation of, 74
verifying, 568
Administration, letters of:
application for, 531
notice of, 538
waiver of citation, 537
issuance of, 539
petition for, 512, 532
forms, 533-535
legal back, 536
renunciation of right to, 537
who has prior rights to, 532
Administrator:
appointment of, 531-539
parties to, 531
defined, 578
executor differentiated from, 511
oath of, 532
forms, 533-535
party to law suit, 242
power to make lease, 475
Admiral, forms of address, salutation,
close, reference, 105
Admission to bar, requirements for, 4
Advances made to clients, record of,
139
Advice, legal, stranger wanting, 24
Affiant:
defined, 193, 244
name of, in affidavit, 194
signature of, 194
Affidavits:
acknowledgments differentiated from,
193
authentication of, 194
by secretary:
notice of meeting mailed, form,
443

Affidavits (Cont.):
by secretary (Cont.):
publication, notice of meeting,
form, 443
copy of will, 515
defined, 578
essentials of, 194
for court use, 312-314
form, 314
parts of, 313
in opposition, form, 314
jurat clause, 194
name of affiant in, 194
nature of, 193
oath, 194
preparation of, 194-196, 313
proving correct copy of will filed for
probate, forms, 516, 517
purpose of, 193
service of citation, 529
signature, 195
of affiant, 194
of notary, 194
statement of facts in, 194
venue, recital of, 194
Affirmation of affidavit, 249
Agenda, directors' meeting, 423
Agent, under power of attorney, 196
Agreement:
between two corporations, seal attested, 173-174
endorsed legal back for, 165
form, 164
partnership, 10
Alabama:
authentication of instruments, 184
court papers, provisions, 264
courts of record, 222
district courts in, 220
Federal circuit covering, 228
incorporating provisions, 396
notaries public, 186
official reports, how cited, 355
parties on appeal, designation, 339
statutes of limitations, 615
will provisions, 203
Alaska:
authentication of instruments, 184
court papers, provisions, 264
Federal circuit covering, 228
notaries public, 186
official reports, how cited, 355
statutes of limitations, 615
will provisions, 203
Alderman, Forms of address, salutation,
close, reference, 98

Allegation:
  defined, 578
  in complaint, 268
Alphabetical filing system:
  how to use, 59
  nature of, 58
  transfer of files to storage, 59
Ambassador:
  American, forms of address, saluta-
    tion, close, reference, 100
  foreign, forms of address, salutation,
    close, reference, 102
Amendment, motion for leave to make,
    309
American court system, 218-228
American Digest, 559-562
  how to use, 560
  table of cases, 561
  units of system, 559
    periods covered by each, 559
Amicus curiae, defined, 241
Ampersand, in address, 71, 72
Ancillary letters, defined, 578
Annexed papers, how to arrange, 304
Announcements:
  filing, 61
  list of persons receiving, 8
    how to keep, 7
  of removal of offices, 7
  to classmates, 8
  to clients, 8
  to county officials, 8
  to members of local bar, 8
  when entering practice, 6
  when resuming practice, 7
  who receives, 8
Annual meeting:
  directors, minutes of, 445
  stockholders, 419
Annual reports:
  to state authority, 439
  to stockholders, 439
Answer, 243, 275-281
  caption, 276
  defined, 275-276
  diary entry, 281
  endorsed back of, 279
  form, 277-278
  number of copies, 276
  paper used, 276
  parts of, 276
  preparation of, 276-279
  secretary's duties, 280
  service of:
    on plaintiff's attorney, 279
    proof of, 280

Answer *(Cont.)*:
  signature, 276
  stipulation extending time to, form,
    290
  verification, 243, 276
Answering court calendar call, 237
Apostolic Delegate, forms of address,
    salutation, close, reference, 106
Appeal *(see also* Appealed cases):
  defined, 336
  Federal courts of, table, 221
  methods of, 336
  parties on, 337
Appealed cases:
  briefs, 344-353 *(see also* Briefs)
  change in caption of case, 337
  citations, 354-365 *(see also* Citation
    of authorities)
  designation of parties, 337-339
    tables, 338, 339
  diary entries, 336
  notice of appeal, 339
  record, 335-344
    assignment of errors, 342
    binding of, 343
    certification of, 343
    defined, 340
    filing of, 343
    format and make-up of, 343
    instructions to clerk, 342
    preparation of, 342
    service of copies, 344
    title of, 343
    volumes of, 343
    who prepares, 342
  review by higher court, 336
  reviewing court, rules of, 335
  service on opposing counsel, 340
Appearance, notice of, 281-284
  in common law case, form, 282
  in equity case, form, 283
  nature of, 281
  preparation of, 281
  secretary's responsibilities, 281
Appellate courts:
  appeals to *(see* Appealed cases)
  designations of, 232
  Federal, table of, 221
  jurisdiction of, 229
  reporters of, 354
  state system, 219
Application for oral argument, 352
Appointment:
  calendar for month, 48
  client calling without, 22
  client early for, 25

Appointment (*Cont.*):
    diary entry, 41
Archbishop:
    Anglican, writing to, 110
    in U. S., writing to, 106
Archdeacon:
    Anglican, forms of address, salutation,
        close, reference, 110
    Protestant Episcopal, writing to, 111
Argument:
    in briefs, 344
    oral, application for, 352
Arizona:
    authentication of instruments, 184
    court papers, provisions, 264
    courts of record, 222
    Federal circuit covering, 228
    incorporating provisions, 396
    notaries public, 186
    official reports, how cited, 355
    parties on appeal, designation, 339
    statutes of limitations, 615
    will provisions, 203
Arkansas:
    authentication of instruments, 184
    court papers, provisions, 264
    courts of record, 222
    Federal circuit covering, 228
    incorporating provisions, 397
    notaries public, 186
    official reports, how cited, 355
    parties on appeal, designation, 339
    statutes of limitations, 615
    will provisions, 203
Army officials, address chart, 104
Articles of incorporation (*see* Incorpo-
    rating procedure: charter)
Assemblyman, State, forms of address,
    salutation, close, reference, 97
Assets, defined, 114
Assignment of errors, in appealed case,
    342
Assistant Secretary of a Department,
    forms of address, salutation, close,
    reference, 94
Associate Justice of United States Su-
    preme Court, forms of address,
    salutation, close, reference, 93
Associate lawyers, 10
Association, in corporation name, 383
Asterisks:
    to indicate enclosure, 81
    spacing between, 159, 160
Atlantic Reporter, 357
Attention line:
    in letter, 80

Attention line (*Cont.*):
    on envelope, 79
Attestation:
    by officer of corporation, 175
    clause:
        distinguished   from   testimonium
            clause, 169
        forms, 174, 175
        instruments, generally, 176
        wills, 200, 202
    defined, 176, 579
Attorney:
    as applicant, 5
    certificate of good faith by, 295
    powers of (*see* Power of attorney)
Attorney General, forms of address, sal-
    utation, close, reference, 97
Attorney-in-fact:
    certificate of acknowledgment by, 181,
        183
    defined, 196
Authentication:
    of affidavit, 194
    of instruments generally, 183
    table of state provisions, 184-185
Author's alterations, charge for, 373

B

Backing sheet, 165
Backs, legal (*see* Legal backs)
Bank account:
    deposits, 115
    firm, 117
        in cash journal, 115
    trust, 117
        in cash journal, 115
    withdrawals, 115
Bank, in name of corporation, 383
Bankruptcy, 580
    involuntary, 580
    proceedings, steps in, 580
    referee in, 580
    schedules filed by bankrupt, 581
    secretary's duties, 581
    voluntary, 580
Bar association, interest in, 8
Bargain-and-sale deed, nature of, 458
Beneficiaries of will, 199
Bequest, 201
Bill:
    in equity, 267 (*see also* Complaints)
        defined, 218
    of complaint (*see* Complaints)
    of discovery, 558
    of particulars, 296-302

Bill (*Cont.*):
 of particulars (*Cont.*):
  demand for (*see* Demand for bill of particulars)
  form, 300
  parts of, 299
  preparation of, 299
  secretary's duties, 302
  verification of, 243
Bills for services:
 bill heads, 138
 disbursements itemized in, 138
 how calculated, 138
 preparation of, 138
Binders, loose-leaf (*see* Loose-leaf binders)
Bishop:
 Anglican, forms of address, salutation, close, reference, 110
 in United States, forms of address, salutation, close, reference, 110
 Methodist, forms of address, salutation, close, reference, 110
 Presiding, Protestant Episcopal Church of America, forms of address, salutation, close, reference, 110
 Protestant Episcopal, forms of address, salutation, close, reference, 110
Blanks, printed (*see* Printed forms)
Blind copy notation, in letters, 81
Block style, envelope address, 79
Blue and white book:
 how to use, 557
 purpose of, 556
Blue book:
 how to use, 557
 purpose of, 556
Bluebooks of states, 8
Bond and mortgage, nature of, 466
Bookkeepers, 11
Bookkeeping, 113-139
 assets, defined, 114
 books required, 113
 cash journal, 115-116
 credits, defined, 114
 debits, defined, 114
 double entry, 114
 entries, defined, 114
 rules to remember, 114-115
 system of, 113
Books (*see also* Library)
 marking, for take-ins, 147, 148
 minute (*see* Minutes of meetings: minute book)

Books (*Cont.*):
 of original entry, 114, 115
 stock certificate, 391, 433
 titles of, typing, 158
Brackets, "sic" in, 162
Briefs:
 appealed cases, 344-353
 argument in, 344, 347
 authorities cited, list of, 345
  illustration of, 349
 contents of, 344
 cover and binding, 350
 drafts of, 345
 filing, 352
  time of, 345
 format of, 345
 index of, 345
  illustration, 348
 manuscript for, marked for printer, 353
 nature of, 344
 number of copies, 345
 preparation of, 345, 350
  preliminaries to, 344
 printed, page from, 347
 printing procedure, 352
 service on opposing counsel, 352
 typed, page from, 346
Brigadier General, forms of address, salutation, close, reference, 103
British Cabinet, member of, forms of address, salutation, close, reference, 103
British Prime Minister, forms of address, salutation, close, reference, 103
Brother (Catholic), forms of address, salutation, close, reference, 107
Bulletins, filing, 61
 nature of, 53
Business corporations, nature of, 380
Business Writing: Theory and Practice, Parkhurst and Davis, 83
By-laws:
 adoption of, minutes, 441
 defined, 582
 familiarity with, 418
 first page of, illustration, 394
 preparation of, 393

C

Cabinet officers, forms of address, salutation, close, reference, 94

Cabinets:
  as room partitions, illustration, 12
  for suit register, 328
  legal blank, 13
Calendars:
  appointment, for month, 48
  corporation, 438-440
  court, 237
    daily and weekly call of, 237
California:
  authentication of instruments, 184
  court papers, provisions, 264
  courts of record, 222
  Federal circuit covering, 228
  incorporating provisions, 397
  notaries public, 186
  official reports, how cited, 355
  parties on appeal, designation, 339
  statutes of limitations, 615
  will provisions, 203
Callers at office:
  clients (see Clients)
  law book salesmen, 26
  magazine salesmen, 27
  peddlers, 27
Canadian Prime Minister, forms of address, salutation, close, reference, 103
Canon, forms of address, salutation, close, reference, 107
Capital:
  account, 117, 132
  defined, 132
Capital stock (see Stock)
Capitalization in wills, 210
Captain:
  Army, forms of address, salutation, close, reference, 104
  Navy, forms of address, salutation, close, reference, 104
Captions (see also under specific paper)
  illustrations, 251-258
  on court papers, 250
    in Federal district courts, 258
  on Tax Court papers, 618
Carbon copies:
  blind copy notation, 81
  court papers, 259, 260
  distribution notation, 81
  duplicate original, 150
  of telegrams, 91
  triplicate original, 150
Card index:
  follow-up file, 43, 47
  for corporation calendar, 438

Card index (Cont.):
  for filing:
    alphabetical files, transfer of, 59
    as cross-index, 53
    cards, 54-57
      forms, 55, 56
Cardinal, in United States, forms of address, salutation, close, reference, 106
Caret, showing omissions by, 162
Cases:
  decided, reports of (see Decided cases, reports of)
  new, report (see New case report)
Cash:
  journal, 115-116
    sheet, items included, 115-116
      posting from, to general ledger, 119
        illustration, 119-129
  payments, entry in books, 115
  received, entry in books, 115
Catalogues:
  as enclosures, 82
  filing, 61
  of printed law blanks, 166
Catholic dignitaries, forms of address, salutation, close, reference, 106-108
Certificate:
  attorney's, of good faith, 295
  county clerk, 163
  of acknowledgment:
    authentication of, 183
    by attorney-in-fact, 181, 183
    by corporation, 179, 183
    by husband and wife, 178, 182
    by partnership, 180, 183
    how to take, 187-189
    notary's seal, 182
    of individual, 177, 182
    post- or ante-dating, 188
  of incorporation (see also Incorporating procedure: charter)
  of good faith, by lawyer, 295
  of title, 487, 490
  stock (see Stock: certificates)
  Torrens, 487, 490
Certificate of incorporation (see Incorporating procedure: charter)
Certification:
  of copies of will, 209
    forms, 209-210
  of defendants, by title companies, 503
  of record, appealed case, 343
Certiorari writs, nature of, 336

Cestui que trustent, party to foreclosure action, 501

Chancellor of a university, forms of address, salutation, close, reference, 112

Chancery courts, 231

Chancery, master in, reference to, in foreclosure action, 509

Chaplain:
Army, forms of address, salutation, close, reference, 104
Navy, forms of address, salutation, close, reference, 105

Character count, estimating length of copy, 371

Charge sheets, 37

Charge to jury, 321

Chargé d'Affaires ad Interim, American, forms of address, salutation, close, reference, 101

Charges:
collection, nature of, 10
made to clients, 138

Charitable institutions, testamentary trusts, 202

Charter, incorporation (*see* Corporation: charter)

Chattel mortgage, nature of, 466

Checking pages, 163

Checklists:
contract of sale:
closing, 491, 492
information for filling in form, 485
payments by seller and purchaser, 496
diary entries, 41-43
errors, in reading proofs, 376
foreclosure action, what to do in, 510
information needed:
to fill in contract of sale, 485
to fill in deed form, 458, 460
to fill in mortgage or deed of trust, 468
to prepare summons and complaint on collection item, 549
material in follow-up files, 44
standard clauses in commercial leases, 479

Chief Justice of the United States, forms of address, salutation, close, reference, 93

Chief of a Division or Bureau, forms of address, salutation, close, reference, 95

"Chinese" copy, 160, 162

Christmas presents:
from clients, 25
reminders, in diary, 40

Circuit courts, 219
states in each circuit, table, 228

Citation of authorities, 354-366
accuracy of, 354
constitutions, 358
errors in, 354
how to type, 364-365
illustrations, 365-366
italicizing, 364
law reviews, 364
named reporters, 363
National Reporter System, 354-357
table, 357-358
nature of, 354
official reports, 354-357
table, 355-356
published decisions, 361-363
slip decisions, 363
statutes and codes, 358, 361
string, 363
taking, in shorthand, 354
treatises, 364
underscoring, 364
unpublished cases, 363

Citation, probate proceedings:
affidavit of service, 529
nature of, 523
service by publication and mailing, 524
waiver of (*see* Waiver: of citation)

City Attorney, forms of address, salutation, close, reference, 98

City Counsel, forms of address, salutation, close, reference, 98

Claims:
collection, acknowledgment of, 542, 544

Clauses:
in deeds, 461-463, 471
in leases, 476, 479
in mortgages, 467, 470
in power of attorney, 196
recurring, 146

Clerk of the court, 235
authentication by, 183
instruction to, on appeal, 342
index system of, 235
secretary's use of, 235
minute books, 236
secretary's use of, 237
permanent record book, 236
writing to, 99

Clerks:
  file, 11
  law, 10
  mail, 11
  managing, 10
Client:
  advances made to, record of, 139
  announcements to, 8
  billing, 138
  charges made to, 138
  contacts with (*see* Contacts with clients)
  files, 52-60
  lawyer's relation with, 9
  ledger, 132
    form of sheet for, 118
    posting time charges to, 136
  toll calls placed by, 29
  when lawyer can see, 23
  when lawyer cannot see, 22
  who call without appointment, 22
  who want to see files, 26
Close punctuation, letters, 70
Closing of title (*see* Contract of sale: closings)
Closings of letters (*see* Complimentary close)
Closing statement (*see* Contract of sale: closing statement)
Codes, statutes and (*see* Statutes and codes)
Codicil to will, 213
Collating, process of, 163
Collections of commercial items:
  acknowledgment of claim, 542, 544
  charges, defined, 10
  commercial law lists, 540
  completed, disposal of, 546
  filing, 541
  follow-up system, 541
  forwarding an item, 546
  installment payments, 545
  lawyer's part in, 540
  letters, 544, 547
    number written, 548
  nature of, 540
  office procedures, 541
  record of, 545
  remitting to forwarder, 546
  reports to forwarder, 545
  uncontested suit, 548-550
    judgment by default, 549
      preparation of, 550
    summons and complaint, 548
      preparation and service of, 548
  when lawyer recommends, 548
    checklist of information needed, 549

College officials, address chart, forms of address, salutation, close, reference, 112
Colonel, writing to, 104
Colorado:
  authentication of instruments, 184
  court papers, provisions, 264
  courts of record, 222
  Federal circuit covering, 228
  incorporating provisions, 397
  notaries public, 186
  official reports, how cited, 355
  parties on appeal, designation, 339
  statutes of limitations, 615
  will provisions, 203
Combing-back procedure, follow-up files, 47
Commander, Naval, forms of address, salutation, close, reference, 105
Commercial collections, files, 53
Commercial Law League of America, collection fees, 546
Commercial law lists, 540
Commercial lease, nature of, 476
Commission, broker's, contract of sale, 485
Commissioners of a city, forms of address, salutations, close, reference, 98
Committee meetings, corporation, 419
Commodore, forms of address, salutation, close, reference, 105
Common law:
  case, notice of appearance in, 282
  defined, 583
  remedies at, 232
Communication, privileged, defined, 4, 9
Community affairs, interest in, 8
Company:
  in corporation name, 383
  writing name of, 71
Complainant, defined, 239
Complaint, bill of:
  allegations, 268
  body of, 268
  captions, 268
  counts, 268
  defined, 267
  diary entry, 275
  in foreclosure action, 503-505
  legal back, 269
  nature of, 267
  number of copies, 269
  paper used, 264-265
  parts of, 268

Complaint, bill of (*Cont.*):
  pleading, initial, 218
  prayer in, 268
  preparation of, 269-271
  secretary's duties, 274
  service on defendant, 275
    table, 264-265
  signature, 268
  verification of, 243, 269
Complimentary close:
  army officers, 104
  Catholic faith, 106-108
  court officials, 99
  foreign officials and representatives, 102-103
  generally, 78
  Jewish faith, 109
  naval officers, 105
  Protestant faith, 110-111
  state and local government officials, 97-98
  U. S. diplomatic representatives, 100-101
  U. S. government officials, 93-96
Comptroller General, forms of address, salutation, close, reference, 96
Conclusions of law (*see* Findings of fact and conclusions of law)
Conforming:
  court papers, 259
  process of, 163
Connecticut:
  authentication of instruments, 184
  court papers, provisions, 264
  courts of record, 222
  Federal circuit covering, 228
  incorporating provisions, 398
  notaries public, 186
  official reports, how cited, 355
  parties on appeal, designation, 339
  statutes of limitations, 615
  will provisions, 203
Consideration:
  in contracts, 586
  in deeds, 461
  in mortgage, 470
Constitutions, citing, 358
Consul General, Consul, or Vice-Consul, forms of address, salutation, close, reference, 101
Contacts with clients, 20-36
  early for appointment, 25
  gifts from, 25
  hysterical, 25
  information to get from, 16
  invitations from, 25

Contacts with clients (*Cont.*):
  irate, telephone call from, 33
  payment for work, 25
  personal contacts with, 21-27
  secretary's introduction to, 20
  stranger, wanting legal advice, 24
  telephone, 27-36
Conference room, law office, 13
"Confidential" notation, in letters, 80
Contingent fee, defined, 9
Continuation sheets, letters, 82
Contract of sale, 484-487
  binder, 486
  closing statement, 492-499
    adjustments, calculating, 494
    illustrative form, 498-499
    insurance adjustment, 495
    interest adjustment, 495
    nature of, 492-494
    payments, miscellaneous, 495-496
    rent adjustment, 495
    suggested form of, 496
    tax adjustment, 494
  closings:
    checklists of preparations:
      by secretary to purchaser's attorney, 492
      by secretary to seller's attorney, 491
    date, 483
    memorandum of figures, form, 493
    preparation for, 491
  defined, 456
  earnest money, 486
  escrowed, 486
  filling in form, checklist of information, 485
  immediate transfer of title, 484
  installment sale, 484
  necessity for, 484
  number of copies, 485
  parties to, 484
  preparation of, 485
  title, evidence of, 487-490
  title closing, 487, 491
  types of, 484
Contractor, use of term, 169
Contracts (*see also* Agreement)
  competent parties, 586
  consideration, 586
  legality of subject matter, 586
  offer and acceptance, 585
  under seal, 587
Control account, accounts receivable, 117
Conventional mortgage, nature of, 467

Copy:
  estimating length of, 370-372
  in copied material, 163
  marked, illustration of, 371
  marking, 369, 370
  "true and exact," 162
Copyholder, described, 14
Copying:
  executed document, 162
  letterheads, 163
  test-writing, 162
  unsigned draft, 162
Corporate forms:
  affidavit of secretary:
    mailing of notice, annual meeting
      of stockholders, 443
    publication of notice, stockholders'
      meeting, 444
  incorporators' meeting, waiver of no-
    tice, 441, 442
  minutes, excerpt showing adoption,
    minutes of previous meeting as
    corrected, 448
  notice:
    annual meeting of stockholders, 443
    mailing of, 443
    publication of, 444
    special meeting of directors, 445
    special meeting of stockholders, 443,
      444
  purpose of meeting, 443, 445
  quorum, annual meeting of directors,
    445
  resolutions (see Resolutions)
  waiver of notice:
    of first meeting of directors, 442
    of first meeting of incorporators, 442
Corporation:
  alien, 382
  business, 380
  by-laws (see By-laws)
  calendar, 438-440
    how to keep, 438
    need for, 438
    sources of dates, 439
  certificate of acknowledgment by, 179,
    183
  charter (see Incorporating procedure:
    charter)
  corporate outfit, 391
  counsel, writing to, 98
  domestic, defined, 381
  foreign, 243, 381
  forms (see Corporate forms)
  incorporating papers, preliminary
    memorandum, 382

Corporation (Cont.):
  incorporators, 381
  information folder, 418
  kinds of, 380
  meetings (see Meetings)
  minutes of meetings, 601
    annual meeting of directors, 445
    first meeting of directors, 395
    minute book, 391
  name:
    change in, 440
    reservation of, 383
  nature of, 379, 587
  officers:
    compensation of, 446
    temporary, 441
  organizing, 379-417 (see Incorporating
    procedure)
  party to deed, 457
  party to instrument, signatures, 171
  party to law suit, 243
  party to lease, 475
  power to make contract of sale, 484-
    485
  private, 380
  public, 380
  public service, 380
  seal of, 172-175, 391
    conforming documents bearing,
      163
  secretary, acting as, 418-449
  specimen forms (see Corporate
    forms; Forms; Resolutions)
  state of incorporation, 381
  stock (see Stock)
  stock certificate book, 391
  stock ledger, 391
  verification of complaint by officer
    of, 246
  who may form, 381
Corpus Juris Secundum System, 566
Corrections of errors:
  on bound pages, 165
  on drafts, 161
Correspondence, 66-89 (see also Let-
    ters):
  arranging in file folders, 63
  general files, 53
  procedure, 60
Cost of professional services, 132-138
Counsel, opposing:
  defined, 266
  service of pleadings on, 263
    table, 264-265
Counter-order, defined, 315
Counts, in complaint, 268

County clerk, certificate of, 163
County courts, 231
County officials, announcements sent to, 8
Court calendar, 237
Court matters:
keeping progress record of, 326-334 (*see also* Suit register)
when case is appealed (*see* Appealed cases)
Court, meanings of word, 217
Court order, 315-320 (*see also* Orders: judge's)
defined, 315
form, 316-317
preparation of, 315, 317
secretary's duties, 317-320
Court papers:
affidavits, 312-314
answer, 243, 275-281 (*see also* Answer)
bill of particulars, 296-302 (*see also* Bill: of particulars)
complaints, 267-271, 274 (*see also* Complaint, bill of)
conforming copies, 259
defined, 168, 239
demurrers, 291-296 (*see also* Demurrers)
filing, in court, 263
findings of fact and conclusions of law, 320 (*see also* Findings of fact and conclusions of law)
folding, 262
instructions to jury, 321
interrogatories, 302
judgments and decrees, 322-325 (*see also* Judgments; Decrees)
motion and notice of motion, 309-312 (*see also* Motions)
motion to make pleading more definite, 301, 302
note of issue, 285
notices (*see* Notices)
number of copies, 259
orders, 315-320 (*see also* Orders)
paper for, 15
pleadings (*see* Pleadings)
secretary's responsibilities, 263
serving, 263
stipulations, 288-291
summons, 271-275 (*see also* Summons)
typing, 249-262
captions, 250
headings, 249
illustrative styles, 251-258

Court papers (*Cont.*):
typing (*Cont.*):
indentations, 259
numbering pages, 259
spacing, 259
verifications, 243-249 (*see also* Verifications)
Court register, secretary's use of, 236
Court work:
entries in diary, 41
reminding lawyer of, 49
Courtesy:
quality of, 20, 21
telephone, 27
Courts:
American system, 218-228
chancery, 231
clerk of the court, 235-237
county, 231
criminal, 231
Federal, 220-221 (*see also* Federal courts)
higher, review by, 336
inferior, 230
judges, 234
jurisdiction (*see* Jurisdiction)
justices, 234
juvenile, 231
municipal, 231
of appellate jurisdiction, 229
of intermediate review, 231
admission to practice before, 5
of original jurisdiction, 219, 229
officials, form, 99
of special jurisdiction, 231
probate, 218, 231
procedure, 218
reviewing, rules of, 355
state (*see* State courts)
superior, 230
Supreme appellate, 232
United States (*see under* United States)
Covenants in deeds, 462
Creditors, notice to, in probate of will, 530
Credits, defined, 114
Criminal courts, 231
Cross-claimant, defined, 240
Cross-complainant, defined, 240
Cross-complaints, parties to, 240
Cross-defendant, 240
Cross-index:
alphabetical filing, 59
numerical filing, 53

Cross-plaintiff, defined, 240
Curator, incompetent represented by, 241
Customs and Patent Appeals, United States Court of, 221
Customs Court, United States, 221

D

Daily follow-up file, 47
Daily time sheet, 132
Date, closing, of title, 483, 487
Date line of letter, typing, 71
Dates entered in diary, 41-43
Davis, Roy, co-author, *Business Writing: Theory and Practice*, 83
Day letters, telegraph service, 89
Deadlines, entered in diary, 39, 41
Dean:
  or Assistant Dean, of college or graduate school, forms of address, salutation, close, reference, 112
  Protestant, forms of address, salutation, close, reference, 111
Death of associate, resolution extending sympathy on, 449
Debits, defined, 114
Debtor, judgment, defined, 550
Debts, provision for in wills, 201
Decedent's estate, defined, 511
Decided cases, reports of:
  by subject, 558
  headnotes to, 554
  National Reporter System, 354-357
  official, 354-357
  organization of, 554
  selected cases series, 558
  syllabus, 554
  use of, 555
Decisions of courts:
  published, 554-559 (*see also* Decided cases, reports of)
  unpublished, 363
Declaration, defined, 267
Decoration of law office, 14
Decrees, 322-325
  defined, 322
  interlocutory, 322
  nature of, 322
  number of copies, 322
  of divorce, form, 323-324
  preparation, 322
  secretary's duties, 325
Deeds, 456-465
  acknowledgment, 465
  bargain-and-sale, 458

Deeds (*Cont.*):
  clauses in (*see* Deeds: statements and clauses in)
  deed poll, nature of, 457
  defined, 456, 589
  description of property, 454
  forms of, 457
    illustration, 459, 460
  indenture, 457
  kinds of, 458
  of gift, 458
  parties to, 456
  preparation of, 464
  printed forms of, 458
    information to fill in, 458, 460
  quit-claim, 458
  recording, 464
  revenue stamps on, 463
    cancelling, 464
  seal, 464
  signature to, 464
  special purpose, 461
  statements and clauses in, 461-463
    consideration, 461
    covenants, 462
    encumbrances, 461
    exceptions and reservations, 463
    habendum clause, 462
    restrictions and conditions, 463
    testimonium clause, 463
  state tax on, 464
  statutory, 457
  trust, 467 (*see also* Mortgages)
    printed forms of, 468
    redemption-of-bonds clause in, 471
  typed, 461, 469
  warranty, 458
    from husband and wife, form, 459
Default:
  in mortgage, 503
  judgment by (*see* Judgment: by default)
Defeasance clause, in mortgage, 467, 470
Defendant:
  as cross-complainant, 240
  defined, 239
Degrees:
  and abbreviations of, 5
  scholastic, in address, 92
Delaware:
  authentication of instruments, 184
  corporation, incorporators' meeting, minutes of, 440
  court papers, provisions, 264
  courts of record, 222

Delaware (*Cont.*):
  Federal circuit covering, 228
  incorporation provisions, 398
  notaries public, 186
  official reports, how cited, 355
  parties on appeal, designation, 339
  statutes of limitations, 615
  tax on stock, 435
  will provisions, 203
Delegate to the United Nations, United
      States, forms of address, saluta-
      tion, close, reference, 101
Demand for bill of particulars:
  caption, 298
  diary entry, 290
  form, 297-298
  nature of, 296
  number of copies, 296
  parts of, 296
  preparation of, 296-299
  secretary's duties, 299
  signature, 299
Demurrers, 291-296
  certificate of good faith, 295
  defined, 291
  endorsed back, 295
  entries in suit register, 295, 296
  forms, first and last pages, 292, 293
  nature of, 291
  number of copies, 295
  paper used, 295
  parts of, 291
  points and authorities supporting,
      form, 294
  preparation of, 291, 295
  secretary's responsibilities, 295
  signature, 291
  title of document, 295
  verification, 295
Departments, law firm, 10
Deponent, defined, 193, 244
Deposition:
  defined, 149
  how to take, 149
  illustration, in question and answer
      form, 151-152
  witnesses to will, 529
Depreciation:
  account, 117
  reserve for, 117
Description of property (*see* Real prop-
      erty description)
Devise, use of term, in will, 201
Devisee, defined, 199
Diagram, follow-up files, 46

Diary:
  daily time sheet combined with, 133
    form, 135
  entries:
    about legal work, 40
    advance entries, 39
    appealed cases, 336
    checklist of, 41-43
    in red, 39, 41-43
    notice of, form, 50
    obtaining information for, 40
    return dates, 273, 275
    work accomplished, checklist, 43
  lawyer's, 39
  making up, 39
  nature of, 37
  page from, form, 38
  return dates in, 273, 275
  secretary's, 39
  tickler card file used with, 43
Dictation, 144-150
  deposition, 149
  errors in, 144
  pairs of words, 145
  recurring phrases, clauses, sentences,
      146
  take-ins, 147
  testimony, 149
  understanding material, 144
  unusual words, 147
Diplomatic representatives, forms of
      address, salutation, close, refer-
      ence, 100-101
Director of an Office, forms of address,
      salutation, close, reference, 95
Director of Bureau of the Budget, forms
      of address, salutation, close, ref-
      erence, 96
Directories, state, 8
Directors:
  election of, in minutes, 441
  fees, for attendance at meetings,
      424
  first meeting of, minutes, 395
  meetings (*see* Meetings: directors)
Disbursements, on client's ledger sheet,
      130
Distributees, defined, 531
Distribution line, legal document, 157
District Attorney, forms of address, sal-
      utation, close, reference, 98
District courts, 219
  admission to practice, 5
  Federal, 220-221
    captions on papers filed in, 258
    divisions of, 221

District courts (*Cont.*):
    state, 219, 220
        divisions of, 220
    United States, 221
District of Columbia:
    authentication of instruments, 184
    court papers, provisions, 264
    courts of, 219
    judicial circuits in, 228
    notaries public, 186
    statutes of limitations, 615
    United States Court of Appeals, 221
    will provisions, 203
Ditto marks, when permissible, 163
Divorcee, form of address, 74
Documentary stamps, 463 (*see also* Revenue stamp tax)
Documents (*see* Legal documents; *also* Court papers)
Domestic corporation (*see* Corporation)
Double entry bookkeeping, 114
Drafts:
    correcting errors in, 161
    crossing out typing, 161
    ditto marks in, 164
    of briefs, 345
    of minutes, 429
    typing, 161
    unsigned, retyping, 162
Drawing account, 130
Due dates, entered in diary, 39, 41, 42
Dummies, incorporators as, 381
Dummy for printer, preparation of, 373
Duplicate originals, 150

E

Earnest money:
    contract of sale, 486
    defined, 590
Ellipses, use of, 159, 160
Emergency Court of Appeals, United States, 221
"Emphasis ours," use of, 159
Enclosures:
    envelopes for, 82
    fastening, to letter, 82, 83
    larger than letter, 82
    mark signifying, in letters, 81
    size of letter, 82
    smaller than letter, 83
Encumbrances against property, in deeds, 461
Encyclopedia of Incorporating Forms, 568
Endorsement on legal backs, 164, 165

Engagements (*see* Appointments)
Envelopes:
    attention line, 79
    combination, 82
    for enclosures, 82
    items in address, 79
    personal or confidential notation, 80
    styles of address, 79
    types of, 16
Equipment:
    for follow-up system, 45
    law office, 14
Equity:
    action:
        notice of appearance in, form, 283
        party defending, 239
        types of, 233
    bill in, 267
        defined, 218
    defined, 232
    law distinguished from, 232-234
    principles of, 233
Error, writ of, review by higher court, 336
Errors:
    assignment of, in appealed case, 342
    copying, in "true and exact" copy, 162
    in citations, 354
    in dictation, 144
    in drafts, correcting, 161
    in minutes, 430
    in proofs, checklist, 376
    in quoted material, 159
    in typed manuscript, 368
    typographical, in proofs, 373
Escrow:
    defined, 591
    for sale of real property, 486
Escrowee, defined, 487
Esquire, use of, in address, 72
Estate:
    administrator (*see* Administrator)
    administration (*see* Probate and estate administration)
    decedent's, 511
    executor (*see* Executor)
    personal or legal representative, 511
    testate or intestate, 511
et al., et ux., et vir, in title of case, 250
Ethics of secretary, 3
Evidence of title, 487-489
Examination for admission to bar, 4
Execution:
    of instruments, 169-176 (*see also* Instruments: execution of)
    of judgment, defined, 592

Executor:
  administrator differentiated from, 511
  appointment of, 200, 202
  oath of, 529
  party to law suit, 242
  petition for letters testamentary, 512
Executrix, 511
Exhibits, ditto marks in, 163
Ex parte:
  defined, 592
  motion, in foreclosure action, 509
Expenses:
  miscellaneous, 117
    in cash journal, 116
  overhead, in cash journal, 116
  tax, in cash journal, 116
Extraordinary writs, defined, 336

F

Family dates, entered in diary, 42
Federal courts:
  admission to practice, 5
  courts of record, and members, table, 221
  district, captions on papers filed in, 258
  system, composition of, 220
  United States, 220-221
Federal government (*see* United States: Government)
Federal Reporter:
  citation of, 357
  courts covered by, 357
Fees:
  collection, disposal of, 546
  Federal registration, on stock, 435
  for services and disbursements, 138
  for telephone call, 34
  income from:
    in cash journal, 116
    in general ledger, 117
  incorporation, payment of, 390
  lawyers', 9
    collection charges, 10
    contingent, 9
    forwarding, 10
    single retainer, 9
    yearly retainer, 9
  of directors, 424
  when fixed, 136
Fiduciary, lawyer as, 9
Figures (*see* Numbers)
File clerk, 11
File room, law office, 13
Files (*see also* Filing):
  broken down into volumes, 63

Files (*Cont.*):
  bulletins, 61
  catalogues, 61
  catch-all, 53
  classification of, 52
  clients', 52, 53-60
  clients who want to see, 26
  closing, 64
  collection, 541
    folder, form, 543
  commercial collections, 53
  equipment, follow-up files, 45
  extra copies, 65
  folders, arranging papers in, 63
  follow-up, 44-47 (*see also* Follow-up files)
  general correspondence, 53
  jackets, 63
    labeled, form, 64
  labels for drawer, typing, 62
  material taken from, control of, 65
  name and subject, 60
  paper, defined, 63
  parts of, 63
  periodicals, bulletins, etc., 53, 61
  personal, 53
  physical setup, 61-65
  printed papers, treatment of, 65
  retired, 57
  storage of, when closed, 57
  tickler card (*see* Tickler card file)
Filing, 52-65 (*see also* Files):
  alphabetical system, 58-60
  bills for clients, 138
  collection matters, 541
  court papers, 263
  cross-index, 53
  incorporation charter, 385
  new case report, 19
  numerical system, 53-58
  of records, appealed case, 344
  of schedules, by bankrupt, 581
  preparation of material, 61
  recording differentiated from, 190
  suit register sheets, 329
Fill-ins:
  on printed form, 167
  spacing for, 158
Findings of fact and conclusions of law:
  defined, 320
  preparation of, 320
  secretary's duties, 321
Firm bank account, 117
Flat rental lease, nature of, 476
Fleet Admiral, forms of address, salutation, close, reference, 105

Florida:
  authentication of instruments, 184
  court papers, provisions, 264
  courts of record, 222
  Federal circuit covering, 228
  incorporation provisions, 399
  notaries public, 186
  official reports, how cited, 355
  parties on appeal, designation, 339
  statutes of limitations, 615
  will provisions, 203
Folders:
  alphabetical filing system, 59
  blue book, defined, 63
  clauses in commercial leases, 479
  corporate meeting, 419
  information, corporate, 418
  labels, typing, 62
  numerical filing system, 56
  personal files, 60
  progress record, 327
Folding court papers, 262
Follow-up files:
  combing-back procedure, 47
  daily, handling material in, 47
  equipment, 45
  folders, arrangement of, 45
  material to be placed in, checklist, 44
  necessity for, 44
  on small scale, 47
  operation of system, 45-47
  tickler card file for follow-up, 47
Follow-up system, collections, 541
Foreclosure action, 500-510
  certification of defendants, 503
  checklist of what to do in, 510
  complaint:
    caption, 504
    filing and service of, 508
    number of copies, 504
    preparation of, 503
  description:
    of mortgage, 502
    of note or bond, 502
    of property, 502
  fictitious names, as defendants, 501
  follow-up of process service, 508
  mortgage, when in default, 503
  notice of lis pendens, 505
    filing and service of, 508
    form, 506-507
    preparation of, 505-507
  notice of pendency of action (see notice of lis pendens)
  papers necessary for, 500
    information for preparing, 500

Foreclosure action (Cont.):
  parties defendant, 501
  parties plaintiff, 501
  party sheet, 508
  procedure, 503-510
  report, 503
  summons:
    filing and service of, 508
    preparation of, 508
  title search, 503
  venue, 501
Foreign Ambassador in United States, forms of address, salutation, close, reference, 102
Foreign corporation:
  defined, 381
  party to law suit, 243
Foreign country, in address, 79
Foreign Diplomatic Representative in United States, forms of address, salutation, close, reference, 102
Foreign Minister in United States, forms of address, salutation, close, reference, 102
Foreign officials and representatives, forms of address, salutation, close, reference, 102-103
Foreign words, when to underscore, 158
Forms:
  acknowledgments:
    by attorney-in-fact, 181
    by corporation, two officers, 179
    by husband and wife, separate examination, 178
    by individual, 177
    by partnership, 180
  adjournment of meeting, 442, 447
  affidavit, 195
    in opposition, 314
    of service of citation, 528
    of service by mail, 341
    proving a correct copy of will, 516, 517
  agreement, 173-174
    endorsed legal back, 164
  answer, 277-278
  bill of particulars, 300
    demand for, 297-298
  bond and mortgage, endorsed back, 474
  brief:
    authorities cited in, 349
    cover for, 350
    index to, 348
    printed, 347
    typed, 346

Forms (*Cont.*):
    by-laws, 394
    certificate of good faith, 295
    certification, wills, 209-210
    charter, 386, 387, 388
    client's ledger sheet, 118
    closing figures, memorandum of, 493
    closing statement, 498, 499
    collection file folder, 543
    complaint, 270
    corporate (*see* Corporate forms)
    court order, 316
    daily time sheet, 134
        combined with diary, 135
    deeds, warranty, from husband and
        wife, 459, 460
    demurrer, 292, 293, 294
    deposition, in question and answer
        form, 151-152
    file index cards, 55, 56
    interlocutory decree of divorce, 323-
        324
    interrogatories, 151-152
    judge's order, 318
    jurat, 194
    lease, commercial, 477, 478
    minutes of meeting, 426, 427, 431
    motion:
        notice of, 311
        to make complaint more definite
            and certain, 301
    new case report, 17, 18
    note of issue, 285
        endorsed back, 286
    notice:
        of appearance in common law case,
            282
        of appearance in equity case, 283
        of filing and entry, 306
        of *lis pendens,* 506-507
        of motion, 311
        of settlement, 307
        of trial, 287
        to take deposition upon oral ex-
            amination, 309
    opinion of title, 480
    orders:
        court, 316-317
        judge's, 318
    page from lawyer's diary, 38
    payroll record, 131
    petition for letters of administration,
        533-536
    power of attorney, endorsed back, 198
    printed (*see* Printed forms)
    progress record sheet, 327

Forms (*Cont.*):
    resolutions (*see* Resolutions)
    service ledger sheet, 136, 137
    stipulation extending time to answer,
        290
    stock certificate, 434, 437
    suit register record, 330
    summons, printed form, 272
    telephone:
        message memos, 30, 31
        toll call, record of, 29
    verifications:
        by attorney for plaintiff, 248
        by individual, 245
        by officer of domestic corporation,
            246
        by officer of foreign corporation,
            247
    wills, 205, 206, 207
        affidavit of service, 528
        affidavits proving correct copy, 516,
            517
        probate of:
            citation, 526
            petition for probate, 519-522
            waiver of citation, 525
            progress record, 514
Forwarding fee, defined, 10
Frailey, L. E., *Handbook of Business
    Letters,* 87
Funeral expenses, payment of, in wills,
    201
Furniture, law office, 13

G

Galley proofs:
    author's alterations, 373
    corrected, illustration, 375
    correcting, 373-376
    reading, with copy, 376
General ledger, 116
    classification of accounts in, 117
    debit and credit, 116
    posting to, 119
General of the Army, forms of address,
    salutation, close, reference, 104
Georgia:
    authentication of instruments, 184
    court papers, provisions, 264
    courts of record, 223
    Federal circuit covering, 228
    incorporating provisions, 399
    notaries public, 186
    parties on appeal, designation, 339
    statutes of limitations, 615
    will provisions, 203

Gift, deed of, nature of, 458
Gifts from clients, 25
Good faith, attorney's certificate of, 295
Government:
  Federal officials, address chart, 93-96
  local officials, address chart, 97-98
  state officials, address chart, 97-98
Governor of State, forms of address, salutation, close, reference, 97
Graded rental lease, nature of, 476
Grantee, party to deed, 456
Grantor, party to deed, 456
Guardian:
  ad litem:
    application for appointment of, 509
    defined, 241
  appointment of, in will, 200, 202
Guides:
  labels, typing, 62
  out, 65
  tabbed, in tickler file, 43

H

Habeas corpus writs, nature of, 336
Habendum clause in deed, 462
Hawaii:
  courts of, 219
  Federal circuit covering, 228
Headings on court papers, 249 (see also Captions)
Hearings:
  foreclosure action, 509
  probate of will, 527
High Commissioner, forms of address, salutation, close, reference, 101
Holidays, entered in diary, 42
Holographic wills, 199
Honorary positions, persons holding, address chart, 92-112
Hours worked, record of, 118
Husband and wife:
  certificate of acknowledgment by, 178, 182
  contract of sale, 484
  examined "separate and apart," acknowledgments, 188
  joint will, 199
  parties to deed, 457
  parties to law suit, 242
  reciprocal will, 199
  warranty deed from, form, 459, 460
Hyphen, use of:
  excessive, 155
  in page numbers, 155

Hysterical clients, 25

I

Idaho:
  authentication of instruments, 184
  court papers, provisions, 264
  courts of record, 223
  Federal circuit covering, 228
  incorporating provisions, 400
  notaries public, 186
  official reports, how cited, 355
  parties on appeal, designation, 339
  statutes of limitations, 615
  will provisions, 203
Identification line, in letters, 80
Illinois:
  authentication of instruments, 184
  court papers, provisions, 264
  courts of record, 223
  Federal circuit covering, 228
  incorporation provisions, 400
  names of corporations, publication, 383
  notaries public, 186
  official reports, how cited, 355
  parties on appeal, designation, 339
  statutes of limitations, 615
  will provisions, 203
In re, in subject line, 70
Income from fees:
  in cash journal, 116
  in general ledger, 117
Incompetents:
  contract of sale and, 485, 586
  defined, 241
  leases on behalf of, 475
  party to law suit, 241
"Incorporated," in corporation name, 383
Incorporating Forms, Encyclopedia of, 393, 568
Incorporating procedure:
  charter:
    acknowledgment, 389
    cover for, 389
    execution of, 389
    state requirements, chart, 396-419
    filing of, 385, 390
    state requirements, chart, 396-419
    first, second, and last pages, illustrated, 386, 387, 388
    nature of, 384
    number of copies, 385
    state requirement, table, 396-417
    paper used for, 385
    preparation of, 385-389
    purpose clause, 382

Incorporating procedure (*Cont.*):
  charter (*Cont.*):
    signing of copies, 389
    stock clause, 383
    title of, 386
    typing, 385-389
  first meeting of incorporators:
    minutes of, 394
      forms, 440-442
  incorporators (*see* Incorporators)
  organization meetings, 391-395
    secretary's preparation for, 391
    terminology for participants, 391
    waiver of notice, 392
  organization records, chart, 396-419
  reservation of name, chart, 396-419
  state department in charge, chart,
    396-417
  state law governing, chart, 396-417
  state provisions, chart, 396-417
  steps in, listed, 380-381
  tax and fees, payment of, 390
Incorporation, state of, 381
Incorporators:
  and subscribers, use of term, 391
  defined, 381
  Delaware corporation, 440
  first meeting, minutes of, 394
    forms, 440-442
  use of word, 391
Indented material (*see also* Quoted
    material):
  in court papers, 259
  in legal documents, paragraphs, 155
  spacing, 157
  take-ins, 147
Indented style:
  envelope address, 79
  letters, 66, 68
Indenture:
  deed, nature of, 457
  defined, 594
  trust, 467
Index:
  number, of court case, 250
  of brief, 345, 348
  of minutes, 432
  of recorded or filed instruments, 190
  system, clerk of the court, 235
  tabs, typing, 62
  visible, for suit register, 328
Indiana:
  authentication of instruments, 184
  court papers, provisions, 264
  courts of record, 223
  Federal circuit covering, 228

Indiana (*Cont.*):
  incorporating provisions, 401
  notaries public, 186
  official reports, how cited, 355
  parties on appeal, designation, 339
  statutes of limitations, 615
  will provisions, 203
Individual:
  certificate of acknowledgment by, 177,
    182
  party to deed, 457
  party to lease, 475
  seal of, 176
Infants (*see* Minors)
Inferior courts, 230
In re, in subject line, 70
Insane persons (*see* Incompetents)
Installment:
  contract of sale, 484
  payments, 545
Instruments (*see also under specific in-*
    strument; also Court papers)
  acknowledgments, 176-183
  affidavits, 193-196
  agreements, 169
  attestation clause, 175, 176
  authentication of, statutory provi-
    sions, 183-185
  bill of sale, 168
  contracts of sale, 169, 484-487
    closing statement, 492-499
  copying, 162
  deeds, 168, 169, 456-465
  defined, 168
  differentiated from court papers, 168
  execution of, 169-176
    defined, 169, 592
    signatures, 170-172
    testimonium clause, 169, 170
  leases, 168, 474-482
  mortgages, 465-474
  notarization of, 169, 183-189
    details to observe, 189
    following letter of law, 187-189
  parties to, 168
  photostat method of copying, 190
  power of attorney, 196-198
  real property descriptions, 451-456
  recording, 189-192
    differentiated from filing, 190
    mailing instrument for, 191
    purpose of, 189
    secretary's part in, 190
  sealing, 172-176
  title closings and evidence of title,
    487

Instruments (*Cont.*):
  typing, 169
  wills, 168, 169, 198-213
  witness clause, 175, 176
Insurance:
  accounts, 117
  adjustment, closing statement, 495
  title, 487
  policies, 490
Interest adjustment, closing statement, 495
Interlocutory judgment or decree, 322
  decree of divorce, 323-324
Intermediate review, courts of, 231
Interrogatories:
  nature of, 302
  preparation of, 302
Intestate, defined, 511
Invitations from clients, 25
Involuntary bankruptcy, 580
Iowa:
  authentication of instruments, 184
  court papers:
    provisions, 264
    typing style, 251
  courts of record, 223
  Federal circuit covering, 228
  incorporation provisions, 401
  notaries public, 186
  official reports, how cited, 355
  parties on appeal, designation, 339
  statutes of limitations, 615
  will provisions, 203
Issue:
  definition and uses of word, 284
  joined, 284
  note of:
    defined, 284
    form, 285
    preparation of, 285
    secretary's duties, 288
Italics:
  in quoted material, 159
  underscoring and, 158
"Italics ours," use of, 159

J

Jewish dignitaries, forms of address, salutation, close, reference, 109
Joint will, made by husband and wife, 199
Jones Legal Forms Annotated, 568
Journal:
  cash, 115-116
  sheet, columns in, 115

Jr., Sr., in address, 71
Judges (*see also* Justices; Orders: judge's)
  designation as judge, 234
  forms of address, salutation, close, reference, 99
  judge's order, 315
Judgment, 322-325 (*see also* Decrees)
  by default, 275, 549, 550
    defined, 598
    foreclosure action, 509
  defined, 597
  execution of:
    defined, 592
    stayed, 322
  nature of, 322
  number of copies, 322
  preparation of, 322
  secretary's duties, 325
Judgment creditor, defined, 550
Junior partner, 10
Jurat:
  defined, 194
  form, 194
  typing, 195
Jurisdiction:
  appellate, 229
  in personam, 229
  in rem, 229
  in title of case, 249
  limitations on, 230
  meanings of term, 229
  original, 229
  special, courts of, 231
Jury, instructions to, 321
Justices:
  designation as justice, 234
  forms of address, salutation, close, reference, 99
  Presiding, forms of address, salutation, close, reference, 99
Juvenile courts, 231

K

Kansas:
  authentication of instruments, 184
  court papers, provisions, 264
  courts of record, 223
  Federal circuit covering, 228
  incorporating provisions, 401
  notaries public, 186
  official reports, how cited, 355
  parties on appeal, designations, 339
  statutes of limitations, 615
  will provisions, 203

Kentucky:
  authentication of instruments, 184
  court papers, provisions, 264
  courts of record, 223
  Federal circuit covering, 228
  incorporating provisions, 402
  notaries public, 186
  official reports, how cited, 355
  parties on appeal, designations, 339
  statutes of limitations, 615
  venue, recital of, 180
  will provisions, 203

L

Labels:
  file drawer, 62
  folder, 62
  guide, 62
  typing, for files, 62
Language:
  in letter writing (*see* Words and phrases)
  legal, understanding, 144
Latin words and phrases, 569-576
Law:
  degrees and abbreviations, 5
  equity distinguished from, 232-234
  governing acknowledgments, 177
  issue of, defined, 284
Law action (*see* Law suits)
Law firms:
  names of, in letters, 71
  organization of, 10
  partnership, 10
Law office:
  decoration, 14
  equipment, 14
  furniture, 13
  layout, 13
  personnel, listed, 10
  stationery supplies, 15
  team spirit in, 20
Law reviews, citation of, 364
Law suits:
  collection, uncontested, 548-550
  object of, 233
  parties to, 239-243
    administrators, 242
    amicus curiae, 241
    complainant, 239
    corporations, 243
    cross-complainant, -claimant, -plaintiff, -defendant, 240
    defendant, 239
    executors, 242
    husband and wife, 242

Law suits (*Cont.*):
  parties to (*Cont.*):
    incompetents, 241
    in cross action, 240
    intervening, 240
    minors, 241
    on appeal, 241
    partnerships, 242
    plaintiff, 239
    respondent, 239
    trustees, 242
  party bringing, 239
  party defending, 239
  title of, typing, 250
Lawyer:
  advertising by, 6
  associate, 10
  building a practice, 6-8
  ethics of, 3, 6, 9
  fees of, 9-10, 136, 138
  outside activities, 8
  partners, 10
  relations with clients, 9
  sole practitioners, 10, 13
  time cost, finding, 132-136
Layout of law office, 13
Leasehold estate in premises, defined, 475
Leases, 474-482
  acknowledgment, 480
  commercial, 476
    form, 477, 478
  contract for, closing statement, 492
  duration of, 475
  execution of, 480
  flat rental, 476
  graded rental, 476
  lawyer's approval of, 482
  ninety-nine year, 475
  parties to, 475
  percentage, 476
  personalty, 475
  preparation of, 481
  printed forms of, 476
  recording, 480
  residential, 476
  short- or long-term, 475
  standard clauses in, 476, 479
    commercial leases, checklist of, 479
  typed, 480
Ledger:
  general (*see* General ledger)
  stock, 391
  subsidiary, 117-119
Legacy, use of term, 201

Legal backs, 164
  agreement, form, 164
  answer, 276
    form, 279
  bond and mortgage, 474
  brief, 350
  charter application, 389
  complaint, 269
  court papers, 259-262
    endorsement on, 260
    style of case, 260
  deed, 465
    form, 460
  demand for bill of particulars, 299
  demurrer, 205
  documents, 164
  endorsement, 165
  findings of fact and conclusions of
    law, 321
  lease, 482
  mortgage, 473
    form, 474
  note of issue, 285
    form, 280
  notice of appeal, 340
  notice of appearance, 281
  notice of *lis pendens*, 507
  notice of motion and affidavit, 312
  notices, 304
  orders, 317
  power of attorney, 197
    form, 198
  preparation of, 164
  record on appeal, 343
  stipulation, 280
  summons, 273
  summons and complaint form, 260
  warranty deed by husband and wife,
    460
  will, 212
    form, 212
Legal blanks:
  cabinet for, 13
  filling in, 166
Legal documents (*see also* Court pa-
    pers; Instruments)
  arranging, in file folders, 63
  bound pages, making corrections on,
    165
  cabinet for, 12
  collating, 163
  conforming copies of, 163
  defined, 143
  ditto marks in, 163
  executed:
    conforming, 163

Legal documents (*Cont.*):
  executed (*Cont.*):
    copying, 162
    legal backs, 164 (*see also* Legal backs)
    marking, for take-ins, 147, 148
    paper used for, 15, 16, 153 (*see also*
      under specific document)
    typing, 150-167 (*see also* Typing)
Legal forms, books of, 567
Legal instruments (*see* Instruments)
Legal paper:
  covers, kinds of, 15
  legal cap, 15
  legal-size, 15
Legal papers (*see* Court papers; Instru-
    ments)
Legal profession, nature of, 4
Legal work, entries in diary, 40
Legatee, defined, 199
Lessee, defined, 475
Lessor, defined, 475
Letterheads:
  copying, 163
  executive, 16
  firm, 16
  marked "copy," 16
  used for billing, 138
Letters:
  address, 71-76 (*see also* Address)
  ancillary, defined, 578
  application for patent, 606
  attention line, 80
  blind copy notation, 81
  carbon copy distribution notation, 81
  collection, 544, 547
  complimentary close, 78
  "confidential," 80
  continuation sheets, 82
  date line, typing, 71
  enclosure mark, 81
  enclosures, 82-83 (*see also* Enclosures)
  envelopes, 79
  identification line, 80
  mailing notation, 80
  model:
    filing of charter, payment of fees,
      390
    mailing instrument for recording,
      191
    opinion of title, 489
    ordering corporate outfit, 392
  of administration (*see* Administra-
    tion, letters of)
  opinion, 70, 489
  personal notation, 80
  postscripts, 81

Letters (*Cont.*):
  punctuation in, 70
  responsibility line, 80
  salutations, 76 (*see also* Salutations)
  second sheets, 82
  signature, 78
  style setups:
    indented, 66, 68
    official, 69, 70
    semi-block, 66, 67
  subject line, 70
  succeeding pages, heading on, 82
  testamentary, 530 (*see also* Probate of wills)
    petition for, 512
  to persons holding honorary or official positions, chart, 93-112 (*see under* Address; Complimentary close; Salutation)
Letter writing:
  favorite words and expressions, 88
  language, suggestions re, 83-89
  sentence length, 88
  trite terms, list of, 83-86
  two words, same meaning, 87
  unnecessary words and phrases, 86-87
Librarian of Congress, forms of address, salutation, close, reference, 96
Library, 553-568
  American Digest, 559
  blue and white book, 556, 557
  blue book, 556, 557
  books that classify the law, 559
  codes, 553
  Corpus Juris Secundum System, 566
  form books, 567
  National Reporter System, 356, 554
    table, 357
  official reports, 355
    table of, 355
  practice manuals, 566
  reference facilities, checking names and addresses, 568
  reports of decided cases, 554-559
  Shepard's Citations, 562-566
  statutes, 553
Lien:
  defined, 598
  tax, 599, 619
Lieutenant:
  Army, forms of address, salutation, close, reference, 105
  Navy, forms of address, salutation, close, reference, 105

Lieutenant Colonel, forms of address, salutation, close, reference, 104
Lieutenant General, forms of address, salutation, close, reference, 104
Lieutenant Governor, forms of address, salutation, close, reference, 97
Line spacing:
  in typing, 157
  quoted or indented material, 159
Lis pendens (*see* Foreclosure action: notice of *lis pendens*)
Lists:
  desk telephone, 34-36
  mailing, 7-8
Litigation papers (*see* Court papers)
Local government officials, address chart, 97-98
Long distance (toll) telephone calls, 29
  placed by clients, 29
Loose-leaf notebook, 143
Lord Chief Justice, forms of address, salutation, close, reference, 103
Louisiana:
  authentication of instruments, 184
  court papers, provisions, 264
  courts of record, 223
  Federal circuit covering, 228
  incorporating provisions, 402
  notaries public, 186
  official reports, how cited, 355
  parties on appeal, designations, 339
  statutes of limitations, 615
  typing style, court papers, 255
  venue, recital of, 180
  will provisions, 203
  witnessing wills in, 209
L. S., meaning and use of, 176

M

Mac, Mc, in address, 71
Mail and mailing:
  clerks, 11
  enclosures, 82, 83
  mailing lists, 7-8
  notation, in letters, 80
  stock certificates, 436
Maine:
  authentication of instruments, 184
  court papers, provisions, 264
  courts of record, 224
  Federal circuit covering, 228
  incorporating provisions, 403
  notaries public, 186
  official reports, how cited, 355
  parties on appeal, designation, 339

Maine (*Cont.*):
  statutes of limitations, 615
  will provisions, 203
Major, forms of address, salutation, close, reference, 104
Major General, forms of address, salutation, close, reference, 104
Manager, office, 10, 11
Managing clerk, 10
Managing partner, 10
Man and wife (*see* Husband and wife)
Mandamus, writ of, nature, 336
Manuscript:
  checking, 368
  consistency, 368
  corrections in, 368
  covers, 15
  estimating length of, 370-372
    by character count, 371
    by word count, 372
  margins, 368, 369
  marked copy, illustration, 371
  marking copy, 369
    procedure, 370
  numbering pages, 369
  page from brief, marked for printer, 353
  planning, 369
  proofreader's marks, 368
  typing, rules for, 367
  use of, in proofreading, 373, 374
Marginal and tabular stops, setting, 155
Margins, 154
  quoted material, 158
Marking books, documents, etc., for take-ins, 147, 148
Married woman:
  form of address, 74
  wife of titled man, form of address, 74
Martindale-Hubbell Law Directory, source for mailing list, 8
Maryland:
  authentication of instruments, 184
  court papers, provisions, 264
  courts of record, 224
  Federal circuit covering, 228
  incorporating provisions, 403
  notaries public, 186
  official reports, how cited, 355
  parties on appeal, designation, 339
  statutes of limitations, 615
  will provisions, 203
Massachusetts:
  authentication of instruments, 184
  court papers, provisions, 264

Massachusetts (*Cont.*):
  courts of record, 224
  Federal circuit covering, 228
  incorporating provisions, 404
  notaries public, 186
  parties on appeal, designation, 339
  statutes of limitations, 615
  venue, recital of, 180
  will provisions, 203
Mayor of a city, forms of address, salutation, close, reference, 97
Meetings:
  committee, 419
  corporate, 419-433
  diary entry, 42
  directors:
    agenda, 423
    fees for attendance, 424
    notice of, 422
      preservation of, 423
    quorum at, 422
    regular, 419
    special, 419
  drafting resolutions before, 425
  kinds of, 419
  materials to take to, 424
  meeting folder, 419
  meeting room, reservation and preparation of, 423
  minutes of, 428-433 (*see also* Minutes of meetings)
  of incorporators, form, 440
  organization, 391-395
  preparations for, 419
  stockholders:
    annual, 419
    notice of, 420
    proxies and proxy statement, 421
    quorum at, 421
    special, 419
    waiver of notice, 420
  supplies for, 424
  taking notes at, 426
    memorandum forms for, 425-427
    preparations for, 425
Mesdames, Mmes., in address, 74
Messrs., in address, 72
Metes and bounds description, 453, 455
Michigan:
  authentication of instruments, 184
  court papers, provisions, 264
  courts of record, 224
  Federal circuit covering, 228
  incorporating provisions, 404
  notaries public, 186

Michigan (*Cont.*):
parties on appeal, designation, 339
statutes of limitations, 615
will provisions, 203
Minister:
American, forms of address, salutation, close, reference, 100
Protestant, forms of address, salutation, close, reference, 111
Minnesota:
authentication of instruments, 184
court papers, provisions, 264
courts of record, 224
Federal circuit covering, 228
incorporation provisions, 405
notaries public, 186
parties on appeal, designation, 339
statutes of limitations, 615
will provisions, 203
Minors:
as distributees of estate, 531
contract of sale and, 485, 586
defined, 241
leases on behalf of, 475
parties to law suit, 241
service of citation on, 524
Minutes of meetings, 601
certified extract of, 430
forms, 431, 432
contents of, 428
draft of, 429
final form of, 429
first meeting:
of directors, 395
of incorporators, 395
indexing, 432
minute book, 428
combined, contents of, 428
inserting corrections in, 430
Mississippi:
authentication of instruments, 184
court papers, provisions, 264
courts of record, 224
Federal circuit covering, 228
incorporating provisions, 405
notaries public, 186
parties on appeal, designation, 339
statutes of limitations, 615
will provisions, 203
Missouri:
authentication of instruments, 184
court papers, provisions, 264
courts of record, 224
Federal circuit covering, 228
incorporating provisions, 406
notaries public, 186

Missouri (*Cont.*):
parties on appeal, designation, 339
statutes of limitations, 615
will provisions, 203
Monsignor, forms of address, salutation, close, reference, 107
Montana:
authentication of instruments, 184
court papers, provisions, 264
courts of record, 224
Federal circuit covering, 228
incorporating provisions, 406
notaries public, 186
parties on appeal, designation, 339
statutes of limitations, 615
will provisions, 203
Monthly appointment calendar, 48
Mortgages, 465-475
acknowledgment, 473
assumed, 497
back, 473
form, 474
bond and, 466
chattel, 466
clauses in (*see* Mortgages: statements and clauses in)
conventional, 467
defeasance clause in, 467
deed of trust, 467
defined, 465
forms of, 466
information to fill in, checklist, 468
nature of, 465
parties to, 466
preparation of, 472
printed forms, 167, 468
property subject to, 497
purchase money, 467
recording, 473
seal, 464
short statutory forms of, 467
signature to, 464
statements and clauses in:
acceleration clause, 470
consideration, 470
defeasance clause, 470
description of debt, 469
description of property, 471
miscellaneous, 472
partial release, 471
state tax, 472
transfer tax, 463
trust, 467
typed, 469
when considered in default, 503

Mother Superior of a Sisterhood (Catholic or Protestant), forms of address, salutation, close, reference, 108
Motions:
  defined, 309
  for change of venue, 309
  for leave to amend, 309
  for new trial, 309
  kinds of, 309
  notice of, 304, 310
    form, 311
    secretary's responsibilities, 312
  oral or written, 309
  to strike, 309
Mr., Mrs., Miss, in address, 73, 74, 75
Municipal courts, 231

N

Names:
  addressees, in letters, 71-76
  checking, reference facilities for, 568
  fictitious, in foreclosure action, 501
  misspelling of, 354
National Reporter System, 354-358
  abbreviations of reporters, table, 357
  American Digest and, 559
  citation of cases in, 361
  citation of reporters, table, 357
  courts covered by, table, 357
Navy officials, forms of address, salutation, close, reference, 105
Nebraska:
  authentication of instruments, 184
  court papers, provisions, 264
  courts of record, 225
  Federal circuit covering, 228
  incorporating provisions, 407
  notaries public, 186
  parties on appeal, designation, 339
  statutes of limitations, 615
  will provisions, 203
Nevada:
  authentication of instruments, 184
  court papers, provisions, 265
  courts of record, 225
  Federal circuit covering, 228
  incorporating provisions, 407
  notaries public, 186
  parties on appeal, designation, 339
  statutes of limitations, 615
  will provisions, 203
New case report, 16-19
  illustrations, 17, 18
  information from client in, 16, 17
  routing of, 19

New Hampshire:
  authentication of instruments, 184
  court papers, provisions, 265
  courts of record, 225
  Federal circuit covering, 228
  incorporating provisions, 407
  notaries public, 186
  parties on appeal, designation, 339
  statutes of limitations, 615
  will provisions, 203
New Jersey:
  authentication of instruments, 184
  court papers, provisions, 265
  courts of record, 225
  Federal circuit covering, 228
  incorporating provisions, 408
  notaries public, 186
  parties on appeal, designation, 339
  statutes of limitation, 615
  will provisions, 203
New Mexico:
  authentication of instruments, 184
  court papers, provisions, 265
  courts of record, 225
  Federal circuit covering, 228
  incorporating provisions, 408
  notaries public, 186
  parties on appeal, designation, 339
  statutes of limitations, 615
  will provisions, 203
New York:
  authentication of instruments, 184
  court papers, provisions, 265
  courts of record, 225
  Federal circuit covering, 228
  incorporating provisions, 409
  notaries public, 186
  parties on appeal, designation, 339
  statutes of limitations, 615
  will provisions, 203
New York Supplement Reporter, 357
Night letter, telegram, 89
Ninety-nine year lease, 475
Noncupative (oral) wills, 199
North Carolina:
  authentication of instruments, 184
  court papers, provisions, 265
  courts of record, 225
  Federal circuit covering, 228
  incorporating provisions, 409
  notaries public, 186
  parties on appeal, designation, 339
  statutes of limitations, 615
  will provisions, 203
North Dakota:
  authentication of instruments, 184

North Dakota (*Cont.*):
court papers, provisions, 265
courts of record, 225
Federal circuit covering, 228
incorporating provisions, 409
notaries public, 186
parties on appeal, designation, 339
statutes of limitations, 615
will provisions, 203
Northeastern Reporter, 357
Northwestern Reporter, 357
Notarial seal:
conforming documents bearing, 163
on certificate of acknowledgment, 182
Notarization of documents, 183-189
administering oath, 246
date of expiration of commission, 182
details to observe in, 189
notarial seal, 182
rules governing, 187-189
statutory provisions, table, 186-187
Notary public:
administration of oath by, 246
defined, 185
powers and duties of, 185
signature of, in affidavit, 194
statutory provisions, table, 186-187
Notebook:
loose-leaf, 143
ruled for testimony, 149
Note of issue, 285
back of, form, 286
form, 285
number of copies, 285
preparation, 285
Notices:
annual meeting of stockholders, form, 443
backing and binding of, 304, 306
in probate of will, 530
kinds of, 303-304
nature of, 303
of appeal, 339
of appearance, 281-284
caption, 281
endorsed back, 281
in common law case, form, 282
in equity case, form, 283
paper used, 281
service on counsel, 284
signature, 281
of application for letters of administration, 538
of diary entry, form, 50
of directors' meetings, 422, 423
of filing and entry, 304, 306

Notices (*Cont.*):
of *lis pendens,* in foreclosure, 505
form, 506-507
of motion, 304, 309-312
diary entries, 312
endorsed back, 312
form, 311
information needed to prepare, 311
of probate of will, 527
of settlement, 304, 307
of stockholders' meeting, 420
waiver of, 420
of trial, 284-288
diary entries, 288
service on counsel, 288
papers annexed or attached to, 304, 306
preparation of, 303
service of, 306
settle order on notice, 315
to creditors:
after letters of administration are granted, 539
after letters testamentary are granted, 503
to take deposition upon oral examination, 304, 308
waiver of:
first meeting of directors, form, 442
first meeting of incorporators, form, 442
Numbering:
clauses in leases, 480
items in wills, 201
pages:
court papers, 259
legal documents, 155
Numbers:
court calendar, 237
streets and avenues, in address, 75
zone, in address, 76
Numerical system of filing, 53-58
advantages and disadvantages, 53
assigning, by type of case, 57
how to use, 53
key numbers, 53-54, 56
nature of, 53
processing, for retirement, 57
procedure, 58

O

Oath:
administering, to person verifying pleading, 246
averment of, in affidavit, 194
of executor, 529

Office (see Law office)
Office boys, 11
Office manager, 10
Officers:
    authentication of instruments by,
        table, 184
    compensation, resolution regarding,
        446
    of armed forces, forms of address,
        salutation, close, reference, 104-
        105
Office supplies:
    entry in general ledger, 117
    list of, 15
Official or honorary positions, per-
        sons holding, forms of address,
        salutation, close, reference, 92-
        112
    Catholic faith, 106-108
    court officials, 99
    foreign officials and representatives,
        102-103
    Jewish faith, 109
    officers of armed forces:
        Army, 104
        Navy, 105
    Protestant faith, 110-111
    state and local government, 97-98
    U. S. diplomatic representatives, 100-
        101
    U. S. government, 93-96
Official reports:
    citation of, 335
        table, 335-336
    finding a case in, 555
Official style, letters, 69, 70
Officials, county, announcements sent
        to, 8
Ohio:
    authentication of instruments, 185
    court papers, provisions, 265
    courts of record, 226
    Federal circuit covering, 228
    incorporating provisions, 410
    notaries public, 186
    parties on appeal, designation, 339
    statutes of limitations, 615
    will provisions, 203
Oklahoma:
    authentication of instruments, 185
    court papers, provisions, 265
    courts of record, 226
    Federal circuit covering, 228
    incorporating provisions, 410
    notaries public, 186
    parties on appeal, designation, 339

Oklahoma (Cont.):
    statutes of limitations, 615
    will provisions, 203
Omissions, showing, by caret, 162
Onion skin paper, 15
Open punctuation, letters, 70
Opinion letters:
    nature of, 70
    of title, form, 480
Oral argument, application for, 352
Orders, 315-320
    counter-orders, 315
    court, 315
        form, 316
    judge's, 315
        form, 318
    preparation of:
        while court is not sitting, 315
        while court is sitting, 315
    secretary's duties:
        counsel to settle order on notice,
            317, 319-320
        counsel to submit order, 320
    settle, on notice, 315
    submit, 315
Oregon:
    authentication of instruments, 185
    court papers, provisions, 265
    courts of record, 226
    Federal circuit covering, 228
    incorporating provisions, 411
    notaries public, 187
    parties on appeal, designation, 339
    statutes of limitations, 615
    will provisions, 203
Organization:
    meeting, corporation, 391-395
    of corporation (see Incorporating pro-
        cedure)
    of law firm, 10
Out guides, in files, 65
Overhead expenses, in cash journal, 116
Oyer & terminer courts, 231

                        P
Page proofs:
    author's alterations, 373
    correcting, 373
    reading, 376
Pages, numbering:
    court papers, 259
    legal documents, 155
Pamphlets, filing, 53
Paper:
    feeding, to typewriter, 153, 154
    for charter, 385

Paper (*Cont.*):
　for continuation sheets, 16
　for court papers, 249 (*see also under
　　specific paper*)
　state requirements, table, 264-265
　for drafts, 161
　for legal instruments, 153 (*see also
　　under specific instrument*)
　for letterheads, 16
　legal cap, 15
　　bond or onion skin, 15
　legal-size, 15
　yellow manifold, 16
　yellow scratch pads, 16
Paragraphing telegrams, 91
Paragraphs:
　indentation, legal documents, 155
　quoted material, 158
　recurring, 146
Parentheses:
　"italics ours" in, 159
　"sic" in, 162
Parties:
　appeal, designation of, 337
　　tables, 338, 339
　to a legal action, 239-243 (*see also
　　Law suits: parties to*)
　to an instrument, 168, 170, 171
　to appointment of administrator, 531
　to deed, 456
　to foreclosure action, 501
　to lease, 475
　to mortgage, 466
　to power of attorney, 196
　to probate of will, 513, 515
　to wills, 198
Partner:
　junior, 10
　managing, 10
　senior, 10
Partnership:
　certificate of acknowledgment by, 180,
　　183
　in law firm, 10
　party to deed, 457
　party to instrument, 171
　party to law suit, 242
　party to lease, 475
Patent Appeals, United States Court of
　Customs and, 221
Patents:
　applications for, 603-606
　　parts of, 604
　assignment of application, 605
　obtaining, 603-604
　secretary's duties, 605

Payment:
　contract of sale, 495
　dates entered in diary, 42
　for overtime, 26
　for work, by clients, 25
Payroll record, 130-132
　form, 131
Peddlers, as callers at office, 27
Pendency of action (*see* Foreclosure
　action: notice of *lis pendens*)
Pennsylvania:
　authentication of instruments, 185
　court papers, provisions, 265
　courts of record, 226
　Federal circuit covering, 228
　incorporating provisions, 411
　notaries public, 187
　parties on appeal, designation, 339
　statutes of limitations, 615
　venue, recital of, 180
　will provisions, 204
Percentage lease, nature of, 476
Periodicals, filing, 53, 61
Personal appearance of secretary,
　11
Personal files, 53, 60
Personal notation, in letters, 80
Personal property, 606
　bequest or legacy, 201
　lease on, 475
　legatee of, 199
　state requirements, wills, 203
　title to, 607
Petition:
　defined, 267
　for letters of administration, 532
　　form, 533-536
　for probate of will, 515
　　form, 519-522
　verification of, 243
Petitioner:
　for letters of administration, 531
　for probate of will, 513
Petty cash account, 117, 139
Phrases:
　recurring, 146
　words and (*see* Words and phrases)
Pica type, marginal and tabular stops
　with, 155
Plaintiff:
　and cross-defendant, 240
　defined, 218, 239
　first pleading, 267
　notice of trial given by, form, 287
Pleadings:
　caption on, 250

Pleadings (*Cont.*):
  copies filed in court, state require-
    ments, table, 264
  defined, 218
  first pleading, by plaintiff, 267
  in practice manuals, 567
  judgment entered on, 322
  motion to make more definite and
    certain, 302
    form, 301
  paper used for, state requirements,
    table, 264
  service on opposing counsel, state re-
    quirements, table, 264
  verification of, 243
  who may verify, 244
Pluries summons, defined, 274
Points and authorities, 291
  form, 294
Points, spacing between, 159
Pope, forms of address, salutation, close,
  reference, 106
Posting:
  defined, 114
  to general ledger, 119
Postscript to letter, 81
Power of attorney:
  acknowledgment, 197
  endorsed back, 197
    form, 44
  forms of, 196
  general, 196
  limited, 196
  nature of, 196
  number of copies, 197
  paper used, 197
  parties to, 196
  preparation of, 197
  recording, 197
  signature, 197
  statements and clauses in, 196
Practice, law, building a, 6-8
Prayer in complaint, 268
Preferred stock certificate, 392
Prentice-Hall Corporation System, Inc.,
  The, 379
Prentice-Hall Federal Tax Service, 559
Prentice-Hall, Inc., loose-leaf tax service, 439
Presents:
  from clients, 25
  reminder of, in diary, 39-40
President:
  of a Board of Commissioners, forms
    of address, salutation, close, ref-
    erence, 98

President (*Cont.*):
  of a Republic, forms of address, salu-
    tation, close, reference, 103
  of the United States, forms of ad-
    dress, salutation, close, reference,
    93
  of a university, forms of address,
    salutation, close, reference, 112
Priest, forms of address, salutation,
  close, reference:
  Catholic, 107
  president of a university, 112
  Protestant, 111
Prime Minister, British or Canadian,
  forms of address, salutation, close,
  reference, 103
Principal, power of attorney, 196
Printed forms:
  closing statement, 493
  contract of sale, 485
  court papers, 262
  deeds, 458
  fill-ins on both sides, 167
  incorporating charter, 385
  judgment by default, 550
  law blanks, 166
  leases, 476
  minutes and by-laws, 391-392
  notice to creditors, 531
  printing date, 166
  proxies, 422
  registration of printing, 166
  summons, 272
  typing, on ruled lines, 166
  wills, 199
  with small blanks, 167
  "Z" ruling on, 167
Printed material:
  manuscript, 367-372 (*see also* Manu-
    script)
  proofs, 373-376 (*see* Galley proofs;
    Page proofs)
Private corporations, nature of, 380
Privileged communication, defined, 4,
  9
Probate and estate administration, 511-
  539 (*see also* Probate of wills)
  appointment of administrator, 531-
    539 (*see also* Administration, let-
    ters of; Administrator of estate)
  executor and administrator differenti-
    ated, 511
  lawyer's part in, 512
  nature of, 511
Probate courts, 218, 231
  proceedings in, 511

Probate of wills:
  citation, 523
    affidavit of service, form, 528
    form, 526
    preparation of, 524
    waiver of, 523, 524, 525
  copy of will, affidavit of, 515
    form, 516, 517
  decree admitting will to, 529
  deposition of witnesses, 529
  executor's right to act, 513
  hearing, preparations for, 527
  letters testamentary, 530
    petition for, 512
  notice of probate, 527
  parties to, 513, 515
  petition for, 515, 517-523
    forms, 519-522
    transfer tax affidavit filed with, 523
  progress record in, form, 514
  waiver of citation, 523, 524, 525
Process, service of:
  by publication, 613
  of citation, 524
  following-up, 508
  nature, 613
Professional woman, form of address, 75
Professor, forms of address, salutation,
    close, reference, 112
Profit and loss:
  account, 117
  statement, 130
Progress record:
  file folder for, 327
  in probate of will, form, 514
  of court matters, 326-334 (see also
    Suit register)
  sheet, form, 327
Prohibition writs, nature of, 336
Proofreaders, 11
Proofreading, 376
  copied material, 162
  standard marks, 374
    use of, in correcting manuscript,
      368
Proofs, 373-376 (see Galley proofs; Page
    proofs)
Proprietorship account, 117
Protestant dignitaries, forms of address,
    salutation, close, reference, 110-
    111
Proxy:
  defined, 421
  secretary's duties, 421
  statement, 421
  typing, 422

Public service:
  corporation, nature of, 380
  legal profession as, 8
Puerto Rico:
  courts of, 219
  Federal circuit covering, 228
Punctuation:
  close, 70
  in letters, 70
  in telegrams, 89, 90
  in wills, 210
  open, 70
Purchase money mortgage, nature of,
    467

Q

Question and answer testimony:
  notebook ruled for, 149
  transcription of, 151, 152
Quit-claim deed, 458
Quorum:
  directors' meetings, 422
  stockholders' meetings, 421
Quotation marks, for title of book,
    158
Quoted material:
  errors in, 159
  exact (Chinese) copy of, 160
  in court papers, indentations, 259
  italics in, 159
  line spacing, 157, 159
  margins, 158
  paragraphs, 158
  showing omissions in, 159
  take-ins, 147, 148
Quo warranto writs, 336

R

Rabbi, forms of address, salutation,
    close, reference, 109
Real estate (see Real property)
Real property:
  description of, 451-456
    checking, 454
    in deeds, 454
    in foreclosure action, 502
    in mortgage, 471
    lot and block, 454
    metes and bounds, 453, 455
    section and township, 451-453
    typing, 454-456
  devise of, 201
  devisee of, 199
  state requirements, wills, 203

Rear Admiral, forms of address, salutation, close, reference, 105
Receivership, application for, in foreclosure action, 509
Reception room, law office, 13
Receptionist, 11
Reciprocal wills, 199
Recording instruments, 189-192
  deeds, 464
  distinguished from filing, 190
  leases, 480
  mailing instruments, 191
    covering letter, form, 191
  mortgages, 473
  secretary's duties, 190
Records:
  appealed cases, 335-344 (*see also* Appealed cases: record)
  of progress in court matters (*see* Progress record; Suit register)
  payroll, 130-132
  record book, of clerk of the court, 236
  toll telephone call, form, 29
Red-inking a will, 213
Referee in bankruptcy, 580
Reference:
  books, in law library, 568
  to persons holding honorary or official positions, last column of address charts, 93-112
Register, suit (*see* Suit register)
Re, in subject line, 70
Reminder systems, 37-51
  appointments, 48
  card tickler, 37, 43
  court work, 49-51
  diary, 37-43
  follow-up files, 37, 44-47
  necessity for, 47
  procedure, 49
  things to be done, 37, 47-51
Renewal dates, entered in diary, 42
Rent:
  accounts, 117
  adjustment, closing statement, 495
Reporters:
  of National Reporter System, 357
  official reports, 354
Reports:
  and reporters, how to use, 555
  annual (*see* Annual reports)
  decided cases, 554-559
  foreclosure, 503
  new case, 16-19 (*see also* New Case report)

Reports (*Cont.*):
  official, 354
  on tax matters, 439
  to Federal and state governments, 439
Representatives, diplomatic, forms of address, salutation, close, reference:
  foreign, 102-103
  U. S. government, 100-101
Representative, United States, forms of address, salutation, close, reference, 95
Reserve:
  for depreciation, 117
  services charged account as, 129
Resident Commissioner, forms of address, salutation, close, reference, 95
Residential lease, nature of, 476
Residuary clause, 200, 202
Resolutions:
  accepting resignation of director, 447
  amending by-law, on stockholders' authorization, 447
  authorizing sale and issue of stock to persons determined by executive committee, 447
  blanket, authorizing issuance of duplicate certificate, 448
  compensation of officers, 446
  drafting, before meetings, 425
  expressing gratitude for services of resigning officer, 448
  extending sympathy on death of associate, 449
  issuance of:
    capital stock, 442
    duplicate stock certificate, 448
  of stockholders, forms, 449
  president, salary of, 446
  resignation of officer, acceptance of, 448
  to satisfy outside person or organization, 425
  verbatim record of, 427
Respondent, defined, 239
Responsibility line, legal document, 156
Restrictions, in deeds, 463
Retainer:
  single, defined, 9
  yearly, defined, 9
Retirement of file, processing for, 57, 58

Retyping:
  test-writing revised page, 162
  unsigned draft, 162
Revenue stamp tax:
  Federal:
    cancellation of stamp, 464
    denominations of stamps, 463
    issuance and transfer of stock, 433
      amount, 435
    stock transfer, 435
    transfer of property, 463
      amount, 463
  state:
    on deed, 464
    on mortgage, 472
Reverend, in address, 73
Revocation clause, in will, 200
Rhode Island:
  authentication of instruments, 185
  court papers, provisions, 265
  courts of record, 226
  Federal circuit covering, 228
  incorporating provisions, 412
  notaries public, 187
  parties on appeal, designation, 339
  statutes of limitations, 615
  will provisions, 204
Routing new case report, 19
Rule days, 273

S

Salaries, in general ledger, 117
Sale, contracts of (*see* Contracts of
  sale)
Salesmen:
  law book, 26
  magazine, 27
  visits from, 26
Salutations:
  abbreviations permitted, 76
  business title not used in, 77
  company, 76
  firm of women, 77
  forms of, 76
  individual, 76
  organization of men and women,
    76-77
  persons holding honorary or official
    positions:
    Army officers, 104
    Catholic faith, 106-108
    court officials, 99
    foreign officials and representatives,
      102-103

Salutations (*Cont.*):
  persons holding honorary or official
    positions (*Cont.*):
    Jewish faith, 109
    Naval officers, 105
    Protestant faith, 110-111
    state and local government officials,
      97-98
    U. S. diplomatic representatives,
      100-101
    U. S. government officials, 93-96
    women, 77
Schedules, ditto marks in, 163
Scholastic degree, in address, 92
ss. (*scilicet*), meaning of, 180
Seal:
  attestation of, 175, 176
  conforming documents bearing, 163
  contracts under, 587
  corporate, 172-175, 391
  notary, 182
    state requirements, 186
  of individual, 176
Secretary:
  corporate:
    acting as, 418-449
    attestation by, 174
  legal:
    as partner, 3
    deportment of, 11, 13
    diary of, 39
    ethics of, 3
    introduction to client, 20
Secretary General of United Nations,
  forms of address, salutation, close,
  reference, 102
Secretary of State, forms of address,
  salutation, close, reference, 97
Secretary to the President, forms of
  address, salutation, close, reference, 95
  assistant, 96
  with military rank, 95
Securities transferred through broker,
  437
Semi-block style, letters, 66, 67
Senator, United States, forms of address, salutation, close, reference,
  95
Senior partner, 10
Sentence length, in letters, 88
Service charges:
  in cash journal, 116
  posting, 136-138
Service ledger sheet, forms, 136, 137

Service of legal papers:
by mail, 340
affidavit of, 341
on opposing counsel (*see also under specific paper*)
brief, 352
notices, 303
pleadings, 263
state requirements, 264
process (*see* Process, service of)
Services charged account, 116, 129
Settlement sheet (*see* Contract of sale: closing statement)
Settle order, judge's instructions to, 315
Shepard's Citations, 562-566
Shorthand, taking citations in, 354
"sic," use of, in typing, 162
Signature (*see also under specific document*):
clause (*see* Testimonium clause)
firm name, 78
in copied material, 163
legal instruments, 170-172
fitting, on page, 171
testimonium clause, guide to, 170
of affiant, 194
of notary public:
to acknowledgment, 181
to affidavit, 194
of witnesses', in wills, 200, 202
Single retainer, 9
Sister, forms of address, salutation, close, reference, 108
Sister Superior, forms of address, salutation, close, reference, 108
Slip decisions, 363
South Carolina:
authentication of instruments, 185
court papers, provisions, 265
courts of record, 226
Federal circuit covering, 228
incorporating provisions, 412
notaries public, 187
parties on appeal, designation, 339
statutes of limitations, 615
will provisions, 204
South Dakota:
authentication of instruments, 185
court papers, provisions, 265
courts of record, 226
Federal circuit covering, 228
incorporating provisions, 413
notaries public, 187
parties on appeal, designation, 339
statutes of limitations, 615
will provisions, 204

Spacing:
between asterisks, 159
court papers, 259
fill-ins, 158
line, 157
quoted material, 159
rules for, 157
Speaker of House of Representatives, forms of address, salutation, close, reference, 93
Specialization in law field, 5
Special meetings:
of directors, 419
notice of, form, 445
of stockholders, 419
notice of, form, 443
proxy for, form, 444
Sr., Jr., in address, 71
Stamps (*see* Revenue stamp tax; Documentary stamps)
Stapling enclosures, 82, 83
State courts:
appellate courts, 219
designation of highest, 232
judicial circuits in which located, table, 228
jurisdictions divided into Parts, 219-220
of record, table, 222-228
relation to Federal courts, 220
superior, or trial, 219
system of, 219
State government officials, forms of address, salutation, close, reference, 97-98
State Representative, forms of address, salutation, close, reference, 97
States:
district courts in, 220
highest court in, 232
inheritance statutes, 512
judicial circuits in which located, table, 228
of incorporation, 381
requirements for admission to bar, 4
statutory forms of mortgage, 467
State transfer tax:
on deed, 464
on mortgage, 472
on stock, 435
Stationery supplies, 15
Statute:
of frauds, 614
of limitations, 614-616
chart, 615

Statutes and codes, 553-554
  citation of, 358
    table, 359
  how to use, 554
  United States, 358
Statutory deed, nature of, 457
Statutory provisions:
  age requirement, wills, 199
  authentication of instruments, 183
  husband and wife examined "separate and apart," 188
  notaries public, 185-187
  wills, 203
Stay writs, nature of, 336
Stenographers, in law office, 11
Stipulations:
  caption, 289
  diary entry, 289, 290
  endorsed back, 289
  extending time to answer, form 290
  nature of, 288
  number of copies, 289
  paper used, 289
  parts of, 288
  preparation of, 289
  secretary's duties, 289
  service on counsel, 289
  signature, 289
Stock:
  assignment, separate form of, 437
  capital, issuance of, form, 442
  certificates:
    and stub, form, 434
    book, 391, 433
    color of, 392
    issuance of, 435
    mailing, 436
    preparation of, 395
    transfer of, 436
      form, 437
  common, 392
  issuance of, authority for, 433
  ledger, 391
  official inspection of books and documents, 435
  original issue of:
    defined, 433
    Federal stamp tax on, 433, 435
  preferred, 392
  preparation of, 395
  stated number of shares, 433
  taxes on:
    Federal stamp tax, 433, 435
    state transfer, 435
  transfer, in blank, 437

Stock (Cont.):
  transferred shares:
    defined, 433
    Federal stamp tax on, 433, 435
Stockholders:
  annual report to, 439
  meetings (see Meetings: stockholders)
  use of term, 391
Storage of retired files, 57
  alphabetical files, 59
  numerical files, 57
  personal files, 60
  preparation for, 64
String citations, 363
Subject line, in letters, 70
Submit order, judge's instructions to, 315
Subscribers (to stock), use of term, 391
Suit register, 326-334
  closing record of case in, 333
  entries, types of, 329, 332
  file folders for, 327
  form and sufficiency of record, 332
  illustration of, 330-331
  loose-leaf binder for, 326
  nature of, 326
  opening case in, when and how, 329
  physical features of, 326
  portable tray or cabinet for, 328
  sheets:
    filing, 329
    form, 327
Summons:
  alias, 274
  and complaint:
    collection suit, 548, 549
    legal back, 261
  caption, 273
  defined, 271
  number of copies, 273
  paper used, 273
  parts of, 271
  pluries, 274
  preparation of, 271-273
  printed form of, 272
  return day of, 273
    computing, 273
  secretary's duties, 274
  service on defendant, 275
  signature, 271
Superior courts, 230
Superior of a Brotherhood, forms of address, salutation, close, reference, 107

Supervisor of secretaries and stenographers, 11
Supplies:
  office, in general ledger, 117
  stationery, 15
Supreme appellate courts, 232
Supreme Court of the United States (*see* United States: Supreme Court)
Surrogate's court, 511 (*see also* Probate court)
Surrogate's Court Act of New York, 523
Swearing to verification of pleading, 246, 249

T

Tables:
  address chart, 92-112
  authentication of instruments, 184-185
  citation of statutes and codes, 359-360
  designation of parties on appeal, 339
  Federal courts, 221
  incorporating chart, 396-417
  in manuscript, 373
  judicial circuits and states in each, 228
  National Reporter System, 357-358
  notaries public, 186-187
  of cases, how to use, 561
  official reports, 355-356
  pleadings, 264-265
  state courts, 222-227
  states, judicial circuit, 228
  wills, 203-204
Tabular stops, setting, 155
Tabulated material, typing, 156
Take-ins, in dictation, 147
Tax and taxation, 6
  accrued withholding, in general ledger, 117
  adjustment, closing statement, 494
  dates entered in diary, 42
  expense:
    in cash journal, 116
    in general ledger, 117
  incorporating, payment of, 390
  lien, 599, 619
  old age benefit, in general ledger, 117
  on stock (*see* Stock: taxes on)
  Prentice-Hall loose-leaf service, 439
  sale, 619
  state:
    on deeds, 464
    on mortgages, 472
  transfer, affidavit filed with will, 523

Tax Court, United States, 221
  papers filed in:
    captions, 618
    fastenings, 618
    number of copies, 618
    printed papers, 617
    signatures, 618
    typed papers, 617
  practice, 617
Telegrams:
  class of service, 89
  how to send, 89
  letters and figures, mixed groups of, 91
  number of copies, 89
  paragraphing, 91
  punctuation in, 89, 90
  same message to multiple addresses, 90
  to person on airplane, 90
  to person on train, 90
  typing, 89
    when other work is in machine, 91
Telephone:
  calls:
    answering, 30
    ascertaining purpose of, 32
    from irate client, 33
    long distance (toll), 29
    making notes of, 30
    message memo forms, 30, 31
    placing, 28
    queries as to lawyer's fee, 34
    screening, 31
  contacts, importance of, 27
  conversation of secretary, 34
  courtesy, rules of, 27
  desk lists:
    law business numbers, 34
    lawyer's personal numbers, 36
    office administration numbers, 35
  operators, 11
Tennessee:
  authentication of instruments, 185
  court papers, provisions, 265
  courts of record, 226
  Federal circuit covering, 228
  incorporating provisions, 413
  notaries public, 187
  parties on appeal, designation, 339
  statutes of limitations, 615
  will provisions, 204
Territorial Delegate, forms of address, salutation, close, reference, 95

Testamentary trusts:
  nature of, 201
  purpose of, 202
Testament, meaning of term, 198
Testate, defined, 511
Testators, 199
  age requirement, 199
  joint, 199
  mental capacity of, 199, 200
Testatrix, 198, 199
Testimonium clause:
  example of, 171
  in deed, 463
  in instruments, 169
  in power of attorney, 196
  in will, 200, 202
  introductory words to, typing, 170
Testimony:
  notebook ruled for, 149
  taking, 149
    transcription of, form, 151-152
Test-writing, in copied material, 162
Texas:
  authentication of instruments, 185
  court papers, provisions, 265
  courts of records, 227
  Federal circuit covering, 228
  incorporation provisions, 413
  notaries public, 187
  parties on appeal, designation, 339
  statutes of limitations, 615
  will provisions, 204
That, repetition of, in dictation, 145
Tickler card file:
  described, 43
  for follow-up, 47
  used with diary, 43
Time:
  charges:
    charge sheets, filing of, 138
    daily time sheet, 133-136
    entries in diary, 44
    finding, 132-136
  records, 37
  sheets, 44
  to answer, stipulation extending, 290
Title:
  abstract of, 487-489
    recertification of, 488
  certificate of, 487, 490
  closings (*see* Contract of sale: closings)
  companies, 503
  evidence of, 487
  insurance, 487
  insurance policies, guaranty title, 490

Title (*Cont.*):
  opinion of, 489
  transfer of, contract of sale, 484
Titles:
  address, 71-74
  business, 73
  honorary or official, 92
    address chart, 92-112
  hyphenation of, 74
  judges, 234
  justices, 234
  personal, foreign diplomatic representative, writing to, 102
  wife of titled man, form of address, 74
Toll (long distance) telephone calls, 28
  placed by clients, 29
Torrens certificate, nature of, 487, 490
Torrens, Sir Robert, 490
Township description, real estate, 451, 453
Transfer of stock (*see* Stock: transferred shares)
Transfer tax (*see* Revenue stamp tax)
Transmittal letters:
  filing of charter, 390
  recording instruments, 191
Tray, portable, for suit register, 328
Treatises, citing, 364
Trial:
  motion to set cause for, 309
  new, motion for, 309
  notice of, 284-288
    given by plaintiff, form, 287
    preparation of, 286, 288
    secretary's responsibilities, 288
Trial balance:
  accounts receivable, 129
  defined, 129
  steps in taking, 129
Triplicate originals, 150
Trust:
  bank account, 117
  deed of (*see* Deeds: trust)
  indenture, 467
  in name of corporation, 383
  mortgage, 467
  provisions, in will, 200, 201
  testamentary, 201
  use of term, 383
Trustee, party to law suit, 242
Tutor, minor represented by, 241
Typewriter:
  electric, 14
  feeding paper to, device for, 153, 154
  marginal and tabular stops, setting, 155
  pica vs. elite type, 14

Typing:
　acknowledgment, 182
　affidavits, 194-196
　aligning paper, 153
　charter, 385-389
　complaints, 269-271
　copying, 162
　court papers, 249-262 (*see also* Court
　　papers: typing)
　crossing out, in drafts, 161
　date line, 71
　deeds, 461
　distribution line, 157
　drafts, 161
　index tabs and labels, 62
　leases, 480
　legal backs, 164, 165
　legal documents, 150-167
　manuscript, for printer, 367
　margins, 154, 155
　marking take-ins for, 147, 148
　mortgages, 469
　numbering pages, 155
　number of copies, 150
　powers of attorney, 196, 197
　printed forms, 166
　quoted material (*see* Quoted mate-
　　rial)
　real property descriptions, 454-456
　responsibility line, 156
　retyping unsigned draft, 162
　salutations, 76
　signatures, 78
　spacing (*see* Spacing)
　street address, 75
　tabulated material, 156
　telegrams, 89, 91
　title of book, 158
　underscoring, 158
　unsigned draft, retyping, 162
　verification, 245-249 (*see also* Verifica-
　　tions: typing)
　wills, 204-209

U

Underscoring, in typing, 158
Under Secretary of a department, forms
　of address, salutation, close, refer-
　ence, 94
Uniform Acknowledgment Act, 177
United Nations:
　Secretary General, forms of address,
　　salutation, close, reference, 102
　United States Delegate to, forms of
　　address, salutation, close, refer-
　　ence, 101

United States:
　delegate to the United Nations, forms
　　of address, salutation, close, ref-
　　erence, 101
　diplomatic representatives, forms of
　　address, salutation, close, refer-
　　ence, 100-101
　Court of Appeals:
　　Emergency, 221
　　for District of Columbia, 221
　　for First District, 221
　Court of Claims, 221
　Court of Customs and Patent Ap-
　　peals, 221
　Customs Court, 221
　District Court:
　　for District of Maryland, 221
　　for Southern District of New York,
　　　221
　Federal courts, 220-221
　Government:
　　loyalty to, 4
　　officials, address chart, 93-96
　Supreme Court, 219, 220, 221
　　admission to practice, 5
　　Justices of, forms of address, salu-
　　　tation, close, reference, 93
　　official reports of, 354
　　rules for appeals, 335
　Tax Court, 221
Unmarried woman, form of address, 74
Unpublished cases, 363
Unusual words, special outlines for, 147
Utah:
　authentication of instruments, 185
　court papers, provisions, 265
　courts of record, 227
　Federal circuit covering, 228
　incorporating provisions, 414
　notaries public, 187
　parties on appeal, designation, 339
　statutes of limitations, 615
　will provisions, 204

V

Venue:
　in acknowledgment, 180
　in affidavit, 194, 195
　foreclosure action, 501
　motion for change of, 309
　title of case, 249
　verifications, 244
Verifications:
　acknowledgments differentiated from,
　　246, 249
　administering oath, 246

Verifications (*Cont.*):
by attorney, 244
form, 248
by individual, form, 245
by officer of domestic corporation, form, 246
by officer of foreign corporation, 247
complaints, 269
forms of, 244
nature of, 243
typing, 245-249
illustrative forms (*see* Forms: verifications)
venue of, 244
Vermont:
authentication of instruments, 185
court papers, provisions, 265
courts of record, 227
Federal circuit covering, 228
incorporating provisions, 415
notaries public, 187
parties on appeal, designation, 339
statutes of limitations, 615
will provisions, 204
Vice Admiral, forms of address, salutation, close, reference, 105
Vice President of the United States, forms of address, salutation, close, reference, 93
Virginia:
authentication of instruments, 185
court papers, provisions, 265
courts of record, 227
Federal circuit covering, 228
incorporating provisions, 415
notaries public, 187
parties on appeal, designation, 339
statutes of limitations, 615
typing style, court papers, 257
will provisions, 204
Virgule, in responsibility and distribution lines, 156, 157
Voluntary bankruptcy, 580

W

Waiver:
defined, 622
of citation:
in probate of will, 523
form, 525
letters of administration, 537
preparation of, 524
of notice:
first meeting of directors, 442
forms, 441, 442
organization meeting, 392

Waiver (*Cont.*):
of notice (*Cont.*):
stockholders' meeting, 420
Warranty deed, 458
from husband and wife, form, 459, 460
Washington:
authentication of instruments, 185
court papers, provisions, 265
courts of record, 227
Federal circuit covering, 228
incorporating provisions, 416
notaries public, 187
parties on appeal, designation, 339
statutes of limitations, 615
will provisions, 204
West Virginia:
authentication of instruments, 185
court papers, provisions, 265
courts of record, 227
Federal circuit covering, 228
incorporating provisions, 416
notaries public, 187
parties on appeal, designation, 339
statutes of limitations, 615
will provisions, 204
Wherefore clause, in complaint, 268
Widow, form of address, 74
Wife:
husband and (*see* Husband and wife)
of titled man, form of address, 74
Wills, 198-213
attestation clause, 200, 202
beneficiaries of, 199
bequests, 200, 201
capitalization in, 210
certifying copies of, 209
codicil, 213
contents, pattern of, 200
control over distribution by executor, 512
debts, payment of, 201
defined, 198
devises, 200, 201
dispositive clauses, 201
executor, appointment of, 200, 202
forms:
first page of, 205
last page of, 206
signature and preceding page of, 206-208
funeral expenses of, 201
guardian, appointment of, 200, 202
handwritten, 199
holographic, 199
introductory paragraph, 200
joint, husband and wife, 199

Wills (*Cont.*):
  kinds of, 199
  noncupative, 199
  numbered articles or items in, 201
  oral, 199
  parties to, 198
  preparation of, 211
  probate of (*see* Probate of wills)
  punctuation in, 210
  reciprocal, 199
  red-inking, 213
  residuary clause, 200, 202
  revocation clause, 200
  signature, 202, 207
  testator or testatrix, 198
  testimonium clause, 200, 202
  text, or body of, 200, 201-202
  title of, 200
  trust provisions, 200, 201
  typing, 204-209
    page length, gauging and testing, 208
  witnessing, 200, 202, 209
Wisconsin:
  authentication of instruments, 185
  court papers, provisions, 265
  courts of record, 227
  Federal circuit covering, 228
  incorporating provisions, 417
  notaries public, 187
  parties on appeal, designation, 339
  statutes of limitations, 615
  typing style, court papers, 253
  will provisions, 204
Witness clause (*see* Attestation: clause)
Witnesses to will, 209
  deposition of, 529
  signatures, 200, 202
Women:
  American Ambassador, forms of address, salutation, close, reference, 100
  American Minister, forms of address, salutation, close, reference, 100
  cabinet officer, forms of address, salutation, close, reference, 94
  firm of, salutation, 77
  forms of address, letters, 74
  forms of salutation, 77
  men and, salutation, 76-77
  Sisters (Catholic), forms of address, salutation, close, reference, 108

Women (*Cont.*):
  U. S. Representative, forms of address, salutation, close, reference, 95
  U. S. Senator, forms of address, salutation, close, reference, 95
Word count, estimating length of copy, 372
Words and phrases:
  favorite, 88
  foreign, when to underscore, 158
  Latin:
    defined, 569-576
    list of, 569-576
  length of words, 88
  padded phrases, 87
  pairs of words, 145
    listed, 146
  trite terms, list of, 83-86
  two words, same meaning, 87
  unnecessary, 86-87
  unusual, special outlines for, 147
Work:
  checklist of diary entries, 43
  for clients, payment for, 25
  overtime and night, payment for, 26
Workroom in law office, 13
Writs:
  extraordinary, 336
  known as citations, 354
  of error, review by higher court, 336
Wyoming:
  authentication of instruments, 185
  court papers, provisions, 265
  courts of record, 227
  Federal circuit covering, 228
  incorporating provisions, 417
  notaries public, 187
  parties on appeal, designation, 339
  statutes of limitations, 615
  will provisions, 204

Y

Yearbooks, standard, 37
Yearly retainer, 9

Z

Zone numbers, in address, 76
"Z" ruling, on printed forms, 167